IGNAZ STEGMILLER

The Pre-Investigation Stage of the ICC

Beiträge zum Internationalen und Europäischen Strafrecht

Herausgegeben von RiLG Prof. Dr. Kai Ambos

Band 8

The Pre-Investigation Stage of the ICC

Criteria for Situation Selection

By

Ignaz Stegmiller

Duncker & Humblot · Berlin

The Faculty of Law
of the University of Göttingen accepted this work
as a thesis in the year 2009.

Bibliographic information of the German national library

The German national library registers this publication in
the German national bibliography; specified bibliographic data
are retrievable on the Internet about http://dnb.d-nb.de.

Typesetting: L101 Mediengestaltung, Berlin
Printing: Berliner Buchdruckerei Union GmbH, Berlin
Printed in Germany

ISSN 1867-5271
ISBN 978-3-428-13350-5 (Print)
ISBN 978-3-428-53350-3 (E-Book)
ISBN 978-3-428-83350-4 (Print & E-Book)

Printed on no aging resistant (non-acid) paper
according to ISO 9706 ♾

Internet: http://www.duncker-humblot.de

I dedicate this work to my parents,
Theresia and Günter Stegmiller,
for their love and support.

Preface

The study at hand was accepted as a dissertation at the University of Göttingen in December 2009.

Without the generous support by several people it would not have been possible to accomplish the writing of this book. First, I would like to thank my supervisor Professor Dr. Kai Ambos, Judge at the State Court Göttingen, for his encouragement and support. Furthermore, I would like to express my thanks to the second referee Professor Dr. Andreas Paulus.

For generous publication subsidies I would like to thank the FAZIT-Stiftung and the German Federal Foreign Office (Auswärtiges Amt).

Warm thanks go to the DAAD and DFG who provided me with stipends during my research. The DFG supported my participation in the ICL Salzburg Summer School 2007, and the DAAD even awarded three stipends: one for the ICL Summer School in Siracusa in 2006, one for my Visiting Professional stay at the ICC's Office of the Prosecutor (OTP) in 2007, and one for my Visiting Researcher stay at Yale University for the Spring Semester 2009.

My stay at the Legal Advisory Section of the OTP was of outstanding importance. I would like to thank Dr. Hans Bevers and Enrique Carnero-Rojo for fruitful discussions. I would also like to thank Paul Seils for letting me interview him on several occasions, and from the Investigation Division I would like to thank Xabier Agirre Aranburu for several interviews. I further thank Abou Abass, Anatole Kabore, Melissa Hacking, Magali Maystre, Renuka Dhinakaran, and Anna Wijsman-Ivanovitch for their help and social support during my stay at the Court. Last but not least, I would like to thank Klaus Rackwitz, who enabled me to do research at the ICC *in situ*. Note however that the views expressed in this study are those of the author alone and do not necessarily represent those of the ICC or the OTP.

At Yale University, I would like to thank two persons who strongly supported my work: Sterling Professor Emeritus of Law and Professorial Lecturer in Law Dr. Mirjan Damaška, and Director of Graduate Programs Maria Dino.

I would also like to thank Prof. Dr. Peter Rackow, Dr. Shahryar Ebrahim-Nesbat, and Robin Sühle who all accompanied me a short way at the university of Göttingen.

For language revisions I have to emphasize the amount of work done by Melissa Hacking, Christina Andersen, Kathleen Claussen, Tom Dannenbaum, Chavi Keeney Nana, Elias Stegmiller, Pascal Hase and Andreas Müller. Special thanks go to Matt Halling for the (time-consuming!) final language revision.

Moreover, I would like to express great thanks to Ousman Njikam who helped me with revisions, many discussions, and a lot of moral support.

Last but by no means least, I thank Sandra, my inspiration, who always cared about me and the completion of this book.

Ignaz Stegmiller

Contents

Annex 2

Country analysis 478

Annex 3

SC-Res. 1593 (2005) 542

Table of Figures

Abbreviations and Terminology

AC	Appeals Chamber
ACCP	Austrian Code of Criminal Procedure
AFRC	Armed Forces Revolutionary Council
AJIL	American Journal of International Law
ALC	Annotated Leading Cases
AMICC	American NGO Coalition for the ICC
APIC	Agreement on Privileges and Immunities of the International Criminal Court
APRD	Armée Populaire pour la Restauration de la République et de la Démocratie
APuZ	Aus Politik und Zeitgeschichte
ASIL	American Society of International Law
ASP	Assembly of State Parties
ASPD	Action Sociale pour la Paix et le Développement
AUILR	American University International Law Review
BJC	British Journal of Criminology
CanLII	Canadian Legal Information Institute
CAR	Central African Republic
CDF	Civil Defence Forces
Cf.	Confer
CICC	Coalition for an International Criminal Court
CJIL	Cornell Journal of International Law
CLR	Criminal Law Review
CNDP	Congrès national pour la défense du peuple
CODEPU	Corporación de Promoción y Defensa de los Derechos del Pueblo
Cp.	Compare
CPS	Crown Prosecution Service
CUP	Cambridge University Press
DDR	Disarmament, Demobilisation and Reintegration
DECIDI	Démocratie et Civisme pour le Développement Intégral
DPP	Director of Public Prosecutions
DRC	Democratic Republic of Congo
ECCC	Extraordinary Chambers in the Courts of Cambodia
ECtHR	European Court of Human Rights
EJCrim	European Journal of Crime, Criminal Law and Criminal Justice
EJIL	European Journal of International Law

EuGRZ	Europäische Grundrechte Zeitschrift
ExCom	Executive Committee OTP
FACA	Forces armées Centrafricaines
FIDH	Fédération International des Ligues des Droits de l'Homme
FNI	Front des Nationalistes et Intégrationistes
FPLC	Forces Patriotiques pour la Libération du Congo
FRPI	Force de résistance patriotique en Ituri
GA	General Assembly
GCCP	German Code of Criminal Procedure
GCICL	German Code of International Criminal Law
GLJ	German Law Journal
GOJIL	Göttingen Journal of International Law
GP	Garde présidentielle
GRULAC	Group of Latin America and Caribbean Countries
HHRL	Harvard's Human Rights Journal
HILJ	Harvard International Law Journal
HRLC	Human Rights Law Commentary
HRLJ	Human Rights Law Journal
HRQ	Human Rights Quaterly
HuV-I	Humanitäres Völkerrecht Informationsschriften
Ibid.	Ibidem
ICC	International Criminal Court
ICCPR	International Covenant on Civil and Political Rights
ICJ	International Court of Justice
ICLQ	International and Comparative Law Quaterly
ICLR	International Criminal Law Review
ICTJ	International Centre for Transitional Justice
ICTR	International Criminal Tribunal for Rwanda
ICTY	International Criminal Tribunal for the Former Yugoslavia
ICWC	International Research and Documentation Center for War Crimes Trials
ID	Investigation Division
IJTJ	The International Journal of Transitional Justice
ILC	International Law Commission
IMT	International Military Tribunal
IMTFE	International Military Tribunal for the Far East
IRRC	International Review of the Red Cross
JAL	Journal of African Law
JCCD	Jurisdiction, Complementarity and Cooperation Division
JICJ	Journal of International Criminal Justice
JuS	Juristische Schulung
KCLJ	King's College Law Journal

LAS	Legal Advisory Section
LRA	Lord's Resistance Army
MichJIL	Michigan Journal of International Law
MJIL	Melbourne Journal of International Law
MLC	Mouvement de libération du Congo
Mn	Marginal number
NDPP	National Director of Public Prosecution
New Eng. ICLA	New England International and Comparative Law Annual
NILR	Netherlands International Law Review
NJIL	Nordic Journal of International Law
NJW	Neue Juristische Wochenschrift
NPWJ	No Peace Without Justice
OHCHR	Office of the High Commissioner for Human Rights
OPCD	Office of Public Counsel for the Defence
OPCV	Office of Public Counsel for Victims
OTP	Office of the Prosecutor
OUP	Oxford University Press
PACE	Police and Criminal Evidence Act
PD	Prosecution Division
POA	Prosecution of Offences Act
PTC	Pre-Trial Chamber
RDI	Rivista di Diritto Internazionale
reg.	Regulation
RGDIP	Revue Générale de Droit International Public
RIDP	Revue International de Droit Pénal
RLP	Refugee Law Project
RPE	Rules of Procedure and Evidence
RS	Rome Statute
RSC	Revue de science criminelle et de droit pénal comparé
SC	Security Council
SCSL	Special Court for Sierra Leone
TC	Trial Chamber
TRC	Truth and Reconciliation Commission
U.C. Davis J. Int. Law and Policy	U.C. Davis Journal of International Law and Policy
UFDR	Union des Forces Démocratiques pour le Rassemblement
UN	United Nations
UNMIBH	UN Mission in Bosnia and Herzegovina
UPC	Union des Patriotes Congolais
UPDF	Uganda Peoples Defence Force
VCLT	Vienna Convention on the Law of Treaties

VJIL	Virginia Journal of International Law
VJTL	Vanderbilt Journal of Transitional Law
VN	Vereinte Nationen (*Journal*)
VPRS	Victims Participation and Reparations Section
VWU	Victims and Witness Unit
WEOG	Western European and Others Group
YIHL	Yearbook of International Humanitarian Law
YLJ	Yale Law Journal
YLS	Yale Law School
ZaöRV	Zeitschrift für ausländisches öffentliches Recht und Völkerrecht
ZIS	Zeitschrift für Internationale Strafrechtsdogmatik
ZStW	Zeitschrift für die gesamte Strafrechtswissenschaft

"There are times when we are told that justice must be set aside in the interests of peace. It is true that justice can only be dispensed when the peaceful order of society is secure. But we have come to understand that the reverse is also true: without justice, there can be no lasting peace."

UN Secretary-General Kofi Annan, Statement at the Inaugural Meeting of the Judges of the International Criminal Court, 11.3.2003, The Hague, The Netherlands.

Part I

Introduction

A. Introduction to the problem

The International Criminal Court (hereinafter ICC) is the first permanent international criminal court of the history of mankind with jurisdiction to prosecute individuals responsible for the most serious crimes of international concern: genocide, crimes against humanity, and war crimes.[1] It was established on 17 July 1998 by more than 120 States at the "United Nations Diplomatic Conference of Plenipotentiaries on the Establishment of an International Criminal Court."[2] The ICC Statute (also known as the Rome Statute)[3] entered into force on 1 July 2002; at present (1 September 2010), 113 States have ratified and 139 signed the Statute.[4]

---

1 For the recently adopted crime of aggression that is now regulated in article 8*bis* see further *infra* notes 418 and 1321. Note that articles in this thesis without further indications are those of the ICC Statute, rules without further indications are those of the ICC's Rules of Procedure and Evidence.

2 See <www.un.org/icc/final.htm> (all websites in this study last visited 1.9.2010); the ICC Statute was adopted by a vote of 120 in favor to 7 against, with 21 abstentions.

3 Rome Statute of the International Criminal Court, adoption 17.7.1998/entry into force 1.7.2000 (A/CONF.183/9) available at: <www2.icc-cpi.int/Menus/ICC/Legal+Texts+and+Tools/>.

4 See for an updated list of signatures and ratifications <www.iccnow.org>; see also <www2.icc-cpi.int/Menus/ASP/states+parties/>.

Meanwhile the ICC has developed into a fully functioning institution[5]: five situations have been opened for investigation (Uganda; Darfur, Sudan; the Central African Republic, hereinafter CAR; the Democratic Republic of Congo, hereinafter DRC; and, most recently, the Republic of Kenya).[6] Moreover, fourteen (unsealed) arrest warrants and three summonses to appear have been issued leading to ten cases before the Court.[7] In the course of its judicial activities, mainly procedural matters had to be solved, and the Court handled approximately 1400 filings until late 2007 (including annexes).[8] International criminal procedural law plays a decisive role in international criminal justice; it forms the framework for punishing the most serious crimes of concern to the international community. A precise procedure is of particular importance with a view to the legitimacy and credibility of the ICC. The discipline of international criminal procedural law has developed from an adversarial to a mixed procedure and can be designated a doc-

---

[5] "The Court is fully operational," cf. Address to the United Nations General Assembly, Judge Philippe Kirsch, President of the International Criminal Court, 1.11.2007, 3; see further Carsten Stahn/Göran Sluiter, "From 'infancy' to emancipation? – A review of the Court's first practice" in Carsten Stahn/Göran Sluiter (eds.), *The Emerging Practice of the International Criminal Court* (Martinus Nijhoff Publishers, Leiden Boston 2009) 1, 1 et seq. On the OTP's activities on a weekly basis see <www.icc-cpi.int/Menus/ICC/Structure+of+the+Court/Office+of+the+Prosecutor/Weekly+Briefings/>.

[6] See <www2.icc-cpi.int/Menus/ICC/Situations+and+Cases/>. On the Kenyan situation see *Situation in Kenya*, Decision pursuant to article 15 of the Rome Statute on the authorization of an investigation into the situation in the Republic of Kenya, 31.3.2010 (ICC-01/09-19).

[7] In the situation of DRC five arrest warrants were issued and resulted in four separate cases: *Prosecutor v. Thomas Lubanga Dyilo* (ICC-01/04-01/06), *Prosecutor v. Germain Katanga and Mathieu Ngudjolo Chui* (ICC-01/04-01/07), *Prosecutor v. Bosco Ntaganda* (ICC-01/04-02/06), and *Prosecutor v. Callixte Mbarushimana* (ICC-01/04-01/10). In the situation of Uganda five arrest warrants resulted in the case of *Prosecutor v. Joseph Kony, Vincent Otti, Okot Odhiambo and Dominic Ongwen* (ICC-02/04-01/05); the arrest warrant against Raska Lukwiya was withdrawn and rendered without effect because of his death, see *Prosecutor v. Kony et al.*, Prosecution's request that the warrant of arrest for Raska Lukwiya be withdrawn and rendered without effect because of his death, 22.3.2007 (ICC-02/04-01/05-230). Three arrest warrants and three summonses to appear were issued in Darfur and resulted in the cases of *Prosecutor v. Ahmad Muhammad Harun ("Ahmad Harun"), Ali Muhammad Ali Abd-Al-Rahman ("Ali Kushayb")* (ICC-02/05-01/07), *Prosecutor v. Omar Al Bashir* (ICC-02/05-01/09), *Prosecutor v. Bahr Idriss Abu Garda* (ICC-02/05-02/09), and most recently *Prosecutor v. Abdallah Banda Abakaer Nourain and Saleh Mohammed Jerbo Jamus* (ICC-02/05-03/09). Last but not least, an arrest warrant was unsealed on 24.5.2008, leading to the first case in the CAR situation of *Prosecutor v. Jean-Pierre Bemba Gombo* (ICC-01/05-01/08). In more detail on the actual situations and cases see Part III, B., I., 1–5.

[8] Report on the activities of the Court, ASP sixth session, 18.10.2007 (ICC-ASP/6/18) para. 10; also Stahn/Sluiter, in Stahn/Sluiter, *supra* note 5, 4–5.

trine of its own. This development has occurred through the various amendments of the International Criminal Tribunal for the Former Yugoslavia's (hereinafter ICTY) Rules of Procedure and Evidence (hereinafter RPE[9]) and the drafting of the ICC Statute, which have merged civil and common law elements into one international procedure.[10] The ICTY's and ICC's mixed procedure contains structural elements or building blocks of both the "adversarial" and the "inquisitorial" system.[11] Having said that, recent developments have led towards "an amalgam of both common law and civil law elements, so as to render it *sui generis*."[12] In contrast, the law of the *ad hoc* tribunals was drafted by common lawyers and the Draft Statute of the International Law Commission for an ICC[13] provided for an adversarial proce-

---

[9] Upcoming reference to the RPE in this study without further indications refers to the ICC Rules of Procedure and Evidence, in contrast to those of the ICTY or ICTR, which will be indicated by adding "ICTY" and "ICTR."

[10] Kai Ambos, "The structure of international criminal procedure: adversarial, inquisitorial or mixed?" in Michael Bohlander (ed.), *International criminal justice: a critical analysis of institutions and procedures* (Cameron May, London 2007) 429, 429; also John Jackson, "Finding the best epistemic fit for international criminal tribunals" (2009) 7 JICJ 17, 18; Karin Calvo-Goller, *The trial proceedings of the International Criminal Court* (Martinus Nijhoff Publishers, Leiden 2006) 147, who calls the adopted system "a combination leading to a *sui generis* system." In international comparative law, it has been acknowledged that the traditional confrontation common vs. civil law does not cope with the reality of modern criminal procedural law anymore, Robert Heuser/Thomas Weigend, *Das Strafprozessgesetz der Volksrepublik China in vergleichender Perspektive* (Calling P.O.D., Hamburg 1997) 40.

[11] Ambos, *supra* note 10, 431; *id.,* "International Criminal Law at the crossroads: from *ad hoc* imposition to a treaty-based universal system" in Carsten Stahn/Larissa van Herik (eds.), *Future Perspectives on International Criminal Justice* (T.M.C. Asser Press, The Hague 2010) 161, 169–70; Claus Kress, "The procedural law of the International Criminal Court in outline: anatomy of a unique compromise" (2003) 1 JICJ 596, 604–5. For a comparative analysis of both traditions see Richard Vogler, *A worldview of criminal justice* (Ashgate, Aldershot 2005). The terms "adversarial" and "inquisitorial" are to be used "with caution and only in the general sense of the still existing common-civil law divide," cf. Kai Ambos, "International Criminal Procedure: 'adversarial', 'inquisitorial' or mixed" (2003) 3 ICLR 1, 2 et seq.; in a similar vein, Alphons Orie, "Accusatorial versus inquisitorial approach in international criminal proceedings" in Antonio Cassese/Paola Gaeta/John Jones (eds.), *The Rome Statute of the ICC: a commentary,* Vol. II (OUP, Oxford 2002) 1440 et seq., with various references. In consequence, Ambos prefers the terms "Anglo-American" and "Romano-Germanic" legal systems, cf. Kai Ambos, " 'Witness proofing' before the ICC: neither legally admissible nor necessary" in Stahn/Sluiter, *supra* note 5, 605 with fn. 31.

[12] *Prosecutor v. Mucić et al. (Čelebići Camp)*, Decision on the motion on presentation of evidence by the accused Esad Landzo, 1.5.1997 (IT-96-21-T), para. 15.

[13] Report of the ILC on its work of its forty-sixth session, 2.5.1994–22.7.1994, GA forty-ninth session, Supplement No. 10 (A/49/10); on the ILC phase see Wil-

dure.[14] Only various amendments of the ICTY's RPE, and a so called "French Draft" presented in 1996,[15] brought about real discussions between common law and civil law, "which finally led to the convergence of both systems in the ICC Statute and the Rules."[16]

But a truly mixed procedure requires staff that have knowledge of both common law and civil law, and individuals who are able and willing to look beyond their own legal systems. The procedural law is affected by the actors within the judicial system – at the ICTY those actors mainly came from a common law background. At the ICC the initial position is slightly different. First of all, the ICC Statute itself is more flexible to both approaches, be it common law or civil law. In addition, there is a statutory obligation to achieve representation of the principal legal systems of the world in the Court's staff members, equitable geographical representation, and a fair representation of women and men for all positions according to the criteria set out in article 36 (8).[17] In reality, however, the Court still struggles to achieve equitable geographical representation. Five regions were identified based on the tradition of the United Nations (hereinafter UN); the five regions are the African,[18] Asian,[19] Eastern European,[20] Latin

---

liam Schabas, *The International Criminal Court: a commentary on the Rome Statute* (OUP, Oxford 2010) 6 et seq.

[14] Cf. Ambos, *supra* note 10, 431; Gilbert Bitti, "Two bones of contention between civil and common law: the record of the proceedings and the treatment of concursus delictorum" in Horst Fischer/Claus Kreß/Sascha Lüder (eds.), *International and national prosecution of crimes under international law* (Berlin Verlag Spitz, Berlin 2001) 273, 273; Vladimir Tochilovsky, "Legal systems and cultures in the ICC: the experience from the ICTY" in *ibid.*, 627, 629; Fabricio Guariglia, "Investigation and prosecution" in Roy Lee (ed.), *The International Criminal Court, the making of the Rome Statute, issues, negotiations, results* (Kluwer Law International, The Hague 1999) 227, 234; Megan Fairlie, "The marriage of common and continental law at the ICTY and its progeny, due process deficit" (2004) 4 ICLR 243, 268 et seq.

[15] Draft Statute of the ICC, Working paper submitted by France, 6.8.1996 (A/AC.249/L.3).

[16] Ambos, *supra* note 10, 433.

[17] These criteria shall be considered with regard to the employment of all staff members; article 44 (2) stipulates their application *mutatis mutandis*.

[18] 53 member States: Algeria, Angola, Benin, Botswana, Burkina Faso, Burundi, Cameroon, Cape Verde, Central African Republic, Chad, Comoros, Republic of the Congo, Côte d'Ivoire, Democratic Republic of the Congo, Djibouti, Egypt, Equatorial Guinea, Eritrea, Ethiopia, Gabon, Gambia, Ghana, Guinea, Guinea-Bissau, Kenya, Lesotho, Liberia, Libyan Arab Jamahiriya, Madagascar, Malawi, Mali, Mauritania, Mauritius, Morocco, Mozambique, Namibia, Niger, Nigeria, Rwanda, Sao Tome and Principe, Senegal, Seychelles, Sierra Leone, Somalia, South Africa, Sudan, Swaziland, Togo, Tunisia, Uganda, United Republic of Tanzania, Zambia, Zimbabwe. For the regional groups see <www.un.org/sc/members.asp>, where it is

American and the Caribbean States – GRULAC,[21] and the Western European and Others Group – WEOG,[22] and the professional staff was classified accordingly. The target was exceeded in Africa, roughly achieved in Eastern Europe and WEOG, but the numbers were below target in Asia and GRULAC.[23] Moreover, the common law influence is – in my opinion –

further indicated if and when the countries were members of the SC. On the development of the UN electoral groups, Sam Daws, "The origins and developments of UN electoral groups" in Ramesh Thakur (ed.), *What is equitable geographic representation in the twenty-first century* (The United Nations University, New York 1999) 11, 11 et seq.

[19] 53 member States: Afghanistan, Bahrain, Bangladesh, Bhutan, Brunei Darussalam, Cambodia, China, Cyprus, Democratic People's Republic of Korea, Fiji, India, Indonesia, Iran, Iraq, Japan, Jordan, Kazakhstan, Kuwait, Kyrgyzstan, Lao People's Democratic Republic, Lebanon, Malaysia, Maldives, Marshall Islands, Federated States of Micronesia, Mongolia, Myanmar, Nauru, Nepal, Oman, Pakistan, Palau, Papua New Guinea, Philippines, Qatar, Republic of Korea, Samoa, Saudi Arabia, Singapore, Solomon Islands, Sri Lanka, Syrian Arab Republic, Tajikistan, Thailand, Timor-Leste, Tonga, Turkmenistan, Tuvalu, United Arab Emirates, Uzbekistan, Vanuatu, Vietnam, Yemen. Kiribati is not a member of any regional group, but geographically located in Asia, and might join this regional group in the future.

[20] 23 member States: Albania, Armenia, Azerbaijan, Belarus, Bosnia and Herzegovina, Bulgaria, Croatia, Czech Republic, Estonia, Georgia, Hungary, Latvia, Lithuania, Poland, The former Yugoslav Republic of Macedonia, Montenegro, Republic of Moldova, Romania, Russian Federation, Serbia, Slovakia, Slovenia, Ukraine.

[21] 33 member States: Antigua and Barbuda, Argentina, Bahamas, Barbados, Belize, Bolivia, Brazil, Chile, Colombia, Costa Rica, Cuba, Dominica, Dominican Republic, Ecuador, El Salvador, Grenada, Guatemala, Guyana, Haiti, Honduras, Jamaica, Mexico, Nicaragua, Panama, Paraguay, Peru, Saint Kitts and Nevis, Saint Lucia, Saint Vincent and the Grenadines, Suriname, Trinidad and Tobago, Uruguay, Bolivarian Republic of Venezuela.

[22] 29 member States (including the special cases of Israel and the USA): Andorra, Australia, Austria, Belgium, Canada, Denmark, Finland, France, Germany, Greece, Iceland, Ireland, Israel (limited competencies only), Italy, Liechtenstein, Luxembourg, Malta, Monaco, The Netherlands, New Zealand, Norway, Portugal, San Marino, Spain, Sweden, Switzerland, Turkey, United Kingdom of Great Britain and Northern Ireland, United States of America (considered to be a member of the group for electoral purposes only).

[23] Cf. Table 3, Chart 1: geographical representation: percentage actual vs. targeted, Annex III to the Report of the Committee on Budget and Finance on the work of its eighth session, ASP sixth session, 29.5.2007 (ICC-ASP/6/2) Africa target: 13.09 percent, actual: 18.14 percent; Eastern Europe target 7.32 percent, actual 7.84 percent; WEOG target 57.74 percent, actual 56.37 percent; Asia target: 7.69 percent, actual 6.37 percent; GRULAC target 14.15 percent, actual 11.27 percent. On the methodology, as well as suggestions for further improvement of equal geographical representation and gender balance, see Report of the Bureau on geographical representation and gender balance in the recruitment of staff of the International Criminal Court, ASP sixth session, 24.10.2007 (ICC-ASP/6/22) para. 8 et seq., 47 et seq.; also OTP Report on the activities performed during the first three years

still stronger than the civil law influence. A large proportion of the working staff tend to take their experience from the ICTY or International Criminal Tribunal for Rwanda (hereinafter ICTR) into consideration. In any case, some problems within the ICC Statute go well beyond considering a more common law or civil law approach. There are various complex problems built into the ICC Statute, which require creative solutions to be developed by the case law and the emerging doctrine on international criminal procedure. The internationalization of criminal law creates new opportunities for comparative work in the field of procedural law.[24]

One important issue of international criminal procedural law addressed by this study is the pre-investigation stage, which essentially deals with the selection of situations for investigation. In contrast to the *ad hoc* tribunals, the ICC explicitly recognizes a preliminary examination procedure as foreseen by article 15 (6).[25] These examinations take place before the (formal) investigation stage in accordance with article 54 begins. Thus, two different procedural stages regarding the ICC procedural law can be identified, namely the pre-investigation stage and the formal investigation stage.[26] During the upcoming survey the stages have to be distinguished carefully, and provisions have to be tested as to whether they apply to pre-investigations or (full) investigations. Accurate distinction is necessary because the powers of the Office of the Prosecutor (hereinafter OTP) in the course of formal investigations go far beyond those during pre-investigations. In terms of terminology, "pre-investigation" and "preliminary examinations" will be used throughout;[27] the former is preferred by the author if reference

---

(June 2003–June 2006), 12.9.2006 (hereinafter OTP Report on activities 2003–2006) 28.

24 Markus Dirk Dubber, "Comparative criminal law" in Mathias Reiman/Reinhard Zimmermann (eds.), *The Oxford handbook of comparative law* (OUP, Oxford 2006) 1287, 1307.

25 See Chapter 3, Section 3 headed "Preliminary examination and evaluation of information," of the Regulations of the OTP, adoption/entry into force 23.4.2009 (ICC-BD/05-01-09) available at: <www2.icc-cpi.int/Menus/ICC/Legal+Texts+and+Tools/Official+Journal/>.

26 In a similar vein, Giuliano Turone, "Powers and duties of the Prosecutor" in Cassese/Gaeta/Jones, *supra* note 11, 1137, 1146; Stefan van Heeck, *Die Weiterentwicklung des formellen Völkerstrafrechts* (Duncker & Humblot, Berlin 2006) 145; Kai Ambos, *Internationales Strafrecht,* 2nd edition (C. H. Beck, München 2008) § 8, mn 20a; Jan Wouters/Sten Verhoeven/Bruno Demeyere, "The International Criminal Court's Office of the Prosecutor: navigating between independence and accountability?" Institute for International Law, Working paper No. 97, July 2006, 19 et seq.

27 The differentiation by *Schabas* of "preliminary examinations," when the Prosecutor is acting *proprio motu,* and "pre-investigative phase," when the matter results from a referral, cf. William Schabas, *An introduction to the International Criminal Court,* 3rd edition (CUP, Cambridge 2007) 239, is not convincing. It is expressly

is made to the procedural stage as a whole, whereas the latter is used by the ICC Statute and the OTP Regulations and refers to the analysis of information[28] and referrals. In order to distinguish the pre-investigations from all-embracing investigations, the term "formal" or "full" investigation, as opposed by the simple term "investigation," is introduced whenever reference is made to investigations under article 54.

B. Research objective, research questions and structure

The overall objective of the study is to clarify the procedure and content of the pre-investigation stage. The dimension of this phase can be described as twofold, that is to say its nature involves procedural and substantive questions. First, an overview of the scope of the entire stage must be given which outlines the beginning, the procedural process and the methods used, and the formal ending of the pre-investigation phase. In my view, the triggering procedure marks the initiation of analysis,[29] followed by the analysis process as laid down in article 15 (2), rules 46, 47, and 104, and a decision as to whether there is a reasonable basis to initiate an investigation according to articles 53 (1) and 15 (3), and finally rule 48, which then formally ends pre-investigation and triggers all-embracing investigations.

On the other hand, the evaluation criteria to determine the reasonable basis for initiating an investigation comprise substantive questions that go to the very heart of the ICC Statute. On what basis are situations selected? Dismissing a situation might have serious impact on the international community. The main criteria are enumerated in article 53 (1), but they are left

---

stated that referrals and communications are basically subjected to the same analysis process, Annex to the "Paper of some policy issues before the Office of the Prosecutor:" referrals and communications (hereinafter Annex paper), September 2003 (ICC-OTP 2003) 7. The terminological distinction is not necessary with regard to the different trigger mechanisms; instead it is submitted that the terms are used interchangeably by the Court.

[28] From a purely legal perspective, the term "information" is preferred *vis-à-vis* "communication," because only the former finds equivalent in the ICC Statute and its supplementary legal texts. For example, the newly drafted OTP Regulations did abolish the term "communication" and use the term "information on crimes" instead, cf. OTP Regulation 2. However, the term "communication" has found its way into numerous other OTP documents, and will therefore be used as the equivalent to information under article 15. For the use of the term "communication" in OTP practice see <www2.icc-cpi.int/Menus/ICC/Structure+of+the+Court/Office+of+the+Prosecutor/Comm+and+Ref/>.

[29] On this matter see Héctor Olásolo, *The triggering procedure of the International Criminal Court* (Martinus Niijhoff Publishers, Leiden 2005).

undefined. The study aims at giving them more substance, particularly with regard to the terms "gravity" and "interests of justice."[30]

The fact that the preliminary examination process is substantially divided between two provisions (articles 15 and 53) and that no coordination within the Statute is given, renders the envisaged analysis very complicated. Taking for granted that a preliminary examination has to be carried out by the Prosecutor no matter whether the source of the *notitia criminis* is the UN Security Council (hereinafter SC), a State Party, or from somewhere else,[31] this study can be subdivided into two essential parts: an analysis of article 15, which deals with the method followed during preliminary examinations, and an analysis of article 53, which focuses on the parameters that are used for situation selection.[32]

As to a more precise overview of the study at hand, first the structure of the OTP is presented [Part II], before an overview of the pre-investigation phase is given [Part III]. In addition, in the course of Part III, core questions, e.gs. the differentiation between situation and case or the relationship between article 15 and article 53, will be discussed and resolved. Country analysis specifically focused on preliminary examinations, which are included in Annex 2, assist with understanding the nature of the ICC preliminary procedure where appropriate. The main result from the screening of national systems is the uniqueness and general incomparableness of the ICC's procedure, but the analysis also shows that certain terminology has been taken from national jurisdictions (e. g. "interests of justice" from "public interest"). Further, Part III deals with article 15 in detail and focuses on the manner in which the preliminary examination is carried out [Part III, B., VI. and C.]. Needless to say, the extent of the preliminary examination and the required authorization of the Pre-Trial Chamber (hereinafter PTC) under article 15 (4) will be of particular importance. Additionally, the criteria for situation selection, mainly "gravity" and "interests of justice," will be approached [Part IV], before final conclusions [Part V] are presented.

This study is not intended to be a purely academic exercise but should also provide a handbook for practitioners at the ICC, in particular analysts

---

30 It is, however, suggested that each criterion deserves and in-depth study on its own due to the complexity and the various legal questions arising from them. The study at hand does not intend to cover all aspects of "gravity" and "interests of justice," but shall provide an outline of the present status and presents initial proposals.

31 Cf. Turone, in Cassese/Gaeta/Jones, *supra* note 26, 1146; Annex paper, *supra* note 27, 7. See further Part III, C., I.

32 A similar distinction (*method* according to article 15 (2) and *parameters* according to article 53 (1)) is made by Turone, in Cassese/Gaeta/Jones, *supra* note 26, 1146–7.

of the Jurisdiction, Complementarity and Cooperation Division (hereinafter JCCD).[33] Given the complexity of the issue at hand it can regrettably not cover all questions that might arise: however, it is aimed at disclosing areas which have not been examined in depth up to now.

C. Methodology

The primary method for examining the procedure and content of the pre-investigation stage is an interpretation of the ICC Statute and the ICC's RPE.[34] In the meanwhile, subsidiary procedural law sources, namely the Regulations of the Court (hereinafter Court Regulations)[35] and the Regulations of the OTP (hereinafter OTP Regulations),[36] have been adopted and have to be taken into consideration accordingly, despite the fact that these sources must be in conformity with the ICC Statute and are complementary in nature. After an outline of applicable law in the style of article 21 [I.], the common interpretation method, also used in this book, is explored [II.]. Moreover, comparative analysis is included in the study with regard to the nature of the pre-investigation; therefore, the preferred comparative methodology is explained below [III.].

I. Applicable law

Whereas the Statutes of the ICTY and ICTR are silent as to the sources of the applicable law, the ICC specifically provides for this in article 21.[37] Article 21 (1) establishes a hierarchy of the sources of applicable law[38] and

---

[33] On the JCCD see OTP Regulation 7; further Part II, B.

[34] Adoption/entry into force 9.9.2002 (ICC-ASP/1/3) available at: <www2.icc-cpi.int/Menus/ICC/Legal+Texts+and+Tools/>.

[35] Adoption/entry into force 26.5.2004 (ICC-BD/01-01-04), amendment 1, 9.3.2005 (ICC-BD/01-01-04/Rev.01-05) and amendment 2, adoption 14.6.2007/ 14.11.2007/entry into force 18.12.2007 (ICC-BD/01-02-07) available at: <www2.icc-cpi.int/Menus/ICC/Legal+Texts+and+Tools/>.

[36] OTP Regulations, *supra* note 25.

[37] Article 21 constitutes the first codification of international criminal law sources, see Margaret McAuliffe deGuzman, "Article 21" in Otto Triffterer (ed.), *Commentary on the Rome Statute of the International Criminal Court,* 2nd edition (C.H. Beck, Hart Publishing, Nomos: München, Oxford, Baden-Baden 2008) article 21, mn 6.

[38] Allain Pellet, "Applicable law," in Cassese/Gaeta/Jones, *supra* note 11, 1051, 1076 et seq.; McAuliffe deGuzman, in Triffterer, *supra* note 37, article 21, mn 1; Gilbert Bitti, "Article 21 of the Statute of the International Criminal Court and the treatment of sources of law in the jurisprudence of the ICC," in Stahn/Sluiter, *supra* note 5, 285, 287–8; Daniel Sheppard, "The International Criminal Court and 'inter-

directs the Court to apply the Statute, the Elements of Crimes[39] (article 9), and the RPE. Though the last two seem, at first sight, to be placed on an equal footing with the Statute, articles 9 (3) and 51 (5) clarify that they are of subsidiary nature. Next, applicable treaties and the principles and rules of international law shall be looked upon. Failing that, general principles of law derived from national laws can be used, provided that those principles are not inconsistent with the Statute and with internationally recognized norms and standards. The Court may also refer to its previous decisions (article 21 (2)). Under the terms of article 21 (3), "The application and interpretation of law pursuant to this article must be consistent with internationally recognized human rights, and be without any adverse distinction founded on grounds such as gender as defined in article 7, paragraph 3, age, race, color, language, religion, or belief, political or other opinion, national, ethnic or social origin, wealth, birth or other status."[40] Across-the-board, a line may be drawn between the ICC's "proper law" and external general law sources,[41] and these twofold categories will henceforth have to be fleshed out.

1. Proper law of the ICC

Four possible sources are listed in article 21: the ICC Statute itself, the Elements of Crimes, the RPE, and, potentially, the case law of the Court. With regard to the procedure to be followed before the ICC, other specific legal provisions complement these four sources.

The Statute consists of 13 parts and 128 articles:

- Part 1: Establishment of the Court (articles 1–4);
- Part 2: Jurisdiction, admissibility and applicable law (articles 5–21);
- Part 3: General principles of criminal law (articles 22–33);
- Part 4: Composition and administration of the Court (articles 34–52);

nationally recognized human rights': understanding article 21 (3) of the Rome Statute" (2010) 10 ICLR 43, 46; Florian Melloh, *Einheitliche Strafzumessung in den Rechtsquellen des ICC-Statuts* (Duncker & Humblot, Berlin 2010) 194.

39 Adoption/entry into force 9.9.2002 (ICC-ASP/1/3) available at: <www2.icc-cpi.int/Menus/ICC/Legal+Texts+and+Tools/>.

40 According to Pellet, in Cassese/Gaeta/Jones, *supra* note 38, 1080, these internationally recognized human rights take precedence over all other applicable rules, and this assumption raises, for example, the problem of defining the formal sources as well the substance thereof.

41 Pellet, in Cassese/Gaeta/Jones, *supra* note 38, 1053. On the procedural law of the ICC cf. Claus Kress, "The procedural texts of the International Criminal Court" (2007) 5 JICJ 537, 537 et seq.

- Part 5: Investigation and prosecution (articles 53–61);
- Part 6: The trial (articles 62–76);
- Part 7: Penalties (articles 77–80);
- Part 8: Appeal and revision (articles 81–85);
- Part 9: International cooperation and judicial assistance (articles 86–102);
- Part 10: Enforcement (articles 103–111);
- Part 11: Assembly of States Parties (articles 112);
- Part 12: Financing (articles 113–118);
- Part 13: Final clauses (articles 119–128).

Three parts (part five, six, and seven), and thus 28 articles, refer directly to the procedure before the Court in a narrow sense. Part two, which embraces the triggering procedure (articles 13–15), jurisdictional provisions (articles 11–12), admissibility (article 17), and the applicable law of article 21, is of particular importance regarding ICC procedural law. Part four has a particular bearing on criminal proceedings, and, for a better understanding of the structure of the Court, is included later in the study at hand.[42] Indirect implications flow from part nine, since the management of investigations largely depends upon cooperation of states.[43]

In addition to the ICC Statute, the Elements of Crimes shall assist the Court in the interpretation and application of articles 6, 7, and 8 pursuant to article 9 (1). The latter provision was included at the last minute to the insistence of the United States.[44] Be that as it may, the Elements and

[42] See Part II.

[43] In a similar vein, van Heeck, *supra* note 26, 91. For the practical difficulties due to the lack of cooperation of the Sudan government see "Prosecutor calls on citizens to push for arrest of Darfur war crimes suspect," 13.10.2007, The Canadian Press; "ICC prosecutor to inform UNSC of Sudan's non-cooperation," 9.10.2007, Sudan Tribune; also Address to the United Nations General Assembly, Judge Philippe Kirsch, President of the International Criminal Court, 1.11.2007, 4 et seq.; Report of the International Criminal Court to the United Nations for 2006/2007, GA sixty-second session, 31.8.2007 (A/62/314) 10 et seq.

[44] The concept of Elements of Crimes does not appear in the Preparatory Committee's Draft Statute (Report of the Preparatory Committee on the Establishment of an International Criminal Court, 14.4.1998 (A/CONF.183/2/Add.1)), and was only introduced by the United States during the last session of the Committee, cf. Pellet, in Cassese/Gaeta/Jones, *supra* note 38, 1059; Otto Triffterer, Otto, "Can the 'elements of crimes' narrow or broaden the responsibility for criminal behavior defined in the Rome Statute," in Stahn/Sluiter, *supra* note 5, 381, 386–7. According to Pellet, in Cassese/Gaeta/Jones, *supra* note 38, 1059, this norm is a "regrettable concession made to that country [the US] by the majority of States participating in the Rome Conference." Critical also David Hunt, "The International Criminal Court.

amendments thereto have to be consistent with the Statute according to article 9 (3). As to the Elements themselves, in its fifth session the Preparatory Commission[45] adopted a report containing the finalized draft text of the Elements,[46] and the Elements were finally approved in the first session of the Assembly of States Parties (hereinafter ASP). With respect to the subject-matter of the Elements, they cannot supply any guidance regarding the pre-investigation phase, and therefore they will be left aside in the subsequent chapters.

The RPE serve as a clarification and as a complement to the procedural framework as laid down in the Statute (article 51). They were prepared by the Preparatory Commission,[47] and adopted on the first session of the ASP.[48] In February 1999, Australia and France had prepared drafts that formed the basis for the ensuing discussions.[49] The drafts reflected the common law and civil law traditions, respectively, and it is remarkable how the final draft harmonized the two approaches.[50] Basically, the Rules flesh out the norms of the Statute, which concern the Court's competence, organization, and procedure. The 225 rules are subdivided into 12 chapters:

- 1. General provisions (rules 1–3);
- 2. Composition and administration of the Court (rules 4–43);
- 3. Jurisdiction and admissibility (rules 44–62);
- 4. Provisions relating to various stages of the proceedings (rules 63–103);

High hopes, 'creative ambiguity' and an unfortunate mistrust in international judges" (2004) 2 JICJ 56, 59 et seq., 65 et seq.

[45] On the work of the Preparatory Commission see <http://untreaty.un.org/cod/icc/prepcomm/prepfra.htm>.

[46] Report of the Preparatory Commission for the International Criminal Court, Addendum Part II, Finalized Draft Text of the Elements of Crimes, 2.11.2000 (PCNICC/2000/1/Add.2).

[47] Report of the Preparatory Commission for the International Criminal Court, Addendum Part I, Finalized Draft Text of the Rules of Procedure and Evidence, 2.11.2000 (PCNICC/2000/1/Add.1).

[48] Report of the First Session (Official Records of the Assembly of States Parties to the Rome Statute of the International Criminal Court), ASP first session (ICC-ASP/1/3) 10 et seq.; further on the RPE, see Fabricio Guariglia, "The rules of procedure and evidence of the International Criminal Court: a new development in international adjudication of individual criminal responsibility" in Cassese/Gaeta/Jones, *supra* note 11, 1111, 1111 et seq.

[49] Proposal submitted by Australia, Draft Rules of RPE of the ICC, 26.1.1999 (PCNICC/1999/DP.1), and Proposal by France, General outline of the RPE, 1.2.1999 (PCNICC/1999/DP.2, DP.3, DP.6, DP.7 and Add.1, DP.8 and Add.1 and 2, and DP.10 and Add.1).

[50] Pellet, in Cassese/Gaeta/Jones, *supra* note 38, 1065.

- 5. Investigation and prosecution (rules 104–130);
- 6. Trial procedure (rules 131–144);
- 7. Penalties (rules 145–148);
- 8. Appeal and revision (rules 149–161);
- 9. Offences and misconduct against the Court (rules 162–172);
- 10. Compensation to an arrested or convicted person (rules 173–175);
- 11. International cooperation and judicial assistance (rules 176–197);
- 12. Enforcement (rules 198–225).

Article 51 (1) grants the ASP the power to modify the RPE by a two-thirds majority. Article 51 is a new approach compared to the systems adopted by the two *ad hoc* tribunals (article 15 ICTY Statute and article 14 ICTR Statute) whereby judges shall adopt the RPE.[51] On the one hand, article 51's clear rejection of the common law "judge-legislator" sacrifices legislative flexibility required to ensure efficient proceedings. Excessive regulation and normative rigidity rule out potential alternatives and limit the scope of interpretation.[52] On the other hand, the ICC approach generates great benefits in terms of legitimacy, stability and transparency which ultimately outweigh potential problems.[53] After all, the judges can draw up provisional rules in urgent cases where the RPE does not provide for a specific situation before the Court (article 51 (3)). The RPE have to be consistent with the Statute (article 51 (4)), and in the event of conflict between the Statute and the RPE, the Statute shall prevail (article 51 (5)).[54] Regarding this research, rules 46–50 and rules 104–110 will be of outstanding importance since they straighten out the procedure of articles 15 and 53.

The reference to the case law of the Court is fairly ambiguous.[55] Article 21 (2) authorizes the ICC to "apply principles and rules of law as interpreted in its previous decisions". This provision does not obligate adherence to prior decisions through a binding rule of *stare decisis,* but rather permits the judges to take their prior decision into consideration.[56] In fact, it re-

---

[51] See ICTY Rules of Procedure and Evidence, 10.12.2009 (IT/32/Rev.44), which have been amended forty-three times. For the ICTR see ICTR Rules of Procedure and Evidence, 14.3.2008, which have been amended seventeen times.

[52] "Excessive regulations and normative rigidity combined can suffocate the Court," cf. Guariglia, in Lee, *supra* note 14, 1123.

[53] Cf. Guariglia, in Lee, *supra* note 14, 1115 et seq., 1133; Ambos, *supra* note 26, § 6 mn 49.

[54] On article 51 (5) see Bitti, in Stahn/Sluiter, *supra* note 38, 290–1.

[55] Pellet, in Cassese/Gaeta/Jones, *supra* note 38, 1054, 1065.

[56] McAuliffe deGuzman, in Triffterer, *supra* note 37, article 21, mn 20.

flects a compromise between the common law approach to binding precedent, and the civil law concept that precedent has no binding effect.[57] As to the scope of the provision, the Court "may" take previous decisions into account and thus acts in a fully discretionary fashion: the case law is a subsidiary means for the determination of the rules of law.[58] Existing case law was applied very soon on the jurisprudence of the ICC; yet, it remains a discretionary choice, and, in particular, the case law of Appeals Chambers does not seem to be placed higher than the case law of other Chambers of the Court.[59]

Numerous other procedural provisions not mentioned in article 21 were drafted and now form part of the Court's criminal procedure. In accordance with article 52, the judges adopted the Regulations of the Court, which consist of 126 regulations.[60] Pursuant to article 52 (1), the Regulations are intended to govern the routine functioning of the Court; the separation of the RPE and Court Regulations is a novelty without precedent in international criminal procedure.[61] The Regulations of the Court are subdivided into nine chapters:

- 1. General provisions (regulations 1–8);
- 2. Composition and administration of the Court (regulations 9–19);
- 3. Proceedings before the Court (regulations 20–66);
- 4. Counsel issues and legal assistance (regulations 67–85);
- 5. Victim participation and reparation (regulations 86–88);

57 McAuliffe deGuzman, in Triffterer, *supra* note 37, article 21, mn 20; Pellet, in Cassese/Gaeta/Jones, *supra* note 38, 1066.

58 Pellet, in Cassese/Gaeta/Jones, *supra* note 38, 1066. However, the former author – at least partly inaccurately – criticizes McAuliffe deGuzman, in Triffterer, *supra* note 37, article 21, mn 20 et seq., when he states that she "ignores the discretionary nature of the recourse of precedent." She [McAuliffe deGuzman] repeatedly acknowledges the discretion of the Court, see article 21, mn 21: "[...], in their discretion, to accord precedential value [...]," mn 22: "[...] international criminal law requires a certain amount of discretion [...]," and mn 7: "[t]he judges are also permitted, though not required, to accord precedential value to their interpretation of law in previous decisions." Yet, Pellet's comparison between articles 21 (2) and 38 (1) (d) ICJ Statute is more convincing then the comparison with article 59 ICJ Statute submitted by McAuliffe deGuzman. Pellet draws a persuasive analogy between common uses of case law as subsidiary means for the rules of law in articles 21 (2) and 38 (1) (d) ICJ Statute.

59 Bitti, in Stahn/Sluiter, *supra* note 38, 292–3.

60 On the Regulations see Kreß, *supra* note 41, 540 et seq.; Report on the activities of the Court, ASP fourth session, 16.9.2005 (ICC-ASP/4/16) para. 39.

61 Hans-Jörg Behrens/Christopher Staker, "Article 52" in Triffterer, *supra* note 37, article 52, mn 3.

- 6. Detention matters (regulations 89–106);
- 7. Cooperation and enforcement (regulations 107–118);
- 8. Removal from office and disciplinary measures (regulations 119–125);
- 9. Adoption of the code of judicial ethics (regulation 126).

The formula "in accordance with the Statute and the RPE" indicates that the Court Regulations are subsidiary and have to be in conformity with this primary set of rules. The drafters saw no need for a repetition of article 51 (5).[62] Most notably for the upcoming inquiry, Court Regulations 45 and 49, which deal with matters around article 15, as well as Court Regulation 48, which addresses questions around article 53, must be examined further.

Additional sets of regulations had to be drafted with regard to the RPE. Rule 9 obliges ("shall put in place") the Prosecutor to generate regulations for the management and administration of his office. In June 2003 the OTP published Draft Regulations,[63] and in April 2009 the OTP Regulations were finalized and subdivided into three chapters: 1. General provisions; 2. Administration of the Office; and 3. Operation of the Office.[64] Diverse OTP Regulations will be of importance for the study at hand, most of all OTP Regulations 21–24 (handling of information and evidence) and 25–31 (preliminary examination and evaluation of information). In addition, the former (provisional) Regulations on Analysis of Referrals and Communications (hereinafter Provisional Analysis Regulations) will be consulted.[65] They partly overlap with the finalized OTP Regulations, but are more precise on matters relating to the procedure of analysis adopted by the OTP and thus, in my view, fill in the gaps.[66]

Rule 14 (1) foresees that the Registrar shall put in place regulations governing the operation of the Registry. In compliance with this rule, the Reg-

62 Behrens/Staker, in Triffterer, *supra* note 61, article 52, mn 7.

63 Draft Regulations of the OTP (hereinafter Draft Regulations OTP 2003), 3.6.2003 (ICC-OTP 2003).

64 For the OTP Regulations see *supra* note 25.

65 For the Provisional Analysis Regulations see Annex paper, *supra* note 27, 7 et seq.

66 The Regulations have been developed for the purpose of governing the handling and analysis of information submitted by referrals and communications only, whereas the OTP Regulations deal with OTP related questions in a more general manner. Although the OTP states that the Analysis Regulation will be applied provisionally, pending completion of the Office regulations (Annex paper, *supra* note 27, 7), it is submitted that the Analysis Regulations can be used to outline the precise procedure adopted by the OTP. In my opinion, they can be applied with regard to issues not dealt with by the OTP Regulations, and to the extent that they are not contradictory to them.

ulations of the Registry were adopted and entered into force on the same day (3 March 2006).[67] They contain 223 provisions divided into five chapters: 1. General provisions; 2. Proceedings before the Court; 3. Responsibilities of the Registrar relating to victims and witnesses; 4. Counsel issues and legal assistance; and 5. Detention matters. By reason that these Regulations mainly address administrative matters they have marginal relevance to this study; only Registry Regulations 20 and 21 might be significant to the differentiation between situations and cases. Their small pertinence for the subsequent analysis notwithstanding, further ancillary instruments have to be mentioned briefly:

- Code of Professional Conduct for Counsel;[68]
- Code of Judicial Ethics;[69]
- Staff Regulations;[70]
- Staff Rules of the ICC (Annex to ICC/AI/2005/03);[71]
- Financial Regulations and Rules;[72]
- Agreement of Privileges and Immunity of the ICC;[73]
- Negotiated Relationship Agreement between the ICC and the UN (hereinafter Relationship Agreement);[74]
- Headquarter Agreement between the International Criminal Court and the Host State;[75]

---

[67] Regulations of the Registry, adoption/entry into force 3.3.2006 (ICC-BD/03-01-06), amended 25.9.2006 (ICC-BD/03-01-06-Rev1), available at: <www2.icc-cpi.int/Menus/ICC/Legal+Texts+and+Tools/>.

[68] Adoption 2.12.2005/entry into force 1.1.2006 (ICC-ASP/4/3/Res.1), available at: <www2.icc-cpi.int/Menus/ICC/Legal+Texts+and+Tools/>.

[69] Adoption/entry into force 9.3.2005 (ICC-BD/02-01-05), available at: <www2.icc-cpi.int/Menus/ICC/Legal+Texts+and+Tools/>.

[70] Adoption/entry into force 12.9.2003 (ICC-ASP/2/Res.2), available at: <www2.icc-cpi.int/Menus/ICC/Legal+Texts+and+Tools/>.

[71] Adoption 3.12.2005/entry into force 21.4.2005 (ICC-ASP/4/3), available at: <www2.icc-cpi.int/Menus/ICC/Legal+Texts+and+Tools/Official+Journal/>.

[72] Adoption/entry into force 9.9.2002 (ICC-ASP/1/3), see also the amendment to the Financial Regulations and Rules, adoption 3.12.2005/entry into force 3.12.2005 (ICC-ASP/4/3/Res.10), available at: <www2.icc-cpi.int/Menus/ICC/Legal+Texts+and+Tools/>.

[73] Adoption 9.9.2002/entry into force 22.7.2004 (ICC-ASP/1/3), available at: <www2.icc-cpi.int/Menus/ICC/Legal+Texts+and+Tools/>. Currently, the APIC has 63 ratifications, see <www.iccnow.org>.

[74] Adoption/entry into force 4.10.2004 (ICC-ASP/3/Res.1), available at: <www2.icc-cpi.int/Menus/ICC/Legal+Texts+and+Tools/>. On the Relationship Agreement see Daniel Heilmann, *Die Effektivität des Internationalen Strafgerichtshofs* (Nomos, Frankfurt a. M. 2006) 67 et seq.

- Regulations of the Trust Fund for Victims;[76]
- Agreement between the ICC and the International Committee of the Red Cross on Visits to Persons deprived of Liberty Pursuant to the Jurisdiction of the ICC;[77]
- Agreement between the ICC and the European Union on Cooperation and Assistance;[78]
- Agreement between the ICC and the Federal Government of Austria on the enforcement of sentences of the International Criminal Court;[79]
- Agreement between the Government of the United Kingdom of Great Britain and Northern Ireland and the International Criminal Court on the enforcement of sentences;[80]
- Memorandum of Understanding regarding Administrative Arrangements between the ICC and the Special Court for Sierra Leone (hereinafter SCSL);[81]
- Memorandum of Understanding between the International Criminal Court and the Asian-African Legal Consultative Organization;[82]
- Security arrangements between the EU Council General Secretariat Security Office (GSCSO) and The European Commission Security Directorate (ECSD) and the International Criminal Court Security and Safety Section (ICC-SSS) for the protection of classified information exchanged between the EU and the ICC.[83]

Only the Statute, the Elements of Crimes and the RPE are mentioned in article 21 (1); however, a procedural framework is put up by secondary

---

[75] Adoption 7.6.2007/entry into force 1.3.2008 (ICC-BD/04-01-08), available at: <www2.icc-cpi.int/Menus/ICC/Legal+Texts+and+Tools/Official+Journal/>.

[76] Adoption/entry into force 3.12.2005 (ICC-ASP/4/3/Res.3), available at: <www2.icc-cpi.int/Menus/ICC/Legal+Texts+and+Tools/Official+Journal/>.

[77] Adoption 29.3.2006/entry into force 13.4.2006 (ICC-PRES/02-01-06), available at: <www2.icc-cpi.int/Menus/ICC/Legal+Texts+and+Tools/Official+Journal/>.

[78] Adoption 10.4.2006/entry into force 1.5.2006 (ICC-PRES/01-01-06), available at: <www2.icc-cpi.int/Menus/ICC/Legal+Texts+and+Tools/Official+Journal/>.

[79] Adoption 27.10.2005/entry into force 26.11.2005 (ICC-PRES/01-01-05), available at: <www2.icc-cpi.int/Menus/ICC/Legal+Texts+and+Tools/Official+Journal/>.

[80] Adoption 8.11.2007/entry into force 8.12.2007 (ICC-PRES/04-01-07), available at: <www2.icc-cpi.int/Menus/ICC/Legal+Texts+and+Tools/Official+Journal/>.

[81] Adoption/entry into force 13.4.2006 (ICC-PRES/03-01-06), available at: <www2.icc-cpi.int/Menus/ICC/Legal+Texts+and+Tools/Official+Journal/>.

[82] Adoption 5.2.2008/entry into force 5.2.2008 (ICC-PRES/05-01-08), available at: <www.icc-cpi.int/Menus/ICC/Legal+Texts+and+Tools/Official+Journal/>.

[83] Entry into force 1.3.2008 (ICC/GSCSO/ECSD), available at: <http://register.consilium.europa.eu/pdf/en/08/st08/st08349-re01.en08.pdf>.

sources like the Court Regulations, the Registry Regulations, and the OTP Regulations. Arranged in a hierarchy, the Statute stands above all and, subsequently, the Elements of Crimes and RPE have to be applied. All secondary sources are not sources in the strict sense of article 21, but assist in the application of the primary sources. Admittedly, neither article 21 nor any other provision of the Statute addresses the question of conflict with regard to the legal system as a whole. But article 51 (5) clarifies the primacy of the Statute *vis-à-vis* the RPE, thereto article 9 (3) determines that the Elements of Crimes have to be in accordance with the Statute, and article 52 (1) states that the Court Regulations shall be in accordance with the Statute and the RPE. The interrelationship of the different regulations is touched upon in article 52 (2), rule 9, and rule 14 (1). Article 52 (2) obliges the judges to consult with the Prosecutor and the Registry for the elaboration of their regulations and any amendments thereto; according to rules 9 and 14 (1), the Prosecutor and the Registry shall consult with each other on any matters that may affect the operation of the opposite organ. In conclusion, the proper law of the ICC is composed of the Statute as the fundamental legal basis, followed by the Elements of Crimes and RPE, and then the Regulations of the Court, Registry and OTP.

2. The external general law sources

Where appropriate, the Court shall apply treaties and the principles and rules of international law, including the principles of the international law of armed conflicts (article 21 (1) (b)). The term "where appropriate" expresses the discretion of the judges in order to determine when treaties or principles and rules are applicable.[84] The applicable treaties are not further indicated, and legal commentators provide conflicting opinions on the issue.[85] With regard to the rules of international law, legal scholars agree that its integral part is more or less equivalent to customary international law in the meaning of article 38 (1) (b).[86] They, however, strongly disagree

[84] In a similar vein, McAuliffe deGuzman, in Triffterer, *supra* note 37, article 21, mn 9; also *Prosecutor v. Lubanga,* Decision regarding the practices used to prepare and familiarise witnesses for giving testimony at trial, 30.11.2007 (ICC-01/04-01/06-1049) para. 44.

[85] McAuliffe deGuzman, in Triffterer, *supra* note 37, article 21, mn 10, who identifies the ICCPR and the Geneva Conventions; Pellet, in Cassese/Gaeta/Jones, *supra* note 38, 1068 et seq., declares this "not very convincing."

[86] Pellet, in Cassese/Gaeta/Jones, *supra* note 38, 1071; McAuliffe deGuzman, in Triffterer, *supra* note 37, article 21, mn 13; Ambos, *supra* note 26, § 6 mn 5; Schabas, *supra* note 27, 196. For the relevance of ICTY and ICTR precedent under this provision see Volker Nerlich, "The status of ICTY and ICTR precedent in proceedings before the ICC" in Stahn/Sluiter, *supra* note 5, 305, 312 et seq.

on the importance of the inclusion of the word "principles," which some consider to be a distinct source of law:[87] a view opposed by one commentator.[88] A modern approach, that acknowledges the twofold origin of principles as deriving from a comparison of national laws and international legal conscience, leads to an assimilation of customary international law and general principles in the sense of "principles and rules of international law" under article 21 (1) (b).[89] Complementary, "general principles of law derived by the Court from national laws of legal systems of the world, including as appropriate, the national laws of States that would normally exercise jurisdiction over the crime" can be utilized (article 21 (1) (c)).[90] Article 21 (1) (b) and (c) thus provide subsidiary second and third sources of law. However, the Appeals Chamber in Lubanga held that the application of both is subject to the same condition: the existence of a gap in the ICC Statute.[91]

Article 21 (3) states that judges must apply the law in consistency with internationally recognized human rights. The norm raises difficult legal problems; it might even create a "super-legality" by codifying (or recognizing) that those human rights take precedence over all other applicable rules.[92] If certain provisions of the Statute or its supplementary texts infringe upon such "internationally recognized human rights," the judges are authorized to hold such a statutory norm inapplicable.[93] Thereby, the judges would first have to define the exact content of article 21 (3), mainly because the ambit is extended beyond fundamental human rights to all internationally recognized human rights.[94] Apart from the controversial interpretation to set aside an article of the Statute, article 21 (3) surely gives the judges a flexible

---

[87] McAuliffe deGuzman, in Triffterer, *supra* note 37, article 21, mn 12; Ambos, *supra* note 26, § 6 mn 7.

[88] Pellet, in Cassese/Gaeta/Jones, *supra* note 38, 1071, holds the opinion that article 21 (1) (b) refers exclusively to customary international law. In the same vein, Melloh, *supra* note 38, 198.

[89] Ambos, *supra* note 26, § 6 mn 7; similarly McAuliffe deGuzman, in Triffterer, *supra* note 37, article 21, mn 12. On general principles see exhaustively Fabián Raimondo, *General principles of law in the decisions of International Criminal Courts and Tribunals* (Martinus Nijhoff Publishers, Leiden 2008).

[90] On this issue see "comparative law methodology," Part I, C., III.

[91] *Prosecutor v. Lubanga,* Judgment of the appeal of Mr. Thomas Lubanga Dyilo against the decision on the defence challenge to the jurisdiction of the court pursuant to article 19 (2) (a) of the Statute of 3 October 2006, 14.12.2006 (ICC-01/04-01/06-772) para. 34; Bitti, in Stahn/Sluiter, *supra* note 38, 294 et seq.

[92] Pellet, in Cassese/Gaeta/Jones, *supra* note 38, 1079 et seq.

[93] Mahnoush Arsanjani, "The Rome Statute of the International Criminal Court" (1999) 93 AJIL 22, 28–9; Pellet, in Cassese/Gaeta/Jones, *supra* note 38, 1081.

[94] Pellet, in Cassese/Gaeta/Jones, *supra* note 38, 1081.

source of law that might, for instance, provide additional procedural remedies.[95] In future practice, the scope of article 21 (3) will depend on the Judges' understanding of "internationally recognized human rights."[96]

3. Intermediary conclusion

The Court's international criminal procedure has now been codified almost completely, and its complexity has no precedent.[97] The ICC has opened five formal investigations on the basis of article 53 (1),[98] its upcoming case law will provide more guidance on the application of divergent legal sources. With regard to this study, the Statute will always be seeded number one, and interpretations will be carried out accordingly. Besides the additional legal texts of the RPE and the three sets of regulations, official OTP policy papers, which are not legal sources but form the overall strategy of the OTP according to OTP Regulation 14 (1) and (2), can be used to approach the practice of pre-investigations.[99] Needless to say, the OTP's

[95] Bitti, in Stahn/Sluiter, *supra* note 38, 304.

[96] Bitti, in Stahn/Sluiter, *supra* note 38, 300 et seq.; Sheppard, *supra* note 38, 48–9, 71.

[97] Kreß, *supra* note 41, 543.

[98] See above Part I, A. and below Part III, B., I. For Kenya (and the relationship article 15–53) see *Situation in Kenya*, Decision pursuant to article 15, *supra* note 6, paras. 24–5, 12–3.

[99] Four position papers have been published by the OTP, namely: (1) the Paper on some policy issues before the Office of the Prosecutor (hereinafter Policy paper), September 2003 (ICC-OTP 2003); (2) the Annex paper, *supra* note 27; (3) the Policy paper on victim participation, and (4) the Policy paper on the interests of justice (hereinafter Interests of justice paper), September 2007 (ICC-OTP-2007), all available at: <www2.icc-cpi.int/Menus/ICC/Struc ture+of+the+Court/Office+of+the+Prosecutor/Policies+and+Strategies/>. These papers are based on OTP regulation 14 (2). An additional policy paper on the Criteria for selection of situations and cases (hereinafter Selection paper), Draft for discussion, 2006 (ICC-OTP), is expected to be published by late 2010. On the policy papers see further Paul Seils, "The selection and prioritization of cases by the Office of the Prosecutor of the International Criminal Court" in Morten Bergsmo (ed.), *Criteria for prioritizing and selecting core international crimes cases,* Forum for International Criminal and Humanitarian Law (FICHL) (International Peace Research Institute, Oslo 2009) 55, 55 et seq.; critical on the current policy practice Nidal Nabil Jurdi, "The prosecutorial interpretation of the complementarity principle: does it really contribute to ending impunity on the national level?" (2010) 10 ICLR 73, 74. In addition, the official transcripts of the first and second public hearing on the Prosecutor's main policies will be screened and included where appropriate, see <www2.icc-cpi.int/Menus/ICC/Structure+of+the+Court/Office+of+the+Prosecutor/Network+with+Partners/Public+Hearings/>. To a certain extent, they form the "drafting history" of the OTP's policy. Further on the OTP strategy see Luis Moreno-Ocampo, "The International Criminal Court in motion," in Stahn/Sluiter, *supra* note 5, 13, 13 et seq.; most recently Prosecutorial Strategy 2009–2012, OTP, The Hague, 1.2.2010; also Part IV, B., II., 4.

strategy as reflected in its policy and strategy papers must be scrutinized carefully *vis-à-vis* the ICC Statute.

II. Rules of interpretation

The interpretation of articles 15 and 53, as with all other provisions of the ICC Statute, must follow the rules of interpretation in article 21 (3) thereof, as well as the general principles of interpretation provided in articles 31, 32, and 33 of the Vienna Convention on the Law of Treaties.[100] According to article 31 VCLT, a Treaty shall be interpreted in "good faith in accordance with the ordinary meaning to be given to the terms of the treaty in their context and in the light of its object and purpose." No greater weight shall be given to one of the three main elements of treaty interpretation to the detriment of the others: the text, its context, and the object and purpose of the treaty.[101] The application of the means of interpretation is understood as "a single combined operation."[102] This combined operation notwithstanding, "the starting point of interpretation is the elucidation of the meaning of the text, and it is not an investigation *ab initio* into the intentions of the parties."[103] It is important to note that the context for the purpose of interpretation shall comprise the text of the treaty, including its Preamble (article 31 (2) VCLT). Other documents connected with the treaty can be taken into consideration of the "context" according to article 31 (2) and (3) VCLT. The RPE, for instance, can be deemed an "instrument which was made between all the parties in connection with the conclusion of the treaty (article 31 (2) (b) VCLT)."

---

[100] Vienna Convention of the Law of Treaties (hereinafter VCLT), adoption 23.5.1969/entry into force 27.1.1980, UN Treaty Series, Vol. 1155, 331. Articles 31 and 32 VCLT reflect customary international law, Anthony Aust, *Modern treaty law and practice* (CUP, Cambridge 2000) 11 with fn. 22, 186 with fn. 8. On the principles of interpretation also Christopher Keith Hall, "Suggestions concerning International Criminal Court prosecutorial policy and strategy and external relations," Contribution to an expert consultation process on general issues relevant to the ICC Office of the Prosecutor, 28.3.2003, 1, 8 et seq.; Kai Ambos, *Der Allgemeine Teil des Völkerstrafrechts,* 2. Aufl. (Duncker & Humblot, Berlin 2004) 378 et seq.; Franziska Eckelmans, "The first jurisprudence of the Appeals Chamber of the ICC" in Stahn/Sluiter, *supra* note 5, 527, 530–1.

[101] Cf. the commentaries on Draft Articles 27 and 28, Draft Articles on the Law of Treaties with commentaries, ILC 18th session, *Yearbook of the ILC,* Vol. II (1966) 218; Aust, *supra* note 100, 185.

[102] Draft Articles on the Law of Treaties with commentaries, *supra* note 101, 219.

[103] Draft Articles on the Law of Treaties with commentaries, *supra* note 101, 220.

Only in a supplementary fashion, the *travaux préparatoires* may be examined in order to confirm the results from an application of article 31 VCLT. The *travaux préparatoires* can also be consulted to determine the meaning when the operation of article 31 VCLT leaves the meaning ambiguous or obscure (article 32 (a) VCLT), or leads to a result, which is manifestly absurd or unreasonable (article 32 (b) VCLT). As a rule, the ordinary meaning of a provision must prevail. Drafting history documents only provide for means of aid, not for alternative or autonomous means of interpretation, and article 32 (a) and (b) of the VCLT have to be seen as very limited exceptions.[104] The *travaux* is not defined further,[105] but is generally understood to include written material.[106]

The ICC Statute has been authenticated in Arabic, Chinese, English, French, Russian, and Spanish (article 128), so that article 33 VCLT applies. In principle, the texts are equally authoritative,[107] except in the case when a comparison of the authentic texts discloses a difference of meaning, which the application of articles 31 and 32 does not remove, the meaning, which best reconciles the texts, having regard to the object and purpose of the treaty, has to be adopted (article 33 (3) VCLT). In this survey, the English text will be used as the point of origin. It will be compared, where appropriate, with the French and Spanish version, but not with the Arabic, Chinese, and Russian version.[108]

---

[104] Draft Articles on the Law of Treaties with commentaries, *supra* note 101, 223.

[105] Draft Articles on the Law of Treaties with commentaries, *supra* note 101, 223.

[106] Such as successive drafts of the treaty, conference records, explanatory statements by an expert consultant at a codification conference, uncontested interpretative statements by the chairman of a drafting committee and ILC Commentaries, cf. Aust, *supra* note 100, 198.

[107] From a factual point of view, it can be argued that the English version must be ranked higher than other "authenticated" versions of the ICC Statute since negotiations and drafting documents were mainly achieved in English and did form the basis for compromise, see Ambos, *supra* note 100, 381. Contrary, Emanuela Fronza/Ezequiel Malarino, "Die Auslegung von multilingualen strafrechtlichen Texten am Beispiel des Statuts für den Internationalen Strafgerichtshof," (2006) 118 ZStW 927, 940–1; *id.,* "Problemas de determinación de la norma penal y soluciones de interpretación en textos penales plurilingües en el ejemplo del Estatuto de Roma" in Kai Ambos/Ezequiel Malarino/Jan Woischnik (eds.), *Temas actuales del derecho penal internacional: contribuciones de América latina, Alemania y Espana* (Konrad-Adenauer-Stiftung, Berlin 2005) 61, 65–6, 79 et seq.

[108] Four different levels of language problems can be encountered, cf. Hans Bevers/Chantal Joubert, *Schengen investigated* (Kluwer Law International, The Hague, London, Boston, 1996) 10 et seq.

III. Comparative law methodology

Article 21 (1) (c) refers to the general principles in a sense of a traditional comparative law perspective and as a subsidiary source. This involves a triple operation: i) a comparison between national systems, ii) a search for common principles, and, iii) their transposition to the international sphere.[109]

The comparison does not necessarily include all national legal systems, but rather a representative majority, which includes the principal legal systems.[110] At first glance, these can probably be reduced to civil law, common law, and perhaps Sharia law.[111] The identification of legal families is, however, far more complex, and one has to pay attention to hybrid systems of law, as well as many particularities. Zweigert/Kötz group the legal systems differently: they distinguish between the Romanistic family, the Germanic family, the Nordic family, and the Common law family.[112] The law of the

---

[109] Pellet, in Cassese/Gaeta/Jones, *supra* note 38, 1073; Jan-Christoph Nemitz, *Strafzumessung im Völkerstrafrecht* (Ed. Iuscrim, Freiburg i. Brsg. 2002) 42 et seq. For an implicit application of the principle of "no appeal unless conferred by statute" see *Prosecutor v. Kony et al.*, Decision on the Prosecutor's position on the decision of Pre-Trial Chamber II to redact factual descriptions of crimes from warrants of arrest, motion for reconsideration and motion for clarification, 28.10.2006 (ICC-01/04-01/05–60) para. 18; reaffirmed in *Prosecutor v. Lubanga,* Decision on the prosecution motion for reconsideration and, in the alternative, leave to appeal, 23.6.2006 (ICC-01/04-01/06-166) para. 10; also Raimondo, *supra* note 89, 159.

[110] The French text is much clearer, referring to "les lois nationales représentant les différents systèmes juridiques de droit." See also *Situation in DRC,* Prosecutor's application for extraordinary review of Pre-Trial Chamber I's 31 March 2006 decision denying leave to appeal, 2.5.2006 (ICC-01/04-143), para. 16; Pellet, in Cassese/Gaeta/Jones, *supra* note 38, 1073; Bitti, in Stahn/Sluiter, *supra* note 38, 299–300; Melloh, *supra* note 38, 209–210. For the ICTY see *Prosecutor v. Erdemović,* Appeal's judgment, joint separate opinion of Judge McDonald and Judge Vohrah, 7.10.1997 (IT-96-22-A) para. 57: "[…] will necessarily not involve a direct comparison of the specific rules of each of the world's legal systems, but will instead involve a survey of those jurisdictions whose jurisprudence is, as a practical matter, accessible to us in an effort to discern a general trend, policy or principle underlying the concrete rules of that jurisdiction […]". However, the survey may not be too limited (citing practice in two countries, and, in addition, the lack of any references from the Romano-Germanic legal system), cf. *Prosecutor v. Lubanga,* Decision regarding the practices used to prepare and familiarise witnesses, *supra* note 84, para. 41.

[111] *Situation in DRC*, Prosecutor's application for extraordinary review, *supra* note 110, para. 16; Pellet, in Cassese/Gaeta/Jones, *supra* note 38, 1074.

[112] Konrad Zweigert/Hein Kötz, *Introduction to comparative law,* 3rd edition (OUP, Clarendon 1998) 73; critical on the families' approach Helmut Heiss, "Hierarchische Rechtskreiseinteilung" (2001) 100 *Zeitschrift für Vergleichende Rechtswissenschaft* (2001) 396, 397 with various references in fn. 5.

People's Republic of China, Japanese law, Islamic law, and Hindu law, as well as a new emerging family of African law, are equally mentioned as possible categories.[113] It is self-evident that not all national systems can be included, but the methodology to achieve a representative sample needs further adjustment.[114] Beyond applying the concrete rules found in national law, the principles underlying these rules have to be identified.[115] The discovered principle has to be transposable to the international legal order. Article 21 (1) (c) permits the judges, as appropriate, to consider the laws of the States that would normally exercise jurisdiction. This specific reference to national laws does not, however, stipulate their direct application. Legal constructs on the basis of national laws should not be applied automatically and imported mechanically into international criminal proceedings.[116] Given the linkage to the former mentioned general principles ("general principles [...] including, [...], the national laws of States"), the reference rather emphasizes preference for an inclusion of the affected State(s)'s laws as part of an over-all comparative analysis in the discretion ("as appropriate") of the judges.[117] As to which States should be considered as "normally exercising jurisdiction" no further guidance is given, but at least two bases of jurisdiction (territoriality and nationality) are widely recognized.[118]

For comparative research the three basic questions can be narrowed down to "why, what and how" do we compare?[119] In spite of the decisive

113 Zweigert/Kötz, *supra* note 112, 63 et seq. On the importance to include African countries Raimondo, *supra* note 89, 161.

114 According to Ambos, in Stahn/van Herik, *supra* note 11, 171, the method of comparative law as employed by international courts and tribunals requires improvement, particulary with regard to the national systems to be examined.

115 Ambos, *supra* note 26, § 5, mn 8; Mireille Delmas-Marty, "The contribution of comparative law to a pluralist conception of international law" (2003) 1 JICJ 13, 18 et seq. ("hybridization"); Carl-Friedrich Stuckenberg, *Vorstudien zu Vorsatz und Irrtum im Völkerstrafrecht* (De Gruyter, Berlin 2007) 25; *Situation in DRC*, Prosecutor's application for extraordinary review, *supra* note 110, para. 17. Contrary to the Prosecutor's application, the Judges did not find a general principle of law allowing for extraordinary review of a lower decision denying leave to appeal, cf. *Situation in DRC,* Judgment on the Prosecutor's application for extraordinary review of Pre-Trial Chamber I's 31 March 2006 decision denying leave to appeal, 13.7.2006 (ICC-01/04-168) para. 32. Most notably, the Judges stated that article 82 does not contain a *lacuna* that needs to be filled in by general principles.

116 *Prosecutor v. Erdemović,* Appeal's judgment, separate and dissenting opinion of Judge Cassese, 7.10.1997 (IT-96-22-A) para. 2; Pellet, in Cassese/Gaeta/Jones, *supra* note 38, 1076; Stuckenberg, *supra* note 115, 26 (no "domestic analogy").

117 McAuliffe deGuzman, in Triffterer, *supra* note 37, article 21, mn 18; van Heeck, *supra* note 26, 98.

118 McAuliffe deGuzman, in Triffterer, *supra* note 37, article 21, mn 18.

119 Esin Örücü, *The enigma of comparative law* (Martinus Nijhoff Publishers, Leiden, Boston 2004) 33 et seq., 41 et seq., 51 et seq.

role of comparative law, no entire comparative study will be conducted at hand. Rather, the procedure as laid down by article 21 is followed, i.e. whenever an interpretation of the international legal sources does not rule out ambiguity, comparative research might fill in the gaps. For the sake of clarity a working hypothesis and the analysis of different countries are included in Annex II, and where appropriate reference is made to the findings of this comparative survey. The "why" can thus be answered with reference to the ICC's primary sources and their partial vagueness. "What" to compare is difficult to answer, bearing in mind the difficulties to arrive at a representative majority of countries. On the macro-comparative level, the distinction between civil law and common law is taken as a general basis, while for the choice of countries additional other factors are taken into consideration (Romanistic, Germanic, and Nordic family; Chinese, Hindu, and Sharia law; African law; current and potential situations pending before the ICC[120]). Regarding the micro-comparative level the question must be addressed: "what is law?" From a traditional approach, a positivist looks at statutory rules, and in addition case law and pertinent legal documents, contrary to a broad approach, which embraces the social, cultural, economic, and political environment.[121] Practically, the positive law is more accessible than broader circumstances, and comparative research is inherently difficult, even if limited to these positivist sources. Broader factors will be included whenever possible, particularly with regard to local justice mechanisms, and for the purpose of comparative research "a legal source is everything that shapes or helps to shape the law."[122] Another question is how to compare, i.e. what method shall be employed in comparative law research.[123] With regard to this survey, the basic methodological principle of functional-

---

[120] In my opinion, the inclusion of this factor is strengthened by article 21 (1) (c), which allows for the consideration of the laws of States which would normally exercise jurisdiction; see *Prosecutor v. Lubanga,* Decision on the practices of witness familiarisation and witness proofing, 8.11.2006 (ICC-01/04-01/06-679) para. 35: "pursuant to article 21 (1) (c) of the Statute, [...] including, as appropriate, the national laws of the Democratic Republic of the Congo ("the DRC")." However, the Judges did not examine the laws of the DRC, which would have contributed to ascertain the content of "appropriateness" under article 21 (1) (c); similarly Raimondo, *supra* note 89, 164.

[121] Örücü, *supra* note 119, 47 et seq. On the difficulties to establish the sources of law of another legal system cf. Stefan Vogenauer, "Sources of law and legal method in comparative law" in Reiman/Zimmermann, *supra* note 24, 877 et seq.

[122] Vogenauer, *supra* note 121, 879, who quotes and translates a statement by Konrad Zweigert. *Prosecutor v. Lubanga,* Decision on the practices of witness familiarisation, *supra* note 120, paras. 38–9, encourages a broad approach because the PTC included codes of conduct of the Bar Council when assessing national laws of article 21 (1) (c).

[123] Örücü, *supra* note 119, 51 et seq.

ity is used.[124] According to this method the point of comparison must be phrased in functional terms, i.e., the *tertium comparationis* is not a legal term or institution, but a pertinent set of issues. All principles that contribute to a solution of the identified problem will thereby be taken into account.

IV. Conclusion

The methodology chosen for this study will rely on the common interpretation of article 21. The ICC Statute, the RPE, and other relevant provisions will be interpreted, following a literal, systematic, and teleological approach. The drafting history may be examined in order to confirm the results or for determining ambiguous meanings. As a complement, principles of international law will be discerned. A twofold analysis will form the basic approach to these rules and principles, first looking at international (criminal) law jurisprudence and secondly conducting a national law comparative research.[125]

[124] On this principle see Zweigert/Kötz, *supra* note 112, 34 et seq.; Melloh, *supra* note 38, 208–9. A critical analysis of the methods is presented by Ralf Michaels Durham, "The functional method of comparative law" in Reiman/Zimmermann, *supra* note 24, 339 et seq.; further Ambos, supra note 26, § 5 mn 8, who links the functional approach to a value based comparison (*wertende Rechtsvergleichung*).

[125] For a similar approach, looking first at the jurisprudence of the ICTY, the ICTR, and the Special Court for Sierra Leone (hereinafter SCSL), and then conducting a comparison of national laws, see *Prosecutor v. Lubanga,* Decision on the practices of witness familiarisation, *supra* note 120, paras. 30 et seq.

Part II

Structure of the Office of the Prosecutor

A. Overview: Structure of the Court

The ICC is an independent, permanent court with the power to exercise its jurisdiction over persons for the most serious crimes of international concern (genocide, crimes against humanity, war crimes) and is seated in The Hague (articles 1, 3). It is not an organ of the UN, but brought into relationship with it through an agreement.[126] The Court is composed of four organs: the Presidency, the Judicial Divisions, the Office of the Prosecutor, and the Registry (article 34).

The Presidency is composed of three judges: the President, First Vice-President, and Second Vice-President, who are responsible for the proper administration of the Court except for the OTP (article 38 (3)). The Judicial Divisions consists of eighteen judges subdivided into the Pre-Trial Division, the Trial Division, and the Appeals Division (article 34 (b)).[127] Articles 35 to 37 govern the election procedure.[128] The judicial functions are carried

---

[126] Cf. *supra* note 74. On the structure and administration of the Court see Schabas, *supra* note 27, 342 et seq.; Medard Rwelamira, "Composition and administration of the Court" in Lee, *supra* note 14, 153 et seq.; HRW, "Courting history. The landmark International Criminal Court's first years" (hereinafter HRW Courting history report), July 2008, 9 et seq.; Kai Ambos, "Zur Rechtsgrundlage des Internationalen Strafgerichtshofs," (1999) 111 ZStW 175, 177.

[127] Thereto Hirad Abtahi, "The Judges of the International Criminal Court and the organization of their work" in José Doria/Hans-Peter Gasser/Cherif Bassiouni (eds.), *The legal regime of the International Criminal Court, Essays in Honour of Professor Igor Blishchenko* (Martinus Nijhoff Publishers, Leiden Boston 2009) 331, 336 et seq.

[128] The first elected judges were the following: Maureen Harding Clark (Ireland, WEOG, List A, female, 9 years), Fatoumata Dembele Diarra (Mali, African regional group, List A, female, 9 years), Adrian Fullford (United Kingdom, WEOG, List A, male 9 years), Karl T. Hudson-Phillips (Trinidad and Tobago, GRULAC, List A, male, 9 years), Claude Jorda (France, WEOG, List A, male, 6 years), Elizabeth Odio Benito (Costa Rica, GRULAC, List A, female, 9 years), Georghios M. Pikis (Cyprus, Asian regional group, List A, male, 6 years), Tuiloma Neroni Slade (Samoa, Asian regional group, List A, male, 3 years), Sang-Hyun Song (Republic of Korea, Asian regional group, List A, male, 3 years), Sylvia H. de Figueiredo Steiner (Brazil, GRULAC, List A, female, 9 years), René Blattmann (Bolivia, GRULAC,

out by the Chambers, which is organized into three divisions: i) the Pre-Trial Division, which is currently composed of the Second Vice-President and five other judges, ii) the Trial Division, which is composed of the First Vice-President and seven other judges, and iii) the Appeals Division, which is composed of the President and four other judges.[129] The assignment is made on the basis of the nature of the functions each division performs and the qualifications and experience of the judges; the Trial and Pre-Trial Divisions should be composed predominantly of judges with criminal trial experience (article 39 (1)). Pursuant to article 39 (2) (b) (iii), the PTC is composed either of a single judge or of a bench of three judges, three judges carry out the judicial functions of the Trial Chamber (Article 39 (2) (b) (ii)), and the Appeals Chamber is composed of all the judges assigned to the Appeals Division (Article 39 (2) (b) (i)).

The Registry is responsible for the non-judicial aspects of the administration and servicing of the Court. It is headed by the Registrar (presently Ms. Silvana Arbia), who exercises his or her function under the authority of the President of the Court (article 43 (2)).[130] The Registrar is elected by an absolute majority by secret ballot, taking into account any recommendation by the ASP, and shall hold office for a term of five years (article 43 (4) and (5)). Within the Registry, a Victims and Witness Unit (VWU) provides for the particular needs of victims and witnesses. The Victims Participation and Reparations Section (VPRS) ensures the Statute's mandate to take into account the views of victims.[131] A number of semi-autonomous offices fall under the Registry for administrative purposes, but these offices otherwise

List B, male, 6 years), Hans-Peter Kaul (Germany, WEOG, List B, male, 3 years), Philippe Kirsch (Canada, WEOG, List B, male, 6 years), Erkki Kourula (Finland, WEOG, List B, male, 3 years), Akua Kuenyehia (Ghana, African regional group, List B, female, 3 years), Navanethem Pillay (South Africa, African regional group, List B, female, 6 years), Mauro Politi (Italy, WEOG, List B, male, 6 years), Anita Ušacka (Latvia, Eastern Europe regional group, List B, female, 3 years); for the up-to-date list of Judges see: <www.2.icc-cpi.int/Menus/ICC/Structure+of+the+Court/Chambers/The+Judges/>. On the election procedure Benjamin Schiff, *Building the International Criminal Court* (CUP, Cambridge 2008) 107–8; Abtahi, in Doria/Gasser/Bassiouni, *supra* note 127, 335–6.

129 Cf. <www2.icc-cpi.int/Menus/ICC/Structure+of+the+Court/Chambers/>. See also article 39 (1), which requires the President to be part of the Appeals Division besides four other judges, and a minimum of six judges to sit on the Pre-Trial and Trial Division.

130 The current Registrar, Ms. Silvana Arbia (Italy), succeded Mr. Bruno Cathala (France); see <www2.icc-cpi.int/Menus/ICC/Structure+of+the+Court/Registry/The+Registrar/>.

131 See Article 43 (6), Rules 16–19, Registry Regulations 79–96 ("Assistance to Victims and Witnesses"), 97–118 ("Victims Participation and Reparations"); Schiff, *supra* note 128, 129 et seq.

function wholly independently. According to Court Regulation 81, the Office of Public Counsel for Victims (OPCV) was established for the purpose of providing support and assistance to victims participating in the proceedings and their legal representatives.[132] Further, the Office of Public Counsel for the Defence (OPCD) was established in accordance with Court Regulation 77.

The ASP is not an organ of the Court, but the management oversight and legislative body of the ICC. Each State Party has one representative at the ASP, who can be accompanied by alternates and advisers (article 112 (1), ASP Rules of Procedure 23 (1)[133]), and each State Party has one vote (article 112 (7)). The ASP shall meet every year at the seat of the Court, or at the Headquarters of the UN (article 112 (6)). Article 112 (2) enumerates the powers of the ASP, among which the budgetary decision is of major importance (article 112 (2) (d)).

The ASP has a Bureau, which consists of a President, two Vice-Presidents, and 18 members elected by the ASP for three-year terms (article 112 (3) (a)).[134] Two working groups in accordance with article 112 (4) have been established, namely the New York Working Group of the Bureau and the Hague Working Group of the Bureau.[135]

---

132 On the OPCV see <www.icc-cpi.int/Menus/ICC/Structure+of+the+Court/Defence/Office+of+Public+Counsel+for+the+Defence/>; Paolina Massidda/Sarah Pellet, “Role and practice of the Office Counsel for Victims” in Stahn/Sluiter, *supra* note 5, 691, 691 et seq.

133 Rules of Procedure of the Assembly of States Parties, ASP first session, 3.–10.9.2002 (ICC-ASP/1/3), 156 et seq. On the ASP see Adriaan Bos, “Assembly of States Parties” in Antonio Cassese/Paola Gaeta/John Jones (eds.), *The Rome Statute of the ICC: a commentary,* Vol. I (OUP, Oxford 2002) 297 et seq.; William Schabas, “Structure and administration of the Court” in Mark Ellis/Richard Goldstone (eds.), *The International Criminal Court: Challenges to achieving justice and accountability in the 21st century* (Idebate Press, New York 2008) 35, 43.

134 The respective Bureau can be found at <www2.icc-cpi.int/Menus/ASP/Bureau/>. The Bureau assumed its functions at the beginning of the seventh session of the ASP, on 14 November 2008, and is composed of the President Mr. Christian Wenaweser (Liechtenstein), Vice-President Mr. Jorge Lomonaco (Mexico), and Vice-President Mr. Zachary D. Muburi-Muita (Kenya). The Rapporteur is Ms. Simona Drenik (Slovenia).

135 For the mandates of these Working Groups, and for the Decisions of the Bureau, see <www2.icc-cpi.int/Menus/ASP/Bureau/>.

B. Office of the Prosecutor

The OTP shall act independently and as a separate organ of the Court: it is one of the four organs of the ICC (articles 34, 42 (1)). It is responsible for receiving referrals and any substantiated information on crimes within the jurisdiction of the Court, for examining them, and for conducting investigations and prosecutions before the Court (article 42 (1)). The Office is headed by the Chief Prosecutor, who has full authority over the management and administration of the Office, including the staff, facilities and other resources thereof (article 42 (2)). Luis Moreno Ocampo (Argentina), who was elected by the States Parties for a term of nine years, is the head of the OTP, and he took office on 16 June 2003; Fatou Bensouda (Gambia) was elected Deputy Prosecutor by the ASP on 8 September 2004.[136]

As a consequence of its mandate, the OTP comprises three operational divisions and two support section: the Jurisdiction, Complementarity and Cooperation Division (hereinafter JCCD), the Investigation Division (hereinafter ID), and the Prosecution Division (hereinafter PD); in addition, the Services Section and Legal Advisory Section (hereinafter LAS) provide critical support (OTP Regulation 5). The Immediate Office of the Prosecutor coordinates the work of the Office. An Executive Committee (hereinafter ExCom), which is comprised of the heads of the three divisions pursuant to OTP Regulation 4 (1), and which is chaired by the Prosecutor, provides advice on major decisions, such as the initiation of investigations, and promotes coordination of activities.[137] ExCom is responsible for the development and adoption of the strategies, policies and budget of the Office (OTP Regulation 4 (2)).

The Immediate Office, the LAS, and the Services Section assist the Prosecutor with the coordination and provision of services to the operational divisions and joint teams.[138] The Immediate Office of the Prosecutor consists of a small team of professional and administrative staff, who directly assist the Prosecutor in carrying out his specific activities.[139] Upon request,

---

136 Cf. <www.icc-cpi.int/Menus/ICC/Structure+of+the+Court/Office+of+the+Prosecutor/>; also Report of the International Criminal Court for 2004, GA sixtieth session, 1.8.2005 (A/60/177) paras. 26 et seq.; Schabas, in Ellis/Goldstone, *supra* note 133, 40.

137 Report of the International Criminal Court for 2004, *supra* note 136, para. 30.

138 Proposed Programme Budget for 2008 of the International Criminal Court, ASP sixth session, 25.7.2008 (ICC-ASP/6/8) para. 96; Proposed Programme Budget for 2009 of the International Criminal Court, ASP seventh session, 29.7.2008 (ICC-ASP/7/9) para. 114; most recently Proposed Programme Budget for 2011 of the International Criminal Court, ASP ninth session, 2.8.2010 (ICC-ASP/9/10 (MPII)) para. 138.

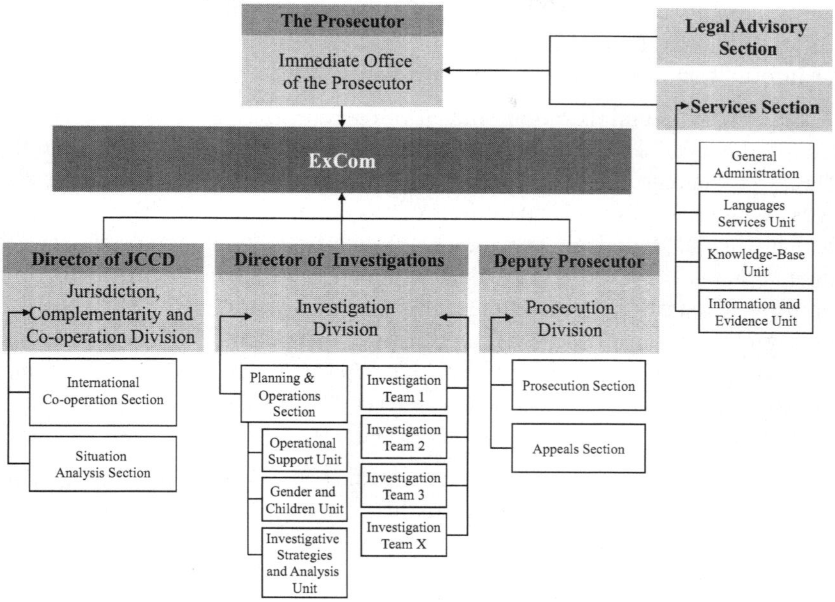

Source: Author.

Figure 1: OTP Organisation Sheet

the LAS is responsible for the provision of legal advice to the Prosecutor, ExCom, and the operational divisions. It coordinates legal training, contributes to the development of the legal tools,[140] and manages the development and coordination of the legal academic network of the OTP (OTP Regulation 11). The Services Section assists in all administrative and technological matters, and it provides the OTP's point of liaison with the Registry. It prepares and controls the Office's budget, provides interpretation services, registers, processes, and stores evidence and information, and develops, introduces, and maintains specific information management tools and practices required by the Office (OTP Regulation 10). The Services

[139] Such as coordinating the divisions' and sections' activities; defining the Office of the Prosecutor's policies, and evaluating their effectiveness through comprehensive lessons learned exercises; coordinating with the other organs of the Court; supervising directly the Office of the Prosecutor's communication strategy; and recording the Prosecutor's decisions and following up on the implementation thereof, see Proposed Programme Budget for 2006 of the International Criminal Court, ASP fourth session, 24.8.2005 (ICC-ASP/4/5) para. 48.

[140] On the legal tools project see <www2.icc-cpi.int/Menus/ICC/Legal+Texts+and+Tools/Legal+Tools/>.

Section comprises four units serving the entire OTP: the General Administration Unit, the Language Services Unit, the Knowledge-Base Unit, and the Information and Evidence Unit (hereinafter IEU).[141]

The General Administration Unit develops and oversees the implementation of the OTP's budget, and handles human resources services for the OTP.[142] Language Services means the provision of all the translation services required during the analysis, investigation, trial, and appeals stages; the Knowledge-Base Unit provides OTP-specific technology-based services and maintains the OTP's databases.[143] IEU ensures "the secure reception, complete registration, confidential and appropriate handling and storage (including electronic) of all physical evidence and potential trial exhibits."[144] Of particular importance is the fact that IEU receives, acknowledges, and stores communications, as well as referrals, during the preliminary examination process.[145] The upcoming survey will come back to this issue.

Regarding the operational divisions, JCCD provides analysis and legal advice on issues pertaining to jurisdiction, complementarity, and cooperation. It analyzes referrals and information on crimes as required under articles 15 and 53, rules 48 and 104, and it prepares reports for assisting ExCom in a decision pursuant to article 53 (1) as to whether there is a reasonable basis to proceed with an investigation (OTP Regulation 7 (a)). JCCD further gives legal advice on jurisdiction and admissibility at all stages of the proceedings, and it makes coordination efforts on cooperation issues (OTP Regulation 7 (b)–(d)). The tasks carried out by JCCD are reflected in the particular subsections: the International Cooperation Section and the Situation Analysis Section. The International Cooperation Section channels all requests for assistance, negotiates cooperation agreements as appropriate, develops information-sharing networks, and provides legal advice on cooperation.[146] The Situation Analysis Section provides objective and systematic analysis of situations of interest; it conducts the initial review of incoming communications, in conjunction with the IEU, and prepares reports and recommendations for ExCom.[147] The Analysis Section provides

141 On the four units see Proposed Programme Budget for 2006, *supra* note 139, para. 63 et seq.

142 Proposed Programme Budget for 2006, *supra* note 139, para. 64.

143 Proposed Programme Budget for 2006, *supra* note 139, paras. 65–6.

144 Proposed Programme Budget for 2006, *supra* note 139, para. 67.

145 Proposed Programme Budget for 2006, *supra* note 139, para. 67. On IEU's involvement in the first phase on analysis (so-called Phase I) see in more detail Part III, C.

146 Proposed Programme Budget for 2006, *supra* note 139, para. 109, Proposed Programme Budget for 2008, *supra* note 138, para. 131; Proposed Programme Budget for 2009, *supra* note 138, para. 142.

advice on complex matters of fact and law regarding jurisdiction, admissibility, and the "interests of justice."[148] The Office of the Director oversees the work performed by the two sections.[149]

The Investigation Division is responsible for the conduct of investigations, which involves the preparation of necessary security plans and protection policies, the provision of investigative expertise and support, the preparation and coordination of field deployment of Office staff, and the factual crime analysis of information and evidence collected (OTP Regulation 8). Headed by the Office of the Deputy Prosecutor for Investigations,[150] the Division comprises Investigation Teams and the Planning and Operation Section.[151] Responsibilities with regard to the Planning and Operation Section are divided into three units: the Operational Support Unit, the Gender and Children Unit, and the Investigative Strategies and Analysis Unit. The Operational Support Unit supports and monitors field operations, liaises with Investigation Teams, ensures that necessary security procedures are developed and applied, and provides the transcripts of interviews and other data entry support. Specialist advice and support in relation to victim and witness issues is given by the Gender and Children Unit (OTP Regulation 12). Last but not least, the Investigative Strategies and Analysis Unit develops and implements new strategies for undertaking investigations.[152]

The Prosecution Division will have principal responsibility for the litigation of proceedings before the Chambers of all three judicial divisions, but further participates in the investigation stage by providing legal advice on issues likely to arise during investigations which may impact on future litigation (OTP Regulation 9). All activities of PD are coordinated, implemented, and supervised by the Office of the Deputy Prosecutor for Prosecution.[153]

---

[147] Proposed Programme Budget for 2006, *supra* note 139, para. 108; Proposed Programme Budget for 2009, *supra* note 138, para. 143. On the preliminary examination process and the involvement of JCCD (as well as IEU) see further Part III, C.

[148] Proposed Programme Budget for 2006, *supra* note 139, para. 109, Proposed Programme Budget for 2008, *supra* note 138, para. 132.

[149] Proposed Programme Budget for 2008, *supra* note 138, para. 134.

[150] It must be noted that the Deputy Prosecutor, Mr. Serge Brammertz, resigned in order to continue to serve as Commissioner of the United Nations International Independent Investigative Commission, cf. Report on the activities of the Court, 18.10.2007, *supra* note 8, para. 58. He is presently the Chief Prosecutor of the ICTY.

[151] Proposed Programme Budget for 2008, *supra* note 138, Graph "Major Programme II: Office of the Prosecutor," 23; Programme Budget for 2009, *supra* note 138, Graph "Major Programme II: Office of the Prosecutor," 28.

[152] In more detail on the tasks carried out by these three units see Proposed Programme Budget for 2006, *supra* note 139, para. 137.

[153] Proposed Programme Budget for 2006, *supra* note 139, para. 178.

PD is divided into a Prosecution Section and an Appeals Section. The Prosecution Section litigates cases before the Pre-Trial and Trial Divisions, as opposed to the Appeals Section, that litigates in appellate proceedings before the Appeals Division. The Prosecution Section gives advice to the Investigation Division on investigative and case preparatory activities, drafts documents containing charges under article 61 (3) (a), and is responsible for legal submissions, especially on questions of evidence and procedure.[154] The Appeals Section prepares legal submissions concerning interlocutory and final appeals proceedings, and has primary responsibility for presenting oral arguments on appeal.[155]

C. Conclusion

The independence of the OTP is an essential interest protected by article 42 and OTP Regulation 13.[156] Article 42 (1) affirms that "a member of the Office shall not seek or act on instructions from external sources." Above all, article 42 (2) gives the Prosecutor exclusive responsibility for the organization of the Office, including its administration. Thereby, the Prosecutor's exercise of authority over management and administration must be in accordance with the Court's financial regulations and rules.[157] The ASP decides on the budget of the Court (article 112 (2) (d)), and provides management oversight to the Prosecutor (article 112 (2) (b)). The potential for the ASP to indirectly influence how resources will be allocated to each investigation through the adoption of a budget is an inherent danger in this arrangement. While this would undermine the Prosecutor's authority and violate article 42 (2), it is interesting to note that the States Parties have already realized how important it is for the Court to have sufficient funds to react promptly in the execution of its duties. For providing additional, unanticipated financial resources in certain circumstances a Contingency Fund was set up in 2004.[158] This fund contains an amount of 10 million Euros

---

[154] Proposed Programme Budget for 2006, *supra* note 139, para. 187.

[155] Proposed Programme Budget for 2006, *supra* note 139, para. 196.

[156] On the constraints of the Prosecutor's independence see Jan Wouters/Sten Verhoeven/Bruno Demeyere, "The International Criminal Court's Office of the Prosecutor: navigating between independence and accountability?" (2008) 8 ICLR 273, 281 et seq.; also Wu Wei, *Die Rolle des Anklägers eines internationalen Strafgerichthofs* (Peter Lang, Frankfurt a. M. 2007) 11 et seq.; recently Carsten Stahn, "Judicial review of prosecutorial discretion: five years on" in Stahn/Sluiter, *supra* note 5, 247, 249.

[157] Financial Regulations and Rules, *supra* note 72.

[158] Resolution ICC-ASP/3/Res.4, Programme budget for 2005, Contingency Fund, Working Capital Fund for 2005, scale of assessments for the apportionment

and aims at covering costs "associated with an unforeseen situation following a decision by the Prosecutor to open an investigation; or unavoidable expenses for developments in existing situations that could not be foreseen or could not be accurately estimated at the time of adoption; or budget costs associated with an unforeseen meeting of the Assembly of States Parties."[159] The Contingency Fund ensures certain flexibility which is indispensable to the work of the OTP. Moreover, it safeguards the Office's independence under article 42 and gives the Prosecutor a useful tool versus unforeseen expenses.

The description of the OTP structure is necessary for understanding how potential situations are analyzed. Three functional divisions (JCCD, ID, and PD) correspond to the three major areas of activity of the OTP. Be that as it may, during the initial phase of pre-investigations the IEU and JCCD – under the supervision of ExCom and the Prosecutor – are the main actors.[160] As appropriate, JCCD may consult PD and LAS.[161] Later, when pre-investigations near completion, ID takes over and may lead joint investigation teams including members from ID, PD, and JCCD.[162] In all situations, analysis culminates in a decision by the Prosecutor to proceed or not to proceed with formal investigations.

---

of expenses of the International Criminal Court and financing of appropriations for the year 2005, 10.9.2004 (ICC-ASP/3/25) 324.

[159] Resolution ICC-ASP/3/Res.4, *supra* note 158, 324.

[160] Cf. Regulations 2–5 of the Provisional Analysis Regulations, Annex paper, *supra* note 27.

[161] Regulations 5.1 and 6.2 of the Provisional Analysis Regulations, Annex paper, *supra* note 27.

[162] Regulation 6.3 of the Provisional Analysis Regulations, Annex paper, *supra* note 27.

Part III

The pre-investigation stage

A. Overview of proceedings before the ICC

Four main procedural stages can be distinguished in the ICC Statute: investigations (part V), trial (part VI), appeal and revision (part VIII), and enforcement (part X). But this fourfold differentiation is not exhaustive, mainly because proceedings before the ICC are not entirely comparable either to ICTY/ICTR proceedings or national proceedings, be they common law or civil law. The Prosecutor has thus identified ten steps he deems decisive:

- preliminary analysis;
- opening an investigation;
- conducting the investigation;
- presenting evidence to the judges and requesting a summons to appear or arrest warrants;
- summonses or arrest warrants (judicial action based on the Prosecutor's evidence);
- appearance of the named individuals (third party action);
- confirmation of charges;
- trial;
- possible appeal;
- sentencing.[163]

Some of these steps mark the transition from one phase to the other (for instance, the formal opening of an investigation draws the line between preliminary steps and full investigative steps). It is particularly the preliminary analysis phase (pre-investigation stage) that makes a more thorough analysis necessary. The investigation is preceded by a pre-procedural stage of the triggering procedure, or "investigation of the situation phase." It is ar-

---

[163] Cf. <www.icc-cpi.int/Menus/ICC/Structure+of+the+Court/Office+of+the+Prosecutor/FAQ/FAQ.htm>.

gued that the issuance of a warrant or summons to appear (article 58) marks the formal commencement of the criminal procedure, which deals with cases as opposed to situations.[164] The previous triggering phase must be subdivided into three types of triggering proceedings, depending on the activation request: a State Party referral (articles 13 (a), 14), a Security Council referral (article 13 (b)), or the OTP's initiation *proprio motu* upon the receipt of information on crimes (articles 13 (c), 15).[165] The innovative inclusion of the triggering procedure in the ICC Statute provided a basis for many ideas which found their way into the present study. It has been proposed by Olásolo that the triggering procedure is an autonomous procedural stage.[166] Most certainly, the triggering procedure marks the commencement of proceedings before the ICC: it "triggers" any criminal procedure before the Court. The author in favor of an autonomous triggering phase describes the object, parties, and proceedings in great detail,[167] but it is not necessary to contrast the triggering procedure with criminal proceedings. Therefore, I suggest a terminological clarification that uses the term "triggering procedure" solely for the initiation of OTP activities (State referrals, SC referrals, and *proprio motu*), and that prefers the term "preliminary examination" or "pre-investigation" for the entire stage before investigations *stricto sensu* are started. In my opinion, the triggering procedure marks the formal commencement of these pre-investigations. Once activation is made the OTP takes over and starts its (criminal) preliminary inquiry in order to determine whether or not to initiate an investigation.[168] The triggering procedure commences the analysis of situations; however, it does not constitute a procedural stage on its own. Complex preliminary investigations are conducted subsequently and result in a decision to continue with a formal investigation or to terminate proceedings (articles 53 (1), 15 (3), and rule 48).[169] At the pre-investigative phase the Prosecutor is not entitled to exercise all of his powers.[170]

---

164 Olásolo, *supra* note 29, 50 et seq.

165 Olásolo, *supra* note 29, 33.

166 Olásolo, *supra* note 29, 35.

167 Olásolo, *supra* note 29, 35 et seq.

168 Schabas, *supra* note 27, 239.

169 See already Part I, A: introduction to the problem, with references in fn. 26; Frank Hoffmeister/Sebastian Knoke, "Das Vorermittlungsverfahren vor dem Internationalen Strafgerichtshof – Prüfstein für die Effektivität der neuen Gerichtsbarkeit im Völkerstrafrecht" (1999) 59 Zeitschrift für ausländisches öffentliches Recht und Völkerrecht 785, 807 ("[...] the authors identify them as constituting a pre-investigation procedure"); Theresa Wilhelmi, "Die Verfahrensordnung des Internationalen Strafgerichtshofs – Modell eines universalen Strafverfahrens?," Institut für Rechtspolitik – Rechtspolitisches Forum Nr. 24, 2004, 38–9.

170 Annex paper, *supra* note 27, 4.

Thus, in a functional sense, pre-investigations may be seen as a separate phase, but not the triggering procedure as such. In the alternative, investigations could be regarded as one stage, subdivided into pre-investigation and full investigations as sub-categories.[171] In sum, pre-investigations have to be valued adequately *vis-à-vis* the procedural system of the ICC as a whole. They need to be designated a procedural stage on their own, or at least a procedural sub-stage of investigations. In a second step, the exact course of action of this newly identified procedural phase and its substantive content need to be addressed by this study.

With regard to the investigation stage, relevant norms can be found in part V: investigation and prosecution. The beginning of formal investigations is marked by a decision under article 53 (1) or an authorization of the PTC under article 15 (4). It is worth noting that there is a supervisory role of the PTC under article 53 (3),[172] which, however, turns into a confirmatory role if the Prosecutor decides not to proceed with an investigation solely based on the "interests of justice" (article 53 (3) (b)). Keeping in mind the obligatory authorization of a *proprio motu* request under article 15 (4), the PTC's involvement during the beginning of an investigation is multifold. Alongside the OTP as the main actor, the PTC becomes the impeding actor during pre- and full investigations.

The Prosecutor uses his powers under article 54 in order to taper off investigations towards one or more persons. If the Prosecutor cannot find a sufficient basis for a prosecution, he suspends proceedings (article 53 (2)), which can be reconsidered at any time based on new facts or information (article 53 (4)). Otherwise, the Prosecutor applies for a warrant of arrest or summons to appear. The PTC issues such a warrant if there are reasonable grounds to believe that a person has committed a crime within the jurisdiction of the Court and the arrest appears necessary (article 58 (1)). According to the jurisprudence of the ICC, a case formally exists after the issuance of a warrant to arrest or a summons to appear.[173] Thus, the formal *investigation of a situation* reaches from the article 53 (1) decision until the issuance of an arrest warrant, which can be distinguished from the investigation

171 Van Heeck, *supra* note 26, 145 with further references in fn. 29. Turone, in Cassese/Gaeta/Jones, *supra* note 26, 1146, calls it "a particular stage, which is not yet an investigation, but can be considered as a sort of pre-investigation carried out by the Prosecutor in order to simply find out whether the real investigation deserves to be started."

172 *Situation in CAR,* Prosecution's report pursuant to Pre-Trial Chamber Ill's 30 November 2006 decision requesting information on the status of the preliminary examination of the situation in the Central African Republic, 15.12.2006 (ICC-01/05-7) para. 1.

173 Cf. the discussion at Part III, B., III.

of a case. The formal *investigation of a case* starts with the article 58 (1) decision and might last as far as the beginning of the confirmation hearing (article 61 (4) spells out: "Before the hearing, the Prosecutor may continue investigations [...]").

The interface between the investigation and trial stage is the confirmation hearing as foreseen in article 61.[174] It has been suggested that – together with the initial proceedings (article 60) and the disclosure of evidence – the confirmation hearing constitutes an intermediate phase which has to be treated a separate phase.[175] Ambos/Miller argue that its beginning is marked by the arrival of the suspect at the Court.[176] Olásolo names the filing of the charging document as the beginning of the intermediate phase.[177] However, it follows from article 61 (1) that the beginning of the confirmation hearing is related to the arrival of the suspect, and not the filing of the charges (article 61 (3)).[178] This is certainly true, yet implies a narrow interpretation of the pre-trial phase exclusively for the part of the proceedings between investigation and trial. A pre-trial phase *stricto sensu* – comparable to the German *Zwischenverfahren*[179] – would basically limit the stage to articles 60 and 61 proceedings. The decisive question is thus to precisely identify the beginning of the pre-trial phase.

Before reaching a decision on this issue a closer look at the PTC and its functions is helpful. Six judges are currently assigned to the Pre-Trial Division,[180] and the Pre-Trial Chambers have significant responsibilities in the

---

[174] Kai Ambos/Dennis Miller, "Structure and function of the confirmation procedure before the ICC from a comparative perspective" (2007) 7 ICLR 335, 336; van Heeck, *supra* note 26, 130. With specific references to the Lubanga confirmation hearing see Gauthier de Beco, "The confirmation of charges before the International Criminal Court: evaluation and first application" (2007) 7 ICLR 469, 470 et seq. Including Lubanga and Katanga/Chui see War Crimes Research Office, "The confirmation of charges process at the International Criminal Court" (hereinafter WCRO confirmation of charges report), International Criminal Court Legal Analysis and Education Project (United States of America, American University Washington College of Law 2008) 1 et seq.

[175] Ambos/Miller, *supra* note 174, 336; also Olympia Bekou, "Pre-Trial procedures before the International Criminal Court," 20th International Conference of the International Society for the Reform of Criminal Law, Brisbane, 2 July–6 July 2006, 2; Michelle Marchesiello, "Proceedings before the Pre-Trial Chambers" in Cassese/Gaeta/Jones, *supra* note 11, 1231, 1239 et seq. On the drafting history of article 61 see WCRO confirmation of charges report, *supra* note 174, 44 et seq.

[176] Ambos/Miller, *supra* note 174, 338; similarly Marchesiello, *supra* note 175, 1239.

[177] Olásolo, *supra* note 29, 51.

[178] Ambos/Miller, *supra* note 174, 338.

[179] Ambos/Miller, *supra* note 174, 354 et seq.

procedural system of the ICC.[181] First of all, it is necessary that the PTC authorizes any investigation *proprio motu* (article 15 (4)). Preliminary rulings on admissibility (article 18 (2)) and reviewing the Prosecutor's decision not to proceed with an investigation/a prosecution (article 53 (3)) are further at the control of the PTC, not to mention the key role of the PTC in relation to a unique investigative opportunity (article 56).

For the operation of the PTC not only its powers have to be noted, but it is crucial to know at what point the PTC becomes involved. According to Court Regulation 46 (2), a situation shall be assigned to a PTC as soon as the Prosecutor has informed the Presidency in accordance with Court Regulation 45, i.e. a situation has been referred to the Prosecutor by a State Party, the Security Council, or an article 15 (3) request. In practice, the Presidency has complied with Court Regulation 46 (2) in all five situations with immediate effect, and assigned the situations in DRC and Darfur to PTC I, the situations in Uganda and Kenya to PTC II, and the situation in the CAR to PTC III.[182]

It has to be noted that Court Regulations 45 et seq. are situated in chapter 3, section 2: "Pre-trial" of the Court Regulations. The nomenclature "pre-trial," as well as the early role of the PTC, favor a vast interpretation of the pre-trial stage that would start with the assignment of a situation and terminate in a confirmation of charges decision under article 61 (7). In contrast, a formal pre-trial phase is not specifically provided for in the ICC Statute. Relevant norms can be found in part V: investigation and prosecution. Article 57 outlines the functions and powers of the PTC. Furthermore, articles 58 and 59 cover the warrant of arrest, summons to appear, and arrest proceedings in the custodial State. Initial proceedings before the Court

---

180 For the up-to-date composition see <www2.icc-cpi.int/menus/icc/structureof the court/chambers/pretrialdivision/pretrialdivision?lan=en-GB>.

181 All-embracing, Olivier Fourmy, "Powers of the Pre-Trial Chamber" in Cassese/Gaeta/Jones, *supra* note 11, 1207–1230; Simon de Smet, "A structural analysis of the role of the Pre-Trial Chamber in the fact-finding process of the ICC" in Stahn/Sluiter, *supra* note 5, 405, 405 et seq.; also Ekaterina Trendafilova, "Fairness and expeditiousness in the International Criminal Court's pre-trial proceedings" in Stahn/Sluiter, *supra* note 5, 441, 441 et seq.; Göran Sluiter, "Human rights protection on the ICC pre-trial phase" in Stahn/Sluiter, *supra* note 5, 459, 459 et seq.

182 *Situation in DRC,* Decision assigning the situation in the Democratic Republic of Congo to Pre-Trial Chamber I, 5.7.2004 (ICC-01/04-1); *Situation in Darfur (Sudan),* Decision assigning the situation in Darfur, Sudan to Pre-trial Chamber I, 21.4.2005 (ICC-02/05-1); *Situation in Uganda,* Decision assigning the situation in Uganda to Pre-Trial Chamber II, 5.7.2004 (ICC-02/04-1); *Situation in CAR,* Decision assigning the situation in the Central African Republic to Pre-Trial Chamber III, 19.1.2005 (ICC-01/05-1); Press Release (Kenya), The situation of the Republic of Kenya assigned to Pre-Trial Chamber II, 6.11.2009 (ICC-CPI-20091106-PR473).

are provided for in article 60, while article 61 governs the confirmation hearing. The term pre-trial is not defined in the Statute, and none of the norms mentioned above refer to such a phase. Some guidance on the length of the pre-trial stage is given in the RPE in chapter 5, section VI, which provides rules 127–130 under the heading "closure of the pre-trial phase." The ending is marked by the confirmation hearing decision under article 61 (7). If the charges are confirmed, the Presidency constitutes a Trial Chamber and refers the case to it (rule 130), formally bringing the pre-trial to an end.

To determine the exact beginning of the pre-trial phase is even more challenging. The practice of the ICC suggests that the issuance of a warrant of arrest (article 58) constitutes not only the demarcation line between situation and case,[183] but also marks the ending of the investigation phase and beginning of the pre-trial phase.[184] However, this ICC website-practice appears difficult to follow from a legal perspective. First appearance and subsequent disclosure being essential parts of the pre-trial *stricto sensu* require the physical presence of the person accused.[185] Yet, there was a lack of surrender or voluntary appearance in the cases of *Prosecutor v. Bashir* and *Prosecutor v. Harun and Kushayb,* which are, nonetheless, designated "pre-trial phase" by the Court.

Three potential starting points for the pre-trial stage have been identified: the assignment of a situation, the issuance of an arrest warrant or summons to appear, and, last but not least, the arrival of the suspect. The assignment of a situation takes place very early, sometimes even long before a formal investigation is opened.[186] The PTC fulfils a supervisory role during early proceedings, which should not be put on the same level with the formal pre-trial phase. Bearing this in mind, it appears hardly possible to reach a clear-cut *substantive* determination. In fact, investigation phase and pre-trial phase may overlap.[187] Therefore, a *terminological* solution is suggested, which picks up all three potential starting points: involvement of the PTC, broad pre-trial phase, and pre-trial phase *stricto sensu.*

---

183 Héctor Olàsolo, "The lack of attention to the distinction between situation and cases in national laws on co-operation with the International Criminal Court with particular reference to the Spanish case" (2007) 20 LJIL 193, 194.

184 On the official website of the ICC the cases *Prosecutor v. Bosco Ntaganda, Prosecutor v. Ahmad Harun and Ali Kushayb,* and *Prosecutor v. Omar Hassan Ahamad Al Bashir* are all designated "pre-trial" phase, see <www2.icc-cpi.int/Menus/ICC/Situations+and+Cases/Cases/>.

185 Marchesiello, *supra* note 175, 2141.

186 In the situation of CAR more than two years passed between the assignment of the situation and the opening of a formal investigation.

187 Ambos/Miller, *supra* note 174, 339.

The PTC becomes involved with the assignment of a situation when no formal pre-trial has started. The role of the PTC during early proceedings should, nevertheless, not be underestimated. An essential supervisory role is performed regarding the assigned situation, and provides for effective checks and balances. Article 58 proceedings mark the beginning of a broader pre-trial phase with cases as its objective. The PTC's role switches from a purely supervisory role to active involvement in the proceedings. However, the formal pre-trial phase in the sense of an intermediate stage is characterized by the arrival of the suspect. The term "pre-trial *stricto sensu*" should be used exclusively with regard to proceedings under articles 60 and 61, which constitute the part of the proceedings between investigation and trial. A detailed pre-confirmation scheme is set out in rule 121.[188] The role of the judges is increasingly active and controlling.[189]

As a result, an approach that schematizes pre-trial in a strict sense is followed. As a refinement, the term pre-trial should be avoided: the term "intermediate phase" should be used at all times. Until now, three phases have been identified: pre-investigations, investigations, and intermediate proceedings.

Once the charges are confirmed in accordance with article 61 (7), the preparation for trial starts.[190] Promptly after the constitution of a Trial Chamber and the referral of the case to it (article 61 (11), rule 130), the Chamber convenes a status conference in order to set a trial date (rule 132). Subsequent status conferences take place to adopt procedures necessary to facilitate the fair and expeditious conduct of the proceedings and to determine the language or languages used at trial (article 64 (3), Court Regulation 54). The trial itself follows a straightforward scheme (article 64 (8), rules 140–142): opening statement, presentation of evidence, closing arguments, deliberations, and judgment.[191]

---

188 Robert Cryer/Håkan Friman/Darryl Robinson/Elizabeth Wilmshurst, *An introduction to International Criminal Law and Procedure* (OUP, Cambridge 2007) 380.

189 Cryer/Friman/Robinson/Wilmshurst, *supra* note 188, 380.

190 Schabas, *supra* note 27, 282; on the exact commencement of the trial see *Prosecutor v. Bemba*, Decision on the admissibility, *infra* note 280, para. 210, 78.

191 Cryer/Friman/Robinson/Wilmshurst, *supra* note 188, 386. See further on the trial stage Calvo-Goller, *supra* note 10, 217 et seq.; Frank Terrier, "Powers of the Trial Chamber" in Cassese/Gaeta/Jones, *supra* note 11, 1259, 1259 et seq.; *id.*, "The Procedure before the Trial Chamber" in *ibid.*, 1277, 1277 et seq.; Hans-Jörg Behrens, "Das Verfahren des Internationalen Strafgerichtshofes nach dem Statut von Rom" (1998) 11 HuV-I 144, 147 et seq.; Robert Heinsch, "How to achieve fair and expeditious trail proceedings before the ICC: is it time for a more judge-dominated approach?" in Stahn/Sluiter, *supra* note 5, 479, 479 et seq.; Reinhold Gallmetzer, "The Trial Chamber's discretionary power to devise the proceedings before it and its exercise in the trial of *Thomas Lubanga Dyilo*" in Stahn/Sluiter, *supra* note 5, 501, 501 et seq. On the ICTY and other tribunals (as well as the ICC) see Antonio

In general, the trial should be held in public (article 64 (7)). Several exceptions are envisaged by the Statute (article 64 (7) and article 68), which deviate from the requirements of human rights treaties. Relevant articles should, however, be interpreted in strict accordance with the principle of a public trial as embodied in human rights law.[192] The presiding judge gives the directions of proceedings at trial (article 64 (8) (b)). If he does not give any directions, the prosecution and the defence must agree on the order and manner in which the evidence is submitted (rule 140 (1)). The Chamber as main actor has inherent powers enumerated in article 64 (6), which go to such lengths as the production of additional evidence (article 64 (6) (d)). The dominant role of the Chamber, specifically the presiding judge, has led to controversies between common law and civil law advocates, which have been described as a *clash of cultures*.[193] Rule 140 (2) reflects the compromise achieved by the parties: a witness is questioned by the prosecution and defence without intervention of the Chamber, and the Chamber can only pose questions before or after the prosecution and defence have taken their turns. Cross-examination is thus implicitly admitted, and its optional use will to a large extent depend on the actors.[194] All in all, the trial phase of the ICC has departed from the (mainly) common law model of the *ad hoc* tribunals, and it features more civil law elements in its criminal proceedings.[195]

The appeal stage starts just after the trial with the launching of an appeal of any of the parties. The grounds for appeal included in article 81 are procedural error, error of fact, error of law, and, as an additional ground in case of conviction, "any other ground that affects the fairness or reliability of the proceedings or decision."[196] On appeal, the Chamber may order a

---

Cassese, *International Criminal Law*, 2nd edition (OUP, Oxford 2008) 409 et seq.; Hans-Jörg Behrens, "The trial proceedings" in Lee, *supra* note 14, 238 et seq.; *id.*, "Investigation, trial and appeal in the International Criminal Court Statute" (1998) 6 EJCrim 113, 113 et seq.; Stefan Kirsch, "The trial proceedings before the ICC" (2006) 6 ICLR 275, 275 et seq.

[192] Christoph Safferling, *Towards an international criminal procedure* (OUP, Oxford 2001) 239.

[193] Ambos, *supra* note 26, § 8 mn 31.

[194] Ambos, *supra* note 26, § 8 mn 31.

[195] Van Heeck, *supra* note 26, 137; differentiated Donald Piragoff, "Article 69" in Triffterer, *supra* note 37, article 69, mn 5; Cryer/Friman/Robinson/Wilmshurst, *supra* note 188, 387.

[196] For a detailed analysis of the ICC's appeal procedure see Ambos, *supra* note 10, 493 et seq.; Robert Roth/Marc Henzelin, "The appeal procedure of the ICC" in Cassese/Gaeta/Jones, *supra* note 11, 1535, 1535 et seq.; Calvo-Goller, *supra* note 10, 303 et seq.; Schabas, *supra* note 27, 306 et seq.; Helen Brady/Mark Jennings, "Appeal and revision" in Lee, *supra* note 14, 294, 294 et seq.

new trial before a different Trial Chamber (article 83 (2)) or affirm, reverse, or revise the appealed decision. In an appeal against sentence the Appeals Chamber may vary the sentence (article 83 (3)). According to article 83 (1)–(2), the Appeals Chamber has all the powers of the Trial Chamber. It may even call evidence itself to determine a factual issue, which leaves the Appeals Chamber with broad discretion.[197] Similarly to the trial phase, the appeals system of the ICC has abandoned the appeals procedure of the *ad hoc* tribunals and rather resembles civil law practice.[198]

Interlocutory appeals against other decisions must be distinguished from the appeal against judgment and sentence (article 82). An interlocutory appeal can be directed against decisions relating to jurisdiction or admissibility, granting or denying release, or against a decision of the PTC to act on its own initiative with regard to a unique investigative opportunity under article 56 (3).[199] Article 82 (1) (d) further provides for an interlocutory appeal that requires leave to appeal by the Chamber issuing the challenged decision. Appeals under article 82 (1) (a)–(c) do not require leave of the Court (rule 154), while the ones under article 82 (1) (d) and article 82 (2) require leave by the PTC or by the Trial Chamber (rule 155). In turn, such a leave requires "a decision that involves an issue that would *significantly affect* the fair and expeditious conduct of the proceedings or the outcome of the trial, and for which, in the opinion of the Pre-Trial or Trial Chamber, an immediate resolution by the Appeals Chamber may *materially advance the proceedings* (emph. added)."[200] Initially, the ICC has adopted a very restrictive approach, and it has underlined the exceptional nature of interlocutory appeals.[201]

Legal formalities are regulated in rules 150–158. A time limit of 30 days must be complied with for any appeal against a decision of conviction or acquittal under article 74, a sentence under article 76, or a reparation order under article 75 (rule 150 (1)). With regard to other decisions, the fixed

---

197 Cryer/Friman/Robinson/Wilmshurst, *supra* note 188, 389.

198 Safferling, *supra* note 192, 334; Ambos, *supra* note 26, § 8 mn 46.

199 Article 82 (1) (a)–(c). See further Eckelmans, in Stahn/Sluiter, *supra* note 100, 537 et seq.

200 Article 82 (1) (d). On interlocutory appeals under 82 (1) (d) see Ambos, *supra* note 10, 495 et seq.

201 *Prosecutor v. Kony et al.,* Decision on Prosecutor's application for leave to appeal in part Pre-Trial-Chamber II's decision on the Prosecutor's application for warrants of arrest under article 58, 19.8.2005 (ICC-02/04-01/05-20-US-Exp), para. 15 et seq.; Cryer/Friman/Robinson/Wilmshurst, *supra* note 188, 390 with fn. 345; Ambos, *supra* note 10, 496–7; Håkan Friman, "Interlocutory appeals in the early practice of the International Criminal Court" in Stahn/Sluiter, *supra* note 5, 553, 558.

time limit is 5 days (rules 154 (1) and 155 (1)), except for an appeal under article 82 (1) (c) which sets a limit of 2 days (rule 154 (2)).

Revision applies to a conviction or sentence (article 84). A final judgment shall be revised if new evidence has been discovered, which

(1) was not available at the time of trial, and such unavailability was not wholly or partially attributable to the party making application;
(2) is sufficiently important that had it been proved at trial it would have been likely to have resulted in a different verdict (article 84 (1) (a)).

In addition, article 84 (1) (b) allows for revision if decisive evidence turns out to be false, forged, or falsified. As a matter of course, serious misconduct or breach of duty by a participating judge are grounds for revision (article 84 (1) (c)).

The enforcement stage under articles 103–111 commences once the final judgment has been delivered.[202] Rules 198–225 complement articles 103 et seq. According to article 103 (1) (a) and rule 200, a list of States, which have indicated their general willingness to accept sentenced persons, shall be maintained by the Registrar. A State designated by the Presidency can nevertheless reject the enforcement *in concreto* (article 103 (1) (c), rule 205). If the State accepts the Presidency's decision, the sentenced person shall be delivered to that State as soon as possible (rule 206 (2)). Transfer to another State is possible at all times according to article 104 and rules 209–210. Furthermore, enforcement is supervised by the Court, and must be in conformity with widely accepted international treaty standards governing treatment of prisoners (article 106 and rule 211). It has to be noted that the sentence of imprisonment is binding and cannot be modified by the State (article 105 (1); the ICC alone decides on any application for appeal or revision (article 105 (2)).

As a final result, it is proposed to designate pre-investigations as its own procedural stage at the ICC, which divides criminal proceedings into the following six stages: pre-investigation stage, investigation stage, intermediate stage, trial stage, appeal stage, and enforcement stage.

---

202 On the enforcement stage see Calvo-Goller, *supra* note 10, 327 et seq.; Ambos, *supra* note 26, § 8 mn 83 et seq.; Cryer/Friman/Robinson/Wilmshurst, *supra* note 188, 401–2; Schabas, *supra* note 27, 320 et seq.; Claus Kress/Göran Sluiter, "Section 8, Enforcement" in Cassese/Gaeta/Jones, *supra* note 11, 1751, 1751 et seq.; Trevor Pascal Chimimba, "Establishing an enforcement regime" in Lee, *supra* note 14, 345, 345 et seq.

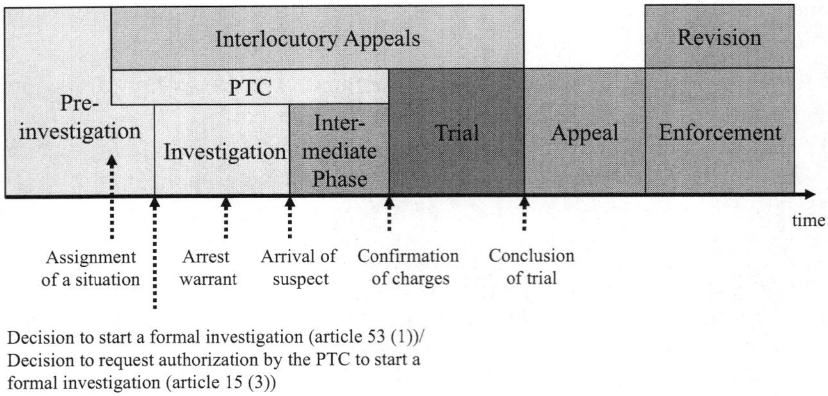

Source: Author – This graph is based partly on the Report on the Court Capacity Model, Assembly of State Parties, 5th session, 21.08.2006, ICC-ASP/5/10, p. 5.

Figure 2: Proceedings before the ICC

B. Initiation of analysis – the triggering procedure

I. Introduction

The term "trigger mechanism" was introduced during the establishment process of the ICC. The Preparatory Committee referred to a trigger mechanism in 1996, still meaning two main clusters of issues: *first,* acceptance of the Court's jurisdiction and the conditions for the exercise of jurisdiction; and *second,* who can trigger the system and the role of the Prosecutor.[203] At hand, only the second cluster is referred to using the term trigger mechanism.[204] Article 13 determines the (trigger) mechanisms on the basis of which the ICC may exercise its jurisdiction. A situation has to be referred to the Court either by a State Party (articles 13 (a), 14), by the SC (article 13 (b)), or the Prosecutor initiates an investigation *proprio motu* on the basis of information received by reliable sources (articles 13 (c), 15).[205] If the Prosecu-

[203] Report of the Preparatory Committee on the Establishment of the International Criminal Court, Vol. 1, Proceedings of the Preparatory Committee during March-April and August 1996, GA fifty-first session, Supplement No. 22, 13.9.1996 (A/51/22) mn 116.

[204] Similarly, Olásolo, *supra* note 29, 33; Christoph Junck, *Die Gerichtsbarkeit des Internationalen Strafgerichtshofs* (Peter Lang, Frankfurt a.M. 2006) mn 434.

[205] Illustrative, Jo Stigen The relationship between the International Criminal Court and national jurisdictions (Martinus Nijhoff Publishers, Leiden, Boston 2008) 90. See already above Part III, A.

tor wants to use his *proprio motu* power to proceed with a formal investigation, he must request authorization by the PTC (article 15 (3)).

Four investigations formally underway have been referred to the Prosecutor by States Parties (Uganda, Democratic Republic of Congo, and Central African Republic) and by the Security Council (Darfur, Sudan).[206] Recently, the Prosecutor has decided to initiate a *proprio motu* request under article 15 (3) in Kenya.[207] The two situation brought before the Court by a declaration of acceptance of jurisdiction – pursuant to article 12 (3) – from Non-States Parties (Côte d'Ivoire and Palestine) remain under analysis.[208] In total, the Pre-Trial Chambers have issued fourteen warrants of arrest and three summonses to appear at the request of the OTP.[209]

1. Democratic Republic of Congo

On 23 June 2004, the Prosecutor publicized his decision to open an investigation on crimes committed on the territory of the DRC, especially in the Ituri region, since 1 July 2002.[210] After receiving information from in-

206 Security Council Resolution 1593 (2005), adopted by vote of 11 in favor to none against, with 4 abstentions (Algeria, Brazil, China, United States) <www.un.org/News/Press/docs/2005/sc8351.doc.htm>. An overview of the ICC's jurisprudence in the aforementioned situations (in German and until September 2008) is given by Eleni Chaitidou, "Rechtssprechungsübersicht: Aktuelle Entwicklung am Internationalen Strafgerichtshof" (2008) 14 ZIS 371, 371 et seq.; see also ICC Outreach Report 2008, 20.11.2008 and ICC Outreach Report 2009, 18.11.2009; Schiff, *supra* note 128, 194 et seq.; Christopher Hall, "Developing and implementing an effective positive complementarity prosecution strategy" in Stahn/Sluiter, *supra* note 5, 219, 223–4.

207 *Situation in Kenya*, Request for authorization of an investigation pursuant to article 15, 26.11.2009 (ICC-01/09-3); see also the authorization by the majority of the PTC, *Situation in Kenya*, Decision pursuant to article 15, *supra* note 6, 83.

208 Report on the activities of the Court, 18.10.2007, *supra* note 8, para. 35; OTP Report on activities 2003–2006, *supra* note 23, 10; Visit of the Minister of Justice of the Palestinian National Authority, 22.1.2009.

209 See <www2.icc-cpi.int/Menus/ICC/Situations+and+Cases/Cases/>. Eight warrants of arrest are outstanding: four in Uganda, three in Darfur, and one in DRC, cf. Report of the International Criminal Court to the United Nations for 2007/2008, GA sixty-third session, 22.8.2008 (A/63/323) 2 (though not yet mentioning the arrest warrant against Al Bashir, which amounts to arrest warrant number eight, and the third warrant in the Darfur situation).

210 OTP-Press Release (DRC), The Office of the Prosecutor of the International Criminal Court opens its first investigation, 23.6.2004 (ICC-OTP-20040623-59). For the background of the conflict see "Democratic Republic of Congo" in HRW, World Report 2008, Events of 2007, 105 et seq.; International Centre for Transitional Justice, Federico Borello, "A first few steps," October 2004, 1, 7 et seq.; Schiff, *supra* note 128, 210 et seq.; Jean-Pascal Obembe, "The International Criminal Court – a

dividuals and non-governmental organizations, the Prosecutor had announced in July 2003 that he would closely follow the situation in Ituri.[211] In September 2003, the Prosecutor informed the ASP that he stood ready to seek authorization from a Pre-Trial Chamber to start an investigation *proprio motu* if necessary. In the light of the current circumstances in the field, however, a consensual division of labor could be an effective approach, for the reason which the Prosecutor emphasized that a referral and active support from the DRC would facilitate the work of the OTP.[212] The Prosecutor received such a (self-)referral signed by the President of the DRC, Joseph Kabila, referring to him the situation of crimes within the jurisdiction of the Court allegedly committed anywhere in the territory of the DRC since the entry into force of the ICC Statute.[213] After careful determination under article 53 and rule 104, the Prosecutor informed the President of the Court that there was a reasonable basis to initiate an investigation, and the Presidency assigned the situation in the DRC to PTC I.[214]

Since that time, four cases have resulted from the DRC situation, the case *Prosecutor v. Thomas Lubanga Dyilo*, which is currently in the trial

work in progress in the Democratic Republic of Congo" (2005) 18 HuV-I 11, 11 et seq.; Hartmut Hamann, "Internationaler Strafgerichtshof und Vereinte Nationen in der Demokratischen Republik Kongo" (2006) 118 ZStW 799, 799 et seq.; Henri Boshoff/Thierry Vircoulon, "Update on Ituri" (2004) 13 African Security Review 65, 65 et seq.; Stephen Elliot Smith, "Inventing the laws of gravity: the ICC's initial *Lubanga* decision and its regressive consequences" (2008) 8 ICLR 331, 332; Jan Wouters/Sten Verhoeven, "Cases identified for investigation and prosecution by the International Criminal Court" in Evelyn Ankumah/Edward Kwakwa (eds.), *African Perspectives on International Criminal Justice,* African Legal Aid Special Series, Vol. 3 (Océ Business Services: Accra 2005) 133, 134–5; Chandra Lekha Sriram/Amy Ross, "Geographies of crime and justice: contemporary transitional justice and the creation of 'zones of impunity'" (2007) 1 IJTJ 45, 52–3; ICTJ, Human Rights Center Berkeley & Payson Center for International Development, "Living with fear, a population-based survey on attitudes about peace, justice, and social reconstruction in Eastern Democratic Republic on Congo" (hereinafter ICTJ DRC population-based survey), August 2008, 1, 6, 10 et seq.

211 OTP-Press Release (DRC), Press Conference of the Prosecutor – Communications, 24.7.2003 (ICC-OTP-20030724-28); Communications received by the Prosecutor since 2002, 24.7.2003 (ICC-OTP-20030724-28) 7.

212 Statement by the Prosecutor of the International Criminal Court, Mr. Luis Moreno-Ocampo, made at the first meeting of the Assembly of its second session, 8.9.2003, 4.

213 OTP-Press Release (DRC), Prosecutor receives referral of the situation in the Democratic Republic of Congo, 19.4.2004 (ICC-OTP-20040419-50). On Kabila's referral and the background thereof, William Burke-White, "Complementarity in practice: The International Criminal Court as part of a system of multi-level global governance in the Democratic Republic of Congo" (2005) 18 LJIL 557, 563 et seq.

214 *Situation in DRC,* Decision assigning the situation in the Democratic Republic of Congo to Pre-Trial Chamber I, 5.7.2004 (ICC-01/04-1) 2–3.

phase; the joint case *Prosecutor v. Germain Katanga and Mathieu Ngudjolo Chui,* which is equally at the trial stage; the *Prosecutor v. Bosco Ntaganda* case, where an arrest warrant has been issued (designated pre-trial phase), and the *Prosecutor v. Callixte Mbarushimana.*[215] Eight persons are currently in custody of the ICC: Thomas Lubanga Dyilo, Germain Katanga, Mathieu Ndgudjolo Chui, Callixte Mbarushimana (all DRC), Jean-Pierre Bemba (CAR),[216] Bar Idriss Abu Garda, Abdallah Banda Abakaer Nourain, and Saleh Mohammed Jerbo Jamus (all Darfur, Sudan).

Pre-Trial Chamber I issued a sealed warrant of arrest against Thomas Lubanga Dyilo on 10 February 2006 and unsealed the warrant on 17 March 2006. In the views of the Chamber, there were reasonable grounds to believe that Mr. Lubanga had committed the war crimes of conscripting and enlisting children under the age of fifteen years and using them to participate actively in hostilities.[217] On 20 March 2006, Mr. Lubanga made his first appearance before PTC I during which his identity was verified. Moreover, Mr. Lubanga's initial appearance started the first intermediate trial of the Court, which climaxed in the confirmation of the three charges. In accordance with article 61 (7), PTC I decided that there was sufficient evidence to establish substantial grounds to believe that Thomas Lubanga Dyilo is criminally responsible as co-perpetrator for the war crimes of enlisting and conscripting children under the age of fifteen years into the *Forces Patriotiques pour la Libération du Congo* (hereinafter FPLC), the military wing of the *Union des Patriotes Congolais* (hereinafter UPC) and using them to participate actively in hostilities in Ituri (eastern region in the DRC) from September 2002 to 13 August 2003.[218] On 6 March 2007, the Presidency rendered a decision constituting Trial Chamber I and referring the case *Prosecutor v. Thomas Lubanga Dyilo* to it.[219] The beginning of

---

215 See <www2.icc-cpi.int/menus/icc/situations+and+cases/>.

216 Moreno-Ocampo, in Stahn/Sluiter, *supra* note 99, 17, 19.

217 *Prosecutor v. Lubanga,* Warrant of arrest, 10.2.2006 (ICC-01/04-01/06-2) 4; *Prosecutor v. Lubanga,* Annex I, Decision on the Prosecutor's application for warrant of arrest, article 58, 10.2.2006 (ICC-01/04-01/06-8-US-Corr., reclassified as public pursuant to decision ICC-01/04-01/06-37); the latter decision was included in the annex to *Prosecutor v. Lubanga,* Decision concerning Pre-Trial Chamber I's decision of 10 February 2006 and the incorporation of documents into the record of the case against Mr. Thomas Lubanga Dyilo, 24.2.2006 (ICC-01/04-01/06-8-US-Corr., reclassified as public pursuant to decision ICC-01/04-01/06-37). On the Lubanga case see Report of the International Criminal Court for 2007/2008, *supra* note 209, para. 8 et seq.

218 *Prosecutor v. Lubanga,* Décision sur la confirmation des charges, 29.1.2007 (ICC-01/04-01/06-803) 133. Critically evaluating the confirmation of charges proceedings in the Lubanga case, WCRO confirmation of charges report, *supra* note 174, 14 et seq.

the trial was scheduled for 31 March 2008,[220] but later this date was suspended.[221] On 13 June 2008, the Trial Chamber imposed a first stay of the proceedings, concluding that the Prosecution had incorrectly used article 54 (3) (e), and therefore withheld significant exculpatory evidence from the accused and inhibited his right to prepare a proper defence.[222] The misuse resulted in an infringement of the fair trial principle and in a decision to release Thomas Lubanga Dyilo.[223] On 7 July 2008, the Appeals Chamber granted suspensive effect of the Prosecution's appeal against the decision to release Mr. Lubanga.[224] On 21 October 2008, the Appeals Chamber remanded the matter to the Trial Chamber for a new determination until which the accused remained in the custody of the Court.[225] The Trial Chamber lifted the stay of proceedings on 18 November 2008 as the reasons for imposing the stay "ha[d] fallen away" and scheduled the trial provisionally for 26 January 2009. Trial Chamber I further decided not to grant the release or provisional release of Thomas Lubanga Dyilo and ordered him to remain in custody until the beginning of the trial. The trial finally commenced on 26 January 2009, but a second stay of proceedings was in place due to non-implementation of an order issued by Trial Chamber I until reversed by the Appeals Chamber very recently.[226] The Lubanga trial may now continue, though the proceedings are expected to take some time.

---

[219] *Prosecutor v. Lubanga,* Decision constituting Trial Chamber I and referring to it the case of The Prosecutor v. Thomas Lubanga Dyilo, 6.3.2007 (ICC-01-04-01-06-842).

[220] *Prosecutor v. Lubanga,* Decision regarding the timing and manner of disclosure and the date of trial, 9.11.2007 (ICC-01/04-01/06-1019) para. 29.

[221] *Prosecutor v. Lubanga,* Decision suspending deadline for final disclosure, 30.1.2008 (ICC-01/04-01/06-1141) para. 4.

[222] *Prosecutor v. Lubanga,* Decision on the consequences of non-disclosure of exculpatory materials covered by Article 54 (3) (e) agreements and the application to stay the prosecution of the accused, together with certain other issues raised at the Status Conference on 10 June 2008, 13.6.2008 (ICC-01/04-01/06-1401) para. 92; confirming *Prosecutor v. Lubanga,* Judgment on the appeal of the Prosecutor against the decision of Trial Chamber I entitled "Decision on the consequences of non-disclosure etc.," 21.10.2008 (ICC-01/04-01/06-1486) para. 51.

[223] *Prosecutor v. Lubanga,* Decision on the release of Thomas Lubanga Dyilo, 2.7.2008 (ICC-01/04-01/06-1418).

[224] *Prosecutor v. Lubanga,* The Appeals Chamber gives suspensive effect to the appeal against the decision on the release of Thomas Lubanga, 7.7.2008 (ICC-CPI-20080707-PR338).

[225] *Prosecutor v. Lubanga,* Judgment on the appeal of the Prosecutor against the decision of Trial Chamber I entitled "Decision on the release of Thomas Lubanga Dyilo," 21.10.2008 (ICC-01/04-01/06-1487) para. 45 (Judge Pikis dissenting).

[226] See *Prosecutor v. Lubanga*, Redacted decision on the Prosecutor's urgent request for variation of the time-limit to disclose the identity of intermediary 143 or alternatively to stay proceedings pending further consultations with VWU, 8.7.2010

On 28 April 2008, upon the request of the Prosecutor, PTC I unsealed a warrant of arrest against Bosco Ntaganda (also known as "the Terminator"), alleged former Deputy Chief of the General Staff of the FPLC, alleged current Chief of Staff of the *Congrès national pour la défense du people* (CNDP) armed group, and former associate of Thomas Lubanga Dyilo.[227] The two arrest warrants against Lubanga and Ntaganda were originally requested together.[228] Bosci Ntaganda allegedly committed war crimes of enlistment and conscription of children under the age of 15 and of using them to participate actively in hostilities in Ituri from July 2002 until December 2003.[229] He is still at large and allegedly continues to be implicated in the commission of crimes in the DRC.[230]

On 17 October 2007, the Congolese authorities surrendered and transferred Germain Katanga (also known as "Simba") to the ICC. The corresponding warrant of arrest was publicly announced and unsealed on 18 October 2007; it was already issued under seal on 2 July 2007.[231] The warrant lists nine counts including three counts of crimes against humanity and six counts of war crimes.[232] On 22 October 2007, PTC I held a public hearing during which Mr. Katanga appeared for the first time before the Court, his identity was verified, and the Chamber provisionally set the confirmation of charges hearing for the 28 February 2008.[233]

Mathieu Ngudjolo Chui was the third detainee of the ICC, and he was transferred on 7 February 2008. On the same day, a warrant of arrest was publicly announced and unsealed (it had been issued under seal on 6 July 2007).[234] The warrant of arrest lists six counts of war crimes and three

(ICC-01/04-01/06-2517-RED) para. 31, 22-3; *Prosecutor v. Lubanga*, Judgement on the appeal of the Prosecutor against the decision of Trial Chamber I of 8 July 2010, 8.10.2010 (ICC-01/04-01/06-2582) para. 62, 26.

227 Press Release (DRC), Warrant of arrest against Bosco Ntaganda unsealed, 29.4.2008 (ICC-CPI-20080429-PR310). The sealed warrant was issued under seal on 22 August 2006.

228 *Prosecutor v. Ntaganda,* Annex II, Decision on the Prosecutor's application for warrants of arrest, article 58 of 10.2.2006, incorporated in the record of the case pursuant to decision ICC-01/04-520, 21.7.2008 (ICC-01-04-02-06-20-Anx2) para 1.

229 *Prosecutor v. Ntaganda,* Mandat d'arrêt, 22.8.2006 (ICC-01/04-02/06-2).

230 OTP-Press Release (DRC), DRC: ICC Warrant of Arrest unsealed against Bosco Ntaganda, 29.4.2008 (ICC-OTP-20080429-PR311).

231 *Prosecutor v. Katanga,* Mandat d'arrêt à l'encontre de Germain Katanga, 2.7.2007 (ICC-01/04-01/07-1).

232 *Prosecutor v. Katanga,* Mandat d'arrêt, *supra* note 231, 6–7.

233 Press Release (DRC), First appearance of Mr. Germain Katanga before the Pre-Trial Chamber I, 22.10.2007 (ICC-20071022-260).

234 Press Release (DRC), Third detainee for the International Criminal Court: Mathieu Ngudjolo Chui, 7.2.2008 (ICC-CPI-20080207-PR284).

counts of crimes against humanity in the territory of Ituri identical to the arrest warrant against Germain Katanga.[235] Mr. Chui's first appearance took place on 11 February 2008, and his identity was verified by the judges.[236]

The Prosecution intended – already since the joint arrest warrant application – to have the cases against Katanga and Chui joined, so that they would be prosecuted together, because of their joint participation in the same attack.[237] PTC I found that there were reasonable grounds to believe that Mathieu Ngudjolo Chui, as the highest ranking *Front des Nationalistes et Intégrationnistes* (hereinafter FNI) commander, and Germain Katanga, as the highest ranking *Force de résistance patriotique en Ituri* (hereinafter FRPI) commander, played an essential role in designing and implementing a joint FNI and FRPI attack against the village of Bogoro, in the territory of Ituri, on or around 24 February 2003.[238] In consequence of the link between the two suspects, the PTC decided to join the cases as initially sought by the Prosecution.[239] The commencement date of the confirmation hearing, previously scheduled to commence on 28 February, then moved to 21 May, was ultimately postponed to 27 June 2008.[240] PTC I opened the hearing on 27 June 2008. Presiding Judge Akua Kuenyehia provided a quick summary to the background of the case and the principles governing the proceedings, emphasizing the presumption of innocence and stating that the burden of proof lies with the Prosecutor.[241] On 26 September 2008, the Chamber decided to commit Katanga and Chui on trial for most of the charges.[242] On 24 October 2008, the Presidency constituted Trial Chamber

---

235 *Prosecutor v. Chui,* Mandat d'arrêt à l'encontre de Mathieu Ngudjolo Chui, 6.7.2007 (ICC-01/04-02/07) 6–7; *Prosecutor v. Chui,* Decision on the evidence and information provided by the Prosecution for the issuance of a warrant of arrest for Mathieu Ngudjolo Chui, 6.7.2007 (ICC-01/04-01/07-262) 29–30.

236 Press Release (DRC), First appearance of Mathieu Ngudjolo Chui before Pre-Trial Chamber I, 11.2.2008 (ICC-CPI-20080211-PR286).

237 *Prosecutor v. Chui,* Prosecution's observations on the joinder of the cases against Germain Katanga and Mathieu Ngudjolo Chui, 14.2.2008 (ICC-01/04-01/07-195).

238 See Press Release (DRC), Second arrest: Germain Katanga transferred into the custody of the ICC, 18.10.2007 (ICC-20071018-250) and Press Release (DRC), Third detainee for the International Criminal Court: Mathieu Ngudjolo Chui, *supra* note 234. It is worth noting that the nine counts in the arrest warrants are identical.

239 *Prosecutor v. Chui,* Decision on the joinder of the cases against Germain Katanga and Mathieu Ngudjolo Chui, 10.3.2008 (ICC-01-04-01-07-257); thereto WCRO confirmation of charges report, *supra* note 174, 33.

240 *Prosecutor v. Katanga and Chui,* Decision on the Defence request for postponement of the confirmation hearing, 25.4.2008 (ICC-01/04-01/07-446) 8.

241 Press Release (DRC), Opening of the confirmation hearing against Germain Katanga and Mathieu Ngudjolo Chui, 27.6.2008 (ICC-CPI-20080627-PR333).

II and referred the pending case to it.[243] The trial's commencement was originally set for 24 September 2009[244] and was postponed until 24 November 2009. On the latter date the trial was opened before Trial Chamber II and is now the second trial in the context of the situation in the DRC.

The OTP completed a first phase of investigations, mainly in Ituri, and is now moving to new cases, paying particular attention to crimes committed by a multiplicity of perpetrators and groups in the North and South Kivu provinces, such as the case of Callixte Mbarushimana, who was arrested recently for crimes committed in the Kivus.[245]

2. Uganda

Closely after the investigation in the DRC was opened, the Prosecutor opened a second investigation with regard to Northern Uganda.[246] In De-

242 Press Release (DRC), Decision on the confirmation of charges in the case of The Prosecutor v. Germain Katanga and Mathieu Ngudjolo Chui, 26.9.2008 (ICC-CPI-20080926-PR357); *Prosecutor v. Katanga and Chui,* Decision on the confirmation of charges in the case of The Prosecutor v. Germain Katanga and Mathieu Ngudjolo Chui, 30.9.2008 (ICC-01/04-01/07-717). Critically evaluating the process, WCRO confirmation of charges report, *supra* note 174, 30 et seq.

243 *Prosecutor v. Katanga and Chui,* Decision constituting Trial Chamber II and referring to it the case of The Prosecutor v. Germain Katanga and Mathieu Ngudjolo Chui, 24.10.2008 (ICC-01-04-01-07-729) 4–5.

244 Press Release (DRC), Trial of Germain Katanga and Mathieu Ngudjolo Chui to commence Thursday, 24 September 2009, 27.3.2009 (ICC-CPI-20090327-PR402).

245 Report of the International Criminal Court for 2007/2008, *supra* note 209, para. 20; OTP-Press Release (DRC), ICC Prosecutor recalls ICC has jurisdiction over crimes against the civilian population in the Kivus, 4.11.2008 (ICC-OTP-20081104-PR369); Press Release (DRC), Callixte Mbarushimana arrested in France for crimes against humanity and war crimes allegedly committed in the Kivus (Democratic Republic of Congo) 11.10.2010 (ICC-CPI-20101011-PR 581).

246 OTP-Press Release (Uganda), Prosecutor of the International Criminal Court opens an investigation into Northern Uganda, 29.7.2004 (ICC-OTP-20040729-65). For the background of the conflict see "Uganda" in HRW, World Report 2008, *supra* note 210, 172 et seq.; OHCHR, Making peace our own, Victims' perceptions of accountability, reconciliation and transitional justice in Northern Uganda, 14.8.2007, 1, 4 et seq.; Schiff, *supra* note 128, 195 et seq.; Tim Allen, *Trial justice, The International Criminal Court and the Lord's Resistance Army* (Zed Books, London, New York 2006) 1 et seq., 25 et seq.; Erin Baines, "The haunting of Alice: local approaches to justice and reconciliation in Northern Uganda" (2007) 1 IJTJ 91, 98 et seq.; Kasaija Phillip Apuuli, "The International Criminal Court (ICC) and the Lord's Resistance Army (LRA) insurgency in Northern Uganda" (2004) 15 CLF 391, 391 et seq.; *id.,* "The ICC arrest warrants for the Lord's Resistance Army leaders and peace prospects for Northern Uganda" (2006) 4 JICJ 179, 180 et seq.; Mohamed El Zeidy, "The Ugandan government triggers the first test of the complementarity principle: as assessment of first State Party's referral to the ICC" (2005)

cember 2003 President Yoweri Museveni referred the situation "concerning the Lord's Resistance Army (hereinafter LRA) in northern and western Uganda" to the Prosecutor.[247] The Prosecutor later responded that "the scope of the referral encompasses all crimes committed in Northern Uganda in the context of the ongoing conflict involving the LRA,"[248] thus indicating a broader interpretation of the situation, which includes all possible perpetrators contrary to a limitation to the LRA only. Despite the modification of the referral by the Prosecutor, it seems apparent enough that the Prosecutor solicited for Uganda's self-referral even though the public record doesn't clearly indicate so.[249] On 16 September 2004, the situation in Uganda was assigned to PTC II.[250] On 6 May 2005, the Prosecutor submitted applications for five arrest warrants. PTC II issued the intended warrants on 8 July 2005 against Joseph Kony,[251] Vincent Otti,[252] Okot Od-

5 ICLR 83, 83 et seq.; Payam Akhavan, "Developments at the ICC: the Lord's Resistance Army case: Uganda's submission of the first state referral to the ICC" (2005) 99 AJIL 403, 403 et seq.; Manisuli Ssenyonjo, "The International Criminal Court and the Lord's Resistance Army Leaders: prosecution or amnesty?" (2007) 7 ICLR 361, 365; H. Abigail Moy, "The ICC's arrest warrants and Uganda's LRA: renewing the debate over amnesty and complementarity" (2006) HHRL 267, 267–8; Phuong Pham/Patrick Vinck/Eric Stover, "The LRA and forced conscription in Northern Uganda" (2008) 30 HRQ 404, 404 et seq.; Wouters/Verhoeven, in Ankumah/Kwakwa, *supra* note 210, 140 et seq.; RLP, Working Paper No. 17, Peace first, justice later: traditional justice in Northern Uganda (hereinafter RLP paper no. 17), Lucy Hovil/Joanna Quinn, July 2005, 3 et seq.; Kasaija Phillip Apuuli, "The ICC's possible deferral of the LRA case to Uganda" (2008) 6 JICJ 801, 801 et seq.; Lekha Sriram/Ross, *supra* note 210, 48–9; Nick Grono/Adam O'Brien, "Justice in conflict? The ICC and peace processes" in Nicholas Waddell/Phil Clark (eds.), *Courting conflict? Justice, peace and the ICC in Africa* (Royal African Society, London 2008) 13, 14 et seq.

[247] Press Release (Uganda), President of Uganda refers situation concerning the Lord's Resistance Army (LRA) to the ICC, 29.1.2004 (ICC-20040129-44); Allen, *supra* note 246, 1; William Burke-White/Scott Kaplan, "Shaping the contours of domestic justice: The International Criminal Court and an admissibility challenge in the Ugandan situation" in Stahn/Sluiter, *supra* note 5, 79, 79; Jurdi, *supra* note 99, 81.

[248] *Prosecutor v. Kony et al.,* Decision to convene a status conference on the investigation in the situation in Uganda in relation to the application of article 53, 2.12.2005 (ICC-02/04-01/05-68) para. 5. See also Remarks by ICC Prosecutor Luis Moreno-Ocampo at the 27th meeting of the Committee of Legal Advisers on Public International Law – CADHI (Strasbourg, France), 18.3.2004, 6.

[249] Schabas, *supra* note 27, 149.

[250] *Situation in Uganda,* Decision assigning the situation in Uganda to Pre-Trial Chamber II, 5.7.2004 (ICC-02/04-1).

[251] *Prosecutor v. Kony et al.,* Warrant of Arrest for Joseph Kony issued on 8 July 2005 as amended on 27 September 2005, 27.9.2005 (ICC-02/04-01/05-53).

[252] *Prosecutor v. Kony et al.,* Warrant of Arrest for Vincent Otti, 8.7.2005 (ICC-02/04-01/05-54). There have been reports by the media, the Uganda Peoples Defence Force (hereinafter UPDF); and other sources, that Vincent Otti was killed,

hiambo,[253] Dominic Ongwen,[254] and Raska Lukwiya.[255] With presumably three of the five indicted dead, the only two remaining commanders might very well be Joseph Kony and Dominic Ongwen.[256] None of the suspects has been apprehended and peace talks in Juba, South Sudan have been consistently accompanied by LRA requests to drop the arrest warrants.[257] In early March 2008, the Prosecutor re-emphasized that four arrest warrants remain in effect and that the LRA would have to follow the judicial process of the ICC before the PTC in order to challenge admissibility.[258] The gov-

---

and the OTP has taken steps to assess the veracity of these reports, *Prosecutor v. Kony et al.,* Submission of information regarding Vincent Otti, 8.11.2007 (ICC-02/04-01/05-250) paras. 1–2. So far the Chamber has not verified the reports or terminated the proceedings against Vincent Otti.

253 *Prosecutor v. Kony et al.,* Warrant of Arrest for Okot Odhiambo, 8.7.2005 (ICC-02/04-01/05-56). According to LRA internal sources Okot Odhiambo was executed, see "Northerners weigh up Odhiambo killing," 15.4.2008, Joe Wacha, ICC – Africa Update 167, Institute for war & peace reporting. These rumors, as well as the killing of Vincent Otti, still need to be verified before the ICC.

254 *Prosecutor v. Kony et al.,* Warrant of Arrest for Dominic Ongwen, 8.7.2005 (ICC-02/04-01/05-57).

255 *Prosecutor v. Kony et al.,* Warrant of Arrest for Raska Lukwiya, 8.7.2005 (ICC-02/04-01/05-55). According to the decision of PTC II, *Prosecutor v. Kony et al.,* Prosecution's request that the warrant of arrest for Raska Lukwiya be withdrawn and rendered without effect because of his death, 22.3.2007 (ICC-02/04-01/05-230), to terminate the proceedings against Raska Lukwiya, the name of Raska Lukwiya has been removed from the case.

256 See "LRA's murky negotiators," 17.4.2008, Emma Mutaizibwa, ICC – Africa Update 167, Institute for war & peace reporting; Kimberly Hanlon, "Now that peace is being negotiated in Uganda, will the ICC still pursue justice?" (2007) 14 Tulsa Journal of Comparative & International Law 295, 296.

257 "Ugandan Rebels to appeal ICC warrants," 12.3.2008, Katy Glassborow/Peter Eichstaedt, ICC – Africa Update 160, Institute for war & peace reporting; "Why the International Criminal Court must withdraw indictments against the top LRA leaders: a legal perspective," 20.8.2006, Zachary Lomo, The Sunday Monitor. On the discussion, with further references, see Schabas, *supra* note 27, 40 with fn. 65. There are voices that regard the peace negotiations as a (partial) result due to the pressure by the ICC arrest warrants, see Kai Ambos, "Die Rolle des Internationalen Strafgerichtshofs" (2006) 41 APuZ 10, 17; OTP-Press Release (Uganda), Statement by Prosecutor Luis Moreno-Ocampo, 6.7.2006 (ICC-OTP-20060706-146); Statement by Luis Moreno-Ocampo: Fifth session of the Assembly of States Parties, 24.11.2006, 2–3: "[...] the loss of their safe haven led the LRA commanders to engage in negotiations, [...]"; also Mr. Sivu Maqungo of South Africa, Session 3: Interested States, Second public hearing of the OTP, 17.10.2006. On the Juba talks cf. Apuuli (2008), *supra* note 246, 804–5; OHCHR, Making peace our own, *supra* note 246, 20 et seq. On the prior peace talks with the LRA cf. Allen, *supra* note 246, 78 et seq.

258 OTP-Statement (Uganda), OTP statement in relation to events in Uganda, 4.3.2008; also "Building a Future on Peace and Justice," Address by Mr. Luis Moreno-Ocampo, Prosecutor of the ICC, Nuremberg, 24.–25.6.2007, 6; Burke-White/Kaplan, in Stahn/Sluiter, *supra* note 247, 82–3.

ernment of Uganda insisted that the peace deal and plans for domestic trials of rebel leaders work hand-in-hand with the ICC.[259] Recently, it is doubtful if the peace talks are fruitful at all since the LRA is reported to be regrouping despite its commitment to peace.[260] Joseph Kony, who was expected to sign the peace agreement on 10 April 2008, never showed up.[261] In the light of new information on attacks by the LRA the Prosecutor called to renew efforts to arrest Kony and his top commanders.[262] He re-emphasized that appeasement is not working with Kony.[263]

From a judicial point of view, the article 19 (1) proceedings, which were initiated in late 2008, affirmed the admissibility of the *Kony et al.* case at the stage of the decision (March 2009), especially with regard to complementarity issues (such as the factual and legal situation in Uganda regarding the Special Division of the High Court and the "inactivity" scenario).[264] The PTC arrived at the conclusion that:

---

[259] "Uganda Insists Peace Not at Odds With ICC," 14.4.2008, Katy Glassborow, ICC – Africa Update 167, Institute for war & peace reporting; *Prosecutor v. Kony et al.*, Annex 2 to the report by the registrar on the execution of the "request for further information from the Republic of Uganda on the status of execution of the warrants of arrest," 10.7.2008 (ICC-02/04-01/05-305-Anx2) 2: "Therefore, with or without the peace agreement, Uganda will continue to provide the Court with all the cooperation it requires."

[260] "LRA prepares for war, not peace," 24.4.2008, Katy Glassborow/Peter Eichstaedt/Emma Mutaizibwa, ICC – Africa Update 168, Institute for war & peace reporting; Michael Otim/Marieke Wierda, "Justice at Juba: international obligations and local demands in Northern Uganda," in Waddell/Clark, *supra* note 246, 21, 27.

[261] *Prosecutor v. Kony et al.*, Annex 2 to the report by the registrar, *supra* note 259, 2. See further the Agreement on accountability and reconciliation between the government of the Republic of Uganda and the Lord's Resistance Army/Movement (hereinafter Agreement on accountability and reconciliation), 29.6.2007, Juba (Sudan).

[262] OTP-Press Release (Uganda), Prosecutor calls for renewed efforts to arrest LRA leader Kony in wake of new attacks, 6.10.2008 (ICC-OTP-20081006-PR359); Report of the International Criminal Court for 2007/2008, *supra* note 209, para. 31.

[263] Prosecutor's statement at the ISS Symposium on "The ICC that Africa wants," 14.12.2009, Cape Winlands 9.11.2009, 4.

[264] *Prosecutor v. Kony et al.,* Decision on the admissibility of the case under article 19 (1) of the Statute, 10.3.2009 (ICC-02/04-01/05-377) paras. 13 et seq. See further *Prosecutor v. Kony et al.,* Decision initiating proceedings under article 19, requesting observations and appointing counsel for the Defence, 21.10.2008 (ICC-02/04-01/05-320); *Prosecutor v. Kony et al.,* Request pursuant to rule 103 (1) of the Rules of Procedure and Evidence for leave to submit observation as amicus curiae in the proceedings under Article 19 (1) of the Rome Statute of the International Criminal Court in the case of The Prosecutor v. Kony and others, 7.11.2008 (ICC-02/04-01/05-335) paras. 11 et seq.; *Prosecutor v. Kony et al.,* Application by the Uganda Victims' Foundation and the Redress Trust for leave to submit observations to the Pre-Trial Chamber II of the International Criminal Court, pursuant to Rule

"Pending the adoption of all relevant legal texts and the implementation of all practical steps, the scenario against which the admissibility of the Case has to be determined remains therefore the same as at the time of the issuance of the Warrants, that is one of *total inaction* on the part of the relevant national authorities; accordingly, there is no reason for the Chamber to review the positive determination of the admissibility of the Case made at that stage (emph. added)."[265]

3. Central African Republic

On 21 December 2004, President Bozizé referred the situation of CAR to the ICC and requested an investigation by the OTP into the crimes committed on its territory since 1 July 2002, which was publicly announced on 7 January 2005.[266] On 19 January 2005, the situation was assigned to PTC III.[267] Considering that in DRC and Uganda preliminary examinations were completed after six months and that almost two years passed in CAR without any information given by the Prosecutor, the Chamber felt obligated to request information on the status of the preliminary investigation.[268] The Prosecutor replied and provided information, but emphasized that he was not under a legal obligation to do so.[269] Be that as it may, the request by

---

103 of the Rules of Procedure and Evidence, 31.10.2008 (ICC-02/04-01/05-330); *Prosecutor v. Kony et al.,* Observations on behalf of victims pursuant to article 19 (1) of the Rome Statute with 55 public annexes and 45 redacted annexes, 18.11.2008 (ICC-02/04-01/05-349); *Prosecutor v. Kony et al.,* Submission of observations on the admissibility of the case under article 19 (1) of the Statute, 18.11.2008 (ICC-02/04-01/05-350); *Prosecutor v. Kony et al.,* Prosecution's observations regarding the admissibility of the case against Joseph Kony, Vincent Otti, Okot Odhiambo and Dominic Ongwen, 18.11.2008 (ICC-02/04-01/05-352); *Prosecutor v. Kony et al.,* Amicus Curiae submitted pursuant to the Pre-Trial Chamber II "Decision on application for leave to submit observations under Rule 103" dated 5 November 2008, 18.11.2008 (ICC-02/04-01/05-353). Thereto William Burke-White/Scott Kaplan, "Shaping the contours of domestic justice" (2009) 9 JICJ 257, 257 et seq.; also *id.,* in Stahn/Sluiter, *supra* note 247.

265 *Prosecutor v. Kony et al.,* Decision on the admissibility of the case under article 19 (1), *supra* note 264, para. 52.

266 William Schabas, "First prosecutions at the International Criminal Court" (2006) 27 HRLJ 25, 38; OTP-Press Release (CAR), Prosecutor receives referral concerning Central African Republic, 7.1.2005 (ICC-OTP-20050107-86).

267 *Situation in CAR,* Decision assigning the situation in the Central African Republic to Pre-Trial Chamber III, 19.1.2005 (ICC-01/05-1).

268 *Situation in CAR,* Decision requesting information on the status of the preliminary examination of the situation in the Central African Republic, 28.3.2006 (ICC-01/05-6) 4–5.

269 *Situation in CAR,* Prosecution's report pursuant to Pre-Trial Chamber III's 30 November 2006 decision requesting information on the status of the preliminary examination, *supra* note 172, para. 1; Mohamed El Zeidy, "The gravity threshold under the Statute of the International Criminal Court" (2008) 19 CLF 35, 54, calls the

the PTC resulted in an investigation, which was opened on 22 May 2007.[270] The Prosecutor indicated that the investigation focuses on violence that occurred during a peak of violence in 2002–2003, including a massive campaign of sexual violence, and that he will continue gathering information and monitoring recent crimes being committed on the territory of the CAR, including in the north of the country (areas of Birao and Paoua), where violence has erupted again since the end of 2005.[271] On the whole, it took the Prosecutor more than two years – referral on 7 January 2005 until the opening of an investigation on 22 May 2007 – to end his pre-investigations and start a formal investigation.[272]

The only case arising from the CAR situation so far concerns Jean-Pierre Bemba Gombo, President and Commander in Chief of the *Mouvement de libération du Congo* (hereinafter MLC), who is allegedly responsible ("*il y a des motifs raisonnables de croire que M. Jean-Pierre Bemba est pénalement responsable*") for war crimes and crimes against humanity committed on the territory of CAR from 25 October 2002 to 15 March 2003.[273] He was arrested on 24 May 2008, and later transferred and surrendered to The Hague by the Belgian authorities on 3 July 2008.[274] After his first appearance on 4 July 2008, the confirmation of charges hearing finally commenced on 12 January 2009.[275] On 3 March 2009, the Chamber adjourned the hearing pursuant to article 67 (7) (c) (ii), and it requested the Prosecu-

---

practice of the OTP "the acceptance of a supervision on a voluntary basis, showing a sort of mutual cooperation between the organs of the Court."

270 OTP-Press Release (CAR), Prosecutor opens investigation in the Central African Republic, 22.5.2007 (ICC-OTP-PR-20070522-220).

271 Background note on the opening by the Prosecutor of an investigation in CAR, 22.5.2007 (ICC-OTP-BN-20070522-220-A); Report of the International Criminal Court for 2007/2008, *supra* note 209, paras. 51–2.

272 Very critical on the long silence on behalf of the OTP, Mr. Antoine Bernard – International Federation for Human Rights (FIDH), Session 2: NGOs and other experts, Second public hearing of the OTP, 26.9.2006.

273 *Prosecutor v. Bemba,* Mandat d'arrêt à l'encontre de Jean-Pierre Bemba Gombo remplaçant le mandat d'arrêt décerné le 23 mai 2008, 10.6.2008 (ICC-01/05-01/08-15) para. 21; Press Release (CAR), Jean-Pierre Bemba Gombo arrested for crimes allegedly committed in the Central African Republic, 24.5.2008 (ICC-CPI-20080524-PR315).

274 Press Release (CAR), Surrender of Jean-Pierre Bemba to the International Criminal Court, 3.7.2008 (ICC-CPI-20080703-PR335). See also "Comment: Bemba is ICC's biggest fish," 18.6.2008, Eugène Bakama Bope, ICC – Africa Update 175, Institute for war & peace reporting.

275 Press Release (CAR), The confirmation of charges hearing in the case of The Prosecutor v. Jean-Pierre Bemba Gombo is postponed, 2.12.2008 (ICC-CPI-20081202-PR378); OTP-Press Release (CAR), Confirmation of charges hearing in the case of The Prosecutor v. Jean-Pierre Bemba Gombo – Opening remarks by Fatou Bensouda, Deputy Prosecutor of the ICC, 12.1.2009.

tor to consider amending the document containing the charges to address article 28 as possible mode of liability.[276] From a legal point of view, this decision entails two interesting points that need to be mentioned briefly. First, PTC III clarified that "notion of a 'different crime' pursuant to article 61 (7) (c) (ii) of the Statute relates both to the crimes as defined in articles 6, 7, and 8 of the Statute, as well as to the mode of liability as referred to in articles 25 and 28 of the Statute."[277] Secondly, the term "adjourn the hearing" should be interpreted broadly so that a hearing "may take place subsequent to the oral sessions and as long as the Chamber has not made its final determination on the merits and issued a decision whether or not to confirm the charges."[278] PTC II committed Mr. Bemba to trial on 12 June 2009. The Chamber thereby confirmed some counts and declined others, referring the case as such to a Trial Chamber for further (trial) proceedings.[279] The trial was set to start on 27 April 2010, but was postponed several times due to an admissibility challenge by the Defence and will now commence shortly.[280]

It is striking that in two situations (DRC, Uganda) the Prosecutor actively encouraged, or even exerted pressure, to receive self-referrals. Rather than using its *proprio motu* powers under article 15, the OTP chose a policy of self-referrals under articles 13 (a) and 14. The legality and inherent dangers of such self-referrals will be discussed below (Part III, B., IV., 3.). Furthermore, it took longer to decide on an investigation into the CAR situation compared to the other situations based on state referrals (DRC, Uganda). Beside the legal question regarding to what extent the Prosecutor can expand pre-investigations before starting a formal investigation (Part III, D.), the reasons *in concreto* are merely speculative. It is, however, certain that there were severe differences in time between the two fast-track situations (DRC, Uganda) on the one hand, and the slow-track situation (CAR) on the

---

[276] *Prosecutor v. Bemba,* Decision adjourning the hearing pursuant to article 67 (7) (c) (ii) of the Rome Statute, 3.3.2009 (ICC-01/05-01/08-388) 19–20.

[277] *Prosecutor v. Bemba,* Decision adjourning the hearing, *supra* note 276, para. 26. For a critical evaluation see Kai Ambos, "Critical issues in the *Bemba* confirmation decision" (2009) 22 LJIL 715, 724 et seq.

[278] *Prosecutor v. Bemba,* Decision adjourning the hearing, *supra* note 276, para. 37.

[279] *Prosecutor v. Bemba,* Decision pursuant to article 61 (7) (a) and (b) of the Rome Statute on the charges of the Prosecutor against Jean-Pierre Bemba Gombo, 15.6.2009 (ICC-01/05-01/08-424).

[280] Press Release (CAR), Commencement of the trial of Jean-Pierre Bemba postponed until 5 July 2010, 8.3.2010 (ICC-CPI- 20100308-PR503); Press release (CAR), The commencement of the trial in the case The Prosecutor v. Jean-Pierre Bemba Gombo is postponed, 7.7.2010 (ICC-CPI-20100707-PR554); see further *Prosecutor v. Bemba,* Decision on the admissibility and abuse of process challenge, 24.6.2010 (ICC-01/05-01/08-802).

other hand. For the sake of transparency further explanations by the OTP would have been recommendable.[281] As an interim result, the practice of self-referrals was solicited for by the Prosecutor. This creative interpretation of article 14 and its consequences will need further discussion.

4. Darfur, Sudan

With regard to Darfur, Sudan, the SC, acting under Chapter VII of the UN Charter, adopted Resolution 1593 referring the situation to the ICC under article 13 (b);[282] the situation in Darfur was assigned to PTC I.[283] On 6 June 2005, the OTP officially decided to open investigations[284] informing the SC and explaining the conducted preliminary analysis.[285] As a consequence of the referral, the Prosecutor had received a sealed envelope containing the conclusions of the International Commission of Inquiry on Darfur as well as a sealed list of 51 individuals named by the International Commission as suspects of grave international crimes in Darfur.[286] On 13 December 2005, the Prosecutor submitted a second report to the SC reporting on the first investi-

---

281 See further Part IV, B., II., 4. and Part IV, B., III., 3., d), aa).

282 OTP-Press-Release (Darfur), Security Council refers situation in Darfur to ICC Prosecutor, 1.4.2005 (ICC-OTP-20050401-96); SC-Res.1593 (2005) was adopted on 31 March 2005 by a vote of 11 in favor, none against with 4 abstentions (Algeria, Brazil, China, United States). For the background of the conflict see "Sudan" in HRW, World Report 2008, *supra* note 210, 166 et seq.; Schiff, *supra* note 128, 226 et seq.; Wouters/Verhoeven, in Ankumah/Kwakwa, *supra* note 210, 145 et seq.; Jakob Pichon, "The principle of complementarity in the cases of the Sudanese nationals Ahmad Harun and Ali Kushayb before the International Criminal Court" (2008) 8 ICLR 185, 214 et seq.; Robert Cryer, "Sudan, Resolution 1593 and international criminal justice" (2006) 19 LJIL 195, 196 et seq.; Alex De Waal, "Darfur, the Court and Khartoum: The politics of State non-cooperation," in Waddell/Clark, *supra* note 246, 29, 29 et seq.

283 *Situation in Darfur (Sudan),* Decision assigning the Situation in Darfur, Sudan to Pre-trial Chamber I, 21.4.2005 (ICC-02/05-1).

284 OTP-Press-Release (Darfur), The Prosecutor of the ICC opens investigation in Darfur, 6.6.2005 (ICC-OTP-0606-104).

285 First Report of the Prosecutor of the International Criminal Court, Mr. Luis Moreno-Ocampo, to the Security Council pursuant to UNSC 1593 (2005), 29.6.2005.

286 *Prosecutor v. Harun and Kushayb,* Background information – Facts regarding the situation in Darfur, Sudan, 2.5.2007 (ICC-PIDS-PR-20070502-214A) 1; OTP-Press-Release (Darfur), Prosecutor receives list prepared by Commission of Inquiry on Darfur, 5.4.2005 (ICC-OTP-20050405-97); OTP-Press-Release (Darfur), List of Names of Suspects in Darfur opened by the ICC OTP, 14.4.2005 (ICC-OTP-20050411-98). See further Report of the International Commission of Inquiry on Darfur to the United Nations Secretary-General, Pursuant to Security Council Resolution 1564 of 18 September 2004, 25.1.2005.

gation phase. Good progress had been made on information gathering related to the universe of crimes in Darfur and a number of alleged criminal incidents were selected for full investigation.[287] Since this report, the OTP continued investigations from the outside in light of continuing insecurity in Darfur.[288] On 14 December 2006, the Prosecutor informed the SC that he had nearly completed investigations into some of the worst crimes committed in Darfur, and that the OTP was finalizing its submissions to the Judges of the PTC.[289] The Prosecutor subsequently reported to the SC every six months on actions taken and upcoming activities.[290]

On 27 February 2007, the PTC received an application requesting the issuance of summonses to appear in respect of Mr. Ahmad Muhammad Harun (hereinafter Ahmad Harun), former Minister of State for the Interior of the Government of Sudan and current Minister of State for Humanitarian Affairs, and Mr. Ali Muhammad Ali Abd-Al-Rahman (hereinafter Ali Kushayb), a Janjaweed/militia leader.[291] After examining the application, the PTC delivered its decision on 27 April 2007, holding that summonses to appear would not be sufficient, and that arrest warrants are necessary to ensure appearance of the two suspects.[292] The Judges consequently issued an arrest warrant against Ahmad Harun and Ali Kushayb after determining that the case falls within the jurisdiction of Court, appears to be admissible, and that article 58 (7) and article 58 (1) are fulfilled.[293] There were reasonable grounds to believe that Mr. Harun had committed twenty counts of crimes against humanity and twenty-two counts of war crimes. Reasonable grounds were also present to believe Mr. Kushayb had committed twenty-two counts of crimes against humanity and twenty-eight counts of war crimes.[294] On 4 June 2007, the Registry issued a request for arrest and sur-

[287] Second Report of the Prosecutor of the International Criminal Court, Mr. Luis Moreno-Ocampo, to the Security Council pursuant to UNSC 1593 (2005), 13.12.2005, 2–3.

[288] Third Report of the Prosecutor of the International Criminal Court, to the Security Council pursuant to UNSC 1593 (2005), 14.6.2006, introduction.

[289] Fourth Report of the Prosecutor of the International Criminal Court, to the Security Council pursuant to UNSC 1593 (2005), 14.12.2006, 1, 7.

[290] Eight Report of the Prosecutor of the International Criminal Court, to the Security Council pursuant to UNSC 1593 (2005), 3.12.2008, para. 5.

[291] Fifth Report of the Prosecutor of the International Criminal Court, to the Security Council pursuant to UNSC 1593 (2005), 7.6.2007, 1.

[292] *Prosecutor v. Harun and Kushayb,* Decision on the Prosecution application under article 58 (7) of the Statute, 27.4.2007 (ICC-02/05-01/07-1-Corr) para. 124.

[293] *Prosecutor v. Harun and Kushayb,* Decision on the Prosecution application under article 58 (7) of the Statute, *supra* note 292.

[294] *Prosecutor v. Harun and Kushayb,* Decision on the Prosecution application under article 58 (7) of the Statute, *supra* note 292, 43 et seq; *Prosecutor v. Harun*

render for Ahmad Harun and Ali Kushayb to Sudan,[295] neighboring States (Arab Republic of Egypt, Eritrea, the Federal Democratic Republic of Ethiopia, and the Libyan Arab Jamahiriya),[296] States Party to the ICC Statute,[297] and all SC members that are not States Parties to the ICC Statute.[298] Neither arrest warrant has been executed to date, which led the Prosecutor to report the failure of the government of Sudan to cooperate.[299] Compliance with SC-Res.1593 (2005) and the full and immediate cooperation of the Sudanese government through the arrest and surrender of Ahmad Harun and Ali Kushayb lies within the hands of the international community and the SC.[300] The OTP then announced its second and third investigation in Darfur; the second case focuses on the pattern of repeated attacks on civilians and the third case focuses on the targeting of AU and UN

---

and Kushayb, Warrant of arrest for Ali Muhammad Ali Abd-Al-Rahman ("Ali Kushayb"), 27.4.2007 (ICC-02/05-01/07-3-Corr); *Prosecutor v. Harun and Kushayb,* Warrant of arrest for Ahmad Muhammad Harun ("Ahmad Harun"), 27.4.2007 (ICC-02/05-01/07-2-Corr).

[295] *Prosecutor v. Harun and Kushayb,* Request to the Republic of the Sudan for the arrest and surrender of Ahmad Harun, 5.6.2007 (ICC-02/05-01/07-13); *Prosecutor v. Harun and Kushayb,* Request to the Republic of the Sudan for the arrest and surrender of Ali Kushayb, 5.6.2007 (ICC-02/05-01/07-14).

[296] *Prosecutor v. Harun and Kushayb,* Request to the Arab Republic of Egypt, Eritrea, the Federal Democratic Republic of Ethiopia and the Libyan Arab Jamahiriya for the arrest and surrender of Ahmad Harun, 5.6.2007 (ICC-02/05-01/07-15-Corr); *Prosecutor v. Harun and Kushayb,* Request to the Arab Republic of Egypt, Eritrea, the Federal Democratic Republic of Ethiopia and the Libyan Arab Jamahiriya for the arrest and surrender of Ali Kushayb, 5.6.2007 (ICC-02/05-01/07-16-Corr).

[297] *Prosecutor v. Harun and Kushayb,* Request to States Parties to the Rome Statute for the arrest and surrender of Ahmad Harun, 5.6.2007 (ICC-02/05-01/07-17); *Prosecutor v. Harun and Kushayb,* Request to States Parties to the Rome Statute for the arrest and surrender of Ali Kushayb, 5.6.2007 (ICC-02/05-01/07-18).

[298] *Prosecutor v. Harun and Kushayb,* Request to United Nations Security Council members that are not States Parties to the Statute for the arrest and surrender of Ahmad Harun, 5.6.2007 (ICC-02/05-01/07-19); *Prosecutor v. Harun and Kushayb,* Request to United Nations Security Council members that are not States Parties to the Statute for the arrest and surrender of Ali Kushayb, 5.6.2007 (ICC-02/05-01/07-20).

[299] Sixth Report of the Prosecutor of the International Criminal Court, to the Security Council pursuant to UNSC 1593 (2005), 5.12.2007, paras. 4, 19 et seq., 83; also Statement of the Prosecutor, ICC Prosecutor: Harun is a fugitive, 25.4.2008; Seventh Report of the Prosecutor of the International Criminal Court, to the Security Council pursuant to UNSC 1593 (2005), 5.6.2008, paras. 30, 40–1; Ninth Report of the Prosecutor of the International Criminal Court, to the Security Council pursuant to UNSC 1593 (2005), 5.6.2009, paras. 22 et seq., 49; recently, Eleventh Report of the Prosecutor of the International Criminal Court, to the Security Council parsuant to UNSC 1593 (2005), 17.6.2010, para. 13, 2, paras. 16 et seq., 3 et seq.

[300] Sixth Report pursuant to UNSC 1593, *supra* note 299, para. 87; Seventh Report pursuant to UNSC 1593, *supra* note 299, para. 10.

peacekeepers.[301] In consequence, the Prosecutor formally submitted his second case against Sudanese President, Hassan Ahmad Al Bashir, for committing genocide, crimes against humanity, and war crimes.[302] PTC I issued a warrant of arrest on 4 March 2009.[303] Most notably, the Chamber held that Omar Al Bashir's official capacity as a sitting Head of State does not exclude his criminal responsibility, nor does it grant him immunity against prosecution before the ICC.[304] Thus, Mr. Al Bashir represents the ICC's first case against a sitting Head of State. However, the majority of the Chamber, Judge Anita Ušacka dissenting, did not uphold the Prosecution's allegations of genocide since the OTP failed to provide reasonable grounds to believe that the Government of Sudan "acted with *dolus specialis*/specific intent to destroy, in whole or in part, the Fur, Massalit and Zaghawa groups [...]," nevertheless [the PTC] "considers that, if, as a result of the ongoing Prosecution's investigation into the crimes allegedly committed by Omar Al Bashir, additional evidence on the existence of a GoS's genocidal intent is gathered, the Majority's conclusion in the present decision would not prevent the Prosecution from requesting, pursuant to article 58 (6) of the Statute, an amendment to the arrest warrant for Omar Al Bashir so as to include the crime of genocide."[305] The crime of genocide was therefore not included in the first warrant, but the Chamber left a (small) backdoor open for its later inclusion. Recently, the Appeal's Chamber reversed the

---

301 Seventh Report pursuant to UNSC 1593, *supra* note 299, para. 56–7.

302 OTP-Press-Release (Darfur), ICC Prosecutor presents case against Sudanese President, Hassan Ahmad Al Bashir, for genocide, crimes against humanity and war crimes in Darfur, 14.7.2008 (ICC-OTP-20080714-PR341); see further Prosecutor's statement on the Prosecutor's application for a warrant of arrest under article 58 against Omar Hassan Ahmad Al Bashir, 14.7.2008; Summary of the case: Prosecutor's application for warrant of arrest under article 58 against Omar Hassan Ahmad Al Bashir, 14.7.2008; Eight Report pursuant to UNSC 1593, *supra* note 290, paras. 23 et seq.

303 Press Release (Darfur), ICC issues a warrant of arrest for Omar Al Bashir, President of Sudan, 4.3.2009 (ICC-CPI-20090304-PR394); *Prosecutor v. Al Bashir,* Warrant of arrest for Omar Hassan Ahmad Al Bashir, 4.3.2009 (ICC-02/05-01/09-1). See the attempt to prevent the Chamber from doing so, *Situation in Darfur (Sudan),* Application on behalf of Citizens' Organizations of The Sudan in relation to the Prosecutor's applications for arrest warrants of 14 July 2008 and 20 November 2008, 11.1.2009 (ICC-02/05-170).

304 *Prosecutor v. Al Bashir,* Decision on the Prosecutor's application for a warrant of arrest against Omar Hassan Ahmad Al Bashir, 4.3.2009 (ICC-02/05-01/09-3) paras. 41–5.

305 *Prosecutor v. Al Bashir,* Decision on the Prosecutor's application for a warrant of arrest against Bashir, *supra* note 304, paras. 206–7; contrary *Prosecutor v. Al Bashir,* Separate and partly dissenting opinion of Judge Anita Ušacka, Decision on the Prosecutor's application for a warrant of arrest against Omar Hassan Ahmad Al Bashir, 4.3.2009 (ICC-02/05-01/09-3) para. 105.

PTC's decision to the extent that the PTC did not issue a warrant of arrest in respect to genocide and it directed the PTC to decide anew, on the basis of the correct standard of proof, and PTC I issued a second warrant of arrest on 12 July 2010 in respect to the crime of genocide.[306]

On 20 November 2008, Luis Moreno-Ocampo presented evidence to the Judges, potentially leading to a third case in Darfur against three rebel commanders for their alleged responsibility for crimes committed against African Union peacekeepers on 29 September 2007 (Haskanita attack).[307] On 17 May 2005, PTC I made public its decision to issue a summons to appear against Bahar Idriss Abu Garda, a rebel commander, who allegedly participated actively in the Haskanita attack.[308] First, the names of the other two rebel commanders remained undiclosed, but Abdallah Banda Abakaer Nourain an Saleh Mohammed Jerbo Jamus arrived voluntarily at the ICC in June 2010.[309] Before, Mr. Abu Garda had been the first person to appear voluntarily before the Court and the first person to appear in the Darfur situation.[310] In the initial appearance on 18 May 2009 the date of the beginning of the confirmation of charges hearing was scheduled for 12 October 2009.[311] It was held on 19 to 30 October 2009. On 8 February 2010 the Chamber declined to confirm the charges.[312] PTC I found that the Prosecu-

---

306 *Prosecutor v. Al Bashir,* Judgment on the appeal of the Prosecutor against the "Decision on the Prosecution's application for a warrant of arrest against Omar Hassan Ahmad Al Bashir," 3.2.2010 (ICC-02/05-01/09-73) 3: *Prosecutor v. Al Bashir*, Second warrant of Arrest for Omar Hassan Ahmad Al Bashir, 12.7.2010 (ICC-02/05-01/09-95).

307 OTP-Press-Release (Darfur), "Attacks on peacekeepers will not be tolerated," ICC Prosecutor presents evidence in third case in Darfur, 20.11.2008 (ICC-OTP-20081120-PR373); Eight Report pursuant to UNSC 1593, *supra* note 290, paras. 12–3, 52 et seq.

308 *Prosecutor v. Abu Garda,* Decision on the Prosecutor's application under article 58, 7.5.2009 (ICC-02/05-02/09-1).

309 Press Release (Darfur), New suspects in the situation in Darfur, Sudan arrive voluntarily at the ICC: First appearance scheduled for tomorrow, 16.6.2010 (ICC-CPI-20100616-PR 547; cf. earlier Tenth Report of the Prosecutor of the International Criminal Court, to the Security Council pursuant to UNSC 1593 (2005), 7.12.2009, para. 35, 5.

310 OTP-Press-Release (Darfur), Abu Garda arrived at the premises of the Court, 17.5.2009 (ICC-CPI-20090517-PR413); OTP-Press-Release (Darfur), Prosecutor: "The attack on African Union peacekeepers in Haskanita was an attack on millions of civilians they had come to protect; we will prosecute those allegedly responsible," 17.5.2009 (ICC-OTP-20090517-PR412).

311 Press Release (Darfur), Confirmation of charges hearing in the case of The Prosecutor v. Bahr Idriss Abu Garda scheduled to start on Monday, 12 October 2009, 19.5.2009 (ICC-CPI-20090519-PR414).

312 *Prosecutor v. Abu Garda,* Decision on the confirmation of charges, 8.2.2010 (ICC-02/05-02/09-243-Red).

tion's allegations that Abu Garda participated in the alleged common plan to attack MGS Haskanita were not supported by sufficient evidence.[313] It now rests upon the OTP to present additional evidence.

5. Article 15 situations (Côte d'Ivoire, Iraq, Venezuela, Palestine, Kenya, etc.)

On 15 February 2005, Côte d'Ivoire accepted the jurisdiction of the ICC for crimes committed on its territory since 19 September 2002 through a declaration, via a note verbal,[314] in accordance with article 12 (3).[315] According to the OTP, the situation in the Côte d'Ivoire appears to involve over a thousand potential victims of willful killing within the jurisdiction of the Court.[316] But no formal investigation has been opened yet, which leads to the conclusion that this declaration of acceptance is treated as *proprio motu* information under article 15.[317] On 22 January 2009, the Palestinian National Authority lodged a declaration pursuant to article 12 (3), thus making it the second *ad hoc* declaration besides Côte d'Ivoire.[318] Nevertheless, the declaration does not "jump the queue," but the OTP carries out an independent legal assessment similar to the other communications received.[319]

---

[313] *Prosecutor v. Abu Garda,* Decision on the confirmation of charges, *supra* note 312, para. 236, 97.

[314] For the note verbal see <www2.icc-cpi.int/NR/rdonlyres/74EEE201-0FED-4481-95D4-C8071087102C/279843/ICDENG.pdf>.

[315] Press Release (Côte d'Ivoire), Registrar confirms that the Republic of Côte d'Ivoire has accepted the jurisdiction of the Court, 15.2.2005 (ICC-20050215-91). See further "Côte d'Ivoire" in HRW, World Report 2008, *supra* note 210, 172 et seq.; Theresa Steinberger-Fraunhofer, *Internationaler Strafgerichtshof und Drittstaaten* (Duncker & Humblot, Berlin 2008) 278–9.

[316] Update on communications received by the Office of the Prosecutor of the ICC (hereinafter Update on communications), 10.2.2006, 4.

[317] The treatment as *proprio motu* information has also been favored by Paul Seils, Former Senior Analyst and Head of the Analysis Section in the JCCD, OTP, The Hague, Interview with Paul Seils on 5.4.2006; see further discussion on the issue at Part III, B., VI., 10.

[318] Visit of the Palestinian National Authority Minister of Foreign Affairs and Minister of Justice, 13.2.2009; for the declaration as such see <www2.icc-cpi.int/NR/rdonlyres/74EEE201-0FED-4481-95D4-C8071087102C/279777/20090122PalestinianDeclaration2.pdf>. See also Yaël Ronan, "ICC jurisdiction over acts committed in the Gaza strip" (2010) 8 JICJ 3, 3 et seq., who questions whether the Palestinian declaration was admissible in the first place (due to the lack of statehood, cf. *ibid.,* 11 et seq., 26); see further Schabas, *supra* note 13, 290.

[319] Visit of the Palestinian National Authority, *supra* note 318; also OTP weekly briefing, 4.–9. August 2010, Issue # 49, 11.8.2010, 3.

With regard to investigations *proprio motu* in practice, 472 communications were already received in the first year,[320] and more keep flooding in daily. Between 1 July 2002 (when the Statute entered into force) and 10 February 2006 a total of 1732 information on crimes within the jurisdiction of the Court ("communications"[321]) from 103 different countries reporting alleged crimes in 139 countries were sent to the Court.[322] Sixty percent of these communications originated in four countries: United States, United Kingdom, France, and Germany.[323] Recently, the OTP mentions that the total number of communications since July 2002 has risen to over 8700 from more than 140 countries.[324] As a matter of fact, no formal investigation pursuant to articles 15 (3) and 53 (1) has been initiated on the basis of these communications at the time the Update Paper was issued.[325] Only recently was an investigation *proprio motu* initiated in Kenya which, however, does not essentially alter the results as we will see later.[326]

According to an OTP update from 2006,[327] 80 percent of these communications were found to be manifestly outside the jurisdiction of the Court. In 5 percent of the communications the Court lacked temporal jurisdiction (article 11) because events before the entry into force of the ICC Statute on

---

320 Schiff, *supra* note 128, 115.

321 The term "communications" can neither be found in the ICC Statute nor the RPE. It was, however, introduced by the OTP (see Update on communications, *supra* note 316, 1). Lately, the newly drafted OTP Regulations seem to depart from the term "communication" from a legal perspective, but the Office still uses the term in its practice, cf. already *supra* note 28. See further Morten Bergsmo/Jelena Pjeić, "Article 15" in Triffterer, *supra* note 37, article 15, mn 13.

322 Update on communications, *supra* note 316, 1. Only a few months later, the numbers had already increased significantly to 1918 communications, see OTP Report on activities 2003–2006, *supra* note 23, para. 6. In 2008 alone, the OTP received and analyzed a total of 4248 communications, see Address to the Assembly of States Parties, Mr. Luis Moreno-Ocampo, Prosecutor of the International Criminal Court, 14.11.2008, 2.

323 Update on communications, *supra* note 316, 1.

324 See <www2.icc-cpi.int/Menus/ICC/Structure+of+the+Court/Office+of+the+Prosecutor/Comm+and+Ref/>; of the newly received Communications, many related to the situation in South Ossetia, Georgia, see Report of the International Criminal Court to the United Nations for 2008/2009, GA sixty-fourth session, 17.9.2009 (A/64/356) 13, para. 44.

325 Cf. Update on communications, *supra* note 316, 1.

326 See, *inter alia,* Part III, B., IV., 3.

327 Update on communications, *supra* note 316, 1 et seq. For the management of referrals and communications in general, see Annex paper, *supra* note 27; also Kai Ambos, "Prosecuting international crimes at the national and international level: between justice and Realpolitik" in Wolfgang Kaleck/Michael Ratner/Tobias Singelnstein/Peter Weiss (eds.), *International prosecution of human rights crimes* (Springer, Berlin 2007) 57.

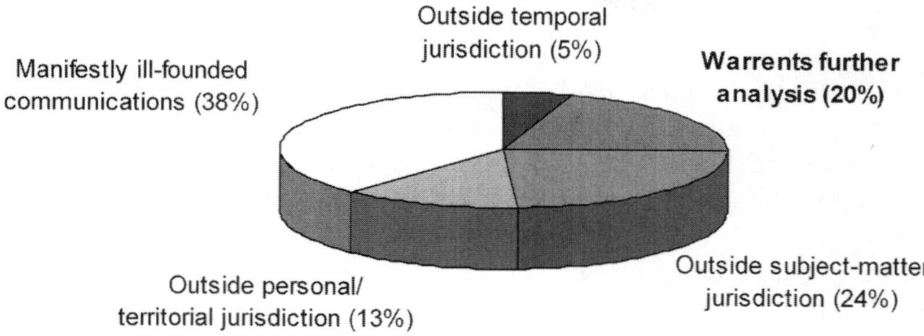

Source: Author.

Figure 3: Communications to the ICC

1 July 2002 were concerned, in 24 percent the allegations did not fall within the subject-matter jurisdiction, that is, did not refer to genocide, crimes against humanity, or war crimes (articles 5–8),[328] 13 percent concerned alleged crimes outside the personal or territorial jurisdiction (article 12),[329] and 38 percent of the communications were manifestly ill-founded.

20 percent of communications, 346 in absolute numbers, were identified as warranting further analysis and were grouped together by situations. The OTP only refers to 23 situations in total,[330] not differentiating between the ones based upon referrals and those based upon communications. In its Provisional Analysis Regulations the OTP notably distinguishes three different phases during preliminary examinations: analysis phase I – initial review, analysis phase II – basic reporting, and analysis phase III – intensive analysis (see further Part III, C., III. on the different phases in more detail).[331] Referrals and communications are basically subjected to the same analysis and accordingly the OTP groups the situations into the levels they have reached.

Of the total 23 situations in 2006, 6 had been dismissed, 7 remained under "basic reporting," and 10 were elevated for "intensive analysis."[332] Taking into account the three State referrals (DRC, Uganda, and CAR), the one Security Council referral (Darfur), and the one *ad hoc* declaration of a

[328] According to article 5 (1), the Court has jurisdiction over the crime of genocide, crimes against humanity, war crimes, and the crime of aggression (on the latter see further *infra* notes 418 and 1321); see also Ambos, *supra* note 327, 57.

[329] Article 12 (2) limits the competence of the ICC to the territory of States Parties (a) or to the accused's State (b).

[330] Update on communications, *supra* note 316, 3.

[331] Provisional Analysis Regulations 4–6, Annex paper, *supra* note 27, 9 et seq.

[332] Update on communications, *supra* note 316, 3. When the OTP reports on situations under analysis, it exclusively refers to the ones under intensive analysis, *ibid.*

Non-State Party (Côte d'Ivoire), it seems as if the OTP reduced the remaining communications to 18 situations (23 minus 5). Of the 10 situations for "intensive analysis" three had led to the initiation of an investigation (DRC, Uganda, Sudan, all outlined above), two had been dismissed (Iraq and Venezuela),[333] and five did remain under analysis.[334] In view of the practice regarding situations that originate from communications, it becomes apparent that *none* had reached the stage of requesting authorization of an investigation pursuant to article 15 (3). In other words, none had successfully passed the pre-investigation stage and entered the formal investigation stage. Thus, the OTP was altogether carrying out investigations into four situations (DRC, Uganda, CAR, and Darfur), dismissed two situations with public notification (Iraq and Venezuela) and kept five situations under analysis at the point of time the update on communications was given (including the Côte d'Ivoire).[335]

More recently,[336] the number has risen to at least six situations under preliminary analysis, including Afghanistan, Colombia,[337] Guinea,[338] Palestine, Côte d'Ivoire, and Georgia.[339] In the future, the OTP's objective is to

---

[333] See the decisions published in the interest of transparency as an annex to the update of communications, *supra* note 316: Iraq response, Annex to the Update on communications received by the Office of the Prosecutor of the ICC, 10.2.2006; Venezuela response, Annex to the Update on communications received by the Office of the Prosecutor of the ICC, 10.2.2006.

[334] In the Update of Communications, *supra* note 316, five situations are designated as remaining under analysis, since the investigation in the situation of CAR was not yet opened when the Update paper was published.

[335] Report of the International Criminal Court to the United Nations for 2006/2007, *supra* note 43, 1, 9. The remaining three situations did involve Afghanistan, Colombia, and Nigeria, cf. Ambos, supra note 327, 58, since the situations in Iraq and Burundi mentioned by Ambos have already been dismissed (Iraq response, *supra* note 333; Burundi has been dismissed to the knowledge of this author). For the limited jurisdiction with regard to war crimes in Colombia – from November 2009 onwards – see Peter Burbidge, "Justice and peace? – The role of law in resolving Colombia's civil conflict" (2008) 8 ICLR 557, 569.

[336] Last checked 1.9.2010. For the latest information see the OTP's weekly briefing at <www.icc-cpi.int/Menus/ICC/Structure+of+the+Court/Office+of+the+Prosecutor/Weekly+Briefings/>.

[337] For an in-depth research of the situation in Colombia with regard to the principle of complementarity under the ICC Statute see Kai Ambos, *The Colombian Peace Process and the principle of complementarity of the International Criminal Court* (Springer, Heidelberg 2010).

[338] OTP-Press Release (Guinea), ICC Prosecutor confirms situation in Guinea under analysis, 14.10.2009 (ICC-OTP-20091014-PR464); OTP weekly briefing, 15.–21. December 2009, Issue # 18, 21.12.2009, 1 and 5.

[339] OTP-Press Release (Georgia), ICC Prosecutor confirms situation in Georgia under analysis, 20.8.2008 (ICC-OTP-20080820-PR346). For Colombia and Côte

conduct up to 10 preliminary examinations in relation to currently examined or new situations.[340]

The Kenyan situation was closely monitored by the OTP as a matter of preliminary examination at first. Rather than making use of his article 15 powers, the Prosecutor articulated a strong preference of national proceedings, and, in the alternative, a self-referral under article 14.[341] However, due to inaction – the efforts to establish a local tribunal stalled due to the lack of quorum in Parliament[342] – the Prosecutor felt obligated to request the opening of an investigation under article 15.[343] On 26 November 2009, the Prosecutor then formally used the *proprio motu* power for the first time.[344] On 31 March 2010, the majority of PTC II authorized the investigation in accordance with article 15.[345]

---

d'Ivoire see also the Prosecutor himself, Address to the Assembly of States Parties, Mr. Luis Moreno-Ocampo, Prosecutor of the International Criminal Court, 30.11.2007, 6. Schabas, *supra* note 27, equally mentions Colombia and Afghanistan. For Kenya, see OTP statement in relation to events in Kenya, 5.2.2008; OTP-Press Release (Kenya), Prosecutor reaffirms that the situation in Kenya is monitored, 11.2.2009; "Kenya: Spokesman – ICC analyses country's situation," 22.4.2008, Hirondelle News Agency (Lausanne); further HRW Courting history report, *supra* note 126, 33; CICC, "Situations," The Monitor, No. 37, Nov. 2008–April 2009, 8–9; Address to the Assembly of States Parties 2008, *supra* note 322, 2; OTP weekly briefing, 15.–22. September 2009, 23.09.2009; OTP weekly briefing, 10.–16. November 2009, Issue # 13, 18.11.2009, 3 et seq.; OTP weekly briefing, 8.–14. December 2009, Issue # 17, 16.12.2009, 3 et seq.; OTP weekly briefing, 4.–9. August 2010, *supra* note 319, 2; Moreno-Ocampo, in Stahn/Sluiter, *supra* note 99, 19; also <www2.icc-cpi.int/Menus/ICC/Structure+of+the+Court/Office+ of+the+Prosecutor>. The only viable non-African candidates are thus Afghanistan, Georgia, Colombia, thereto Kevin Jon Heller, "Situational gravity under the Rome Statute" in Carsten Stahn/Larissa van Herik (eds.), *supra* note 11, 227, 227, and, most recently, Palestine.

340 Prosecutorial Strategy 2009–2012, *supra* note 99, para. 36, 10.

341 Agreed Minutes of the meeting between Prosecutor Moreno-Ocampo and the delegation of the Kenyan government, The Hague, 3 July 2009, 1–2; *Situation in Kenya*, Request for authorization, *supra* note 207, para. 14, 8. On the Kenyan efforts see Antonina Okuta, "National legislation for prosecution of international crimes in Kenya" (2009) 7 JICJ 1063, 1063 et seq.

342 "Tribunal bill debate halted over quorum," 18.11.2009, Daily Nation; *Situation in Kenya*, Request for authorization, *supra* note 207, para. 12, 7.

343 OTP, Kenyan authorities committed to cooperate as ICC Prosecutor informs them that in December he will request ICC Judges to open an investigation into post-election violence, 6.11.2009, 1–2; OTP-Press Release (Kenya), Prosecutor's statement at the press conference in Kenya, 26.11.2009, Nairobi and The Hague; OTP weekly briefing, 24.–30. November 2009, Issue # 15, 2.12.2009, 1. On the background of the Kenyan situation see *Situation in Kenya*, Request for authorization, *supra* note 207, paras. 3 et seq., 4 et seq.

344 CICC, "Prosecutor request opening of ICC investigation in Kenya," 26.11. 2009, Media advisory.

II. Definition of the term "referral"

The term "referral" is used to define the trigger mechanism, more precisely the action by which the Security Council or a State Party can trigger the exercise of jurisdiction by the Court. In order to determine whether the exercise of jurisdiction is triggered by a specific referral, the term "situation" also plays a decisive role. Both terms are nowhere defined in the ICC Statute. Their legal nature will be discussed before coming to the three trigger mechanisms in particular. A number of related questions will be discussed in the analysis, e.g. to what extent the Prosecutor is bound to the definition of a situation or may redefine such a situation – as he did in the Ugandan situation.[346] The inherent problems of self-referrals – and whether the withdrawal of the referral by the referring entity has legal consequences – are addressed below.[347]

The determination of the precise nature of referrals requires an interpretation "in accordance with the ordinary meaning to be given to the terms of the treaty in their context and in the light of its object and purpose," supplemented by the drafting history if necessary.[348] "Referral" is mentioned several times throughout the ICC Statute and the RPE without a specific definition. It is used to circumscribe the action by a State Party or the SC to trigger the ICC's jurisdiction. OTP Regulation 2 states more precisely:

> "Referral" refers to a request from a State Party under article 14 or from the Security Council under article 13 paragraph (b) to the Prosecutor to investigate a situation in which one or more crimes under the jurisdiction of the Court appear to have been committed.

According to article 42 (1), the OTP is the responsible entity for receiving and examining referrals. A referral must be in written form (rule 45). The formal requirements regarding SC and State Party requests are slightly different, because only the latter requires specifying relevant circumstances with supporting documentation (article 14 (2)). In addition, referrals contrast with information required under article 15; what is needed is equally unspecified by the ICC Statute.

In the lights of a broader contextual interpretation, however, formal preconditions converge. The seriousness of information received (article 15 (2)) and referrals (rule 104 (1)) has to be analyzed carefully. Additional in-

---

345 *Situation in Kenya*, Decision pursuant to article 15, *supra* note 6; for the dissenting opinion see *ibid.*, Dissenting opinion of Judge Hans-Peter Kaul, 31.3.2010 (ICC-01/09-19).

346 Cf. Part III, B., I., 2.

347 Part III, B., IV.

348 Part I, C., II.

formation can be demanded for this purpose, and regarding both, communications (15 (2)) and referrals (rule 104 (2)), from States, organs of the UN, intergovernmental and non-governmental organizations, or other reliable sources the Prosecutor deems appropriate. The standard for seriousness is thus identical in all three triggering procedures and the preliminary examination process is – at least theoretically – almost identical.[349] It is therefore submitted that any SC referral requires the same specific information as a State referral and communications do. In practice, a SC referral is preceded by intense negotiations and is most likely accompanied by in-depth reports. Nonetheless, a hypothetical frivolous SC referral can be rejected due to insufficient specificity. Likewise, information provided under article 15 cannot be too broad and unspecific.[350] To sum up, the standard of seriousness is the same for all three trigger mechanisms and shall be applied equally.

There are, however, important procedural differences concerning the threshold to start an investigation through a referral. Surely, the criteria for the determination of a reasonable basis to proceed are the same (article 15 (3), rule 48, and article 53 (1)). But the starting point for communications *vis-à-vis* referrals is reversed: when the Prosecutor receives a referral, article 53 provides that the Prosecutor *shall* initiate an investigation *unless* he determines that there is no reasonable basis to proceed under the Statute. Further, the PTC reviews a determination not to proceed, but does not review a decision to proceed (article 53 (3)). If the Prosecutor receives information and acts *proprio motu,* he needs an authorization of the PTC to start an investigation (article 15 (3)). In other words, the Prosecutor must show the PTC that there is a reasonable basis to proceed.[351] As a result, SC and State referrals are privileged and "jump the queue."[352]

Coming to the drafting history, the ILC Draft Statute uses the term "referral of a matter" in article 23 (1) with respect to crimes referred to the Court by the SC.[353] For the triggering of States the term "complaint" was

---

349 Cf. Part III, C.

350 Annex paper, *supra* note 27, 2.

351 Annex paper, *supra* note 27, 1–2.

352 Schabas, *supra* note 266, 32, who states that, in the case of Uganda, the self-referral put the situation on the top of the Prosecutor's agenda, where it might not belong if it was treated as a *proprio motu* situation. See also Wouters/Verhoeven/Demeyere, *supra* note 156, 284. Regarding "fast track" proceedings following a SC referral, Turone, in Cassese/Gaeta/Jones, *supra* note 26, 1144.

353 Draft statute for an International Criminal Court 1994, Report of the International Law Commission on the work of its forty-sixth session, 2 May–22 July 1994, GA forty-ninth session, 1.9.1994 (A/49/10 (Supp.)) 84. On the drafting history, Sharon Williams/William Schabas, "Article 13" in Triffterer, *supra* note 37, article 13, mn 2 et seq.

mentioned (articles 21, 25 ILC Draft Statute),[354] and it was further explained:

> "The complaint is the mechanism that invokes this facility and initiates the preliminary phase of the criminal procedure."[355]

The ILC even digs deeper into the matter elsewhere and particularizes the complaint:

> "The complaint is intended to bring to the attention of the Court the apparent commission of a crime. The complaint must as far as possible be accompanied by supporting documentation."[356]

As to the content of a complaint, the Preparatory Committee in 1996 outlined the proposals as follows:

> "As far as possible a complaint shall [specify] [provide as much information as possible to assist the Prosecutor in deciding whether an investigation should be initiated, including]:
>
> (a) [the facts which indicate] the basis of jurisdiction relied upon in making the complaint;
>
> (b) the specific crime or crimes within the jurisdiction of the Court, which the complainant State believes has been committed;
>
> (c) the circumstances of the alleged crime;
>
> (d) the identity and location of any persons suspected of committing such crime, [if known];
>
> (e) the identity and location of any witnesses, if known;
>
> (f) a description of evidence or believed sources of evidence pertinent to the investigation; and
>
> (g) whether the complaint State, or other States to its knowledge, may be investigating or prosecuting the matter, and the details of such investigation or prosecution; and be accompanied by such supporting documentation as is available to the complaint State."[357]

The reference to a complaint was still used in article 45 [25] of the so-called Zutphen Draft, though in brackets another terminological option was already included: "[referring a [matter] [situation]."[358] It was then sug-

---

[354] ILC Draft Statute 1994, *supra* note 353, 79, 89.

[355] ILC Draft Statute 1994, *supra* note 353, Commentary on article 25, para. 1, 89.

[356] ILC Draft Statute 1994, *supra* note 353, Commentary on article 25, para. 5, 90.

[357] Report of the Preparatory Committee on the Establishment of the International Criminal Court, Vol. 2, Compilation of Proposals, GA fifty-first session, Supplement No. 22A, 13.9.1996 (A/51/22) 110.

gested by the United Kingdom that States refer situations rather than single cases,[359] and the newly revised article was drafted as follows:

> "Article 45 [25]. Referral of a situation by a State
>
> 1. A State Party may refer to the Prosecutor a situation in which one or more crimes within the jurisdiction of the Court appear to have been committed, requesting the Prosecutor to investigate the situation for the purpose of determining whether one or more specific persons should be charged with the commission of such crimes.
> 2. As far as possible, a referral shall specify the relevant circumstances and be accompanied by such supporting documentation as is available to the complainant State.
> 3. The Prosecutor shall notify the Security Council of all situations referred under this article."

This option was included in the Preparatory Committee's Draft Statute as a further option for article 6,[360] and in a discussion paper issued by the Bureau of the Rome Conference the draft article 45 [25] of the UK proposal was transferred as a whole into article 11.[361]

The change in terminology has to be seen in connection with the discussion of situations as opposed to cases,[362] and one can assume that the nomenclature, though not the substance, was changed by removing "complaint."[363] However, it must be noted that the complaints procedure was converted into a referral procedure (*Verweisungsverfahren*).[364] The neutral term referral was preferred by some delegations due to the fear of politicization by selecting individual suspects and lodging complaints against them.[365]

---

358 Report of the inter-sessional meeting from 19 to 30 January 1998 in Zutphen, the Netherlands, Preparatory Committee on the Establishment of an International Criminal Court, 4.2.1998 (A/AC.249/1998/L.13) article 45 [25], option 1, 109–10.

359 Proposal by the United Kingdom of Great Britain and Northern Ireland – Trigger mechanism, Preparatory Committee on the Establishment of the International Criminal Court, 25.3.1998, Working group on complementarity and trigger mechanism, 16 March–3 April 1998 (A/AC.249/1998/WG.3/DP.1) para. 2.

360 Draft Statute, April 1998, *supra* note 44, "further option for articles 6, 7, 10, and 11," 38.

361 Bureau Discussion Paper, Part 2. Jurisdiction, Admissibility and Applicable Law, United Nations Diplomatic Conference of Plenipotentiaries on the Establishment of an International Criminal Court, 15 June–17 July 1998, 6.7.1998 (A/CONF.183/C.1/L.53) article 11, 14. The sole variation was the inclusion of option 2 under para. 3, viz. no paragraph 3.

362 Part III, B., III.

363 Schabas, *supra* note 27, 146–7; Junck, *supra* note 204, mn 456.

364 Hoffmeister/Knoke, *supra* note 169, 788.

365 Van Heeck, *supra* note 26, 147; Schabas, *supra* note 27, 146.

Self-referrals were not envisaged during the drafting period;[366] another related question is their legality under the current ICC system.[367] With regard to the one-dimensional legal definition of a referral the answer is simpler: the referral in the ICC Statute was designed after the concept of a complaint and resembles a *notitia criminis* in domestic systems.[368] It initiates the preliminary examination of the Prosecutor and must be assessed in the context of the ICC's legal framework. Analogies that can be drawn to complaints and *notitia criminis* notwithstanding, the ICC Statute alone defines the precise legal parameters of a referral. For instance, the object of referrals is broader compared to complaints: "situations" are referred, and they are generally defined in terms of temporal, territorial, and in some cases personal parameters.[369] To conclude, OTP Regulation 2 rightly states that the SC or a State Party *requests* the OTP to investigate a situation and thus triggers the OTP's legal evaluation. The outcome of the analysis and possible acceptance of the situation is yet solely vested with the Prosecutor. Therefore, a referral can be viewed – together with the *proprio motu* information according to articles 13 (c) and 15 (1) – as the ICC's *notitia criminis*.

III. Distinguishing situation v. case

The triggering procedure mentions "situations" as its objects as opposed to "cases."[370] This was the result of long-lasting discussions throughout the meetings of the Preparatory Committee for an ICC. During the meetings many delegations feared excessive politicization and preferred the term "situation" or "matter" in order to avoid the lodging of complaints against one particular crime or individual.[371] However, the term "situation" is nowhere

---

366 Schabas, *supra* note 27, 147; see also Part III, B., IV., 1.

367 Part III, B., IV., 3.

368 Turone, in Cassese/Gaeta/Jones, *supra* note 26, 1144; Héctor Olásolo, "The prosecutor of the ICC before the initiation of investigations: a quasi-judicial or a political body?" (2003) 3 ICLR 87, 92; Matthew Brubacher, "Prosecutorial discretion within the International Criminal Court" (2004) 2 JICJ 71, 77.

369 See Part III, B., III., 1.

370 Olásolo, *supra* note 29, 39 et seq.; Carsten Stahn/Héctor Olásolo/Kate Gibson, "Participation of victims in pre-trial proceedings of the ICC" (2006) 4 JICJ 219, 227; Jann Kleffner, *Complementarity in the Rome Statute and national criminal jurisdictions* (OUP, Oxford/New York 2008) 198; War Crimes Research Office, "The relevance of 'a situation' to the admissibility and selection of cases before the International Criminal Court" (hereinafter WCRO report "situation" and case selection), International Criminal Court Legal Analysis and Education Project (United States of America, American University Washington College of Law 2009) 1; also Ignaz Stegmiller, "The pre-investigation stage of the ICTY and ICC compared" in Thomas Kruessmann (ed.), *ICTY: towards a fair trial?* (Neuer Wissenschaftlicher Verlag, Wien, Graz 2008) 311, 319.

defined in the ICC Statute or the RPE.[372] It is essential to define the concept of a situation and its parameters to determine the ICC's jurisdictional reach. The ICC cannot extend its jurisdiction to crimes committed outside the triggered situation.[373]

The concept of situations will be interpreted by looking at the ICC's legal framework, taking into account the drafting history. The word "situation" can be found in articles 13 (a), (b), 14 (1), (2), 15 (5), (6), 18 (1), and 19 (3). First, the term is opposed by the terms "case" and "crime." Crime generally stands for either conduct prohibited by law or the criminal activity itself.[374] A case comprises "a specific incident in which crimes within the jurisdiction of the Court have been committed by identified perpetrators."[375] One major problem is that the term "situation" was used in articles 13 and 14, but is not consequentially followed throughout the ICC Statute, against what the term "case" or "crime" is used frequently in the Statute, though the term "situation" would sometimes make more sense and was probably meant.[376] With regard to article 17 there was simply no time at the Rome Conference to adjust the definition of the concepts of admissibility and inadmissibility to the new distinction between situations and cases.[377] Moreover, as already mentioned, neither the term case nor situation is defined in the ICC Statute and its auxiliary documents. It can only be reasoned from arti-

---

371 Phillipe Kirsch/Darryl Robinson, "Referral by States Parties" in Cassese/Gaeta/Jones, *supra* note 133, 621; Olásolo, *supra* note 29, 43; Lionel Yee, "The International Criminal Court and the Security Council: articles 13 (b) and 16" in Lee, *supra* note 14, 147–8; Florian Razesberger, *The ICC, the principle of complemetarity* (Peter Lang, Frankfurt a.M. 2006) 31; Mahnoush Arsanjani, "Reflections on the jurisdiction and trigger mechanism of the International Criminal Court" in Herman Hebel/Johan Lammers/Jolien Schukking (eds.), *Reflections on the International Criminal Court, Essays in honour of Adriaan Bos* (Asser Press, The Hague 1999) 57, 65; Jörg Meißner, *Die Zusammenarbeit mit dem Internationalen Strafgerichtshof nach dem Römischen Statut* (C.H. Beck, München 2003) 53; Williams/Schabas, in Triffterer, *supra* note 353, article 13, mn 13; Heilmann, *supra* note 74, 152; WCRO report "situation" and case selection, *supra* note 370, 12. See already above fn. 365.

372 WCRO report "situation" and case selection, *supra* note 370, 20-1.

373 Junck, *supra* note 204, mn 472.

374 Cf. "crime" as defined at <http://dictionary.lp.findlaw.com>.

375 Third Report pursuant to UNSC 1593, *supra* note 288, 2; Fourth Report pursuant to UNSC 1593, *supra* note 289, 7.

376 See, as an example, article 15 (4). It is submitted that the term "case" in article 15 (4) should be interpreted as referring to a "situation" in line with article 15 (5) and (6), cf. Héctor Olásolo, "The triggering procedure of the International Criminal Court, procedural treatment of complementarity and the role of the Office of the Prosecutor" (2005) 5 ICLR 121, 127 with fn. 11; Christopher Hall, "Article 19" in Triffterer, *supra* note 37, article 19, mn 3 with fn. 13.

377 Olásolo, *supra* note 376, 127 with fn. 11.

cles 13 (a), (b), and 14 that a situation is a broader image "in which one or more of such crimes appears to have been committed." A textual, contextual, and teleological interpretation *per se* does not shed light on the issue. For this reason, the drafting history must be consulted.

Article 23 (1) ILC Draft Statute envisaged that the Security Council would refer a "matter," that is to say, a situation to which Chapter VII of the UN Charter applies. It is the responsibility of the Prosecutor to determine which individuals should be charged with crimes in relation to that matter.[378] The *Ad Hoc* Committee on the Establishment of an ICC emphasized that the referral of a general matter or situation by the SC would preserve the independence and autonomy of the court in the exercise of its investigative, prosecutorial, and judicial functions.[379] With regard to complaints by States (article 25 ILC Draft Statute) the object was an alleged "crime," but the drafters already mentioned concerns that the jurisdiction should not be invoked "on the basis of frivolous, groundless, or politically motivated complaints."[380] The International Law Commission did not yet provide for the Prosecutor to initiate investigations *proprio motu*.

During the Preparatory Committee's meetings the terms "matter," "case," and "situation" were discussed heavily. Some delegates suggested replacing "matter" with "case," while others did not agree and held the view that specific individuals should not be referred by the SC.[381] Regarding State complaints delegations similarly feared politicization of the complaint procedure and did not want the States to select individual suspects.[382] As a result both alternatives ("case" *vis-à-vis* "situations" for action by the SC; "situation" *vis-à-vis* "crimes" for action by States) were included as alternative proposals.[383] The United States' delegation recommended the introduction of the more neutral term "situation" for SC referrals and State complaints.[384]

---

378 ILC Draft Statute 1994, *supra* note 353, Commentary on article 23, para. 2, 85.

379 Report of the *Ad Hoc* Committee on the Establishment of an International Criminal Court, GA fiftieth session, Supplement No. 22, 6.9.1995 (A/50/22) para. 120, 27.

380 ILC Draft Statute 1994, *supra* note 353, Commentary on article 25, para. 5, 90. Later also Report of the *Ad Hoc* Committee 1995, *supra* note 379, para. 136, 30.

381 Report of the Preparatory Committee 1996, Vol. 1, *supra* note 203, para. 136, 32; Proceedings of the Preparatory Committee during the period 25 March–12 April 1996, Draft Summary, Trigger Mechanism, 8.4.1996 (A/AC.249/CRP.5) para. 19, 5–6.

382 Report of the Preparatory Committee 1996, Vol. 1, *supra* note 203, para. 146, 34; Proceedings of the Preparatory Committee during the period 25 March–12 April 1996, *supra* note 381, para. 29, 8. See also Silvia Fernández de Gurmendi, "The role of the international prosecutor" in Lee, *supra* note 14, 180.

383 Report of the Preparatory Committee 1996, Vol. 2, *supra* note 357, 75–7 (action by the SC), 108–110 (action by States).

On 14 August 1997, the Preparatory Committee took note of the reports of the Working Group on Complementarity and Trigger Mechanism and only listed the options "matter" and "situation" with regard to action by the SC.[385] For State action the "lodging of a complaint" was still the first option, but "[referring a [matter] [situation] in which one or more crimes within the jurisdiction of the Court appear to have been committed]" was inserted to show further possibilities.[386]

It was also during Preparatory Committee sessions that the idea of a third trigger mechanism, namely the possibility of the Prosecutor initiating investigations *proprio motu,* was seriously approached for the first time.[387] In this context the term "matter" was used: "[(c) the matter is brought by the Prosecutor, in accordance with article 25*bis*.]."[388]

In the Zutphen Draft Statute of early 1998 the mentioned proposals were included in brackets, which led to the alternatives "situation" or "matter" for SC action (article 6 [21] (1) (a), 10 [21] (1) Zutphen Draft Statute). "Lodging of complaint," "referring a matter," or "referring a situation" were proposed for State action (article 6 [21] (1) (b), 45 [25] Option 1 Zutphen Draft Statute), and, last but not least, "matter" was proposed for initiatives by the Prosecutor (article 6 [21] (1) (c), 46 [25*bis*] Option 1 Zutphen Draft Statute).[389] The Draft Statute of April 1998 likewise listed the same bracketed options,[390] but included an alternative proposal by the United

384 United States Delegation, Preparatory Committee on ICC, Proposed amendments pertaining to the trigger mechanism ILC Draft Statute for International Criminal Court, 1.4.1996; United States Delegation, Preparatory Committee on ICC, "Trigger Mechanism," Second question, The role of the Security Council and of complaints by States articles 23 and 25, 1.4.1996, 4, 6. The word "situation" was however considered too broad by some delegations, cf. Report of the Preparatory Committee 1996, Vol. 1, *supra* note 203, para. 136, 32. See also Fernández de Gurmendi, in Lee, *supra* note 382, 180–1.

385 Decision taken by the Preparatory Committee at its session held from 4 to 15 August 1997, 14.8.1997 (A/AC.249/1997/L.8/Rev.1) 3, article 21 (1) (a): "the [matter] [situation] is referred to the Court by the Security Council," and 7, article 23 (1): "[on the basis of a [formal] decision to refer] a [matter] [situation] in which one or more crimes appear to have been committed to [...]."

386 Decision taken by the Preparatory Committee, *supra* note 385, 9.

387 Proceedings of the Preparatory Committee during the period 25 March–12 April 1996, *supra* note 381, para. 32, 8; Report of the Preparatory Committee 1996, Vol. 1, *supra* note 203, para. 149, 35. Further on the drafting history of the *proprio motu* power, see Part III, B., VI., 2.

388 Decision taken by the Preparatory Committee, *supra* note 385, 3.

389 Zutphen Draft Statute 1998, *supra* note 358, article 6 [21], 46; article 10 [23], 52; article 45 [25], 109; article 46 [25*bis*], 110.

390 Draft Statute April 1998, *supra* note 44, article 6, 30; article 10, 34; article 11, 35–6; article 12, 37.

Kingdom as "further option for articles 6, 7, 10 and 11," which only used the term "situation" for SC referrals and State referrals.[391] During the Rome Conference this proposal was generally supported, and delegations preferred the broader notion of a "situation" to the term "matter" or "case."[392] The Report of the Committee of the Whole accordingly used the term "situation" with regard to SC referrals and State referrals:

"Article 13 [6] Exercise of jurisdiction

The Court may exercise its jurisdiction with respect to a crime referred to in article 5 in accordance with the provisions of this Statute if:

(a) A situation in which one or more of such crimes appears to have been committed is referred to the Prosecutor by a State Party in accordance with article 14 [11];

---

[391] Draft Statute April 1998, *supra* note 44, further option for articles 6, 7, 10 and 11, 38. For the proposal itself, see Proposal by the United Kingdom of Great Britain and Northern Ireland, *supra* note 359. See also Official Records, Vol. III, Reports and other documents, United Nations Diplomatic Conference of Plenipotentiaries on the Establishment of an International Criminal Court, 15 June–17 July 1998, UN, New York 2002 (A/CONF.183/13 (Vol. III)) 26–7.

[392] See statements in Official Records, Vol. II, Summary records of the plenary meetings and of the meetings of the Committee of the Whole, United Nations Diplomatic Conference of Plenipotentiaries on the Establishment of an International Criminal Court, 15 June–17 July 1998, UN, New York 2002 (A/CONF.183/13 (Vol. II)): Ms. Johnson (Norway) para. 21, 65; Ms. Freivalds (Sweden) para. 55, 68; Mr. van Mierlo (Netherlands) para. 53, 100; Ms. Wilmshurst (United Kingdom of Great Britain and Northern Ireland), para. 43, 183; Mr. Saland (Sweden) para. 68, 185 ("He also preferred that entire situations, such as a situation involving genocide, be referred rather than individual crimes"); Mr. Nyasulu (Malawi) para. 1, 186 ("The word 'situation' was preferable to a word such as 'matter' "); Mr. Garcia Labajo (Spain) para. 11, 187 ("A referral to the Court by States Parties or by the Security Council should relate to a situation, not an individual case"); Mr. Tomka (Slovakia) para. 25, 188; Mr. Manongi (United Republic of Tanzania) para. 28, 188; Mr. Stigen (Norway) para. 35, 188; Mr. Perrin de Brichambaut (France) para. 45, 189 ("Article 6 should be formulated in the broadest terms, with referral to the Court of questions, complaints and situations"); Mr. Cede (Austria) para. 53, 190 ("He noted with satisfaction that, in article 6, the word 'situation' had replaced 'matter' "); Mr. Piragoff (Canada) para. 12, 194; Mr. Politi (Italy), para. 19, 194; Mr. Scheffer (United States of America) para. 21, 195; Ms. Diop (Senegal) para. 54, 197; Ms. Kamaluddin (Brunei Darussalam) para. 60, 197; Mr. Koffi (Côte d'lvoire) para. 65, 197; Mr. Bazel (Afghanistan) para. 79, 198; Mr. Shariat Bagheri (Islamic Republic of Iran) para. 83, 199; Ms. Chatoor (Trinidad and Tobago) para. 2, 211. Contrary, Mr. Mahmood (Pakistan) para. 43, 189 ("He preferred the word 'matter' to 'situation', which was a wider term and might bring within the jurisdiction of the Prosecutor issues not directly connected with the case"); Mr. Palacios Trevino (Mexico) para. 63, 191 ("as a general rule, States Parties should refer situations, but they should not be prevented from submitting cases involving individual persons"); Mr. Giiney (Turkey) para. 42, 196; thereto also Schabas, *supra* note 13, 298.

(b) A situation in which one or more of such crimes appears to have been committed is referred to the Prosecutor by the Security Council acting under Chapter VII of the Charter of the United Nations; or

(c) The Prosecutor has initiated an investigation in respect of such a crime in accordance with article 15 [12]."[393]

As an intermediary conclusion, the drafting history clarifies that a loose concept of situations was preferred for SC and State referrals. This suggests a very broad interpretation. One can distinguish "situation" from "cases" in negative terms, i.e. situations cannot identify specific individuals for specific crimes. State delegations feared political misuse of the triggering procedure, thus they favored a vast concept that leaves the ultimate choice to the Prosecutor instead of the referring party.

Coming to the *proprio motu* power, the drafting history is not as explicit as for SC and State referrals. Articles 13 (c) and 15 (1) allow any individual or legal person to communicate concrete facts to the Prosecutor. Article 15 (4) even speaks of the jurisdiction of the "case." On the other hand, article 15 (5) and (6) mention "the same situation," which seems to be in line with a general preference for situations. Thus, Article 15 (4) has to be read in context with article 15 (5) and (6). This suggests poor drafting of article 15 (4), and, in spite of the literal reference to "case," that situations are the objects of article 15 proceedings.[394] In view of the fear of politically motivated investigations – especially with the adoption of a *proprio motu* triggering power[395] – the OTP has to group the facts together to general situations.[396]

To conclude, all three trigger mechanisms have situations as their objects, and during the preliminary examination the OTP is concerned with situations and not cases.[397] What remains to be answered are the precise definitions of situations and cases, as well as the exact point of time when cases arise out of situations. In its decision of 17 January 2006 PTC I clarified the distinction between situations and cases stating:

"Situations, which are *generally defined in terms of temporal, territorial and in some cases personal parameters*, such as the situation in the territory of the De-

[393] Report of the Committee of the Whole, 17.7.1998 (A/CONF.183/8) in Official Records, Vol. III, *supra* note 391, 99.

[394] Olásolo, *supra* note 29, 44 with fn. 67. See already *supra* note 376.

[395] Part III, B., VI., 2.

[396] In the same vein, Olásolo, *supra* note 29, 44. For the practice of the OTP in accordance with this finding see Update on communications, *supra* note 316, 2; Iraq response, *supra* note 333, 1, where the OTP grouped 240 communications together; Venezuela response, *supra* note 333, 1, where the OTP refers to 12 communications.

[397] Olásolo, *supra* note 29, 46; Razesberger, *supra* note 371, 33.

mocratic Republic of the Congo since 1 July 2002, entail the proceedings envisaged in the Statute to determine whether a particular situation should give rise to a criminal investigation as well as the investigation as such. Cases, *which comprise specific incidents during which one or more crimes within the jurisdiction of the Court seem to have been committed by one or more identified suspects*, entail proceedings that *take place after the issuance of a warrant of arrest or a summons to appear* (emph. added)."[398]

The three essential findings of this paragraph, i. e. defining a situation, defining a case, and setting a demarcation line between the two (issuance of a warrant of arrest or summons to appear), will be evaluated as follows.

1. Defining a situation

It can be concluded from the drafting history that situations have to be defined in a very vague manner in order to avoid biased referrals and that they are opposed by the legal notion of cases. The Chamber accordingly lists the objective criteria of temporal and territorial parameters in the first place. From the outset, the ICC Statute limits the jurisdiction to crimes committed after the Statute's entry into force on 1 July 2002 (article 11 (1)), and to the territory or national(s) of a State Party (article 12 (2)). If a State becomes a party after 1 July 2002, the Statute only enters into force after the accession of the State in question (article 11 (2)). Temporal and territorial parameters must be within these statutory boundaries. With regard to a SC referral this statement has to be put into perspective, since article 12 (2) does not refer to article 13 (b), hence excluding SC referrals from any territorial limitations.[399] However, the SC must act in accordance with other constraints imposed by the ICC Statute, such as express limitations of its jurisdiction *ratione materiae* (article 5), *ratione temporis* (article 11 (1)), and its jurisdiction *ratione personae* under articles 25 (1) and

[398] *Situation in DRC,* Decision on the applications for participation in the proceedings of VPRS 1, VPRS 2, VPRS 3, VPRS 4, VPRS 5 and VPRS 6, 17.1.2006 (ICC-01/04-101-Corr) para. 65; also *Prosecutor v. Lubanga,* Decision on the Prosecutor's application for warrant of arrest, article 58, *supra* note 217, para. 21; *Prosecutor v. Katanga,* Decision on the evidence and information provided by the Prosecution for the issuance of a warrant of arrest for Germain Katanga, 5.11.2007 (ICC-01/04-01/07-55) para. 9. Thereto Cyril Laucci, *The annotated digest of the International Criminal Court,* 2004–2006 (Martinus Nijhoff Publishers, Leiden 2007) 15–6; Olàsolo, *supra* note 183, 193 et seq.; Kleffner, *supra* note 370, 198–9. See already earlier, naming temporal and geographical parameters as significant, Kirsch/Robinson, in Cassese/Gaeta/Jones, *supra* note 371, 625.

[399] Heilmann, *supra* note 74, 160 et seq.; Michael Kurth, *Das Verhältnis des Internationalen Strafgerichthofes zum UN-Sicherheitsrat* (Nomos, Frankfurt a. M. 2006) 62. Likewise, article 18 (1) expressly refers only to articles 13 (a) and (c), and shall also not apply regarding SC referrals.

26.[400] Since it is left to the Prosecutor to screen the referral and its consistency with statutory norms, the SC would otherwise act *ultra vires* in terms of the ICC Statute.[401] A modification of the jurisdictional reach of the ICC through a SC referral must therefore be denied.[402]

Having said so, a situation cannot be broader than statutory limits. An ordinary, straight-forward situation would be the referral of a conflict on the territory of one State during a specified time period.[403] The situation in the CAR can serve as an example, since the letter of the CAR's government refers "the situation of crimes within the jurisdiction of the Court committed anywhere on the territory of the Central African Republic since 1 July 2002."[404]

Due to statutory limits, the following short survey will first concentrate on the broadest possible situation under the ICC Statute. A comparison of the trigger mechanism as a whole with regard to the ICTY or the ICTR is foreclosed, since no comparable procedure exists in the *ad hoc* tribunals. Nevertheless, their jurisdiction is explicitly delineated in their founding documents, which is comparable to the act of defining a situation.[405] Article 1 ICTY Statute holds:

---

[400] Williams/Schabas, in Triffterer, *supra* note 353, article 13, mn 16; Junck, *supra* note 204, mn 539, 603; Heilmann, *supra* note 74, 154–5; Flavia Lattanzi, "The Rome Statute and State sovereignty. ICC competence, jurisdictional links, trigger mechanism" in Flavia Lattanzi/William Schabas (eds.), *Essays on the Rome Statute of the International Criminal Court,* Vol. 1 (Il Sirente, Ripa Fagnano 1999) 63. Contrary, regarding *ratione temporis* and *ratione materiae* limitations, Héctor Olásolo, "Reflections on the International Criminal Court's jurisdictional reach" (2005) 16 CLF 279, 292; *id., supra* note 29, 129. See also Luigi Condorelli/Santiago Villalpando, "Referral and deferral by the Security Council" in Cassese/Gaeta/Jones, *supra* note 133, 634 et seq.: these authors submit that, in principle, the limits of the Court's jurisdiction apply. They argue, however, that article 11 presents a number of loopholes and can be interpreted in a manner as not precluding the SC from referring a situation in which crimes where committed before the entry into force of the ICC Statute (at 636–7).

[401] For such an *ultra vires* determination of a situation under article 16 – such as when a specific person is singled out – see Cherif Bassiouni, *The legislative history of the International Criminal Court: Introduction, analysis, and integrated text,* Vol. 1 (Transnational Publishers, Ardsley, NY 2005) 132.

[402] Heilmann, *supra* note 74, 153 et seq.; Junck, *supra* note 204, mn 578 et seq.; Luigi Condorelli/Santiago Villalpando, "Can the Security Council extend the ICC's jurisdiction?" in Cassese/Gaeta/Jones, *supra* note 133, 573 et seq.

[403] All pending referrals before the ICC have included at least a starting date and a geographical area, cf. WCRO report "situation" and case selection, *supra* note 370, 22.

[404] Prosecutor receives referral concerning Central African Republic, *supra* note 266.

> "The International Tribunal shall have the power to prosecute persons responsible for serious violations of international humanitarian law committed in the territory of the former Yugoslavia since 1991 in accordance with the provisions of the present Statute."[406]

Comparing the CAR situation with ICTY article 1, certain similarities can be identified. In both situations, reference to a vast territory and a specific time-frame is made. Differences can be found in terms of accurateness. The CAR situation sets a precise starting date, i. e. the entry into force of the ICC Statute on 1 July 2002, whereas for the ICTY the wording "since 1991" is less accurate. Moreover, the ICTY Statute refers to "the territory of the former Yugoslavia," thus the basis is provided by a former State that does not exist anymore. Coming further to the ICTR, article 1 ICTR Statute states:

> "The International Tribunal for Rwanda shall have the power to prosecute persons responsible for serious violations of international humanitarian law committed in the territory of Rwanda and Rwandan citizens responsible for such violations committed in the territory of neighboring States between 1 January 1994 and 31 December 1994, in accordance with the provisions of the present Statute."[407]

Here the time-frame is even more precise than in the CAR situation. It sets an exact start and ending date of the situation under scrutiny. The territorial scope is indeed wider; it extends the tribunal's jurisdiction to the territory of neighboring States. With this short comparison, three problems have been disclosed concerning the broadness of a situation:

(1) Can a situation be defined by a former State's territory?

(2) Are future crimes within the defined situation if no cessation date is set and the conflict is on-going or recurs?

(3) Is the territory limited to the territory of one State, or can transborder conflicts be referred as well?

Concerning the territory of a former State, successive States may cause some difficulties. Those States might – in contrast to the former State – not join the ICC Statute and oppose the Court. An easy answer would be to point to public international law, since each of those States will be subject

[405] Olásolo, *supra* note 29, 46–7. However, Juan Yanez-Barnuevo, Session 3: Transcript, First public hearing OTP 17.6.2003, differentiates three or four potential situations in the Former Yugoslavia: the crisis in Croatia, the crisis in Bosnia, the crisis in Kosovo, and, maybe, the crisis in Macedonia. This demonstrates how difficult – and yet important – it is to develop a legal working definition of the term situation.

[406] ICTY Statute, adopted 25.5.1993 by SC-Res. 827/last amended 29.6.2010 by SC-Res.1931.

[407] ICTR Statute, adopted 8.11.1994 by SC-Res. 955/last amended 13.10.2006 by SC-Res.1717.

to the international obligations that bound their predecessor according to the theory of succession of States.[408] The ICC could simply refer to the undisputed territory at the point of commission of the alleged crimes, viz. the "former territory of the State XY."

With respect to temporal requirements, the beginning is set out by article 11, but the expiration of a situation is not fixed by the ICC Statute explicitly. Article 13 (b) conflicts with the inclusion of future crimes because it refers to a "situation in which one or more of such crimes appears to *have been committed* (emph. added)." In sharp contrast, the Prosecutor shall consider, according to article 53 (1), if there is a "reasonable basis to believe that a crime within the jurisdiction of the Court has been or *is being committed* (emph. added)." Taking into consideration the desired deterrent effect of the ICC and the intended prevention of crimes,[409] on-going crimes fall within the scope of predefined situations.[410]

With regard to future crimes, I suggest that a certain nexus is required to include these crimes in a pending situation. If the conflict has been terminated then a new, totally unrelated spread of violence – coincidentally located within the same State – cannot be investigated. The suggested nexus will become clearer if we take a look at the CAR situation once more. In the CAR, the conflict between government forces and rebels took place during a peak of violence in 2002–2003, mainly in and around the capital city of Bangui.[411] Since the end of 2005 violence erupted in the north of the country, in particular the areas of Birao and Paoua.[412] The three named

---

[408] On the succession of States see Ian Brownlie, *Principles of Public International Law,* 6th edition (OUP, Oxford 2003) 621 et seq.

[409] The OTP emphasizes that the announcement of an investigation could have a preventative impact, and that the mere monitoring of a situation could deter future crimes from being committed, see OTP Report on prosecutorial strategy (hereinafter OTP strategy), 14.9.2006, 6. With concrete examples of deterrence (Côte d'Ivoire, Colombia, Uganda) see "Building a Future on Peace and Justice," Address by Mr. Luis Moreno-Ocampo, *supra* note 258, 8. For Colombia and Côte d'Ivoire, also Mr. Juan E Méndez, President of the International Center of Transitional Justice, Session 4: NGOs and other experts, Second public hearing of the OTP, 18.10.2006. On the deterrent effect of the ICC in practice, see Schabas, *supra* note 27, 57; *id.*, *supra* note 13, 298.

[410] It is submitted that on-going crimes are crimes that started before or during the referral of the situation and continued after the situation had been referred to the ICC. Future crimes are those where violence erupted again after the conflict was considered over. For a return of violence in the CAR see the Background note on the opening by the Prosecutor of an investigation in CAR, *supra* note 271, 4.

[411] Background note on the opening by the Prosecutor of an investigation in CAR, *supra* note 271, 1–2.

[412] Background note on the opening by the Prosecutor of an investigation in CAR, *supra* note 271, 4.

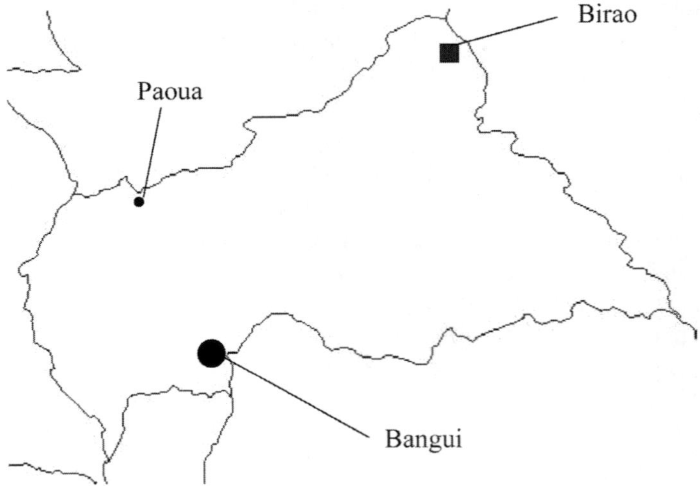

Source: Author.

Figure 4: Map of Central African Republic

cities (Bangui, Paoua, and Birao) form a triangle on the outer boarders of the country and are far apart.

This could object an adjunctive situation for all events. On the other hand, the parties of the conflict are largely the same.[413] Thus, the unstable "situation" is spread throughout the entire country and involves congruent actors. It is submitted that a nexus between different peaks of violence exists if the principal actors are the same. The nature of the conflict needs to be assessed by the OTP. If a nexus can be identified, then future crimes can be investigated as part of the pending situation. If closely monitoring potential on-going or future crimes is truly a deterrent,[414] then surveillance might help the ICC to fulfill its mandate more efficiently. However, to

[413] In a simplified description, Ange-Félix Patassé and his recruited rebels and foreign mercenaries versus François Bozizé and his troops, "Central African Republic: ICC Opens Investigation," 22.5.2007, Human Rights News; *Prosecutor v. Bemba,* Mandat d'arrêt, supra note 273, para. 12. More detailed on the involved parties, i.e. the two rebel movements of the *Armée Populaire pour la Restauration de la République et la Démocratie* (hereinafter APRD) and the *Union des Forces Démocratiques pour le Rassemblement* (hereinafter UFDR), as well as the government *Forces armées Centrafricaines* (hereinafter FACA) and elite *Garde presidentielle* (hereinafter GP), see "Central African Republic" in HRW, World Report 2008, *supra* note 210, 88 et seq.

maximize the deterrent impact more situations under analysis must be made available to the public and the OTP must adopt a more proactive role.[415]

Last but not least, transborder conflicts are exceptionally important with regard to every current situation because the situations in the CAR, the DRC, Uganda, and Darfur all affect neighboring countries.[416] Article 12 (2) (b) clearly allows for jurisdiction of the ICC for nationals of the pending situation even if the person carries the conflict across the border. In the same vein, nationals of neighboring countries, who commit crimes on a member state's territory, whose situation is pending, fall under the Court's jurisdictional reach according to article 12 (2) (a). The remaining issue to be solved concerns a situation that refers to a number of States; for example, a hypothetical situation regarding crimes committed on the border territory between Uganda and Sudan. If the alleged crimes take place on the territory of one State, such a referral is unnecessary. However, if two States have a conflict where crimes are committed on both sides, such a referral makes sense. Assuming that both States are States Parties, the Court could approve a situation "referring alleged crimes committed in the conflict between State A and State B and on the territory of the aforementioned States."[417] Here again, a nexus in order to avoid frivolous referrals is deemed necessary. The nexus could, for example, be linked to the crime of aggression, or a referral of a transborder situation could be allowed only for SC referrals.[418] In any event, the referral of a transborder situation should not be approved with regard to self-referrals due to the large conflict potential. Further, a situation referring "alleged crimes committed in States A, B, C and D" is not within the ambit of the Court, since the reference

---

414 Mr. Gareth Evans of the International Crisis Group, Session 1: Interested States, Second public hearing of the OTP, 25.9.2006.

415 Mr. Antoine Bernard – International Federation for Human Rights (FIDH), *supra* note 272.

416 As an example, regarding the Ituri region, see Wouters/Verhoeven, in Ankumah/Kwakwa, *supra* note 210, 136–7. They outline the involvement of Rwanda, Uganda, and the DRC, all supporting local armed groups. For Sudan and Chad see WCRO report "situation" and case selection, *supra* note 370, 26–7.

417 In the same vein, Dominic McGoldrick, "The Permanent International Criminal Court: An end to the culture of impunity?" (1999) CLR 627, 640 ("[...] extend across a number of States").

418 The crime of aggression has been defined in accordance with article 5 (2) at the Review Conference in Kampala; cf. Resolution RC/Res. 6, The Crime of Aggression, ASP Review Conference 13th plenary meeting, 11.6.2010. See further Discussion paper on the crime of aggression proposed by the Chairman (revision June 2008), ASP resumed sixth session, 2.–6.6.2008, 14.5.2008 (ICC-ASP/6/SWGCA/2); further CICC, "ASP Highlights," The Monitor, Journal of the CICC, Issue No. 38, May–October 2009, 4; see also <www.icc-cpi.int/Menus/ASP/Crime+of+Aggression/>.

does not show traceable parameters. If the latter was approved, the ICC could identically be mandated to exercise universal jurisdiction, monitoring any conflicts world-wide. Reference to large regions or continents is not permitted under the current system.

Having discussed the broadest possible approach towards a situation, henceforth the narrowest potential situation will be addressed. Coming first to the familiar territorial and temporal parameters, the posed question is how narrow these parameters can be phrased. A State's frontier is, for example, a very clear-cut territorial determination. In practice, situations are often framed by distinguishable areas within the respective country. In the DRC Ituri was particularly analyzed,[419] Uganda was sometimes reduced to Northern Uganda,[420] and Sudan is commonly known as the "Darfur situation."[421] This is nothing out of the ordinary, since core crimes under article 5 (1) are complex and must be classified somehow. In any event, it is difficult – if not impractical – to draw a distinct theoretical line. The massacres of My Lai, for instance, would most certainly qualify as one situation under the ICC Statute due to their gravity, albeit they took place in only one single village.[422] On the other hand, downsizing could adulterate the comparability of gravity. Breaking down a situation into various smaller situations and comparing them individually face to face with one larger situation of an entire State causes falsification. While the OTP can to a certain extent define narrow situations, States are not allowed to do so. Rule 44 (2) RPE, though only relating to declarations under article 12 (3), can be used as an argument favoring this hypothesis. It states that a declaration causes the acceptance of jurisdiction with respect to any crimes referred to in article 5. In other words, if a State declares acceptance of the ICC's jurisdiction, it accepts that the OTP is investigating into all crimes within the State equally, and the OTP might even extend the situations (predefined by the State) in order to achieve objectivity.[423] Bearing this in mind, States themselves can only define situations in regards to State boundaries.

419 OTP-Press Release (DRC), Prosecutor receives referral of the situation in the Democratic Republic of Congo, *supra* note 213; Lekha Sriram/Ross, *supra* note 210, 57.

420 OTP-Press Release (Uganda), Prosecutor of the International Criminal Court opens an investigation into Northern Uganda, *supra* note 246.

421 Critically on the geographic limitation, Lekha Sriram/Ross, *supra* note 210, 57; similarly Schabas, *supra* note 13, 299.

422 More than 500 Vietnamese civilians were killed by American soldiers in the My Lai massacre, which took place on the morning of 16 March 1968, see "Murder in the name of war – My Lai," 20.7.1998, BBC News.

423 Junck, *supra* note 204, mn 491; Ruth Wedgwood, "The United States and the ICC: achieving a wider consensus through the Ithaca Package" (1999) 32 CJIL 535, 541 ("State must be willing to have its own conduct scrutinized as well"); Christian

With regard to SC referrals, some authors propose that the SC should be granted the exceptional right to refer isolated acts and even one individual.[424] It is a peculiar idea to allow the referral of cases through the backdoor by such a broad interpretation. During the drafting process some parties feared politically biased referrals and expressly introduced the concept of situations as opposed to cases. If individuals or individual cases could be referred, the whole concept is sold down the river. This danger is self-evident with regard to self-referrals, and such a "referral from a State Party need not be limited to specific cases, in the sense of an allegation against a named individual or individuals for having committed a specific crime or crimes."[425] A privileged SC referral of an individual finds no support in the ICC Statute or in the drafting history. Quite the opposite is the case: the power of the Prosecutor to decide "if" and "how" to investigate is in no way infringed upon by whatever kind of referral, even if individuals are named.[426] Referrals constitute *notitia criminis,* which leaves any further determinations to the Prosecutor. Prejudicial determination must be avoided in the first place, hence individuals cannot be referred to the Court under article 13 (b).[427] The SC does, however, enjoy wider discretion than a State based on its powers under Chapter VII, and it can delimit a situation more specifically than referring to a States' boundaries, if appropriate.[428] There

---

Tomuschat, "Das Statut von Rom für den Internationalen Strafgerichtshof" (1998) 73 Friedenswarte 335, 343.

424 Condorelli/Villalpando, in Cassese/Gaeta/Jones, *supra* note 400, 633; Kurth, *supra* note 399, 65; Junck, *supra* note 204, mn 492 et seq., who even extends this right to all referrals. Contrary, Chris Gallavin, "Prosecutorial discretion within the ICC: under the pressure" (2006) 17 CLF 43, 48.

425 Daniel Ntanda Nsereko, "Article 18" in Triffterer, *supra* note 37, article 18, mn 6; also Hoffmeister/Knoke, *supra* note 169, 788; Ulrich Fastenrath, "Der Internationale Strafgerichtshof" (1999) 39 JuS 632, 634 ("[...] Situationen (= Tatkomplexe, nicht einzelne Strafverfahren)"); Wei, *supra* note 156, 55; Daniela Stagel, *Sicherheitsrat und Internationaler Strafgerichtshof: Zur Abgrenzung ihrer Kompetenzen nach der Charta der Vereinten Nationen und dem Römischen Statut* (Kovač, Hamburg 2008) 71.

426 Condorelli/Villalpando, in Cassese/Gaeta/Jones, *supra* note 400, 633; Kurth, *supra* note 399, 65; Corinna Contag, *Der Internationale Strafgerichtshof im System kollektiver Sicherheit* (Nomos, Baden-Baden 2009) 112.

427 The inclusion of names in a list, which leads to a mixed referral, should also be avoided. The Prosecutor is under no obligation to rely on the names, but the political effect has to be taken into account, cf. Mahnoush Arsanjani, "ICC and trigger mechanism by a State" in Perakis, S. (ed.), *International Criminal Court, A new dimension in international justice. Questions and prospects for a new humanitarian order,* Colloqium, Santorini 14–16 September 2000 (Ant. N. Sakkoulas Publishers, Athens 2002) 149; also Stagel, *supra* note 425, 66.

428 Jens David Ohlin, "Peace, security, and prosecutorial discretion" in Stahn/Sluiter, *supra* note 5, 185, 186 et seq., argues that the SC's discretion overrides the

is room for a SC referral concerning a limited region within a State if the SC already holds particularized knowledge.

As an intermediary conclusion, the referral of a clear-cut territory of a State should be the norm. Large areas or even locations, such as towns, villages, and rescue camps, can circumscribe a situation, but must be referred by the SC or be identified by the Prosecutor himself in the course of investigations. In general, those locations form one part of a broader situation under scrutiny rather than being situations on their own.

As stated above, temporal parameters are objective and essential for a predetermination. On-going and future crimes can be included. On the other hand, a time-frame cannot be set too narrow. If the period is limited to one specific incident committed by one specific group, it is invalid. In consequence, the Prosecutor can simply delete the dates and set the entry into force of the Statute with respect to the affected State as a starting date. This option of redefining referrals is proposed regarding any referrals that would bring about a one-sided investigation. To conclude, the scaling down of a situation entails dangers when it is conducted by external actors. Under the *proprio motu* power, the Prosecutor has discretion to narrow down situations to larger areas, or even towns, villages, and rescue camps, where peaks of violence occurred, as long as some objective comparability based on gravity exists.

The Chamber's definition of a situation further mentions in "some cases personal parameters." While the reference to temporal and geographical parameters is undisputed, other parameters are less clear.[429] Jurisdiction *ratione personae* is admittedly limited by statutory provisions: persons under the age of eighteen do not fall within the ambit of the ICC (article 26). Moreover, article 12 (2) (b) limits the jurisdiction *ratione personae* if crimes occur in a non-member state and are committed by nationals of a non-member state and a member state. In this event, the ICC is barred from exercising jurisdiction over any non-member citizens and can bring to trial only the nationals of member states.[430]

Prosecutor's discretion, even adjusting it to "zero discretion" if a situation is referred based on the SC's Chapter VII powers. With all due respect to Ohlin's arguments, I do not agree that the SC has the power to abrogate the ICC Statute. If the SC refers or defers situations, it must do so within the ambits of the ICC Statute, cf. further Part III, B., V.

[429] Kirsch/Robinson, in Cassese/Gaeta/Jones, *supra* note 371, 625; WCRO report "situation" and case selection, *supra* note 370, 21; critical also Schabas, *supra* note 13, 299.

[430] Communications received by the Prosecutor since 2002, *supra* note 211, 5; Iraq response, *supra* note 333, 3.

Beyond statutory boundaries, the setting of limits by the referring party must be evaluated with a sound degree of skepticism. One author identifies three major issues open for discussion: personal limitations, legal limitations, and factual limitations.[431] However, he does not address the follow-up matter: How should the OTP, as the institution receiving referrals, deal with these possible limitations? If limitations are permitted or denied, the respective consequences need to be explained.

Personal parameters naturally cause subjective classification. The ICTR's jurisdiction was, for instance, limited to Rwandan nationals for crimes committed outside Rwanda (article 1 ICTR Statute). Allegations of victor's justice could result if mandates focus on those acting on behalf of only one side.[432] One-sided investigations must therefore be avoided. Article 54 calls for an investigation into all facts and evidence, thus scrutinizing all potentially involved parties. Therefore, a referral defined in part by nationality or limiting the jurisdiction to just one ethnic group in a conflict is not permissible under the ICC Statute.[433]

Another aspect is the threshold of "persons who bear the greatest responsibility," which might limit the personal jurisdictional scope from the outset. The SCSL contains this jurisdictional barrier in article 1 (1) of its Statute:

> "The Special Court shall, except as provided in subparagraph (2), have the power to prosecute *persons who bear the greatest responsibility* for *serious violations of international humanitarian law and Sierra Leonean law committed in the territory of Sierra Leone since 30 November 1996*, including those leaders who, in committing such crimes, have threatened the establishment of and implementation of the peace process in Sierra Leone (emph. added)."[434]

A similar provision can be found in the mandate of the Extraordinary Chambers in the Court of Cambodia (hereinafter ECCC), i.e. "to bring to trial senior leaders of Democratic Kampuchea and those who were most responsible."[435] The Prosecutor of the ICC similarly introduced a policy of

---

[431] Junck, *supra* note 204, mn 481 et seq.

[432] Kirsch/Robinson, in Cassese/Gaeta/Jones, *supra* note 371, 625.

[433] Junck, *supra* note 204, mn 482. In a reserved manner, Kirsch/Robinson, in Cassese/Gaeta/Jones, *supra* note 371, 625: "[...] leaves open the question as to whether a referral defined in part by nationality would be appropriate."

[434] SCSL Statute, 16.1.2002, annexed to the Agreement between the United Nations and the Government of Sierra Leone on the Establishment of the Special Court for Sierra Leone, signed on 16.1.2002. See further the SCSL's Rules of Procedure and Evidence, 28.5.2010.

[435] Article 1 Law on the Establishment of the Extraordinary Chambers in the Courts of Cambodia for the prosecution of crimes committed during the period of Democratic Kampuchea (hereinafter ECCC Law), with inclusion of amendments as promulgated on 27.10.2004.

focusing on those who bear the greatest responsibility.[436] However, there is a decisive difference between a statutory jurisdictional – and thus legal – constraint to those bearing the greatest responsibility and a policy that introduces such limitations.[437] Moreover, it is the OTP that selects the persons, and a predetermination by the referring party certainly infringes upon that right.

In the same vein, legal limitations must be rejected. A complaint which solely focuses on genocide allegations and intentionally leaves out other crimes could cause trouble for the Court if it turns out that evidence is not sufficient. The threshold is lower for crimes against humanity and might, in the worst case scenario, be excluded by a legally limited referral. Not only is there no basis in the ICC Statute for legal limitations, but the possibility of State complaints was also abrogated in favor of the more neutral term "referral of a situation."[438]

Turning to factual limitations, facts are necessarily limited in temporal and territorial respect for limiting the situation under analysis. However, factual limitations which go beyond the outlined ambit of these two parameters must be rejected. If specific facts are singled out, the referred situation is prejudiced. A government that refers a situation of a certain time-period in which air raids on its cities took place, but allegedly committed preceding or successive attacks, presumably aims at one-sided investigations against its opponents.[439] The Ugandan referral serves as a good example. The President of Uganda – despite the government's involvement in the conflict – only referred the situation "concerning the LRA."[440] Although the Prosecutor later responded that the scope of the referral encompasses all crimes committed in Northern Uganda,[441] thus redefining the

---

436 Policy paper, *supra* note 99, 3, 7; OTP Report on activities 2003–2006, *supra* note 23, 11, 16, 20; OTP strategy, *supra note* 409, 3, 5; Seils, in Bergsmo, *supra* note 99, 55. See further Part IV, C., IV., 4., b), aa) and ee).

437 A policy does not equal a legal limitation and is open for changes. It may be set aside if the OTP so decides, and is merely a guideline than an obligatory test, see in more detail Part IV, C., IV., 4., b), ee).

438 Junck, *supra* note 204, mn 486; see already Part III, B., II.

439 Junck, *supra* note 204, mn 490.

440 Press Release (Uganda), President of Uganda refers situation concerning the Lord's Resistance Army (LRA) to the ICC, *supra* note 247; Lekha Sriram/Ross, *supra* note 210, 56.

441 *Prosecutor v. Kony et al.,* Decision to convene a status conference on the investigation in the situation in Uganda, *supra* note 248, para. 5; *Prosecutor v. Kony et al.,* Prosecution's observations regarding the admissibility, *supra* note 264, para. 4; also Charles Chernor Jalloh, "Regionalizing International Criminal Law" (2009) 9 ICLR 445, 486; WCRO report "situation" and case selection, *supra* note 370, 2–3, 25–6.

situation in broader terms, up-to-date five arrest warrants only against LRA leaders were unsealed. Amnesty International and HRW felt compelled to question the one-sided approach that ignored the government forces.[442] One author even conjectures that the Prosecutor has a tacit understanding with the Ugandan government to prosecute rebel leaders only.[443] This shows how dangerous limited referrals are to the impartial work of the OTP. Not even going as far as others and assuming biased investigations, the allegations alone demonstrate how the narrow predefinition of the Ugandan situation by the Ugandan President influenced the OTP's reputation.

For the moment, it is submitted that factual limitations – similarly to legal and to a large extent personal limitations – cannot be permitted to predefine a situation. We will now turn to the follow-up question, i. e. how the OTP can proceed with a situation that is not predefined in the referral as wanton.

The situation under pre-investigation has to reach the "reasonable basis" standard to proceed to full investigations (articles 15 (3), 53 (1), rule 48).[444] From the ICC Statute, it is not yet clear whether the Prosecutor can modify a situation he receives or even declare it void. The handling of a predefinition of a situation which the OTP wishes to change must be solved. One could consider the phrasing in the referral letter binding. Yet, article 42 (1) stands strongly against such a binding force, calling for the independence of the Prosecutor and stating that a member of the Office shall not seek or act on instructions from any external source. In addition, the OTP has to cover all facts and evidence relevant to an assessment whether there is criminal responsibility under the ICC Statute (article 54 (1) (a)). OTP Regulation 24 furthermore states:

> "In the analysis of information and evidence regarding alleged crimes, the Office shall develop and apply a consistent and objective method for the evaluation of sources, information and evidence."

---

442 "Uganda: First ever arrest warrants by International Criminal Court – a first step towards addressing impunity," 14.10.2005, Amnesty International (AFR 59/ 008/2005): "Although the steps taken by the ICC are to be supported, it must be noted that ICC trials will only cover a handful of the thousands of persons responsible for crimes against humanity and war crimes in Northern Uganda and only members of the LRA, but none of the members of the government armed forces or their civilian superiors." See also "ICC takes decisive step for justice in Uganda," 14.10.2005, HRW: "The ICC must also look into abuses committed by the Ugandan army."

443 Schabas, *supra* note 27, 149.

444 Statement of the Prosecutor of the International Criminal Court, Mr. Luis Moreno-Ocampo to the Security Council on 29 June 2005 pursuant to UNSCR 1593 (2005), 29.6.2005, 1–2.

One-sided investigations would undermine the duty to establish the truth in accordance with article 54 (1) (a). Hence, the wording of a referral cannot oblige the OTP to continue exclusively within the paraphrased ambit.

Another option would be to redefine the situation as the Prosecutor did in Uganda. He concluded that "the scope of the referral encompasses all crimes committed in Northern Uganda in the context of the ongoing conflict involving the LRA."[445] Another possibility would have been to simply reject the referral as legally invalid. Taking for granted that referrals are merely *notitia criminis*, the approach of redefinition seems convenient at first sight. *Notitia criminis* inform the Prosecutor of crimes, and he may – on this basis – expand or specify the concrete situation. Regarding information under article 15 (1), the OTP may do so trouble-free. The information must be grouped together, and it is the Prosecutor who shapes the situation. Article 42 (1) names the Prosecutor as the receiving entity for examining referrals and substantiated information equally. On the other hand, article 13 stipulates that the Court may exercise jurisdiction *if* a situation is referred or a *proprio motu* investigation is initiated. Whenever the OTP receives a referral, there will be a referring party interested to see its situation analyzed. As highlighted above, a rephrasing sometimes may not do away with criticism since the redefined situation will always be viewed in relation to the original referral. Nevertheless, the OTP can narrow down the referred situation without any legal concerns if done organically during investigation: investigating a situation, identifying relevant incidents, and ultimately bringing cases with individuals before the Court. The broadening of a situation is legally unclear: one author draws a line between symmetric interpretation and correction, holding that the former is unproblematic, against what the latter is disputable.[446] Another author states, with respect to SC referrals, that the OTP may not transgress the parameters set by the SC.[447] Most recently, the WCRO suggested that the Prosecutor can either reject the referral and start investigations *proprio motu* or ask for a revised referral.[448]

The OTP cannot touch the substantial part of the referral, and generally a line between symmetric interpretation and correction should be adopted. Marginal changes can be conducted by the OTP with regard to State referrals. However, a modification of the parties – as in the Ugandan situation –

445 *Prosecutor v. Kony et al.,* Decision to convene a status conference on the investigation in the situation in Uganda, *supra* note 248, para. 5.

446 Claus Kress, "'Self referrals' and 'waivers of complementarity'" (2004) 2 JICJ 944, 947.

447 Olásolo, *supra* note 29, 94.

448 WCRO report "situation" and case selection, *supra* note 370, 2, 25.

is significant and amounts to a correction of the referral. Thanks to article 54 (1), the Prosecutor could have chosen not to accept the original Ugandan referral, which otherwise would have resulted in one-sided investigations. Needless to say that this alternative, i.e. rejecting the entire referral, was not desired by the Prosecutor. In conclusion, the redefinition of referrals, though legally possible under the ICC Statute to a certain extent, is not the ideal solution. The answer how to treat referrals, which do not correspond with the statutorily required objectivity, was given by the OTP in its Annex paper:

> "The Prosecutor's *proprio motu* power to initiate an investigation with authorization from a Pre-Trial Chamber is a very important mechanism under the Statute. This procedure provides the legal basis to carry out investigations even where states have failed to refer an objectively serious situation."[449]

Instead of rejecting or redefining a referral, the OTP can treat the referral as *proprio motu* information. Together with his information on other facets of the respective matter, the Prosecutor can then define his own situation and submit it to the PTC for authorization under article 15 (3). In fact, *proprio motu* proceedings are likely to be the least politicized trigger mechanism and back up a decision to dismiss ill-conceived referrals from States Parties.[450] Statutory provisions demand objective investigations and prosecutions. A feasible tool was given to the Prosecutor to navigate through ill-defined situations by providing for the *proprio motu* power. He has regrettably not used it in the Uganda situation.[451] In the future, the OTP should alter this unfortunate policy decision in order to avoid any frivolous investigations – or accusations thereof – caused by the trap of self referrals.

To sum up, the Prosecutor is not bound by predefinitions, be it by States or the SC, and may adopt an expansive interpretation of a situation if otherwise the result would be a violation of the duty to conduct an objective investigation.[452] Judicial review at two levels, through the PTC and the Ap-

---

449 Annex paper, *supra* note 27, 4. On the possibility of expanding the scope via *proprio motu,* see Junck, *supra* note 204, mn 476; Bassiouni, *supra* note 401, 166. Kirsch/Robinson, in Cassese/Gaeta/Jones, *supra* note 371, 625 with fn. 31, name two possibilities to controvert inappropriate politically motivated referrals that include some crimes but exclude others: a remedy by another State through a broader referral or *proprio motu* proceedings by the Prosecutor.

450 Phillipe Kirsch/Darryl Robinson, "Initiation of proceedings by the Prosecutor" in Cassese/Gaeta/Jones, *supra* note 133, 663.

451 Most likely, the Prosecutor wanted to avoid the demanding threshold of authorization by the PTC. For the OTP's public perception, a *proprio motu* modification would nevertheless be the best solution. Allegations of bias can only be ruled out if the OTP takes this path in the future.

452 In the same vein, Gallavin, *supra* note 424, 53, 55, 57 ("[...] the Prosecutor ought to adopt an expansive interpretation of the referral and once again apply the

peals Chamber, guarantees the integrity of the process.[453] Thereby, the Prosecutor must act within the boundaries of the ICC Statute, meaning that an enlargement to Non-States Parties is not possible without the backup of the SC.[454] The SC has considerably more power to influence the work of the OTP than a State, and could *de facto* limit the persons under scrutiny.[455] On the other hand, it is the political power of the SC that allows the ICC to enlarge its powers to Non-States Parties in the first place. The possible misuse is unavoidable as long as universal ratification is not achieved. If the SC, however, obviously refers a one-sided, narrow situation,[456] the OTP has to reject it due to lack of impartiality.

Temporal and territorial parameters, as well as personal and any other thinkable parameters, have clarified the term "situation" to a certain extent. A situation before the ICC is framed by statutory provisions, though perhaps in a very broad way. Ongoing crimes – and to a certain extent future crimes – are within the scope of such a vast notion. It is further recommended to permit definitions through the use of former State boundaries, as well as to allow for transborder situations. Having said so, it is ultimately left to the Prosecutor to identify frivolous situations that are phrased too loosely.[457] While a discretionary redefinition is legally possible to some extent, it is advisable to reassess the current practice and switch to applying the *proprio motu* device more frequently.[458] Kenya is a good start into this direction, yet it will be interesting to see the Prosecutor's choice in more controversial situation countries where the support of the State's government is not as explicit as in Kenya.

---

provisions of the Statute in accordance with the evidence available from the entire 'situation'."); also Bassiouni, *supra* note 401, 131 ("The appropriate meaning of the term 'situation' […] must be determined contextually by the Prosecutor."); Hall, *supra* note 100, 23 ("[…] the Prosecutor should […] give the broadest possible interpretation to the situation referred.").

453 Bassiouni, *supra* note 401, 131.

454 Stagel, *supra* note 425, 78 et seq.

455 Stagel, *supra* note 425, 79; similarly, Oliver Fixon, "Der IStGH: Seine Entstehung und seine Stellung im Völkerrecht" in Stefan Kirsch (ed.), *Internationale Strafgerichtshöfe* (Nomos, Baden-Baden 2005) 207, 217.

456 For an example, see Stagel, *supra* note 425, 78 et seq.

457 McGoldrick, *supra* note 417, names the possibility of a counter-referral by a "referred" State against the referring State. In such a scenario, it would equally be up to the Prosecutor to evaluate both – referral and counter-referral – and a counter-referral could be a leeway for any State to put both sides of the conflict on the Prosecutor's agenda.

458 Even stricter, WCRO report "situation" and case selection, *supra* note 370, 27–8. The WCRO arrives at the conclusion that the Prosecutor cannot *sua sponte* expand the parameters of a situation and *must* follow the procedures laid out in article 15 in such a scenario.

2. Defining a case

The distinction between situations and cases is a core feature of the ICC. As compared to "situations," the assessment of a case was – at first – less disputed, but has similarly led to recent controversies, in particular with regard to the "same conduct-test" (*critère du même comportement*) as part of the admissibility determination.[459] A case is formed by the following elements of law and fact: (1) the facts or criminal events; (2) the suspect or accused; (3) the charges, i. e. the legal characterization of the facts; (4) the mode of responsibility; and (5) the standard of evidence (depending on the phase of development of the case).[460] The definition of a case has been further simplified in the way that a case comprises "specific incidents during which one or more crimes within the jurisdiction of the Court seem to have been committed by one or more identified suspects."[461] Not much later, PTC I recalled the decision of 17 February 2006 and identified a case in the same manner.[462] In this regard, it is interesting to note that the PTC also held that:

> "[…] a case arising from the investigation of a situation will fall within the jurisdiction of the Court only if the specific crimes of the case do not exceed the territorial, temporal and possibly personal parameters defining the situation under investigation and fall within the jurisdiction of the Court."[463]

---

[459] *Prosecutor v. Katanga and Chui,* Motion challenging the admissibility of the case by the Defence of Germain Katanga, pursuant to article 19 (2) (a) of the Statute, 11.3.2007 (ICC-01/04-01/07-949) paras. 39 et seq.; *Prosecutor v. Katanga and Chui,* Public redacted version of the 19th March 2009 Prosecution response to motion challenging the admissibility of the case by the Defence of Germain Katanga, pursuant to article 19 (2), 30.3.2009 (ICC-01/04-01/07-1007) paras. 50 et seq.; *Prosecutor v. Katanga and Chui,* Motifs de la décision orale relative à l'exception d'irrecevabilité de l'affaire (article 19 du Statut), 16.6.2009 (ICC-01/04-01/07-1213) paras. 11 et seq., 17 et seq., 95. See further on the "same conduct-test" Part IV, B., III., 2., b), cc), (1). The Appeals Chamber did not address the correctness of the test because it noticed inactivity and therefore did not have to deal with the secondary prongs of unwillingness and inability, cf. *Prosecutor v. Katanga and Chui,* Judgment on the appeal of Mr. Germain Katanga against the oral decision of Trial Chamber II of 12 June 2009 on the admissibility of the case, 25.09.2009 (ICC-01/04-01/07OA8) para. 81.

[460] Xabier Agirre Aranburu, "Gravity of crimes and responsibility of the suspect" in Bergsmo, *supra* note 99, 147, 147.

[461] *Situation in DRC,* Decision on the applications for participation in the proceedings of VPRS 1 etc., *supra* note 398, para. 65; Olásolo, *supra* note 29, 40, 74. See further on the definition of a case from the OTP's point of view *Prosecutor v. Katanga and Chui,* Public redacted version of the 19th March 2009 Prosecution response to motion challenging the admissibility, *supra* note 459, paras. 58 et seq., 61.

[462] *Prosecutor v. Lubanga,* Decision on the Prosecutor's application for warrant of arrest, article 58, *supra* note 217, para. 21.

It is thus re-emphasized that the initial definition of a situation is quite important. Once parameters are set by the OTP, and a formal investigation has been opened regarding the situation, the Prosecutor has to stay within his predefined boundaries. He can only identify cases falling within the specific situation. The Chamber found *in concreto* that the case against Thomas Lubanga Dyilo falls within the DRC situation currently under investigation as the Prosecutor referred to *conduct* that allegedly took place between July 2002 and December 2003 in certain camps and areas located in the region of Ituri in the territory of the DRC.[464]

Regarding admissibility, PTC I held that it is "*a condition sine qua non* for a case arising from the investigation of a situation to be inadmissible that national proceedings *encompass both the person and the conduct which is the subject of the case before the court* (emph. added)."[465] In other words, the Chamber established a "same person, same conduct-test" to determine whether a State is inactive, and thus whether the case is admissible before the ICC.[466] We will have to come back to this controversial decision with regard to admissibility, in particular inactivity ("specificity test").[467] As an intermediary conclusion, it must be emphasized that the definition of a "case" is not a minor technical question, but has significant influence of the admissibility determination.[468]

In accordance with the Chamber, the Prosecutor assessed the legal notion of a case as representing "a specific incident in which crimes within the jurisdiction of the Court have been committed by identified perpetrators."[469] In other words, the term "cases" should be understood as "being

---

463 *Prosecutor v. Lubanga,* Decision on the Prosecutor's application for warrant of arrest, article 58, *supra* note 217, para. 21.

464 *Prosecutor v. Lubanga,* Decision on the Prosecutor's application for warrant of arrest, article 58, *supra* note 217, para. 23. The DRC situation has been defined as encompassing the territory of the DRC since 1 July 2002.

465 *Prosecutor v. Lubanga,* Decision on the Prosecutor's application for warrant of arrest, article 58, *supra* note 217, para. 31, 37; *Prosecutor v. Harun and Kushayb,* Decision on the Prosecution application under article 58 (7) of the Statute, *supra* note 292, para. 24; *Prosecutor v. Bemba,* Décision relative à la requête du procureur aux fins de délivrance d'un mandat d'arrêt à l'encontre de Jean-Pierre Bemba Gombo, 10.6.2008 (ICC-01/05-01/08-14) para. 21; also Fifth Report pursuant to UNSC 1593, *supra* note 291, 7; Rod Rastan, "What is a 'case' for the purpose of the Rome Statute?" (2008) 19 CLF 435, 436, who calls this the "specificity test."

466 *Prosecutor v. Katanga and Chui,* Motion challenging the admissibility of the case by the Defence, *supra* note 459, para. 30; further on the "same conduct-test" Part IV, B., III., 2., b), cc), (1).

467 See Part IV, B., III., 2., b), cc), (1).

468 Darryl Robinson, "The mysterious mysteriousness of complementarity" (2010) 21 CLF 67, 100–1.

469 Third Report pursuant to UNSC 1593, *supra* note 288, 2.

constituted by the underlying event, incident and circumstances – i. e. in the criminal context, the conduct of the suspect in relation to a given incident."[470] The OTP thus identifies that a case must be based on particular facts, incidents, and conduct related to a crime within the ICC's jurisdiction.[471]

Furthermore, when selecting situations and cases, the Prosecutor adopted a policy of focused investigations (with those "bearing the greatest responsibility" as his ultimate targets), meaning that the OTP will pursue a limited number of cases and a limited number of persons.[472] Situations before the ICC typically entail mass crimes and massive victimization and it is practically impossible to prosecute all perpetrators or all crimes. The OTP also follows a sequential approach,[473] investigating specific cases within a situation one after another rather than all at once, whereby cases inside the situation are selected according to gravity.[474] Upon completion of each case, the Office examines whether other cases in the situation warrant investigation – bearing in mind the gravity and admissibility thresholds of the ICC Statute.[475] In principle, situations and cases provide a sample that is reflec-

---

470 *Prosecutor v. Katanga and Chui,* Public redacted version of the 19th March 2009 Prosecution response to motion challenging the admissibility, *supra* note 459, para. 58.

471 *Prosecutor v. Katanga and Chui,* Public redacted version of the 19th March 2009 Prosecution response to motion challenging the admissibility, *supra* note 459, para. 60.

472 Prosecutorial Strategy 2009–2012, *supra* note 99, para. 19, 5–6; Annex to the Three Year Report and the Report on the prosecutorial strategy, 20.9.2006, 1: "[...] need for a selective, focused approach (based on gravity and taking into account resources and practical constraints)." Such a focused approach was already recommended by an Informal Expert Paper: Fact-finding and investigative functions of the Office of the Prosecutor, including international co-operation, ICC-OTP 2003, para. 20. On the OTP policy see further Part IV, B., II., 4.

473 Update on communications, *supra* note 316, 1, 5; OTP Report on activities 2003–2006, *supra* note 23, 8; Outlining the Three-Year Report – Ms. Olivia Swaak-Goldman, Session 1: Interested States, Second public hearing of the OTP, 25.9.2006; Guariglia, in Stahn/Sluiter, *supra* note 1215, 215. Sceptical, Ms. Géraldine Mattioli – HRW, Session 2: NGOs and other experts, Second public hearing of the OTP, 26.9.2006, who fears "delays in the investigations and consequences for the preservation of evidence or serious problems of perception for the Office;" similarly, Mr. Antoine Bernard – International Federation for Human Rights (FIDH), *supra* note 272; Mr. Richard Dicker – HRW, Session 4: NGOs and other experts, Second public hearing of the OTP, 18.10.2006 ("selective justice"); Schiff, *supra* note 128, 118–9.

474 OTP Report on activities 2003–2006, *supra* note 23, 2, 8; Third Report pursuant to UNSC 1593, *supra* note 288, 2. Welcoming the way the criterion of "gravity" is laid out, Ms. Géraldine Mattioli, HRW, *supra* note 473.

475 Update on communications, *supra* note 316, 1, 5.

tive of the gravest incidents and the main types of victimization.[476] In practice, however, the OTP does not always cope with expectations.[477] The charges against Mr. Lubanga Dyilo, which focus exclusively on conscripting, enlisting, or using children under the age of fifteen in hostilities, do not cover as many incidents as they otherwise could have.[478] The follow-up cases in the DRC show improvement in this respect and offer a broader variety of counts.[479]

Prima facie, the selection process can be described as follows: selecting situations, selecting geographic regions, selecting incidents, selecting groups, selecting persons most responsible for most serious crimes, selecting a case (decision to request a prosecution), and selecting charges.[480] The selection process is a crucial aspect of this study, yet here we are concentrating mainly on the selection of situations and their respective criteria. One of the most important strategic questions for the Court as a whole is, in my opinion, how it selects its situations and subsequently its cases, and if those decisions are objective.

Finally returning to the initial problem of the ambit of a case, a clear-cut case is *Prosecutor v. Lubanga Dyilo,* which comprises the criminal responsibility of Thomas Lubanga Dyilo for war crimes (conscripting and enlisting children under the age of fifteen years and using them to participate actively in hostilities) in the territory of the DRC since July 2002.[481] A case might also incorporate more identified suspects where appropriate (for instance *Prosecutor v. Germain Katanga and Mathieu Ngudjolo Chui*).[482]

---

476 OTP Report on activities 2003–2006, *supra* note 23, 8. Thereto see Ms. Géraldine Mattioli, HRW, *supra* note 473.

477 On unrealistic expectations *vis-à-vis* the ICC see Burke-White, *supra* note 1218, 59 et seq.

478 Ms. Mariana Getz – Redress, Session 2: NGOs and other experts, Second public hearing of the OTP, 26.9.2006. Ms. Getz fears that the "gravity test" is being replaced with something more akin to an "expediency test." Whereas focused charges – contrary to the policy of the ICTY – are an advancement, it has to be emphasized that the OTP should not overshoot the mark. A special accentuation of crimes against children is excellent, but not to the detriment of leaving out severe crimes as murder.

479 Above Part III, B., I., 1.

480 Stahn, in Stahn/Sluiter, *supra* note 156, 249; Selection paper, *supra* note 99, para. 34 et seq.

481 For similar examples taken from the ICTY (Dario Kordic; Radislav Krstic), see Olàsolo, *supra* note 183, 194.

482 For the ICTY, see *Prosecutor v. Kupreskic et al.,* Trial judgment, 14.1.2000 (IT-95-16), that names even six accused: Zoran Kupreskic, Mirjan Kupreskic, Vlatko Kupreskic, Drago Josipovic, Dragan Papic, and Vladimir Santic. For the ICTR, see *Prosecutor v. Nahimana et al.,* Trial judgment, 3.12.2003 (ICTR-96-11), that lists Ferdinand Nahimana, Jean-Bosco Barayagwiza, and Hassan Ngeze.

Filtering cases from pending situations, however, will be the real challenge for the OTP. The design of a solid case hypothesis during the initial stage is fundamental for the subsequent process, and it must cover: (1) the status of authority or role of the suspect; (2) the structure of the organization instrumental to the crime and subordinated to or associated with the suspect; (3) the pattern and *modus operandi* of the criminal events; and (4) a conclusion on the mode of responsibility.[483]

3. Demarcation line between situation and case

Last but not least, PTC I held that cases entail proceedings that take place after the issuance of a warrant of arrest or a summons to appear, thus setting a strict demarcation line at article 58 proceedings.[484] Formally, a case now only exists after the issuance of a warrant of arrest. As a consequence, it follows that the object of article 15 (3) and 53 (1) proceedings are situations defined by temporal, territorial, and sometimes personal parameters.[485] The process from situations to cases can be sketched as follows:

(1) the OTP obtains *notitia criminis*;

(2) starts pre-investigating;

(3) identifies a situation;

(4) checks the criteria enshrined in articles 53 (1), 15 (3), rule 48 with regard to the situation as a whole;

(5) starts a formal investigation (in the case of a referral), or asks for authorization of a formal investigation (under article 15) pursuant to article 54;

(6) investigates and identifies individual suspects;

(7) ultimately applies for a warrant of arrest or summons to appear if the reasonable grounds standard of article 58 is met; and

(8) the PTC issues a warrant of arrest or summons to appear.

Once the last step has been reached, a formal case exists according to the Chamber. In practice, however, the stages are blurry since the OTP will

---

483 Agirre Aranburu, in Bergsmo, *supra* note 460, 148–9. Similarly, cf. OTP Regulation 34.

484 *Situation in DRC,* Decision on the applications for participation in the proceedings of VPRS 1 etc., *supra* note 398, para. 65; already before *Situation in DRC,* Decision following the consultation held on 11 October 2005 and the Prosecution's submission on jurisdiction and admissibility filed on 31 October 2005, 9.11.2005 (ICC-01/04-93) 4; Olàsolo, *supra* note 183, 194; Rastan, *supra* note 465, 442–3.

485 Anticipated by Olásolo, *supra* note 29, 44–5.

most likely focus on individuals before a formal case exists. Therefore, a case could begin at three potential stages: (1) during pre-investigation and investigation stages; (2) at the moment the Prosecutor makes an application for an arrest warrant or summons to appear; or (3) when the PTC issues a decision to issue a warrant of arrest or summons to appear.[486] As presented above, there are dangers that the *notitia criminis* of the referral entails reference to individuals or that information under article 15 (1) will contain some case-related information. Most countries foresee a broader pre-investigation or preliminary investigation into the crime scene contrasted by the full investigation that aims at specific suspects.[487] Therefore, it might be argued that cases are the object on which the decision to initiate a formal investigation is based.

Some aspects have been resolved by the Chamber: *prima facie,* a theoretical line has been drawn between situations and cases. Nevertheless, the PTC's decision is not entirely convincing. Interpretations which were not anticipated by the founders of the ICC Statute have reared their heads. Whereas discrepancy to the drafting history is nothing out of the ordinary, it is remarkable nonetheless that the term "situation" has resulted in a "demarcation line between proceedings concerning the situation and the case at the issuance of a warrant of arrest or a summons to appear." While focusing on the term "case" and "situation," the basic structure of the ICC Statute was not sufficiently taken into consideration. First of all, article 53 (1) (b) speaks of "the case is or would be admissible." A literal argument could be made that article 53 (1) (b) therefore refers to cases and not situations. However, as noted above, the ICC Statute does not use stringent terminology. The reference to "case" seems rather to be the result of an incoherent drafting process.[488] Then again, articles 13–15 are situated within part II of the ICC Statute on jurisdiction, admissibility, and applicable law. Most importantly, they deal with the triggering procedure, one essential part of a newly introduced pre-investigation stage. In this regard, the term "situation" was introduced in order to avoid politically motivated complaints.[489] In contrast, article 53 is situated within part V on prosecution and investigation. At this stage, the triggering procedure has already taken place. It is not entirely persuasive to enlarge the concept of situations vastly into the pre-investigation stage and even into the formal investigation stage. At this point, the Prosecutor alone is responsible for starting an investigation, and the original concern, i.e. the danger of politically motivated com-

[486] Rastan, *supra* note 465, 440.

[487] Cf. Annex 2.

[488] Rastan, *supra* note 465, 441.

[489] See Part III, B., III., with references in fn. 371.

plaints, does not exist anymore. In my view, the differentiation causes problems in the application of the criteria within article 53 (1), which was intended to deal with ordinary investigations, i. e. cases and not situations. It is nothing out of the ordinary that the Prosecutor discovers a certain crime scene, then initiates an investigation, and subsequently narrows down the investigation until he can present a case, in the narrow sense, with one or more suspects for prosecution. If this is labeled a "case hypothesis,"[490] it is yet closer to being a case than a situation. The selection process is the following: selecting a situation, selecting a geographic region, selecting incidents, selecting groups, selecting persons, selecting charges, case.[491] At the very beginning, the Prosecutor starts investigating, and the essential parts of his selection process are the criteria he applies in order to filter out a suspected person. If the criteria remain unclear, the differentiation between situation and case is not helpful for avoiding politicized prosecutions, and the OTP will most certainly face criticism. It has to be apparent who is selected for which reasons based on non-discriminatory choices. The differentiation of situation and case with regard to articles 15 (3) and 53 (1) is not imperative. It is more important to disentangle the criteria within article 53 (1) and (2) for achieving smooth functioning of the pre-investigation phase. A transparent, comprehensible procedure must be accomplished by the OTP and be made public. Applying the criteria of article 53 (1) to situations and cases is the main challenge for the future, and a first approach shall be completed in the course of this study. This formal differentiation of case and situation notwithstanding, the terms may overlap because an accurate disjuncture seems practically impossible.

4. Conclusion

During the pre-investigation phase the OTP is concerned with situations and not cases.[492] The main purpose of the investigation of a situation is to identify cases.[493] The two notions may overlap, but the formal demarcation line is now set at article 58 proceedings as decided by PTC I in the DRC situation on 17 January 2006.

Situations are generally defined by temporal, territorial, and sometimes personal parameters. The exact situation may be framed by the OTP, whereas the starting point is marked by the three trigger mechanisms refer-

490 Rastan, *supra* note 465, 441; Burke-White/Kaplan, *supra* note 264, 260; recently also OTP Regulation 34.

491 See already Part III, B., III., 2.

492 Razesberger, *supra* note 371, 33.

493 Stigen, *supra* note 205, 93.

ring *notitia crimines* to the ICC. It is worth noting that neither referrals nor private communications automatically trigger the powers of the Prosecutor.[494] The Prosecutor is not entirely bound by predefinitions and may reinterpret the definition of a situation. For achieving more objectivity the Prosecutor must, however, increasingly use his *proprio motu* power.

The concept of situations has led to increasing ICC case law and academic debate on the participation of victims, especially their participatory rights, at the different procedural stages, distinguishing between victims of a situation (e. g. all natural persons, organizations, and institutions that have suffered harm as a result of the commission of crimes within the jurisdiction of the Court in a specific territory), or victims of a case (e. g. natural persons, organizations, and institutions that have suffered harm as a result of the conduct of one or several identified accused or suspects).[495] Upcoming developments in the area of participation of victims will be interesting to watch and are closely linked to the differentiation between situations and cases. In this context, it must be noted that extensive interpretation of article 68 (3) has been limited in so far as victim participation cannot be granted during the procedural phase of an investigation, but only during later stages (pre-trial, trial, and appeal).[496]

---

[494] Annex paper, *supra* note 27, 1.

[495] *Situation in DRC,* Decision on the applications for participation in the proceedings of VPRS 1 etc., *supra* note 398, paras. 23 et seq.; HRW, "A summary of the case law of the International Criminal Court," March 2007, 1, 3 et seq.; Ambos, in Bohlander, *supra* note 10, 444 et seq.; Stahn/Olásolo/Gibson, *supra* note 370, 221; Jérôme De Hemptinne/Francesco Rindi, "ICC Pre-Trial Chamber allows victims to participate in the investigation phase of proceedings" (2006) 4 JICJ 342, 344; A.H. Guhr, "Victim participation during the pre-trial stage at the International Criminal Court" (2008) 8 ICLR 109, 134 et seq.; also War Crimes Research Office, "Victim participation before the International Criminal Court" (hereinafter WCRO Report Victim Participation), International Criminal Court Legal Analysis and Education Project (United States of America, American University Washington College of Law 2007); International Bar Association, "Balancing rights: The ICC at a procedural crossroads," May 2008, 1 et seq.; FIDH, "Victims' rights before the ICC," 23.4.2007; Mariana Goetz, "The International Criminal Court and its relevance to affected communities" in Waddell/Clark, *supra* note 246, 65, 68 et seq.; Sergey Vasiliev, "Article 68 (3) and personal interest of victims in the emerging practice of the ICC" in Stahn/Sluiter, *supra* note 5, 635, 635 et seq.; Nino Tsereteli, "Victim participation in ICC proceedings" in Stahn/van Herik, *supra* note 11, 625, 637 et seq.

[496] *Situation in DRC,* Judgment on victim participation in the investigation stage of the proceedings in the appeal of the OPCD against the decision of Pre-Trial Chamber I of 7 December 2007 and in the appeals of the OPCD and the Prosecutor against the decision of Pre-Trial Chamber I of 24 December 2007, 19.12.2008 (ICC-01-04-556) paras. 57–9; Policy paper on victim participation under article 68 (3) of the ICC Statute, OTP Draft December 2009, 7.12.2009, 7–8.

The task of selecting situations and cases surely goes to the heart of the ICC model. Even if the Office comes to a negative conclusion on "reasonable basis," it is not precluded from considering further information regarding the same situation and re-evaluating its former decision (articles 15 (6) and 53 (4)). In conclusion, it has to be noted that the Prosecutor distinguishes between a *case driven approach,* which implies that the OTP must act in every situation involving crimes that appear to fall within the Court's jurisdiction, and a *resource driven approach,* according to which the Prosecutor may only take two or three situations each year, focusing on the worst crimes.[497] The Chief Prosecutor pointed out:

> "Determining the correct model is a legal, financial and strategic question that will require dialogue between many actors. It has a *legal* dimension, namely the interpretation of Article 53, and therefore involves the OTP and ultimately the judges. It has a *budgetary* dimension and therefore involves the States Parties. It also has a *strategic* dimension – what is the desired scope and role of the Court? – and therefore involves all stakeholders."[498]

The best answer lies in the middle of the two mentioned – case driven and resource driven – approaches. The OTP has the policy tool to focus its investigations, and the gravity matter is the Office's key criterion. In addition, and in order to not lose sight of ending impunity as emphasized in the Preamble of the ICC Statute, a new 106*bis* RPE must be introduced which allows for a referral of situations and cases back to national jurisdiction where feasible.[499]

IV. State referral

State referrals are provided for in article 13 (a), and defined in more detail in article 14, but were thought to have little potential for use.[500] As a matter of fact, three of five situations pending before the Court were referred under articles 13 (a) and 14. The mechanism has not, however, operated as intended; instead of inter-State actions, the three situations of Uganda, DRC, and CAR embrace the borders of the referring State itself, which became quickly known as self-referrals.[501] State Party referrals can

[497] Statement by Luis Moreno-Ocampo: Informal meeting of Legal Advisors of Ministries of Foreign Affairs, 24.10.2005, 9–10.

[498] Statement by Luis Moreno-Ocampo: Informal meeting, *supra* note 497, 10.

[499] See further Part V, C.

[500] Schabas, *supra* note 27, 143; Kress, *supra* note 446, 944; Matthew Happold, "The ICC and the LRA" (2007) 87 MJIL 1, 7 with fn. 60. As an example for the expectation that State referrals would be a rare tool, see Hoffmeister/Knoke, *supra* note 169, 788, 793. The law-in-action has proven them wrong, cf. Razesberger, *supra* note 371, 60.

[501] Schabas, *supra* note 27, 143; Kress, *supra* note 446, 944; Akhavan, *supra* note 246, 405.

accordingly be divided into two separate forms: third party referrals and self-referrals.[502] This section begins with a short survey of the drafting history of the relevant provisions (1.) and an outline of the preconditions of State referrals (2.) before approaching the problematic practice of self-referrals (3.). It concludes with a discussion of two related issues: the withdrawal of a referral (4.) and the waiver of complementarity (5.).

1. Drafting history

Article 25 of the ILC Draft Statute allowed States Parties to lodge a complaint with the Prosecutor,[503] an innovation that was thought at the time to encourage States to join the Statute and to share in the financial burden of its implementation.[504] As a further requirement, article 25 ILC Draft Statute states that the Complainant State must be a party to the 1948 Genocide Convention if the complaint concerns a genocide case. Supporting documentation (article 25 (3) ILC Draft Statute) should prevent "frivolous, groundless or politically motivated complaints" and, moreover, should provide the Prosecutor with sufficient information to begin an investigation.[505]

Ad Hoc Committee meetings in 1995 led to further discussion on the trigger mechanism, in particular with regards to State referrals. Some delegates advocated for an expansive procedure in which any State Party would be able to refer any crimes within the jurisdiction of the Court, rejecting the distinction between genocide and other crimes. Other delegations favored a restrictive procedure that only allowed interested States to file a complaint.[506] During the Preparatory Committee's meetings in 1996 some voices equally wanted to limit the right to lodge a complaint to States with an interest in the case.[507] In response to this position, some delegations argued that crimes under the Statute were of interest to the international community as a whole and that any State should be able to lodge a com-

502 Gallavin, *supra* note 424, 49.

503 ILC Draft Statute 1994, *supra* note 353, 89. See already Part III, B., II.; also Cherif Bassiouni, *The legislative history of the International Criminal Court: An article-by-article evolution,* Vol. 2 (Transnational Publishers, Ardsley, NY 2005) 132–3; WCRO report "situation" and case selection, *supra* note 370, 8 et seq.; Schabas, *supra* note 13, 305-6.

504 ILC Draft Statute 1994, *supra* note 353, 89.

505 ILC Draft Statute 1994, *supra* note 353, 90.

506 Report of the *Ad Hoc* Committee 1995, *supra* note 379, para. 112, 25.

507 Report of the Preparatory Committee 1996, Vol. 1, *supra* note 203, para. 147, 34. Back then, interested States were identified as the custodial State, the State where the crime was committed, the State of nationality of the suspect, the State whose nationals were victims, and the State which was the target of the crime.

plaint.[508] Another proposal would have required more than one State to lodge a complaint "in order to signify that a serious crime of interest to the international community was at issue."[509] As a result, numerous options were included in brackets in article 45 [25] of the Zutphen Draft,[510] which later was transferred without substantial changes into article 11 of the Preparatory Committee's Draft Statute of 1998.[511]

However, an alternative draft of the United Kingdom, entitled "Referral of a situation by a State," was included in the Preparatory Committee's Draft Statute 1998 as a "further option for articles 6, 7, 10, and 11." The United Kingdom suggested that States refer situations rather than single cases. This proposal essentially departed from the restrictive complaint procedure and simplified the triggering procedure:[512] the idea was widely supported during the Rome Conference[513] and finally found its way into article 14 of the ICC Statute with two changes. First, the word "complainant State" in the UK draft was changed to "State referring the situation;" second, the duty to notify the SC of each referred situation was not included.

No reference to self-referrals or voluntary referrals can be found in the discussions.[514] From the drafting history it can be concluded that the delegates were more concerned with the delineation between a situation and case than the terminological change from complaint to referral.[515]

It was the OTP that changed the course of developments in 2003[516] by adopting a policy of inviting and encouraging voluntary referrals.[517] The

---

[508] Report of the Preparatory Committee 1996, Vol. 1, *supra* note 203, para. 147, 34.

[509] Report of the Preparatory Committee 1996, Vol. 1, *supra* note 203, para. 147, 34.

[510] Zutphen Draft Statute 1998, *supra* note 358, article 45 [25], 109–10.

[511] Draft Statute, April 1998, *supra* note 44, article 11, 35–6.

[512] See above Part III, B., II.; also Mr. Kourula (Finland) in Official Records, Vol. II, *supra* note 392, para. 37, 183.

[513] Cf. the statements at *supra* note 392.

[514] Official Records, Vol. II, *supra* note 392. Further, no specific reference to the change in terminology from "complaint" to "referral" can be found in the Committee of the Whole summary records (Summary records of the 29th meeting, United Nations Diplomatic Conference of Plenipotentiaries on the Establishment of an International Criminal Court, 15 June–17 July 1998, 20.11.1998 (A/CONF.183/C.1/SR.29), Summary records of the 30th meeting, 20.11.1998 (A/CONF.183/C.1/SR.30), Summary records of the 31st meeting, 20.11.1998 (A/CONF.183/C.1/SR.31)), and the main commentaries on the ICC Statute did also not envisage an option of self-referrals (Schabas, *supra* note 27, 147); *id.*, *supra* note 13, 309–11).

[515] See above Part III, B., II. and III., 1.

[516] Policy paper, *supra* note 99, 6; Annex paper, *supra* note 27, 5; Kress, *supra* note 446, 945.

Presidency obviously allowed the practice of self-referrals and assigned three self-referred situations to the PTCs.[518] Moreover, PTC I held that the self-referral in the DRC is consistent with the ultimate purpose of the complementarity regime.[519]

2. Preconditions of a State referral

Article 14 (1) states that "a State Party may refer to the Prosecutor a situation in which one or more crimes within the jurisdiction of the Court appear to have been committed requesting the Prosecutor to investigate the situation for the purpose of determining whether one or more specific persons should be charged with the commission of such crimes." The legal consequences of a State referral are spelled out in the chapeau of article 13, namely "[...] the Court may exercise jurisdiction with respect to a crime referred to in article 5 [...]." As to the relationship between article 13 (a) and 14, article 14 is merely a repetition of article 13 (a) (article 14 (1) clause 1) or adds a self-evident phrase (article 14 (1) clause 2).[520]

As to the general preconditions of a State referral, *any* State Party may refer a situation. A restrictive proposal to limit the right to complain to interested States, i.e. the territorial or custodial State or national State of victim of the alleged perpetrator(s), was eventually not approved.[521] Therefore, a State need only be party to the ICC Statute to call on the right to refer a situation. Third States cannot make use of articles 13 (a) and 14, even if they lodge a declaration of acceptance of the Court's jurisdiction under article 12 (3).[522]

The object of the referral must be a situation.[523] "Requesting the Prosecutor to investigate" does not denote a legal obligation to start a full inves-

---

[517] OTP Report on activities 2003–2006, *supra* note 23, 7; Happold, *supra* note 500, 8; William Schabas, "Complementarity in practice: creative solutions or a trap for the Court?" in Mauro Politi/Federica Gioia (eds.), *The International Criminal Court and national jurisdictions* (Ashgate, Hampshire 2008) 25, 28 et seq.

[518] *Situation in DRC,* Decision assigning the situation in the DRC, *supra* note 214; *Situation in Uganda,* Decision assigning the situation in Uganda, *supra* note 250; *Situation in CAR,* Decision assigning the situation in the CAR, *supra* note 267.

[519] *Prosecutor v. Lubanga,* Decision on the Prosecutor's application for warrant of arrest, article 58, *supra* note 217, para. 35.

[520] Junck, *supra* note 204, mn 458.

[521] See above Part III, B., IV., 1; Antonio Marchesi, "Article 14" in Triffterer, *supra* note 37, article 14, mn 8 et seq.; Williams/Schabas, in Triffterer, *supra* note 353, article 13, mn 15; Kirsch/Robinson, in Cassese/Gaeta/Jones, *supra* note 371, 623.

[522] Olásolo, *supra* note 29, 142; Junck, *supra* note 204, mn 459. On article 12 (3) declarations see Part III, B., VI., 10.

tigation. In fact, if read in conjunction with the chapeau of article 13 ("may exercise jurisdiction"), the referral constitutes the *notitia criminis*. The Prosecutor shall then decide whether there is "reasonable basis to proceed" as a consequence of the notification by the State. Article 53 requires the Prosecutor to evaluate the information made available to him *vis-à-vis* the criteria of subparagraphs a, b, and c.[524] The article 53 determination lies in the hands of the OTP alone, but the referring State – or, in the alternative, the SC – has a right to be informed of any decision not to initiate an investigation (rule 105 (1)) or not to prosecute (rule 106 (1)), and can subsequently ask the Prosecutor to reconsider his decision (article 53 (3) (a)). If the decision is solely based on the "interests of justice" the PTC might even conduct a review on its own and must then confirm the decision of the Prosecutor (article 53 (3) (b)).

The purpose of the request to the Prosecutor under article 14 (1) is to determine whether persons should be charged with the commission of crimes under the ICC Statute. In conformity with the statutory system, the Prosecutor is free to investigate all persons who may be responsible.[525] Despite his wide discretion, significant limits have been placed on his prosecutorial power. As outlined above, the Prosecutor must inform the triggering parties – article 15 (6) also foresees a duty to inform under *proprio motu* proceedings[526] – of a decision not to proceed. Inaction of the Office is thus not allowed and the Prosecutor is under a duty to analyze the situation. Moreover, he *shall* initiate an investigation (article 53 (1)) and *shall* submit a request for authorization (article 15 (3)), if there is a reasonable basis to proceed.[527] In a nutshell, the referring parties cannot obligate the Prosecutor to investigate a specific case, but do, as parties, enjoy certain rights under article 13.

Regrettably, the formal regulation of article 14 (2) was not further clarified in the RPE.[528] Article 14 (2) is largely based on article 25 (3) ILC Draft Statute, and changed little during negotiations.[529] Under article 14 (2)

---

523 On the definition of a situation see Part III, B., III., 1.

524 Whether one of the crimes under article 5 has been committed, whether the case would be admissible, and whether an investigation would be in the "interests of justice;" see Kirsch/Robinson, in Cassese/Gaeta/Jones, *supra* note 371, 624. On the criteria see Part IV, B., III.

525 Marchesi, in Triffterer, *supra* note 521, article 14, mn 12.

526 Thereto Part III, B., VI., 8.

527 Part IV, B., II., 1.

528 In the same vein, Junck, *supra* note 204, mn 458.

529 See already Part III, B., IV., 1; also Marchesi, in Triffterer, *supra* note 521, article 14, mn 13–4; Kirsch/Robinson, in Cassese/Gaeta/Jones, *supra* note 371, 624.

States have the duty ("shall") to specify relevant circumstances and provide supporting documentation. Such information should assist the Prosecutor in his evaluation of a "reasonable basis" to proceed with a full investigation. However, two phrases allow for variation of the strict duty, in particular "as far as possible" and "as is available." The terms "relevant" circumstances and "supporting" documentation are similarly open to interpretation. As noted above, the information provided marks the starting point of pre-investigative steps by the OTP. It can be reasoned that the referral needs to be accompanied by some further information which, however, depends on the circumstances of the particular situation. During the negotiations an exact list was proposed,[530] albeit with reference to the information needed to file a complaint, and not to make a referral. Rule 45 gives a further technical clarification stating that a referral must be in writing. As a whole, however, the current procedural system does not specify what qualifies as sufficient additional information in accordance with article 14 (2). It is therefore submitted that article 14 (2) – aside from the fact that its significance is as yet unknown[531] – ultimately leaves it to the Prosecutor to decide on the adequate level of elaborateness. If referrals fail to comply with formal and material requirements they should not be rejected, but should rather be treated as article 15 (1) information.[532]

3. Self-referrals

Despite the fact that State referrals were originally not anticipated,[533] a practice of self-referrals evolved (DRC, Uganda, and CAR).[534] Even in Kenya, which was now initiated as an investigation *proprio motu,* the Prosecutor clearly favored a self-referral.[535] In fact, Kenya agreed that:

---

530 See already Part III, B., II. with fn. 357.

531 Marchesi, in Triffterer, *supra* note 521, article 14, mn 14.

532 Olásolo, *supra* note 29, 105.

533 Mahnoush Arsanjani/Michael Reismann, "Developments at the International Criminal Court: The law-in-action of the ICC" (2005) 99 AJIL 385, 386–7; Matthew Happold, "The ICC and the LRA" (2007) 87 MJIL 1, 7 with fn. 60. See also the drafting history at Part III, B., IV., 1.

534 Cherif Bassiouni, "The ICC – *Quo vadis*?" (2006) 4 JICJ 421, 424–5; Kleffner, *supra* note 370, 213; Burke-White/Kaplan, in Stahn/Sluiter, *supra* note 247, 85–6; Ronald Slye/Beth van Schaack, Beth, *International criminal law* (Wolters Kluwer/Aspen Publishers, Austin 2009) 56–7; Payam Akhavan, "Self-referrals before the International Criminal Court: Are States the villains or the victims of actrocities" (2010) 21 CLF 103, 106; Schabas, *supra* note 13, 307 et seq.

535 Agreed Minutes of the meeting between Prosecutor Moreno-Ocampo and the delegation of the Kenyan government, *supra* note 341, 2; also Prosecutor's statement at the ISS Symposium, *supra* note 263, 5–6; Akhavan, *supra* note 534, 107.

> "in the alternative, if there is no parliamentarian agreement, and in accordance with the Kenyan commitment to end of impunity of the most responsible of the most serious crimes, the Government of Kenya will refer the situation to the Prosecutor *in accordance with article 14* of the Rome Statute (emph. added)."[536]

The Prosecutor only switched to the last resort of the *proprio motu* tool after national proceedings failed and a self-referral appeared unrealistic. There is no public explanation as yet as to why Kenya strayed from the agreed minutes and did not self-refer their situation, but the Kenyan situation has not changed the *policy* of the OTP to prefer self-referrals over *proprio motu*.

Before or during the Rome negotiations, no one expected that governments would want to invite the ICC to investigate and prosecute crimes that occurred on their territory.[537] A so-called self-referral (or "auto-referral"[538]) takes place when a State Party refers a situation that has taken place in its territory or in which its nationals have played a substantial role.[539] However, the issue needs to be discussed more precisely, given that the drafting history did not discuss it and given the inherent danger that exists if the ICC becomes instrumentalized by the referring State's governments for political gain.[540] Two questions – legal and policy-related – are particularly relevant.

First addressing the legal issue, it has already been mentioned that the drafting history did not specifically envisage a self-referral by the affected State. Academics offer a broad variety of views on self-referrals, from "firmly grounded in law and commendable as a matter of legal policy"[541]

---

536 Agreed Minutes of the meeting between Prosecutor Moreno-Ocampo and the delegation of the Kenyan government, *supra* note 341, 2.

537 Mahnoush Arsanjani/Michael Reismann, "The International Criminal Court and the Congo: from theory to reality" in Leila Sadat/Michael Scharf (eds.), *The theory and practice of International Criminal Law, Essays in honor of M. Cherif Bassiouni* (Martinus Nijhoff Publishers: Leiden 2008) 325, 327–8; Schabas, in Mauro/Gioia, *supra* note 517, 32.

538 Jann Kleffner, "Auto-referrals and the complementarity nature of the ICC," in Stahn/Sluiter, *supra* note 5, 41, 41 et seq.

539 Olásolo, *supra* note 29, 169; El Zeidy, *supra* note 545, 213.

540 Paola Gaeta, "Is the practice of 'self-referrals' a sound start for the ICC?" (2004) 2 JICJ 949, 952; Schabas, *supra* note 27, 143–4; Schiff, *supra* note 128, 199. In each situation, the referring State asked the Prosecutor to investigate crimes allegedly committed by rebels fighting against the central authorities, cf. Antonio Cassese, "Is the ICC still having teething problems?" (2006) 4 JICJ 434, 436; William Schabas, "Complementarity in practice: some uncomplimentary thoughts" (2008) 19 CLF 5, 19; Carsten Stahn, "Complementarity: a tale of two notions" (2008) 19 CLF 87, 111; HRW Courting history report, *supra* note 126, 41.

541 Kress, *supra* note 446, 945.

to "certainly superfluous."[542] As a matter of fact, the change in terminology from "complaint" to "referral" did not provoke a single comment, it was even designated a "technical issue."[543] On the other hand, the matter was marginally touched upon in discussion on the complementarity regime. In the report of the *Ad Hoc* Committee of 1995 it was suggested "that the draft statute should provide for the possibility that a State might voluntarily decide to relinquish its jurisdiction in favor of the international criminal court in respect of crimes expressly provided for under its statute."[544] In 1997, the matter was addressed in a more precise manner when the drafters inserted a footnote stating: "The present text of article [x] is without prejudice to the question whether complementarity-related admissibility requirements of this article may be waived by the State or States concerned."[545] Yet, the question was not discussed in Rome, and when the RPE were finalized, the matter of self-referral was left to the Court's interpretation.[546] In sum, the drafting history does not substantially touch upon the issue of self-referrals. Those analyzing the *travaux préparatoires* are divided into two camps with opposing views, alternatively finding that the *travaux* favors or disfavors self-referrals. Since the *travaux* may be examined only supplementary and is, in any event, inconclusive, a definitive answer in either direction is not possible.

Articles 13 and 14 mention "referrals" and "refer." A complaint can only be lodged against another State. In contrast, the term "refer" leaves room for a creative interpretation, and certainly does not prohibit defining a situation as the State's own territory.[547] Given the Preamble's call for an end to impunity, it seems recommendable to allow any possible trigger of *notitia criminis* which the ICC Statute does not outlaw specifically. No provision in the ICC system contradicts the newly-arranged triggering via self-referrals. In fact, the ICC Statute offers space for creative ambiguity that was thought to provide flexibility for the actors. The law-in-action may even prove quite different from that envisaged by its creators.[548] Legality concerns can thus be rejected, in spite of the unclear drafting history. In conclusion, and only legally speaking, self-referrals are a valid triggering mechanism for the Court.[549]

---

542 Schabas, *supra* note 27, 149; *id.*, *supra* note 13, 309 ("invention of the Office of the Prosecutor").

543 Summary records of the 29th meeting, *supra* note 514, para. 6, 2.

544 Report of the *Ad Hoc* Committee 1995, *supra* note 379, para. 47, 9.

545 Quoted from Mohamed El Zeidy, *The principle of complementarity in international criminal law* (Martinus Nijhoff Publishers, Leiden, Boston 2008) 213.

546 El Zeidy, *supra* note 545, 213.

547 Kress, *supra* note 446, 945; also acknowledged by Schabas, *supra* note 540, 17; *id.*, *supra* note 13, 311.

548 Arsanjani/Reismann, *supra* note 533, 386.

Another more substantial objection concerns the policy of soliciting self-referrals. The Prosecutor put forward a policy of inviting and welcoming voluntary referrals.[550] The OTP has noted that the method of initiating investigations by voluntary referral has been beneficial, increasing the likelihood of important cooperation and on the ground support.[551] However, there are also two inherent dangers. First, the State's request may be motivated by a wish to expose internationally the crimes by the other side. Second, full cooperation may only be achieved where crimes have been allegedly committed by the other side and investigations steer clear of state agents.[552] If the OTP only conducts investigations against members of resistance groups at the exclusion of government forces, the legitimacy of the Court may be questioned.[553] Despite potential advantages – for instance, *prima facie* willingness of the State Party's authorities to cooperate – dangers to the perception of the independence and impartiality of the OTP cannot be overestimated.[554]

On the other hand, referrals are subject to pre-investigation as well as judicial review and can be rejected; they only "trigger" ICC jurisdiction.[555] But accusations of biased investigations[556] cannot be countered easily. Uganda provides a good case in point: while crimes committed by one

---

549 In the same vein, *Prosecutor v. Lubanga,* Decision on the Prosecutor's application for warrant of arrest, article 58, *supra* note 217, para. 35; Giorgio Gaja, "Issues of admissibility in case of self-referrals" in Mauro/Gioia, *supra* note 517, 49, 49–50; Akhavan, *supra* note 534, 107 et seq.

550 OTP Report on activities 2003–2006, *supra* note 23, 7; critical Jurdi, *supra* note 99, 94. See already *supra* notes 516 and 517.

551 OTP Report on activities 2003–2006, *supra* note 23, 7.

552 Gaeta, *supra* note 540, 951–2. The State could be using the Court as a political weapon, see further references in *supra* note 540; also Schabas, *supra* note 27, 144.

553 Arsanjani/Reismann, *supra* note 533, 394; Mr. Christopher Keith Hall – Amnesty International, Session 2: NGOs and other experts, Second public hearing of the OTP, 26.9.2006. On the crimes of government forces, see Apuuli (2004), *supra* note 246, 402 et seq.; *id.* (2006), *supra* note 246, 186.

554 Mr. Richard Dicker, HRW, *supra* note 473; Ms. Jeanne Sulzer, Coordination of the FIDH Legal Action Group, Session 4: NGOs and other experts, Second public hearing of the OTP, 18.10.2006; Lekha Sriram/Ross, *supra* note 210, 61; Jurdi, *supra* note 99, 94. On the implication of the ICC's involvement in Uganda, see Refugee Law Project's position paper on the announcement of formal investigations of the LRA by the Chief Prosecutor of the ICC and its implications on the search for peaceful solutions to the war in Northern Uganda, 28.7.2004, 6 et seq.; also HRW Courting history report, *supra* note 126, 41.

555 Akhavan, *supra* note 246, 411. See also the results at Part III, B., III., 4.

556 See, for instance, Apuuli (2006), *supra* note 246, 185, with further references; Hall, in Stahn/Sluiter, *supra* note 206, 223; for the DRC Richard Dicker, "Making justice meaningful for victims" in Bergsmo, *supra* note 99, 187, 189; see also the

party (the LRA) are already under investigation, no formal investigations against State agents have been opened as yet. Several critics urged the Prosecutor to investigate both sides of the conflict and presented leads for crimes allegedly committed by Ugandan government agents.[557] PTC II noted a statement by the Prosecutor "that OTP investigations and assessments of allegations made against the military forces of the Government of Uganda are ongoing."[558] The Chamber felt obligated to ask the Prosecutor for information on the pending DRC and Uganda situations based on a statement of the Prosecutor that one is nearing completion and another is well advanced; in the Chamber's words "the interpretation of article 53 [...] involves the OTP and ultimately the judges."[559] In the very same statement, it was also emphasized by the Prosecutor that the gravity of all crimes committed in Northern Uganda by all groups (LRA, UPDF and other forces) was being analyzed.[560] The crimes committed by the LRA thereby proved to be of dramatically higher gravity, and the investigation started with these violations.[561] However, the Judges did recall article 54 (1) (a) and the duty of the OTP to conduct impartial investigations. The Chamber also noted that rule 106 and article 53 (2) (b) impose a duty to inform Chambers in writing of any decision concluding that there is no sufficient basis for prosecution under article 53 (2) and to give the reasons for this decision. The Chamber also emphasized that such a decision "shall be effective only if confirmed by the Pre-Trial Chamber."[562] In light of this decision, the OTP provided the Chamber with the information that it had not made such a decision yet.[563] The OTP further pointed out that "nearing completion" is not the same as "has completed the investigation."[564]

Defence in *Prosecutor v. Bemba*, Decion on the admissibility, *supra* note 280, para. 75, 27.

557 Cf. the references at *supra* notes 442 and 443; also Dicker, in Bergsmo, *supra* note 556, 190. Further examples of implicit criticism are mentioned by Akhavan, *supra* note 246, 411.

558 *Prosecutor v. Kony et al.*, Decision to convene a status conference on the investigation in the situation in Uganda, *supra* note 248, para. 7.

559 *Prosecutor v. Kony et al.,* Decision to convene a status conference on the investigation in the situation in Uganda, *supra* note 248, para. 8; Statement by Luis Moreno-Ocampo: Informal meeting, *supra* note 497, 1, 9.

560 Statement by Luis Moreno-Ocampo: Informal meeting, *supra* note 497, 7.

561 Statement by Luis Moreno-Ocampo: Informal meeting, *supra* note 497, 7.

562 *Prosecutor v. Kony et al.,* Decision to convene a status conference on the investigation in the situation in Uganda, *supra* note 248, paras. 10, 12, 13.

563 *Prosecutor v. Kony et al.,* OTP submission providing information on status of the investigation in anticipation of the status conference to be held on 13 January 2006, 11.1.2006 (ICC-02/04-01/05-76) paras. 1, 8.

564 *Prosecutor v. Kony et al.,* OTP submission providing information on status of the investigation, *supra* note 563, paras. 3, 6.

The Ugandan situation also involves follow-up problems regarding waivers of complementarity (4.) and a (subsequent) withdrawal of a referral (5.), which will be discussed accordingly. As a provisional result, it is a matter of fact that no charges against government forces have yet been made. Even if we presume that the crimes of the LRA were dramatically weightier in gravity, the allegation of biased investigations hangs in the air due to the self-referral by the government.

Returning to the matter of cooperation, the referring party expresses a *prima facie* political will to cooperate. But articles 86 et seq. already oblige all States Parties to cooperate. In addition, as stated above, the government will certainly advance proceedings against its opponents, although it is unlikely to fully cooperate in an investigation against state agents.[565] The Ugandan President Museveni, for instance, initially expressed his good will to help investigating war crimes by the ICC, but has also stated: "And in any case, if such cases are brought to our attention, we will try them ourselves."[566]

Having said that, the Prosecutor can make use of the *proprio motu* power for the sake of clarity and to avoid criticism, supposedly at the expense of *prima facie* cooperation with local governments. After careful consideration, the Prosecutor has chosen to open the gateway for self-referrals as a policy decision.[567] The only way out is yet an application of the Prosecutor's power *proprio motu,* and by that I mean not a *proprio motu* initiation as we have seen in Kenya. While the request under article 15 (3) is certainly a historically remarkable point as it constituted the first *formal* investigation *proprio motu,* the Prosecutor negotiated for a self-referral before switching to *proprio motu.* At the starting phase of the Court, it makes sense that the OTP solicited for self-referrals; this policy allowed the Court to start working properly, where *proprio motu* investigations without any factual consequences (for instance, no arrests at all) would have been fatal to the ICC. Presumably, there would have been no first case due to lack of cooperation, although the *proprio motu* power served as a powerful incentive to gain the self-referrals.[568] The encouraging of self-referrals thus allowed the Court to operate in a cooperative setting.[569] At present, the ICC is working at full capacity and has proven to be a functioning institution.

---

565 Gaeta, *supra* note 540, 951–2; Schabas, *supra* note 27, 149; Kleffner, *supra* note 370, 216.

566 Remarks by ICC Prosecutor, *supra* note 248, 6; Jurdi, *supra* note 99, 81, calls this "selective" willingness.

567 It is ultimately left to the Chief Prosecutor to make such decision, and a future Prosecutor might refine or even change policy issues.

568 Rod Rastan, "The responsibility to enforce – connecting justice with unity" in Stahn/Sluiter, *supra* note 5, 163, 172.

569 Jurdi, *supra* note 99, 92.

More probably than not, there must be some situations out of the various communications that reach the established gravity threshold and should warrant investigations.

In a nutshell, the decision in favor of self-referrals has to be evaluated in the context of an emerging ICC; henceforth the Prosecutor should re-evaluate his policy and seriously consider making more use of *proprio motu* investigations, especially if it comes down to a decision of acting *proprio motu* or self referring a situation. Without re-evaluation, the Prosecutor might lose sight of his own prosecutorial priorities.[570]

4. Waivers of complementarity (including articles 18 and 19 proceedings)

A waiver of complementarity has been defined as a formal declaration by the State most directly concerned (normally the territorial State), acknowledging that it is not carrying out, or has not carried out, any investigation or prosecution concerning the crimes allegedly committed in the situation at hand.[571] In other words, the State deliberately waives any further admissibility deliberations under article 17, meeting the expectation that "[...] it may be appropriate for the State concerned to simplify the admissibility proceedings by expressly acknowledging that it is not investigating or prosecuting particular cases, in favor of ICC jurisdiction."[572] It could then be argued that self-referrals always constitute such a voluntary, *a priori* and *ab initio* relinquishment of the right to exercise jurisdiction by the referring State.[573] This would mean that every self-referral inherently contains a waiver of the admissibility requirements.

On the other hand, self-referrals and waivers of complementarity might have similarities, but are not identical. The former goes to the triggering of jurisdiction, while the latter is a matter of admissibility.[574] A State may wave admissibility no matter how the situation was triggered.[575] Based on this assumption, a waiver may occur without a self-referral and *vice versa*.[576] It remains to be seen whether the concept of waivers is accepted at all.

---

570 In the same vein, Schabas, *supra* note 27, 36. Contrary, Mr. Sivu Maqungo of South Africa, *supra* note 257, who prefers the Prosecutor inviting the States to participate rather than using his *proprio motu* power.

571 Olásolo, *supra* note 29, 169; Kress, *supra* note 446, 946.

572 Informal expert paper: The principle of complementarity in practice, ICC-OTP 2003, para. 62.

573 Kleffner, in Stahn/Sluiter, *supra* note 538, 42.

574 El Zeidy, *supra* note 545, 212.

575 Schabas, *supra* note 27, 148; *id.*, *supra* note 19, 311.

576 El Zeidy, *supra* note 545, 214.

The discussion of waivers of complementarity and self-referrals can be divided into three pertinent questions: first, whether the concept of waivers is legally permitted under the ICC Statute; second, whether a waiver and/or self-referral precludes the application of complementarity in general; and third, whether a specific State making use of a waiver and/or self-referral deliberately waives his rights to challenge admissibility under articles 18 and 19.

No provision within the Statute explicitly provides for a waiver, but it is also not prohibited. In fact, article 54 (c) and (d) allow for arrangements with States as long as they are not inconsistent with the Statute. In addition, the OTP could seek express and written statements from a State not to exercise jurisdiction and to leave the situation to the ICC.[577]

The waiver issue first arose in 1995.[578] At the time, some delegations found the idea of a waiver inconsistent with the principle of complementarity and feared that it would undermine the effectiveness of national justice systems.[579] This opposition notwithstanding, the matter found its way into a footnote of the Draft Statute 1998: "[T]he present text of article 15 is without prejudice to the question whether complementarity-related admissibility requirements of this article may be waived by the State or States concerned."[580] The issue was not dealt with further during the Rome Conference and many delegations preferred to defer the discussion to the RPE.[581] However, the RPE is silent on the matter, which suggests that the interpretation was left to the ICC judges.[582]

The drafting history does not clarify the matter. Waivers of complementarity were marginally addressed, but never resolved. The complementarity regime can be interpreted in a strict or liberal fashion. The former focuses on the positive obligations of States under preambular paragraphs 4 and 6, which would not permit the granting of a waiver, whereas the latter is based on articles 1, 17, and on preambular paragraph 10, which leave room for alternative ICC intervention.[583] The ICC Statute certainly favors national proceedings and sees itself as a court of last resort. Above all, impu-

577 Informal expert paper: complementarity, *supra* note 572, para. 66.

578 Cf. Part III, B., IV., 3. with fn. 544; El Zeidy, *supra* note 246, 100, 217.

579 Report of the *Ad Hoc* Committee 1995, *supra* note 379, para. 47; recently Jurdi, *supra* note 99, 76.

580 Draft Statute, April 1998, *supra* note 44, article 15, 40 with fn. 38.

581 John Holmes, "The principle of complementarity" in Lee, *supra* note 14, 41, 78; El Zeidy, *supra* note 246, 100.

582 El Zeidy, *supra* note 246, 100 with fn. 90; *id., supra* note 545, 213.

583 El Zeidy, *supra* note 246, 101 et seq.; *id., supra* note 545, 218 et seq.

nity must be fought by whatever means available. An interpretation *e contrario* of article 17 (1) (a)–(c) suggests that, in the case of inactivity from the outset, the situation or case is admissible by implication (inaction scenario).[584] Where there are no domestic investigations, the ICC is technically allowed to proceed even without a finding on unwillingness or inability (concept of uncontested admissibility).[585] Therefore, burden sharing – despite potential ability of the concerned State – is not forbidden by the complementarity regime. The OTP can proceed with investigations if the referring State remains inactive.

A different question is if any concept of a waiver is necessary at all. A self-referral by a State and its inactivity could be regarded as an implicit waiver. The line between wanton inaction and inability might, however, be less clear in practice. Explicit waivers would ease further admissibility proceedings, and could even contain explicit waiving of the State's rights under articles 18 (2) and 19 (2) (b). However, the legal barrier of article 19 (5) – the earliest opportunity requirement – was included to strike a balance between the protection of the state's rights and the need for a proper functioning of the Court.[586] An additional concept of "waivers" appears not necessary under the ICC Statute. With regard to the legality of waivers, it is sufficient to acknowledge that the ICC may proceed with investigations and prosecutions even if the State might be able to act itself. It is therefore put forward that explicit waivers are not required under the complementarity threshold if one follows the outlined approach of uncontested admissibility.[587] The decisive question is whether the State takes action regarding the situation or case. Having said so, this is only the strict legal side of the coin. One cannot fail to note that, on the other hand, there is the dilemma that the Court might be forced to take situations or cases simply by reason

---

[584] *Prosecutor v. Lubanga,* Decision on the Prosecutor's application for warrant of arrest, article 58, *supra* note 217, para. 29; El Zeidy, *supra* note 246, 103; Stahn, *supra* note 540, 105–6; Happold, *supra* note 500, 10. See also Part IV, B., III., 2., b), cc), (1).

[585] Informal expert paper: complementarity, *supra* note 572, para. 61; Stahn, *supra* note 540, 109–10. See further Part IV, B., III., 2., b), cc), (1).

[586] Burke-White/Kaplan, *supra* note 264, 275–6.

[587] It has been argued by the Trial Chamber that self-referrals may indicate inability or unwillingness in a concrete analysis of article 17, see, for example, *Prosecutor v. Katanga and Chui,* Motifs de la décision orale, *supra* note 459, para. 91. This understanding of article 17 is misconceived. It does not appropriately pay attention to the principle of inactivity; the question of inability or unwillingness does not arise if there were no domestic investigations or prosecutions, *Prosecutor v. Katanga and Chui,* Judgment on the appeal of Mr. Germain Katanga against the oral decision of Trial Chamber II of 12 June 2009 on the admissibility of the case, *supra* note 459, para. 97.

that a State remains wholly inactive or even abandons proceedings.[588] Trial Chamber II has even acknowledged that a sovereign State may waive its jurisdiction and may choose not to challenge admissibility.[589] This approach favors a concept of waivers under the ICC regime, especially implicit waivers of admissibility. However, if a State decides to refrain from its own proceedings because it is opportune,[590] the concept of complementarity is turned into ICC primacy at the election of States. This is just another argument to discourage self-referrals and trigger situations by way of *proprio motu*. At the same time, an express regulation of self-referrals and their relation to complementarity appears desirable.[591] In any event, the basic complementarity scheme does apply to self-referrals,[592] and due to the inactivity concept the OTP does not need to approve (explicit or implicit) waivers. Even if the concept of waivers is adopted, the Trial Chamber has clarified that parts of the admissibility testing, namely *ne bis in idem* and gravity, remain untouched and must be tested notwithstanding a waiver.[593]

Nonetheless, turning to the possible consequences of a self-referral, the rights of the State to challenge admissibility and jurisdiction might be affected. Challenges under articles 18 (2) and 19 (2) (b) have two dimensions: a *procedural right* to challenge ICC action and a *substantive dimension* that examines whether the challenge is legally well-grounded. Notwithstanding the fact that challenges under these articles seem contradictory to the nature of a self-referral, nothing within the Statute would prevent a State that has referred the situation on its own territory from making an admissibility or a jurisdictional challenge.[594] In addition, the rights of the accused under article 19 (2) (a) cannot be affected by State action. The accused's procedural right to challenge should not be waived by State action; an entirely different question is, of course, whether the person will in fact invoke admissibility.[595] In any event, the referring State may become able

---

588 Kleffner, *supra* note 370, 222; *id.*, in Stahn/Sluiter, *supra* note 538, 53.

589 *Prosecutor v. Katanga and Chui,* Motifs de la décision orale, *supra* note 459, para. 78.

590 As suggested by Trial Chamber II in *Prosecutor v. Katanga and Chui,* Motifs de la décision orale, *supra* note 459, para. 79.

591 Kleffner, *supra* note 370, 222–3.

592 Kleffner, in Stahn/Sluiter, *supra* note 538, 47–8.

593 *Prosecutor v. Katanga and Chui,* Motifs de la décision orale, *supra* note 459, paras. 81, 87.

594 Regarding article 19 (2), cf. Hall, in Triffterer, *supra* note 376, article 19, mn 14.

595 Kleffner, *supra* note 370, 222; Burke-White/Kaplan, in Stahn/Sluiter, *supra* note 247, 112–3; recent ICC practice yet limits the rights to challenge admissibility, cf. Gilbert Bitti/Mohamed El Zeidy, "The *Katanga* Trial Chamber Decision: selected issues" (2010) 23 LJIL 319, 328.

Article 18 – Article 19

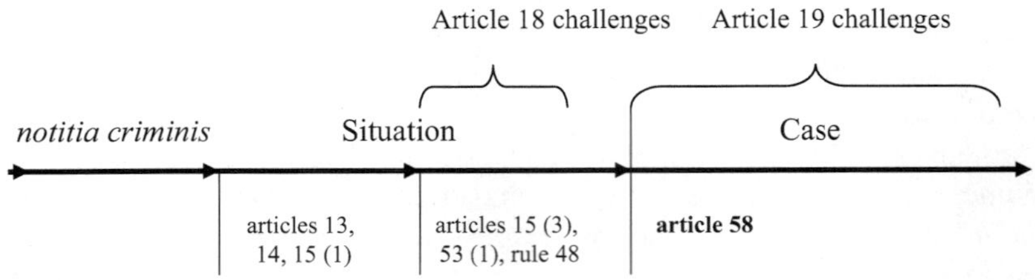

Source: Author.

Figure 5: Article 18 – Proceedings

and willing as a matter of fact,[596] and denying the procedural right to challenge admissibility from the outset seems too rigorous.

It is worth noting that there are considerable procedural hurdles for a challenging State that might lead to a dismissal. Once the Prosecutor opens an investigation, States must be notified under article 18 (1) and may – within one month – seek a deferral unless the PTC authorizes the investigation (article 18 (2)). The State may appeal a decision by the PTC (article 18 (4)). A State which has challenged a ruling of a PTC may only bring challenges under article 19 on grounds of additional significant facts or a significant change of circumstances (article 18 (7)), limiting the possibilities for frivolous challenges.[597] Article 18 applies at an early stage of investigations, in contrast to article 19 which applies at later stage and only to cases.[598] Because article 19 applies to a case, its provisions cannot apply prior to the issuance of a warrant of arrest or summons to appear.[599]

---

[596] *Prosecutor v. Lubanga,* Decision on the Prosecutor's application for warrant of arrest, article 58, *supra* note 217, para. 36. In the same vein, but critical on the cursory observations of the PTC, Hall, in Triffterer, *supra* note 376, article 19, mn 14 with fn. 46.

[597] Hall, in Triffterer, *supra* note 376, article 19, mn 6.

[598] Hall, in Triffterer, *supra* note 376, article 19, mn 1; Schabas, *supra* note 27, 278; Steinberger-Fraunhofer, *supra* note 315, 196; El Zeidy, *supra* note 246, 110; *id.,* "Some remarks on the question of the admissibility of a case during arrest warrant proceedings before the International Criminal Court" (2006) 19 LJIC 741, 742. Contrary Razesberger, *supra* note 371, 121.

[599] *Situation in DRC,* Decision following the consultation held on 11 October 2005, *supra* note 484, 4; Schabas, *supra* note 27, 280–1. On the differentiation situation and case already Part III, B., III.

Article 19 is thus narrower than article 18, because it only covers cases and not entire situations. However, it is much broader than article 18 in that it concerns all issues arising from admissibility and jurisdiction until the commencement of a trial.[600] In exceptional circumstances, a challenge may even be brought after the commencement of the trial.[601] Under article 18, in contrast, States have one month to put the Prosecutor on notice that they are investigating or have investigated the crime in question – in other words, that they consider the situation inadmissible in the sense of article 17. Article 18 applies only to investigations initiated by the Prosecutor or a State Party; article 19 applies to all three trigger mechanisms.[602] Arguably, a self-referring State could be denied article 18 rights.[603] On the other hand, the Statute is based on a notion of complementarity and favors State investigations. To date, not a single country has made an article 18 challenge. Even if the PTC allows for article 18 challenges by self-referring States, it will be difficult for the State to substantiate its request. Article 18 motions are only allowed one month after the OTP's notification. The period between the referral and the opening of an investigation is too short to demonstrate genuine investigations. In any event, the determination should be left to the PTC, which should grant any country the opportunity to reassert jurisdiction. The PTC must decide on the *merits* instead of denying the procedural right in the first place.[604]

Article 19 (5), on the other hand, requires the State to bring such a challenge "at the earliest opportunity." The PTC may deny action due to the procedural reasons of article 19 (5)[605] or because the challenge is unfounded. The challenging State must conduct genuine proceedings; it has to prove that circumstances have changed and that it is now able and willing to investigate and prosecute.[606] In light of a prohibition of shielding persons

---

600 Schabas, *supra* note 27, 279; Hall, in Triffterer, *supra* note 376, article 19, mn 6 et seq.

601 Article 19 (4); thereto Hall, in Triffterer, *supra* note 376, article 19, mn 22; more restrictively *Prosecutor v. Katanga and Chui,* Motifs de la décision orale, *supra* note 459, para. 49 (yet the Judges did grant the Motion, *ibid.,* paras. 56–8); a detailed analysis of Katanga case law (Trial Chamber and Appeals Chamber) is given by Dov Jakobs, "The Importance of being earnest: the timeliness of the challenge to admissibility in *Katanga*" (2010) 23 LJIL 331, 333 et seq.

602 Cf. article 18 (1); Schabas, *supra* note 27, 278.

603 El Zeidy, *supra* note 246, 107 et seq.

604 In the same vein, El Zeidy, *supra* note 246, 109.

605 On the earliest opportunity, see Razesberger, *supra* note 371, 118–9, who states that non-action of a State under article 18 (2) introduces the standard of article 18 (7) ("additional significant facts or significant change of circumstances") into article 19 (5); also Burke-White/Kaplan, in Stahn/Sluiter, *supra* note 247, 90.

606 Hall, in Triffterer, *supra* note 376, article 19, mn 14.

from criminal liability, and considering the general principle of estoppel, such an argument is difficult to make for a self-referring State.[607] As a basic rule, the burden of proof lies on the party making the allegations (*onus probandi actori incumbit*),[608] which renders the merits of the challenge open for dispute and hardly defendable for the State.

In conclusion, article 18 and 19 procedural rights are not limited by a self-referral. The Court and the Prosecutor should therefore retain in the article 18–19 framework.[609] The disadvantages of this approach might be increasing the length of proceedings, as well as increasing workload for the OTP and the PTCs. That said, one big advantage is consistency within the ICC Statute; these provisions apply even in the self-referral context. The alternative of endorsing a broad concept of waivers would bring about even more follow-up problems concerning several provisions (articles 53, 18, 19, 58, etc.).[610] Self-referrals are at least treated the same way as "normal" State referrals. Above all, it is important not to close the door to the possibility that future cases could be deferred to national jurisdictions by an article 18 or 19 challenge if circumstances in the State have actually changed. Consequently, self-referrals should never be viewed as *automatic* waivers of the right to challenge admissibility.[611] If the Court decides to approve a concept of waivers, which I find not particularly necessary in the light of the inactivity concept, the Judges must assess the referral document of the State.[612] The State's will must then be inferable from the document wording without doubt.

5. Withdrawal of a referral

The question whether a State referral can be legally withdrawn arose in the broader context of the Ugandan situation. In Uganda, there were many discussions about how to avoid OTP action in favor of local initiative,

---

607 Burke-White/Kaplan, in Stahn/Sluiter, *supra* note 247, 90–1, 109 et seq.

608 Hall, in Triffterer, *supra* note 376, article 19, mn 7; Kleffner, *supra* note 370, 203.

609 Kleffner, *supra* note 370, 219; also *Prosecutor v. Chui,* Mandat d'arrêt, *supra* note 235, 3: "[...] without prejudice to the filing of any challenge to the admissibility of the case under articles 19 (2) (a) and (b) of the Statute and without prejudice to any subsequent decision in this regard [...]."

610 On the consequences of self-referrals and waivers of complementarity *vis-a-vis* articles 18, 19 and 53, see El Zeidy, *supra* note 545, 274 et seq.

611 Stigen, *supra* note 205, 249–50, who lists five reasons why an automatic waiver would be inconsistent with the purpose of the ICC Statute.

612 Thereto *Prosecutor v. Katanga and Chui,* Motifs de la décision orale, *supra* note 459, paras. 92 et seq.

mainly because of on-going peace negotiations.[613] From a purely legal perspective, this discussion revolved around whether the State has a right to withdraw a referral, as well as the possible legal effects of such withdrawal.

The ICC Statute does not provide for a withdrawal. A concept of "withdrawal of complaints" was discussed in 1990 in the ILC, but the title has appeared nowhere in the drafting history since then, and, more importantly, the final package does not include a provision on withdrawals.[614] Article 127 (2) states that a State that withdraws from the Statute shall not be discharged from the obligations arising from the Statute while it was a party. Therefore, the withdrawal of a referral is not consistent with the ICC's procedural system, which provides for State challenges with regard to jurisdiction and admissibility. Moreover, from a contextual point of view, the SC has the explicit right to defer an investigation or prosecution for a period of 12 months under article 16. This option was introduced as an exclusive measure and was not undisputed.[615] If a deferral for States is introduced through the backdoor, the ICC's complex procedural system could be turned upside down.

The right to withdraw can be based on five points: the concept of State sovereignty, the principle of complementarity, the interests of justice, the legitimacy of the right of withdrawal, and the relevant practice followed by national legal systems.[616] First, state sovereignty is not a very strong argument in this case. States transfer sovereignty partly to the ICC by ratifying the Statute. They have to act in accordance with the ICC Statute, especially article 127 (2) which stipulates that a State cannot withdraw from its obligations while it is a party. Second and third, the principle of complementarity and the "interests of justice" are part of the procedural gateway of the ICC. They provide for methods to dismiss ICC action, but these methods do not include a State withdrawal. Dismissals under articles 53 (1), (2), 18, or 19 are the options under the current procedural system. Complementarity

613 See Part III, B., I., 2.; also "ICC May Drop LRA Charges," 15.11.2004, New Vision: Museveni himself even said: "The Konys can come out and engage in internal reconciliation mechanisms put in place by the Acholi community such as mata-oput or blood settlement. The state could then withdraw its case and we could inform the ICC that we have a solution to the Kony problem. That is what the ICC wants. No cover-up, no impunity."; recently Mohamed El Zeidy, "The legitimacy of withdrawing State Party referrals and *ad hoc* declarations under the Statute of the International Criminal Court" in Stahn/Sluiter, *supra* note 5, 55, 55–6.

614 El Zeidy, in Stahn/Sluiter, *supra* note 613, 57 et seq.

615 Part III, B., V., 3.

616 Adel Maged, "Withdrawal of referrals – a serious challenge to the function of the ICC" (2006) 6 ICLR 419, 422. Differentiated, but critical, see "Interview with Daniel Nsereko," 16.10.2007, Phone Interview, 10:30–11 AM NY time, CICC, 3: "[...] As of now I don't think a referral can be withdrawn."

and "interests of justice" do not provide for an explicit withdrawal of a State referral and thus do not favor such an approach. Fourth, with regard to the practice of national legal systems, the transfer of national proceedings to the ICC cannot be conducted easily.[617] Despite some considerable arguments drawn from findings on the national withdrawal procedures of criminal complaints,[618] it is submitted that the ICC's trigger mechanism differs from the common complaint procedure. The ICC regards situations as its procedural objects, and the exact content of a referral is defined by the ICC Statute only.[619] Drawing a comparison with the English and Welsh criminal justice system, "[i]t follows for the foregoing that the English criminal justice system, despite the fact that it does not recognize explicitly the right to withdrawal, it recognizes the right of discontinuance of criminal complaints and legalize[s] it when the public interest or the interests of justice so warrant."[620] In line with this finding, the concept of an explicit State deferral was intentionally not included. Instead, a complex procedural system that allows for several avenues of discontinuance was agreed upon.

In sum, a State withdrawal does not have any legal consequences for an investigation that has already been launched based on the referral.[621] Before the initiation of an investigation, the OTP could prefer to switch to *proprio motu* proceedings if the State articulates its unwillingness through a withdrawal,[622] notwithstanding the fact that the withdrawal has no legal effect.

The ICC Statute deals with deferral of proceedings in four places: articles 53 (1) and (2), 16, 18, and 19. The determination under article 53 is left to the OTP, and PTC supervision is foreseen only in the "interests of justice." In any event, States cannot use this as a gateway to challenge OTP action. After the initiation of a formal investigation, the OTP has to inform concerned States (article 18 (1), rule 52). These States can request a deferral based on admissibility within one month after the notification (article 18 (2), rules 53–55). Once an arrest warrant has been issued, article 19 (2) (b) and (c) enables the concerned States to file a challenge to admissibility or jurisdiction.[623] Furthermore, article 16 gives the SC the exclusive right to

---

617 See Part I, C., III.

618 Maged, *supra* note 616, 426 et seq.

619 Cf. Part III, B., II.

620 Maged, *supra* note 616, 432. On the English and Welsh criminal procedure see Annex 2, B., XVII.

621 In the same vein, Schabas, *supra* note 27, 151: "Once the jurisdiction has been 'triggered' it cannot be 'untriggered'."

622 Similarly, Maged, *supra* note 616, 437.

623 On articles 19 and 18 see already Part III, B., IV., 4., and the graph *ibid.* On the differences between article 19 (2) (b) and (c) see Hall, in Triffterer, *supra* note 376, article 19, mn 13–5.

defer investigations or prosecutions. Focusing on the Ugandan situation, the period for article 18 has already expired. Since the Prosecutor has re-emphasized that four arrest warrants remain in effect, an article 53 (2) suspension appears unlikely. The remaining options for Uganda are to challenge admissibility under article 19 (2) (c) and to persuade the Chamber thereof, or a deferral of the SC in relation to article 16, with the former being the preferable course of action. Should it choose this route, the Court would be able to scrutinize Uganda's justice system, its willingness to prosecute, and any available alternative justice mechanisms *vis-à-vis* article 17.[624]

In conclusion, a State cannot withdraw a referral with any legal effect. The ICC's procedural system shows linear coherency and provides for sophisticated options regarding referrals in articles 16, 18, 19, and 53. This renders the implementation of a non-statutory[625] concept of withdrawing State referrals superfluous. A different question is whether to give the ICC's actors an active tool to defer cases on their own motion if domestic actors become able to prosecute. In this regard, the Statute shows a *lacuna*, and an explicit deferral rule (a new rule 106*bis* – similar to rule 11*bis* ICTY RPE) should be drafted, enabling the Court to defer to national authorities if, for example, admissibility determinations change over time.[626]

6. Conclusion

Critical evaluation of the OTP's early practice shows that the policy of self-referrals is legally possible under the ICC Statute, but it is not a choice that will enjoy sustained success. This policy should be re-evaluated. The Prosecutor could otherwise be caught in a trap of having a suspect relationship with the referring State,[627] as well as follow-up problems in the application of the law. The current system of admissibility does not sit easily with self-referrals.[628] Therefore, a codification of waivers of complementar-

---

624 In this regard, note the PTC's new admissibility check in Uganda, cf. Part III, B., I., 2. and Part IV, B., III., 2., b), cc), (1). According to this finding, the PTC can analyze admissibility again, if circumstances change in a given situation.

625 Misleading, El Zeidy, in Stahn/Sluiter, *supra* note 613, 77–8. There is no withdrawal *lacuna* in the ICC Statute with regard to States that wish to withdraw, and jurisprudence on withdrawals of complaints by human rights bodies cannot be transferred to the ICC's system. The independence of the OTP must be ensured, and withdrawals of referrals would exactly go in the opposite direction. It would then be the State that ultimately decides who is prosecuted. Apparently, the potential of misuse is too high as to approve a concept of (State) withdrawals.

626 Further on this idea see Part V, C.

627 See, for example, Schabas, *supra* note 540, 33.

628 Kleffner, *supra* note 370, 222; *id.*, in Stahn/Sluiter, *supra* note 538, 53.

ity and/or withdrawals goes into the wrong direction and must be regarded with an attitude of regulatory modesty. ICC supporters are well advised to await the sure-to-come evolvement of the case law on self-referrals rather than lobbying for statutory arrangements.

State referrals played an important role in the early years of ICC practice, a development that was not expected by the drafters. In fact, three of the five pending situations were referred by States. However, the Prosecutor pushed actively for at least two of these three State referrals (DRC and Uganda),[629] and, moreover, would have preferred a self-referral in Kenya over the *proprio motu* device.[630] In the DRC and Uganda, the Prosecutor could very well have chosen a different path in relation to the *proprio motu* trigger mechanism. Making a policy decision, however, he did not do so. In future, the Prosecutor should rely more heavily on article 15. The *prima facie* cooperation and support on the ground does not outweigh the perception of the OTP's independence and impartiality. No tool other than article 15 rightly ensures the portrayal of the Prosecutor in such situations.

V. Security Council referral

Article 13 (b) provides for a second type of triggering procedure when the SC refers a situation to the ICC. Pursuant to this provision, the Council may create jurisdiction over crimes committed on the territory of a Non-State Party.[631] In so doing it must respect the parameters of the ICC Statute.[632]

---

629 See Part III, B., I., 1. and 2.

630 Agreed Minutes of the meeting between Prosecutor Moreno-Ocampo and the delegation of the Kenyan government, *supra* note 341, 2.

631 Williams/Schabas, in Triffterer, *supra* note 353, article 13, mn 16; Pietro Gargiulo, "The controversial relationship between the International Criminal Court and the Security Council" in Lattanzi/Schabas, *supra* note 400, 81; Kenneth Gallant, "The International Criminal Court in the system of States and International Organizations" (2003) 16 LJIL 553, 580 et seq.; Gabriël Oosthuizen, "Some preliminary remarks on the relationship between the envisaged International Criminal Court and the UN Security Council" (1999) XLVI NILR 313, 317; Cherif Bassiouni, "Note explicative sur le Statut de la Cour Pénale Internationale (CPI)" (2000) 70 RIDP 1, 18; Steinberger-Fraunhofer, *supra* note 315, 132; Franklin Berman, "The relationship between the International Criminal Court and the Security Council," in Hebel/Lammers/Schukking, *supra* note 371, 176; Pascal Arnold, *Der UNO-Sicherheitsrat und die strafrechtliche Verfolgung von Individuen* (Helbing und Lichtenhahn, Basel, Genf, München 1999); Fixon, in Kirsch, *supra* note 455, 217; Vera Gowlland-Debbas, "The relationship between political and judicial organs of international organisations: the role of the Security Council in the new International Criminal Court," in Laurence Boisson de Chazournes/Cesare Romano/Ruth Mackenzie (eds.), *Inter-*

In Darfur the SC referred a situation to the ICC for the first time, stating in § 1 of SC-Res. 1593 (2005) that the SC "*[d]ecides* to refer the situation in Darfur since 1 July 2002 to the Prosecutor of the International Criminal Court."[633] Article 17 of the Agreement between the UN and the ICC regulates details concerning the cooperation between the ICC and the SC. This Agreement gained practical importance in view of § 8 of SC-Res. 1593 (2005) which requested the Prosecutor to report to the SC every six months. The Prosecutor complied accordingly while indicating that he is under no legal obligation to do so.[634]

1. Preconditions of a referral under article 13 (b)

According to article 13 (b) the Court may exercise its jurisdiction with respect to a crime referred in article 5 if

> "a situation in which one or more of such crimes appears to have been committed is referred to the Prosecutor by the Security Council acting under Chapter VII of the Charter of the United Nations."[635]

The parameters of article 13 (b) can be subdivided into (1) a referral; (2) of a situation; (3) by the SC acting under Chapter VII of the UN Charter. The definitions of a referral and a situation have been clarified above,[636] thus remains the criterion of "the SC action under Chapter VII of the UN Charter." To act under Chapter VII the SC must determine that the situation

---

national organisations and international dispute settlement: trends and prospects (Transnational Publishers, Ardsley, New York 2002) 195, 200–1. See already fn. 399.

632 See above Part III, B., III., 1. with fn. 400; see also Schabas, *supra* note 13, 301.

633 For SC-Res. 1593 (2005) see Annex 4. On the resolution *as such* also Williams/Schabas, in Triffterer, *supra* note 353, article 13, mn 16; Heilmann, *supra* note 74, 245 et seq.; Luigi Condorelli/Annalisa Ciampi, "Comments of the Security Council referral of the situation in Darfur to the ICC" (2005) 3 JICJ 590, 590 et seq.; Nigel White/Robert Cryer, "The ICC and the Security Council: an uncomfortable relationship" in Doria/Gasser/Bassiouni, *supra* note 127, 455, 473; Kurth, *supra* note 399, 72 et seq.; Lutz Oette, "Peace and justice, or neither?" (2010) 8 JICJ 345, 347. On the problematic financing of SC referrals see Michael Reismann, "On paying the piper: financial responsibility for Security Council referrals to the International Criminal Court" (2005) 99 AJIL 615, 615 et seq.

634 Williams/Schabas, in Triffterer, *supra* note 353, article 13, mn 16; Heilmann, *supra* note 74, 250–1. On the reports themselves see Part III, B., I., 4.

635 The provision can be traced back to article 23 ILC Draft Statute 1994, *supra* note 353. On the drafting history see already Part III, B., II.; further Williams/Schabas, in Triffterer, *supra* note 353, article 13, mn 2 et seq.; Gargiulo, in Lattanzi/Schabas, *supra* note 631, 70 et seq.; Hoffmeister/Knoke, *supra* note 169, 789.

636 Cf. Part III, B., II. and III.

in question poses a threat to peace, is a breach of the peace, or is an act of aggression.[637] Secondly, the SC must choose a particular measure to maintain or restore international peace and security.[638] An explicit reference to Chapter VII is not absolutely necessary, but it has to be clear that a Chapter VII-determination is intended.[639] The decision of the SC has to be transmitted to the Prosecutor in writing.[640]

"Threat to peace," "breach of the peace," or "act of aggression" are all undefined in the UN Charter. These notions provide the SC with a large degree of discretion when reaching a determination on these matters.[641] Similarly, the SC enjoys wide discretion in the choice of measures taken under Chapter VII.[642] It has been argued by some authors that – besides a formal resolution – a less formal recommendation could suffice under article 13 (b).[643] In analogy to founding the *ad hoc* tribunals a referral under article 13 (b) should be regarded as a non-military measure under article 41 of the UN Charter.[644]

It has to be emphasized that the SC's discretion is not unfettered. It has to act within the boundaries of the UN Charter, *ius cogens*, and in accordance with the principle of proportionality.[645] Decisions of the SC are

---

637 See Jochen Frowein/Nico Krisch, "Article 39" in Bruno Simma (ed.), *The Charter of the United Nations: a commentary,* Vol. 1 (OUP, Oxford 2002) article 39, mn 3 et seq; Arnold, *supra* note 631, 193 et seq., 211 et seq.; Contag, *supra* note 426, 112–3.

638 Frowein/Krisch, in Simma, *supra* note 637, article 39, mn 7.

639 Frowein/Krisch, in Simma, *supra* note 637, article 39, mn 27; Stagel, *supra* note 425, 88, 91; Heilmann, *supra* note 74, 91; undecided Junck, *supra* note 204, mn 547.

640 Article 17 (1) Agreement between the UN and the ICC; rule 45.

641 Frowein/Krisch, in Simma, *supra* note 637, article 39, mn 4; Heilmann, *supra* note 74, 91.

642 Frowein/Krisch, in Simma, *supra* note 637, article 39, mn 4.

643 Ruth Philips, "Jurisdiction and admissibility" (1999) 10 CLF 61, 72; Junck, *supra* note 204, mn 552.

644 Heilmann, *supra* note 74, 97, 153. In a similar vein, Roberto Lavalle, "A vicious storm in a teacup: the action by the United Nations Security Council to narrow the jurisdiction of the International Criminal Court" (2003) 14 CLF 195, 201, 209.

645 Frowein/Krisch, in Simma, *supra* note 637, introduction to chapter VII, mn 25 et seq.; Ioana Peteculescu, "The review of the United Nations Security Council decisions by the International Court of Justice" (2005) LII NILR 167, 170 et seq.; Arnold, *supra* note 631, 200 et seq.; 273–4, 284–5; Heilmann, *supra* note 74, 109; Mehrdad Payandeh, "Rechtskontrolle des UN-Sicherheitsrates durch staatliche und überstaatliche Gerichte" (2006) 66 ZaöRV41, 44 et seq.; White/Cryer, in Doria/ Gasser/Bassiouni, *supra* note 633, 458; Schabas, *supra* note 27, 159. Admittedly, the boundaries *ius cogens* and proportionality are disputable, cf. thereto Arnd Dü-

nevertheless *prima facie* binding for UN member states (article 25 of the UN Charter),[646] and, in the event of conflict, obligations under the Charter shall prevail over any other obligations for member states (article 103 of the UN Charter).[647] Priority of SC decisions *vis-à-vis* the ICC Statute can, however, not be reasoned with regard to the ICC itself as an independent international organization,[648] but for its member states. Article 103 of the UN Charter only applies to states, which is further clarified by article 48 (2) of the UN Charter. Article 48 (2) of the UN Charter makes clear that only member states, not intergovernmental organizations, are bound by the Charter.[649] The ICC enjoys its own, independent legal personality (article 4 ICC Statute). Moreover, the inherent jurisdiction any judicial tribunal possesses to determine its own jurisdiction (*Kompetenz-Kompetenz*; *compétence de la compétence*) emerges in articles 19 and 119 of the ICC Statute,[650]

---

ker, *Die Strafverfolgung von Angehörigen einer Friedenstruppe der Vereinten Nationen* (Kovač, Hamburg 2008) 230 et seq.

646 Certain Expenses of the United Nations, Advisory Opinion, 20.7.1962, 168; Legal Consequences for States of the Continued Presence of South Africa in Namibia (South West Africa) notwithstanding Security Council Resolution 276 (1970), Advisory Opinion, 21.6.1971, para. 113; Questions of Interpretation and Application of the 1971 Montreal Convention Arising from the Aerial Incident at Lockerbie (Request for Indication of Provisional Measures), Libyan Arab Jamahiriya v. United States of America, Order, 14.4.1992, para. 42.

647 Thereto White/Cryer, in Doria/Gasser/Bassiouni, *supra* note 633, 459–60.

648 Oosthuizen, *supra* note 631, 325; Gallant, *supra* note 631, 569, 573; Heilmann, *supra* note 74, 126; Hoffmeister/Knoke, *supra* note 169, 805; Matthias Neuer, "The Darfur referral of the Security Council and the scope of jurisdiction of the International Criminal Court" (2005) 8 YIHL 320, 338. Contrary, Brian MacPherson, "Authority of the Security Council to exempt peacekeepers from International Criminal Court proceedings" (July 2002) ASIL Insights; Meißner, *supra* note 371, 102–3; Ohlin, in Stahn/Sluiter, *supra* note 428, 189–90.

649 Brun Otto Bryde/August Reinisch, "Article 48" in Simma, *supra* note 637, article 48, mn 10; Dan Sarooshi, "The peace and justice paradox: The International Criminal Court and the Security Council" in Dominic McGoldrick/Peter Rowe/Eric Donnelly (eds.), *The Permanent International Criminal Court* (Hart Publishing, Oxford 2004) 95, 107–8; also Sebastian Heselhaus, "Resolution 1422 (2002) des Sicherheitsrates zur Begrenzung der Tätigkeit des Internationalen Strafgerichtshofs" (2002) 62 ZaöRV 907, 910.

650 Condorelli/Villalpando, in Cassese/Gaeta/Jones, *supra* note 400, 640–1; Anne Kindt, *Menschenrechte und Souveränität,* Beiträge zum Internationalen und Europäischen Strafrecht Bd. 3 (Duncker & Humblot, Berlin 2009) 169 et seq.; Heilmann, *supra* note 74, 146; Gallant, *supra* note 631, 573; Frank Jarasch, "Errichtung, Organisation und Finanzierung des Internationalen Strafgerichtshofs und die Schlußbestimmungen des Statuts" (1999) 12 HuV-I 10, 18; Kai Ambos, "The legal framework of transitional justice. A systematic study with a special focus on the role of the ICC" in Kai Ambos/Judith Large/Marieke Wierda (eds.), *Building a future on peace and justice. Studies on Transitional Justice, Conflict Resolution and Development* (Springer, Berlin et al. 2009) 19, 82, para. 50; Gowlland-Debbas, in de Cha-

resulting in a right to review SC decisions if the ICC is directly affected.[651] Such an incident control mechanism is limited; it cannot involve political motives of the SC. In other words, the power of the ICC only embraces control of the *legality* of SC actions – the Court cannot deal with questions of appropriateness and effectiveness of SC resolutions.[652] Nevertheless, the SC cannot act *legibus solutus* (unbound by law).[653] Under article 53 the Prosecutor could, in any event, dismiss any given situation, even those referred by the SC.[654]

Several authors have argued that operative § 6 of SC-Res. 1593 (2005) concerning Darfur and § 7 of SC-Res. 1497 (2003) concerning Liberia[655] are *ultra vires* and incompatible with the ICC Statute.[656] Resolutions 1497

---

zournes/Romano/Mackenzie, *supra* note 631, 201; Contag, *supra* note 426, 127; *Prosecutor v. Bemba,* Decision pursuant to article 61 (7) (a) and (b), *supra* note 279, para. 23.

651 Ambos, in Ambos/Large/Wierda, *supra* note 650, 82, para. 50; Mohamed El Zeidy, "The principle of complementarity: a new machinery to implement international criminal law" (2002) 23 MichJIL 869, 960 with fn. 368, 966; Sarooshi, in McGoldrick/Rowe/Donnelly, *supra* note 649, 114–5; Heilmann, *supra* note 74, 147; Steinberger-Fraunhofer, *supra* note 315, 248–9; Oosthuizen, *supra* note 631, 319 et seq.; Salvatore Zappalà, "The reaction of the US to the entry into force of the ICC Statute: comments on UN SC Resolution 1422 (2002) and article 98 agreements" (2003) 1 JICJ 114, 119; Stagel, *supra* note 425, 113; Amnesty International, "International Criminal Court: The unlawful attempt by the Security Council to give US citizens permanent impunity from international justice" (hereinafter Amnesty International, Deferral Report) 1 May 2003, 39. For the ICTY, *Prosecutor v. Tadić,* Decision on the defence motion for interlocutory appeal on jurisdiction, 2.10.1995 (IT-94-1-AR72) mn 18.

652 Condorelli/Villalpando, in Cassese/Gaeta/Jones, *supra* note 400, 641–2; Heilmann, *supra* note 74, 148; Meißner, *supra* note 371, 261; Gallant, *supra* note 631, 572; Olásolo, *supra* note 29, 179; Oosthuizen, *supra* note 631, 318 et seq., 322 ("substantive review not possible"); *Prosecutor v. Kanyabashi,* Decision on the Defence Motion on Jurisdiction, 18.6.1997 (ICTR-96-15-T) para. 20. Regarding judicial control by the ICJ, see Michael Fraas, *Sicherheitsrat der Vereinten Nationen und Internationaler Gerichtshof* (Peter Lang, Frankfurt a.M. 1998) 159 et seq. On the disputed question whether the ICC can review the legality of SC action under Chapter VII see further Part III, B., V., 3., b), ee).

653 Neha Jain, "A separate law for peacekeepers: The clash between the Security Council and the International Criminal Court" (2005) 16 EJIL 239, 243.

654 El Zeidy, *supra* note 651, 960.

655 SC-Res. 1497 (2003), 1.8.2003.

656 Williams/Schabas, in Triffterer, *supra* note 353, article 13, mn 16; Schabas, *supra* note 27, 156 et seq.; *id., supra* note 13, 300; Heilmann, *supra* note 74, 239 et seq. (SC-Res. 1497), 248 et seq. (SC-Res.1593); Condorelli/Ciampi, *supra* note 633, 596–7; Neuer, *supra* note 648, 338–9; Salvatore Zappalà, "Are some peacekeepers better than others? UN Security Council Resolution 1497 (2003) and the ICC" (2003) 1 JICJ 671, 674 et seq.

and 1593 exclude jurisdiction over "nationals, current or former officials or personnel from a contributing State [...] which is not a party to the Rome Statute" and presume exclusive jurisdiction of that contributing State. Barring the ICC and all States other than the contributing State permanently from jurisdiction is plainly contrary to the ICC Statute.[657] What remains to be seen is whether the ICC makes use of its *Komptenz-Kompetenz* and declares a SC resolution or a paragraph thereof inconsistent with the ICC Statute.[658]

2. Application of the principle of complementarity to SC referrals

Whether the SC must meet admissibility criteria and respect the principle of complementarity was left (intentionally) unresolved at the Rome Conference.[659] With reference to the *ad hoc* tribunals some authors hold that the principle of complementarity does not apply or only applies subsidiarily to the determinations made by the SC.[660] From a contextual point of view, it is argued that article 18 (1), a principal feature of complementarity, only refers to article 13 (a) and (c), leaving out SC referrals.[661] Furthermore, article 19 makes no direct reference to SC referrals.[662]

---

[657] Schabas, *supra* note 27, 156–7; Condorelli/Ciampi, *supra* note 633, 596–7. See further Part III, B., V., 3., c), bb) and cc).

[658] In the same vein, Heilmann, *supra* note 74, 251; Kurth, *supra* note 399, 199; Noëlle Quénivet, "Who changed the road rules? The ICC and the Security Council hammering in conflict road signs" (2003) 78 Friedenswarte 29, 46.

[659] Williams/Schabas, in Triffterer, *supra* note 353, article 13, mn 16; Philips, *supra* note 643, 73 with fn. 40. The question was marginally raised but not resolved in the Report of the *Ad Hoc* Committee 1995, *supra* note 379, para. 120, 27; Report of the Preparatory Committee 1996, Vol. 1, *supra* note 203, para. 132, 31.

[660] Andreas Zimmermann, "Die Schaffung eines ständigen Internationalen Strafgerichtshofs" (1998) 58 ZaöRV 47, 94; similarly, Morten Bergsmo, "Occasional remarks on certain state concerns about the jurisdictional reach of the ICC, and their possible implications for the relationship between the Court and the Security Council" (2000) 69 NJIL 87, 110; Hans-Peter Kaul/Claus Kreß, "Jurisdiction and cooperation in the Statute of the International Criminal Court: principles and compromises" (1999) 2 YIHL 143, 172; George Fletcher/Jens David Ohlin, "The ICC – two courts in one?" (2006) 4 JICJ 428, 431 ("[...] 'security cases' are placed on a separate track, with greater weight given to the legal determinations made by the Council under its law-making authority.").

[661] Fletcher/Ohlin, *supra* note 660, 431; Damir Arnaut, "When in Rome...? The International Criminal Court and avenues for U.S." (2003) 43 VJIL 525, 541 with fn. 85. The idea is also raised (but not followed) by Williams/Schabas, in Triffterer, *supra* note 353, article 13, mn 16; Gowlland-Debbas, in de Chazournes/Romano/Mackenzie, *supra* note 631, 203.

[662] Fletcher/Ohlin, *supra* note 660, 431.

However, further contextual and teleological interpretation of the relevant norms of the ICC Statute leads to the conclusion that Articles 19 and 53 clearly apply to SC referrals.[663] In addition, no exception to the principle of complementarity for SC referrals was envisaged in the drafting history.[664] The importance of complementarity as a central animating principle is emphasized in preambular paragraph 10, article 1, and article 17.[665] Furthermore, article 53 (1) (b) refers to article 17 and all trigger mechanisms have to pass this threshold, suggesting that complementarity applies to SC referrals.[666] Rule 105 (1) corroborates this finding: when the Prosecutor decides not to initiate an investigation he "shall promptly inform in writing the State or States that referred the situation under article 14, or the Security Council in respect of a situation covered by article 13, paragraph (b)." Although there is not one cross-reference to article 53 in articles 17 and 19, article 19 by itself suggests that it embraces SC referrals.[667] Article 19 (3) explains that "in proceedings with respect to jurisdiction or admissibility, *those who have referred the situation under article 13,* as well as victims, may also submit observations to the Court (emph. added by the author)." Therefore, at least implicitly, article 19 favors the application of complementarity for SC referrals.

Articles 17 and 19 do not indicate an exception for the SC as they are silent on the matter. Where appropriate, the ICC Statute "contemplates and addresses the interaction of ICC procedures and Security Council actions,

---

663 Pichon, *supra* note 282, 189; with regard to article 53, cf. Contag, *supra* note 426, 117, 122.

664 Condorelli/Villalpando, in Cassese/Gaeta/Jones, *supra* note 400, 637 with fn. 37.

665 Condorelli/Villalpando, in Cassese/Gaeta/Jones, *supra* note 400, 637; Wouters/Verhoeven, in Ankumah/Kwakwa, *supra* note 210, 147–8; Stagel, *supra* note 425, 95–6; Philips, *supra* note 643, 63; Lattanzi, in Lattanzi/Schabas, *supra* note 400, 63.

666 Pichon, *supra* note 282, 189; Kleffner, *supra* note 370, 164 et seq.; Wouters/Verhoeven, in Ankumah/Kwakwa, *supra* note 210, 148; Gargiulo, in Lattanzi/Schabas, *supra* note 631, 84; Philips, *supra* note 643, 73; Stagel, *supra* note 425, 96; Wei, *supra* note 156, 58; Junck, *supra* note 204, mn 617; van Heeck, *supra* note 26, 179–80; John Holmes, "Complementarity: national courts *versus* the ICC" in Cassese/Gaeta/Jones, *supra* note 133, 667, 683; Turone, in Cassese/Gaeta/Jones, *supra* note 26, 1164; Gowlland-Debbas, in de Chazournes/Romano/Mackenzie, *supra* note 631, 203.

667 Gargiulo, in Lattanzi/Schabas, *supra* note 631, 84; Heilmann, *supra* note 74, 158; Junck, *supra* note 204, mn 616; Wouters/Verhoeven/Demeyere, *supra* note 156, 305; Stagel, *supra* note 425, 97 et seq. (who discusses whether article 18 (7) stands against such a finding, but neglects it in the end). Taking into consideration the significant differences between article 18 and 19 proceedings, including the time gap between the two challenges (cf. above Part III, B., IV., 4.), article 18 (7) is merely a safeguard to avoid misuse of the principle of complementarity by states.

including the extent to which procedures are affected by a Security Council action (Articles 13, 16, 18)."[668] Articles 12 (2) and 18 (1) explicitly refer only to articles 13 (a) and (c), which suggests that 13 (b) was intentionally left out. Regarding articles 17 and 19, a clear *e contrario* inference implies that complementarity generally applies to SC referrals.[669] The practice of the OTP confirms this result. In reports and statements to the SC on the situation in Darfur the Prosecutor made clear that he believes a determination of admissibility is required.[670] Chief Prosecutor Luis Moreno-Ocampo pointed out:

> "In light of the complementarity regime and article 53 (1) (b) of the Statute, I am required to consider whether there could be cases that would be admissible within the situation in Darfur."[671]

The decision to go forward is essentially a result of the absence of criminal proceedings related to the cases under scrutiny and is not an assessment of the Sudanese criminal justice system as such.[672] To date, no SC member has objected to this OTP practice.[673] PTC I has not challenged the application of the issue of admissibility to the case *Prosecutor v. Harun and Kushayb,*[674] which supports the prevailing view[675] that the

---

[668] Informal expert paper: complementarity, *supra* note 572, para. 68.

[669] Informal expert paper: complementarity, *supra* note 572, para. 68; Wei, *supra* note 156, 58; Stigen, *supra* note 205, 238–40.

[670] First Report pursuant to UNSC 1593 (2005), *supra* note 285, 3; Second Report pursuant to UNSC 1593 (2005), *supra* note 287, 5; Third Report pursuant to UNSC 1593, *supra* note 288, 4–5; Fourth Report pursuant to UNSC 1593, *supra* note 289, 5–7; Fifth Report pursuant to UNSC 1593, *supra* note 291, 7–9; Sixth Report pursuant to UNSC 1593, *supra* note 299, paras. 10 et seq.; Seventh Report pursuant to UNSC 1593, *supra* note 299, paras. 20 et seq.; Prosecutor's statement on the Prosecutor's application for a warrant of arrest under article 58 against Omar Hassan Ahmad Al Bashir, *supra* note 302, 2; Summary of the case: Prosecutor's application for warrant of arrest under article 58 against Omar Hassan Ahmad Al Bashir, *supra* note 302, 2–3; Moreno-Ocampo, in Stahn/Sluiter, *supra* note 99, 14; recently, Phani Dascalopoulou-Livada, "The principle of complementarity and security council referrals" in Politi/Gioia, *supra* note 517, 57, 61; Schabas, *supra* note 13, 301.

[671] Statement pursuant to UNSCR 1593 (2005), *supra* note 444, 2.

[672] Statement pursuant to UNSCR 1593 (2005), *supra* note 444, 3; Address by the Prosecutor to the United Nations Security Council, 13.12.2005, 3.

[673] Until March 2008, see Williams/Schabas, in Triffterer, *supra* note 353, article 13, mn 16.

[674] *Prosecutor v. Harun and Kushayb,* Decision on the Prosecution application under article 58 (7) of the Statute, *supra* note 292, paras. 19 et seq.

[675] From the large amount of literature coming to the same conclusion see – in addition to the already mentioned authors – Giuseppe Palmisano, "The ICC and third States," in Lattanzi/Schabas, *supra* note 400, 417 with fn. 58; Paolo Benvenuti, "Complementarity of the International Criminal Court to national jurisdic-

principle of complementarity applies to SC referrals. It is concluded that – regardless of the trigger mechanism – admissibility has to be assessed by the Prosecutor.[676]

3. Deferral according to article 16

Article 16 allows the SC to defer investigations and prosecutions in the interests of peace and security. This provision applies to all three trigger mechanisms, in other words, the SC can defer *any* situation that has been "triggered" before the ICC. The SC may request the ICC to defer an investigation or prosecution in a resolution adopted under Chapter VII UN Charter for a period of 12 months, and it can renew the request under the same conditions. As in the case of article 13 (b), article 16 demonstrates the potentially oppositional relationship between the political organ SC and the judicial entity ICC.[677] That said, article 16 does have the advantage of removing the difficult question of peace and justice to another actor; recognizing that peace is to some extent a political decision beyond the scope of law.[678] At the time the provision was drafted it was thought unlikely that the SC would make frequent use of it.[679] Before addressing the requirements and pitfalls of the deferral norm, a short survey into its drafting history is necessary.

---

tions," in *ibid.*, 41; Hoffmeister/Knoke, *supra* note 169, 798; Meißner, *supra* note 371, 106; Antonio Cassese, "The Statute of the International Criminal Court: some preliminary reflections" (1999) 10 EJIL 144, 159; Claus Kress, "Der Internationale Strafgerichtshof und der Sicherheitsrat der Vereinten Nationen" in Eberhard Kempf/Gabriele Jansen/Egon Müller (eds.), *Festschrift für Christian Richter II* (Nomos, Baden-Baden 2006) 319, 328; Mauro Politi, "Le Statut de Rome de la Cour pénale internationale. Le point de vue d'un négociateur" (1999) 103 RGDIP 817, 839; White/Cryer, in Doria/Gasser/Bassiouni, *supra* note 633, 463; Contag, *supra* note 426, 120–1.

676 Kleffner, *supra* note 370, 165–6.

677 Report of the *Ad Hoc* Committee 1995, *supra* note 379, para. 125, 28; Sandra Bartelt, "Die Zulässigkeit von Wahrheitskommissionen im Lichte des neuen Internationalen Strafgerichtshofs" (2005) 43 Archiv des Völkerrechts 187, 213–4.

678 Thomas Unger/Marieke Wierda, "Pursuing justice in ongoing conflict: a discussion of current practice" in Ambos/Large/Wierda, *supra* note 650, 263, 281.

679 Claudia Fritsche, "Security Council Resolution 1422: peacekeeping and the International Criminal Court" in Jochen Frowein et al. (eds.) *Verhandeln für den Frieden – Negotiating for peace, Liber Amicorum Tono Eitel* (Springer, Berlin 2003) 107, 112; Helmut Gropengießer/Jörg Meißner, "Amnesties and the Rome Statute of the ICC" (2005) 5 ICLR 267, 289. Academics, however, envisaged and feared the development under SC-Res. 1422 (2002), cf. Düker, *supra* note 645, 217.

a) Drafting history

The present wording emerged only in the last stages of the Rome Conference.[680] Article 16 has its origins in article 23 (3) ILC Draft Statute.[681] Article 23 (3) ILC Draft Statute reads as follows:

> "No prosecution may be commenced under this Statute arising from a situation which is being dealt with by the Security Council as a threat to or breach of the peace or an act of aggression under Chapter VII of the Charter, unless the Security Council otherwise decides."

Rather than giving the SC a power to defer proceedings, article 23 (3) ILC Draft Statute obligated the Court to refrain from prosecuting situations that the SC deals with. In other words, it was the SC who must expressly authorize the Court to take action and, through the exercise of its veto power, any permanent member could have blocked ICC action.[682] Different positions on the issue were discussed within the *Ad Hoc* Committee[683] and the Preparatory Committee,[684] and can be grouped into three basic views.[685] First, the ILC Draft article 23 (3) should have been retained in light of the SC's primary responsibility under Chapter VII for the maintenance of international peace and security.[686] Second, the article should have been deleted since it undermines the independence and impartiality of the Court.[687] A third view found that some form of safeguard clause was necessary, but not as currently foreseen because the text was too va-

---

680 Morten Bergsmo/Jelena Pjeić, "Article 16," in Triffterer, *supra* note 37, article 16, mn 1; Bureau Proposal, *supra* note 695, article 10, option 1, 11.

681 ILC Draft Statute 1994, *supra* note 353, 85; Bassiouni, *supra* note 503, 130; Yee, in Lee, *supra* note 371, 149; Gargiulo, in Lattanzi/Schabas, *supra* note 631, 85 et seq.; Aly Mokhtar, "The fine art of arm twisting: The US, Resolution 1422 and the Security Council deferral power under the Rome Statute" (2003) 3 ICLR 295, 302 et seq. Very critical regarding the original draft El Zeidy, *supra* note 651, 961.

682 Report of the *Ad Hoc* Committee 1995, *supra* note 379, paras. 123, 125, 28; Bergsmo/Pjeić, in Triffterer, *supra* note 680, article 16, mn 2, 9; Christopher Keith Hall, "The third and fourth sessions of the UN Preparatory Committee on the Establishment of the International Criminal Court" (1998) 92 AJIL 124, 131; Steinberger-Fraunhofer, *supra* note 315, 233.

683 Report of the *Ad Hoc* Committee 1995, *supra* note 379, paras. 122 et seq., 28–9.

684 Report of the Preparatory Committee 1996, Vol. 1, *supra* note 203, paras. 140 et seq., 33–4.

685 Bergsmo/Pjeić, in Triffterer, *supra* note 680, article 16, mn 3; Yee, in Lee, *supra* note 371, 150; Olásolo, *supra* note 29, 172–3; Kurth, *supra* note 399, 76.

686 Report of the *Ad Hoc* Committee 1995, *supra* note 379, para. 124, 28; Report of the Preparatory Committee 1996, Vol. 1, *supra* note 203, para. 141, 33.

687 Report of the *Ad Hoc* Committee 1995, *supra* note 379, para. 125, 28; Report of the Preparatory Committee 1996, Vol. 1, *supra* note 203, para. 142, 33.

gue.[688] It was suggested to amend the provision so that the ICC could proceed if the SC did not take action "within a reasonable time."[689]

Despite these divergent opinions a Singaporean proposal of August 1997 became the basis of a second option for article 23 (3) ICL Draft Statute and sparked a breakthrough, providing that:

> "No investigation or prosecution may be commenced or proceeded with under this Statute where the Security Council has, acting under Chapter VII of the Charter of the United Nations, given a direction to that effect."[690]

Canada added a 12 month renewable period,[691] and it was finally UK support for the Singaporean proposal that broke the deadlock.[692] Furthermore, it was an all-embracing UK proposal on the trigger mechanisms that served as a basis for the final wording of article 16, introducing a new article 10 (former article 23 (3) ILC Draft Statute), which found its way into the Preparatory Committee's Draft Statute 1998 as a further option:

> "No investigation or prosecution may be commenced or proceeded with under this Statute [for a period of twelve months] after the Security Council [, acting under Chapter VII of the Charter of the United Nations,] has requested the Court to that effect; that request may be renewed by the Council under the same conditions."[693]

Achieving a widely acceptable balance on the ICC – SC relationship was one of the main political problems during the Rome Conference.[694] The Bureau of the Committee of the Whole circulated two papers narrowing

---

688 Report of the *Ad Hoc* Committee 1995, *supra* note 379, para. 126, 29; Report of the Preparatory Committee 1996, Vol. 1, *supra* note 203, para. 143, 33–4.

689 Report of the Preparatory Committee 1996, Vol. 1, *supra* note 203, para. 143, 34.

690 Proposal by Singapore on article 23, Preparatory Committee on the Establishment of the International Criminal Court, 8.8.1997 (Non-Paper/WG.3/No.16). On the importance of the Singapore plan Jennifer Joakim, "The Singapore plan: maximising the power of the ICC" (1998) 4 New Eng. ICLA 211, 218 et seq.; El Zeidy, *supra* note 651, 962; Gargiulo, in Lattanzi/Schabas, *supra* note 631, 89.

691 Proposal submitted by Canada for article 23, Preparatory Committee on the Establishment of the International Criminal Court, 18.8.1997 (Non-Paper/WG.3/No.18).

692 Bergsmo/Pjeić, in Triffterer, *supra* note 680, article 16, mn 5; Kurth, *supra* note 399, 79; Olásolo, *supra* note 29, 173.

693 Proposal by the United Kingdom of Great Britain and Northern Ireland, *supra* note 359, article 10 [23], 3; Draft Statute, April 1998, *supra* note 44, further option for articles 6, 7, 10 and 11, article 10 (2), 39; Bassiouni, *supra* note 503, 110.

694 Bergsmo/Pjeić, in Triffterer, *supra* note 680, article 16, mn 8; White/Cryer, in Doria/Gasser/Bassiouni, *supra* note 633, 464; Kurth, *supra* note 399, 80 et seq. Herta Däubler-Gmelin, "Die Stärke des Rechts im Zeitalter der Globalisierung – Beginn der Arbeit des Internationalen Strafgerichtshofs" in Festschrift für Albin Eser, *Menschengerechtes Strafrecht* (C.H. Beck, München: 2005) 725, who mentions that

down three options:[695] the first option's wording was based upon the UK proposal and was later transferred into article 16 of the ICC Statute as part of the "final package-deal."[696] In conclusion, political considerations were given more weight than legal arguments during the negotiations, and the SC ended up being given a critical role when it comes to dealing with situations where peace and justice seem to be in conflict.[697] The latter question will be addressed in more detail elsewhere.[698] The drafting history has shown that article 16 was one of the most difficult and sensitive provisions to be included in the ICC Statute.[699]

b) *Interpretation of elements*

Six constituent elements can be classified and interpreted with regard to an application of article 16:

(1) investigation or prosecution;

(2) commence or proceed;

(3) period of twelve months;

(4) resolution adopted under Chapter VII UN Charter;

(5) SC request; and

(6) renewal of the request.

---

article 16 was a concession to ICC critical States in order to enhance affirmative votes.

[695] Bureau Discussion Paper, *supra* note 361, 13–4; Bureau Proposal, Part 2. Jurisdiction, Admissibility and Applicable Law, United Nations Diplomatic Conference of Plenipotentiaries on the Establishment of an International Criminal Court, 15 June–17 July 1998, 10.7.1998 (A/CONF.183/C.1/L.59) 11–2; thereto Bergsmo/Pjeić, in Triffterer, *supra* note 680, article 16, mn 6; Gerhard Hafner/Kristen Boon/Anne Rübesame/Jonathan Huston, "A response to the American view as presented by Ruth Wedgwood" (1999) 10 EJIL 108, 114–5.

[696] Draft Statute for the International Criminal Court, United Nations Diplomatic Conference of Plenipotentiaries on the Establishment of an International Criminal Court, 15 June–17 July 1998, 16.7.1998 (A/CONF.183/C.1/L.76/Add.1-Add.14; see, in particular, Add.2 on "Part 2. Jurisdiction, Admissibility and Applicable Law," article 16 [10], 12). On the "final package deal" Phillipe Kirsch/John T. Holmes, "The Rome conference on an ICC: the negotiating process" (1999) 93 AJIL 2, 9–10; Kurth, *supra* note 399, 82; Arsanjani, *supra* note 93, 23 et seq.; Kress, *supra* note 675, 323–4.

[697] Bergsmo/Pjeić, in Triffterer, *supra* note 680, article 16, mn 7; concurring, El Zeidy, *supra* note 651, 963.

[698] See Part IV, B., III., 3.

[699] Ademola Abass, "The competence of the Security Council to terminate the jurisdiction of the International Criminal Court" (2005) 40 Texas International Law Journal 263, 269; also Schabas, *supra* note 13, 327-8.

aa) Investigation or prosecution

Coming first to the normative content of "investigation or prosecution," it is worthwhile to note that article 23 (3) ILC Draft Statute referred only to prosecutions, in contrast to the inclusion of both terms in article 16. The ICC Statute does not define the terms "investigation" or "prosecution." An investigation involves action that may be taken with respect to both a situation and/or an individual, whereas a prosecution comprises only actions taken with respect to a specific person.[700] Despite the theoretical line between situations and cases in article 58 proceedings,[701] investigations and prosecutions may largely overlap. Due to the *sequenced approach* of case selection within a situation according where cases inside the situation are selected based on their gravity,[702] investigations will continue even after a particular case has been picked for prosecution. It is submitted that the line between situations and cases should be drawn at the issuance of an arrest warrant, which appears coherent with the jurisprudence to date.[703]

In order to determine the scope of article 16 it is essential to ascertain when formal investigations exactly begin and at what point prosecutions end. An investigation commences when the Prosecutor reaches a decision on the "reasonable basis" standard, initiates an investigation (article 53 (1)), or submits a request for authorization which needs to be approved by the PTC (article 15 (3) and (4)). The determination of a "reasonable basis" legally separates pre-investigations and formal investigations.[704] Although the line between the two could be quite hazy,[705] two different stages can be distinguished. It can be deduced from articles 15, 53 (1), and rule 47 that preliminary measures are conducted *before* a formal investigation is initiated.[706] However, the scope does cover situations and cases as article 16 explicitly mentions "investigations *and* prosecutions."[707]

---

700 Bergsmo/Pjeić, in Triffterer, *supra* note 680, article 16, mn 11; Mohamed El Zeidy, "The United States dropped the atomic bomb of article 16 of the ICC Statute: Security Council power of deferrals and resolution 1422" (2002) 35 VJTL 1503, 1512.

701 See Part III, B., III., 3.

702 OTP strategy, *supra note* 409, 5.

703 Bergsmo/Pjeić, in Triffterer, *supra* note 680, article 16, mn 14, who prefer the approach that prosecutions start once charges have been confirmed in accordance with article 61.

704 See already Part III, A.; in the same vein, Bergsmo/Pjeić, in Triffterer, *supra* note 680, article 16, mn 12; El Zeidy, *supra* note 700, 1513.

705 Oosthuizen, *supra* note 631, 336.

706 In more detail Part III, C. and E.

707 Contrary, Annalisa Ciampi, "The proceedings against President Al Bashir and the prospects of their suspension under article 16 ICC Statute" (2008) 6 JICJ 885,

From a textual point of view, article 16 solely refers to "investigations" and not to the "preliminary examination" measures referenced in article 15 (1), (2), (6) and rule 104. A contextual and teleological interpretation confirms this finding. Article 16 was inserted after, and not before, articles 14 and 15. The deferral request was thus not conceived as an instrument for preventive action by the SC, but it requires the existence of some sort of situation which gives rise to the level of further investigations.[708] The authority to even bar the commencement of investigations does not support a different conclusion.[709] As stated above, a formal investigation only starts once a determination on "reasonable basis" has been reached. Hence, the SC can block the Prosecutor from commencing formal investigations, but the latter should still be allowed to continue with all steps that can be considered as preliminary to the formal investigative phase.[710] Moreover, the SC cannot interfere with the receiving and examination of referrals (article 42 (1)), since such an intervention is not explicitly provided for under the ICC Statute.

In a nutshell, an investigation in the sense of article 16 only starts when the Prosecutor has determined that a "reasonable basis" (articles 15 (3) and 53 (1)) exists.[711] The remaining question is how long prosecutions might last. Prosecution comes to an end after rendering the final judgment (article 74), which includes appeals according to articles 81 (1) and 83, or the expiry of the time-limit for the right to appeal (30 days according to rule 150 (1)). A wider interpretation, embracing sentencing (article 76) and enforcement of sentencing (articles 103 et seq.), finds no sufficient support in the ICC Statute or the RPE. Article 16 therefore does not extend the SC's deferral power to the totality of activities of the OTP.[712] In sum, article 16 applies to all steps after the decision to proceed on a "reasonable basis" until the rendering of a final judgment.

---

889. Ciampi's approach may be desirable given the potential influence on target selection by the SC, but the wording precisely refers to both stages, and therefore leaves no room for opposite findings.

708 Carsten Stahn, "The ambiguities of Security Council Resolution 1422" (2003) 14 EJIL 85, 90.

709 Stahn, *supra* note 708, 90.

710 Bergsmo/Pjeić, in Triffterer, *supra* note 680, article 16, mn 15; Stahn, *supra* note 708, 90; Condorelli/Villalpando, in Cassese/Gaeta/Jones, *supra* note 400, 651; Oosthuizen, *supra* note 631, 336.

711 El Zeidy, *supra* note 651, 964; Bergsmo/Pjeić, in Triffterer, *supra* note 680, article 16, mn 17; Heilmann, *supra* note 74, 167.

712 Bergsmo/Pjeić, in Triffterer, *supra* note 680, article 16, mn 15; Sarooshi, in McGoldrick/Rowe/Donnelly, *supra* note 649, 106.

bb) Commence or proceed

If the SC files a deferral under article 16, the investigation or prosecution shall not be commenced or continued. As discussed above, an investigation commences after the Prosecutor has made a decision on "reasonable basis," thus the SC can block only formal investigations. Another, related question is how the SC becomes aware of the commencement of an investigation. Article 18 (1) obliges the Prosecutor to inform States Parties and States that would normally exercise jurisdiction if he opens an investigation based on article 13 (a) or articles 13 (c) and 15. Furthermore, rule 105 (1) states that if the Prosecutor decides not to open an investigation he must promptly notify the State(s) referring the situation or the SC in respect of a referral under article 13 (b). For harmonizing the notification duties, OTP Regulation 30 now fills in the gap:

> "When a situation has been referred to the Prosecutor pursuant to article 13, paragraph (b), and the Prosecutor has determined that there would be a reasonable basis to initiate an investigation, the Office shall notify the Security Council through the Secretary-General of the United Nations."

Nevertheless, no duty can be found within the statutory framework that the SC shall be notified of commencements based on State referrals or the *proprio motu* power. Practice of the OTP in all situations has shown that it will announce the opening of any investigation through a press release.[713] In addition, the Relationship Agreement guarantees proper flow of information.[714] Article 3 of the Relationship Agreement frames a reciprocal duty to cooperate and coordinate efforts. The interrelationship regarding the SC and the ICC via the Secretary General is codified in article 17 (1) of the Relationship Agreement for SC referrals (and article 17 (2) for SC deferrals respectively).

Early practice of the ICC and the Relationship Agreement *de facto* ensure that the SC becomes aware of all investigations. An obligation to notify the SC of investigations based upon articles 13 (a), 13 (c), and 15 was, however, not specified. For the sake of clarity a new rule 50*bis,* including exactly such a duty, should be inserted. Rule 50*bis* could be phrased:

> When a situation has been referred to the Prosecutor under article 13, paragraph (a), or under articles 13 (c) and 15, and the Prosecutor has determined that there

[713] OTP-Press Release (DRC), The Office of the Prosecutor of the International Criminal Court opens its first investigation, *supra* note 210; OTP-Press Release (Uganda), Prosecutor of the International Criminal Court opens an investigation into Northern Uganda, *supra* note 246; OTP-Press Release (CAR), Prosecutor opens investigation in the Central African Republic, *supra* note 270; OTP-Press-Release (Darfur), The Prosecutor of the ICC opens investigation in Darfur, *supra* note 284. See also Bergsmo/Pjeić, in Triffterer, *supra* note 680, article 16, mn 18.

[714] Heilmann, *supra* note 74, 167.

is a reasonable basis to initiate an investigation, the Prosecutor shall inform the Security Council through the Secretary General of the United Nations.

Under article 16, the SC can also stop proceedings that are already under way. The effects of a stay of proceedings for an accused (must that person be set free?) as well as for the preservation of evidence are unclear but have to be addressed.[715]

Neither the ICC Statute nor its ancillary documents present an answer to the posed questions. If the case is still at the investigation stage, it is clear that a deferral will suspend any further investigations and no arrest warrant can be issued. If a warrant has already been issued it cannot be executed, because this would violate the deferral by the SC. If a person has already been arrested, further procedural steps are banned. Less clear is the question of whether a person under arrest must be set free due to the deferral. One author suggests that, according to a strict literal reading, article 16 is limited to the blocking of investigations and prosecutions only, but does not mean that the accused is no longer incriminated.[716] Others focus on the person's right to "be tried without undue delay" (articles 67 (1) (c), 64 (2)), and therefore argue that a deferral would entail an imperative review of the Chamber on the interim release of the person.[717] Taking into account the right of a person not to be subjected to arbitrary arrest or detention, and the possible continuation of the deferral if renewed, I do prefer the latter view. In any event, the PTC can release the person with conditions (article 60 (2)).

No further explanation is given as to what shall happen with potential witnesses and the preservation of evidence in the case of a deferral under article 16. In the last draft version of article 10, option 1, a *nota bene* was incorporated, saying that "[t]he question of the need for preservation of evidence requires further discussion."[718] Be that as it may, no regulation resulted from the further discussions addressing the matter. In general, the SC may regulate how measures shall be taken and could provide guidance.[719] Absent any instructions the Prosecutor may still take limited steps under article 15 (2) and rule 104. However, these measures are strictly limited,

[715] El Zeidy, *supra* note 700, 1514; Bergsmo/Pjeić, in Triffterer, *supra* note 680, article 16, mn 19.

[716] El Zeidy, *supra* note 700, 1514.

[717] Condorelli/Villalpando, in Cassese/Gaeta/Jones, *supra* note 400, 653 with fn. 104. The deferral does not imply *ipso facto* the release of the accused, but an imperative revision similar to article 60 (3).

[718] Bureau Proposal, *supra* note 695, 11; Bergsmo/Pjeić, in Triffterer, *supra* note 680, article 16, mn 19.

[719] Bergsmo/Pjeić, in Triffterer, *supra* note 680, article 16, mn 20; Condorelli/Villalpando, in Cassese/Gaeta/Jones, *supra* note 400, 651 et seq.

and they cannot be delayed in order to avoid entering the formal investigation phase. Some authors argue that, absent SC guidance, the Prosecutor may apply article 54 (3) (f) to take steps necessary for the preservation of evidence.[720] Under this provision the Prosecutor may take "necessary measures, or request that necessary measures be taken, to ensure [...] the protection of any person or the preservation of evidence." On the other hand, textual and contextual interpretation militates against this application of article 54. In its heading article 54 lists the duties and powers of the Prosecutor "with respect to investigations." A deferral under article 16 has the effect of suspending those investigations. In addition, article 54 is situated within part V ("investigation and prosecution"). It contains typical investigation measures. As such, the norm cannot apply outside formal investigation, be it pre-investigations or suspended investigations under article 16. A teleological interpretation only changes this finding marginally and enables the OTP to take steps only to preserve what was done prior to the deferral.[721] Therefore, in the absence of a norm giving permission to preserve evidence after a SC deferral, and if the SC does not give further guidelines *in casu,* in-depth preservation of evidence is not possible.[722]

In order to redress this deficiency it is suggested to revisit two proposals made during the Rome Conference for amending draft article 10 (Role of the Security Council). Belgium proposed the inclusion of the following sentence in paragraph 2: "Without prejudice to article 86, paragraph 4, such request shall not affect the right of the Prosecutor to take the necessary measures to preserve evidence."[723] Furthermore, Spain presented a proposal that allowed the Prosecutor to take all "necessary measures for the preservation of the evidence and any other precautionary measures in the interests of justice."[724] It is recommended to open the floor for discussions on the unresolved matter of preservation of evidence in the case of article 16 deferrals at a Review Conference.[725]

---

[720] Bergsmo/Pjeić, in Triffterer, *supra* note 680, article 16, mn 20.

[721] El Zeidy, *supra* note 700, 1515.

[722] Condorelli/Villalpando, in Cassese/Gaeta/Jones, *supra* note 400, 652, who conclude that article 56, as presently worded, cannot be applied; further Heilmann, *supra* note 74, 168.

[723] Proposal submitted by Belgium, Committee of the Whole, United Nations Diplomatic Conference of Plenipotentiaries on the Establishment of an International Criminal Court, 15 June–17 July 1998, 19.6.1998 (A/CONF.183/C.1/L.7); thereto, El Zeidy, *supra* note 700, 1515 with fn. 72; Gargiulo, in Lattanzi/Schabas, *supra* note 631, 90.

[724] Proposal for article 10 submitted by Spain, Committee of the Whole, United Nations Diplomatic Conference of Plenipotentiaries on the Establishment of an International Criminal Court, 15 June–17 July 1998, 25.6.1998 (A/CONF.183/C.1/L.20) para. 7 (3).

A new rule 50*ter* could be included with the following wording:

(1) When an investigation or prosecution has been deferred by the Security Council in accordance with article 16, the Security Council may regulate what measures can be taken by the Court in response to the procedural and evidentiary implications of such a deferral.

(2) In the absence of guidance by the Security Council, the Prosecutor shall take all necessary measures for the preservation of the evidence and any other precautionary measures in the "interests of justice."

cc) Period of twelve months

The SC can request the deferral of proceedings for a period of twelve months. A request under article 16 is thus a temporary device.[726] The wording might suggest a specific period of twelve months, but the period can be shorter.[727] Twelve months is merely the upper limit, whereas the SC may fix a shorter time period below this barrier.[728]

With respect to the beginning of the period two different views are held by Bergsmo/Pjeić and Heilmann. It is argued that the 12 month period starts running on the date the deferral request is received by the Court.[729] Heilmann opposes this argument and refers to the current practice of the SC that sets a date itself as part of the particular resolution.[730] SC-Res. 1422 (2002) of 12 July 2002 states that the ICC shall not commence or proceed with investigations or prosecutions "for a twelve-month period starting 1 July 2002." In the same vein, SC-Res. 1487 (2003) of 12 June 2003 names a "twelve-month period starting 1 July 2003." Setting a date and the receiving of the deferral request will go hand-in-hand in practice. After passing the resolution it will be transmitted to the Court shortly after.

---

725 Review Conferences are foreseen by article 122 (2). The first Review Conference was supposed to take place seven years after the entry into force (article 123 (1)); thereafter, any State Party can request a Conference and a majority of States Parties has to approve the convening thereof (article 123 (2)). The first review conference finally took place in the second quarter of 2010 in Kampala, see CICC, "ASP Highlights," The Monitor, No. 38, *supra* note 418, 4; also <www2.icc-cpi.int/Menus/ASP/ASP+Events/ASP+Calendar+2010/Review+Conference.htm>.

726 Carsten Stahn, "Complementarity, amnesties and alternative forms of justice: some interpretative guidelines for the International Criminal Court" (2005) 3 JICJ 695, 699.

727 Bergsmo/Pjeić, in Triffterer, *supra* note 680, article 16, mn 21; Condorelli/Villalpando, in Cassese/Gaeta/Jones, *supra* note 400, 648 with fn. 85; Contag, *supra* note 426, 155.

728 Heilmann, *supra* note 74, 168.

729 Bergsmo/Pjeić, in Triffterer, *supra* note 680, article 16, mn 21.

730 Heilmann, *supra* note 74, 169.

The Relationship Agreement ensures a smooth course of events. In response to the merely academic question the latter view is more coherent with the SC's practice and therefore preferable.

dd) Resolution adopted under Chapter VII of the UN Charter

Like the referral power under article 13 (b), the power to request a deferral flows from Chapter VII of the UN Charter. The reference to Chapter VII clarifies that not any SC action, but a specific Chapter VII-resolution is necessary. In other words, the preconditions of Chapter VII of the UN Charter have to be met (*Rechtgrundverweisung*).[731] The SC should therefore respect both the conditions set up by the UN Charter and those deriving from article 16 itself.[732]

First, the SC must determine that one of the essential preconditions – threat to peace, breach of peace, or an act of aggression – exists; however, this does not have to be mentioned expressly in the decision.[733] A disputed question is whether this threat to peace must be the direct cause for the investigations or prosecutions *per se*. The preferred opinion is that the SC need not do so; a reference to a larger factual or political background related to the ICC's proceedings can justify a deferral decision.[734] According to this interpretation, the SC can decide that the suspension of ICC proceedings effectively contributes to the maintenance or restoration of peace. It could, for instance, be argued that suspension of the ICC facilitates the achievement of a peace agreement.[735] On the other hand, it would not be easy for the SC to reverse its previous decisions[736] insofar as the SC has

---

731 Heilmann, *supra* note 74, 172; also Bergsmo/Pjeić, in Triffterer, *supra* note 680, article 16, mn 23; Contag, *supra* note 426, 146.

732 Condorelli/Villalpando, in Cassese/Gaeta/Jones, *supra* note 400, 646; see further Part III, B., V., 3., b), ee).

733 On the preconditions of Chapter VII of the UN Charter, see already Part III, V., 1. On the necessity of a determination under article 39 of the UN Charter to invoke Chapter VII, see Amnesty International, Deferral Report, *supra* note 651, 60 et seq., with various references in fn. 182–4; also Oette, *supra* note 633, 351.

734 Condorelli/Villalpando, in Cassese/Gaeta/Jones, *supra* note 400, 647; Oosthuizen, *supra* note 631, 333. Contrary, Cassese, *supra* note 675, 163; Zappalà, Salvatore, "Il procuratore della Corte Penal Internazionale: luci e ombre" (1999) 82 RDI 39, 66.

735 Condorelli/Villalpando, in Cassese/Gaeta/Jones, *supra* note 400, 647; Fixon, in Kirsch, *supra* note 455, 218. See further Part IV, B., III., 3., e), aa).

736 Bergsmo/Pjeić, in Triffterer, *supra* note 680, article 16, mn 10; Jochen Herbst, "Immunität für Angehörige der U.S.-Streitkräfte vor der Strafverfolgung durch den IStGH?" (2002) 29 EuGRZ 581, 587.

established international criminal jurisdictions (ICTY and ICTR) for the maintenance and restoration of peace.[737] Be that as it may, it is sufficient for the SC to show that ICC action could undermine the SC's efforts to maintain international peace and security rather than to reach a determination that the ICC' action in itself constitutes a threat to international peace and security.[738] A margin of appreciation regarding factual determinations certainly remains for the SC.[739]

Second, the SC has to comply with the voting procedure as foreseen by article 27 (3) of the UN Charter, requiring an affirmative vote of nine members, including the concurring votes of the five permanent members.[740] Instead of allowing the negative vote of one permanent member to block ICC action, article 16 requires positive action through a resolution by a majority vote (and no permanent member vetoes) to defer proceedings.[741] The veto power cannot be used to block the work of the ICC, but, conversely, only to prevent the obstruction of that work.[742]

ee) SC request

A request should be made through a formal resolution adopted under Chapter VII of the UN Charter and has to be submitted in writing.[743] Article 17 (2) Relationship Agreement further provides that "this request shall immediately be transmitted by the Secretary-General to the President of the Court and the Prosecutor." As in the event of a referral under article 13 (b), the ICC's jurisdictional organs have a limited right to review the SC's action under article 16.[744] Assuming that a limited review is feasible, two

---

737 Cf. SC-Res. 808 (1993), 22.2.1993, preambular para. 9; SC-Res. 955 (1994), 8.11.1994, preambular para. 7.

738 Olásolo, *supra* note 29, 178.

739 Anja Seibert-Fohr, "The relevance of the Rome Statute of the International Criminal Court for amnesties and truth commissions" (2003) 7 Max Planck Yearbook of the UN 553, 584.

740 Olásolo, *supra* note 29, 177; Gowlland-Debbas, in de Chazournes/Romano/Mackenzie, *supra* note 631, 205.

741 Olásolo, *supra* note 29, 177; Slye/van Schaack, *supra* note 534, 57; Gerd Seidel/Carsten Stahn, "Das Statut des Weltstrafgerichtshofs. Ein Überblick über Entstehung, Inhalt und Bedeutung" (1999) 21 Jura 14, 16–7; Heilmann, *supra* note 74, 173; Daniel Ntanda Nsereko, "The relationship between the International Criminal Court and the United Nations Security Council" (2007) 13 ZIS 500, 502; Contag, *supra* note 426, 147.

742 Seidel/Stahn, *supra* note 741, 17; Oosthuizen, *supra* note 631, 333.

743 Olásolo, *supra* note 29, 176.

744 Condorelli/Villalpando, in Cassese/Gaeta/Jones, *supra* note 400, 650; Olásolo, *supra* note 29, 178; Oosthuizen, *supra* note 631, 331.

pertinent questions need further deliberations: first, the review standard has to be addressed, i.e. against which legal background (UN Charter; ICC Statute?) do we evaluate the particular resolution. Second, the procedure for such a review by the ICC has not been regulated in article 16 or the RPE and requires fine-tuning.

Beginning with the review standard, the ICC could satisfy itself (a) that the correct voting procedure was followed by the SC, (b) that it indeed did adopt a resolution under Chapter VII of the UN Charter, and, (c) that the SC in fact did request the Court to defer its proceedings in accordance with article 16.[745] Another author concurs in these three points and adds that the request has to be limited to a maximum of twelve months (d).[746]

The phrasing "in a resolution adopted under Chapter VII" in article 16 embodies the idea that the SC takes a formal vote instead of merely discussing a Chapter VII situation.[747] Therefore, the ICC is able to scrutinize the correct voting procedure. Clearly, the SC has to adopt a resolution under Chapter VII; other measures of the SC do not fall within the scope of article 16. A formal resolution is therefore inevitable. It is, though, controversial to which extent the ICC can examine the nature of the resolution *vis-à-vis* the UN Charter and other international law. The SC must act in accordance with Chapter VII; thus, a situation under article 39 of the UN Charter must exist and the SC must act in accordance with the principles and purposes of the United Nations (article 24 (2) of the UN Charter).[748] It cannot act *ultra vires*, i.e. beyond the powers conferred by the UN Charter. Yet, it is a different matter if and how the actions by the SC can be checked by the ICC. The SC enjoys wide discretion when reaching a decision under article 39 of the UN Charter;[749] this begs the question as to the degree which the ICC's judges could possibly control its acts. A substantive review of the basis underlying the SC's determination pursuant to article 39 of the UN Charter is rejected by some authors.[750] In contrast, Amnesty In-

[745] Oosthuizen, *supra* note 631, 331; in the same vein Zsuzsanna Deen-Racsmány, "The ICC, peacekeepers and Resolution 1422: will the Court defer to the Council?" (2002) XLIX NILR 353, 362, 370, 382 with fn. 155.

[746] Kurth, *supra* note 399, 195; who further mentions that the last point alone cannot render a request invalid. In the case of a 24 month period, for example, the ICC shall continue its proceedings after twelve months, and shall solely halt proceedings for twelve months before.

[747] Oosthuizen, *supra* note 631, 333. On the voting procedure see already Part III, B., V., 3., b), dd).

[748] Yasmin Naqvi, "Amnesty for war crimes: defining the limits of international recognition" (2003) 851 IRRC 583, 593.

[749] Deen-Racsmány, *supra* note 745, 380, with further references in fn. 145 ("almost absolute discretion"); also Part III, B., V., 1.

ternational favors an all-embracing review power of the ICC.[751] Taking into account the margin of discretion of the SC, and the fact that its decision centers around political evaluations, it is submitted that a review by the ICC be limited to legality only and should exclude political analysis of whether article 39 of the UN Charter was properly triggered.[752]

A request for deferral that is inconsistent with the ICC Statute would not bind the Court.[753] It has been argued that SC resolutions can only be scrutinized in light of the UN Charter.[754] Such a restrictive view is not persuasive, since it conceals the twofold nature of a resolution under article 16. A resolution under article 16 constitutes *first* a resolution under Chapter VII, which naturally has to be checked in light of the UN Charter, and *second* it inherently generates a deferral request, which has to be evaluated in the light of article 16. The choice of the word "requests" suggests that at least the preconditions of article 16 must be fulfilled besides the prerequisites of the UN Charter. While supposedly the word "request" in article 16 does not mean that the ICC has discretion to halt its proceedings,[755] it was inserted deliberately because the SC has no power to simply order a cease of action regarding the ICC.[756] Therefore, there must be an express petition to defer proceedings.[757]

---

750 Oosthuizen, *supra* note 631, 334; Deen-Racsmány, *supra* note 745, 383 with fn. 157.

751 Amnesty International, Deferral Report, *supra* note 651, 39 et seq.; AI even favors determining whether a threat to peace and security, breach of peace and security, or a case of aggression exists, *ibid.* Similarly, Bernd Martenczuk, "The Security Council, the International Court and judicial review: What lessons from Lockerbie?" (1999) 10 EJIL 517, 543–4.

752 Kurth, *supra* note 399, 196 with various references in fn. 950. See also fn. 652.

753 Zappalà, *supra* note 651, 119; Sarooshi, in McGoldrick/Rowe/Donnelly, *supra* note 649, 118; Amnesty International, Deferral Report, *supra* note 651, 36 et seq.; Olásolo, *supra* note 29, 17; Deen-Racsmány, *supra* note 745, 382.

754 Herbst, *supra* note 736, 586; Gallant, *supra* note 631, 575.

755 Oosthuizen, *supra* note 631, 331–2; Kurth, *supra* note 399, 200; Lavalle, *supra* note 644, 200–1; Heselhaus, *supra* note 649, 910; Nabil Elaraby, "The role of the Security Council and the independence of the International Criminal Court: some reflections" in Mauro Politi/Giuseppe Nesi (eds.), *The Rome Statute of the International Criminal Court – A challenge to impunity* (Ashgate, Aldershot 2001) 45. Contrary, Amnesty International, Deferral Report, *supra* note 651, 37.

756 Amnesty International, Deferral Report, *supra* note 651, 37; Naqvi, *supra* note 748, 592.

757 Olásolo, *supra* note 29, 177; Oosthuizen, *supra* note 631, 333; Stahn, *supra* note 708, 88; Elizabeth Wilmshurst, "The International Criminal Court: The role of the Security Council" in Politi/Nesi, *supra* note 755, 40 ("positive decision to ask for deferral").

In sum, a resolution must comply with the UN Charter and article 16. *Ius cogens* and the principle of proportionality are thereby to be taken into account.[758] Moreover, a resolution not in accordance with article 39 of the UN Charter would automatically violate article 16, which presupposes a valid resolution under Chapter VII.[759] The ICC would then not be required to halt its proceedings.

A follow-up question concerns the legal implications of a hypothetical resolution in violation of article 16 and/or the UN Charter. Any resolution not in accordance with the UN Charter would neither bind the ICC nor State Parties to the UN Charter. A resolution not in line with article 16 is also not binding on the ICC.[760] However, it has to be noted that article 16 regulates the powers of the SC only in relation to the ICC and does not touch upon the obligations of states under the UN Charter.[761] In the event a resolution is invalid under article 16, but is valid under the UN Charter, the disputed resolution would have to be accepted as binding and therefore valid for UN member states. This situation would prevent UN member states from cooperating with the ICC.[762] Due to the precedence of the UN Charter over other international agreements (articles 103 and 25 of the UN Charter) UN members are under an obligation to follow the SC rather than the ICC.[763] A dispute on this point could then be referred to the ICJ under article 119 (2).[764] In conclusion, the SC could bind ICC States Parties through a deferral that is inconsistent with article 16 but in accordance with the UN Charter.

This brings us to another concern regarding the review procedure: the Relationship Agreement does not provide for a specific manner of dispute settlement. If the ICC is directly affected, the fact it has review power over the dispute is accepted by the majority of academic voices.[765] Article 22 of

---

758 See thereto the references in fn. 645.

759 Mokhtar, *supra* note 681, 311; Fritsche, in Frowein, *supra* note 679, 116.

760 Deen-Racsmány, *supra* note 745, 382; Stahn, *supra* note 708, 101–2; Kurth, *supra* note 399, 119, 200–1.

761 Deen-Racsmány, *supra* note 745, 384; Kurth, *supra* note 399, 201.

762 Deen-Racsmány, *supra* note 745, 385.

763 Andreas Paulus, "Legalist groundwork for the International Criminal Court" (2003) 14 EJIL 843, 853; Yee, in Lee, *supra* note 371, 152 with fn. 31; Sarooshi, in McGoldrick/Rowe/Donnelly, *supra* note 649, 108; Zappalà, *supra* note 651, 121. Stagel, *supra* note 425, 235, who emphasizes that resolutions are only binding if they were adopted *in accordance* with the UN Charter, not if the SC acted *ultra vires*.

764 Paulus, *supra* note 763, 855; Deen-Racsmány, *supra* note 745, 385. Kurth, *supra* note 399, 190, negates this possibility for SC-Res. 1422, because questions of jurisdiction cannot be referred under article 119 (2). In detail on judicial review by the ICJ, Quénivet, *supra* note 658, 48 et seq.

765 Olásolo, *supra* note 29, 178; see already Part III, B., V., 1. with fn. 650 and 651.

the Relationship Agreement states that any dispute shall be settled by "appropriate means." A dispute settlement by the ICJ seems to be only the second best option compared to a review by the ICC itself.[766] However, a review power denotes the competence of the Court to satisfy itself that it can exercise jurisdiction over a situation, including situations referred by the SC.[767] Therefore, the competence to review any article 16 request might be located within articles 119 (1) and/or 19 (1).[768]

Article 19 cannot be set in motion by the SC, but rather provides an opportunity for the Court to satisfy itself of its jurisdiction or admissibility (paragraph 1). Challenges to the latter can be brought by the accused, a person for whom a warrant has been issued or by States (paragraph 2). Moreover, the ambit of article 19 is very limited.[769] Article 119 is a general norm for disputes about the Court's judicial functions. It seems too broad for the specific question of the Court's competence to review a deferral under article 16, especially because the interrelationship between the Court and the SC must be addressed. For this reason, a proposal for an amendment of the RPE specifically regulating the reviewing procedure under article 16 must be adopted.[770] A new rule 50*quater* could be drafted as follows:

(1) The Prosecutor may ask the Pre-Trial Chamber or the Trial Chamber, depending on the stage of proceedings, to review a deferral request of the Security Council under article 16.

(2) For such a review the Judges shall evaluate the procedure of articles 27 and 39 of the UN Charter, and the requirements of article 16.

ff) Renewal of the request

The wording that a "request may be renewed by the Council under the same conditions" does not indicate any express limitation of the number of times the SC may renew the request under article 16.[771] A broad interpre-

---

[766] It is unlikely that the ICJ will assume jurisdictional review of the SC' determination, see Bassiouni, *supra* note 401, 142.

[767] Oosthuizen, *supra* note 631, 319.

[768] Oosthuizen, *supra* note 631, 335; Meißner, *supra* note 371, 261–2; Kurth, *supra* note 399, 192 et seq.; Gropengießer/Meißner, *supra* note 679, 294.

[769] Cf. Part III, B., IV., 4.

[770] Olásolo, *supra* note 29, 178–9; also Contag, *supra* note 426, 162–3.

[771] Bergsmo/Pjeić, in Triffterer, *supra* note 680, article 16, mn 25; Hafner/Boon/Rübesame/Huston, *supra* note 695, 113–4; Meißner, *supra* note 371, 101; El Zeidy, *supra* note 700, 1515; Marten Zwanenburg, "The Statute of the International Criminal Court and the United States: peacekeepers under fire?" (1999) 10 EJIL 124, 138; Heselhaus, *supra* note 649, 911 with fn. 20. Contrary, Ruth Wedgwood, "The

tation allows the SC to defer even indefinitely.[772] An indefinite deferral would, however, result in a permanent estoppel of ICC procedures, which would be contrary to the balance of interests article 16 is based on.[773] The SC's power is indeed subject to time limits.[774] Therefore, the SC must renew a request every twelve months through a new formal resolution in accordance with the voting procedure of article 27 of the UN Charter and a re-evaluation of article 39 of the UN Charter.[775] This requires a renewed debate within the SC and creates some degree of accountability.[776] If the SC does not adopt a new resolution, the ICC is free to continue its proceedings.

This means that a resolution purporting to dispense with the temporal requirement of an obligatory twelve month renewal would run contrary to article 16 and, therefore, would not bind the ICC.[777] Endless renewals would "deny victims their right to reparations, deny an accused the right to a prompt trial and, if the accused were in custody, lead to indefinite detention without trial."[778] Nevertheless, the SC is not limited in the number of renewals, leaving open the possibility that it could hamper the efficiency of the Court.[779]

c) *Practice of the SC under article 16*

The practice of the SC since 2002 with regard to article 16 needs to be analyzed in the light of the interpretation of its elements above. These reso-

International Criminal Court: an American view" (1999) 10 EJIL 93, 97–8, who assumes a limitation of 24 months and argues that this is a serious arrogation of power regarding the SC (from the US perspective).

772 Gargiulo, in Lattanzi/Schabas, *supra* note 631, 91; El Zeidy, *supra* note 700, 1515; Sarooshi, in McGoldrick/Rowe/Donnelly, *supra* note 649, 105; Nabil, in Politi/Nesi, *supra* note 755, 45; Stagel, *supra* note 425, 197; Lavalle, *supra* note 644, 205; Gropengießer/Meißner, *supra* note 679, 289.

773 Bergsmo/Pjeić, in Triffterer, *supra* note 680, article 16, mn 25; Jessica Gavron, "Amnesties in the light of developments in international law and the establishment of the International Criminal Court" (2002) 51 ICLQ 91, 109.

774 Dwight Newman, "The Rome Statute, some reservations concerning amnesties, and a distributive problem" (2005) 20 AUILR 293, 318.

775 Fixon, in Kirsch, *supra* note 455, 218; Condorelli/Villalpando, in Cassese/Gaeta/Jones, *supra* note 400, 649; Stagel, *supra* note 425, 196; El Zeidy, *supra* note 700, 1526.

776 Condorelli/Villalpando, in Cassese/Gaeta/Jones, *supra* note 400, 649.

777 Sarooshi, in McGoldrick/Rowe/Donnelly, *supra* note 649, 107; Amnesty International, Deferral Report, *supra* note 651, 49 et seq.

778 Amnesty International, Deferral Report, *supra* note 651, 50.

779 Similarly, Stagel, *supra* note 425, 198; El Zeidy, *supra* note 700, 1515.

lutions have to be seen in the broader context of the United States' "unsigning" of the ICC Statute in May 2002[780] (Israel also "unsigned" on 28 August 2002),[781] the American Service-members' Protection Act (ASPA) of 2002,[782] as well as so-called Bilateral Immunity Agreements,[783] and general US opposition towards the ICC as an independent international institution.[784] As a matter of fact, the United States was one of only seven States

780 "Press Statement Richard Boucher, Spokesman," 6.5.2002, Washington DC, International Criminal Court: Letter to UN Secretary General Kofi Annan from Under Secretary of State for Arms Control and International Security John R. Bolton, that reads as follows:

"This is to inform you, in connection with the Rome Statute of the International Criminal Court adopted on July 17, 1998, that the United States does not intend to become a party to the treaty. Accordingly, the United States has no legal obligations arising from its signature on December 31, 2000. The United States requests that its intention not to become a party, as expressed in this letter, be reflected in the depositary's status lists relating to this treaty."

781 On 28 August 2002 the Secretary-General received, from the Government of Israel, the following communication: "[...] in connection with the Rome Statute of the International Criminal Court adopted on 17 July 1998, [...] Israel does not intend to become a party to the treaty. Accordingly, Israel has no legal obligations arising from its signature on 31 December 2000. Israel requests that its intention not to become a party, as expressed in this letter, be reflected in the depositary's status lists relating to this treaty.," see endnote 3 of the Rome Statute (Registration Number I-38544) at the UNTC database <http://treaties.un.org/>.

782 American Service-members' Protection Act, 30.7.2003; Steinberger-Fraunhofer, *supra* note 315, 272 et seq.

783 The US started seeking Bilateral Immunity Agreements, purportedly based on article 98 (2) ICC Statute, to avoid the surrender of particular persons (current or former government officials, military personnel, and US employees – including contractors – and nationals). See further CICC, Factsheet, "Status of U.S. Bilateral Immunity Agreements by region," 14.12.2006; Claus Kress/Kimberly Prost, "Article 98," in Triffterer, *supra* note 37, article 98, mn 7; Steinberger-Fraunhofer, *supra* note 315, 253 et seq., 260 et seq. These agreements do not meet the criteria of article 98 (2), see Björn Sendel, "Bilaterale Nichtüberstellungsabkommen der Vereinigten Staaten und Art. 98 Abs. 2 des Römischen Statuts zur Errichtung eines ständigen Internationalen Strafgerichtshofs" (2007) 3 ZIS 118, 128; Ambos, *supra* note 26, § 8 mn 68; Schabas, *supra* note 27, 74; David Scheffer, "Article 98 (2) of the Rome Statute: America's original intent" (2005) 3 JICJ 333, 335 ("diverges from the original intent"), 353; Harmen van der Wilt, "Bilateral agreements between the United States and States Parties to the Rome Statute: are they compatible with the object and purpose of the Statute?" (2005) 18 LJIL 93, 93 et seq., 108.

784 John Cerone, "Dynamic equilibrium: The evolution of US attitudes toward International Criminal Courts and Tribunals" (2007) 18 EJIL 277, 293 et seq.; Sarah Sewall/Carl Kaysen/Michael Scharf, "The United States of America and the International Criminal Court: An overview" in Sarah Sewall/Carl Kaysen (eds.), *The United States and the International Criminal Court* (Rowan & Littlefield Publishers, Oxford 2000) 1, 8 et seq.; Allen, *supra* note 246, 20–1; Schiff, *supra* note 128, 170 et seq.; Mokhtar, *supra* note 681, 296 et seq.; Deen-Racsmány, *supra* note 745, 354

(besides China, Iraq, Libya, Yemen, Qatar and Israel) to vote against the ICC Statute in 1998.[785] Nevertheless, during negotiations the US delegation tried to influence the Statute for the US' good and did not want it to fail.[786] With George W. Bush junior becoming president the attitude towards the ICC changed drastically.[787] Recently, the US position has been more pragmatic (*moderate stance*), supporting the ICC where it is within the ambit of US interests, such as with referring the Darfur situation to the ICC.[788] After new presidential elections on 4 November 2008 and the replacement of President Bush by President Barack Obama on 20 January 2009, the American position towards the ICC is slightly friendlier, the ad-

---

et seq.; Dominic McGoldrick, "Political and legal responses to the ICC," in McGoldrick/Rowe/Donnelly, *supra* note 649, 442 et seq.; Andreas Zimmermann/Holger Scheel, "Zwischen Konfrontation und Kooperation. Die Vereinigten Staaten und der Internationale Strafgerichtshof" (2002) 50 VN 137, 137 et seq.; Ambos, *supra* note 26, 1st edition, § 6 mn 55–7; William Schabas, "United States hostility towards the International Criminal Court: it's all about the Security Council" (2004) 15 EJIL 701, 703, with numerous references – favorable and critical – to the US position in fn. 5 and 6; also Daryl Mundis, "The United States of America and International Justice" (2004) 2 JICJ 2, 3–4; Dennis Nitsche, *Der Internationale Strafgerichtshof ICC und der Frieden* (Nomos, Baden-Baden 2007) 222 et seq.; Michael Reismann, "Learning to deal with rejection: The International Criminal Court and the United States" (2004) 2 JICJ 17, 17–8; Patricia Wald, "Is the United States" opposition to the ICC intractable?" (2004) 2 JICJ 19, 19 et seq.; Giovanni Conso, "The basic reasons for US hostility to the ICC in light of the negotiating history of the Rome Statute" (2005) 3 JICJ 314, 314 et seq.; Düker, *supra* note 645, 217 et seq. On the legal opposition (31 et seq.) and political concerns (87 et seq.), see Philipp Meißner, *The International Criminal Court controversy* (LitVerlag, Münster 2005).

785 Meißner, *supra* note 784, 31.

786 Schabas, *supra* note 784, 708–9; Cerone, *supra* note 784, 291 ("constructive approach"); David Scheffer, "How to turn the tide using the Rome Statute's temporal jurisdiction" (2004) 2 JICJ 26, 27–8; *id.*, "The U.S. perspective on the ICC" in Sewall/Kaysen, *supra* note 784, 115, 115–6; Steinberger-Fraunhofer, *supra* note 315, 251–2; Gerhard Hafner, "An attempt to explain the position of the USA towards the ICC" (2005) 3 JICJ 323, 323; all-embracing, on the Rome process and the U.S. position, Lawrence Weschler, "Exceptional cases in Rome: The United States and the struggle for an ICC" in Sewall/Kaysen, *supra* note 784, 85, 85 et seq.

787 Cerone, *supra* note 784, 293 ("outright opposition"); Ambos, *supra* note 26, 1st edition, § 6 mn 55; Scheffer, *supra* note 786, 26; *id., supra* note 783, 344 et seq.; Hans-Heinrich Jescheck, "The general principles of International Criminal Law set out in Nuremberg, as mirrored in the ICC Statute" (2004) 2 JICJ 38, 55.

788 Cerone, *supra* note 784, 302 et seq.; "Bellinger says International Court flawed but deserving of help in some cases," 10.7.2007, Interview with John Bellinger, Legal Adviser to the Secretary of State, Council of Foreign Relations. On the moderate stance, Ambos, *supra* note 26, 1st edition, § 6 mn 57; CICC, "Comments by US Officials on Situations before the ICC and Cooperation with ICC Investigations," 1 December 2006.

ministration shows support for Darfur, but it still lacks full, active engagement for the ICC.[789]

aa) SC-Res. 1422 (2002), 1487 (2003)

SC-Res. 1422 (2002)[790] – which was renewed by SC-Res. 1487 (2003)[791] with identical wording – was adopted by the SC only eleven days after the entry into force of the ICC Statute. Its operative part reads as follows:

> *The Security Council,*
>
> [...]
>
> *Acting* under Chapter VII of the Charter of the United Nations,
>
> 1. *Requests*, consistent with the provisions of Article 16 of the Rome Statute, that the ICC, if a case arises involving current or former officials or personnel from a contributing State not a Party to the Rome Statute over acts or omissions relating to a United Nations established or authorized operation, shall for a twelve-month period starting 1 July 2002 not commence or proceed with investigation or prosecution of any such case, unless the Security Council decides otherwise.
> 2. *Expresses* the intention to renew the request in paragraph 1 under the same conditions each 1 July for further twelve-month periods for as long as may be necessary;
> 3. *Decides* that Member States shall take no action inconsistent with paragraph 1 and with their international obligations [...].

Shortly before the UN Mission in Bosnia and Herzegovina (hereinafter UNMIBH) was due to expire, the United States bargained to obtain immunity for its nationals.[792] As the United States could not reach a majority for

---

[789] CICC, "Obama administration on the record: show of support for Darfur investigation significant, but full engagement still lacking," The Monitor, Journal of the CICC, Issue No. 38, May–October 2009, 20. Barack Obama answered in a Candidate Questionnaire Response, Citizens of Global Solutions, 2004, to the question: "Should the United States ratify the "Rome Statute of the International Criminal Court"?" – "Yes. The United States should cooperate with ICC investigations in a way that reflects American sovereignty and promotes our national security interests."

[790] SC-Res. 1422 (2002), 12.7.2002.

[791] SC-Res. 1487 (2003), 12.6.2003. For the final texts of SC-Res. 1422 and 1487, as well as several draft proposals, see CICC, "History and analysis of UN Security Council Resolutions 1422/1487," August 2004, 1 et seq.

[792] Deen-Racsmány, *supra* note 745, 356; Amnesty International, Deferral Report, *supra* note 651, 10; Heilmann, *supra* note 74, 218 et seq.; Steinberger-Fraunhofer, *supra* note 315, 256–7; Mokhtar, *supra* note 681, 307–8.

their proposals, it vetoed the extension of the UNMIBH.[793] In cooperation with the United Kingdom, the United States introduced a new proposal that included a clause to automatically extend the resolution for additional twelve month periods unless the SC decides otherwise.[794] Unanimously, governments participating in the Preparatory Commission for the ICC opposed this approach, mainly because the proposal was an attempt to amend article 16 and would have undermined the integrity of the ICC Statute.[795] In light of this severe criticism, the SC could not come to an understanding, and the UNMIBH was only provisionally extended until 15 July 2002.[796] Ever persistent, the United States started a new attempt on 10 July 2002, sparking a French counter-proposal,[797] before a public debate on the issue sought by Canada highlighted again the critical views of many governments towards the US proposal.[798] The representative of Canada, Mr. Heinbecker, mentioned first that "[...] in the absence of a threat to international peace and security, the Council's passing a Chapter VII draft resolution on the ICC of the kind currently circulating would in our view be *ultra vires*." These concerns notwithstanding, a last draft was circulated by the United States on 11 July 2002; following a draft amendment with minor changes submitted by Mauritius, the US proposal was adopted with minor changes on 12 July 2002 as SC-Res. 1422.[799] Subsequently, the UNMIBH was extended.[800] The renewal after twelve months proved to be difficult since three members (France, Germany, and Syria) abstained in the vote.[801] An envisaged prolongation in 2004 did, however, not gain the required support in the SC and the

---

793 The situation in Bosnia and Herzegovina, Security Council, 4563rd meeting, 30.6.2002 (S/PV.4563) 2; Amnesty International, Deferral Report, *supra* note 651, 15; Kurth, *supra* note 399, 135; White/Cryer, in Doria/Gasser/Bassiouni, *supra* note 633, 467.

794 Amnesty International, Deferral Report, *supra* note 651, 15–6.

795 CICC, Government responses to US – proposed Security Council Resolution on ICC and peacekeeping, Special Plenary Session, Preparatory Commission for the ICC, 3 July 2002; Amnesty International, Deferral Report, *supra* note 651, 17 et seq.; Kurth, *supra* note 399, 136; Deen-Racsmány, *supra* note 745, 359.

796 SC-Res. 1421 (2002), 3.7.2002.

797 Amnesty International, Deferral Report, *supra* note 651, 25, with the wording of the two proposals in fn. 77 and 78.

798 The situation in Bosnia and Herzegovina, Security Council, 4568th meeting, 10.7.2002 (S/PV.4568); Amnesty International, Deferral Report, *supra* note 651, 26 et seq.; Kurth, *supra* note 399, 136 et seq.; Deen-Racsmány, *supra* note 745, 359–60; Schabas, *supra* note 13, 328-9.

799 Amnesty International, Deferral Report, *supra* note 651, 34–5; Heilmann, *supra* note 74, 221.

800 SC-Res. 1423 (2002), 12.7.2002.

801 United Nations Peacekeeping, Security Council, 4772nd meeting, 12.6.2003 (S/PV.4772) 24–5.

United States withdrew its demand, allegedly because of the publicized pictures of US troops torturing and abusing Iraqi prisoners in Abu Ghraib.[802]

I will now turn to a legal assessment of SC-Res. 1422. From a purely legal viewpoint, two main arguments can be advanced: first, that Resolution 1422 lacked a "threat to the peace" due to its abstract reference ("acting under Chapter VII"), and therefore the SC was acting *ultra vires*. Second, the ICC is only bound if article 16 requirements are complied with, and with regard to Resolution 1422 this matter is disputable.

The conformity of the Resolution with the UN Charter is doubtful. No reference to a determination of a threat to peace can be found and only a marginal reference to Chapter VII was included. This is, however, not *per se* a violation of the Charter.[803] Three possible determinations under Chapter VII, potentially constituting a threat to peace, have been identified by authors:

- the potential jurisdiction of the ICC over UN personnel from non-member states;[804]
- the threat by the United States to withdraw its UN troops;[805]
- the threat of the United States to block all future peacekeeping missions by its veto.[806]

After rejected the mentioned reasons and other variations thereof,[807] several authors have come to the conclusion that the SC did not comply with

---

802 "BBC News: Q&A International Criminal Court," 20.3.2006; Cerone, *supra* note 784, 296; Kurth, *supra* note 399, 142–3; Bassiouni, *supra* note 401, 144.

803 Herbst, *supra* note 736, 587; Düker, *supra* note 645, 227; Heilmann, *supra* note 74, 227. Sceptical, Zimmermann/Scheel, *supra* note 784, 142. See further the references in fn. 639.

804 Identified, but strongly rejected, by Heilmann, *supra* note 74, 228; Stagel, *supra* note 425, 217; very critical also Kai Ambos, "International criminal law has lost its innocence," The original German version of this article was published in the German newspaper Süddeutsche Zeitung 16 July 2002, 13, translated by Frank Schorkopf (2002) 3 GLJ, paras. 1 et seq.

805 In favor of this argument, Gallant, *supra* note 631, 575. Contrary Herbst, *supra* note 736, 587; Stahn, *supra* note 708, 87 ("[...] would render article 39 borderless"). Differentiated Stagel, *supra* note 425, 217 et seq.; Fritsche, in Frowein, *supra* note 679, 113 et seq.

806 This argument was introduced by Zappalà, *supra* note 651, 118–9, who, however, does not adhere to it, and holds that the Resolution was consistent with the UN Charter. Critical – with regard to the veto threat – also Amnesty International, Deferral Report, *supra* note 651, 3; Mokhtar, *supra* note 681, 313. The argument is, however, adopted by Contag, *supra* note 426, 171.

807 See, for example, Mokhtar, *supra* note 681, 314, who could not find a basis for a threat to peace *at all* due to the vague references in the context of Resolution

article 39 of the UN Charter and therefore acted *ultra vires*.[808] However, an *ultra vires* claim is difficult to justify in legal terms.[809] One must consider the broad discretion the SC enjoys under article 39 and the compatibility with UN practice, which suggest an outcome that the SC acted within the scope of article 39 of the UN Charter.[810] Another question is the check of SC–Res. 1422 *vis-à-vis* article 16. Paragraph 1 clearly makes a reference to a request "consistent with the provisions of Article 16 of the Rome Statute," which indicates the interpretation of the SC. But the interpretation of the Council is not necessarily authoritative; rather a concrete survey has to be carried out.[811]

Resolution 1422 states that "if a case arises involving current or former officials or personnel from a contributing State not a Party to the Rome Statute" the ICC shall not commence or proceed with investigation or prosecution of any such case. The SC assumes that it is able to request a deferral even in the absence of a specific conflict. It *ab initio* defers hypothetical situations and cases that involve Non-States Parties contributing personnel to UN missions.

An interpretation of article 16, including its drafting history, might shed some more light into the issue of blanket deferrals. From its wording, article 16 does not prohibit such an approach.[812] On the other hand, a blanket

---

1422; also Darryl Robinson, "Serving the interests of justice: amnesties, truth commissions and the International Criminal Court" (2003) 14 EJIL 481, 503 with fn. 86. For an overview of the pros and cons Matthias Goldmann/Cornelia Schneider, "ICC case simulation exercise: *Prosecutor v. Five Pilots from Blueland and Whiteland*" (2003) 4 GLJ 815, 819–20.

808 White/Cryer, in Doria/Gasser/Bassiouni, *supra* note 633, 469–70; Kurth, *supra* note 399, 170–1; Herbst, *supra* note 736, 588; Zimmermann/Scheel, *supra* note 784, 142; Stagel, *supra* note 425, 222; Steinberger-Fraunhofer, *supra* note 315, 258; Lavalle, *supra* note 644, 209; Amnesty International, Deferral Report, *supra* note 651, 51 et seq.; El Zeidy, *supra* note 700, 1540; differentiated, Fritsche, in Frowein, *supra* note 679, 115; Andreas Zimmermann, "'Acting under Chapter VII (...)' – Resolution 1422 and possible limits of the powers of the Security Council" in Frowein, *supra* note 679, 262 et seq.

809 Stahn, *supra* note 708, 98; Jochen Frowein, "Issues of legitimacy around the United Nations Security Council," in Frowein, *supra* note 679, 135.

810 Heilmann, *supra* note 74, 229; Deen-Racsmány, *supra* note 745, 377, 381; Gallant, *supra* note 631, 575; Zappalà, *supra* note 651, 119; Zimmermann, in Frowein, *supra* note 808, 266–7. Similarly, Heselhaus, *supra* note 649, 934; Stahn, *supra* note 708, 98 et seq.

811 Stahn, *supra* note 708, 88; Heselhaus, *supra* note 649, 923; Heilmann, *supra* note 74, 231; Amnesty International, Deferral Report, *supra* note 651, 5; Contag, *supra* note 426, 174 et seq.

812 Stahn, *supra* note 708, 88; MacPherson, *supra* note 648; Deen-Racsmány, *supra* note 745, 363; Heselhaus, *supra* note 649, 921; Düker, *supra* note 645, 222.

prohibition of the ICC's exercise of jurisdiction was not the intent or understanding of the drafters.[813] The provision was rather thought to apply to a specific situation or on a case-by-case basis.[814] Article 16 is an exceptional feature under the ICC Statute and must be interpreted narrowly.[815] Thus, a blanket deferral not linked to a particular situation or case is not coherent with article 16.[816] Systematic interpretation confirms a case-by-case (or situation-by-situation) deferral. Article 16 was inserted after articles 13, 14, and 15. This illustrates that – instead of an instrument of preventive action – the SC was supposed to step in once a situation exists.[817] Preliminary inquires cannot be subjected to article 16 deferrals.[818] A teleological approach corroborates the hypothesis that blanket deferrals are not possible. *Ex ante* blanket immunities for a multiplicity of cases are in sharp contrast to the ICC construct. The interpretation of article 16 envisaged by Resolution 1422 would shift practice towards article 23 (3) ILC Draft Statute, enabling the SC to control the ICC's exercise of jurisdiction and turning the careful drafting of article 16 upside down.[819] This amounts to a doubtful modification of the ICC Statute.[820] In sum, despite the notional consistency with article 16, operative paragraph 1 of Resolution 1422 does not fall

---

[813] Young Sok Kim, *The law of the International Criminal Court* (William S. Hein & Co., Buffalo, New York 2007) 142; Bassiouni, *supra* note 401, 131, 141; Sarooshi, in McGoldrick/Rowe/Donnelly, *supra* note 649, 116; Scheffer, *supra* note 783, 351; Stahn, *supra* note 708, 89; Amnesty International, Deferral Report, *supra* note 651, 45 et seq.; Mr. MacKay (New Zealand), The situation in Bosnia and Herzegovina (S/PV.4568), *supra* note 798, 5; Deen-Racsmány, *supra* note 745, 364 et seq.

[814] Mokhtar, *supra* note 681, 329; Deen-Racsmány, *supra* note 745, 366; Heselhaus, *supra* note 649, 924; Frowein, in Frowein, *supra* note 809, 134; Claus Kress, "The International Criminal Court and the United States. Reflections on Resolution 1422 of the UN Security Council" (2003) 77 Art & Thought 56, 58; Mr. Heinbecker (Canada), The situation in Bosnia and Herzegovina (S/PV.4568), *supra* note 798, 4.

[815] Amnesty International, Deferral Report, *supra* note 651, 42 et seq.; Stagel, *supra* note 425, 224; differentiated, however coming to the same result, Deen-Racsmány, *supra* note 745, 364 et seq.

[816] Mokhtar, *supra* note 681, 312–3; Robert Cryer, *Prosecuting international crime: selectivity and the international criminal law regime* (CUP, Cambridge 2005) 227; Heselhaus, *supra* note 649, 939; Zimmermann, in Frowein, *supra* note 808, 271; White/Cryer, in Doria/Gasser/Bassiouni, *supra* note 633, 468–9; Steinberger-Fraunhofer, *supra* note 315, 259; Düker, *supra* note 645, 223; Contag, *supra* note 426, 177. Contrary, Gallant, *supra* note 631, 575.

[817] Stahn, *supra* note 708, 90.

[818] Zimmermann, in Frowein, *supra* note 808, 270. See also Part III, B., V., 3., b), aa).

[819] Heilmann, *supra* note 74, 233; similarly, Heselhaus, *supra* note 649, 930; Ambos, *supra* note 804, para. 4.

[820] Quénivet, *supra* note 658, 45–6.

within the scope of the mentioned article because it grants blanket immunity.[821] A modification or reinterpretation of article 16 is not within the bounds of the powers of the SC.[822] The first operative paragraph of SC-Res. 1422 is therefore not binding on the Court.[823] From the comments above, it can be concluded that pre-emptive application of article 16 is barred in general, not only concerning Resolution 1422.[824]

The legality of paragraph 2 of SC-Res.1422 has also been raised.[825] Operative paragraph 2 "*expresses* the intention to renew the request [...] each 1 July." The "intention clause" is a relict of previous proposals by the US to achieve automatic extension.[826] Since the present wording does not bind SC members, but rather requires a new vote in accordance with article 16, operative paragraph 2 does not legally delimit the ICC's jurisdiction in an improper way.[827] Considerable *de facto* pressure as identified by one author certainly is politically questionable,[828] but SC members are *de jure* free to decide. From the Statute's perspective the intention clause is irrelevant.

It is worthwhile to note that the legality of Resolution 1422 is highly doubtful and, in my view, at least paragraph 1 violates article 16 and as such does not bind the Court. However, no objections to the binding force of Resolution 1422 have been raised before the ICC. Assuming that SC-Res. 1422 was still in force, it would be an ideal case to apply new rule 50*quarter*.[829] As a matter of fact, the disputed Resolution 1422 has expired in 2004,[830] which presently renders further considerations unnecessary.

---

821 Sarooshi, in McGoldrick/Rowe/Donnelly, *supra* note 649, 118; Deen-Racsmány, *supra* note 745, 366; Heilmann, *supra* note 74, 234; Kurth, *supra* note 399, 171 et seq.; Heselhaus, *supra* note 649, 931; Jain, *supra* note 653, 247; Nsereko, *supra* note 741, 503; undecided, Zappalà, *supra* note 651, 120–1; contrary, MacPherson, *supra* note 648.

822 Deen-Racsmány, *supra* note 745, 366 et seq.

823 On the binding force of requests that are invalid under article 16 see already the references in fn. 760.

824 Stahn, *supra* note 708, 90; Stagel, *supra* note 425, 226; Zappalà, *supra* note 651, 119–20.

825 Stahn, *supra* note 708, 92–3; Mokhtar, *supra* note 681, 314 et seq.; El Zeidy, *supra* note 700, 1528–9.

826 Kurth, *supra* note 399, 176; Stagel, *supra* note 425, 226.

827 Kurth, *supra* note 399, 177; Heselhaus, *supra* note 649, 911; Zimmermann, in Frowein, *supra* note 808, 269; contrary, Stagel, *supra* note 425, 227.

828 Stahn, *supra* note 708, 92–3.

829 Thereto Part III, B., V., 3., b), ee).

830 Welcoming the decision not to seek renewal, Amnesty International and Citizens for Global Solutions in CICC, "History and analysis of UN Security Council Resolutions 1422/1487," *supra* note 791, 110–1; also White/Cryer, in Doria/Gasser/Bassiouni, *supra* note 633, 471.

bb) SC-Res. 1497 (2003)

SC-Res. 1497 (2003) authorized the critical deployment of a multinational stabilization force in Liberia and was passed with a 12-0 vote, with France, Germany, and Mexico abstaining.[831] These three abstaining countries argued that operative paragraph 7 was not in accordance with international and national law.[832] The disputed paragraph reads:

The Security Council

[...]

7. *Decides* that current or former officials or personnel from a contributing State, which is not a party to the Rome Statute of the International Criminal Court, shall be subject to the exclusive jurisdiction of that contributing State for all alleged acts or omissions arising out of or related to the Multinational Force or United Nations stabilization force in Liberia, unless such exclusive jurisdiction has been expressly waived by that contributing State.

This provision grants exclusive jurisdiction to States, which are not party to the ICC Statute, and as such bars the ICC from exercising jurisdiction. It goes even as far as giving those States exclusive jurisdiction over its own nationals. This deprives all other States of being able to exercise jurisdiction, including the State of the *locus commissi delicti* (Liberia) and the State of passive nationality (Victim State).[833] First of all, such a regulation is contrary to the principles of passive personality, nationality, and universal jurisdiction.[834] On the other hand, the Draft UN Model Status of Forces Agreement for Peacekeeping Operations recognizes jurisdiction of contributing States.[835] However, as a matter of principal such agreements only grant primary jurisdiction, not exclusive jurisdiction.[836]

The question is again whether the SC acted *ultra vires* or contrary to the ICC Statute. In general, the same arguments mentioned above in the context of SC-Res. 1422 (2002) can be transposed to SC-Res. 1497 (2003). There have been many voices, within the SC as mentioned above and also by legal academics, which question the legality of SC-Res. 1497, in particular regard-

---

831 The situation in Liberia, Security Council, 4803rd meeting, 1.8.2003 (S/PV.4803) 5.

832 The situation in Liberia (S/PV.4803), *supra* note 831, Mr. Aguilar Zinser (Mexico) 2; Mr. Pleuger (Germany) 4; Mr. Duclos (France) 7.

833 Zappalà, *supra* note 656, 673.

834 HRW, "The adoption of Security Council Resolution 1497: A setback for international justice," 1 September 2003, 2; differentiated, Cryer, *supra* note 282, 209.

835 Draft Model Status of Forces Agreement for Peacekeeping Operations, Annex Report of the Secretary General, 9.10.1990 (A/45/594) para. 47 b); Jain, *supra* note 653, 245.

836 Zappalà, *supra* note 656, 673.

ing the immunity provisions that were included.[837] Resolution 1497 further tries to amend the ICC Statute by doing away with the jurisdiction over non-member states under article 12 (2) (a).[838] Nothing in the Charter authorizes the SC to amend another treaty.[839] The exclusion of jurisdiction is not a form of request under article 16.[840] A request under article 16 must be limited for a period of twelve months and asks for a stay of proceedings. In contrast, Resolution 1497 grants absolute immunity from an ICC prosecution.[841]

Since the SC did not act in conformity with article 16, paragraph 7 of Resolution 1497 is not binding on the ICC.[842] In any event, the legality of Resolution 1497 has not been challenged before the ICC or the ICJ so far. Regarding the review power, Resolution 1497 paragraph 7 clearly falls outside the ambit of article 16. In contrast, SC-Res. 1422 was formally phrased as a request under article 16 that could have been reviewed under a new rule 50*quater*.[843] As a consequence, SC-Res. 1497 should be ignored rather then being tested under a new rule 50*quater*. However, if the ICC's jurisdiction is challenged under article 19 (2) with reference to SC-Res.1497, the Judges are able to designate the disputed operative paragraph 7 to be not in conformity with the ICC Statute.

cc) SC-Res. 1593 (2005)

The Darfur Resolution 1593 has been called an initial sign of cooperation between the SC and the ICC.[844] It constitutes the first SC referral under article 13 (b) in the history of the ICC.[845] Operative paragraph 6, drafted in the style of paragraph 7 of SC-Res. 1497, is, however, troubling:

> *The Security Council*
>
> [...]
>
> 6. *Decides* that nationals, current or former officials or personnel from a contributing State outside Sudan which is not a party to the Rome Statute of the International Criminal Court shall be subject to the exclusive jurisdiction of that contri-

---

[837] See, *inter alia,* Jain, *supra* note 653, 244; Heilmann, *supra* note 74, 240 et seq.; Zappalà, *supra* note 656, 674 et seq; Düker, *supra* note 645, 240.

[838] Heilmann, *supra* note 74, 242–3.

[839] Jain, *supra* note 653, 250; contrary Düker, *supra* note 645, 229–30.

[840] Jain, *supra* note 653, 241, 247; Abass, *supra* note 699, 272.

[841] HRW, "The adoption of Security Council Resolution 1497," *supra* note 834, 3.

[842] Coming to the same result, Jain, *supra* note 653, 252–3; Heilmann, *supra* note 74, 243.

[843] Thereto Part III, B., V., 3., b), ee) and c), aa).

[844] Kress, *supra* note 675, 325 et seq.

[845] See already Part III, B., I., 4. and Part III, B., V., 1.

buting State for all alleged acts or omissions arising out of or related to operations in Sudan established or authorized by the Council or the African Union, unless such exclusive jurisdiction has been expressly waived by that contributing State.

Concerns regarding operative paragraph 6 and its consistency with international law and the ICC Statute were mentioned in statements following the formal voting procedure for SC-Res. 1593.[846] In general, the same remarks regarding SC-Res. 1422 and 1497 apply in this context.[847] An additional aspect raised by one author – one that also applies to SC-Res. 1497 above[848] – is this paragraph's consistency with the grave breaches provisions of the Geneva Conventions[849] and the Convention against Torture.[850] These provisions embody *jus cogens* norms[851] and oblige virtually all UN Member States to exercise universal jurisdiction over those responsible for these crimes or to extradite them to a country that will.[852] Assuming that a duty of *jus cogens* character exists, Resolution 1593 abrogates this obligation and asks States to do exactly the opposite. If, for instance, the contributing State has not enacted proper legislation or is not willing to prosecute, the third State is, nevertheless barred from jurisdiction by reason of operative paragraph 6. In this respect, Mr. De La Sablière (France) clarified in his statement after the adoption of Resolution 1593:

---

846 Reports of the Secretary General on the Sudan, Security Council, 5158th meeting, 31.3.2005 (S/PV.5158), Mr. Sardenberg (Brazil) 11; Mr. Baja (Philippines) 6; Mr. De La Sablière (France) 8.

847 In great detail on SC-Res. 1593, see Cryer, *supra* note 282, 209 et seq.; Contag, *supra* note 426, 131 et seq.

848 See, for instance, HRW, "The adoption of Security Council Resolution 1497," *supra* note 834, 2.

849 Articles 49–50 Geneva Convention (I) for the Amelioration of the Condition of the Wounded and Sick in Armed Forces in the Field, 12.8.1949; articles 50–51 Geneva Convention (II) for the Amelioration of the Condition of Wounded, Sick and Shipwrecked Members of Armed Forces at Sea, 12.8.1949; articles 129–130 Geneva Convention (III) relative to the Treatment of Prisoners of War, 12.8.1949; articles 146–147 Geneva Convention (IV) relative to the Protection of Civilian Persons in Time of War, 12.8.1949; article 85 (1) Protocol Additional (I) to the Geneva Conventions of 12 August 1949, and relating to the Protection of Victims of International Armed Conflicts, 8.1.1977.

850 Article 5 Convention against Torture and Other Cruel, Inhuman or Degrading Treatment or Punishment, 26.6.1987.

851 Alexander Orakhelashvili, *Peremptory norms in international law* (OUP, Oxford 2006) 61 et seq.; Stefan Kadelbach, *Zwingendes Völkerrecht* (Duncker & Humblot, Berlin 1992) 71 with numerous references in fn. 15, 249; Andreas Zimmermann, "The exercise of universal jurisdiction in criminal matters" in Christian Tomuschat/Jean-Marc Thouvenin (eds.), *The fundamental rules of the international legal order* (Martinus Nijhoff Publishers, Leiden, Boston 2006) 335, 348–9.

852 Schabas, *supra* note 27, 156; Williams/Schabas, in Triffterer, *supra* note 353, article 13, mn 16; similarly Düker, *supra* note 645, 240.

> "Here, I must emphasize that the jurisdictional immunity provided for in the text we have just adopted obviously cannot run counter to other international obligations of States and will be subject, where appropriate, to the interpretation of the courts of my country."[853]

Irrespective of an *ultra vires* claim, paragraph 6 is in other ways incompatible with the ICC Statute. In its Preamble, SC-Res. 1593 recalls "article 16 of the Rome Statute under which no investigation or prosecution may be commenced or proceeded with by the International Criminal Court for a period of 12 months after a Security Council request to that effect." This express reference might imply article 16 as the SC's legal basis, and a possible interpretation to reconcile the SC's decision with the ICC Statute would be that operative paragraph 6 applies in relation to the ICC for twelve months only.[854] However, article 16 cannot be identified as the SC's legitimate basis. Neither the Resolution itself nor the SC comments indicate any action was taken pursuant to article 16.[855] A request has to be made *specifically* under article 16; a general reference does not suffice. As stated above, a general exclusion of jurisdiction is not a form of request anticipated by article 16.[856] Therefore, paragraph 6 does not constitute a request under article 16. Further, the bar of exercise of jurisdiction by domestic courts of all states (except the national state of the alleged offender) runs counter to the principle of complementarity.[857] For these reasons, operative paragraph 6 is inconsistent with the ICC Statute, and, consequently, is not binding on the ICC.

Resolutions 1422, 1497, and 1593 have not been challenged as a whole or in parts. Scholars preferred that the matter of operative paragraph 6 be resolved as a preliminary matter before any prosecutions were to have taken place.[858] For the sake of clarity such a determination seems desirable at the earliest opportunity. However, the ICC Statute does not explicitly provide for an article 16 review mechanism, for the reason which a new rule 50*quater* is suggested above. If need be, a determination is possible under article 19 (1) according to which the Judges can satisfy themselves that the ICC has jurisdiction. The jurisdictional assessment is limited to "any case brought before it." In other words, article 19 (1) implies that, generally speaking, the Judges test jurisdiction after the issuance of a war-

---

853 Reports of the Secretary General on the Sudan (S/PV.5158), *supra* note 846, 8.

854 Condorelli/Ciampi, *supra* note 633, 596.

855 Heilmann, *supra* note 74, 250; White/Cryer, in Doria/Gasser/Bassiouni, *supra* note 633, 475.

856 See Part III, B., V., 3., c), bb).

857 Condorelli/Ciampi, *supra* note 633, 597.

858 Williams/Schabas, in Triffterer, *supra* note 353, article 13, mn 16.

rant of arrest.[859] Moreover, Resolution 1593 can be subdivided precisely into operative paragraphs 1, 2, and 6. Paragraph 1 provides for the referral of a clear-cut situation in Darfur, paragraph 2 emphasizes a duty of cooperation, and paragraph 6 is the attempt to exclude jurisdiction over certain persons. The paraphrasing of the situation in operative paragraphs 1 and 2 is coherent with the ICC Statute. In sharp contrast, paragraph 6 does not even fall within the ambit of article 16. Instead of being tested under a new rule to review the legality of deferrals, the paragraph should be put aside until, as the case may be, it is invoked under article 19 (2).

In sum, the practice of SC-Resolutions *vis-à-vis* the ICC has been influenced strongly by the early opposition of the United States. Serious attempts to limit the scope of application of the ICC Statute have been proposed, and the conflict relationship can be summarized as the preservation of power for SC members against an independent ICC. Fortunately, SC-Res. 1422 was not extended, putting aside some legality problems. Yet, in particular, operative paragraph 6 of the pending Darfur situation might cause problems. A potential review of operative paragraph 6 is "floating" in the academic world. In reality, a legality review still appears to be a long way off. It remains to be seen how the SC handles article 16 requests in the future, primarily whether the SC uses this tool for its intended purpose – a specific conflict of peace and justice linked to a particular situation or case.

4. Conclusion

In conclusion, article 16 can be seen as the statutory complement to article 13 (b),[860] yet taking into consideration that article 16 can be applied to any situation no matter how it was originally triggered. Articles 16 and 13 (b) grant the SC undeniable possibilities to influence the work of the ICC. However, both norms have to be assessed in the light of the ICC Statute and how the SC's action is embedded in the ICC system. Article 13 (b) is one of three equal trigger mechanisms. While acknowledging the strong mandate under a SC referral, the basic procedure is identical. First and foremost, the principle of complementarity applies to SC referrals. Before initiating a formal investigation, article 53 (1) has to be tested by the Prosecutor. In any event, SC referrals still constitute the ICC's fast-track proceed-

---

[859] Part III, B., IV., 4.; similarly, Hall, in Triffterer, *supra* note 376, article 19, mn 3.

[860] Of course, article 16 applies to all investigations and prosecutions, no matter how the situation was originally triggered (State referral, SC referral, and *proprio motu*).

ings – they avoid article 18 determinations, for example – and provide for stronger cooperation enforcement mechanisms.

Article 16 allows the SC to defer ICC proceedings for a period of twelve months. In making use of this power, the SC does not operate in a legal vacuum and is constrained by the requirements of article 16.[861] Some loopholes with regard to article 16 have been identified, and could be closed by new rules 50*bis, ter,* and *quarter*. The introduction of an explicit review norm, in particular, would change things for the better. Article 16 was thought to be an exceptional norm, operated carefully by the SC. Practice has shown the opposite. None of the adopted Resolutions 1422, 1497, and 1593 are entirely in conformity with the UN Charter and the ICC Statute. The expansion of ICC States Parties, as well as the newly elected US government, hopefully will improve the relationship of the SC and ICC. Resolution 1593 was a first step towards complementing each other and interacting in a mutual fight against impunity, ideally leaving judicial matters to the Court and political sensitive issues to the SC.

VI. *Proprio motu* power – article 15 analysis

1. Introduction

Article 15 deals with one of the three ways of initiating an investigation established under article 13 (c). It provides for the Prosecutor's *proprio motu* power and sets out the manner in which a preliminary examination initiated pursuant to this power is carried out.[862] The expression *proprio motu* may be understood as "on his own motion." The Prosecutor is solely responsible for an investigation of a situation referred by a State Party or the Security Council, but if the Prosecutor acts *proprio motu* the decision to proceed with an investigation must be authorized by the PTC (article 15 (3)).[863]

The exact preconditions of article 15 are complex and require a precise analysis of its subparagraphs (see below 3.–8.). Article 15 is one of the most delicate provisions of the ICC Statute.[864] Moreover, article 15 is a gateway to both the preliminary examination process with regard to all three trigger mechanisms (Part III, C.) and the evaluation for opening a full

[861] Kleffner, *supra* note 370, 289. On the legality of article 16 *vis-à-vis* the UN Charter Steinberger-Fraunhofer, *supra* note 315, 234 et seq.

[862] Art. 15 (2); similarly rule 104, which deals with SC referrals and State referrals; see further Part III, C., I.

[863] Calvo-Goller, *supra* note 10, 157.

[864] *Situation in Kenya*, Decision pursuant to article 15, *supra* note 6, para. 17, 7.

investigation (Part III, C., II.). For the moment, four preconditions for the *proprio motu* trigger mechanism can be identified:

(1) information analysis conducted through the OTP;

(2) a positive determination of "reasonable basis to proceed" by the Prosecutor;

(3) a request for authorization of the investigation;

(4) authorization through the PTC upon examination of the "reasonable basis to proceed."

2. Drafting history

Initial International Law Commission discussions did not provide for prosecutorial *proprio motu* power and provided only for State Party and SC referrals.[865] Only one member suggested that "the Prosecutor should be authorized to initiate an investigation in the absence of a complaint if it appears that a crime apparently within the jurisdiction of the Court would otherwise not be duly investigated."[866] This view changed slightly during the 1995 *Ad Hoc* Committee debates, when it was suggested that the Prosecutor should be given the power to initiate investigations and prosecutions.[867] Some delegations held the view that such an expanded role would "enhance the independence and autonomy of the prosecutor, who would be in a position to work on behalf of the international community rather than a particular complainant State or the Security Council."[868]

A first draft proposal of the article was adopted at the Preparatory Committee's 1996 session,[869] followed by article 25*bis*,[870] which was subse-

[865] ILC Draft Statute 1994, *supra* note 353, article 21, 79–80; article 23, 84–5; article 25, 89; also Kirsch/Robinson, in Cassese/Gaeta/Jones, *supra* note 450, 658; Fernández de Gurmendi, in Lee, *supra* note 382, 175; Bergsmo/Pjeić, in Triffterer, *supra* note 321, article 15, mn 1; Danner, *supra* note 953, 513. See recently on the drafting history WCRO report "situation" and case selection, *supra* note 370, 14 et seq., 18–9; Schabas, *supra* note 13, 315 et seq.

[866] ILC Draft Statute 1994, *supra* note 353, Commentary on article 25, para. 4, 90.

[867] Report of the *Ad Hoc* Committee 1995, *supra* note 379, para. 25, 5; Kirsch/Robinson, in Cassese/Gaeta/Jones, *supra* note 450, 659; Fernández de Gurmendi, in Lee, *supra* note 382, 176–7.

[868] Report of the *Ad Hoc* Committee 1995, *supra* note 379, para. 113, 25–6; Bergsmo/Pjeić, in Triffterer, *supra* note 321, article 15, mn 2.

[869] Report of the Preparatory Committee 1996, Vol. 2, *supra* note 357, 109, article 25*quat* which reads: "The Prosecutor shall initiate investigations *ex officio* or on the basis of information obtained from any source, particularly from Governments, United Nations organs, intergovernmental and non-governmental organizations. The

quently reproduced without change in article 46 of the Zutphen Draft Statute.[871] But the Preparatory Committee's 1996–1998 sessions were characterized by opposing and sometimes intractable debates,[872] finally resolved by a joint Argentine-German proposal of 25 March 1998[873] which found general support by the majority of States. This proposal limited the Prosecutor's preliminary examinations to information received from other parties (e. g. States, organizations, victims, or other reliable sources) to determine whether there was a reasonable basis for investigation.[874] In addition, the PTC would have to approve the matter if it was satisfied that i) there was a "reasonable basis to proceed," ii) that the case "appears to fall within the jurisdiction of the Court," and iii) that it was admissible, "having regard to article 11."[875] The current version of article 15 is largely identical to the Argentine-German proposal, except that is leaves out the duty to assess admissibility.[876]

While the idea of a trigger mechanism for the Prosecutor initially received tentative support, this support steadily increased and was identified as a "cornerstone" objective of the so-called like-minded States by 1997.[877] By the time of the last Preparatory Committee meetings from March to

Prosecutor shall assess the information received or obtained and decide whether there is sufficient basis to proceed."

870 Decision taken by the Preparatory Committee, *supra* note 385, 9–10. Article 25*bis* states: "The Prosecutor [may] [shall] initiate investigations [ex officio] [proprio motu] [or] on the basis of information [obtained] [he may seek] from any source, in particular from Governments, United Nations organs [and intergovernmental and non-governmental organizations]. The Prosecutor shall assess the information received or obtained and decide whether there is sufficient basis to proceed. [The Prosecutor may, for the purpose of initiating an investigation, receive information on alleged crimes under article 20 (a) to (d) from Governments, intergovernmental and non-governmental organizations, victims and associations representing them, or other reliable sources.]"

871 Zutphen Draft Statute 1998, *supra* note 358, article 46 [25*bis*], 110–1.

872 Proceedings of the Preparatory Committee during the period 25 March–12 April 1996, *supra* note 381, paras. 32–34, 8–9; Report of the Preparatory Committee 1996, Vol. 1, *supra* note 203, paras. 149–151, 35; Fernández de Gurmendi, in Lee, *supra* note 382, 177–8.

873 Proposal submitted by Argentina and Germany, article 46, Information submitted to the Prosecutor, 25.3.1998, Preparatory Committee on the Establishment of the International Criminal Court, 25.3.1998, Working group on procedural matters, 16 March–3 April 1998 (A/AC.249/1998/WG.4/DP.35).

874 Kirsch/Robinson, in Cassese/Gaeta/Jones, *supra* note 450, 660; Fernández de Gurmendi, in Lee, *supra* note 382, 183–4; Danner, *supra* note 953, 514–5.

875 Proposal submitted by Argentina and Germany, *supra* note 873, para. 2; Bergsmo/Pjeić, in Triffterer, *supra* note 321, article 15, mn 5.

876 Bergsmo/Pjeić, in Triffterer, *supra* note 321, article 15, mn 5.

877 Kirsch/Robinson, in Cassese/Gaeta/Jones, *supra* note 450, 659; Ambos, in Bohlander, *supra* note 10, 434; Schabas, *supra* note 27, 160.

April 1998, there were still two solid, opposing positions: the like-minded States supporting the issue of a *proprio motu* power and the delegations with concerns about a separate prosecutorial triggering power.[878]

It is worth noting that the idea of judicial review was introduced during the 1996 Preparatory Committee session.[879] The Prosecutor would have to submit the matter to the Chamber, which would then decide in an *in camera* and confidential procedure whether the issue should be pursued or dropped.[880]

The Argentine-German proposal was incorporated into article 13 of the Draft Statute submitted to the Rome Conference.[881] During the Rome Conference, 76 percent of the participating countries – in total numbers 61 States – supported a *proprio motu* power.[882] Yet, it was unclear until the end of the negotiations whether the proposition would survive.[883] The first of two Bureau papers attempted to narrow down the drafting options, and presented two alternatives: option 1 included a *proprio motu* trigger under PTC supervision and option 2 did away with the entire article.[884] The second Bureau paper retained option 1, suggesting the drafting of an additional provision containing further safeguards on the Prosecutor's ability to act.[885] Notwithstanding opposition by some States, e.g. the United States, China, India, and Japan,[886] article 15 was adopted.[887] The negotiating history,

---

878 Bergsmo/Pjeić, in Triffterer, *supra* note 321, article 15, mn 4.

879 Proceedings of the Preparatory Committee during the period 25 March–12 April 1996, *supra* note 381, para. 33, 8–9.

880 Report of the Preparatory Committee 1996, Vol. 1, *supra* note 203, para. 150, 35; Fernández de Gurmendi, in Lee, *supra* note 382, 182–3; Bergsmo/Pjeić, in Triffterer, *supra* note 321, article 15, mn 3.

881 Draft Statute, April 1998, *supra* note 44, article 13, 37–8. Article 12 still contained the draft version based on article 46 [25*bis*] Zutphen Draft Statute.

882 CICC, "The numbers, NGO coalition special report on country positions," The Monitor, No. 36, May – October 2008, 11.

883 Bergsmo/Pjeić, in Triffterer, *supra* note 321, article 15, mn 6.

884 Bureau Discussion Paper, *supra* note 361, 14–5.

885 Bureau Proposal, *supra* note 695, 12–3.

886 See the statements opposing a *proprio motu* power in Official Records, Vol. II, *supra* note 392: Mr. Owada (Japan) para. 46, 67; Mr. Lahiri (India) para. 50, 86; Mr. Rubinstein (Israel) para. 40, 99; Mr. Vengadesan (Malaysia) para. 50, 109; Mr. Al-Thani (Qatar) para. 66, 110; Mr. Sayyid Said Hilal Al-Busaidy (Oman) para. 70, 110; Mr. Liu Daqun (China) para. 39, 124; Mr. Güney (Turkey) para. 44, 124; Mr. Alhadi (Sudan) para. 77, 126; Mr. Ayub (Pakistan) para. 95, 128; Mr. Nathan (Israel) para. 111, 201; Mr. Scheffer (United States of America) para. 125 et seq., 202; Mr. Gevorgian (Russian Federation) para. 133, 203, para. 114, 301; Mr. Gadyrov (Azerbaijan) para. 71, 299; Mr. Nguyen Ba Son (Viet Nam) para. 52, 308; Mr. Kerma (Algeria) para. 76, 309; Mr. Al-Shaibani (Yemen) para. 82, 310; Mr. de Saram (Sri Lanka) para. 11, 314; Mr. Mahmood (Pakistan) para. 18, 315; Mr. Ahmed (Iraq)

especially US opposition to the Prosecutor's triggering power, may explain the restrictions imposed on the Prosecutor. It does not, however, explain why the Prosecutor had not invoked its *proprio motu* until initiating the Kenyan situation in late 2009.

3. Initiation of pre-investigations (paragraph 1)

Article 15 (1) states that the Prosecutor "may initiate investigations *proprio motu*." The term "may" suggests discretion at first sight. Some commentators have therefore stated that the Prosecutor's initiation right is "unconditional and discretionary, but carefully balanced by the need for authorization by a Pre-Trial Chamber."[888]

---

para. 22, 315; Mr. Hadi (United Arab Emirates) para. 30, 316; Mr. Mirzaee Yengejeh (Islamic Republic of Iran) para. 42, 317; Mr. Peraza Chapeau (Cuba) para. 69, 331; Mr. El Masry (Egypt) para. 6, 335; Mr. Nega (Ethiopia) para. 63, 341.

[887] See the statements in favor of a *proprio motu* power in Official Records, Vol. II, *supra* note 392, Mr. Axworthy (Canada) para. 65, 68; Mr. Telička (Czech Republic) para. 24, 74; Mr. Wako (Kenya) para. 66, 77; Ms. Nagel Berger (Costa Rica) para. 77, 78; Mr. Baja (Philippines) para. 9, 82; Mr. Dabor (Sierra Leone), para. 53, 87; Mr. Tjiriange (Namibia) para. 58, 87; Mr. Sommaruga (Observer for the International Committee of the Red Cross) para. 71, 89; Mr. Dini (Italy) para. 3, 91; Mr. Hashim (Brunei Darussalam) para. 14, 91; Mr. Fall (Guinea) para. 19, 92; Mr. Görög (Hungary) para. 21, 92; Mr. van Mierlo (Netherlands) para. 53, 100; Mr. Frieden (Luxembourg) para. 69, 101; Mr. Jensen (Denmark) para. 4, 114; Mr. Slade (Samoa) para. 62, 109; Mr. Adamou (Niger) para. 76, 110; Mr. Agius (Malta) para. 14, 115; Ms. Kleopas (Cyprus) para. 43, 117; Mr. Dorsen (Observer for the Lawyers Committee for Human Rights) para. 79, 119; Mr. Perrin de Brichambaut (France) para. 47, 189; Mr. Rowe (Australia) para. 116, 201; Ms. Wong (New Zealand) para. 120, 202; Mr. Stigen (Norway) para. 136, 203; Mr. Manongi (United Republic of Tanzania) para. 7, 204; Mr. Kaul (Germany) para. 15, 204; Ms. Blokar (Slovenia) para. 20, 205; Mr. Brown (Trinidad and Tobago) para. 24, 296; Ms. Fernández de Gurmendi (Argentina) para. 39, 297; Mr. Wenaweser (Liechtenstein) para. 93, 300; Mr. Moussavou Moussavou (Gabon) para. 104, 300; Mr. Arevalo (Chile) para. 119, 301; Mr. Rwelamira (South Africa) para. 123, 301; Mr. Maiga (Mali) para. 154, 303; Prince Zeid Ra'ad Zeid Al Hussein (Jordan) para. 159, 303; Mr. Choi Seunghoh (Republic of Korea) para. 165, 303; Mr. Da Gama (Guinea-Bissau) para. 171, 303; Mr. da Costa Lobo (Portugal) para. 20, 306; Mr. Hafner (Austria) para. 24, 307; Ms. Shahen (Libyan Arab Jamahiriya) para. 32, 307; Ms. Mokitimi (Lesotho) para. 40, 307; Ms. O'Donoghue (Ireland) para. 55, 308; Ms. Daskalopoulou-Livada (Greece) para. 63, 309; Mr. Deguenon (Benin) para. 72, 309; Mr. Vergne Saboia (Brazil) para. 86, 310; Ms. Lento (Finland) para. 97, 311; Mr. Tafa (Botswana) para. 4, 313; Ms. Wyrozumska (Poland) para. 12, 314; Ms. Peralba Garcia (Andorra) para. 13, 314; Mr. Larrea Dávila (Ecuador) para. 14, 315; Ms. Simone (Armenia) para. 23, 215; Ms. Reffi (San Marino) para. 32, 316; Mr. Onkelinx (Belgium) para. 40, 330; Mr. Jurgelevičius (Lithuania) para. 60, 340; Mr. Jeichande (Mozambique) para. 71, 341; Ms. Talvet (Estonia) para. 76, 342; Mr. Zappalà (Bosnia and Herzegovina) para. 40, 347.

The drafting history provides little clarification: article 25*quat* of the Preparatory Committee's Draft of 1996 used the word "shall;"[889] in contrast, the later draft of article 25*bis* and article 46 Zutphen Draft Statute 1998 respectively bracketed both words "shall" and "may."[890] The Draft Statute of April 1998 incorporated the version with both terms in brackets ("[may] [shall]") into article 12, whereas the version of article 13 did not contain the part that currently forms the first paragraph of article 15.[891] Once again, the Bureau papers set the course by including only the word "may" in option 1 of both papers.[892]

However, the discretion granted has to be seen in the context of the terms "initiate investigations" and "*proprio motu*." The Prosecutor may not start *full* investigations, but can only initiate *pre-investigations* on his own.[893] "Investigations" within paragraph 1 should not be misconstrued; paragraph 6 refers to "the preliminary examination referred to in paragraphs 1 and 2."[894] Article 15 (1) investigations are distinguishable from the (full) investigation stage governed by article 54. The expression "*proprio motu*" thus allows the Prosecutor to act on his own initiative without any formal referral or duty to initiate.[895] Furthermore, article 13 (c) names article 15 as one of three trigger mechanisms, on equal footing with articles 13 (a), 14, and article 13 (b). Therefore, the discretion meant by paragraph 1 covers the right of the Prosecutor to initiate pre-investigations only.

The discretionary right under paragraph 1 must further be assessed in the context of the following subparagraphs of article 15. Subparagraph 2 requires the Prosecutor to analyze information received ("shall analyse"). If, after careful evaluation, the Prosecutor concludes that there is a reasonable basis to proceed with a full investigation, he must ("shall") submit a request for authorization to the PTC pursuant to article 15 (3). In addition, if a reasonable basis is not satisfied, the Prosecutor must ("shall") inform the information providers of this fact in accordance with article 15 (6). Determining what constitutes a "reasonable basis" is partially determined by rule 48,

---

888 Bergsmo/Pjeić, in Triffterer, *supra* note 321, article 15, mn 9.

889 Report of the Preparatory Committee 1996, Vol. 2, *supra* note 869, 357, 109, article 25*quat*.

890 Cf. already fn. 870 and fn. 871 with the corresponding text.

891 Draft Statute, April 1998, *supra* note 44, articles 12 and 13.

892 Bureau Discussion Paper, *supra* note 361, article 12, option 1, 14–5; Bureau Proposal, *supra* note 695, article 12, option 1, 12–3.

893 Bergsmo/Pjeić, in Triffterer, *supra* note 321, article 15, mn 9–10.

894 Bergsmo/Pjeić, in Triffterer, *supra* note 321, article 15, mn 10; Razesberger, *supra* note 371, 61. Surprisingly, the latter author argues elsewhere (at 70–1) that "initiation of investigation" is the same under article 15, 18, and 53.

895 Bergsmo/Pjeić, in Triffterer, *supra* note 321, article 15, mn 11.

linking article 15 (3) to the criteria of article 53 (1).[896] These provisions ensure, in addition to article 42 (1), a careful preliminary inquiry by the OTP. Inaction or arbitrary exercise is clearly out of bounds.[897] It has to be noted that the pre-investigation stage, i.e. the phase in which information is analyzed to assess whether there is a reasonable basis to proceed (articles 15 (3) and 53 (1), rules 48 and 104), has to be conducted with respect to all three trigger mechanisms.[898] For some, these procedural mandates create a general duty to commence preliminary examinations.[899]

The balance between unconditional discretion on the one hand and a duty to start pre-investigations on the other can be found at the midway point between the two. The OTP enjoys substantial discretion to start inquiries on its own initiative (article 15 (1)). However, this power should, as shown above, be interpreted narrowly in view of articles 15 (2)–(6) and 53 (1). Unfettered discretion applies only to pre-investigations initiated on the Prosecutor's own authority, in other words, if he decides to start autonomous inquiries on information he gained knowledge of, but that was not formally submitted under article 15 (2).[900] Here, the Prosecutor enjoys a wide range of discretion. However, the Prosecutor is still bound to reach a determination of reasonable basis at some point. In this respect, the OTP emphasizes its independence and holds rigid timetables on when to reach such a "reasonable basis" determination as not being in conformity with the statutory framework.[901] The Prosecutor is in the difficult position of finding an operable balance between capacity overload and the duty to prosecute "the most serious crimes of concern to the international community," as reflected in preambular paragraph 4, articles 1 and 5 (1). Additional facets of this question will be addressed in the different context of choosing situations and cases for full investigation and prosecution.[902] With regard to pre-investigations, however, the Prosecutor is obliged to operate thorough examinations of communications ("information received") and referrals.[903] Discretion can be located in paragraph 1, but must be limited to that same

[896] See further Part III, C.

[897] Bergsmo/Pjeić, in Triffterer, *supra* note 321, article 15, mn 9.

[898] OTP Regulation 25; Annex paper, *supra* note 27, 3–4, 7; see already fn. 27. In more detail Part III, C.

[899] Wouters/Verhoeven/Demeyere, *supra* note 156, 294.

[900] On autonomous information (liberal interpretation) against information received as embracing only formally submitted information (narrow interpretation) see Part III, B., VI., 4.

[901] Annex paper, *supra* note 27, 3.

[902] See the discussion at Part IV, B. II., 1.–6.

[903] Besides the already mentioned statutory provisions, OTP Regulations 25 and 26 strengthen this argument. Coming to the same conclusion, van Heeck, *supra* note 26, 154–5.

paragraph. The discretionary power is confined by a contextual interpretation, and thus cannot be extended to the initiation of pre-investigations as a whole.

As mentioned above, "investigations" refers only to preliminary examination. To bring the evaluation of paragraph 1 to a close, this finding needs to be further dismantled and put into perspective *vis-à-vis* articles 53 (1) and 18. On their face, article 53 ("initiate an investigation") and article 18 ("initiates an investigation pursuant to articles 13 (c), 15") use identical wording to article 15 (1). But article 18 only applies *after* a determination of reasonable basis has been made.[904] The Prosecutor does not have to notify States when he initiates preliminary examinations.[905] Article 53 is systematically located in part 5 dealing with (full) investigations and prosecutions. Moreover, article 42 (1) distinguishes between "examining them" (referrals and substantiated information) and "conducting investigations and prosecutions."[906] Article 15 deals with the *initiation* of investigations, while article 53 concerns the decision to *start* investigations and prosecutions.[907] On the other hand, a purely literal interpretation renders both articles equal.[908] The latter view can be rebutted by adopting a systematic interpretation with reference to article 15 (6), as already outlined above. Nonetheless, the differentiation of *initiating* investigations in opposition to *starting* investigations is insufficiently precise. When the preliminary examination is concluded, the Prosecutor moves towards the realm of formal investigations under article 15 (3), and the decision of the PTC to authorize full investigations under article 15 (4) is on equal footing with article 53 (1). Article 15 therefore embraces two different levels: first, the pre-investigation method referred to in paragraphs 1, 2, and 6, and second, a stage to start full investigations and formally cease pre-investigations, as indicated by paragraphs 3, 4, and 5. One should therefore speak of pre-investigations versus full investigations, but not strictly link these stages to articles 15 *vis-à-vis* 53. These articles (partly) overlap and form one pre-investigation phase that applies to all three trigger mechanisms and culminates in a determination to start a (full) investigation.[909] Be that as it may, the terminology of article 15 (1) has to be interpreted, in light of article 15 (6), as referring to pre-investigation steps only.

---

904 Nsereko, in Triffterer, *supra* note 425, article 18, mn 7. See also Part III, B., IV., 4.

905 Stigen, *supra* note 205, 126.

906 Morten Bergsmo/Pieter Kruger, "Article 53" in Triffterer, *supra* note 37, article 53, mn 5.

907 Bergsmo/Kruger, in Triffterer, *supra* note 906, article 53, mn 10.

908 Razesberger, *supra* note 371, 70–1.

909 On the relationship between article 15 and 53 see further Part III, C., I.

4. Analysis of communications (paragraph 2)

According to article 15 (2), "the Prosecutor shall analyze the seriousness of the information received." In its early practice, the OTP used the term "communication" as shorthand for "information on crimes within the jurisdiction of the Court."[910] The term "communications" is not statutory language, and it should not be interpreted as limiting the neutral term "information received." The newly drafted OTP Regulations depart from the term "communication" from a legal perspective; thus, the OTP seems to acknowledge the legal notion of "information received" while still using the term "communications" in practice.[911]

Moreover, the term "shall" indicates a legal duty to analyze all information received by the OTP. A qualified member of the OTP must, therefore, analyze all incoming communications.[912] If the information justifies invoking article 15, the OTP is under a statutory obligation to conduct a preliminary examination.

Assuming such a duty, it is necessary to specify the possible types of communications. In order to make this determination, we must ask two questions: first, whether there is a minimum requirement to qualify as a "communication," and second, how to assess the term "seriousness." The ICC Statute is silent on the required content of the communication.[913] The sender cannot be required to make an extensive inquiry, but overly general and broad information might not allow the Prosecutor to successfully launch a full investigation.[914] Article 42 (1) speaks of "substantiated information," which could indicate a specific threshold. However, the term "information" appears to be more neutral and broad than "complaint" or "communication." In this respect, the term "information" should take precedence over the term "communication," that was introduced by the OTP as a working term. From a textual interpretation, "information" includes *inter alia* "knowledge derived from study, experience, or instruction" and "knowledge of specific events or situations that has been gathered or received by communication, intelligence or news."[915] Contextually, article 15 (1) speaks of

---

910 Annex paper, *supra* note 27, 1. See also the references in fn. 321.

911 Cf. fn. 321.

912 Annex paper, *supra* note 27, 4; Bergsmo/Pjeić, in Triffterer, *supra* note 321, article 15, mn 13; Stigen, *supra* note 205, 102. For an interpretation of article 15 (1) in the light of article 15 (2) and (6) see already Part III, B., VI., 3.

913 Wouters/Verhoeven/Demeyere, *supra* note 156, 294.

914 Annex paper, *supra* note 27, 2; Wouters/Verhoeven/Demeyere, *supra* note 156, 294.

915 Cf. Free Online Dictionary by Farlex, "information," <www.thefreedictionary.com/information>.

"information on crimes," article 15 (6) mentions "information provided" and "information submitted," article 42 refers to "substantiated information of crimes," and rule 46 names "information provided." Therefore, it is clear that the Prosecutor needs some sort of information as a basis. However, we need to determine whether the information has to be submitted to the Prosecutor by external sources or whether he can also start preliminary investigations based on information gathered by the OTP through other means, e.g. through the media without any formal submission. To provisionally summarize, the term "information" could be interpreted as:

(1) involving a minimum legal threshold;

(2) embracing all information formally submitted;

(3) covering any information on crimes that comes to the knowledge of the OTP.

A minimum threshold comparable to the articles 15 (3) and 53 (1) "reasonable basis" standard or the article 58 (1) (a) "reasonable grounds" standard was not explicitly included. The fact that the "seriousness" *shall be analyzed* implies some degree of action by the OTP instead of an *ex ante* legal threshold. In addition, the gathered information is thought to form the basis for a decision of the Prosecutor under article 15 (3) and does not require precise reference to an entire situation. From a teleological approach, a narrow interpretation that introduces a legal threshold before the initiation of a preliminary inquiry must be rejected. In the same vein, commentators have concluded that "information" is a broad term that covers *all* incoming information.[916] OTP practice strengthens this finding; so far the OTP has adopted a policy of approving all communications at least to the initial review phase and sending a minimum response to all information providers.[917] Taking a glance at the country analysis,[918] the competent national organs generally carry out some form of pre-investigation with regard to complaints received and only decide subsequently whether to dismiss the complaints or start full investigations.

It remains to be decided whether information must be formally submitted. In general, communications shall be addressed to the IEU by mail, email, or facsimile.[919] All received referrals, information on crimes, and declarations are registered and stored by the OTP (OTP Regulation 26). The

---

916 Bergsmo/Pjeić, in Triffterer, *supra* note 321, article 15, mn 13.

917 Update on communications, *supra* note 316, 1 et seq. On the preliminary examination process, in particular the OTP's phases, see further Part III, C.

918 Annex 2.

919 See <www2.icc-cpi.int/Menus/ICC/Structure+of+the+Court/Office+of+the+Prosecutor/Comm+and+Ref/>.

Services Section, in particular the IEU, is responsible for information management.[920] All information provided shall be treated as confidential (rule 46). Nevertheless, article 15 (1) allows for a broader interpretation, since the Prosecutor may initiate investigations on the basis of "information on crimes." On the other hand, it could be argued – in the context of article 15 (2) and (6) – that the Prosecutor's activity at the preliminary stage is limited only to passively "seeking" and "receiving" information.[921] "Information received" would thus only cover information submitted by a natural or legal person. In my view, the latter approach is too stringent. If the Prosecutor gains knowledge of information on crimes through the media, he should not be restricted to a formal receipt. It would be an unnecessary formality to bargain for some form of submission. The purpose of article 15 was to enable the Prosecutor to initiate an investigation on his own. Under article 15 (2) clause 2, the OTP can seek additional information from appropriate sources. As a result, a very broad interpretation is suggested according to which "information" amounts to any information of which the OTP becomes aware.

When starting a preliminary examination, the first main task will be to analyze the seriousness of the information. The question is how "seriousness" can be defined. Synonyms and related words regarding "seriousness" are "thoughtfulness," "importance," "significance," "severity," "weightiness," and "gravity."[922] Antonyms worth mentioning are "frivolousness"[923] and "triviality, unimportance."[924] In its analysis, the OTP shall apply a consistent and objective methodology for source evaluation and the evaluation of information. This methodology includes taking into account *inter alia* the reliability of the source and the credibility of the information and examining information from multiple sources as a means of bias control (OTP Regulation 24). Accordingly, the OTP must conduct quality source evaluation, based on the terms "reliability" and "credibility." In assessing these terms, it is necessary to consider the literal dimension. Starting with "reliability," reliable evidence is synonym to "dependable, good, well founded, well grounded, authentic, definitive, attested, valid, genuine, from the horse's mouth, sound, true" as opposed by "unreliable," "untrustworthy," or "dodgy."[925] Similarly, "credibility" lists synonyms of "plausibility," "be-

920 OTP Regulation 10; Provisional Analysis Regulations 3 and 4, Annex paper, *supra* note 27, 9.

921 Stigen, *supra* note 205, 102; Olásolo, *supra* note 29, 58.

922 Oxford Thesaurus of English, 2nd revised edition (OUP, Oxford 2006) "seriousness," 781.

923 Free Online Dictionary by Farlex, "seriousness," <www.thefreedictionary.com/information>.

924 Oxford Thesaurus of English, *supra* note 922, *ibid.*

lievability," "weight," "authenticity," or "trustworthiness."[926] The underlying test has been described as a "purely evidentiary test, as opposed to one of appropriateness."[927]

From a terminological perspective, the three terms "seriousness," "reliability," and "credibility," cannot be distinguished easily and their characterizations overlap. However, these terms clearly oppose frivolousness, unimportant, and untrustworthy information. The statutory term used with regard to information underlying all three trigger mechanisms (article 15 (2), rule 104 (1)) is seriousness, while the two terms of reliability and credibility were mainly introduced by the OTP through its regulations.[928] It might be questioned whether the implementation provides substantive assistance in determining "seriousness," and whether the terms can be legally differentiated. The inspection of both – the source and the information itself – admittedly refines the test.

From a literal interpretation, it seems necessary to proceed to systematic and teleological considerations. A stated above, the term "seriousness" does not constitute an additional *ex ante* threshold to initiating a preliminary examination, but rather circumscribes the steps taken by the OTP upon receipt of information. Within the preliminary examination, the OTP has to reach a conclusion whether there is a "reasonable basis" to proceed. If the information does not provide sufficient guidance for such a determination, the analysis will be concluded and the information provider shall be informed.[929] Therefore, seriousness should not be evaluated in an isolated manner, but must instead be seen in the context of the factors in article 53 (1), i.e. there is a reasonable basis to believe that a crime has been or is being committed, that the crime is within the ICC's jurisdiction, that the case is admissible (and sufficiently grave), and that the "interests of justice" are served. Seriousness is thus systematically linked to article 53 (1) and forms the evidentiary basis to approach its legal criteria.

Furthermore, the OTP has taken the teleological approach that "analysis occurs at different levels, depending on the seriousness of the information."[930] In its early practice, the OTP has differentiated three stages of analysis with regard to communications and two (corresponding) stages for

---

925 Oxford Thesaurus of English, *supra* note 922, "reliable," 722–3.

926 Oxford Thesaurus of English, *supra* note 922, "credibility," 184–5.

927 Bergsmo/Pjeić, in Triffterer, *supra* note 321, article 15, mn 13.

928 Yet, the term "other reliable sources" was already used in article 15 (2) and rule 104 (2).

929 Annex paper, *supra* note 27, 3; Wouters/Verhoeven/Demeyere, *supra* note 156, 295.

930 Update on communications, *supra* note 316, 3.

referrals.[931] Hence, the OTP introduced a system of three consecutive phases based on the seriousness of information.[932] The OTP's newly introduced permanent regulations contain no corresponding phases (OTP Regulation 27). A formal distinction between three different stages solely based on seriousness is, therefore, supported by neither the Statute nor ancillary documents. While a broad analysis of the OTP's phases *vis-à-vis* the ICC Statute is conducted elsewhere,[933] it appears legally difficult to interpret "seriousness" as generating a three-tiered test. The OTP's approach should be interpreted solely as a description of the OTP's internal working process. In the course of action, all factors of article 53 (1) need to be taken into consideration sequentially, and the phases overlap.[934]

In conclusion, "seriousness" provides a tool for screening and evaluating the information. It is an evidentiary assessment linked to the legal factors of article 53 (1). Moreover, from the literal approach it can be deduced that "seriousness" implies some degree of sincerity.[935]

The second sentence of article 15 (2) spells out that the Prosecutor "may seek additional information from States, organs of the United Nations, intergovernmental or non-governmental organizations, or other reliable sources that he or she deems appropriate, and may receive written or oral testimony at the seat of the Court." The Prosecutor enjoys discretion ("may") in his decision to seek further information; he is absolutely free to decide whether additional information should be requested from the source that provided the information, from other sources, or from both.[936] This discretion notwithstanding, the investigative steps mentioned in article 15 (2) are limited. These steps have to be taken into account when analyzing the seriousness of the information received and their object has to be additional information on the initial, insufficient allegations.[937] Rule 104 (2) repeats the measures of article 15 (2), introducing the same method for State referrals and SC referrals. For this reason, inquiries into the exact content of the methods (e.g. the scope of receiving testimony at the seat of the Court) are located within the preliminary examination process as a whole.[938]

---

931 Annex paper, *supra* note 27, 7.

932 Regulations 4–6 of the Provisional Analysis Regulations, Annex paper, *supra* note 27.

933 Cf. Part III, C., III. and IV.

934 Update on communications, *supra* note 316, 3 with fn. 5 and 7.

935 For "seriousness," as allowing the OTP to deal with manifestly ill-founded communication on an expedited basis, see Part III, C., IV.

936 Turone, in Cassese/Gaeta/Jones, *supra* note 26, 1149.

937 Bergsmo/Pjeić, in Triffterer, *supra* note 321, article 15, mn 14.

938 Part III, C.

5. Submission to the PTC/Victim's representations (paragraph 3)

When the Prosecutor concludes preliminary investigations and wishes to proceed, he shall request PTC authorization of an investigation pursuant to article 15 (3). Paragraph 3 of article 15 refers to a full investigation, in other words, the Prosecutor continues the inquiry into alleged criminal conduct by means of a full investigation with the associated powers under article 54.[939] If the situation was triggered by article 13 (c), article 15 (3) and (4) are mandatory steps to proceed from a preliminary investigation to the stage of a formal investigation. However, if the situation was triggered through articles 13 (a) or (b), paragraphs (3) and (4) of article 15 do not apply and the Prosecutor proceeds to a full investigation through article 53 (1).[940] In practice, the reliance on self-referrals had made it unnecessary to seek approval under article 15 (3).[941] The recent Kenyan situation has now clarified article 15 proceedings to some extent.[942]

The Prosecutor's determination is one of "reasonable basis." Although the determination is left entirely to the Prosecutor, he must be aware of the fact that the PTC will subsequently apply the same test under article 15 (4).[943] The content of reasonable basis is the same under article 15 (3), (4) and article 53 (1), which is restated by rule 48.[944] If the Prosecutor has found that a reasonable basis exists, the term "shall submit [...] a request" implies that such a submission is mandatory.[945] This however, is only partially correct. If the Prosecutor concludes that there is a reasonable basis to proceed then he has no discretion in applying to the PTC. On the other hand, the incorporation of article 53's criteria, above-all the "interests of justice," into the Prosecutor's final determination provides an opening for prosecutorial discretion.[946]

---

939 Bergsmo/Pjeić, in Triffterer, *supra* note 321, article 15, mn 18.

940 Bergsmo/Pjeić, in Triffterer, *supra* note 321, article 15, mn 18.

941 Stahn, in Stahn/Sluiter, *supra* note 156, 273.

942 Cf. *Situation in Kenya*, Decision pursuant to article 15, *supra* note 6.

943 Bergsmo/Pjeić, in Triffterer, *supra* note 321, article 15, mn 19.

944 Olásolo, *supra* note 29, 67; *Situation in Kenya*, Decision pursuant to article 15, *supra* note 6, para. 21, 10; also Part III, C., I. and II. Although rule 48 explicitly only mentions article 15 (3), it is implied that the standard of paragraph 4 is identical with the one set by paragraph 3, see Bergsmo/Pjeić, in Triffterer, *supra* note 321, article 15, mn 27. See further on the reasonability standard Part IV, B., II., 3.

945 Stigen, *supra* note 205, 105; Bergsmo/Pjeić, in Triffterer, *supra* note 321, article 15, mn 22; contrary Schabas, *supra* note 13, 321-2.

946 Stigen, *supra* note 205, 105; Bergsmo/Pjeić, in Triffterer, *supra* note 321, article 15, mn 22. See further the discussion on discretion at Part IV, B., II.

A request for authorization shall be made in writing (rule 50 (2)). Court Regulation 49 (1) (a) mandates that the request shall contain "a reference to the crimes which the Prosecutor believes have been or are being committed and a statement of the facts being alleged to provide the reasonable basis to believe that those crimes have been or are being committed," and under Court Regulation 49 (1) (b) there must be "a declaration of the Prosecutor with reasons that the listed crimes fall within the jurisdiction of the Court." According to Court Regulation 49 (2), the statement of facts referred to in Court Regulation 49 (1) (a) shall indicate:

(a) the places of the alleged commission of the crimes, e.g. country, town, as precisely as possible;

(b) the time or time period of the alleged commission of the crimes; and

(c) the persons involved, if identified, or a description of the persons or groups of persons involved.

If possible, the annex to the activation request should include a chronology of relevant event, maps detailing relevant information (including the location of the alleged crimes), and an explanatory glossary of relevant names of persons, locations and institutions (Court Regulation 49 (3)). Court Regulation 38 (1) (e) established a 100 page limit for the document requesting the authorization of an investigation under article 15 (3).

Together with the request for an authorization, the OTP shall submit "any supporting material collected" (article 15 (3)). The collected material will be primarily gathered pursuant to article 15 (2), and "collected" does not exclude initial information received.[947] If construed narrowly, the phrase "any supporting material" does not necessarily mean "any and all." Under this interpretation, the Prosecutor would only be obliged to forward as much supporting material as is required to show the PTC that the conclusion under article 15 (3) is well-founded.[948] However, "supporting material" cannot be reduced to cover only material that supports the OTP's findings, which would allow for purposeful withholding of information that does not support the OTP's conclusion.[949] This would be inconsistent with article 54 (1) (a) that requires the Office to investigate "incriminating and exonerating circumstances equally." Article 15 (3) requires the OTP to attach to its request all the information gathered through the preliminary examination.[950] Therefore, the Prosecutor has to forward all relevant information to the PTC that supports – or potentially disproves – his conclusion

947 Bergsmo/Pjeić, in Triffterer, *supra* note 321, article 15, mn 23.

948 Bergsmo/Pjeić, in Triffterer, *supra* note 321, article 15, mn 23.

949 Stigen, *supra* note 205, 105.

950 Olásolo, *supra* note 29, 66.

under article 15 (3). In accordance with rule 46, supporting material can be submitted as a confidential attachment to the request.[951]

A particular important feature of article 15 (3) is that it permits victims to make representations, helping the victims to have a voice in proceedings.[952] It is clear that victims may bring information to the attention of the OTP under article 15 (1) and (2).[953] As a logical corollary of the role of victims in *proprio motu* investigations generally, article 15 (3) provides for a specific participation tool during early proceedings.[954] The second sentence of article 15 (3) enables victims to address the PTC during the authorization process in accordance with rule 50. When the Prosecutor intends to seek a request under article 15 (3), all victims known to the Prosecutor or to the Victims and Witnesses Unit must be informed under rule 50 (1). Such a notice was given for the first time in the situation of Kenya.[955] Rule 50 (1) places an extensive obligation on the Prosecutor, who might ultimately be required to notify a broad number of victims.[956] The notification duty placed on the Prosecutor is thus greater than that found in many domestic jurisdictions.[957] However, the Prosecutor can refrain from informing any victims at all if he decides "that doing so would pose a danger to the integrity of the investigation or the life or well-being of victims and witnesses."[958] The Prosecutor may also give notice by general means in order to reach groups of victims. Although the term "general means" was intentionally left undefined, thus giving full discretion to the Prosecutor, such notice could include a media communiqué or informing victim's groups, civil communities, or organizations representing victi-

951 Informal expert paper: Fact-finding and investigative functions, *supra* note 472, para. 34; Olásolo, *supra* note 29, 66.

952 Kirsch/Robinson, in Cassese/Gaeta/Jones, *supra* note 450, 662; Schabas, *supra* note 13, 322.

953 WCRO Report Victim Participation, *supra* note 495, 20; Bergsmo/Pjeić, in Triffterer, *supra* note 321, article 15, mn 24; Stahn/Olásolo/Gibson, *supra* note 370, 226; Alison Marston Danner, "Enhancing the legitimacy and accountability of prosecutorial discretion at the International Criminal Court" (2003) 97 AJIL 510, 516; Holmes, in Cassese/Gaeta/Jones, *supra* note 666, 667, 680.

954 Stahn/Olásolo/Gibson, *supra* note 370, 225; *Situation in Kenya*, Order to the Victims Participation and Reparations Section concerning victims' representations pursuant to article 15 (3) of the Statute, 10.12.2009 (ICC-01/09-4) 3.

955 OTP public notice: victims of post-election violence in Kenya have 30 days to make representations to ICC in the Hague, 23.11.2009; OTP weekly briefing, 17.–23. November 2009, Issue # 14, 25.11.2009, 1; *Situation in Kenya*, Order to the VPRS, *supra* note 954, para. 4, 3.

956 Stahn/Olásolo/Gibson, *supra* note 370, 227.

957 Stahn/Olásolo/Gibson, *supra* note 370, 228.

958 Guhr, *supra* note 495, 135; *Situation in Kenya*, Order to the VPRS, *supra* note 954, para. 4, 3.

mized communities.[959] Following notification under rule 50 (1), victims may make representations in writing according to rule 50 (2) and (3). They have to adhere to a time limit of 30 days following the notification under rule 50 (1), pursuant to rule 50 (3) and Court Regulation 50 (1).[960] In addition, Court Regulation 38 (2) (a) limits the documents submitted by victims under article 15 (3) and rule 50 (3) to 50 pages. Under rule 50 (4), the Chamber may request additional information from the Prosecutor and from any of the victims who have made representations and "if it considers appropriate, may hold a hearing.[961]" It is worth noting that, at this participation stage, situations as opposed to cases form the object of proceedings.[962] Given the importance of the victims' views within the statutory framework, newly introduced OTP Regulation 16 points out that "[t]he Office shall, in coordination with the Victims Participation and Reparations Section of the Registry, as appropriate, seek and receive the views of the victims *at all stages* of its work in order to be mindful of and to take into account their interests (emph. added)."[963] As a result, victims already play an important role during pre-investigations and their views are taken into consideration from the start of OTP action. Thereby, article 15 (3) and rule 50 ensure that victims have an adequate say in the important PTC authorization decision. Beyond these rights, however, formal victim participation during pre-investigations should be limited to those proceedings specifically provided for in the ICC Statute.[964] In a similar vein, the Appeals Chamber has established that victims are not entitled to participate generally in the investigation of a situation.[965] Most recently, Pre-Trial Chamber II re-emphasized the limited scope of victims' participation during authorization procedures under article 15.[966]

---

959 John Holmes, "Jurisdiction and admissibility" in Roy Lee (ed.), *The International Criminal Court: Elements of Crimes and Rules of Procedure and Evidence* (Transnational Publishers, Ardsley 2001) 321, 333.

960 *Situation in Kenya*, Order to the VPRS, *supra* note 954, para. 5, 4.

961 See, for a request from the Prosecutor, *Situation in Kenya*, Decision requesting clarification and additional information, 18.2.2010 (ICC-01/09-15).

962 Stahn/Olásolo/Gibson, *supra* note 370, 227. On the differentiation situation v. case, see already Part III, B., III.

963 Accordingly, the Prosecutor has expressed his intent to systematically seek the views of victims and local communities during all stages of proceedings in its OTP strategy, *supra note* 409, 8.

964 For an endorsement of limiting victim participation during the whole investigation (embracing pre- and full investigations), see Guhr, *supra* note 495, 139, and De Hemptinne/Rindi, *supra* note 495, 347 et seq., who both outline the dangers inherent to a broad interpretation of article 68 (3); also Policy paper on victim participation, *supra* note 496, 8.

965 *Situation in DRC*, Judgment on victim participation in the investigation stage, *supra* note 496, para. 59; Policy paper on victim participation, *supra* note 496, 8.

966 *Situation in Kenya*, Order to the VPRS, *supra* note 954, para. 9, 5.

6. Authorization to commence the full investigation (paragraph 4)

The power to authorize a full investigation based upon *proprio motu* initiation lies with the PTC alone. While the Prosecutor may initiate the pre-investigation, it is the PTC's prerogative to start a formal investigation.[967] From the moment the PTC authorizes the formal investigation, the OTP is entitled to use its powers under article 54.[968] Decisions under article 15 (4) can be appealed by the Prosecutor in accordance with article 82 (1) (a) or (d), but not by States or victims.[969]

The PTC is either composed of three Judges or a single Judge in accordance with article 39 (2) (b) (iii). A ruling issued under article 15 requires a majority of Judges pursuant to article 57 (2) (a), and therefore all three Judges must decide on the authorization request. Under rule 50 (5), the Chamber may issue a decision, including its reasons, authorizing "all or any part of the request of the Prosecutor." The PTC must also give notice to victims who have made representations. The applied test is one of reasonableness, which is identical to the standard set by articles 15 (3) and 53 (1).[970] Since the underlying purpose of the PTC check is to control for frivolous or politically motivated charges, there is a presumption in favor of a reasonable basis to proceed to a full investigation if the Prosecutor demonstrates the application of basic standards and an objective investigation strategy.[971] Article 15 (4) is primarily a filtering mechanism to distinguish those situations that should form the subject of investigations from those that should not.[972]

The phrase "considers that the case appears to fall within the jurisdiction of the Court" causes confusion. First, the provision was drafted in an imprecise manner because, at the given stage, the OTP is concerned with situations as opposed to cases. The term "case" should not be read in isolation from the rest of article 15 and must be put into perspective regarding the preliminary phase. From a systematic and teleological interpretation, I suggest that – contrary to its wording – article 15 (4) deals with situations and that the term "case" is simply misplaced.[973] Second, the phrase "ap-

[967] Bergsmo/Pjeić, in Triffterer, *supra* note 321, article 15, mn 25.

[968] Olásolo, *supra* note 29, 69.

[969] Olásolo, *supra* note 29, 70.

[970] See already *supra* note 944. Further Part IV, B., II., 3.

[971] Bergsmo/Pjeić, in Triffterer, *supra* note 321, article 15, mn 25; Stigen, *supra* note 205, 107 ("quality check").

[972] See *Situation in Kenya*, Request for authorization, *supra* note 207, para. 111, 40, with various references in fn. 106.

[973] See the references in *supra* note 376.

pears to fall within jurisdiction of the Court" could suggest a second measuring stick along with the "reasonable basis to proceed" standard given in articles 15 (3) and 53 (1). Similarly, 15 (4) could go beyond 15 (3), as the jurisdictional requirements are wider. The Chamber need not find all jurisdictional requirements satisfied due to the wording "the case *appears* to fall within the jurisdiction (emph. added)."[974] In addition, since the PTC's determination will be "without prejudice to subsequent determinations by the Court with regard to the jurisdiction and admissibility of a case" under article 15 (4) *in fine,* a thorough examination is not required at this stage and can take place at a later stage via article 19.[975] Yet, the reasonable basis standard is used for all three trigger mechanisms to move from pre-investigations to full investigations. "Reasonable basis" appears in articles 15 (3), (4), and 53 (1). Rule 48 introduces the criteria of article 53 (1) into article 15 (3), which strongly suggests that the "reasonable basis" standard is identical in article 15 (4).[976] PTC II recently clarified the procedure to some extent. It applied the exact standard on the basis of which the Prosecutor arrived at his conclusion.[977] The Chamber therefore saw no need to duplicate its assessment of jurisdiction and was satisfied by a review of article 53 (1).[978] In conclusion, the Judges decided not to give any particular meaning and weight to the additional clause "[...] and that the case appears to fall within the jurisdiction of the Court [...]."

7. Subsequent requests (paragraph 5)

Article 15 (5) deals with the PTC's refusal to accept the Prosecutor's request to authorize a full investigation. According to this provision, the OTP may bring subsequent requests "based on new facts or evidence regarding the same situation." When the PTC denies an authorization according to article 15 (4), the preliminary examination is generally terminated. If the Prosecutor discovers new facts or evidence, article 15 (5) enables him to analyze the seriousness in accordance with article 15 (2) and, if he concludes that there is a reasonable basis, to submit a new request to the PTC pursuant to article 15 (5).[979] Rule 50 (6) clarifies that the new request is subject to the same procedure as the original request.

---

974 Bergsmo/Pjeić, in Triffterer, *supra* note 321, article 15, mn 25–6; *Situation in Kenya*, Request for authorization, *supra* note 207, para. 107, 38–9.

975 Bergsmo/Pjeić, in Triffterer, *supra* note 321, article 15, mn 26; *Situation in Kenya*, Request for authorization, *supra* note 207, para. 107, 38–9.

976 Similarly, Olásolo, *supra* note 29, 67.

977 *Situation in Kenya*, Decision pursuant to article 15, *supra* note 6, para. 24, 12.

978 *Situation in Kenya*, Decision pursuant to article 15, *supra* note 6, paras. 68–9, 30.

One might argue that the PTC has to authorize the OTP to continue monitoring the situation at hand, and that, without authorization, the OTP is prevented from reopening preliminary examinations *proprio motu.*[980] However, this reading is too strict and does not find support in the wording of article 15 (5), which leaves to the discretion of the Prosecutor whether new information gathered justifies re-evaluating the situation. Such newly discovered facts and evidence must relate to the criteria in article 53 (1) and must have the potential of convincing the PTC that a reasonable basis now exists.[981] The PTC has to ensure that the request is based on new information; in other words, case law must give substance to the term "new" facts or evidence regarding the same situation. A stricter approach would impermissibly limit the OTP's ability to collect and examine important evidence. If violence erupts in a situation that has not been authorized, the OTP needs certain flexibility to organize its own procedural agenda. In such a case, the OTP should be able to monitor the old situation, undertake an evaluation, and file a new request for authorization under article 15 (5). Systematically, no provision gives the PTC the power to authorize or deny monitoring as such. This would amount to direct interference in the preliminary examination process that is the Prosecutor's domain.

To summarize, the PTC has to authorize the Prosecutor's proceeding from pre-investigation to full investigation, and thereby the Chamber has a strong supervision power. Any new request for formal investigations is subject to the same procedure, granting the PTC ultimate decision-making power. That the OTP must convince the PTC of its findings is self-evident, be these original pursuant to article 15 (3), or be it subsequent requests under article 15 (5). Misuse of the tool under article 15 (5) is, therefore, unlikely, especially given how article 42 (2) grants the OTP the right to decide how to use its resources. The integrity of pre-investigations must be respected and the monitoring of situations is solely the Prosecutor's decision.

8. Duty to notify information providers (paragraph 6)

Final paragraph 6 regulates the procedure if the Prosecutor concludes – after preliminary examinations – that there is no reasonable basis to proceed. In the case of a negative decision, "he or she shall inform those who provided the information." The duty to notify those who provide information is a statutory obligation. Pursuant to rule 49 (1), such notification must be given promptly and must include reasons for the decision. Rule 105 (2)

---

979 Bergsmo/Pjeić, in Triffterer, *supra* note 321, article 15, mn 29.

980 Olásolo, *supra* note 29, 69.

981 Stigen, *supra* note 205, 108.

emphasizes the application of rule 49 if the Prosecutor decides not to submit a request under article 15 (4).[982] Safeguards are provided in rule 49 (1), which provides that the Prosecutor shall give notice "in a manner that prevents any danger to the safety, well-being and privacy of those who provided information to him or her under article 15, paragraphs 1 and 2, or the integrity of investigations or proceedings." In accordance with OTP Regulation 28, the OTP may decide to make public negative decisions in relation to a preliminary examination. To date, the Prosecutor has published two such responses in Iraq and Venezuela.[983] According to rule 49 (2), the OTP has to formally advise the informant that further information regarding the same situation can be submitted if new facts and evidence come into play. Victims, however, have no right to legal remedy against a decision under article 15 (3) or (4),[984] nor can they participate in a review procedure of a negative decision of the Prosecutor under article 15 (3).[985] A proposal by the French delegation aimed at granting victims the status of a procedural party *stricto sensu,*[986] but was rejected.[987] On the other hand, the PTC may review a decision of the Prosecutor not to proceed with an investigation or prosecution, either at the request of a referring party, or on its own initiative pursuant to article 53 (3).[988] Despite the fact that the form of participation for victims in article 53 (3) proceedings is not expressly determined by rules 89–91, victims should be granted a minimum of participatory rights given that their views ("interest of the victims") shall be taken into account when the "interests of justice" is determined.[989] To conclude, while victims

---

[982] It is submitted that rule 105 (2) is unnecessary given the fact that – if the Prosecutor reaches a final negative decision on reasonable basis under article 15 (3) – a negative decision on the authorization request is logically the next step and triggers the notification duty under article 15 (5) and rule 49 (1).

[983] See *supra* note 333 and corresponding text.

[984] Hoffmeister/Knoke, *supra* note 169, 801; Olásolo, *supra* note 29, 115; Håkan Friman, "Investigation and prosecution," in Lee, *supra* note 959, 493, 498.

[985] For considerable pro- and con arguments regarding a review power, see Stahn/Olásolo/Gibson, *supra* note 370, 229–30. Elsewhere, Olásolo, *supra* note 29, 65, comes to the conclusion that the con arguments prevail. See further Part III, C., I.

[986] Proposal submitted by France concerning part 2 of the Rome Statute of the International Criminal Court, jurisdiction, admissibility and applicable law, 23.11.1999 (PCNICC/1999/WGRPE/DP.43) rules concerning article 15, 2–5; cf., for instance, rule 2.9 (a) that states: "It [the PTC] may, acting on its own motion or at the request of the Prosecutor *or the victims,* hold a hearing (emph. added)."

[987] Olásolo, *supra* note 29, 115; Holmes, in Lee, *supra* note 959, 332–3. In favor of a more limited formal victim participation, see Guhr, *supra* note 495, 124.

[988] This review is, however, limited to proceedings based on SC and State referrals, and cannot be extended to reviews of a decision not to request authorization, cf. Part III, C., I.

that have given information under article 15 have to be informed, they have no right to legal remedy and limited participatory rights.

Another question relates to the breadth of the statutory obligation under article 15 (6). "Those who provided the information" could be interpreted narrowly as to refer only to the original providers of information under article 15 (1).[990] The duty under article 15 (6) would then only pertain to the party that filed the communication; but nothing would prevent the Prosecutor from notifying other parties simultaneously.[991] To the knowledge of this author, the OTP has taken a wider approach, even if such a statutory obligation might not exist. It addresses notification letters to all of the following:

(1) the individual or organization submitting the initial communication;

(2) any other person or organization from whom the Chief Prosecutor has sought additional information under article 15 (2); and

(3) any other person who has given written or oral testimony at the seat of the Court under article 15 (2).

The latter OTP approach is welcomed. From a literal interpretation, the phrase "those who provided the information" is not clear. Rule 49 (1) names article 15 (1) and (2), which systematically favors an inclusion of all information providers. A teleological interpretation, however, only supports the minimum finding that at least the party that filed the communication under article 15 (1) must be notified. The broad information policy followed by the OTP guarantees statutory compliance on the one hand while providing further information to other parties as well.

9. Intermediary conclusion regarding article 15

The alternative trigger mechanism under article 15 has been called a "very valuable and welcome addition to the Statute."[992] This independent mechanism ensures the OTP's independence from States and the SC.[993] The Prosecutor has been given a tool to initiate investigations himself, yet he has not made sufficient use of it so far; this has been criticized.[994] His reluctance must be seen in connection with the checks and balances that were

---

989 Stahn/Olásolo/Gibson, *supra* note 370, 233 et seq. See further Part IV, B., III., 3., d), bb).

990 Bergsmo/Pjeić, in Triffterer, *supra* note 321, article 15, mn 30.

991 Stigen, *supra* note 205, 109.

992 Kirsch/Robinson, in Cassese/Gaeta/Jones, *supra* note 450, 664.

993 Kirsch/Robinson, in Cassese/Gaeta/Jones, *supra* note 450, 662–3.

994 Part III, B., IV., 6.

introduced to ensure the responsibility in its exercise.[995] The PTC's approval was understood as a safeguard against politically motivated investigations by the OTP. In the light of the practice of self-referrals and given the political nature of the SC, it would seem that the *proprio motu* trigger mechanism is actually the least politicized triggering procedure.[996] Nevertheless, the PTC's check imposes restrictions on the OTP that cannot be bypassed easily. Moreover, the exact content and scope of PTC intervention remains blurry and creates considerable insecurity for the Prosecutor. Triggering procedures provided for in article 15 are unusually long and complex, in contrast with the fast-track triggering when the SC or a State makes a referral.[997] It remains to be seen if and how the Prosecutor's first article 15 investigation in Kenya resolves some sore spots. In any event, the future development of the case law on article 15, especially that dealing with the relationship between PTC and the OTP, will be interesting to watch.

10. Article 12 (3) declarations

Article 12 (3) refers to *ad hoc* acceptance of jurisdiction by a Non-State Party of the ICC. The provision requires such a State to lodge a declaration with the Registrar. At the request of the Prosecutor, the Registrar may even inquire on a confidential basis as to whether a State intends to make such a declaration (rule 44 (1)). The Registrar shall then inform the State of the consequences in accordance with rule 44 (2) and, more importantly, that their acceptance of jurisdiction entails the obligation of the State to cooperate with the Court.[998]

With regard to the trigger mechanism, the manner in which declarations fit in the threefolded triggering system (State referral, SC referral, *proprio motu*) needs to be addressed. In a second step, the ambiguous term "crime in question" requires clarification.

Declarations under article 12 (3) do not trigger ICC action, but rather provide for a supplementary mechanism to attribute jurisdiction.[999] As a re-

---

[995] On the checks and balances see Kirsch/Robinson, in Cassese/Gaeta/Jones, *supra* note 450, 663; Bergsmo/Pjeić, in Triffterer, *supra* note 321, article 15, mn 7; Cassese, *supra* note 675, 161; Guariglia, in Lee, *supra* note 14, 233 et seq.

[996] In the same vein, Kirsch/Robinson, in Cassese/Gaeta/Jones, *supra* note 450, 663.

[997] Olásolo, *supra* note 29, 89–90, who also makes some proposals for reform.

[998] This flows from article 12 (3) and rule 44 (1).

[999] Olásolo, *supra* note 29, 138 et seq.; Steinberger-Fraunhofer, *supra* note 315, 184; also Visit of the Palestinian National Authority, *supra* note 318, 1; Ronan, *supra* note 318, 10; for the Palestinian declaration see Schabas, *supra* note 13, 290.

sult, "the main effect of article 12 (3) declarations is the extension of the personal, temporal and territorial scope of the Court's dormant jurisdiction."[1000] Declarations are lodged with the Registrar as opposed to the Prosecutor. The declarations themselves do not constitute State referrals or communications under article 15 (1).[1001] Moreover, SC referrals are not bound by article 12 (3) because the SC has the power to refer any possible situation.[1002]

To classify the norm properly, the distinction between a State and Non-State Party is essential. A referral under articles 13 (a) and 14 can only be made by "a State Party." This does not include States who have accepted the ICC's jurisdiction on an *ad hoc* basis.[1003] It is hence clear that Non-States Parties have to report crimes under article 15, which leads to a treatment as *proprio motu* information by the OTP.

States Parties are free to refer situations in third States that might not be a party to the ICC Statute. In this case, the Prosecutor may ask the Non-State Party under scrutiny if it is willing to lodge a declaration under article 12 (3).[1004] However, it must be re-emphasized that "self-referrals" by Non-States Parties can only be treated as *proprio motu* information under article 15 (1), since the right to make State referrals is limited to member States only. In practice, the question arose in the situation of the Côte d'Ivoire that accepted the jurisdiction of the ICC for crimes committed on its territory since 19 September 2002. The Côte d'Ivoire situation is treated as *proprio motu* information,[1005] despite imprecise terminology used by the OTP.[1006] OTP Regulation 25 (1) states that the preliminary examination and evaluation of a situation may be *initiated* by information on crimes, referrals and declarations. The term "declarations" should be deleted in OTP Regulation 25 (1) which covers the initiation of analysis. Preliminary

---

1000 Olásolo, *supra* note 400, 296; Carsten Stahn/Mohamed El Zeidy/Héctor Olásolo, "Developments at the International Criminal Court: The International Criminal Court's *ad hoc* jurisdiction revisited" (2005) 99 AJIL 421, 423.

1001 Olásolo, *supra* note 29, 142; Stahn/El Zeidy/Olásolo, *supra* note 1000, 424.

1002 See Part III, B., V. with fn. 631. Similarly, Junck, *supra* note 204, mn 150.

1003 Olásolo, *supra* note 29, 142; Sharon Williams/William Schabas, "Article 12" in Triffterer, *supra* note 37, article 12, mn 17.

1004 Thereto Stéphan Bourgon, "Jurisdiction *ratione loci*" in Cassese/Gaeta/Jones, *supra* note 133, 559, 566.

1005 Williams/Schabas, *supra* note 1003, article 12, mn 17; Visit of the Palestinian National Authority, *supra* note 318; also Part III, B., I., 5. with corresponding fn. 317.

1006 Instead of naming the exact trigger, the Office refers to one situation under analysis "pursuant to a declaration of acceptance" (Côte d'Ivoire). See Update on communications, *supra* note 316, 4; OTP Report on activities 2003–2006, *supra* note 23, 10; OTP strategy, *supra note* 409, 7.

analysis is started on the basis of one of the three triggers (information on crimes, SC referral, or State referral), but is never *based* on a declaration as such.

In closing, the declaration of a State Party, expanding the Court's temporal jurisdiction under articles 11 (2), 12 (3), has to be integrated into the triggering procedure. For instance, let us take a look at the declaration lodged by Uganda,[1007] which names two distinguishable time periods. The first is the time period after the entry into force for the relative State, which is unproblematic since Uganda is a State Party with all statutory rights from 1 September 2002 onwards. The second is the period between 1 July 2002 (entry into force of the ICC Statute) and 1 September 2002 (entry into force for the State in question), during which Uganda was a Non-State-Party. If it were not now a State Party, the crimes committed in Uganda between 1 July 2002 and 1 September 2002 would be regarded as *proprio motu* information, but equally the crimes committed after 1 September 2002 would have to be based on an additional declaration accepting the Court's jurisdiction. One might therefore assume that, in general, article 12 (3) declarations are treated as *proprio motu* triggering.[1008]

The phrase "accept the exercise of jurisdiction by the Court with regard to the crime in question" has given rise to concerns with regard to the effect of article 12 declarations. From a purely literal interpretation, it was feared that a scenario could arise in which a State could make a declaration with respect to a specific crime while other crimes, i.e. crimes committed by its own nationals, were not included and therefore would not fall within the jurisdiction.[1009] Such a narrow interpretation could only be supported if the "crime is question" is understood to mean a "specific incident" or a "single crime."[1010] It can, however, be said that a purely literal understanding is contrary to a systematic and teleological interpretation, especially in light of articles 13, 14, 15, 18, and 53, and the careful introduction of the

---

1007 Uganda has lodged a "Declaration on Temporal Jurisdiction" with respect to crimes committed in between 1 July 2002 and 1 September 2002 (entering into force of the Statute for Uganda), cf. *Prosecutor v. Kony et al.*, Warrant of Arrest for Joseph Kony, *supra* note 251, para. 32; Williams/Schabas, *supra* note 1003, article 12, mn 17; Schabas, *supra* note 13, 290.

1008 Stahn/El Zeidy/Olásolo, *supra* note 1000, 426.

1009 Holmes, in Lee, *supra* note 959, 326; Olásolo, *supra* note 29, 138–9; Junck, *supra* note 204, mn 156. The United States argued that article 12 (3) would allow Saddam Hussein to invoke the Court's jurisdiction for crimes committed by the United States in Iraq, yet prevent it from doing the same with crimes committed by the regime itself, see Williams/Schabas, *supra* note 1003, article 12, mn 17.

1010 Hans-Peter Kaul, "Preconditions of the exercise of jurisdiction," in Cassese/Gaeta/Jones, *supra* note 133, 583, 611; Williams/Schabas, *supra* note 1003, article 12, mn 17.

triggering procedure, whose targets are situations as opposed to specific incidents.[1011] In addition, the drafters clearly aimed at an interpretation in the sense of a "situation in question."[1012] A sensible reading of article 12 (3) thus rules out any abusive and one-sided use of declarations; article 12 (3) refers to a category of conduct rather than to a specific incident.[1013]

In any event, previous concerns are allayed by the newly drafted rule 44 (2).[1014] Rule 44 (2) clarifies that "[...] the declaration under article 12, paragraph 3, has as a consequence the acceptance of jurisdiction with respect to the crimes referred to in article 5 of relevance to the situation [...]." As a result, the ICC is now able to exercise jurisdiction over entire situations, not specific incidents or crimes, if a declaration under article 12 (3) is lodged.[1015]

VII. Conclusion on the trigger mechanisms

The threefold trigger mechanism before the ICC is a complex feature and no such procedure was provided for at the *ad hoc* tribunals. Self-referrals have dominated early practice. A critical evaluation of early OTP practice shows that self-referrals are *legally* possible under the statutory framework. The *policy* decision, however, to actively seek such referrals has been rightly criticized by several authors. It could seriously damage the reputation of the ICC in the certain countries, especially if the impression arises that the Court's investigations are one-sided.

It might be argued that a hierarchy between the three different triggers has emerged. If one emphasizes the importance of cooperation with the Court, one may draw a line from the strongest mandate (SC referral) to a less secure mandate (State referrals), and finally to the least secure mandate (*proprio motu* authority).[1016] This would equal three different categories:

1011 Olásolo, *supra* note 29, 139.

1012 Kaul, in Cassese/Gaeta/Jones, *supra* note 1010, 611.

1013 Wedgwood, *supra* note 423, 102.

1014 In the same vein, Olásolo, *supra* note 29, 139; Stahn/El Zeidy/Olásolo, *supra* note 1000, 427 et seq.; Holmes, in Lee, *supra* note 959, 327; Junck, *supra* note 204, mn 162. See further Williams/Schabas, *supra* note 1003, article 12, mn 17, that name one author (Jack Goldsmith) who still claims that – even with rule 44 (2) – the problem persists; also Schabas, *supra* note 13, 288-9.

1015 Critically evaluating the compatibility of rule 44 (2) *vis-à-vis* the ICC Statute (and answering the question in the affirmative), see Junck, *supra* note 204, mn 166 et seq.

1016 Chris Gallavin, "Prosecutorial discretion within the ICC: under the pressure" (2006) 17 CLF43, 49–50. Gallavin further states that self-referrals provide the OTP with a greater mandate than third State referrals.

first class of *notitia criminis* (SC referral), second class of *notitia criminis* (State referral), and third class of *notitia criminis* (*proprio motu*).[1017] Arguments in favor of such a formal hierarchy include embracing the strong control position of the SC.[1018] Indeed, SC referrals are procedurally different and can be described as a "fast-track" procedure (limitations of article 12 (2) do not apply, for example) *vis-à-vis proprio motu* triggering (specific authorization required).[1019]

Some advance the argument that cooperation issues favor self-referrals over *proprio motu* triggering. I do not find this argument persuasive as the cooperation amounts to *prima facie* cooperation which evaporates as soon as the Prosecutor decides to investigate against State officials. These arguments notwithstanding, this potential *de facto* hierarchy is merely a consideration of *Realpolitik*. The ICC Statute did not intend to create a legal hierarchy (or priority) amongst the three trigger mechanisms that are available to the Prosecutor. Articles 13, 14, and 15 distinguish the trigger mechanisms by the origin of the referral, i.e. State Parties, SC, or any other source. Nowhere can one find an obligation or even an incentive for the Prosecutor to prioritize one mechanism over another.[1020] From a statutory approach, a *legal* hierarchy does not exist. In practice, the Prosecutor has welcomed the SC referral for Darfur, he has preferred self-referrals over *proprio motu* triggering in Uganda and DRC, and he had negotiated for a self-referral in Kenya before considering a *proprio motu* investigation.[1021] A self-referral even allows a State to position itself at the top of the Prosecutor's agenda: the referral "jumps the queue."[1022] Considering the fact that the *proprio motu* power is likely to be the least politicized mechanism,[1023] it would most certainly be better for the OTP's reputation and independence if the Prosecutor re-evaluated his initial practice. The establishment of a transparent process of the treatment of article 15 communications would certainly enhance such a policy change.[1024]

1017 Turone, in Cassese/Gaeta/Jones, *supra* note 26, 1144–5.

1018 Turone, in Cassese/Gaeta/Jones, *supra* note 26, 1144, also Brubacher *supra* note 368, 77.

1019 Turone, in Cassese/Gaeta/Jones, *supra* note 26, 1144–5; concurring Razesberger, *supra* note 371, 59–60.

1020 Ms. Jeanne Sulzer, Coordination of the FIDH Legal Action Group, *supra* note 554; FIDH, FIDH statement on the prosecutorial strategy of the OTP of the ICC, Ms. Jeanne Sulzer, 18.10.2006, 3.

1021 See *supra* note 536 and corresponding text.

1022 Wouters/Verhoeven/Demeyere, *supra* note 156, 284; see already fn. 352.

1023 Kirsch/Robinson, in Cassese/Gaeta/Jones, *supra* note 450, 663; see already above Part III, B., VI., 9.

1024 In a similar vein ("[…] the OTP would gain credit by establishing a transparent process of the treatment of article 15 communications and by deciding on guid-

C. Preliminary examination process

Regardless of the trigger mechanism, the first duty of the Prosecutor is to reach a determination about whether there is a reasonable basis to start a full investigation. It is the pre-investigation stage at which this determination is made.[1025] This raises two additional questions for consideration: first, we must outline the *method* of preliminary examination, taking into account potential differences with regard to the three trigger mechanisms. Here, the relationship between article 15 and 53 must be addressed (I.), because the general method and criteria are laid out in article 15 (2) and 53 (1).[1026] Second, the evaluation *criteria* have to be outlined (II.; further Part IV). The OTP has, moreover, adopted OTP Regulations and Provisional Analysis Regulations laying down the process of how communications and referrals are treated. This preliminary OTP examination process will be explained (III.) and scrutinized *vis-à-vis* statutory provisions (IV.).

I. Relationship between article 15 and article 53

It is not clear from the statutory language how articles 15 and 53 are meant to be applied together. Their interrelationship has several dimensions and will be addressed as follows. First, the method described in article 15 (2) and the factors (or criteria) described in article 53 (1) have to be distinguished. Second, delving deeper into the relationship, the review process for when the Prosecutor decides not to initiate an investigation must be examined. With regard to the first point, the RPE, specifically rules 48 and 104, are instructive. Rule 48 states:

> "In determining whether there is a reasonable basis to proceed with an investigation under article 15, paragraph 3, the Prosecutor shall consider the factors set out in article 53, paragraph 1 (a) to (c)."

Rule 104 further clarifies:

> "1. In acting pursuant to article 53, paragraph 1, the Prosecutor shall, in evaluating the information made available to him or her, analyze the seriousness of the information received.
>
> 2. For the purposes of sub-rule 1, the Prosecutor may seek additional information from States, organs of the United Nations, intergovernmental and non-governmental organizations, or other reliable sources that he or she deems appropriate, and

---

ing guidelines [...]"), see FIDH, FIDH statement on the prosecutorial strategy of the OTP, *supra* note 1020, 4.

1025 Part III, B., VI., 3.

1026 Wouters/Verhoeven/Demeyere, *supra* note 156, 295.

may receive written or oral testimony at the seat of the Court. The procedure set out in rule 47 shall apply to the receiving of such testimony."

Rule 48 introduces the criteria of article 53 (1) into article 15 (3) such that it creates a uniform application of "reasonable basis" in both articles.[1027] Jurisdiction, admissibility, and "interests of justice" are thus valid inquiries for pre-investigations irrespective of how they are triggered. Rule 104 inserts the procedure of article 15 (2) into article 53 (1). The Prosecutor is required to analyze the seriousness of information based on referrals and he is given the power to seek additional information. Rule 47 makes it clear that testimony during preliminary investigation is congruent under article 15 (2) and rule 104. The method described in article 15 (2), as well as the working method established by the OTP,[1028] is therefore binding with respect to investigations under all three trigger mechanisms.[1029]

As an intermediary conclusion, rules 48 and 104 show that the relationship between articles 15 and 53 was not clear at the time the ICC Statute was adopted.[1030] The general method and parameters of the pre-investigation are laid down in articles 15 (2) and 53 (1). By clarification through the above-mentioned rules, the method established in article 15 (2) is applicable to article 53 and vice-versa.[1031]

Turning to the second inquiry, namely whether the PTC could review a decision by the Prosecutor not to request an investigation under article 15 (3), it is unclear from the ICC Statute and the RPE whether the review pro-

---

1027 Turone, in Cassese/Gaeta/Jones, *supra* note 26, 1147; Friman, in Lee, *supra* note 984, 495–6; Kleffner, *supra* note 370, 164–5; Ambos, *supra* note 26, § 8 mn 20 b; Bergsmo/Pjeić, in Triffterer, *supra* note 321, article 15, mn 19; Olásolo, *supra* note 29, 72; Razesberger, *supra* note 371, 68; most recently *Situation in Kenya*, Request for authorization, *supra* note 207, para. 45, 17; *Situation in Kenya*, Decision pursuant to article 15, *supra* note 6, paras. 21–25, 10–13.

1028 Thereto Part III, C., III.

1029 Turone, in Cassese/Gaeta/Jones, *supra* note 26, 1147; Friman, in Lee, *supra* note 984, 496; Bergsmo/Kruger, in Triffterer, *supra* note 906, article 53, mn 9; van Heeck, *supra* note 26, 153; Visit of the Palestinian National Authority, *supra* note 318.

1030 Bergsmo/Kruger, in Triffterer, *supra* note 906, article 53, mn 9. The (later) introduction of rules 48 and 104 might also explain the discrepancy between the current version and the former Triffterer commentary of 1999, when the rules were not yet in force. Bergsmo/Pjeić and Bergsmo/Kruger now take the rules into consideration, and they move away from the cumulative model formerly supported; for an illustrative discussion on the cumulative *vis-à-vis* a substitutive model (supporting the latter) Olásolo, *supra* note 29, 71–2. On the drafting history see further *Situation in Kenya*, Decision pursuant to article 15, *supra* note 6, paras. 22–23, 10–12.

1031 Coming to the same result, Wouters/Verhoeven/Demeyere, *supra* note 156, 295.

visions of article 53 (3) apply to *proprio motu* investigations. Initially, the provisions were drafted and arranged in a way that purposefully failed to give a definite answer to the question ("constructive ambiguity").[1032]

A strict interpretation, based on an argument *e contrario* regarding rules 48 and 104, speaks against a complete overlap between article 15 and 53. The links between the articles were expressly formulated in rules 48 and 104 with regard to the method and criteria of the preliminary examination. In contrast, no provision explicitly imports the *proprio motu* review power of the PTC from article 53 (3) (b) into article 15 procedures. There is nothing in any of the corresponding rules that would support a hypothesis that the PTC has the competence to review a decision against seeking authorization for an investigation.[1033] However, based on a wider interpretation, it could be argued that rules 48 and 104 were meant to lead to an all-embracing overlap of articles 15 and 53, merging the two articles into one congruent procedure.[1034]

Both interpretations are legally possible. Article 53 (3) (b) speaks of a review power if the Prosecutor decides not to proceed based solely on the "interests of justice." The decision shall be effective only if confirmed by the PTC and there is no distinction made based on the trigger mechanism used. Approaching the matter systematically is quite complex: first, article 53 (3) (a) gives the State or the SC referring the situation the right to request a PTC review if the Prosecutor decided not to proceed. No such right is given to the information provider under article 15. Article 15 (6) and rule 105 (2), in connection with rule 49, only provide for notification of those who have submitted information.[1035] Since article 53 (3) (a) was drafted in connection with article 53 (3) (b), it could be argued that paragraph (b) only embraces State referrals and SC referrals. However, the Rules of Procedure and Evidence lead us to a different conclusion. Whereas rule 105 (1) and (2) admittedly distinguish between the triggering parties, paragraph 4 of the rule blurs the line by failing to differentiate between the trigger mechanisms and employing rather general wording ("in case the Prosecutor decides not to investigate based solely on the basis of article 53, paragraph 1 (c) [...]"). One might therefore come to the conclusion that the original ambiguity was reduced, but not eliminated, due to the fact that rule 105 (4) does not explicitly exclude application in the situation when the Prosecutor decides not to seek an authorization under article 15.[1036] None-

1032 Friman, in Lee, *supra* note 984, 498; Robinson, *supra* note 807, 483.

1033 Guhr, *supra* note 495, 136.

1034 In this vein, *Situation in Kenya*, Decision pursuant to article 15, *supra* note 6, paras. 24–5, 12–3.

1035 Friman, in Lee, *supra* note 984, 498.

theless, an argument in favor of review power is hard to maintain given the fact that such a review would require the Prosecutor to actually take a *decision* not to request an authorization.[1037] However, rule 109 dealing with the review under article 53 (3) (b) is open to both interpretations as it solely makes reference to "notification given under rule 105 or 106." Systematically, an interpretation in favor of a *proprio motu* review power regarding all trigger mechanisms remains possible.

A teleological line of argument would deny the PTC a *proprio motu* review because such a review power would make the PTC both judge and jury.[1038] In addition, one major procedural difference between referrals and communications needs to be stressed:

> "Where the Prosecutor receives a referral, article 53 provides that the Prosecutor *shall* initiate an investigation *unless* he determines that there is no reasonable basis to proceed under the Statute. Initiation of investigation is further simplified in that the Pre-Trial Chamber may only review his determination *not to proceed*, but does not review an affirmative decision to proceed.
>
> When the Prosecutor receives a communication, the test is the same but the starting point is reversed: the Prosecutor shall not seek to initiate an investigation unless he first concludes that there is a reasonable basis to proceed. In addition, when the Prosecutor acts *proprio motu*, he needs an authorization of the Pre-Trial Chamber to start an investigation. This means that he does not take the decision to investigate alone, but needs to convince the Pre-Trial Chamber that the threshold of a *reasonable basis* to proceed has been met (article 15)."[1039]

To summarize, the Prosecutor is under an assumption to initiate full investigations in the case of SC referrals or State referrals. If he denies doing so, he must justify his decision before the PTC, and the PTC may even overrule him in the case of "interests of justice" deliberations. In the case of *proprio motu* investigations, the onus is reversed. It is now up to the Prosecutor to convince the PTC of the existence of a "reasonable basis" under article 15 (4). How he evaluates the reasonable basis remains within his discretion, and early interference by the PTC appears contrary to the differentiated statutory framework. A positive control over *proprio motu* proceed-

---

1036 Friman, in Lee, *supra* note 984, 498 with fn. 13.

1037 Håkan Friman, "The Rules of Procedure and Evidence in the investigative stage," in Horst Fischer/Claus Kreß/Sascha Rolf Lüder (eds.) *International and national prosecution of crimes under international law* (Berlin Verlag Arno Spitz, Berlin 2001) 191, 194 with fn. 11. Friman then correctly emphasizes that the ICC Statute and the RPE do not impose a duty to take such a formal decision. On the contrary, the Prosecutor may choose to keep the file open, awaiting or seeking additional information. For the problems involved in keeping the file open (e.g. time-limits), see further Part III, E.

1038 Olásolo, *supra* note 29, 65.

1039 Annex paper, *supra* note 27, 1–2.

ings would significantly weaken the prosecutorial independence provided for in article 42 (1).[1040] Furthermore, it must be noted that France submitted a proposal during the drafting of the RPE that aimed at a codification of an explicit review power regarding the OTP's decisions not to seek authorization.[1041] This proposal gained some support, but was rejected by a number of delegations, which argued that the discretion vested in the Prosecutor must not be compromised and that such a direct control would be inconsistent with the Statute.[1042]

All-in-all, the teleological arguments and the drafting history of the RPE speak against a wide interpretation that would grant the PTC an early right of review. Therefore, article 53 (3) (b) cannot be applied under article 15.[1043] Nevertheless, a different approach is not entirely ruled out, and could be introduced through a rule (or paragraph) clarifying the matter. The Judges, for instance, could propose a rule in accordance with article 51 (2) (b), and a two-thirds majority of the ASP's members would have to adopt the new rule.

For the moment, it can be asserted that rules 48 and 104 lead to a partial overlap of articles 15 and 53,[1044] merging the triggering mechanisms into one pre-investigation procedure. All three triggers are *basically* subjected to the same method and criteria which secures consistency. Conformity must, however, stop where carefully drafted statutory differences are otherwise abrogated.

[1040] Stigen, *supra* note 205, 112.

[1041] Proposal by France (PCNICC/1999/DP.6) *supra* note 49, rule 56 (Supervision by the Pre-Trial Chamber of decisions of the Prosecutor taken in the interests of justice) reads in excerpts: "In cases in which the decision of the Prosecutor is based exclusively on the considerations referred to in article 53, paragraph 1 (c) or 2 (c), the Pre-Trial Chamber may, at its own initiative, review this decision [...]," and, more clearly including *proprio motu* investigations into the review power: "[...] should the Pre-Trial Chamber overrule the decision of the Prosecutor not to open an investigation, or, in the case referred to in article 15, not to submit to the Pre-Trial Chamber a request for authorization of an investigation, or not to proceed, the Prosecutor shall comply with the ruling of the Pre-Trial Chamber as soon as possible."

[1042] Friman, Friman, in Lee, *supra* note 984, 497; Stahn/Olásolo/Gibson, *supra* note 370, 230.

[1043] Contrary, *Situation in Kenya*, Decision pursuant to article 15, *supra* note 6, para. 24 with fn.35, 12–3.

[1044] In the same vein, Ambos, *supra* note 26, § 8 mn 20 b ("[...] teilweisen Überlagerung der Tatbestandsmerkmale [...]").

II. Overview of evaluation criteria

After having established a relationship between articles 15 and 53, in particular that rule 48 introduces the criteria of article 53 (1) into article 15 (3), a general overview of the evaluation criteria shall be given. The problems in the application of these criteria will be discussed exhaustively in Chapter IV.[1045]

The effect of rules 48 and 104 is that the "reasonable basis" standard under articles 15 (3), (4), and 53 (1) is applied in the same manner. The threshold can be subdivided into equal parameters, which either provide for a reasonable basis to proceed or not. The Prosecutor has to be satisfied that he has met the criteria of subparagraphs (a), (b), and (c) of article 53 to proceed into the realm of a full investigation.[1046] There is, though, one procedural difference the Prosecutor must bear in mind. If he uses the *proprio motu* power, the OTP has to convince the PTC of its findings on the "reasonable basis to proceed," whereas in the case of referrals the investigation may simply proceed *unless* the Prosecutor determines that there is no basis to proceed. Be that as it may, the verbal phrase "*reasonable basis to proceed*" in the chapeau of article 53 (1) determines that a reasonability test has to be conducted by the OTP.[1047] Thereby, the Prosecutor is required to consider the following three criteria:[1048]

1. first, the available information must provide a reasonable basis to believe that a crime within the jurisdiction of the Court has been or is being committed (article 53 (1) (a));
2. second, the admissibility must be examined taking into account the gravity and complementarity as to national proceedings (article 53 (1) (b), article 17); and

---

1045 See Part IV.

1046 Bergsmo/Kruger, in Triffterer, *supra* note 906, article 53, mn 12.

1047 On the reasonability test see Part IV, B., II., 3.

1048 Or "factors," or "elements," or "parameters" (at hand, the terms are used *vice versa*). On the criteria for the reasonability test, see Turone, in Cassese/Gaeta/Jones, *supra* note 26, 1151 et seq; Bergsmo/Kruger, in Triffterer, *supra* note 906, article 53, mn 7 et seq.; Razesberger, *supra* note 371, 99 et seq.; Ambos, *supra* note 10, 438; Brubacher, *supra* note 368, 78 et seq.; Olásolo, *supra* note 368, 132; Mireille Delmas-Marty, "Interactions between national and international criminal law in the preliminary phase of trial at the ICC" (2006) 4 JICJ 2, 8 et seq.; also the French version thereof *id.,* "La CPI et les interactions entre droit international pénal et droit pénal interne à la phase d'ouverture du procès pénal" (2005) RSC 473, 478 et seq.; Schabas, *supra* note 27, 242 et seq.; Informal expert paper: Fact-finding and investigative functions, *supra* note 472, para. 20; Ray Murphy, "Gravity issues and the International Criminal Court" (2006) 16 CLF 281, 285; James Goldstone, "More candour about criteria" (2010) 8 JICJ 383, 391–2.

3. third, the "interests of justice" taking into account "gravity of the crime and the interests of the victims" (article 53 (1) (c)) must be analyzed.

The first criterion is composed of two sub-elements, the "reasonable basis to believe that a crime exists" and the jurisdiction of the ICC.[1049] In addition to the legal criteria, the Prosecutor takes into account the published Prosecutorial Strategy as reflected in the strategy papers and the policy papers where appropriate.[1050] Neither the principle of legality nor the principle of political discretion has been chosen as the guiding principle governing the overall activity of the Prosecutor,[1051] requiring a close examination of the different criteria of article 53 (1) to evaluate whether or not they embrace discretion.[1052]

III. Preliminary examination method – OTP practice

The OTP has adopted OTP Regulations and Provisional Analysis Regulations detailing how to deal with communications, referrals, and declarations under article 12 (3).[1053] For a better understanding of the whole process, and in the interest of a critical examination of the statutory framework, the practice of the OTP in particular must be outlined. The following description gives an overview of the different phases and shows the way the OTP approaches each phase at present.[1054] Thereby, the official OTP Regulations apparently rank before the Provisional Analysis Regulations; the latter were thought to be only provisionally applied until completion of the former.[1055] However, the OTP Regulations do not delineate the precise preliminary examination process. OTP Regulation 27 speaks of a preliminary distinction between information manifestly outside the Court's jurisdiction (a), information relating to a situation already under analysis (b), and "new" information relating to matters not manifestly outside the jurisdiction, thus potentially forming the basis for newly-discovered situations (c). But the exact phases are mentioned nowhere. It is my understanding that the Provisional

---

1049 Turone, in Cassese/Gaeta/Jones, *supra* note 26, 1151–2; Olásolo, *supra* note 368, 132.

1050 Annex paper, *supra* note 27, 3; OTP Regulation 14. See further Schabas, *supra* note 27, 244; also Part IV, B., II., 4.

1051 Olásolo, *supra* note 368, 132; see further Part IV, B., 5.

1052 Turone, in Cassese/Gaeta/Jones, *supra* note 26, 1151 et seq., and Olásolo, *supra* note 368, 132 et seq., commenced an inquiry into the criteria, checking if the respective criterion entails discretion. A similar, though farther reaching analysis is conducted in Part IV.

1053 In a similar vein, Wouters/Verhoeven/Demeyere, *supra* note 156, 298.

1054 For a detailed graph see Annex 1, C.

1055 Annex paper, *supra* note 27, 7.

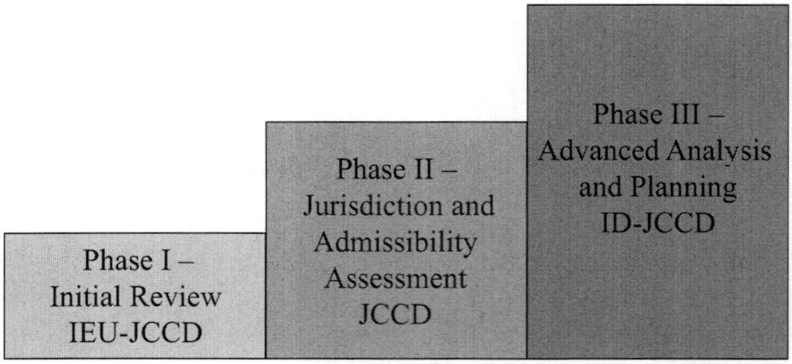

Source: Author.

Figure 6: OTP Pre-Investigations – Three Tiered Process

Analysis Regulations still provide the basis for the working method currently applied by the OTP, and therefore can be consulted to fill in the gaps.[1056] Their hierarchy in the ICC's legal framework is nevertheless very low. They certainly have to comply with the ICC Statute, the RPE and the OTP Regulations, and can be modified continuously by the Office itself, bearing in mind the statutory framework.

The Provisional Analysis Regulations provide for an examination of all communications in three stages: phase I (initial review of communications), phase II (jurisdiction and admissibility assessment), and phase III (advanced analysis and planning).[1057]

According to the OTP, referrals are generally subject to the same process and the same basic standard, except that phase I is unnecessary "given the treatment of referrals under the Statute (article 13 and 53) and the comparative volume of communications."[1058] The OTP mentions a further refinement by differentiating phase II-A ("basic reporting") and a phase II-B which merges with phase III ("more thorough and intensive analysis").[1059]

[1056] See already *supra* note 66 and corresponding text.

[1057] Provisional Analysis Regulations 4–6, Annex paper, *supra* note 27, 9–12. On the three-phased procedure Wouters/Verhoeven/Demeyere, *supra* note 156, 298 et seq.; Stegmiller, *supra* note 370, 325 et seq.; also Stigen, *supra* note 205, 103 with fn. 383; War Crimes Research Office, "The gravity threshold of the International Criminal Court" (hereinafter WCRO report gravity), International Criminal Court Legal Analysis and Education Project (United States of America, American University Washington College of Law 2008) 22 et seq.; and Schiff, *supra* note 128, 111–2.

[1058] Annex paper, *supra* note 27, 7.

Provisional Analysis Regulations 2 and 3 deal with the receipt of referrals and communications. The IEU shall receive, register, and secure all incoming information. Upon receipt of referrals, the head of IEU must inform the heads of JCCD (Provisional Analysis Regulation 2.2). In addition, the Prosecutor is to promptly inform the Presidency in accordance with Provisional Analysis Regulation 2.3. One main difference is that communications proceed through phase I, contrary to referrals, which directly move to phase II.[1060]

The initial review phase aims at distinguishing i) communications that manifestly provide no basis for further action, ii) those that appear to relate to a situation already under analysis, investigation, or prosecution, and iii) those communications warranting further analysis in order to assess whether further action may be appropriate (Provisional Analysis Regulation 4.1 (a)–(c)). The content of this regulation found its way into official OTP Regulation 27, while leaving out paragraph 2 (outlining the duty of the IEU to prepare reports on the volume, frequency, and patters of communications relating to particular situations) and paragraph 3 (outlining how JCCD shall review IEU reports and confirm or amend preliminary identifications made by IEU). In general, phase I is conducted by the IEU under supervision of the JCCD. The largest amount of the received communications is sorted out during this stage.[1061]

The term used in Provisional Analysis Regulation 4.1 (a) "manifestly do not provide any basis" is not further defined. It can be reasoned from the "Update on communications" that the OTP looks at four (jurisdictional) parameters: temporal jurisdiction (article 11), subject matter jurisdiction (article 5), personal/territorial jurisdiction (article 12), and "manifestly ill-founded."[1062] Moreover, the "Update on communications," as well as OTP Regulation 27 (a), use the terminology "manifestly outside the jurisdiction of the Court" instead of "manifestly do not provide any basis." The former wording appears more precise and appropriate, since article 53 (1) (a) names the factors jurisdiction and reasonable basis that a crime has been or is being committed.

Jurisdiction can be subdivided into three elements: temporal, subject-matter, and personal/territorial jurisdiction. Temporal jurisdiction is missing if

1059 Update on communications, *supra* note 316, 3 with fn. 5 and 7.

1060 Provisional Analysis Regulations 2.5: "The seriousness of the information contained in the referral shall be analyzed in accordance with Regulation 5 (Analysis Phase II), *mutatis mutandis*.," and 3.2: "The seriousness of the information contained in the communications shall be analyzed in accordance with Regulation 4 (Analysis Phase I)."

1061 Part III, B., I., 5.

1062 Update on communications, *supra* note 316, 2.

events occurred prior to 1 July 2002. Subject-matter jurisdiction embraces genocide, crimes against humanity, and war crimes. Topics such as immigration, including claims for asylum, medical negligence, social security and pension complaints, employment law (particularly unfair dismissal), and the crime of aggression were mentioned as general examples for communications that were rated outside the subject-matter jurisdiction during initial review.[1063] Besides, the ICC has jurisdiction only (1) over crimes committed on the territory of, or by nationals of, States Parties; (2) over crimes on the territory of, or by nationals of, States submitting a declaration of acceptance of jurisdiction; and (3) over crimes referred by the UN Security Council.[1064] The five present situations are jurisdictionally either based on a States Party's territory (DRC, Uganda, CAR, Kenya), or on a SC referral (Sudan). Of the two dismissed situations based on communications that were made publically available, Venezuela had a territorial basis,[1065] whereas in Iraq the inquiry rested upon nationality concerning nationals of the United Kingdom committed on the territory of a Non-State Party.[1066] In sum, 42 percent of the received communications were sorted out due to a lack of jurisdiction.[1067]

Another question is the nature and definition of the "manifestly ill-founded" communications, which constitute 38 percent of the total.[1068] This "adequate filtering mechanisms" was established with regard to the fear of being flooded with complaints.[1069] It is explained that the ill-founded com-

[1063] Update on communications, *supra* note 316, 2.

[1064] Update on communications, *supra* note 316, 2 with fn. 4; Williams/Schabas, in Triffterer, *supra* note 353, article 13, mn 16; Williams/Schabas, in Triffterer, *supra* note 1003, article 12, mn 14 et seq.

[1065] Venezuela response, *supra* note 333, 2: "Venezuela ratified the ICC Statute on 7 June 2000 and pursuant to articles 11 (1) and 126 (1), the ICC has jurisdiction over crimes perpetrated in the territory or by nationals of Venezuela after 1 July 2002, when the Statute entered into force. The events alleged in the communications occurred on the territory of Venezuela."

[1066] Iraq response, *supra* note 333, 3: "The events in question occurred on the territory of Iraq, which is not a State Party to the Rome Statute and which has not lodged a declaration of acceptance under article 12 (3), thereby accepting the jurisdiction of the Court. Therefore, in accordance with Article 12, acts on the territory of a Non-State Party fall within the jurisdiction of the Court only when the person accused of the crime is a national of a State that has accepted jurisdiction (article 12 (2) (b)). As I noted in my first public announcement on communications, we do not have jurisdiction with respect to actions of Non-State Party nationals on the territory of Iraq." See further Williams/Schabas, *supra* note 1003, article 12, mn 16.

[1067] Cf. Part III, B., I., 5.

[1068] Cf. Part III, B., I., 5.

[1069] Rod Rastan, "The power of the Prosecutor in initiating investigations," International Centre for Criminal Law Reform and Criminal Justice Policy, A paper pre-

munications "faltered on multiple jurisdictional grounds or otherwise did not provide a basis for analysis."[1070] The OTP supposedly developed the idea of a "manifestly ill-founded" barrier in accordance with international law. International law instruments apply a similar standard to avoid time-consuming examinations of complaints. Article 35 (3) of the European Convention for the Protection of Human Rights and Fundamental Freedoms spells out: "The Court shall declare inadmissible any individual application submitted under article 34 which it considers incompatible with the provisions of the Convention or the protocols thereto, *manifestly ill-founded,* or an abuse of the right of application (emph. added)."[1071] In a similar manner, the American Convention on Human Rights states that the Commission shall consider inadmissible any petition or communication in accordance with article 47 (c) if "the statements of the petitioner or of the state indicate that the petition or communication is *manifestly groundless or obviously out of order* (emph. added)."[1072] The OTP must therefore dismiss "frivolous, vexatious or otherwise manifestly unfounded" communications.[1073] "Frivolous" can be circumscribed as "unworthy of serious attention; characterized by lack of seriousness, sense, or reverence; given to trifling, silly."[1074] "Vexatious" means "full of trouble or uneasiness; vexed, annoyed."[1075] It is, however, the OTP's task to develop the precise content for such a standard. If it is obvious for someone without legal training that the information is outside the ICC's jurisdiction, such a communication could be deemed manifestly unfounded.

To reach an intermediary conclusion, the "manifestly ill-founded" standard is unavoidable as a matter of policy. The OTP's effectiveness would be seriously undermined by a flood of frivolous information if no fast-track procedure were available. As stated above, the start of a preliminary examination, as well as a response to the information provider, are mandatory and the notice must be prompt and include reasons for the decision (rule 49

pared for the symposium on the International Criminal Court, 3.–4.2.2007, Bejing, 6.

1070 Update on communications, *supra* note 316, 2: "Examples include general conspiracy claims without specific details; general concerns about local or national politics; or communications failing to provide facts susceptible to analysis."

1071 European Convention for the Protection of Human Rights and Fundamental Freedoms, 3.9.1953, CETS No. 005, article 34.

1072 American Convention on Human Rights, 18.7.1978, article 47.

1073 To the knowledge of the author this phrasing is used by the OTP for the assessment of "manifestly unfounded" communications.

1074 Cf. Oxford English Dictionary, "frivolous," <www.oed.com>.

1075 Cf. Oxford English Disctionary, "vexatious," <www.oed.com>; Black's Law Dictionary, Bryan Garner (ed.), 7th edition (Thomson West, St. Paul 1999) 1559, "vexatious" – "without reasonable or probable cause of excuse; harassing; annoying."

(1) RPE). Further minimum requirements are an analysis of "seriousness" in light of the reasonable basis standard of article 53 (1). From a teleological perspective, it seems possible that "seriousness" was thought to provide for an early separation of obviously ill-founded information from profound allegations. Information that is misplaced on its face, or, in the OTP's words "frivolous, vexatious or otherwise manifestly unfounded," should be rejected based on a fast-track initial review.

Coming back to phase I as such, communication reports during this phase are of a preliminary nature. They are subject to JCCD review that confirms or amends the IEU's (preliminary) findings (Provisional Analysis Regulation 4.3). For communications relating to a situation already under analysis, IEU sends acknowledgement to JCCD and JCCD briefs the relevant staff of the OTP (Provisional Analysis Regulation 4.4). In any event, a communication identified as "manifestly not providing any basis for the Office of the Prosecutor to take further action" or "warranting further analysis" must be included in a report to the Prosecutor and ExCom with recommendations how to continue (or discontinue) proceedings. This recommendation report must be made electronically available to ID and PD, and members of ExCom may request clarifications or make comments. After considering comments, it is ultimately the Chief Prosecutor who reaches a final decision whether further analysis is necessary or whether the communication shall be dismissed. In the latter case, acknowledgements are sent by IEU and the information is archived (Provisional Analysis Regulation 4.5 (a)); otherwise, the communication shall be further analyzed in accordance with Provisional Analysis Regulation 5 and transferred to phase II (Provisional Analysis Regulation 4.5 (b)). In a nutshell, phase I is thought to be a quick screening test that allows the OTP to separate clearly unfounded information from potentially relevant information.

The second phase is a stage of more detailed legal and factual analysis of significant communications and referrals carried out by JCCD, with support from ID, under supervision of the ExCom and the Chief Prosecutor. Where appropriate, JCCD may also consult with PD and LAS; ExCom may further advise ID to gather information about alleged crimes identified by referrals and communications according to Provisional Analysis Regulation 5.2. Phase II requires a more intensive analysis, "including issues of jurisdiction, admissibility, interests of justice, and credibility and sufficiency of information" (Regulation 5.1). Measures taken by JCCD in assessing these issues are enumerated in Regulation 5.3:

(a) identify situations to be monitored on an ongoing basis;

(b) contact the State or States that would normally exercise jurisdiction and seek additional information about *inter alia* the existence and progress of national proceedings, unless there is reason to believe that such consultations may prejudice the future conduct of an analysis or investigation;

(c) take appropriate steps to assess the progress of national proceedings relating to crimes within the jurisdiction of the Court;

(d) seek additional information as appropriate, and establish and maintain contacts with States and organizations for provision of information and cooperation.

In the end, JCCD prepares a report summarizing its analysis and submits it to ExCom. JCCD may choose one of the following three recommendations under Provisional Analysis Regulation 5.4: first, that there is no reasonable basis for further analysis; second, that further analysis and monitoring under Regulation 5 is required; or third, that advanced analysis under Regulation 6 is warranted.

Taking into account the reports and recommendations by JCCD and the advice of ExCom, the Chief Prosecutor may determine that there is no reasonable basis for further analysis (Provisional Analysis Regulation 5.5). In such a case, the senders will be informed. The duty to notify all information providers of decisions is not only laid down in the Provisional Analysis Regulations, but can be found directly in article 15 (6). There is thus a mandatory obligation imposed upon the OTP during the entire pre-investigation stage regarding all final decisions. Having said that, the Prosecutor has two alternatives at the end of phase II instead of terminating procedures; he can either i) determine that further analysis and monitoring relating to jurisdiction, admissibility, and "interests of justice" is required under Provisional Analysis Regulation 5, or ii) determine that advanced analysis is warranted in the next phase III under Provisional Analysis Regulation 6 (Provisional Analysis Regulation 5.6).

Another aspect introduced by the Update on communications is the distinction between phase II-A and phase II-B/III, which is not foreseen in either the Provisional Analysis Regulations or in the OTP Regulations. After initial review (phase I), the OTP differentiated phase II-A (basic reporting) from phase II-B, and a final phase III (more thorough and intensive analysis, presented together with phase II-B for the purpose of simplicity).[1076] The OTP states that "basic reporting" is merely a simple factual and legal analysis, and that the "intensive analysis" involves collecting information from open sources, conducting systematic crime analysis, examining factors such as gravity, complementarity, and the "interests of justice," seeking additional information, and conducting the planning for potential investigations.[1077] The manner in which phases II and III overlap

[1076] Update on communications, *supra* note 316, 3.

remains unclear, as does the point at which article 53 (1) criteria are actually analyzed. Moreover, it may be questioned if seriousness allows for such phases.[1078]

Returning to the Provisional Analysis Regulations, the most serious situations will proceed to phase III of "advanced analysis and planning." According to Provisional Analysis Regulation 6.1 the Prosecutor may, taking into account reports and recommendations submitted by JCCD and ExCom, authorize and instruct his staff:

(a) to seek additional information;

(b) to receive written or oral testimony at the seat of the Court;

(c) to assess the progress of national proceedings relating to crimes within the jurisdiction of the Court;

(d) to prepare reports on jurisdiction, admissibility, the interests of justice and any other matter relevant to the determination under article 53;

(e) to prepare an investigation plan on the situation or the case(s);

(f) to take other appropriate measures to facilitate analysis and prepare for possible investigation.

The confidential article 53 reports mentioned in paragraph d) are of major importance prior to the initiation of formal investigations in accordance with article 53 (1) or to seeking authorization of the PTC in the case of *proprio motu* investigations. OTP Regulation 29 (1) foresees an article 53 report that contains an evaluation pursuant to rules 48 and 104 and a recommendation on whether to investigate a situation. Jurisdiction, admissibility (including gravity), and the "interests of justice" are carefully analyzed in these reports since JCCD will be responsible for "any reports on jurisdiction, admissibility, 'the interests of justice' and any other matter relevant to the determination under article 53" (Provisional Analysis Regulation 6.2). If necessary, JCCD will obtain additional information on the alleged crimes from ID and may consult with PD and LAS. It can be assumed that the given recommendations form the factual and legal basis for the Chief Prosecutor to reach a decision. According to Provisional Analysis Regulation 6.5 and 6.6, the Prosecutor – "taking into account any reports and recommendations submitted by JCCD and the joint analysis team, and the advice of the Executive Committee" – may either determine that there is no reasonable basis to initiate an investigation (in which case the sender will be informed under Regulation 6.5), decide to initiate an investigation under article 53, or seek PTC authorization under article 15 (3) (6.6).

[1077] Update on communications, *supra* note 316, 3.

[1078] For a critical analysis of the OTP's practice see Part III, C., IV.

The Prosecutor may further mandate the preparation of an investigation plan, in which case a joint team will be created by ExCom, led by ID, and include members of ID, PD, and JCCD (Regulation 6.3). A joint team refers to an interdivisional team (OTP Regulation 2). However, it can be asked whether such a team should be composed during pre-investigations or at the beginning of a full investigation after the formal initiation procedures. All divisions are represented in the team in an effort to ensure that the process runs smoothly.[1079] The fact that ID leads the team favors locating the measure within full investigations. Moreover, the joint team is responsible for establishing an investigation plan. Recently, OTP Regulation 32 turned away from the use of joint teams during pre-investigations stating: "A joint team shall be formed *upon a decision to proceed with an investigation* in a situation, for the purpose of conducting the investigation (emph. added)." Since there is no provision within the ICC Statute or the RPE that would allow the OTP to prepare investigation plans during pre-investigations, the measure should not be undertaken during early procedures. In accordance with OTP Regulation 32 (1), which deals with joint teams during investigations, the measure has to be carried out after the pre-investigation phase. Otherwise the stages of pre-investigations and full investigations would be needlessly blurred.

To summarize, for the OTP's pre-investigation method three phases were introduced at the very outset to circumscribe the Office's working process. In the OTP's later practice, phases II and III were not clearly differentiated. The OTP Regulations of April 2009 subsequently omitted the phases in favor of more general rules. Nevertheless, the working process outlined here is still applied by the OTP with regard to all three trigger mechanisms. In addition to the formal process, however, insight into the OTP's application of factors like jurisdiction, admissibility, and "interests of justice" is important. Precise information about the "various factors," "methods and criteria applied," or "criteria of the Statute" would certainly be enlightening. The OTP should give more guidance concerning the terms it employs in the future. For this reason, part IV will exhaustively address the selection criteria.

[1079] OTP Regulation 32 (2): "Each joint team shall be composed of staff from the three Divisions in order to ensure a coordinated approach throughout the investigation."

IV. Preliminary examination method – statutory basis

The manner in which the preliminary examination is carried out by the OTP has been described above, though the question remains whether this procedure for dealing with communications and referrals is in accordance with the ICC Statute and the RPE. First and foremost, it must be noted that the statutory framework leads to an overlap between *proprio motu* proceedings on the one hand, and SC and State referrals on the other hand. This overlap reaches not only the evaluation criteria, but also the general preliminary examination method. As stated above,[1080] article 15 (2) and rule 104 establish the same basic procedure. Article 15 (2) requires the Prosecutor to analyze the seriousness of information received and allows him to seek additional information as appropriate. The identical procedural tools are introduced for referrals through rule 104. Rule 104 (2) even repeats the wording of article 15 (2), second sentence as a remedy to the original lack of coordination between article 53 (1) and 15 (2).[1081] In accordance with the procedure in rule 47, the OTP is enabled to receive written or oral testimony at the seat of the Court pursuant to article 15 (2) and rule 104 (2). In a nutshell, articles 15 (2) and 53 (1), in connection with rules 48 and 104, oblige the OTP to analyze information received through communications and referrals equally.[1082] Consequently, the OTP is not barred from applying the same general procedure for all three trigger mechanisms.

However, specific preliminary examination *measures* and the potential *course of action* need to be further addressed. Starting with early examination measures, the OTP states that during pre-investigations "the Prosecutor is not entitled to exercise all of his powers."[1083] In particular, article 54 powers with respect to full investigations cannot be exercised. Three explicit powers during the pre-investigative analysis phase are mentioned in the ICC Statute and the RPE, which allow the Prosecutor to:

- analyze the seriousness of the information received (article 15 (2), rule 104 (1));
- seek additional information from States, organs of the United Nations, intergovernmental and non-governmental organizations, or any other reliable source (article 15 (2), rule 104 (2));

1080 Cf. Part III, C., I.

1081 Turone, in Cassese/Gaeta/Jones, *supra* note 26, 1149.

1082 Contrary, Olásolo, *supra* note 29, 60: "[...] the scope of a rule 104 OTP preliminary examination should be far more limited than of an article 15 (2) OTP preliminary examination."

1083 Annex paper, *supra* note 27, 4.

– receive oral and written testimony at the seat of the Court, in accordance with the procedure in rule 47 (article 15 (2) rule 104 (2)).

Regarding the course of action, the OTP's basic approach was the introduction of three consecutive phases based on the seriousness of information.[1084] Neither the Statute nor the RPE specify the manner in which information must be gathered for preliminary examination. Yet, we must still ask if seriousness alone renders such a pedantic differentiation possible. An informal expert group described the preliminary examination steps in the following manner:

> "In conducting the article 15 preliminary examination, the Prosecutor needs to analyze the seriousness of the information received (article 15 (1)) and determine whether there is a reasonable basis to proceed with an investigation (article 15 (2)). To this end, the Prosecutor must consider, in accordance with rule 48 and article 15 (3) (a), whether there is a reasonable basis to believe that a crime has been or is being committed, (b) that the crime is within the Court's jurisdiction, (c) that the case is or would be admissible under Article 17, and (d) that the interests of justice would be served by the investigation."[1085]

Accordingly, the term "seriousness" has to be evaluated in connection with "reasonable basis." Thus, when taking action, article 53 (1) criteria must be evaluated in light of the seriousness of all the information received. As already stated above, the OTP's approach must be interpreted as an internal working process rather than three strict phases.[1086] Moreover, these phases might overlap and are not strictly distinguishable procedural steps. At present, no alternative interpretation could refer to concrete statutory provisions because no provision, not even the OTP Regulations, mentions pre-investigation phases.

On the other hand, the *substantive* content of the OTP's process can be scrutinized with regard to the ICC Statute and the RPE. The Prosecutor is required to consider the three criteria listed in article 53 (1). From open sources it can be reasoned that the OTP carefully adheres to this prerequisite since the Prosecutor stated:

> "I am required to consider three factors. First, I must consider whether the available information provides a reasonable basis to believe that a crime within the jurisdiction of the Court has been or is being committed. Where this requirement is satisfied, I must then consider admissibility before the Court, in light of the requirements relating to gravity and complementarity with national proceedings. Third, if these factors are positive, I must give consideration to the interests of justice. (original fn. omitted)."[1087]

[1084] See Part III, B., VI., 4. and C. III.

[1085] Informal expert paper: Fact-finding and investigative functions, *supra* note 472, para. 20.

[1086] Part III, C., IV.

Nevertheless, more guidance on the criteria themselves would improve transparency and traceability. While the OTP has improved its policy on making information publicly available, especially if one compares ICC-OTP practice to ICTY-OTP practice, there are still methodological gaps. In particular, the statutory link for all legal approaches should take centre stage, instead of providing selective information. For instance, the initial review to identify those *proprio motu* communications that manifestly do not provide any basis for further action can be deemed firmly grounded in the statutory term of "seriousness."[1088] If, however, the Prosecutor develops such an additional guideline, the legal basis must be explicitly stated. In my view, the three phases initially introduced by the OTP should not be upheld, and phases two and three in particular must be merged. Therefore, from a statutory standpoint, the OTP cannot create distinct legal sub-phases during the pre-investigation stage. Of course, the OTP may distribute the work in accordance with its mandate and can establish working phases for internal purposes.

Before concluding on the preliminary examination method, further analysis is necessary of the measures available to the Prosecutor, especially with regard to potential limitations imposed upon the OTP during pre-investigations. On the one hand, the Prosecutor has to make a sound evaluation before reaching a decision to start a full investigation. On the other hand, the powers given to him are limited to article 15 (2) and rule 104 respectively. The question is whether the catalogue of pre-investigation measures is exhaustive. One might argue that measures are not exhaustive and that the Prosecutor should be able to take any necessary investigative steps, turning to the PTC for further guidance on article 15 (2).[1089] With respect to "receiving written or oral testimony at the seat of the Court" for instance, the term "seat of the Court" could include possible field offices and temporary arrangements.[1090] However, the limited wording of "the seat of the Court" seems to suggest that the Prosecutor must call witnesses to The Hague, since the interview of a potential witness takes place at a stage in which no investigation is open, although such an interview is a typical investigation step.[1091] A strong presumption therefore favors a strict interpretation of the "seat of the Court" as to exclude field offices, and of the term "testimony" to require a very detailed procedure for the collection of evidence (as opposed by gathering normal information provided by individuals).[1092]

[1087] Venezuela response, *supra* note 333, 1; Iraq response, *supra* note 333, 2.

[1088] For the author's interpretation see Part III, C., III.

[1089] Bergsmo/Pjeić, in Triffterer, *supra* note 321, article 15, mn 17.

[1090] Bergsmo/Pjeić, in Triffterer, *supra* note 321, article 15, mn 16; Turone, in Cassese/Gaeta/Jones, *supra* note 26, 1150; also Schabas, *supra* note 13, 320-1.

[1091] Turone, in Cassese/Gaeta/Jones, *supra* note 26, 1150.

On the one hand, it would be too restrictive to read the provision literally and only admit testimony *taken* at the seat in The Hague. Testimony could alternatively be taken by national authorities and be transmitted to The Hague. Nevertheless, a record in accordance with rules 111 and 112 is obligatory. The remaining question is whether field offices, like the ones established by the ICTY in Belgrade, Sarajevo, and Zagreb, could also be admitted as locations for taking testimony during the pre-investigation stage. There is a fundamental difference between the ICTY Prosecutor acting under Chapter VII of the UN Charter and the ICC Prosecutor acting under the ICC Statute. According to article 3 (1), the seat of the Court is The Hague. Investigative steps outside the Hague can be carried out in exceptional cases only;[1093] as a general rule they will be conducted by competent national authorities in accordance with articles 54 (3) (c), 86, 87 (1) (a), and 99 (1).[1094] Field offices – which are neither mentioned in the ICC Statute nor the RPE – will therefore not form a routine procedural setup during early investigations. Instead, the majority of activities must be performed and coordinated in The Hague during preliminary examinations, and field offices should only play a decisive role once formal investigations have been started.

A related question is whether part 9 of the ICC Statute on "cooperation obligations of States Parties" applies during pre-investigations. A broad interpretation extends article 86 to all activities of the Court, including preliminary examinations.[1095] Indeed, article 86 states that States Parties "shall, in accordance with the provisions of this Statute, cooperate fully," which seems to cover preliminary examinations.[1096] However, the wording refers to "investigation and prosecution," which would exclude the pre-investigation stage.[1097] For a number of reasons, a narrow interpretation is preferable, which would state that a full investigation must be commenced in order to provide the OTP with the powers of article 54 (2) and cooperation

1092 Razesberger, *supra* note 371, 62 et seq.

1093 Cf. articles 57 (3) (d), 99 (4).

1094 Olásolo, *supra* note 29, 60; Morten Bergsmo/Pieter Kruger, "Article 54," in Triffterer, *supra* note 321, article 54, mn 28.

1095 Olásolo, *supra* note 29, 61; Phakiso Mochochoko, "International cooperation and judicial assistance," in Lee, *supra* note 14, 309, who takes a broad approach ("[...] must provide full cooperation without delay to the Court at all stages of the proceedings"). Arguably, the latter author did not (yet) recognize the inherent question of pre-investigations *vis-à-vis* full investigations, since the matter is not explicitly mentioned.

1096 Informal expert paper: Fact-finding and investigative functions, *supra* note 472, para. 24; Olásolo, *supra* note 29, 61.

1097 Informal expert paper: Fact-finding and investigative functions, *supra* note 472, para. 25.

obligations under articles 86 and 93 respectively.[1098] First and foremost, investigations and prosecutions are both explicitly mentioned, while the terms preliminary examinations or pre-investigations are not. Without an express obligation, on-site activities can hardly be enforced. From a teleological perspective, two lines of argument must be weighed against each other: article 86 creates a general obligation duty to facilitate the Court's work at all times; but the measures taken by the OTP during preliminary examination are thought to be of a non-coercive nature and should only initiate all-embracing investigations. If article 86 obligations are denied, further limits are set for pre-investigations, and the danger of vast pre-investigations is limited. In any event, the OTP's staff need a certain degree of security, especially for on-site measures, which is not ensured by the rather unclear wording of article 86. States have been very sensitive to overly broad powers of the Prosecutor, which suggests that the obligatory cooperation scheme comes into play only after the confirmation of the PTC.[1099] Thus, staff insecurity, vagueness of the statutory language, and the danger of prolonging pre-investigations seem to outweigh the desire for a proper support of the Court at all times. Therefore, in my view, part 9 of the ICC Statute does not apply before a formal investigation has been started. This conclusion notwithstanding, the OTP is free to seek cooperation on a voluntary basis during early proceedings.

Returning to the listing of preliminary examination measures, the lax manner in which some authors handle article 15 (2) is quite surprising. At this stage of proceedings, the Prosecutor has not opened a formal investigation and there are few judicial checks. The sophisticated procedural interplay between PTC and OTP only applies after an authorization request has been submitted. For example, the taking of testimony is a typical investigative step that is introduced into pre-investigations through article 15 (2) and rule 104 (2). There is no indication that the word "testimony" is to be employed in a broad sense.[1100] On the contrary, general submission of information is already covered by the preceding wording that allows for "additional information from [...] other reliable sources." Individuals may at all times give information to the OTP in the form of communications, whereas testimony refers to evidence that is given by a competent witness under established procedure.[1101] Moreover, rule 47 introduces the rather technical

---

[1098] At the moment, this can be deemed the prevailing opinion, cf. Claus Kress/Kimberly Prost, "Article 86," in Triffterer, *supra* note 321, article 86, mn 11; Informal expert paper: Fact-finding and investigative functions, *supra* note 472, paras. 25–6; Meißner, *supra* note 371, 54–5. Contrary, Olásolo, *supra* note 400, 288. Differentiated Schabas, *supra* note 13, 320.

[1099] Kress/Prost, in Triffterer, *supra* note 1098, article 86, mn 11.

[1100] Such a broad view is taken by Turone, in Cassese/Gaeta/Jones, *supra* note 26, 1149.

provisions of rules 111 and 112 into article 15 (2) and rule 104 respectively.[1102] Rule 47 (2) even provides that the Prosecutor must ask the PTC to appoint a counsel or a judge to be present during the taking of the testimony, in order to protect the rights of the defence, if the Prosecutor wishes to present the evidence at later procedural stages. Given the foregoing, testimony must be interpreted strictly, since this measure has been transferred to the pre-investigation phase by way of exception.

Similarly, there is no clear legal basis to show that the Prosecutor could turn to the PTC for further guidance on article 15 (2).[1103] The enumerated measures are exhaustive and cannot be stretched. However, to the extent that we are dealing solely with an interpretation of the existing article 15 (2) tools, the PTC can advise the Prosecutor during an authorization request. The PTC will most certainly follow the narrow interpretation taken here, since full investigations cannot be conducted as disguised pre-investigations. To recapitulate, I have argued that:

- the majority of OTP activities during pre-investigations must be performed in The Hague;
- "testimony" refers to a narrow, technical term during pre-investigations, but testimony can be taken by national authorities on a voluntary basis and can be delivered to The Hague;
- part 9 of the ICC Statute does not apply to pre-investigations;
- preliminary examination measures are limited to the ones mentioned within article 15 (2), rule 104.

D. Seizure of pre-investigations

The OTP Regulations do not specify an end point for preliminary analysis and a start of full investigations. OTP Regulation 19 (4) states, rather generally, that "[t]he evaluation shall continue for as long as the situation remains under investigation." However, it can be reasoned that a preliminary investigation culminates in a decision by the Prosecutor either to proceed or not to proceed to an investigation.[1104] In other words, the decision on "reasonable basis" marks the line between pre- and full investigations. Of course, in the case of *proprio motu* proceedings, the line is only crossed after PTC authorization pursuant to article 15 (4).

1101 Razesberger, *supra* note 371, 64–5.

1102 On this procedure see Holmes, in Lee, *supra* note 959, 330.

1103 See *supra* note 1089 and corresponding text.

1104 For the sake of clarity, and upon suggestion by this author, a similar wording was included in the newly drafted paragraph (3) of OTP Regulation 29.

The extent of pre-investigations generates further issues and has already led to a clash between OTP and PTC in the CAR situation. Even before this controversy, one author asked how long the pre-investigative stage can be continued before invading into the territory of the formal investigation stage ("[…] how far can the Prosecutor proceed his/her gathering of additional information and 'testimonies' under article 15 (2) without entering the field of an 'investigation'?").[1105] Focusing on article 15 (3), the practical question is how long the Prosecutor can continue without requesting the authorization to start a formal investigation. Neither article 15 (2) nor rule 47 establish any express time limit for preliminary examination. In general, the Prosecutor can keep gathering information until the reasonable basis is reached and he feels sufficiently confident to submit a request under article 15 (3).[1106] The ICC Statute does not impose rigid time-limits to carry out a preliminary examination; at the same time, however, it does not give the OTP unlimited flexibility.[1107] Investigative measures must be interpreted in a restrictive manner and must be limited to the ones enumerated in article 15 (2). The pre-investigation is not an all-embracing investigation and the measures of article 15 (2) (oral or written testimony, etc.) only serve the purpose of analyzing the seriousness of the information received in order to determine the reasonability standard. The "reasonable basis" standard is less than those of "sufficient basis" in article 53 (2), the "reasonable grounds" of article 58 (1) (a), or the "substantial grounds" of article 61 (7). In fact, the "reasonable basis" can be described as the first step of a stairway, which becomes stricter with every step taken towards trial and requires more profound evidence on each level.[1108] Article 15 aims only at information gathering for the purpose of establishing the threshold of "reasonable basis." If the Prosecutor seeks to use investigative measures other than those enumerated there is no reason to avoid the beginning of a formal investigation. Limiting the measures to article 15 (2) would function as a safeguard to avoid vast enlargement of the pre-investigation for gathering more information without supervision of the PTC.[1109] In sum, if the OTP wishes to gather more profound evidence, the start of a formal investigation is unavoidable, after which point the Prosecutor can use all his powers pursuant to article 54. The undeniable risk that the OTP may abuse its powers to carry out article 54 investigations disguised as pre-investigation measures

---

1105 Turone, in Cassese/Gaeta/Jones, *supra* note 26, 1150.

1106 Turone, in Cassese/Gaeta/Jones, *supra* note 26, 1151.

1107 Olásolo, *supra* note 29, 62 with fn. 182.

1108 See further Part IV, B., II., 3.

1109 On the danger of not notifying at all, see El Zeidy, *supra* note 269, 54–5 ("justice delayed is justice denied").

remains.[1110] Avoiding this problem depends on the high moral character of the Prosecutor (article 42 (3)).

In practice, though, the problematic time-frame remains unresolved, since neither the ICC Statute nor the RPE give the PTC a legal handle. It has been suggested that the OTP must complete preliminary examinations within a reasonable period of time.[1111] As outlined above, the object and purpose of article 15 (2) inquiries is aimed at gathering sufficient information for the purposes of an authorization request. Disguised article 54 investigations would be contrary to the limited scope of preliminary examinations.[1112] The article 15 (6) rights of informants, regardless of the fact that the provision does not lay down a precise time limit, would also be abrogated if the OTP were able to indefinitely prolong its examination.[1113]

In the CAR situation, a vast OTP investigation led to just this type of controversy. After the Prosecutor received a referral from the Government of the CAR and announced his preliminary examination, almost two years passed without any information of the status of the situation under scrutiny.[1114] Because the DRC and Uganda examinations were completed within six months, the PTC requested a report on the current status of the preliminary investigation, "including an estimate of when the preliminary examination of the CAR situation will be concluded and when a decision pursuant to article 53 (1) of the Statute will be taken."[1115] Regardless of its complexity, the examination of a situation must be completed within a reasonable time.[1116] The Chamber bases this demand for completion within a "reasonable time" on a systematic interpretation of the ICC Statute in that it refers to rule 105 (1), according to which the Prosecutor shall "promptly" inform the State when he decides not to initiate an investigation.[1117] In ad-

---

1110 Olásolo, *supra* note 29, 62; El Zeidy, *supra* note 269, 54–5.

1111 Olásolo, *supra* note 29, 61–2.

1112 Olásolo, *supra* note 29, 61.

1113 Olásolo, *supra* note 29, 62. On the reasons in favor of a time-limit from the standpoint of the individual and States see Federica Gioia, "The complementarity role of the International Criminal Court: Are there any time-limits?" in Politi/Gioia, *supra* note 517, 71, 72 et seq.

1114 *Situation in CAR,* Decision requesting information on the status of the preliminary examination, *supra* note 268, 4; HRW Courting history report, *supra* note 126, 23; Schabas, *supra* note 13, 667.

1115 *Situation in CAR,* Decision requesting information on the status of the preliminary examination, *supra* note 268, 4. See already Part III, B., I., 3.

1116 *Situation in CAR,* Decision requesting information on the status of the preliminary examination, *supra* note 268, 4; Olásolo, *supra* note 29, 61–2; Stahn, in Stahn/Sluiter, *supra* note 156, 276.

1117 *Situation in CAR,* Decision requesting information on the status of the preliminary examination, *supra* note 268, 3.

dition, it enumerates a number of provisions that embrace the "reasonable time" standard, as well as other related standards, such as "without delay," "promptly," or "in an expeditious manner" (articles 61 (1), (3), 64 (2), 67 (1) (c), 82 (1) (d); rules 24 (2) (b), 49 (1), 101 (1), 106 (1), 114 (1), 118 (1), 121 (1), (6), 132 (1)).[1118] On the one hand, the PTC's sense of urgency in reviewing the progress made in the CAR situation after two years of silence is understandable. On the other hand, no precise provision enables the Chamber to convene status conferences during pre-investigations, and no provision expressly states that the OTP shall conclude its preliminary examinations within a reasonable time. Starting with the latter question, a reasonable time standard could possibly be deduced from systematic and teleological interpretations. Nevertheless, all previous approaches fail to set an exact time-frame for reasonableness. What would be a "reasonable" time period? First, the DRC and Uganda examinations lasted less than six months. Second, pre-investigations are thought to provide for a *prima facie* investigation solely for the purpose of establishing a reasonable basis to initiate a full investigation. In practice, the particularities of one situation might require a more probing examination than another, making it difficult to set an exact time-frame. One solution could be a newly drafted rule 48*bis* with a twofold nature: in paragraph 1 it should provide for a maximum time-table of 18 months; paragraph 2 could then allow for a submission to the PTC for an extension of the time-frame if the OTP needs and can justify the additional time.

The Prosecutor's position in the CAR situation was somewhat different. From his point of view, the PTC is without authority to review or control his activities until he makes a decision to proceed. Although he was under no legal obligation to do so, he replied and provided information, but emphasized that:

> "The Pre-Trial Chamber' supervisory role, under article 53 (3), only applies to the review of a decision under article 53 (1) and (2) by the Prosecutor not to proceed with an investigation or a prosecution. The OTP submits that to date no decision under article 53 (1) has been made, and that accordingly there is no exercise of prosecutorial discretion susceptible to judicial review by the Chamber."[1119]

The OTP's statement is, in essence, correct, but leads us in the wrong direction. A review power by the PTC is only foreseen in article 53 (3),

---

[1118] *Situation in CAR,* Decision requesting information on the status of the preliminary examination, *supra* note 268, 4 with fn. 5.

[1119] *Situation in CAR,* Prosecution's report pursuant to Pre-Trial Chamber III's 30 November 2006 decision requesting information on the status of the preliminary examination, *supra* note 172, 2; El Zeidy, *supra* note 269, 53–4. In contrast, Schabas, *supra* note 27, 247–8, calls this reasoning "flimsy."

and a prerequisite for the exercise thereof is a negative decision of the Prosecutor under article 53 (1) or (2). But the decisive question is whether the PTC can demand information on the status of the examination after a certain period of inaction. The follow-up question is whether and how the Chamber can convene such an early status conference or status report. With regard to the first question, only a new rule or future case law could solve the issue of a time-frame. In my view, a specific time period should be fixed, during which the OTP can pre-investigate freely, in accordance with its statutory independence. If, after more than 18 months, no notification has been provided, the PTC should be able to intervene and ask for information on the status of the investigation.

Yet, it remains unclear which legal basis allows for such an early status check. The problems of article 53 were left unresolved in the situation of the CAR.[1120] The drafting shows an apparent gap in this respect.[1121] In the situation of the CAR, PTC III linked its right to be informed to Court Regulation 46 (2), pursuant to which the Chamber "shall be responsible for any matter, request or information arising out of the situation assigned to it."[1122] Regulation 46 (2) must, however, be seen in connection with statutory provisions (articles 18 and 53 (1), rules 104 and 105 (1)), and provides no independent legal basis for judicial supervision.[1123] In the CAR situation the Chamber asked for a report, while in the DRC and Uganda it only held status conferences. With respect to Uganda, the PTC convened a status conference to discuss a potential decision under article 53 (2).[1124] However, it is important to note that this decision took place after a full article 53 (1) investigation had been initiated for the whole Ugandan situation, and thus involved a later procedural phase than that of the CAR. Nevertheless, the Chamber's underlying purpose was the same: to get information on the status of the OTP's inquiry. For Uganda, the Chamber used Court Regulation 30 as the legal basis which to assert its right to convene such a status conference[1125] and the Prosecutor did not contest this legal foundation.[1126] In-

---

1120 Stahn, in Stahn/Sluiter, *supra* note 156, 276.

1121 El Zeidy, *supra* note 269, 55.

1122 *Situation in CAR,* Decision requesting information on the status of the preliminary examination, *supra* note 268, 3.

1123 El Zeidy, *supra* note 269, 53.

1124 *Prosecutor v. Kony et al.,* Decision to convene a status conference on the investigation in the situation in Uganda, *supra* note 248.

1125 *Prosecutor v. Kony et al.*, Decision to convene a status conference on the investigation in the situation in Uganda, *supra* note 248, para. 15. In the first-ever decision in the DRC, the PTC convened a status conference noting Court Regulations 46 (2) and 30, see *Situation in DRC,* Decision to convene a status conference, 17.2.2005 (ICC-01/04-9) 2; thereto HRW Courting history report, *supra* note 126, 21.

stead, the OTP informed PTC II that no decision pursuant to article 53 (2) had been made and that inquiries involving the UPDF are ongoing.[1127] Court Regulation 30, however, is a rather vague provision and says nothing about the convocation of such status conferences.[1128] In fact, the OTP seems to have adopted an ethic of mutual cooperation, accepting supervision on a voluntary basis.[1129] From a legal point of view, however, one must conclude that no provision clearly allows the PTC to convene status conferences or ask for status reports during pre-investigations. It is therefore submitted that the only feasible solution would be to include the possibility of status conferences and reports in the newly envisaged rule 48*bis*.[1130]

The CAR situation, therefore, generated the first signs of conflict between the PTC and the OTP in this area.[1131] It has to be emphasized that pre-investigations and investigations are primarily the Prosecutor's domain. The Prosecutor correctly emphasized that the "interplay between Pre-Trial Chamber and Prosecution is a sensitive matter that lies at the heart of the compromises reached in Rome between different legal traditions and values and must be approached with the utmost caution."[1132] Ideally, checks by the Chamber have to be codified in the ICC Statute, or at least the RPE, to avoid undue interference into the competences of the Prosecutor. However, the request by PTC III did put the Prosecutor under pressure and resulted in the opening of a formal investigation on 22 May 2007.[1133] On the surface, the CAR situation seemed to fit the profile of a situation that should

---

1126 The OTP did, however, file a submission in response to the first status conference in the DRC situation and opposed the idea of PTC intervention during the investigation stage as being unauthorized, *Situation in DRC,* Prosecutors position on Pre-Trial Chamber I's 17 February 2005 decision to convene a status conference (redacted version), 11.3.2005 (ICC-01/04-12) para. 4. This position was rejected on procedural grounds, then was appealed by the Prosecutor in order to suspend the scheduled status conference, and was finally rejected again, cf. thereto Ambos, in Bohlander, *supra* note 10, 443.

1127 *Prosecutor v. Kony et al.,* OTP submission providing information on status of the investigation, *supra* note 563, paras. 1, 6.

1128 Schabas, *supra* note 27, 246; *Situation in DRC,* Prosecutors position on Pre-Trial Chamber I's 17 February 2005 decision, *supra* note 1126, para. 18.

1129 El Zeidy, *supra* note 269, 54.

1130 El Zeidy, *supra* note 269, 55–6, suggests that reliance on the "implied powers" of the Court could be a possible solution to remedy the gap. Instead, it is put forward that a matter, being as important as the one at hand, thus going to the very heart of the balance OTP *vis-à-vis* PTC, has to be explicitly regulated.

1131 Schabas, *supra* note 27, 246.

1132 *Situation in DRC,* Prosecutors position on Pre-Trial Chamber I's 17 February 2005 decision, *supra* note 1126, para. 3.

1133 See *supra* note 270 and corresponding text.

be heard by this Court and one could ask why the pre-investigation took such a long time. The gravity-related policy of situation selection was arguably in question, as the CAR situations involved a far lower numbers of incidents than Darfur, Uganda, and the DRC.[1134]

To prevent this type of conflict in future, a new rule should be drafted to balance prosecutorial independence against necessary checks.[1135] The following draft is submitted as a basis for discussion:

Rule 48bis

Status requests during preliminary examinations

(1) The Prosecutor shall conclude his preliminary investigation pursuant to article 15 (2), rule 104, within a reasonable time period of no more than 18 months.

(2) If the Prosecutor needs to continue preliminary examinations and cannot yet determine the reasonable basis in accordance with articles 15 (3), 53 (1), rule 48, the Prosecutor may submit reasons to the Pre-Trial Chamber who shall then grant a continuation for an additional period of 6 months.

(3) The Pre-Trial Chamber may request status conferences or reports during preliminary examinations. Before the reasonable time period has expired the Prosecutor may answer *ex aequo et bono*, afterwards he or she shall provide sufficient information.

The introduction of draft rule 48*bis* cannot, however, resolve all concerns. In case law, the PTC has consolidated status conferences during investigation procedures, which could shift the balance between the OTP and the PTC in the direction of more judicial supervision.[1136] On the other hand, unfettered prosecutorial discretion goes against the interests of other parties in the proceedings and is unacceptable.[1137] Judicial intervention during the pre-investigation stage should therefore be possible, but limited. In my opinion, a *legality* decision is strictly forbidden during pre-investigations, and the envisaged rule should only function to *expedite* proceedings. As outlined above, a decision not to initiate *proprio motu* proceedings cannot be controlled by the PTC; in particular, the reasonable basis can only be evaluated by the PTC if the Prosecutor asks for authorization under article 15 (4).[1138] Moreover, the current approach of status conferences during

---

[1134] For the problematic quantitative approach, see Part IV, B., III., 2., c), cc), (2).

[1135] A positive control over *proprio motu* proceedings would significantly weaken prosecutorial independence, Stigen, *supra* note 205, 112.

[1136] Michela Miraglia, "The first decision of the ICC Pre-Trial Chamber" (2006) 4 JICJ 188, 192–3.

[1137] Ambos, in Bohlander, *supra* note 10, 444.

[1138] See Part III, C., I.; coming to the same conclusion Wei, *supra* note 156, 82.

investigations, as well as the demand for a status report in the CAR situation during pre-investigations, is legally slippery. Given this danger, I suggest the initiation of a discussion process based on draft rule 48*bis* for upcoming review conferences, understanding of course that it will be difficult to find the right balance between prosecutorial independence and essential checks. This complicated task must involve all the actors, including States Parties through the ASP.

E. Concluding observations Part III

Chapter III has examined the trigger mechanism, which is embedded in the pre-investigation phase as a whole. State referrals, SC referrals, and *proprio motu* investigations all form essential tools for the Prosecutor to initiate investigations, and there is no legal hierarchy between the three. Due to the OTP policy and the *Realpolitik* interests, however, a factual hierarchy has evolved favoring State self-referrals and SC referrals over third-party referrals and *proprio motu* initiations. In my view, the OTP should change its policy and promote *proprio motu* investigations, which are likely to be the least politicized triggering procedure.

A thorough analysis of the preliminary examination process of the OTP with reference to the statutory language reveals that ICC pre-investigations constitute a distinct procedural stage that lasts from the triggering of a situation until a decision has been taken to either initiate a formal investigation (through PTC authorization) or to refuse further proceedings. Moreover, the demarcation line between situations and cases has been set at the issuance of an arrest warrant. The general process regarding situations can be sketched as follows:

The OTP...

(1) ... obtains *notitia criminis* through one of the three trigger mechanisms;

(2) ... starts pre-investigating;

(3) ... identifies a situation;

(4) ... checks the criteria enshrined in articles 53 (1), 15 (3), rule 48, with regard to the situation as a whole;

(5) ... starts a formal investigation (in the case of a referral), or asks for authorization of a formal investigation (in the case of information under article 15);

(6) ... investigates all-embracingly and ideally identifies individual suspects (individualizes);

(7) ... ultimately applies for a warrant of arrest or summons to appear, if the reasonable grounds standard of article 58 (1), (7), is answered in the affirmative.

As such, situations form the basis of pre-investigations, and step (5) marks the formal ending of the pre-investigation stage. Formal article 54 investigations take place with respect to situations until the OTP applies for a warrant. After a warrant has been issued, cases in the strict sense are brought to trial. Yet, this is only one side of the coin. On the other hand, the OTP advances a process of individualization during the whole case selection procedure. The Prosecutor has described the sequence of the case selection process as follows: selecting situations, selecting geographic regions, selecting incidents, selecting groups, selecting persons most responsible for most serious crimes, selecting charges, and bringing a case.[1139] Two overarching categories – "situations" (including selecting regions and selecting incidents) and "cases" (including selecting groups and selecting persons) – encompass all steps in the selection procedure.[1140] However, pre-investigations can be deemed their own procedural stage at the ICC, for reasons described in Chapter III. They can neither be compared to the *ad hoc* tribunals' initiation procedure nor to national proceedings. As noted above, the ICC's initiation procedures are far more complex and innovative. Moreover, an interpretation of the method and criteria has shown that all three triggers are subject to the same basic procedure. An important aspect for pre-investigations is the relationship between articles 15 and 53, which favors uniform application of the evaluation criteria with regard to SC referrals, State referrals, and *proprio motu* proceedings.

At the pre-investigation phase, the Prosecutor is not, however, entitled to exercise all of his powers. Pursuant to articles 15 (2), 53 (1), and rule 48, preliminary examinations include the following four components:

(a) analyzing the seriousness of the information received;

(b) seeking additional information as deemed appropriate by the Prosecutor;

(c) receiving written or oral testimony at the seat of the Court;

(d) considering whether the information available provides a reasonable basis with careful observance of the criteria mentioned in article 53 (1) (a)–(c).

[1139] See already Part III, B., III., 2. On case selections see also OTP Regulations 33 and 34. Recently, PTC II requested more information on the incidents and groups involved in the Kenyan situation, *Situation in Kenya*, Decision requesting clarification and additional information, *supra* note 961, 6.

[1140] Stahn, in Stahn/Sluiter, *supra* note 156, 268.

In this chapter, I have identified several risks associated with a wide interpretation of available pre-investigation measures. In addition, concerns have been raised that the Prosecutor indefinitely prolongs pre-investigations as disguised full investigations. Therefore, preliminary examination measures must be interpreted narrowly and they must be limited to those enumerated above. For further terminological clarification, I suggest that the terms "pre-investigations" and "preliminary examinations" be used. I prefer the latter term for the process and method applied by the OTP, while the former term more precisely covers the newly identified entire procedural stage. The pre-investigation stage starts with one of the trigger mechanisms, followed by the analysis process as laid down in article 15 (2), rules 46, 47, and 104, and – last but not least – the decision whether there is a reasonable basis to initiate an investigation according to articles 53 (1), 15 (3), and rule 48. This last decision formally ends pre-investigation and triggers a full investigation.

Part IV

Selection criteria

A. Introduction

The Chief Prosecutor of the ICC stated:

> "I will apply the law without political considerations and I should not adjust to political considerations."[1141]

This proclamation reflects the difficult position of the ICC Prosecutor who finds himself in the area of conflict between evolving international criminal law and politics. Indeed, the ICC Prosecutor sits at a critical juncture where the pressure of law and politics converge.[1142] His most important decisions are selecting situations for investigation and choosing cases for prosecution. The outcome surely has explosive impact. Nevertheless, the Prosecutor emphasized that he has the power to "independently select situations.[1143]"

The ICC is meant to punish the most serious crimes of concern to the international community as a whole, thus bringing people to justice even if they are heads of States. Tough decisions have to be made, priorities set, and situations and specific perpetrators selected.[1144] The Prosecutor will have to justify every decision not to get involved in a situation.[1145] For his

---

[1141] Statement by Luis Moreno-Ocampo: Commemoration of the 10th anniversary of the adoption of the Rome Statute of the International Criminal Court, 17.7.2008, 6; similarly, Address to the Assembly of States Parties 2008, *supra* note 322, 6: "I have to apply the law. Nothing more, nothing less."

[1142] Danner, *supra* note 953, 510.

[1143] Prosecutor's speech to the Eighth Session of the Assembly of States Parties, 18.11.2009, 5.

[1144] Graham Blewitt, "Exercising independence: the ICTY and ICC prosecutors" in Stelios Perrakis (ed.), *International Criminal Court, A new dimension in international justice. Questions and prospects for a new humanitarian order,* Colloqium, Santorini 14–16 September 2000 (Ant. N. Sakkoulas Publishers, Athens 2002) 155, 158; James Hamilton, Session 3: General input on ICC-OTP questions (paper), First public hearing of the OTP, 19.3.2003, 2.

[1145] Stigen, *supra* note 205, 339. It must be clear why specific crimes and situations are addressed by the OTP, Jennifer Schense, Session 5: Transcript, First public hearing of the OTP, 17.6.2003, 3.

choice, a clear conception based on objective, transparent criteria is required. Formal criteria can be an essential tool for a more rational and coherent prioritization of cases.[1146] So far, the OTP lacks all-embracing guidelines, notwithstanding serious efforts to develop a prosecutorial strategy in its strategy papers and policy papers.[1147] Sometimes, there is a lack of statutory support for the taken avenue; on the other hand, the question may be posed whether the normative framework for the selection process is sufficient.[1148] At least, the statutory support is ambiguous, and one might wonder about the substantive content of various norms. This uncertainty requires the Prosecutor to generate precise selection criteria by himself. Thereby, a clear distinction between situations and cases is necessary. Generally speaking, the legal criteria for the selection process are rooted in article 53 (1) and (2).[1149] They can be roughly grouped in jurisdictional, admissibility, and "interests of justice" considerations. Article 53 (1)'s criteria are taken into account during pre-investigations when selecting situations. A positive decision with respect to all three legal criteria marks the end of pre-investigations and brings the OTP into the realm of full investigations. In contrast, article 53 (2) is applied at a later stage when the Prosecutor must decide whether there is a sufficient basis for a prosecution. The objects under article 53 (2) are, in principle, cases. However, only if the OTP concludes that there is no sufficient basis, shall it inform the PTC pursuant to article 53 (2) (c) *in fine*. Otherwise the Prosecutor is free to bring his case. To sum up, article 53 (1) covers the legal parameters with regard to situations,[1150] while article 53 (2) constitutes the case selection criteria. The selection process can therefore be divided into two distinct stages: first, the identification of situations and second, the selection of cases.[1151]

1146 Morten Bergsmo, "The theme of selection and prioritization criteria and why it is relevant" in Bergsmo, *supra* note 99, 15, 16.

1147 OTP strategy, *supra note* 409; Prosecutorial Strategy 2009–2012, *supra* note 99; see also *supra* note 99 with corresponding text. In more detail, Schabas, *supra* note 27, 32 et seq., and Part IV, B., II., 4.

1148 Stahn, in Stahn/Sluiter, *supra* note 156, 267.

1149 Selection paper, *supra* note 99, para. 2; also Avril McDonald/Roelof Haveman, "Prosecutorial discretion – some thoughts on objectifying the exercise of prosecutorial discretion by the Prosecutor of the ICC," Contribution to an expert consultation process on general issues relevant to the ICC OTP, 15 April 2003, 2 et seq.

1150 At first sight, this finding appears problematic with regard to the wording of article 53 (1) (b) referring to cases, but it is submitted that purely literal interpretations have shown great deficits, in particular when the differentiation of situations vs. cases is involved, see further Part IV, B., III., 2., c), bb), (5) and *supra* note 376; recently, coming to the same conclusion, Schabas, *supra* note 13, 660.

1151 William Schabas, "Prosecutorial discretion v. judicial activism at the International Criminal Court" (2008) 6 JICJ 731, 734; Ohlin, in Stahn/Sluiter, *supra* note 428, 190.

Moreover, several additional criteria have been suggested by the OTP and academic authors. Most of those are missing an explicit basis within article 53. It will be my hypothesis that most additional (unwritten) criteria must be applied under the "interests of justice" criterion. The latter proposition is justified by the open nature of the "interests of justice" clause in connection with the opening clause of article 53 (2) (c). Article 53 (2) (c) provides, *inter alia,* that the Prosecutor shall take into account "all the circumstances," suggesting a wide scope of potential factors.

The gravity issue (and its range) is highly disputed and needs further analysis. It will be shown that gravity has two dimensions: first, there is it is a legal standard under articles 53 (1) (b), 17 (1) (d); second, gravity under article 53 (1) (c) entails discretionary considerations. Gravity is at the heart of each determination finding out which situations and cases merit international adjudication.[1152] Be that as it may, these questions will be readdressed below and for the moment it can be concluded that the explicit criteria mentioned in article 53 (1) and (2) will form a general basis for the survey. The analysis will therefore be guided by the framework provided for in article 53: the decision-making process to start an investigation (paragraph 1) or prosecution (paragraph 2), the review power of the PTC of a decision not to proceed (paragraph 3), and the power of the Prosecutor to reconsider a decision whether to initiate an investigation or prosecution based on new facts or information (paragraph 4). The decision to start full investigations or prosecutions is governed by the substantive criteria mentioned within the first two paragraphs,[1153] whereas paragraph 3 deals with the scope of and procedural requirements for the Prosecutor's discretionary power not to proceed.[1154] This Chapter will first focus on the beginning of a full investigation (B.), before subsequently dealing with the decision-making process regarding prosecutions (C.). Thereafter, the PTC's review power will be revisited (D. and E.). Last but not least, the OTP's policy approach *vis-à-vis* the elaborated criteria have to be evaluated and a preliminary recommendation for the future will conclude the survey (F.).

1152 Margaret McAuliffe deGuzman, "Gravity and the Legitimacy of the International Criminal Court" (2008) 69 YLS Student Scholarship Series 1, 4; William Schabas, "Prosecutorial discretion and gravity," in Stahn/Sluiter, *supra* note 5, 229, 229.

1153 As already mentioned, the substantive determination basically follows a three-stage scheme (jurisdiction, admissibility, interests of justice); contrary, Frank Meyer, "Complementing complementarity" (2006) 6 ICLR 549, 553, who omits the first criterion of jurisdiction and falsely refers to a two-stage procedure.

1154 Bergsmo/Kruger, in Triffterer, *supra* note 906, article 53, mn 1; Hoffmeister/Knoke, *supra* note 169, 801.

B. The initiation of an investigation, article 53 paragraph 1

Article 53 (1) covers the start of a formal investigation with regard to an entire situation. First, the Prosecutor has to decide whether to launch a situation for further investigations taking into account the relevant criteria of paragraph 1. The OTP gathers and evaluates information during pre-investigations as outlined in Part III of this study, and its pre-investigations culminate in an article 53 (1) determination. After taking a glance at article 53's drafting history (I.), the chapeau will be dismantled (II.). The latter analysis will include core questions of the OTP's prosecutorial discretion and the OTP's early prosecutorial policy. Thereafter, the evaluation criteria can be addressed one by one (III.).

I. Drafting history of article 53

The final version of article 53 is a result of a compromise reached at the Rome Conference and during the Preparatory Committee stage.[1155] It is fair to say that substantial work was achieved by the Conference itself.[1156] In any event, a short glance through the drafting history might be helpful with regard to the "reasonable basis" and "sufficient basis" standards to commence an investigation and prosecution.

First attempts to define investigation and prosecution proceedings can be found in articles 26 and 27 ILC Draft Statute of 1994. Article 26 ILC Draft Statute has the heading "investigation of alleged crimes," and, in its most relevant paragraphs 1, 4, and 5, spells out:

> "1. On receiving a complaint or upon notification of a decision of the Security Council referred to in article 23 (1), the Prosecutor shall *initiate an investigation unless* the Prosecutor decides that there is *no possible basis for a prosecution* under this Statute, in which case the Prosecutor shall so inform the Presidency.
>
> [...]
>
> 4. If, upon investigation and having regard inter alia to the matters referred to in article 35, the Prosecutor *concludes that there is no sufficient basis for a prosecution* under this Statute, the Prosecutor shall so inform the Presidency giving details of the nature and basis of the complaint and of the reasons for not filing an indictment.
>
> 5. At the request of a complainant State or, in a case to which article 23 (1) applies, at the request of the Security Council, the Presidency *shall review a deci-*

[1155] Guariglia, in Lee, *supra* note 14, 229.

[1156] Bergsmo/Kruger, in Triffterer, *supra* note 906, article 53, mn 3; Turone, in Cassese/Gaeta/Jones, *supra* note 26, 1138–9.

sion of the Prosecutor not to initiate an investigation or not to file an indictment, and may request the Prosecutor to reconsider the decision.

[...] (emph. added)."[1157]

It is interesting to note that the drafters envisaged the complainant State to conduct preliminary investigations "which may substitute for the process of initial inquiry an investigation to some degree."[1158] Investigations shall be initiated *unless* there is no possible basis for a prosecution. The drafters thus preferred an assumption in favor of investigations ("shall initiate") and introduced an exemption thereto ("unless") in the case of an insufficient basis for further proceedings. The very same construct (*Regel-Ausnahme-Prinzip*) found its way into article 53 (1) ("shall [...] initiate an investigation, unless [...]"). However, the "possible basis" standard is not further commented on. Upon investigation the Prosecutor must evaluate the information obtained and decide whether there is a *sufficient basis* to proceed with a prosecution. The same standard can be found in current article 53 (2). If the Prosecutor does not initiate an investigation or proceed with the case, a judicial review power is foreseen, leaving the ultimate decision to the Prosecutor.[1159] Nevertheless, the general need to provide some form of judicial control over the Prosecutor's activities was emphasized.[1160] The ILC Report further indicates what factors should be taken into account to determine the sufficient basis standard:

"The phrase "sufficient basis" in paragraph 4 is intended to cover a number of different situations where further action under the Statute would not be warranted: first, where there is no indication of a crime within the jurisdiction of the Court; second, where there is some indication of such a crime but the Prosecutor concludes that the evidence available is not strong enough to make a conviction likely; third, where there is *prima facie* evidence of a crime within the jurisdiction of the Court, but the Prosecutor is satisfied that the case would probably be inadmissible under article 35."[1161]

Hence, the drafters already mentioned jurisdiction, admissibility (complementarity and gravity),[1162] and evidentiary issues. Article 27 ICL Draft Statute further spelled out:

1157 ILC Draft Statute 1994, *supra* note 353, 90–1; Bassiouni, *supra* note 503, 363–4.

1158 ILC Draft Statute 1994, *supra* note 353, 92.

1159 ILC Draft Statute 1994, *supra* note 353, 93.

1160 ILC Draft Statute 1994, *supra* note 353, 93.

1161 ILC Draft Statute 1994, *supra* note 353, 94.

1162 Article 35 ILC Draft Statute 1994 states:

"[...] that a case before it is inadmissible on the ground that the crime in question:

(a) has been duly investigated by a State with jurisdiction over it, and the decision of that State not to proceed to a prosecution is apparently well-founded;

"1. If upon investigation the Prosecutor concludes that there is a *prima facie* case, the Prosecutor shall file with the Registrar an indictment containing a concise statement of the allegations of fact and of the crime or crimes with which the suspect is charged.

[...]."

The complaint should be the document that initiates the investigation of a crime and the indictment should formally initiate a prosecution.[1163] The standard for commencing such a prosecution was determined to be a *prima facie* case, which was understood "to be a credible case which would – if not contradicted by the defence – be a sufficient basis to convict the accused on the charge."[1164]

Coming to the Preparatory Committee of 1996, various suggestions were made as regards the initiation of an investigation providing for a minimum threshold and a screening mechanism.[1165] *Inter alia* the standard to initiate an investigation or to file an indictment was further discussed:

"It was suggested that the Prosecutor should, for example, have broad discretion to decide not to initiate or to discontinue an investigation or prosecution in the interests of justice owing to the age or illness of an individual or a national investigation or prosecution, or to have the authority to decline to investigate or to prosecute certain cases which were not of sufficient gravity and to select the most important cases when crimes were committed on a massive scale."[1166]

For the judicial review power, a number of bodies were proposed as being the one most appropriate to review the Prosecutor's decision not to initiate an investigation: a Trial Chamber, an Investigations Chamber, a Judge at the request of the Complainant State, the SC, or even the victims. According to some, the review should be based on a specific legal standard such as "manifestly inappropriate," and others suggested that the controlling body should be limited to only requesting the Prosecutor to reconsider a decision[1167] The latter idea found its way into article 53 (3) (a), in contrast to which article 53 (3) (b) requires confirmation by the PTC if the Prosecu-

(b) is under investigation by a State which has or may have jurisdiction over it, and there is no reason for the Court to take any further action for the time being with respect to the crime; or (c) is not of such gravity to justify further action by the Court."

1163 ILC Draft Statute 1994, *supra* note 353, 95.

1164 ILC Draft Statute 1994, *supra* note 353, 95.

1165 Report of the Preparatory Committee 1996, Vol. 1, *supra* note 203, para. 224, 49.

1166 Report of the Preparatory Committee 1996, Vol. 1, *supra* note 203, para. 229, 50.

1167 Report of the Preparatory Committee 1996, Vol. 1, *supra* note 203, para. 230, 50.

tor's decision is based solely on the "interests of justice" criterion. All proposals were included into article 26 in several paragraphs and brackets:

"1. [...] the Prosecutor shall:

[...]

[(b) determine prior to initiating an investigation

(i) whether the complaint provides or is likely to provide a [possible] [reasonable basis] [in law or on the facts] for proceeding with a prosecution under this Statute; and

(ii) whether the case is, or would be admissible under article 35; and

(iii) whether an investigation would be consistent with the terms of any relevant Security Council decision; and

(iv) whether to seek a preliminary ruling from the Court regarding the Court's jurisdiction if the case could later be challenged under article 34.

[...]

3. (a) At the request of a complainant State or, in a case to which article 23 (1) applies, at the request of the Security Council, the Presidency [Preliminary Investigations Chamber] [Indictment Chamber] shall review a decision of the Prosecutor not to initiate an investigation and may request the Prosecutor to reconsider his decision. [...]."[1168]

For prosecutions, it was emphasized that the standard, on which the indictment would ultimately be based, "should be sufficiently high to justify trial proceedings."[1169] Article 27 Draft Statute included proposals with regard to reviewing the indictment:

"[...]

2. [The Presidency] [the Indictment Chamber] [the Pre-trial Chamber] shall [constitute an Indictment Chamber comprising (a single judge/three judges) who are not members of the Trial Chamber to] examine the indictment and any supporting material and determine:

(a) whether a *prima facie* case exists with respect of a crime within the jurisdiction of the Court; [and]

(b) whether, having regard, *inter alia*, to the matters referred to in article 35, the case should on the information available be heard by the Court; and

[(c) whether it is desirable in the interests of justice that the case should proceed].

[...]."

[1168] Report of the Preparatory Committee 1996, Vol. 2, *supra* note 357, 112 et seq.

[1169] Report of the Preparatory Committee 1996, Vol. 1, *supra* note 203, para. 235, 51.

For the first time, the "interests of justice" was mentioned as a potential factor. In 1998 the two separate provision of articles 26 and 27 ICL Draft Statute were merged into one article: article 47 Zutphen Draft Statute and article 54 Draft Statute of April 1998 respectively.[1170] The provisions relevant to final article 53 appeared in the mentioned draft articles with multiple brackets and tentative language.[1171] Article 54 Draft Statute of April 1998 reads in its decisive paragraphs:

"1. On receiving a complaint [or upon notification of a decision of the Security Council referred to in article 10, paragraph 1,] [or ex officio upon any other substantiated information], the Prosecutor shall [subject to paragraphs 2 and 3] initiate an investigation unless the Prosecutor concludes that there is no reasonable basis for a prosecution under this Statute and decides not to initiate an investigation, in which case the Prosecutor shall so inform the [Presidency] [Pre-Trial Chamber].

N. B. The term "reasonable basis" in the opening clause is also used in the criteria listed in paragraph 2 (i). If the latter is retained, a broader term in the opening clause might be necessary in order to cover all the criteria listed under paragraph 2.

[2. Prior to initiating investigation the Prosecutor shall: (a) [notify the States Parties of any complaint [or any decision of the Security Council referred to in article 10, paragraph 1], and those States Parties shall so inform the persons within their jurisdiction who are referred to by name in the submission; and]

(b) determine whether:

(i) the complaint provides or is likely to provide a reasonable basis [in law or on the facts] for proceeding with a prosecution under this Statute; and

(ii) the case is or would be admissible under article 15; and

[(ii) *bis* a prosecution under this Statute would be [in the interests of justice] [taking into account the gravity of the offences] [and the interests of victims];

(iii) [an investigation would be consistent with the terms of any relevant Security Council decision]; and

(iv) to seek a preliminary ruling from the Court regarding the Court's jurisdiction if the case could later be challenged under article 17.]

[3. The Prosecutor shall not initiate an investigation where the submission of the case to the Court is challenged under article 15 within one month of notification under article 54, paragraph 2 (a) until the final ruling of the Court.]

[…]

6. If, upon investigation and having regard, inter alia, to the matters referred to in article 15, the Prosecutor concludes that [a case is inadmissible under article 15

[1170] Zutphen Draft Statute 1998, *supra* note 358, article 47, 112–3; Draft Statute April 1998, *supra* note 44, article 54; also Bassiouni, *supra* note 503, 338 et seq.

[1171] Bergsmo/Kruger, in Triffterer, *supra* note 906, article 53, mn 3.

or] there is [not a sufficient basis for a prosecution] [no *prima facie* case] under this Statute [or a prosecution would not be in the interests of justice] [taking into account the interests of victims] and decides not to file an indictment, the Prosecutor shall so inform the [Presidency] [Pre-Trial Chamber], as well as the complainant State [or the Security Council, in a case to which article 10, paragraph 1, applies], giving details of the nature and basis of the complaint and of the reasons for not filing an indictment.

[7. A decision referred to in paragraph 6 based on considerations of the interests of justice shall only become effective upon its having been confirmed by the [Presidency] [Pre-Trial Chamber] under paragraph 8 of this article.] [...]."

The Working Group on Procedural Matters left several formulations in draft article 54 open "until the larger issues are resolved in the Committee of the Whole," thereby referring to questions regarding the trigger mechanism, the *proprio motu* powers of the Prosecutor, and procedures regarding admissibility.[1172] Therefore, the drafting of article 53 – at that time labeled article 54 Draft Statute of April 1998 – has to be seen in close connection to the drafting of the triggering mechanisms, in particular the *proprio motu* controversy.[1173] The investigative powers of the Prosecutor and the process and procedures to be followed caused strong concerns among delegations. Delegations coming from a common law background, for instance, felt that any judicial intervention during investigations could affect the Prosecutor's independence. On the other hand, delegates with a civil law background held that some degree of judicial supervision was inevitable to avoid an abuse of powers.[1174]

On 25 June 1998 a new proposal finally broke the ice and led to the current version of article 53.[1175] Decisive modification was included in this proposal, and specific criteria were built in the "interests of justice" clause. The proposal highlights relevant changes by underlining them as follows:

[1172] Official Records, Vol. II, *supra* note 392, 272 with fn. 103; Working Paper on article 54, Working Group on Procedural Matters, Committee of the Whole, United Nations Diplomatic Conference of Plenipotentiaries on the Establishment of an International Criminal Court, 15 June–17 July 1998, 18.6.1998 (A/CONF.183/C.1/WGPM/L.1) 1 with fn. 1, 2 with fn. 2.

[1173] Cf. Part III, B., VI., 2.

[1174] Guariglia, in Lee, *supra* note 14, 228.

[1175] Working Paper on article 54, paragraphs 1 (c) and 3 (c), submitted by the informal working group composed of the delegations of Argentina, Belgium, Canada, Finland, France, Germany, Israel, Italy, Japan, Malawi, Mexico, New Zealand, Poland, Portugal, Sweden, Switzerland, The United Kingdom of Great Britain and Northern Ireland, and the United States of America, Working Group on Procedural Matters, Committee of the Whole, United Nations Diplomatic Conference of Plenipotentiaries on the Establishment of an International Criminal Court, 15 June–17 July 1998, 25.6.1998 (A/CONF.183/C.1/WGPM/L.18).

"1. The Prosecutor shall, *having evaluated the information made available to him*, initiate an investigation unless he or she determines that there is no reasonable basis to proceed under this Statute. In deciding whether to initiate an investigation, the Prosecutor shall consider whether:

(a) The information available to him provides a reasonable basis to believe that a crime within the jurisdiction of the Court has been or is being committed;

(b) The case is or would be admissible under article 15; and

(c) *Taking into account the gravity of the crime and the interests of victims, there are nonetheless substantial reasons to believe that an investigation would not serve the interests of justice*; [and

(d) An investigation would be consistent with the terms of any Security Council decision.]

If the Prosecutor determines that there is no reasonable basis to proceed, he shall inform the Pre-Trial Chamber.

2. ****

3. If, upon investigation, the Prosecutor concludes that there is not a sufficient basis for a prosecution because:

(a) There is not a sufficient legal or factual basis to seek a warrant or summons under article 58;

(b) The case is inadmissible under article 15; or

(c) *A prosecution is not in the interests of justice, taking into account all the circumstances, including the gravity of the crimes, the interests of victims and the age or infirmity of the alleged perpetrator, and his role in the alleged crime*,

He or she shall inform the Pre-Trial Chamber and the State making a referral under article 11 [or the Security Council in a case under article 10, paragraph 1,] of his or her conclusion and the reasons for the conclusion.

4. (a) *At the request of the State making a referral under article 11 [or the Security Council under article 10], the Pre-Trial Chamber may review a decision of the Prosecutor not to proceed under paragraph 1 or 3 of this article and may request the Prosecutor to reconsider that decision.*

(b) *In addition, the Pre-Trial Chamber may, on its own initiative, review a decision of the Prosecutor not to proceed if it is based solely on paragraph 1 (c) or 3 (c). In such a case, the decision of the Prosecutor shall be effective only if confirmed by the Pre-Trial Chamber.*

5. The Prosecutor may at any time reconsider a decision whether to initiate an investigation or prosecution based on new facts or information."

It can be deduced from the drafting history that the delegations tried to construe an acceptable compromise for the two opposing positions. They maintained the broad, potentially discretionary term of "interests of justice," yet added further criteria to it: gravity of the crimes, the interests of victims, all the circumstances, the age or infirmity of the alleged perpetrator, and his role in the alleged crime. Besides these substantive add-ons, a procedural review power of the PTC was inserted, requiring a confirmation decision if the Prosecutor decides not to proceed solely based on "interests of justice" considerations. This proposal was generally accepted and included in the report of the Working Group on Procedural Matters during the last week of the Conference.[1176] It is worth noting that some delegates expressed concern regarding the reference to the "interests of justice."[1177]

The final language of article 53 is thus based on a consensus reached during the last gasp of the Rome Conference. On the one hand, delegations were reluctant to grant broad prosecutorial discretion, but realized that some discretionary authority was necessary for the Prosecutor to fulfill his functions effectively.[1178] On the other hand, delegations that had opposed judicial review of the Prosecutor's powers accepted that supervision by the PTC could provide an adequate balance.[1179] The convergence of interests rendered the proposal of 25 June 1998 possible, but the proposal did not resolve the question what substantive content a decision to investigate or prosecute has. Neither the ICC Statute nor the follow-up RPE clarify article 53's criteria. In other words, rather than reaching a compromise on the substance and resolving the degree of discretion involved, particularly how to apply the "interests of justice" criterion, the delegations reached a *procedural compromise* by giving a review power to the PTC whenever the Prosecutor decides not to investigate or prosecute based solely on the "interests of justice."[1180] The content of the clause was left to the interpretation of the ICC's actors. It is therefore a great challenge to fill in the content of article 53's criteria – a task the drafters, in the end, did not accomplish.

[1176] Report of the Working Group on Procedural Matters, Committee of the Whole, United Nations Diplomatic Conference of Plenipotentiaries on the Establishment of an International Criminal Court, 15 June–17 July 1998, 13.7.1998 (A/CONF.183/C.1/WGPM/L.2/Add.7).

[1177] Report of the Working Group on Procedural Matters, *supra* note 1176, 2 with fn. 1. At least, the debate at the Rome Conference reflected rhetorical consensus that legal criteria should prevail rather than "political decision-making," see Alexander Greenawalt, "Justice without politics? Prosecutorial discretion and the International Criminal Court" (2007) 39 NYU Journal of International Law and Politics 583, 593.

[1178] Guariglia, in Lee, *supra* note 14, 230.

[1179] Guariglia, in Lee, *supra* note 14, 230.

[1180] Ambos, in Bohlander, *supra* note 10, 439; in the same vein, Memorandum of Law, Interpretation and scope of "interests of justice" in article 53 of the Rome Statute (hereinafter MoL Interests of Justice), 7.5.2004 (MoL 19-040507-1).

II. Chapeau

The chapeau of article 53 (1) deals with the initiation of a full investigation. It contains the elements "shall," "having evaluated the information," "initiate an investigation," followed by the second fragment of "unless," "reasonable basis," and "shall consider." The first three elements clarify that the Prosecutor shall initiate an investigation after carefully evaluating his information. "Information" refers to that which accompanies the referral of a situation or that which was submitted pursuant to articles 15 (1) and (2). The evaluation of information is an analysis of its seriousness, which is identical regarding all three trigger mechanisms.[1181] It has already been developed that article 53 (1) refers to the commencement of a full investigation as opposed to pre-investigations.[1182] With regard to the remaining elements of the chapeau, it is my hypothesis that a general duty to start formal investigations is imposed upon the Prosecutor, but with the adjunct that a differentiated procedural system derogates this general obligation. Just after the duty to initiate investigations emerges ("shall"), the chapeau introduces an exemption thereto ("unless […] there is no reasonable basis"). The Prosecutor shall not proceed if he sees no reasonable basis in favor of investigations, and in order to reach a determination on the reasonable basis he "shall consider" the criteria of article 53 (1) (a)–(c). Legal scholars disagree on what concept has been chosen as the guiding principle of the overall activity of the Prosecutor – the principle of legality or the expediency principle (principle of opportunity). Generally, as already mentioned, the Prosecutor "shall" initiate an investigation, which simply means he is under an obligation to proceed when a "reasonable basis to proceed" is found. However, it cannot be argued that a strict principle of legality was adopted given the selective prosecution strategy of the ICTY and ICTR and, moreover, the ICC's statutory implementation of discretion through the "interests of justice" clause in article 53 (1) (c) and (2) (c).[1183] In addition, the ICC Prosecutor has largely taken into account his published Prosecutorial Strategy as reflected in the strategy papers and the policy papers.[1184] Before de-

---

[1181] Cf. Part III, C., IV.; also Bergsmo/Kruger, in Triffterer, *supra* note 906, article 53, mn 9.

[1182] See Part III, B., VI., 3.; Bergsmo/Kruger, in Triffterer, *supra* note 906, article 53, mn 5.

[1183] Wei, *supra* note 156, 175 et seq.; Stigen, *supra* note 205, 342. For a comparison of the ICTY and ICC procedure see Stegmiller, *supra* note 370, 328 et seq.

[1184] Annex paper, *supra* note 27, 3; OTP Regulation 14; Prosecutorial Strategy 2009–2012, *supra* note 99; see already the references at *supra* note 99. See further Part IV, B., II., 4.; Brubacher *supra* note 368, 72, who states that it is crucial for the credibility and success of the ICC that the Prosecutor develops a framework that accommodates both *legal* and *policy* considerations.

ciding on the merits, the structure of the chapeau will be further assessed. First, the general duty to investigate is annotated (1.), before the exception thereto is revealed (2.). Thereafter, I will address the important standard of reasonability (3.). The OTP's strategy approach is then outlined (4.), followed by academic approaches with respect to discretion (5.). An intermediary conclusion on the discretionary powers of the ICC Prosecutor will complete part II (6.).

1. Duty to investigate

It is interesting to note that article 53 (1) is drafted in mandatory terms:

> "The Prosecutor *shall*, having evaluated the information made available to him or her, initiate an investigation *unless* he or she determines that there is no reasonable basis to proceed under this Statute."

Whenever the Prosecutor finds a reasonable basis to proceed, he is therefore under an obligation to start a formal investigation. In the same vein, article 15 (3) obliges the Prosecutor to submit a request for authorization if a reasonable basis exists with regard to *proprio motu* information.[1185] The mandatory language of both provisions ("shall") suggests *prima facie* mandatory investigations, i.e. strict adherence to the principle of legality.

It has been suggested further that the drafters of the ICC Statute had chosen the principle of legality over the principle of political discretion for the early stages before the initiation of investigations.[1186] The intermediary conclusion of obligatory investigations is affirmed by the Preamble of the ICC Statute which seeks "that the most serious crimes of concern to the international community as a whole must not go unpunished" and desires to "put an end to impunity for the perpetrators of these crimes." Authors therefore erroneously base the ICC's procedural law as a whole on the principle of legality.[1187] The truth is, however, that the duty is only established insofar as there is a reasonable basis to proceed. Through the backdoor, the apparent legality principle is softened and linked to the three criteria enlisted in article 53 (1) (a)–(c) and article 53 (2) (a)–(c) respectively.

[1185] Part III, B., VI., 5.

[1186] Olásolo, *supra* note 368, 131.

[1187] Tomuschat, *supra* note 423, 335; Van Heeck, *supra* note 26, 190, who later, however, recognizes the exemptions thereto.

2. Exception to the duty to investigate

The duty to start a formal investigation is not absolute. In fact, the chapeau of article 53 (1) states that an obligation arises "unless" the Prosecutor determines that there is no reasonable basis for pursuing a full investigation. A duty to investigate thus occurs only when all three criteria listed in article 53 (1) (a)–(c) are fulfilled, the third being the discretional finding whether or not a matter serves the "interests of justice."[1188] If one of the criteria is not met, there is no reasonable basis to proceed. The Prosecutor must consider all of them, since they are cumulative.[1189] Moreover, the exercise of prosecutorial discretion covers the two phases of investigations and prosecutions equally.[1190] Therefore, the different criteria and the reasonable basis have to be clarified, also looking for possible margins of discretion embedded in the criteria. First, the reasonability test of the chapeau needs refinement (3.), before the all-embracing survey (III.) to come addresses the criteria one by one. I will thereby reveal that the "interests of justice" clause embraces broader discretionary determinations, whereas jurisdiction and admissibility require primarily legal analysis.

3. Determination of reasonable basis to proceed

No definition of "reasonable basis" is provided in article 53.[1191] In the ILC Draft 1994 the criterion was "no possible basis;" in the Draft Statute of 1996 the options possible and reasonable basis were both included in brackets.[1192] Today, the term "reasonable basis" appears three times in article 15, three times in article 53, and once in article 18 (1).[1193] Two questions must be asked: first, whether the test is basically the same under all those provisions, and second, how stringent the reasonability threshold is and what is its substantive content.

1188 Stigen, *supra* note 205, 342.

1189 McDonald/Haveman, *supra* note 1149, 3; Wei, *supra* note 156, 78.

1190 The "interests of justice" criterion appears in article 53 (1) and! (2) (c). See also McDonald/Haveman, *supra* note 1149, 2; Luc Côte, "Reflections on the exercise of prosecutorial discretion in international criminal law" (2005) 3 JICJ 162, 166; Delmas-Marty, *supra* note 1048, 8.

1191 Geert-Jan Alexander Knoops, "Challenging the legitimacy of initiating contemporary international criminal proceedings: rethinking prosecutorial discretionary powers from a legal, ethical and political perspective" (2004) 15 CLF 365, 375.

1192 See the drafting history of article 53 at Part IV, B., I.

1193 Similarly, Bergsmo/Kruger, in Triffterer, *supra* note 906, article 53, mn 11. It is yet submitted that article 58 (1) (a) refers to "reasonable grounds" as opposed to "reasonable basis," which is later similarly evaluated by the mentioned authors themselves.

In general, all mentioned provisions refer to the reasonable basis with respect to the stage in-between preliminary and full investigation. Article 53 (1) (a) addresses the "reasonable basis to believe" whether a crime within the Court's jurisdiction exists and is therefore dealt with separately.[1194] Nevertheless, if the "reasonable basis to believe" is fulfilled, it can be assumed that the "reasonable basis to proceed" of the chapeau is equally met. In this respect, PTC II held that

> "[...] the "reasonable basis to believe" test set out in article 53 (l) (a) of the Statute is subsumed by the "reasonable basis to proceed" standard referred to in the opening clause of article 53 (1) of the Statute, since the former is only one element of the latter. Thus, if upon review of the three elements embodied in article 53 (l) (a)–(c) of the Statute and on the basis of the information provided, the Chamber reaches an affirmative finding as to their fulfillment, the "reasonable basis to proceed" standard will consequentially be met."[1195]

Rule 48 further clarifies the interrelationship between articles 15 and 53 to a large extent.[1196] It states that the reasonable basis under article 53 (1) and 15 (3) is the same at its core. Pursuant to rule 48, the criteria of article 53 (1) (a)–(c) have to be applied no matter which trigger mechanism is used at the outset. There is a strong presumption that the test of "reasonable basis" under the ICC Statute has to be understood as being essentially the same, be it for the Prosecutor (pursuant to articles 15 (3) or 53 (1)), or for the PTC (pursuant to article 15 (4)).[1197]

Coming to the substantive content of the reasonable basis, the terminology used is phrased vaguely. Due to the lack of clarity, the term "reasonable basis" is not a predefined law term and certainly entails some discretion.[1198] The ICC Statue contains different levels of suspicion to bet met; starting with the "reasonable basis to believe" (articles 15 (3), (4), and 53 (1) (a)), followed by the "sufficient basis" (article 53 (2)), the "reasonable grounds" (article 58 (1) (a)), and the "substantial grounds" (article 61 (5)). The highest standard is finally contained in article 66 (3), which refers to "beyond reasonable doubt" in order to secure a conviction. In fact, the "reasonable basis" can be described as the first step of a stairway, which becomes stricter with every step taken towards trial and requires more profound evidence on each level.[1199] Surely, the test for starting an investiga-

---

1194 Part IV, B., III., 1., a).

1195 *Situation in Kenya*, Decision pursuant to article 15, *supra* note 6, para. 26, 13.

1196 See already Part III, C., I.

1197 Bergsmo/Pjeić, in Triffterer, *supra* note 321, article 15, mn 27, who come to the same conclusion.

1198 Wei, *supra* note 156, 67; Stigen, *supra* note 205, 95.

1199 In the same vein recently *Situation in Kenya*, Request for authorization, *supra* note 207, para. 103, 36–7: "The test of reasonable basis is the lowest found in

tion must be less onerous than the one regarding the commencement of a prosecution.[1200] From a teleological perspective, the former standard of "reasonable basis" requires less certainty than the latter test of "sufficient basis," and a mere probability test could suffice.[1201] Authors have argued that the Prosecutor must evaluate the probability of a *prima facie* case after conducting full investigations.[1202] But the "reasonable basis" is not the same as a "*prima facie* case," the latter being a higher standard that is used at the confirmation of the indictment.[1203] Reasonable basis is not a very high burden, and the Prosecutor may merely show, in the words of one author, "that there is smoke," and there can be "no smoke without fire."[1204] On the other hand, it has been submitted elsewhere that the reasonability test is stringent compared to national commencements of investigations.[1205] Unfortunately, the OTP has not elaborated on the "reasonable basis" of article 53's chapeau as such. However, the Office has developed a chart with the axes "certainty" and "specificity" with regard to the "reasonable grounds" standard pursuant to articles 53 (2) (a) and 58 (1) (a).[1206] According to the OTP's chart, the specificity increases from article 53 (1) to article 53 (2), while the certainty remains the same. Certainty is estimated to rise only drastically in-between article 58 (1) (a) proceedings and a conviction in accordance with article 66 (3). However, a "reasonable basis" requires less certainty than a "sufficient basis."[1207]

For achieving a first, practicable predefinition of the term, further interpretation of the term "reasonable basis" is deemed necessary. "Reasonable" is "rational," "reason or sound thinking," "in the bounds of common sense"

---

the Rome Statute, which applies four escalating tests for the progressive phases of the proceedings."

1200 Draft Regulations OTP 2003, *supra* note 63, Section 4, Part 2, Draft Regulation 12.3, fn. 80; Brubacher *supra* note 368, 79–80; Bergsmo/Kruger, in Triffterer, *supra* note 906, article 53, mn 12.

1201 Stigen, *supra* note 205, 95–6.

1202 Wouters/Verhoeven/Demeyere, *supra* note 156, 296; Stigen, *supra* note 205, 96; Brubacher *supra* note 368, 79–80.

1203 Nsereko, in Triffterer, *supra* note 425, article 18, mn 7. For the replacement of the *prima facie* expression by the "substantial grounds" standard, see *Prosecutor v. Katanga and Chui,* Decision on the confirmation of charges, *supra* note 242, para. 62 with fn. 90; Guariglia, in Lee, *supra* note 14, 236; also WCRO confirmation of charges report, *supra* note 174, 68–9 (suggesting a low standard of proof at the confirmation of charges procedure).

1204 Daniel Ntanda Nsereko, "Prosecutorial discretion before the national courts and international tribunals" (2005) 3 JICJ 124, 139.

1205 Wei, *supra* note 156, 67.

1206 Agirre Aranburu, in Bergsmo, *supra* note 460, 148.

1207 Stigen, *supra* note 205, 95.

and "not excessive or extreme; fair."[1208] Alternative languages use similar expressions as the English version of the ICC Statute: "base raisonnable" in the French version, "fundamento razonable" in the Spanish version. All-in-all, the literal interpretation reveals the broad scope of reasonability, but little more.

From a systematic perspective, it has already been shown that the reasonability standard is the lowest standard within the ICC Statute. It constitutes the first formal procedural step.

Last but not least, the teleological interpretation might bring about a clear solution. The danger of disguised pre-investigations has been emphasized elsewhere.[1209] On the other hand, the standard of "reasonable basis" has to be very low and not too stringent. Pre-investigations are meant to lessen the burden on the OTP, and must allow for an initial pre-screening. However, they should not replace full investigations. Moreover, the standard increases via articles 53 (2), 58 (1) (a), 61 (5) to 66 (3). Teleologically, one can assume that the reasonability standard is the lowest level within the ICC Statute.[1210] Different conclusions sometimes rest upon the language used,[1211] or simply do not address the provision's intent.

Furthermore, the axes designed by the OTP lead in the right direction. When investigations continue the specificity advances; as the process gets more individualized the line rises on the "specificity" axis. However, certainty does not necessarily have to be revealed during (pre-)investigation, but is a prerequisite for conviction. Nevertheless, it may be assumed that certainty rises during pre-investigations and full investigations.

To sum up, the Prosecutor must take into consideration the three criteria of article 53 (1) (a)–(c) for determining the "reasonable basis," and he must look at the three criteria of article 53 (2) (a)–(c) for evaluating the "sufficient basis." For the latter standard, the degree of specificity has to be greater. Nonetheless, the exact shape of "reasonable basis" and "sufficient basis" requires further adjustment resulting in one single predefinition in

[1208] Free Online Dictionary by Farlex, "reasonable," <www.thefreedictionary.com/reasonable>; similarly Oxford English Dictionary, "reasonable," <www.oed.com>; also *Situation in Kenya*, Decision pursuant to article 15, *supra* note 6, para. 30, 15.

[1209] Part III, D.

[1210] Recenlty, in the same vein, *Situation in Kenya*, Decision pursuant to article 15, *supra* note 6, para. 27, 13.

[1211] For example, the German translation as "hinreichende Grundlage" does not differentiate between article 53 (1) and (2). The proposed alternative of Wei, *supra* note 156, 67, as "begründete Grundlage" equally suggests an overly high standard and does not cope with the envisaged purpose. Alternative translations such as "angemessen," "vernünftig," and "zumutbar" seem to be more appropriate.

the OTP guidelines. The Prosecutor himself is empowered to determine the existence of a reasonable basis.[1212] In the context of Kenya, the OTP suggested the following minimum standard as a first definition of reasonable basis:

> "This would require the existence of some facts or information which would satisfy an objective observer that crimes within the jurisdiction of the Court appear to have been committed, but without identification of the persons who may have committed such offences."[1213]

The PTC, bearing in mind that the "reasonable basis" standard under article 15 is even lower than that provided under article 58, arrived at the following phrasing:

> "[...] the Chamber must be satisfied that there exists a sensible or reasonable justification for a belief that a crime falling within the jurisdiction of the Court "has been or is being committed". A finding on whether there is a sensible justification should be made bearing in mind the specific purpose underlying this procedure."

But the more precise content of the test will only emerge through increasing PTC practice. Moreover, the ICC actors must adopt one all-embracing definition. It is important to bear in mind that the term "*prima facie* case" should not be used, since it was deliberately excluded from the ICC Statute. The definitions should rather be drafted as follows:

- A reasonable basis exists if *initial suspicion* is presumed by the Prosecutor and *realistically* leads to specific cases for prosecution.
- A sufficient basis exists if *specific cases* for prosecution have been identified and *potentially* lead to a conviction if not successfully rebutted during trial.

4. OTP selection strategy approach

The OTP deemed it necessary to establish a policy that covered the entire investigation process, including preliminary examinations.[1214] Three important principles govern the present selection of situations and cases: independence, impartiality, and non-discrimination.[1215] Regional balance is not a criterion.[1216]

1212 Knoops, *supra* note 1191, 375.

1213 *Situation in Kenya*, Request for authorization, *supra* note 207, para. 104, 37.

1214 Håkan Friman, Session 3: Transcript, First public hearing of the OTP, 17.6.2003, 2.

1215 Eight Report pursuant to UNSC 1593, *supra* note 290, para. 20; Fabricio Guariglia, "The selection of cases by the Office of the Prosecutor of the International Criminal Court" in Stahn/Sluiter, *supra* note 5, 209, 212–3, who additionally mentions "objectivity;" HRW, "The selection of situations and cases for trial before

The Prosecutor does not yet have investigative powers during situation selection; the situation analysis phase is of a pre-investigative nature. During situation selection available resources must be maximized; the budget proposal reflects anticipated situations and unforeseen situations may be covered by a so-called contingency fund.[1217]

Regarding case selection, it is suggested that the Prosecutor must set priorities, especially with regard to available resources.[1218] The OTP, while certainly setting priorities, does not explicitly refer to resources as a selection filter.[1219] On the other hand, limited resources provided by the ASP reflect a practical reality and only allow for a certain number of simultaneous investigations.[1220]

Mass crimes entail large numbers of perpetrators, typically numbering in the thousands, and it is impossible to prosecute all of them. The overwhelming workload might otherwise lead to a total paralysis of the Court.[1221] In this respect, the Prosecutor has *focused investigations and prosecutions* on those individuals who bear the greatest responsibility for the most serious crimes, generally those occupying the highest level of political and military authority.[1222] In other words, the OTP has adopted a practice

---

the International Criminal Court. A Human Rights Watch Policy Paper" (hereinafter HRW selection policy paper), October 2006, 2 (alike Guariglia, referring to "objectivity" as the fourth principle). With regard to self-referrals *HRW* stresses the negative implications on the Prosecutor's independence and promotes the *proprio motu* power, *ibid.*, 3–4.

1216 Address to the Assembly of States Parties 2008, *supra* note 322, 6; OTP Report on activities 2003–2006, *supra* note 23, 2.

1217 On the contingency fund see Part II, C.

1218 Nsereko, *supra* note 1243, 125; Danner, *supra* note 953, 520; *id.*, "Navigating law and politics: The Prosecutor of the International Criminal Court and the independent counsel" (2003) 55 Stanford Law Review 1633, 1652; also William Burke-White, "Proactive complementarity: The International Criminal Court and national courts in the Rome system of international justice" (2008) 49 HILJ 53, 54.

1219 Yet, limited resources have been mentioned; see, for instance, the Statement by Luis Moreno-Ocampo: Informal meeting, *supra* note 497, 5.

1220 Burke-White, *supra* note 1218, 66.

1221 Umberto Leanza – Professor of International Law at the Rome University, Session 1: Transcript, First public hearing of the OTP, 17.6.2003, 1; Fabricio Guariglia, Session 3: Transcript, First public hearing OTP, 17.6.2003, 2. The ICC already operates at full capacity, see Ambos, *supra* note 257, 16.

1222 Policy paper, *supra* note 99, 7; Prosecutorial Strategy 2009–2012, *supra* note 99, para. 19, 5–6; Statement by Luis Moreno-Ocampo: Informal meeting, *supra* note 497, 5; Statement by Fatou Bensouda, Deputy Prosecutor of the International Criminal Court, Report on the conference held in Turin from 14.–18.5.2007, ASP sixth session, 30.11.–14.12.2007 (ICC-ASP/6/INF.2) para. 5, 47; Moreno-Ocampo, in Stahn/Sluiter, *supra* note 99, 15 et seq.; Seils, in Bergsmo, *supra* note 99, 55–6; Greenawalt, *supra* note 1177, 627; Wouters/Verhoeven/Demeyere, *supra* note 156,

of exemplary prosecution, targeting some preselected persons. It is the policy of the OTP to bring only a few cases from each situation.[1223] Against those individuals, the Office brings *representative charges* only.[1224] In addition to this narrow focus on those most responsible, the OTP follows a *sequential approach,* investigating specific cases within a situation one after another rather than all at once.[1225] In sum, the four guiding principles for the OTP's strategy have been described as (i) (positive) complementarity; (ii) focused investigations and prosecutions; (iii) addressing the interests of victims; and (iv) maximizing the impact of the OTP's work.[1226]

In my view, the policy choice to limit the number of cases must be strictly distinguished from the legal threshold of admissibility. The latter is not as stringent as the former; otherwise the admissibility threshold would become a legal barrier providing permanent *ex ante* impunity to entire classes of perpetrators. In other words, the OTP has decided as a *policy matter* that not every admissible case will be prosecuted.[1227] It is further worth noting that focused investigations might lead to an impunity gap if national authorities do not step in.[1228]

291; Schabas, *supra* note 27, 33; El Zeidy, *supra* note 269, 42; Vladimir Tochilovsky, Session 3: Transcript, First public hearing OTP, 17.6.2003, 1; Minna Schrag, Session 4: Lessons learned form ICTY experience: Notes for the ICC Prosecutor (paper), First public hearing of the OTP, 20.3.2003, 4; Elizabeth Wilmshurst. Session 5: Transcript, First public hearing of the OTP, 17.6.2003, 1.

1223 On this selective approach see Hamilton, *supra* note 1144, 2; Hall, *supra* note 100, 20, who names the approach a "multiple, variable size situation model."

1224 Prosecutorial Strategy 2009–2012, *supra* note 99, para. 20, 6; FIDH, "Comments on the Office of the Prosecutor's draft policy paper on 'Criteria for selection of situations and cases'," 15.9.2006, 2.

1225 See already Part III, B., III., 2.; also Schabas, *supra* note 1151, 735–6; *id.*, "The role of the Prosecutor of the International Criminal Court" (2008) 83 Friedenswarte 11, 20. Critically, HRW selection policy paper, *supra* note 1215, 5; FIDH, "Comments on the Office of the Prosecutor's draft policy paper on 'Criteria for selection of situations and cases'," *supra* note 1224, 3.

1226 Prosecutorial Strategy 2009–2012, *supra* note 99, para. 15, 4. See earlier Mr. Michel De Smedt, Session 1: Interested States, Second public hearing of the OTP, 25.9.2006; OTP strategy, *supra note* 409, 5–6; Schiff, *supra* note 128, 141. Critically evaluating the OTP's approach to complementarity, see Dan Sarooshi, "Prosecutorial policy and the ICC: Prosecutor's *proprio motu* action or self-denial?" (2004) 2 JICJ 940, 940 et seq.

1227 Prosecutorial Strategy 2009–2012, *supra* note 99, para. 19–20, 5–6.

1228 Policy paper, *supra* note 99, 7; Wouters/Verhoeven/Demeyere, *supra* note 156, 291; András Vámos-Goldman – Institute of Global Issues at the University of British Columbia, Session 5: Transcript, First public hearing of the OTP, 17.6.2003, 2. On the "zones of impunity" in contemporary practice see Lekha Sriram/Ross, *supra* note 210, 45 et seq.

Having outlined the basic selection strategy, the basis of the OTP's overall strategy needs further clarification. OTP Regulation 14 spells out:

(1) The Office shall make public its Prosecutorial Strategy and shall contribute to the Court's Strategic Plan.

(2) As appropriate, the Office shall make public policy papers that reflect the key principles and criteria of the Prosecutorial Strategy.

In accordance with OTP Regulation 14 (2), four papers have been published: The general Policy paper, the Annex paper thereto on referrals and communications, the Policy paper on victim participation, and the Policy paper on the "interests of justice."[1229] More policy papers are in the consultation process and will be published in the near future.[1230] In addition, the Prosecutor published a report according to which the OTP had developed its envisaged Prosecutorial Strategy for three years (late 2006–2009)[1231] and a follow-up Prosecutorial Strategy (2009–2012).[1232] It seems as if the OTP uses the terms "strategy" and "policy" interchangeably. However, it has chosen the terminology "Prosecutorial Strategy" for the overall goals and fixed this expression in OTP Regulation 14 (1).[1233] In accordance with this OTP Regulations, the term "Prosecutorial Strategy" appears preferable when reference is made to the overall guidance by the OTP. Policy papers form the basis of this all-embracing strategy and are subject to unlimited revision. In the policy paper on the "interests of justice," the OTP stresses the paper's policy nature, emphasizing that it does not give rise to any rights in litigation and that it is subject to revision based on experience and legal determinations by the Chambers of the Court.[1234]

Furthermore, it is interesting to note that the Prosecutor established a tradition of promoting public discussions of his main policies. To date he conducted two sets of public hearings. From 17.–18. June 2003, the first public hearing was hosted in The Hague to discuss his first policies. A second public hearing was convened in September and October 2006 to discuss the

---

[1229] Cf. *supra* note 99 and *supra* note 496 with corresponding text. On the OTP policy see Wouters/Verhoeven/Demeyere, *supra* note 156, 290 et seq.; Schabas, *supra* note 27, 32 et seq.

[1230] See Policy paper on victim participation, *supra* note 496. Further, the publication of various policy papers was announced by the OTP in its Prosecutorial Strategy 2009–2012, *supra* note 99, para. 28, 8.

[1231] OTP strategy, *supra note* 409, 2.

[1232] Prosecutorial Strategy 2009–2012, *supra* note 99.

[1233] This expression can also be found on the up-dated OTP website at <www.icc-cpi.int/Menus/ICC/Structure+of+the+Court/Office+of+the+Prosecutor/Policies+and+Strategies/>.

[1234] Interests of justice paper, *supra* note 99, 1.

report on the OTP's activities during the first three years and the above mentioned Prosecutorial Strategy for the next three years.[1235] The dialogue initiated by the Prosecutor has to be welcomed and should be upheld in the future. Through this process, the OTP gains external expert knowledge, aligns expectations, and provides transparency that is inevitable for its selection process. A coherent prosecution strategy is an indispensable tool for investigations and prosecutions.[1236] Moreover, it might be necessary to open case files in their entirety one day in order to justify decisions taken and to rebut any political claims.[1237]

5. Academic approaches towards prosecutorial discretion at the ICC

The question of selecting some situations and individuals over others is a core question of international criminal justice. Since neither the statutory provisions nor OTP policy exhaustively clarify the issue, several authors have criticized the present status and have developed their own proposals. Starting from the outset, there are two pertinent questions that must be addressed if one seriously tries to solve this controversial problem: first of all, it has to be decided which organ is most suitable for prosecutorial selection. Second, there must be a common basis to decide who gets tried and who does not. In other words: who prosecutes and who is prosecuted?[1238] One may therefore differentiate the decision whether or not to act (*Entschließungsermessen*), and the type of action required (*Handlungsermessen*), i.e. whom to prosecute, when to prosecute, and how to sequence cases.[1239]

For the ICC, the Prosecutor – under supervision of the PTC – was designated the adequate acting organ. An important policy choice was thus made in giving the authority to select situations and cases to the Prosecutor rather than other entities such as the PTC, the SC, or States Parties.[1240] The Prosecutor further applies a test which is based on both legal criteria and policy considerations. States Parties and the SC may clearly not instruct the Prosecutor to investigate or prosecute, while the PTC might force the Pro-

---

1235 See <www.icc-cpi.int/Menus/ICC/Structure+of+the+Court/Office+of+the+Prosecutor/Network+with+ Partners/Public+Hearings/>.

1236 Mohamed Othman – Former Chief of Prosecutions of the ICTR and the UN administration in East Timor, Session 1: Briefing Note (Paper), First public hearing of the OTP, 3.2.2003, 3; Friman, *supra* note 1214, 1.

1237 Otto Triffterer, Session 2: Transcript, First public hearing of the OTP, 17.6. 2003.

1238 Wouters/Verhoeven/Demeyere, *supra* note 156, 290–1.

1239 Stahn, in Stahn/Sluiter, *supra* note 156, 252.

1240 Stigen, *supra* note 205, 343.

secutor to proceed under the rare circumstances of article 53 (3).[1241] To sum up, the Prosecutor is the organ at the ICC vested with the power to decide whether or not to act.

But no matter how the Prosecutor selects his situations and cases, pressure and criticism will come from various angles. The prioritization process touches upon political considerations, which brings NGOs, legal commentators, victims, and States into the action.[1242] Having briefly outlined the basic statutory framework and the OTP's selection approach, some aspects remain vague. In particular, it is unclear how far-reaching the OTP's discretion within the selection process is. For this reason, academic approaches *vis-à-vis* the margin of discretion will be delineated, with some suggesting how to improve upon the current exercise of discretion by the Prosecutor. Subsequently, I will integrate the main ideas into one congruent approach which I derive from all of these proposals.

The pertinent question is to locate discretion within the statutory framework and to stipulate its exact scope. Discretion can be defined as "the faculty of deciding or determining in accordance with circumstances and what seems just, right, equitable, and reasonable in those circumstances."[1243] It entails both risks and benefits.[1244] Whilst in most legal traditions the exercise of prosecutorial discretion has become relatively well defined through jurisprudence, international criminal justice is still emerging.[1245] Nevertheless, there is a need for selective prosecution in transitional situations, which is in principle accepted.[1246] However, the exercise of discretion poses the risk of arbitrariness and may threaten the principle of equality before the law.[1247] On the other hand, it is not the existence of discretion *per se* that may be questioned, but the extent to which it should be guided by principles.[1248]

[1241] Stigen, *supra* note 205, 344.

[1242] Stigen, *supra* note 205, 345.

[1243] Definition according to the Oxford Companion of Law, quoted from Nsereko, *supra* note 1204, 124; also Côte, *supra* note 1190, 164. For the different usages of discretion see Rosemary Pattenden, *The Judge, discretion, and the criminal trial* (Clarendon Press, Oxford 1982) 3 et seq.

[1244] Danner, *supra* note 953, 518.

[1245] Hassan Jallow, "Prosecutorial discretion and international criminal justice" (2005) 3 JICJ 145, 146.

[1246] Greenawalt, *supra* note 1177, 620 with further references in fn. 121; Diane Orentlicher, "Settling accounts: The duty to prosecute human rights violations of a prior regime" (1991) 100 YLJ 2537, 2601–2.

[1247] Orentlicher, *supra* note 1246, 2602; Danner, *supra* note 953, 521.

[1248] Tim Quigley, *Procedure in Canadian criminal law,* 2nd edition (Thomson Carswell, Toronto 2005) 16–2.

With regard to the ICC Statute, particularly article 53, the margin of discretion is not clearly defined. There could be unlimited prosecutorial discretion as known to common-law systems and applied by the ICTY/ICTR,[1249] or the ICC Prosecutor could potentially adhere to the principle of legality. As outlined above, the chapeau of article 53 (1) favors the principle of legality as the point of origin. Nonetheless, in a second step, the chapeau waters down a strict application thereof and introduces the broad term "reasonable basis" linked to the criteria of article 53 (1) (a)–(c). The procedural system of the ICC therefore gives the OTP a wide margin of discretion. In particular, the terms "reasonable basis" as used in the chapeau and the "interests of justice" as included in article 53 (1) (c) allow for broad considerations on behalf of the Prosecutor.

In this regard, it has been stated that the Prosecutor cannot exercise discretion in the pure common-law sense (*keine echte Opportunität*), but rather enjoys a broad degree for judgment evaluation (*Beurteilungsspielraum*), inherent to the reasonable basis to proceed with an investigation and prosecution respectively.[1250] It has further been noted that the sole discretionary theme of the chapeau is whether there is a reasonable basis to proceed, and that the provision does not give room to arbitrary decision-making.[1251] Elements, which are of an opportunity nature, are located within article 53 (1) (c) and (2) (c).[1252] The general obligation to prosecute is mitigated by article 53 (1) (c) and (2) (c), essentially a discretionary decision that "needs to balance the interests and to prioritize the overall limited resources of time and personnel."[1253] The system can therefore be best described as based on the legality maxim, tempered by substantial opportunity elements.[1254]

Power is allocated to both the Prosecutor and the PTC as the latter may review the formers decision not to proceed.[1255] Discretion is thus not unfettered; it is procedurally controlled by the PTC pursuant to article 53 (3).[1256]

1249 Kenneth Rodman, "Is peace in the interests of justice? The case of broad prosecutorial discretion at the International Criminal Court" (2002) 22 LJIL 99, 111 ("[...] injecting political prudence into his discretion in order to be effective without foreclosing negotiated solutions or disrupting fragile peace processes.").

1250 Wilhelmi, *supra* note 169, 48–9; similarly, Bergsmo/Kruger, in Triffterer, *supra* note 906, article 53, mn 7; van Heeck, *supra* note 26, 191.

1251 Bergsmo/Kruger, in Triffterer, *supra* note 906, article 53, mn 7.

1252 Wilhelmi, *supra* note 169, 48.

1253 Röben, *supra* note 1254, 524.

1254 Volker Röben, "The procedure of the ICC: Status and functions of the Prosecutor" (2003) 7 Max Planck Yearbook of the UN 513, 523.

1255 Röben, *supra* note 1254, 524.

1256 El Zeidy, *supra* note 246, 107; Robinson, *supra* note 807, 487; Nsereko, *supra* note 1204, 141; Dražan Dukić, "Transitional Justice and the International Crim-

One can therefore not speak of "unlimited discretion." Precise terminology favors the usage of "judicially controllable evaluation of the margin of judgment." Nevertheless, as the term is basically unknown to common law countries, the term "margin of discretion" may be used with regard to the ICC.[1257] It is more important to note the procedurally limited nature of the notion of discretion, and, more importantly, that some margin of judgment evaluation/discretion is introduced through the chapeau ("unless [...] there is no reasonable basis"), and that opportunity deliberations can only be found in article 53 (1) (c) and (2) (c).

Nevertheless, different proposals have been made suggesting changes for the better. The principle of prosecutorial discretion has been linked to the prerequisites "sufficient gravity" and "interests of justice."[1258] From this point of view, the OTP has been turned into a policy-maker.[1259] The Prosecutor is practically given the broadest possible scope of political discretion.[1260] Instead of retaining unlimited prosecutorial discretion, one author suggests to redraft articles 15 (3) and (4), 53 (1) (c) and (2) (c), 17 (d) and rule 48, while striking out article 53 (3) (b). As the second best option, a new rule 104*bis* with a short but exhaustive list of precise and binding criteria on gravity and "interests of justice" could be incorporated.[1261] ICC State Parties should carry out their responsibilities as legislators by limiting the personal scope of Court's jurisdiction to leaders and masterminds from the outset, hand-in-hand with a substitution of the principle of political discretion through the principle of legality.[1262]

For giving article 53 more substantial content, other authors have advocated a guideline-based approach.[1263] The principle idea is demanding *ex*

---

inal Court: in the 'interests of justice'?" (2007) 89 IRRC 691, 716. In more detail Part IV, D. and E.

1257 As the study at hand is written in English, the term "margin of discretion" is used as a tantamount to "margin of judgment evaluation." Rather than sticking to the terminological difference, it is more important to note that discretion is linked to article 53 (1) (c) and (2) (c), and that the PTC may intervene in clear abuse cases according to article 53 (3).

1258 Olásolo, *supra* note 29, 182 et seq.; *id., supra* note 368, 110, 135–6.

1259 Olásolo, *supra* note 29, 188.

1260 Olásolo, *supra* note 368, 111.

1261 Olásolo, *supra* note 29, 190; *id., supra* note 368, 143–4.

1262 Olásolo, *supra* note 29, 193.

1263 McDonald/Haveman, *supra* note 1149, 9; Danner, *supra* note 953, 552; Ambos, in Bohlander, *supra* note 10, 440; Hall, *supra* note 100, 11; Stigen, *supra* note 205, 413 et seq.; Meyer, *supra* note 1153, 581; Nsereko, *supra* note 1204, 143–4; HRW, "Policy paper: the meaning of the 'interests of justice' in article 53 of the Rome Statute" (hereinafter HRW, policy paper article 53), June 2005, 1, 25; Freiburg Declaration on the position of the prosecutor of a Permanent International

ante guidelines that will protect the Prosecutor's independence and enhance the legitimacy of the ICC.[1264] Information should be provided about the factors that the Prosecutor does consider when making his discretionary choices.[1265] Publication of the guidelines, i.e. transparency, is critical for ensuring that the Prosecutor complies with set boundaries.[1266] If the Prosecutor declines to promulgate such guidelines, he must somehow demonstrate that legal, not political, criteria guide his decision-making.[1267] This is not an easy task, assuming that the criteria of article 53 mostly rely on subjective decision-making by the Prosecutor.[1268] Only prosecutorial guidelines beforehand can rebut criticism. With such guidelines in place, actors would be able to better predict and accept the Prosecutor's selection.[1269] They will promote fairness and consistency, and the elaboration of such guidelines is encouraged by international law.[1270]

Furthermore, it has been recommended to re-conceptualize prosecutorial discretion within international criminal law as a whole.[1271] Two main avenues are thereby favored: first, the implementation of a special review procedure to allow the accused to challenge the claim that political considerations influenced the decision to prosecute, and second, the promulgation of criteria to initiate international criminal proceedings.[1272] A special review procedure depends *inter alia* on the scope the PTC will adopt for its review power and whether it will allow for the principle of equality as a valid ground for individual challenges.[1273] The second aspect adds nothing substantial to the already outlined demand for prosecutorial guidelines.

As an alternative, a political deference model has been proposed.[1274] The potential assistance of *ex ante* guidelines is critically observed, coming to the conclusion that authors in favor of such guidelines fail to suggest any model how these criteria can be objectified into decisional rules.[1275] A le-

---

Criminal Court (1998) 6 EJCrim 301, 302, principle 7; differentiated Goldstone, *supra* note 1048, 402 et seq. For the ICTY/ICTR, see Côte, *supra* note 1190, 172. For the exercise of discretion at the ICTR, see Jallow, *supra* note 1245, 147 et seq.

1264 Danner, *supra* note 953, 511, 541 et seq.

1265 Danner, *supra* note 953, 542.

1266 Danner, *supra* note 953, 547.

1267 Danner, *supra* note 1218, 1656.

1268 McDonald/Haveman, *supra* note 1149, 3.

1269 Stigen, *supra* note 205, 413.

1270 Stigen, *supra* note 205, 414.

1271 Knoops, *supra* note 1191, 384.

1272 Knoops, *supra* note 1191, 384–5.

1273 Part IV, B., III., 3., a), dd) and Part IV, E.

1274 Greenawalt, *supra* note 1177, 651 et seq.

1275 Greenawalt, *supra* note 1177, 654–5.

gal test authorizing the Judges to resolve the most pressing question of prosecutorial discretion shifts policymaking from the Prosecutor to the Judges, who are institutionally less competent to address such matters.[1276] In a final step, a political deference model is vindicated: the Prosecutor could explicitly defer to the decision-making authorities of political actors, such as the SC.[1277] This deference model amounts to an outsourcing of policy questions, placing the policy dilemmas of transitional justice in the political area "where they belong, where they can be considered as such, and where they can be subject to public debate and scrutiny."[1278]

Another alternative draft proposes reconsidering the structure of the Pre-Trial Phase, thus creating Pre-Trial Chambers with investigative powers.[1279] The creation of true investigative chambers must be rejected, as it has been exhaustively dealt with during the drafting process. It would endanger the compromise formula of article 53. On the other hand, a modest option aims at enabling the existing PTCs to exercise control after a reasonable time period.[1280] This would leave investigations in the hands of the Prosecutor and, at the same time, improve judicial oversight during pre-investigations. If the State Parties decide to address the matter of reasonable time limits for pre-investigations and full investigations,[1281] this approach is worth being pursued. It should therefore be discussed in the context of a broader revision regarding time limits by the ASP.

The ICC cannot deal with every case due to its limited capacity.[1282] In reality, national jurisdictions must fill the "impunity gap." The Court can, on the other hand, exert pressure on States and it can deal with the most serious crimes committed by the most responsible persons. As a necessary consequence, the Prosecutor is given discretion for exercising selective prosecution. For the credibility and success of the ICC, it will be crucial to develop a feasible framework that accommodates both legal and policy considerations.[1283] Setting up a checks and balances system between the Prosecutor and the PTC will be helpful to serve the "interests of justice."[1284] Discretion cannot be arbitrary: it must be exercised in the legal framework

---

1276 Greenawalt, *supra* note 1177, 660.

1277 Greenawalt, *supra* note 1177, 664–5.

1278 Greenawalt, *supra* note 1177, 672.

1279 Jérôme De Hemptinne, "The creation of investigating chambers at the ICC: an option worth pursuing?" (2007) 5 JICJ 402, 413 et seq.

1280 De Hemptinne, *supra* note 1279, 416–7.

1281 See my proposal regarding pre-investigations at Part III, D.

1282 Wouters/Verhoeven/Demeyere, *supra* note 156, 289.

1283 Brubacher *supra* note 368, 72.

1284 Kim, *supra* note 813, 199.

provided for by the ICC Statute.[1285] Article 53 constitutes a compromise formula which includes discretionary terms and judicial oversight. Rightly so, some authors have described article 53 as a compromise between the choice of strict legality and prosecutorial discretion.[1286]

Coming back to the different proposal outlined above, it has to be emphasized that the provision of article 53 should not be questioned in its entirety. Long negotiations led to a procedural compromise, unfortunately not touching upon the substantive content. It would have been desirable if State Parties gave more substance to article 53 by themselves. At present, the discussion should not be re-opened *ab initio*; rather, a new rule 104*bis* and prosecutorial guidelines can solve most problems. The framework of article 53 is not useless as a whole, but it does need further refinement.[1287] One hypothesis is that discretion finds its origin solely in the "interests of justice" clause and all other criteria should be interpreted from a purely legal point of view. Article 17, for instance, constitutes a legal threshold, in contrast to which article 53 (1) (c) was meant to allow for wider considerations. By originating and limiting broad discretionary choices to article 53 (1) (c) and (2) (c), the framework of article 53 is implemented in a proper manner. In particular, the drafters wanted to reach a feasible procedural compromise on the matter of discretion: some preferred broad discretion and others wanted no discretion at all. This led to the compromise where discretionary considerations are included *solely* under article 53 (1) (c) and (2) (c) and are under the potential supervision of the PTC pursuant to article 53 (3). In my opinion, judicial oversight through articles 15 (4) and 53 (3) is a tool which ensures sustainable control and hopefully leads to open questions being solved by case-law. SC involvement is strongly rejected, as it threatens the independence of the Prosecutor and the ICC. Within the current UN system, deferring the matter of selection to the SC would certainly put an end to the ICC's independence and objectivity.

6. Intermediary conclusion

The critical task is to select situations for investigations, followed by screening potential cases and deciding which individuals to charge with

---

[1285] Stigen, *supra* note 205, 341.

[1286] Schabas, *supra* note 27, 242; Delmas-Marty, *supra* note 1048, 4. Critically on the whole interests of justice construct, see Alfred Rubin, "The International Criminal Court: possibilities for prosecutorial abuse" (2001) 64 Law & Contemporary Problems 153, 162–3.

[1287] In the same vein, Kim, *supra* note 813, 199 ("[...] strikes a good balance between the necessity of the Prosecutor's discretionary power and the necessity of judicial review of that power.").

which crimes.[1288] This task rests upon the Prosecutor and involves discretionary determinations within the statutory framework of article 53. The framework for discretion is embedded in article 53, in particular article 53 (1) (c) and (2) (c).[1289] However, this discretion is subject to the PTC's authority to check a decision not to investigate or prosecute.[1290] Discretion is therefore not unfettered, nor irreversible.[1291] Nevertheless, articles 53 (1) (c) and (2) (c) create some leeway to not investigate and/or prosecute.[1292]

With regard to whether the decision is to start an investigation or a prosecution, the ICC Statute makes a different choice between the principle of legality and political discretion for each set of functions rather than choosing one principle over the other.[1293] Indeed, article 53 can be best described as a procedural compromise between the choice of strict legality and prosecutorial discretion.[1294] Therefore, the different criteria of article 53 must be identified, and must be looked at closely in order to evaluate whether they embrace discretionary considerations or not. Letter (a) of paragraph 1 actually contains two parameters, the "*reasonable basis that a crime exists*" and "*jurisdiction.*" Keeping this in mind, the following criteria emerge:

- The Prosecutor shall not initiate an investigation if there is no reasonable basis to believe that a crime exists (first criterion);
- when there is a reasonable basis to believe a crime exists, he shall not initiate an investigation if the crime does not belong to the jurisdiction of the court (second criterion);
- when both reasonable basis and jurisdiction exist, he shall not initiate the investigation if the case is *prima facie* inadmissible under Article 17 (third criterion);
- when both reasonable basis and jurisdiction exist, and the case is *prima facie* admissible under Article 17, he may decide not to initiate an investigation if there are substantial reasons to believe that it would not serve the interests of justice (fourth criterion);

1288 Danner, *supra* note 953, 520.

1289 In the same vein, Stigen, *supra* note 205, 340.

1290 Article 53 (3). On the authority to check the Prosecutor's discretion, see *Prosecutor v. Kony et al.*, Decision to convene a status conference on the investigation in the situation in Uganda, *supra* note 248, para. 13.

1291 Kleffner, *supra* note 370, 290. Article 53 (4) grants the Prosecutor the possibility to reconsider his previous decision under article 53 (1) and (2).

1292 Kleffner, *supra* note 370, 290–1; further Part IV, B., III., 3., a), ee).

1293 Olásolo, *supra* note 368, 132. In a similar vein, Contag, *supra* note 426, 62 ("Mischform zwischen Opportunitäts- und Legalitätsprinzip").

1294 Delmas-Marty, *supra* note 1048, 9; Schabas, *supra* note 27, 242; Nsereko, *supra* note 1204, 137 ("most progressive and fair prosecutorial regime").

- if all parameters exist, the Prosecutor shall initiate an investigation.[1295]

Another important factor is the accountability of the Prosecutor. This issue is addressed within the concluding parts D and E, when the PTC's judicial review power is examined. As submitted by several academics, the pre-definition of prosecutorial guidelines is a crucial aspect for selection procedures. The Prosecutor's decisions would be more predictable and acceptable if such guidelines were in place.[1296] On the other hand, guidelines beforehand would confine the Prosecutor's flexibility to a certain extent. The OTP has stressed its situation- and case-specific approach.[1297] Nonetheless, only a combination of measures that involves three actors – the Prosecutor, the Judges, and the States Parties – could actually ameliorate the selection process:

1. The Prosecutor should develop a newly-arranged, transparent prosecutorial policy;
2. The Prosecutor must design prosecutorial guidelines, consulting the Judges and external experts;
3. Some core questions (i.e. sub-criteria for gravity and "interests of justice," thus giving them more substantive content) should be included in a new draft rule 104*bis,* adopted by the States Parties.

The threefold nature of the proposal above is thought to strike a balance between foreseeability and equality on the one hand, and flexibility and specificity on the other hand. Draft rule 104*bis* provides a new substantive examination on behalf of the ASP (article 51 (2)). Prosecutorial guidelines provide for a second measure that fleshes out the draft rule 104*bis* and promotes consistency in the selections. However, prosecutorial guidelines go beyond the OTP Regulations and should specifically address the issue of selection procedures. Last but not least, the Prosecutor has to integrate all policy and strategy papers into one transparent strategy model. So far, the OTP has only published strategy approaches. It has not published one congruent, permanent model in accordance with OTP Regulation 14 (1).[1298] The Prosecutor must develop a comprehensive Prosecutorial Strategy paper

---

[1295] See already Part III, C., II., in particular the references in *supra* note 1048.

[1296] Stigen, *supra* note 205, 413; Hall, *supra* note 100, 11.

[1297] Interests of justice paper, *supra* note 99, 7 with fn. 9; also Goldstone, *supra* note 1048, 404.

[1298] See Part IV, B., II., 4. The OTP's strategy (at *supra* note 99 and *supra note* 409) mentions, on the one hand, that a prosecutorial strategy has been developed, but, on the other hand, only gives a brief strategy report for the upcoming three years. It is strongly suggested that the OTP should publish one congruent strategy paper pursuant to OTP Regulation 14 (1). Thereby, all existing policy document should be integrated and rearranged.

that incorporates the major published and unpublished policy papers.[1299] By doing so, the Prosecutor will have to revisit "gravity" and the "interests of justice." Both criteria are of key importance to the ICC, and so far policy papers reflect initial ideas, but do not ensure a real *leitmotif*.

The OTP's Prosecutorial Strategy also safeguards flexibility and case-specific reactions. A transparent strategy would enhance legitimacy, thereby reducing criticism (claims of "selective justice"[1300]), and maintaining the Prosecutor's margin of discretion. It is emphasized that the OTP should further pursue its adopted policy of transparency,[1301] meaning that the newly designed guidelines, as well as a newly arranged prosecutorial strategy, should be made publicly available.[1302]

III. Evaluation criteria (subparagraphs a–c)

Following, the status quo of the evaluation criteria will be analyzed, thereby bearing in mind the three envisaged measures of a new rule 104*bis*, prosecutorial guidelines, and a newly-drafted prosecutorial strategy. Whenever feasible, I will try to reach own approaches in this regard.

1. Subparagraph a – jurisdiction

The first test under article 53 is whether a situation falls within the jurisdiction of the Court. Article 53 (1) (a) can be subdivided into whether there is a reasonable basis to believe that a crime exists (first sub-criterion), and whether the potential crime is within the jurisdiction of the Court (second sub-criterion). This process can be further subdivided into four steps; there must be a reasonable basis to believe that:

1. the event in question occurred,
2. the event constitutes criminal activity under article 5 of the ICC Statute,

---

[1299] Prosecutorial strategies on a three year basis, such as the new Prosecutorial Strategy 2009–2012, *supra* note 99, are not sufficient.

[1300] Unger/Wierda, in Ambos/Large/Wierda, *supra* note 678, 297.

[1301] Seils, in Bergsmo, *supra* note 99, 60. Yet, the "indicating" of criteria, as mentioned by the latter author, is not sufficient. Even with regard to discretion, the principal criteria must be clear.

[1302] Danner, *supra* note 953, 548–9, who stresses that an enforcement of the new guidelines is best ensured through "the weapons of transparency and accountability," meaning publication, monitoring of NGOs and States, and exerting pressure on the Prosecutor if he fails to conform to his own guidelines. Recently, the OTP has announced the publication of various policy papers, see Prosecutorial Strategy 2009–2012, *supra* note 99, para. 28, 8.

3. the crime falls within the temporal jurisdiction of the Court,
4. the crime falls within the personal or territorial jurisdiction of the Court.

a) Reasonable basis to believe that a crime exists

The reasonable basis that a crime exists is the first criterion under article 53 (1) (a) and has to be distinguished from the reasonable basis of the chapeau. Some have questioned if the test under letter (a) is necessary or is merely a repetition of the reasonable basis of the chapeau.[1303] On the one hand, a line can be drawn between the more general test of a "reasonable basis to proceed" and the crime specific test of a "reasonable basis to believe." On the other hand, as PTC II has stated, there is a strong presumption that the "reasonable basis to proceed" of the chapeau will be met if the Chamber reaches an affirmative finding as to the "reasonable basis to believe" and the other elements embodied in article 53 (1) (a)–(c).[1304] In any event, the reasonable basis to believe is not further explained, nor is the reasonability test of the chapeau. It has been suggested that the decision based on the first parameter is non-discretionary since it depends on an objective assessment of the *notitia criminis.*[1305] Coming to the required standard, the Prosecutor must believe that a crime naturally exists and does not have to prove all elements of the crime.[1306] This is an evidentiary standard, but nevertheless a quite low one due to considerable parallels to the "reasonable basis to proceed." The term "reasonable basis" must be interpreted as suggesting a very low and not too stringent standard; in fact it is the lowest threshold within the ICC Statute.[1307] The OTP deemed "reasonability" to be of a legal, non-discretionary nature, but it was undecided on the specific definition.[1308] Potential factors to be considered are whether the information received contains facts about crimes within the jurisdiction of the Court, the reliability of the source, the credibility of the information, the incriminating weight of material, and the availability of evidence.[1309] The process is designed to accomplish an "assessment based on objective and

---

1303 Bergsmo/Kruger, in Triffterer, *supra* note 906, article 53, mn 16.

1304 *Situation in Kenya*, Decision pursuant to article 15, *supra* note 6, para. 26, 13.

1305 Turone, in Cassese/Gaeta/Jones, *supra* note 26, 1152.

1306 Bergsmo/Kruger, in Triffterer, *supra* note 906, article 53, mn 15.

1307 Cf. Part IV, B., II., 3.; *Situation in Kenya*, Decision pursuant to article 15, *supra* note 6, para. 27, 13.

1308 Draft Regulations OTP 2003, *supra* note 63, Section 4, Part 2, Draft Regulation 12.3, fn. 80; based on Turone, in Cassese/Gaeta/Jones, *supra* note 26, 1152.

1309 Regulation 12, Section 4, Part 2 of the Draft Regulations OTP 2003, *supra* note 63.

specific indicia on whether there is a realistic prospect that an investigation would lead to a *prima facie* case about a given crime and its perpetrators."[1310] The OTP takes into account the German *Anfangsverdacht* (primary suspicion), and therefore asks for "a degree of certainty more than mere suspicion."[1311] As alternative formulations, the Office included the phrasing "if there is a realistic prospect that the investigation will produce evidence that will lead to a *prima facie* case against the potential accused" and "if there is a clear indication that a person has participated in a crime within the jurisdiction of the Court."[1312] In fact, the OTP has not been able to adopt one congruent pre-definition.

One can imagine that *prima facie* evidence is sufficient for the "reasonable basis to believe that a crime exists."[1313] On the other hand, the first sub-criterion's effects in practice should not be underestimated: it can easily lead to a rejection, as shown in the Venezuelan situation. In the Venezuelan situation, the Prosecutor held that the requirements to seek authorization of an investigation were not satisfied, in particular, the stringent threshold of article 7 (1) requiring a "widespread or systematic attack against any civilian population" was said to be unfulfilled.[1314] In the same manner, the OTP assessed the Iraq situation and tested the particular thresholds for genocide and crimes against humanity.[1315] In the outcome, both situations were basically rejected on sub-paragraph (a). The information did not provide a reasonable basis that a crime within the jurisdiction of the Court had been committed.[1316] The exact elements – including the specific build-in thresholds – of genocide, crimes against humanity, and war crimes are merely tested (not proven) under the procedural step asking whether "the event constitutes criminal activity under article 5;" they are also elaborated upon as part of the jurisdiction assessment. For the moment, it is sufficient to note that the OTP – already in its early proceedings – considers all elements of the crimes under article 5. While it is not yet necessary to identify

1310 Turone, in Cassese/Gaeta/Jones, *supra* note 26, 1152; Wouters/Verhoeven/Demeyere, *supra* note 156, 296.

1311 Draft Regulations OTP 2003, *supra* note 63, Section 4, Part 2, Draft Regulation 12.3, fn. 80. On the notion of "Anfangsverdacht" see also Annex 2, B., Germany.

1312 Draft Regulations OTP 2003, *supra* note 63, Section 4, Part 2, Draft Regulation 12.3, fn. 80.

1313 McDonald/Haveman, *supra* note 1149, 4.

1314 Venezuela response, *supra* note 333, 4; thereto WCRO report gravity, *supra* note 1057, 22.

1315 Iraq response, *supra* note 333, 4.

1316 Venezuela response, *supra* note 333, 4; Iraq response, *supra* note 333, 4, 7. According to the OTP, the Iraq situation was also partly rejected due to legal gravity issues.

suspects, there must be a reasonable basis that the event occurred and that it amounts to criminal activity under article 5. Nevertheless, it would be desirable to establish a more specific definition for the threshold of "reasonable basis to believe." A feasible approach could be to define the test as follows:

> "If there is *initial evidence* that the event in question occurred and the Prosecutor deems the event to be within the jurisdiction of the Court, the Prosecutor should not decline further proceedings."

Such an evaluation must bear in mind the following findings mentioned above:

- "reasonable basis to proceed" and "reasonable basis to believe" have to be distinguished (although the later presupposes the former);
- the "reasonable basis to believe" test is a very low test and should not set up a too high legal threshold;
- the OTP should objectively assess the available evidence at this stage;
- neither all elements of the crime have to be proven nor must the OTP identify a particular suspect.

b) Jurisdiction of the Court

The second parameter is non-discretionary and refers to jurisdiction, which must be established in a strictly legal way. In accordance with article 19 (1), the Judges have the power to determine the Court's jurisdiction.[1317] The jurisdiction assessment is threefold and can be subdivided into subject-matter jurisdiction (articles 5, 6, 7, and 8), temporal jurisdiction (article 11), and territorial jurisdiction (article 12). In addition, the ICC exercises its personal jurisdiction over natural persons (articles 1, 25) over the age of eighteen (article 26) and irrespective of their official position (article 27 (1)); thus, immunities do not bar the ICC's jurisdiction (article 27 (2)).[1318] In its early case law PTC I spelled out the basic threefold testing:

[1317] PTC III emphasized that "irrespective of the terms of article 19 (1) of the Statute, every international court has power to determine its own jurisdiction, even when there is no explicit provision to that effect," see *Prosecutor v. Bemba,* Décision relative à la requête du procureur, *supra* note 465, para. 11. See further Part IV, B., III., 2.

[1318] Ambos, *supra* note 26, § 8 mn 4; Calvo-Goller, *supra* note 10, 182 et seq.; Meißner, *supra* note 371, 51; Iain Cameron, "Jurisdiction and admissibility under the ICC Statute," in McGoldrick/Rowe/Donnelly, *supra* note 649, 65, 71; also Elizabeth Wilmshurst, "Jurisdiction of the Court" in Lee, *supra* note 14, 127, 127 et seq.

"To fall within the Court's jurisdiction, a crime must meet the following conditions: it must be one of the crimes mentioned in article 5 of the Statute, that is to say, the crime of genocide, crimes against humanity and war crimes; the crime must have been committed within the time period laid down in article 11 of the Statute; and the crime must meet one of the two alternative conditions described in article 12 of the Statute (fn. omitted)."[1319]

Article 5 limits the subject-matter jurisdiction to the core crimes of genocide, crimes against humanity, and war crimes.[1320] In accordance with articles 5 (2), 121 and 123, the crime of aggression was inserted into article 8*bis* at the Review Conference in Kampala.[1321] All definitions of crimes have some build-in thresholds – limiting the discretion of the Prosecutor – that will help to focus decisions.[1322] Every crime entails contextual and specific elements.[1323] For crimes against humanity, the criterion "widespread or systematic attack" was included.[1324] The phrasing excludes random or isolated acts of violence; the adjective "widespread" connotes the large-scale nature of the attack and the number of targeted persons, whereas

---

1319 *Situation in DRC,* Decision on the applications for participation in the proceedings of VPRS 1 etc., *supra* note 398, para. 85; concurring *Prosecutor v. Lubanga,* Decision on the Prosecutor's application for warrant of arrest, article 58, *supra* note 217, para. 24; *Prosecutor v. Chui,* Decision on the evidence and information, *supra* note 235, para. 11; *Prosecutor v. Bemba,* Décision relative à la requête du procureur, *supra* note 465, para. 12; Hoffmeister/Knoke, *supra* note 169, 794 et seq.; Olásolo, *supra* note 400, 289 et seq.; *Situation in Kenya*, Request for authorization, *supra* note 207, para. 47, 17; *Situation in Kenya*, Decision pursuant to article 15, *supra* note 6, para. 39, 18.

1320 See further Steinberger-Fraunhofer, *supra* note 315, 24 et seq., 48 et seq.

1321 Resolution RC/Res. 6, *supra* note 418. The exercise of jurisdiction foresees a Security Council referral in article 15*ter*, or – under elevated circumstances – a state referral or *proprio motu* action in article 15*bis*. For an all-embracing discussion on these new articles see the symposium in (2010) 2 GOJIL, 649, 649–811. For earlier discussions before Kampala see Daniel Ntanda Nsereko, "The International Criminal Court: Jurisdictional and related issues" (1999) 10 CLF 87, 94; Olásolo, *supra* note 400, 289; also <www2.icc-cpi.int/Menus/ASP/Crime+of+Aggression/>.

1322 Schabas, *supra* note 27, 86; Olásolo, *supra* note 400, 290–1; *id., supra* note 376, 133.

1323 *Prosecutor v. Harun and Kushayb,* Decision on the Prosecution application under article 58 (7) of the Statute, *supra* note 292, para. 29; *Prosecutor v. Katanga,* Decision on the evidence and information, *supra* note 398, para. 26; *Prosecutor v. Chui,* Decision on the evidence and information, *supra* note 235, para. 27; *Prosecutor v. Abu Garda,* Decision under article 58, *supra* note 308, para. 6.

1324 Schabas, *supra* note 27, 86; Calvo-Goller, *supra* note 10, 177; Antonio Cassese, "Crimes against humanity" in Cassese/Gaeta/Jones, *supra* note 133, 353, 356 et seq.; Cassese, *supra* note 191, 98; Wouters/Verhoeven/Demeyere, *supra* note 156, 297; Gerhard Werle, *Völkerstrafrecht,* 2. Aufl. (Mohr Siebeck, Tübingen 2007) mn 755. See further *Situation in Kenya*, Decision pursuant to article 15, *supra* note 6; para. 79, 32, para. 94, 40. On the requirement of a State or organizational policy see *ibid.*, paras. 83 et seq., 34 et seq.

the adjective "systematic" refers to the organized nature of the acts of violence and the improbability of their random occurrence.[1325] In the case of genocide, the very high level of *dolus specialis* is part of the definition of genocide; it requires that the offender intends to destroy the targeted group in whole or in part.[1326] An additional objective threshold seems to be introduced through the Elements of Crimes, which indicates that "the conduct took place in the context of a manifest pattern of similar conduct directed against that group or was conduct that could itself effect such destruction."[1327] Genocidal acts are typically both systematic and widespread.[1328] It has been argued that, while the Elements of Crimes cannot be part of the objective definition of genocide, they nevertheless limit the jurisdiction of the ICC to systematic attacks.[1329] However, the Elements can neither restrict the substantive content of genocide nor the jurisdictional reach of the ICC; this information is solely contained in articles 5 and 6 with regard to the crime of genocide (article 9 (3)).[1330] It is therefore submitted that the Elements of Crimes hint at the quantitative scale of genocide, but that the sole threshold *per definitionem* is the special intent. In conclusion, the manifest pattern or large-scale commission cannot be considered an obligatory threshold for genocide on its own, but it could prove to be an important indicator for special intent.[1331]

While crimes against humanity have a quantitative dimension, war crimes do not, in a definitional sense, require the same quantitative scale.[1332] For

---

[1325] *Prosecutor v. Harun and Kushayb,* Decision on the Prosecution application under article 58 (7) of the Statute, *supra* note 292, para. 62; *Prosecutor v. Katanga,* Decision on the evidence and information, *supra* note 398, para. 33; *Prosecutor v. Chui,* Decision on the evidence and information, *supra* note 235, para. 34; *Prosecutor v. Bemba,* Décision relative à la requête du procureur, *supra* note 465, para. 33.

[1326] Ambos, *supra* note 26, § 7 mn 145; Calvo-Goller, *supra* note 10, 176; Werle, *supra* note 1324, mn 702.

[1327] Article 6 (a) lit. 4, article 6 (b) lit. 4, article 6 (c) lit. 5, article 6 (d) lit. 5, article 6 (e) lit. 7 of the Elements of Crimes.

[1328] Wouters/Verhoeven/Demeyere, *supra* note 156, 297; Calvo-Goller, *supra* note 10, 176.

[1329] Werle, *supra* note 1324, mn 705; Cassese, *supra* note 191, 140–1, who differentiates between article 6 (a), (b) and (c) to (e).

[1330] They cannot be equated with binding rules, but rather have the value of auxiliary means, see Antonio Cassese, "Genocide," in Cassese/Gaeta/Jones, *supra* note 133, 335, 348.

[1331] Schabas, *supra* note 27, 86; Ambos, *supra* note 26, § 7 mn 145, 151. Contrary the majority opinion in *Prosecutor v. Al Bashir,* Decision on the Prosecutor's application for a warrant of arrest against Bashir, *supra* note 304, paras. 123 et seq., 133. Against this see the dissent *Prosecutor v. Al Bashir,* Separate and partly dissenting opinion of Judge Anita Ušacka, *supra* note 305, paras. 16 et seq.; thereto Claus Kress, "The crime of genocide and contextual elements" (2009) 7 JICJ 297, 297 et seq.

narrowing the scope of war crimes the phrasing "in particular when committed as part of a plan or policy or as part of a large-scale commission of such crimes" was introduced into the chapeau of article 8.[1333] In practice, however, the PTC analyzes only the context element "whether the crime arose in an international armed conflict or of an armed conflict not of an international character."[1334] The plan or policy or large-scale element only gives discretionary guidance to determine gravity, and it is not a strict requirement of the definition of war crimes since article 8 states "in particular."[1335] The requirement of a plan, policy, or large-scale commission is part of the admissibility determination and not of the definition of war crimes as such.[1336] The application of the legal gravity threshold for excluding isolated crimes is therefore a feasible way to take the "plan or policy or large-scale" requirement into consideration.

As a result, it cannot be maintained in a generalized manner that any isolated activity, i.e. criminal activity that does not take place in a systematic or widespread manner, falls outside the jurisdictional reach of the ICC *per se*.[1337] One has to differentiate between crimes in the ICC Statute. Isolated activity only falls outside the jurisdiction of the Court for crimes against humanity. For war crimes, there is no such obligatory build-in threshold. Isolated war crimes fall within the ICC's subject-matter jurisdiction, but they could later prove not to be admissible or outside the "interests of justice." For genocide, it is submitted that acts could either fall outside the jurisdiction due to the specific intent requirement, or isolated acts could be deemed inadmissible if they were not committed in a manifest pattern. However, it can be argued that a genocide case always fulfils the gravity threshold, and as such cannot be inadmissible, even if constituting an isolated crime.[1338]

1332 Schabas, *supra* note 27, 86; Wouters/Verhoeven/Demeyere, *supra* note 156, 297; Richard John Galvin, "The ICC Prosecutor, collateral damage and NGOs: evaluating the risk of politicized prosecution" (2005) 13 University of Miami International and Comparative Law Review 1, 16–7.

1333 Schabas, *supra* note 27, 87. Further on the state plan or policy element, see William Schabas, "Crimes against humanity: The State plan or policy element" in Sadat/Scharf, *supra* note 537, 347 et seq.

1334 *Prosecutor v. Bemba,* Décision relative à la requête du procureur, *supra* note 465, paras. 46 et seq.

1335 Andreas Schüller, "Gravity under the Rome Statute: Procedural filter or instrument of shaping criminal policy?" (2008) 21 HuV-I 73, 79–80; McAuliffe deGuzman, *supra* note 1152, 7; Hall, *supra* note 100, 13; Calvo-Goller, *supra* note 10, 180.

1336 Ambos, *supra* note 26, § 7 mn 228, who, moreover, values the criterion as being over-restrictive; Michael Cottier, "Article 8, para. 1" in Triffterer, *supra* note 37, article 8, mn 9; also Gerhard Werle/Florian Jessberger, "Unless otherwise provided" (2005) 3 JICJ 35, 50–1, who do, however, not clearly distinguish jurisdiction and admissibility issues.

1337 In such a way, however, Olásolo, *supra* note 400, 291.

The temporal jurisdiction of the ICC is framed by article 11. Only crimes committed after the entry into force (1 July 2002) fall within the Court's jurisdiction *ratione temporis* pursuant to article 11 (1).[1339] With regard to States that ratify or accede after this date, the ICC does not have complete jurisdiction. According to article 11 (2), the Court's temporal jurisdiction begins only after the entry into force for the particular State. The State though has the possibility to lodge a declaration accepting jurisdiction for the crimes within the time gap in-between general and particular entry into force pursuant to articles 11 (2) and 12 (3).[1340] Moreover, the SC can bypass articles 11 (2), 12 (2), and 12 (3), by referring a situation to the ICC. However, it can only refer situations that took place after the general entry into force in accordance with article 11 (1).[1341]

Article 12 deals with the preconditions of the exercise of jurisdiction. It regulates a complex threefold model. In a first step, a State automatically accepts the Court's jurisdiction if it becomes a Party to the Statute pursuant to article 12 (1). In a second step, the links for the exercise of jurisdiction are identified as the territorial State or the nationality of the accused pursuant to article 12 (2) (a), (b). In a third step, article 12 (3) foresees the possibility of *ad hoc* acceptance of jurisdiction through a declaration.[1342] In other words, the jurisdiction *ratione loci* requires one of following two elements to be met: the relevant crime was committed on the territory of a State Party (or a State which has made a declaration under article 12 (3)), or the relevant crime was committed by a national of a State Party (or a

---

1338 Ambos, in Ambos/Large/Wierda, *supra* note 650, 73–4, para. 38 with further references in fn. 356. See further Part IV, B., III., 2., c), cc), (4).

1339 Sharon Williams, "Article 11," in Triffterer, *supra* note 37, article 11, mn 9; Schabas, *supra* note 13, 273 et seq.; *Prosecutor v. Lubanga,* Decision on the Prosecutor's application for warrant of arrest, article 58, *supra* note 217, para. 26; Kim, *supra* note 813, 112; Thomas Hethe Clark, "The Prosecutor of the International Criminal Court, amnesties, and the 'interests of justice:' striking a delicate balance" (2005) 4 Washington University Global Studies Law Review 389, 395; Remarks by Luis Moreno-Ocampo, Prosecutor of the ICC, Conference on "Justice in post armed conflicts and the ICC: Reduction of impunity and a support to international justice," 15.1.2009, 3.

1340 Williams, in Triffterer, *supra* note 1339, article 11, mn 10. Such a declaration was lodged in Uganda, *Prosecutor v. Kony et al.*, Warrant of Arrest for Joseph Kony, *supra* note 251, para. 32; see already the explanations within this study at Part III, B., VI., 10.

1341 Stéphan Bourgon, "Jurisdiction *ratione temporis,*" in Cassese/Gaeta/Jones, *supra* note 133, 543, 553.

1342 Kai Ambos, "Der neue Internationale Strafgerichtshof – Ein Überblick" (1998) 51 NJW 3743, 3744; Morten Bergsmo, "The jurisdictional regime of the International Criminal Court" (1998) 6 EJCrim 29, 30 et seq.; Kim, *supra* note 813, 124; Bassiouni, *supra* note 401, 136; Slye/van Schaack, *supra* note 534, 52 et seq.; Steinberger-Fraunhofer, *supra* note 315, 33 et seq.

State which has made a declaration under article 12 (3)).[1343] Four of the five pending situations (DRC, Uganda, CAR, and Kenya), and the cases resulting from these situations, were based upon the principle of territoriality pursuant to article 12 (2) (a),[1344] and so were the preliminary examinations of crimes committed in Colombia, Afghanistan, and Georgia.[1345] Only the Darfur situation results from another jurisdictional basis, namely the SC's power to refer situations even of States not party to the ICC Statute. Article 12 (2) does not apply where the SC refers pursuant to article 13 (b).[1346]

To sum up, for the first and second parameter the OTP evaluates whether there is a reasonable basis to believe that a crime within the jurisdiction of the Court may have been committed, namely there must be a reasonable basis to believe that:

- the event in question occurred;
- the event constitutes criminal activity under article 5 of the ICC Statute;
- the crime falls within the temporal, personal, and territorial jurisdiction of the Court.

1343 *Situation in DRC,* Decision on the applications for participation in the proceedings of VPRS 1 etc., *supra* note 398, para. 91; concurring *Prosecutor v. Lubanga,* Decision on the Prosecutor's application for warrant of arrest, article 58, *supra* note 217, para. 27; *Prosecutor v. Katanga,* Decision on the evidence and information, *supra* note 398, para. 14; *Prosecutor v. Chui,* Decision on the evidence and information, *supra* note 235, para. 14; also Meißner, *supra* note 371, 55–6; Cassese, *supra* note 675, 159; Philips, *supra* note 643, 66–7; Nsereko, *supra* note 1321, 105; Olásolo, *supra* note 400, 294; Schabas, *supra* note 13, 277; Remarks by Luis Moreno-Ocampo, *supra* note 1339, 2.

1344 *Prosecutor v. Lubanga,* Decision on the Prosecutor's application for warrant of arrest, article 58, *supra* note 217, para. 23; *Prosecutor v. Ntaganda,* Mandat d'arrêt, *supra* note 229, 2–3; *Prosecutor v. Chui,* Mandat d'arrêt, *supra* note 235, 3; *Prosecutor v. Chui,* Decision on the evidence and information, *supra* note 235, para. 15; *Prosecutor v. Katanga,* Mandat d'arrêt, *supra* note 231, 3; *Prosecutor v. Katanga,* Decision on the evidence and information, *supra* note 398, para. 15; *Prosecutor v. Kony et al.,* Decision on the Prosecutor's application for warrants of arrest under article 58, 8.7.2005 (ICC-02/04-01/05-52) 2; *Prosecutor v. Kony et al.,* Warrant of Arrest for Joseph Kony, *supra* note 251, paras. 34, 38; *Prosecutor v. Bemba,* Mandat d'arrêt, *supra* note 273, para. 10; *Prosecutor v. Bemba,* Décision relative à la requête du procureur, *supra* note 465, para. 15. For Kenya see *Situation in Kenya,* Request for authorization, *supra* note 207, para. 50, 18; *Situation in Kenya,* Decision pursuant to article 15, *supra* note 6, para. 178, 68.

1345 Remarks by Luis Moreno-Ocampo, *supra* note 1339, 2.

1346 *Prosecutor v. Harun and Kushayb,* Decision on the Prosecution application under article 58 (7) of the Statute, *supra* note 292, paras. 16–7; *Prosecutor v. Abu Garda,* Decision under article 58, *supra* note 308, para. 2; Remarks by Luis Moreno-Ocampo, *supra* note 1339, 3; *Prosecutor v. Al Bashir,* Decision on the Prosecutor's application for a warrant of arrest against Bashir, *supra* note 304, paras. 36–7.

2. Subparagraph b – admissibility (article 17)

Article 17, which deals with admissibility, is the cornerstone of the ICC Statute.[1347] The issues of admissibility have to be distinguished from jurisdiction;[1348] the principle of complementarity does not relate to the existence of jurisdiction, but establishes the conditions under which it may be exercised.[1349] Admissibility arises at a number of stages in any investigation and prosecution and it involves both the OTP and the PTC.[1350]

The third parameter of admissibility has been called "fluctuating,"[1351] which indicates how challenging it is to find a solid legal interpretation and application. Article 1 and preambular paragraph 10 describe the complementary nature of the ICC, and the chapeau of article 17 explicitly links admissibility to this principle of complementarity.

1347 Sharon Williams/William Schabas, "Article 17" in Triffterer, *supra* note 37, article 17, mn 1; Schabas, *supra* note 13, 336; Philips, *supra* note 643, 63; Razesberger, *supra* note 371, 29; *Prosecutor v. Kony et al.,* Decision on the admissibility of the case under article 19 (1), *supra* note 264, para. 34. There have been numerous contributions on the admissibility issue in general, see *inter alia* Arsanjani, in Hebel/Lammers/Schukking, *supra* note 371, 68, 68 et seq.; Wei, *supra* note 156, 70 et seq.; Cameron, in McGoldrick/Rowe/Donnelly, *supra* note 1318, 83 et seq.; Cassese, *supra* note 675, 158–9; Nsereko, *supra* note 1321, 114 et seq.; Benvenuti, in Lattanzi/Schabas, *supra* note 675, 38 et seq.; Stahn, *supra* note 540, 87 et seq.; Seibert-Fohr, *supra* note 739, 563 et seq.; Pierre-Marie Dupuy, "Principe de complémentarité et droit international général" in Politi/Gioia, *supra* note 517, 17, 17 et seq.; Oscar Solera, "Complementary jurisdiction and international criminal justice" (2002) 84 IRRC 145, 145 et seq.; Manuela Melandri, "The relationship between State sovereignty and the enforcement of international criminal law under the Rome Statute (1998): a complex interplay" (2009) 9 ICLR 531, 537 et seq.; Meißner, *supra* note 371, 66 et seq.; Megan Fairlie, "Establishing admissibility at the International Criminal Court: does the buck stop with the prosecutor, full stop?" (2005) 39 International Lawyer 817, 817 et seq.; Ada Sheng, "Analysing the International Criminal Court complementarity principle through a Federal Courts lens" (2006) 1249 bepress Legal Series 1, 1 et seq.; David Rhys Evans, "Amnesties, pardons and complementarity: does the International Criminal Court have the tools to end impunity?" (2005) 1 HRLC 1, 2 et seq.; Harmen Van der Wilt/Sandra Lyngdorf, "Procedural obligations under the European Convention of Human Rights: useful guidelines for assessment of "unwillingness" and "inability" in the context of the complementarity principle" (2009) 9 ICLR 39, 39 et seq.

1348 *Situation in Kenya*, Decision pursuant to article 15, *supra* note 6, para. 40, 18.

1349 Markus Benzing, "The complementarity regime of the International Criminal Court: international criminal justice between State sovereignty and the fight against impunity" (2003) 7 Max Planck Yearbook of the UN 591, 594.

1350 Burke-White/Kaplan, in Stahn/Sluiter, *supra* note 247, 87; Burke-White, *supra* note 1218, 77. For a limited application of article 17 to cases only cf. WCRO report "situation" and case selection, *supra* note 370, 31.

1351 Turone, in Cassese/Gaeta/Jones, *supra* note 26, 1152.

The admissibility analysis has two prongs: complementarity and gravity.[1352] In practice, the OTP applies gravity first, and it does not address complementarity if the former provides a basis for rejecting the situation. In the Iraq situation the Prosecutor reached a negative conclusion on "gravity," and therefore found it unnecessary to elaborate on complementarity.[1353] Both criteria will be examined below.

PTC I distinguished between two parts of the admissibility test in the arrest warrant decisions against *Lubanga* and *Ntaganda,* the first part being the complementarity test, in particular whether States remained inactive, and only the second part amounting to the gravity threshold:

> "The Chamber considers that the admissibility test of a case arising from the investigation of a situation has two parts. The first part of the test relates to national investigations, prosecutions and trials concerning the case at hand insofar as such case would be admissible only if those States with jurisdiction over it have remained inactive in relation to that case or are unwilling or unable, within the meaning of article 17 (1) (a) to (c), (2) and (3) of the Statute. The second part of the test refers to the gravity threshold which any case must meet to be admissible before the Court. Accordingly, the Chamber will treat them separately (fn. omitted)."[1354]

Judges appear to favor a twofold test that starts with complementarity and subsequently addresses gravity. Although PTC I's decision was successfully appealed,[1355] the outline of the testing mechanism creates a strong presumption in favor of a twofold test starting with complementarity. Yet, the testing order might prove to be less significant and valid arguments can also be made to reverse the order. Most significantly, it might be easier to arrive at a negative finding on gravity before going into the difficult complementarity merits. In any event, gravity is a mandatory component of ad-

---

1352 PTC has acknowledged this twofold test in *Prosecutor v. Lubanga,* Decision on the Prosecutor's application for warrant of arrest, article 58, *supra* note 217, para. 29; see also *Situation in Darfur (Sudan),* Prosecutor's application under article 58 (7), 27.2.2007 (ICC-02/05-56) para. 251; *Prosecutor v. Abu Garda,* Decision on the confirmation of charges, *supra* note 312, para. 28; HRW, A summary of the case law of the ICC, *supra* note 495, 1; HRW Courting history report, *supra* note 126, 38; Ambos, in Ambos/Large/Wierda, *supra* note 650, 73–4, para. 38; Meißner, *supra* note 371, 66–7; Guariglia, in Stahn/Sluiter, *supra* note 1215, 214.

1353 Iraq response, *supra* note 333, 9. The avenue of application in Iraq – based on gravity, leaving out the potentially delicate assessment of articles 17 (a)–(c), 20 (3), – was similarly envisaged by Meißner, *supra* note 371, 79.

1354 *Prosecutor v. Ntaganda,* Annex II, Decision on the Prosecutor's application for warrants of arrest, *supra* note 228, para. 29; *Prosecutor v. Lubanga,* Decision on the Prosecutor's application for warrant of arrest, article 58, *supra* note 217, para. 29.

1355 See Part IV, B., III., 2., c), bb), (3).

missibility and cannot be left aside.[1356] In other words, for reaching a *positive finding* on admissibility, both gravity and complementarity must be fulfilled.

In the following, it must be noted that article 17 is analyzed consistent with article 53. Instead of an all-embracing analysis of admissibility, I will focus on disputed main issues and recent developments, such as the inactivity criterion. A more general listing and basic explanation of all the sub-elements will be provided.[1357]

Last but not least, it is worth noting that the Court itself has the responsibility and statutory authority to assess admissibility issues (*Kompetenz-Kompetenz* in German and *la compétence de la compétence* in French).[1358] In accordance with article 19 (1), it "may" even determine admissibility on its own motion.[1359] On the other hand, this *proprio motu* power to determine admissibility was interpreted restrictively by the Appeals Chamber in its *obiter dicta* in the DRC situation.[1360] The Chamber held that where ad-

---

1356 *Situation in Kenya*, Decision pursuant to article 15, *supra* note 6, para. 57, 25–6.

1357 The procedural phases of complementarity – articles 53, 18, and 19 – are exhaustively addressed by Kleffner, *supra* note 370, 163 et seq.

1358 Holmes, in Cassese/Gaeta/Jones, *supra* note 666, 667, 672; Kleffner, *supra* note 370, 102 ("*the Court*"); *Prosecutor v. Kony et al.,* Decision on the admissibility of the case under article 19 (1), *supra* note 264, para. 45; *Prosecutor v. Kony et al.,* Observations on behalf of victims pursuant to article 19 (1), *supra* note 264, para. 19; *Prosecutor v. Bemba,* Decision pursuant to article 61 (7) (a) and (b), *supra* note 279, para. 23; Benvenuti, in Lattanzi/Schabas, *supra* note 675, 42; El Zeidy, *supra* note 651, 913–4; Meißner, *supra* note 371, 62. On the burden and standard of proof regarding admissibility, see Fairlie, *supra* note 1347, 840, and Kleffner, *supra* note 370, 194 et seq. See also *supra* note 650.

1359 *Prosecutor v. Kony et al.,* Decision initiating proceedings under article 19, *supra* note 264, 5. It is, however, less clear if the Court may do so *in absentia* of the accused, see *Prosecutor v. Kony et al.,* Submission of observations on the admissibility (by the Counsel for the Defence), *supra* note 264, paras. 41 et seq. Against the latter concerns articulated by Defence Counsel Jens Diekmann one might simply refer to the plain reading of article 19 (4) which states that admissibility "may be challenged only once by any person or State referred to in paragraph 2." If the Chamber thus uses its *proprio motu* right under article 19 (1) – be that even *in absentia* – any accused may still use the right under article 19 (2) to challenge. Notwithstanding any former determination, the Chamber has to re-examine admissibility, and therefore I cannot see a risk of judicial pre-determination. Quite the contrary, as admissibility is an ongoing assessment, things might even change for the better for the accused. See *Prosecutor v. Kony et al.,* Decision on the admissibility of the case under article 19 (1), *supra* note 264, paras. 25 et seq.

1360 *Situation in DRC,* Judgment on the Prosecutor's appeal against the decision of Pre-Trial Chamber I entitled "Decision on the Prosecutor's application for warrants of arrest, article 58," 13.7.2006 (ICC-01-04-169) paras. 52–3, reclassified as public on 23.9.2008 pursuant to *Situation in DRC,* Decision on the unsealing of

missibility was not raised by the Prosecution in *ex parte* applications there must be an "ostensible cause" or a "self-evident factor" that impels the exercise of *proprio motu* review under article 19 (1).[1361] In other words, it is not appropriate for the PTC to address admissibility in *ex parte* applications during early proceedings, such as during the issuance of an arrest warrant stage, unless there are exceptional circumstances.[1362] On the other hand, PTC II highlighted the broad discretionary power under article 19 (1) in *Kony et al.,* clarifying that the (just mentioned) judgment by the Appeals Chamber referred to the "very specific procedural scenario of a Prosecutor's application for a warrant of arrest, by its nature triggering *ex parte* proceedings where the suspect is not represented," and, in any event, the lack of clarity as to the judicial authority of Uganda amounts to "an ostensible cause impelling the exercise of *proprio motu* review."[1363] In other words, PTC II saw limited relevance in the self-restraint that was established by the Appeals Chamber, which supposedly applies only to the arrest warrant stage and has little bearing on later stages.[1364] In conclusion, the exact admissibility testing mechanism is far from settled and in future case law will surely evolve.

a) Drafting history overview

Besides preambular paragraph 3, the main article dealing with admissibility during the ILC was article 35 ILC Draft Statute.[1365] In short, the grounds of inadmissibility were that "the crime in question has been or is

judgment of the Appeals Chamber issued on 13 July 2006, 22.9.2008 (ICC-01-04-538-PUB-Exp).

[1361] *Situation in DRC,* Judgment on the Prosecutor's appeal against the decision of Pre-Trial Chamber I, *supra* note 1360, para. 53; concurring *Prosecutor v. Abu Garda,* Decision under article 58, *supra* note 308, para. 4.

[1362] *Situation in DRC,* Judgment on the Prosecutor's appeal against the decision of Pre-Trial Chamber I, *supra* note 1360, paras. 52–3; *Prosecutor v. Al Bashir,* Decision on the Prosecutor's application for a warrant of arrest against Bashir, *supra* note 304, para. 47; see in more detail Part IV, B., III., 2., c), bb), (3).

[1363] *Prosecutor v. Kony et al.,* Decision on the admissibility of the case under article 19 (1), *supra* note 264, paras. 14, 21, and 44.

[1364] In a similar vein, *Prosecutor v. Abu Garda,* Decision on the confirmation of charges, *supra* note 312, para. 27.

[1365] ILC Draft Statute 1994, *supra* note 353, 105–6; Bassiouni, *supra* note 503, 152–3. Going back even further, and addressing the origin and development of the law of complementarity between 1919 and 1937, as well as 1941, and 1998, see El Zeidy, *supra* note 545, 11 et seq.; 59 et seq. See also Kleffner, *supra* note 370, 70 et seq.; Stigen, *supra* note 205, 30 et seq.; Solera, *supra* note 1347, 147 et seq.; Sophie Morel, *La mise en œuvre du principe de complémentarité par la cour pénale internationale le case particulier des amnisties* (Editions bis et ter, Lausanne 2005) 13 et seq.; Schabas, *supra* note 13, 336 et seq.

being duly investigated by any appropriate national authorities or is not of sufficient gravity to justify further action by the Court."[1366] Article 42 (1) affirmed the *ne bis in idem* principle.[1367] The *Ad Hoc* Committee of 1995 called the ILC's approach essential, since the proposed Court did not intend to replace national criminal courts.[1368] Some delegates thought that the principle of complementarity should create a strong presumption in favor on national proceedings. Others propose the opposite view, and a third position suggested a balanced approach "not only to safeguard the primacy of national jurisdictions, but also to avoid the jurisdiction of the court becoming merely residual to national jurisdiction."[1369] From March to April 1996 a first discussion on complementarity arose in the Preparatory Committee and from the very outset widely divergent views existed on the issue.[1370] Several proposals were included in the Preparatory Committee's Report,[1371] but the issue was only substantially dealt with in the August 1997 session.[1372] One of the greatest achievements of the 1997 meeting was a consensus text on complementarity.[1373] The draft article uses almost no brackets – except for paragraph 1 – for the compromise provision; however, a text box was inserted at the beginning explaining the article's origin and footnotes.[1374] In its wording, draft article 35 of 1997 is similar to the final version of the ICC Statute:

> "1. [On application of the accused or at the request of [an interested State] [a State which has jurisdiction over the crime] at any time prior to [or at] the commencement of the trial, or of its own motion], the Court shall determine whether a case before it is inadmissible.
>
> 2. Having regard to paragraph 3 of the Preamble, the Court shall determine that a case is inadmissible where:
>
> (a) the case is being investigated or prosecuted by a State which has jurisdiction over it, unless the State is unwilling or unable genuinely to carry out the investigation or prosecution;

1366 ILC Draft Statute 1994, *supra* note 353, 106; Williams/Schabas, in Triffterer, *supra* note 1347, article 17, mn 4; Holmes, in Lee, *supra* note 581, 44.

1367 ILC Draft Statute 1994, *supra* note 353, 117 et seq.; Williams/Schabas, in Triffterer, *supra* note 1347, article 17, mn 5.

1368 *Ad Hoc* Committee 1995, *supra* note 379, para. 29.

1369 *Ad Hoc* Committee 1995, *supra* note 379, paras. 31 et seq.

1370 Holmes, in Lee, *supra* note 581, 45; Williams/Schabas, in Triffterer, *supra* note 1347, article 17, mn 9.

1371 Report of the Preparatory Committee 1996, Vol. 2, *supra* note 357, 159 et seq.

1372 Holmes, in Lee, *supra* note 581, 45; Williams/Schabas, in Triffterer, *supra* note 1347, article 17, mn 9.

1373 Williams/Schabas, in Triffterer, *supra* note 1347, article 17, mn 10.

1374 Holmes, in Lee, *supra* note 581, 46.

(b) the case has been investigated by a State which has jurisdiction over it and the State has decided not to prosecute the person concerned, unless the decision resulted from the unwillingness or inability of the State genuinely to prosecute;

(c) the person concerned has already been tried for conduct which is the subject of the complaint, and a trial by the Court is not permitted under paragraph 2 of article 42;

(d) the case is not of sufficient gravity to justify further action by the Court.

3. In order to determine unwillingness in a particular case, the Court shall consider whether one or more of the following exist, as applicable:

(a) the proceedings were or are being undertaken or the national decision was made for the purpose of shielding the person concerned from criminal responsibility for crimes within the jurisdiction of the Court as set out in article 20;

(b) there has been an undue delay in the proceedings which in the circumstances is inconsistent with intent to bring the person concerned to justice;

(c) the proceedings were not or are not being conducted independently or impartially and they were or are being conducted in a manner which, in the circumstances, is inconsistent with intent to bring the person concerned to justice.

4. In order to determine inability in a particular case, the Court shall consider whether, due to a total or partial collapse or unavailability of its national judicial system, the State is unable to obtain the accused or the necessary evidence and testimony or otherwise unable to carry out its proceedings (fn. omitted)."[1375]

This article refers to the terms "unwillingness" and "inability" for the first time. During the Rome Conference in 1998 some delegations, including China, Egypt, Mexico, Indonesia, India, Uruguay, and Kenya, wanted to reopen the discussions.[1376] While the compromise was not opened for substantial change, admissibility was refined in article 15 of the Draft Statute 1998.[1377] For the sake of clarity, the final package contained a reference to preambular paragraph 10 and article 1 where complementarity is mentioned.[1378] It needs to be emphasized that without reaching a consensus on the complementarity regime there would most likely not have been an agreement, and thus no ICC.[1379]

[1375] Decision taken by the Preparatory Committee 1997, *supra* note 385, 10 et seq.; Bassiouni, *supra* note 503, 144–5. For the French version, see Morel, *supra* note 1365, 83 et seq.

[1376] Holmes, in Lee, *supra* note 581, 52; Williams/Schabas, in Triffterer, *supra* note 1347, article 17, mn 17.

[1377] Holmes, in Lee, *supra* note 581, 51 et seq.; Williams/Schabas, in Triffterer, *supra* note 1347, article 17, mn 17–8; Draft Statute, April 1998, *supra* note 44, article 15, 40 et seq.

[1378] Williams/Schabas, in Triffterer, *supra* note 1347, article 17, mn 18.

[1379] Williams/Schabas, in Triffterer, *supra* note 1347, article 17, mn 20.

b) Complementarity

Complementarity as such is not defined in the ICC Statute.[1380] Article 17 (1) (a)–(c) rather sets out the non-discretionary requirements of complementarity.[1381] Rule 51 is the only provision within the RPE that addresses complementarity issues, but this rule does not add anything substantial to the ICC Statute.[1382] In conclusion, the ICC Statute and the RPE do not provide a road map for complementarity.[1383] Nonetheless, some preliminary remarks can be drawn from statutory interpretation. The principle of complementarity obligates the Prosecutor to defer to national legal systems where the State that normally exercises jurisdiction is in the process of investigating or prosecuting the crime. It also requires the OTP to defer in a situation where the crime has been investigated but the State has decided not to prosecute or when a national prosecution is completed and ICC action would lead to double jeopardy (articles 17 (1) (a)–(c), 20 (3)). The Prosecutor can – in principle – only intervene when territorial States are unwilling or unable to genuinely investigate or prosecute.[1384] One of the core principles is positive complementarity, thus an approach that encourages national proceedings wherever possible.[1385] In this regard, the OTP distinguishes complementarity as an admissibility test, i. e. how to assess the existence of national pro-

---

[1380] Benzing, *supra* note 1349, 592; Stigen, *supra* note 205, 187; André Klip, "Complementarity and concurrent juridiction" (2004) 19 Nouvelles études pénal 173, 173; Olympia Bekou, "Complementarity and the ICC: a dangerous gamble?" in George Ulrich (ed.), *The International Criminal Court: challenges and prospects, Proceedings of an international conference organised by the European Inter-University Centre for Human Rights and Democratisation (EIUC)* (Marsiolio Editori, Venice 2005) 61, 64–5.

[1381] Hall, *supra* note 100, 15.

[1382] Razesberger, *supra* note 371, 55–6.

[1383] Bassiouni, *supra* note 401, 133.

[1384] Louise Mallinder, *Amnesty, human rights and political transition* (Hart Publishing, Oxford/Portland 2008) 283.

[1385] Géraldine Mattioli/Anneke Van Woudenberg, "Global catalyst for national prosecutions? The ICC in the Democratic Republic of Congo" in Waddell/Clark, *supra* note 246, 55, 57; Hitomi Takemura, "A critical analysis of positive complementarity," XVth International Congress of Social Defense, Toledo, 20.–22.9.2007, 1 et seq.; Schiff, *supra* note 128, 116–7; William Burke-White, "Implementing a policy of positive complementarity in the Rome system of justice" (2008) 19 CLF 59, 59 et seq.; *id., supra* note 1218, 53 et seq.; Hall, in Stahn/Sluiter, *supra* note 206, 220; Stahn, *supra* note 540, 100 et seq., who, moreover, differentiates the classic concept and the positive concept of complementarity (at 95). See also the Chief-Prosecutor himself, Prosecutor's speech to the Eighth Session of the Assembly of States Parties, *supra* note 1143, 5. In the context of Katanga see Ben Batros, "The *Katanga* admissibility appeal: judicial restraint at the ICC" (2010) 23 LJIL 343, 358 et seq.

ceedings and their genuineness, and the positive complementarity concept, i.e. how to promote national proceedings.[1386]

As a starting point, the admissibility of each situation and case is presumed by the Court.[1387] Article 17 (1) then regulates exceptions to the principle of admissibility ("the Court shall determine that a case is inadmissible where"), and exceptions to the exception (unwillingness and inability to investigate or prosecute).[1388] Thus, articles 17 and 20 set forth the material elements of complementarity,[1389] which will now be dealt with in more detail.

aa) Complementarity regarding situations – "in a general manner" (degree and standard of specificity)

In 2003 an informal expert group noticed that complementarity issues could arise during early phases of ICC proceedings and that the admissibility assessment must then be more generalized.[1390] The expert group identified the problem that circles around the term "case" frequently used throughout article 17.[1391] Despite the expert paper, authors have taken a "case" related complementarity approach according to which the Court would always assess the situation in relation to a specific case.[1392] According to these views, the degree of specificity would have to be very high.[1393] This approach is supported by the wording both of articles 17 and 53. Article 53 (1) (b) clearly refers to the "case" which "is or would be" admissible, and so does article 17 on several occasions. Article 17 (2) and

---

1386 Prosecutorial Strategy 2009–2012, *supra* note 99, para. 17, 5; thereto Susana Sá Couto/Katherine Cleary, "The *Katanga* complementarity decisions: sound law but flawed policy" (2010) 23 LJIL 363, 372 et seq.

1387 Claudia Cárdenas, "The admissibility test before the International Criminal Court under special consideration of amnesties and truth commissions" in Jan Kleffner/Gerben Kor (eds.), *Complementary views on complementarity* (T.M.C. Asser Press, The Hague 2006) 115, 116. This article is basically an English summary of her German dissertation: Claudia Cárdenas, *Die Zulässigkeitsprüfung vor dem Internationalen Strafgerichtshof* (BWV, Berlin 2005); also Meißner, *supra* note 371, 70–1; Kleffner, *supra* note 370, 104; Kindt, *supra* note 650, 142.

1388 Stahn, *supra* note 540, 105.

1389 Kleffner, *supra* note 370, 99.

1390 Informal expert paper: complementarity, *supra* note 572, para. 24.

1391 Informal expert paper: complementarity, *supra* note 572, para. 26 with fn. 10; also Olásolo, *supra* note 376, 135 ("[...] against the backdrop of either situations or cases").

1392 Benzing, *supra* note 1349, 603; Philips, *supra* note 643, 77; Razesberger, *supra* note 371, 71.

1393 Kleffner, *supra* note 370, 195.

(3) link unwillingness and inability to a "particular case."[1394] The term "situation" is not even mentioned. However, the subject of pre-investigations are situations, and thus article 53 (1) deals with situations as opposed to cases. During this early procedural stage the OTP and the PTC operate with entire situations; such an understanding finds support from a plain reading of articles 13 (a), (b), 14 (1), 15 (5), (6), and 18 (1).[1395] When making the admissibility determination in the context of initiating an investigation, it is unlikely that the Prosecutor has already identified a particular individual.[1396] In this sense, the Prosecutor has to test admissibility with regard to an entire situation involving potential cases. Since article 53 (1) further includes the hypothetical phrasing "would be admissible," and article 18 equally uses a broad phrase ("criminal acts which may constitute crimes"), the starting admissibility assessment is conducted in a more "generalized" manner. It therefore stands to reason that the specificity increases from a comparatively general standard (article 53 (1)) – via article 18 – to selecting individual cases (article 53 (2)), until it reaches the highest level of cases in the strict sense (article 19).[1397]

It needs to be further analyzed what such a "general" standard entails: What is the exact level of proof? What are the objects of the analysis? First of all, it has to be re-emphasized that challenges by individuals or States under article 19 (2) can only be brought against cases. At this point, the object is without doubt a case, and a State or individual cannot be given the right to challenge an entire situation. But can the Prosecutor assess an entire *situation's* admissibility at the article 53 (1) stage? It has been reasoned that admissibility must be assessed both at the case and situation stage.[1398] Even the sufficient gravity threshold should be taken into account as part of admissibility *prima facie* at the early situation stage.[1399] Although an admissibility test must take place at the early *situation stage* of article 53 (1), it remains unclear how an entire *situation* can be checked with regard to admissibility.

According to Stahn, the admissibility assessment forces the Prosecutor to inquire, *inter alia,* "whether national proceedings extend to *all parties* that

1394 Recently, such a narrow understanding of the term "case" has been adopted by the OTP in *Prosecutor v. Katanga and Chui,* Motifs de la décision orale, *supra* note 459, para. 17.

1395 *Situation in Kenya*, Decision pursuant to article 15, *supra* note 6, paras. 43–4, 19–20.

1396 Kleffner, *supra* note 370, 195.

1397 Kleffner, *supra* note 370, 197.

1398 Stahn, *supra* note 540, 106.

1399 Schüller, *supra* note 1335, 74. In favor of *prima facie* admissibility see Turone, in Cassese/Gaeta/Jones, *supra* note 26, 1151.

might have been involved in the committal of the alleged crimes and whether national proceedings cover *those incidents that may result in cases* where the Court might likely be interested in investigating and prosecuting."[1400] The OTP has chosen a similar, nuanced phrasing – not referring explicitly to situations – but to "potential cases" that "would be admissible."[1401] In a similar vein, it has been suggested that the Prosecutor will scarcely have singled out individual cases, but rather "incidents" comprising cases, and therefore the determination under article 53 (1) (b) is of a preliminary and wider nature.[1402] On the other hand, the OTP has recently argued that article 17 has a detailed character and that the term "case" must be interpreted narrowly for the purpose of the admissibility test.[1403] It remains to be seen how the Prosecutor harmonizes his narrow view of article 17 with his former broad practice regarding an analysis of "potential cases" within situations.

In the context of a *prima facie* determination of admissibility it has also been argued that an early determination may sometimes not be possible due to an insufficient factual and legal basis on which to decide.[1404] On the other hand, the different form of unwillingness and inability lend themselves to different degrees of specificity, and article 53 (1) (b) requires a *prima facie* determination of evidence.[1405]

Unfortunately, the Chambers did – for a long time – not shed light on this issue. While PTC II in the *Kony et al.* case intended to limit itself to a *prima facie* determination regarding admissibility ("appears to be admissible"),[1406] PTC I only referred to "is admissible" and not to "appears to be admissible" in the *Lubanga* case.[1407] Only recently, PTC II affirmed that the admissibility determination under articles 53 (1) (b), 17 should in prin-

---

[1400] Stahn, *supra* note 540, 106–7.

[1401] *Prosecutor v. Kony et al.,* Prosecution's observations regarding the admissibility, *supra* note 264, para. 6; also *Situation in Kenya,* Request for authorization, *supra* note 207, para. 51, 18.

[1402] Stigen, *supra* note 205, 212.

[1403] *Prosecutor v. Katanga and Chui,* Public redacted version of the 19th March 2009 Prosecution response to motion challenging the admissibility, *supra* note 459, paras. 64 et seq.; *Prosecutor v. Katanga and Chui,* Motifs de la décision orale, *supra* note 459, para. 17.

[1404] El Zeidy, *supra* note 598, 748.

[1405] Kleffner, *supra* note 370, 202, 209–10.

[1406] *Prosecutor v. Kony et al.,* Decision on the Prosecutor's application for warrants of arrest, *supra* note 1344, 2; *Prosecutor v. Kony et al.,* Warrant of Arrest for Joseph Kony, *supra* note 251, para. 38.

[1407] *Prosecutor v. Lubanga,* Decision on the Prosecutor's application for warrant of arrest, article 58, *supra* note 217, para. 18; also *Prosecutor v. Chui,* Mandat d'arrêt, *supra* note 235, 3 ("l'affaire [...] est recevable").

ciple be related to a situation (admissibility of a situation).[1408] But the Chamber held that the admissibility assessment can not be conducted in the abstract and thus departed from the phrasing "appears to be admissible" as used before. At the situation phase, admissibility must be assessed against certain criteria defining a "potential case," such as:

(i) the *groups of persons* involved that are likely to be the focus of an investigation for the purpose of shaping the future case(s); and

(ii) the crimes within the jurisdiction of the Court allegedly committed during the *incidents* that are likely to be the focus of an investigation for the purpose of shaping the future case(s).[1409]

Furthermore, PTC II found the Prosecutor's selection of incidents or groups to be preliminary in nature and not binding, meaning that "the Prosecutor's selection on the basis of these elements for the purposes of defining a potential 'case' for this particular phase may change at a later stage, depending on the development of the investigation."[1410] Admissibility is thus an on-going assessment, and may be revisited several times by the OTP, or pursuant to article 19 (1) if the Chamber so decides. One may therefore consider that there is a congruent, elevating line via articles 53 (1) – 18 – 53 (2) – 19 with regard to both the *specificity* required and the *standard* of proof. Practice of the ICC might further elucidate the relevant standards.[1411] In any event, the OTP currently operates on the basis of a case hypothesis (likely set of cases that would arise from the investigation of a situation), and examines admissibility – thus complementarity and gravity – only in a "generalized manner" during early pre-investigations.[1412] PTC II labeled this procedure an analysis of "potential cases." It thus screens the admissibility of one or more potential cases within the context of a situation.[1413] With regard to the parameters the Chamber held that

> "the admissibility assessment requires an examination as to whether the relevant State(s) is/are conducting or has/have conducted national proceedings in relation

---

[1408] *Situation in Kenya*, Decision pursuant to article 15, *supra* note 6, paras. 44–5, 20.

[1409] *Situation in Kenya*, Decision pursuant to article 15, *supra* note 6, para. 50, 23.

[1410] *Situation in Kenya*, Decision pursuant to article 15, *supra* note 6, para. 50, 23; also *Prosecutor v. Bemba*, Decision on the admissibility, *supra* note 290, para. 217, 81.

[1411] Kleffner, *supra* note 370, 213. On the rather unclear practice – from a defence perspective – see *Prosecutor v. Katanga and Chui,* Motion challenging the admissibility of the case by the Defence, *supra* note 459, paras. 31 et seq.

[1412] Stahn, in Stahn/Sluiter, *supra* note 156, 268–9.

[1413] *Situation in Kenya*, Decision pursuant to article 15, *supra* note 6, para. 182, 69.

to the *groups of persons* and the crimes allegedly committed *during those incidents*, which together would *likely* form the object of the Court's investigations. If the answer is in the negative, the "case would be admissible," provided that the gravity threshold is also met (emph. added)."[1414]

bb) Grounds for inadmissibility

The Chapeau of article 17 (1) clarifies that cases and situations are in principle inadmissible ("shall determine that the case is inadmissible where") if one of the reasons in paragraph (a) – (d) is present. This, however, is not a *per se* presumption in favor of inadmissibility, but rather a presumption in favor of action at the State level.[1415] As already mentioned, admissibility is presumed as a starting point, meaning that any case is admissible before the ICC and only becomes inadmissible when one of the criteria for inadmissibility is satisfied.[1416] The enumerated substantive criteria are applied alternatively; i.e., one of the mentioned four is sufficient to render a case or situation inadmissible.[1417] According to article 17 (1) (a)–(d) a case is inadmissible if:

(a) The case *is being investigated or prosecuted* by a State which has jurisdiction over it [...];

(b) The case *has been investigated* by a State which has jurisdiction over it and the State has decided not to prosecute the person concerned [...];

(c) The person concerned *has already been tried* for conduct which is the subject of the complaint, and a trial by the Court is not permitted under article 20, paragraph 3;

(d) The case is not of *sufficient gravity* to justify further action by the Court.

Furthermore, no opening clause can be identified, and the four listed criteria and their sub-elements are as such exhaustive.[1418] Distinct temporal criteria can be revealed from article 17 (1). The provision distinguishes be-

1414 *Situation in Kenya*, Decision pursuant to article 15, *supra* note 6, para. 52, 24; para. 182, 69.

1415 Benzing, *supra* note 1349, 600–1 with fn. 48; Jann Kleffner, "Complementarity as a catalyst for compliance" in Kleffner/Kor, *supra* note 1387, 79, 82.

1416 Cárdenas, 2005, *supra* note 1387, 57; Darryl Robinson, "Comments on chapter 4 of Claudia Cárdenas" in Kleffner/Kor, *supra* note 1387, 141, 141–2; Kindt, *supra* note 650, 142–3.

1417 El Zeidy, *supra* note 651, 898; contrary, Solera, *supra* note 1347, 165 ("cumulative").

1418 At first glance, the text does not point in either direction. However, no inclusive language was used and the word "considers" has been interpreted as deliberately limiting the criteria to the mentioned factors, Benzing, *supra* note 1349, 606; Meißner, *supra* note 371, 72–3; Gropengießer/Meißner, *supra* note 679, 282.

tween i) investigations and prosecutions (article 17 (1) (a) and (b)), ii) trial (article 17 (1) (c)), iii) when an investigation (or prosecution) is either taking place (article 17 (1) (a)) or iv) is already completed (article 17 (1) (b)).[1419] The first ground of inadmissibility under article 17 (1) (a) requires two elements: i) an investigation or prosecution and ii) a State that has jurisdiction.[1420] For the requirements of the second ground of inadmissibility in article 17 (1) (b), the State must have undertaken a systematic inquiry and have decided not to prosecute the case. The broad wording seems to allow for any decision ending the procedure.[1421] The third ground of article 17 (1) (c) refers to double-jeopardy and must be read in conjunction with article 20 (3). For differentiating article 17 (1) (b) and (c), the distinct procedural stages have to be emphasized: article 17 aims at covering all procedural steps without gaps. Article 17 (1) (b) therefore deals with the investigation stage, whereas article 17 (1) (c) refers to the trial stage. The decisive moment is the change of the decision-making authority to a qualified judge.[1422] The last and fourth ground of inadmissibility, namely gravity, will be dealt separately due to its importance and complexity in recent OTP practice.

The core question under article 17 (1) is how strictly the terms "investigations" and "prosecutions" should be interpreted. The text may cover only criminal investigations or may also allow for alternative forms of justice such as truth commission and conditional (or even general) amnesties.[1423] The genuineness of the specific alternative mechanism would then be a question of "unwillingness" and/or "inability." Article 53 (1) and (2) (c) could permit the Prosecutor to consider other justice mechanisms than criminal investigations. I prefer a narrow interpretation of the terms "investigation" and "prosecution" in the sense of criminal investigations *stricto sensu*; alternative justice mechanisms and amnesties should be considered under

---

[1419] Ambos, in Ambos/Large/Wierda, *supra* note 650, 73–4, para. 38.

[1420] Cárdenas, in Kleffner/Kor, *supra* note 1387, 117; Klip, *supra* note 1380, 180. On the definition of "a State which has jurisdiction" see Morel, *supra* note 1365, 97–8.

[1421] Meißner, *supra* note 371, 77. Note that a decision by the national courts to refer a case to the ICC does not qualify as a "decision not to prosecute" in the sense of article 17, cf. *Prosecutor v. Bemba*, Decision on the admissibility, *supra* note 280, para. 242, 90.

[1422] Meißner, *supra* note 371, 77.

[1423] Cameron, in McGoldrick/Rowe/Donnelly, *supra* note 1318, 90; El Zeidy, *supra* note 651, 941; Hoffmeister/Knoke, *supra* note 169, 799–800; Benvenuti, in Lattanzi/Schabas, *supra* note 675, 45–6; Declan Roche, "Truth Commission, amnesties and the International Criminal Court" (2005) 45 BJC 565, 568; Cárdenas, 2005, *supra* note 1387, 58; Marta Valiñas, "Interpreting complementarity and interests of justice in the presence of restorative-based alternative forms of justice" in Stahn/van Herik, *supra* note 11, 267, 273–4.

the "interests of justice" clause. Hence, the following pages will deal with the interpretation of "investigations" and "prosecutions" under article 17 (1), whereas the amnesty issue will be addressed below in more in the section on "interests of justice."[1424] Delegations before and during the Rome Conference were not able to reach a consensus on the issue of amnesties under the ICC Statute.[1425] The Statue's provisions rather reflect "creative ambiguity," which would potentially allow recognizing amnesties.[1426] The ICC Statute as such is not opposed to alternative mechanisms, and it has been argued that the Court could take into consideration flexible restorative mechanisms.[1427] In this regard, the gateways of articles 53 (1) and (2) (c), 17, 16, and 20 have been abundantly mentioned.[1428] Amnesties and truth commissions, whose primary purpose is addressing and resolving armed conflicts rather than shielding a perpetrator from criminal responsibility, could possibly qualify as valid attempts at "investigating" crimes.[1429] Whether amnesties (and/or truth commissions) fall under article 17 depends on the interpretation of "investigation," "decisions," and "unwillingness or inability." The more narrowly they are interpreted, the more unlikely amnesties are to fall under its scope.[1430]

The wording of article 17 (1) refers to "investigations" and "prosecutions," which are criminal law terminology taken from national laws.[1431] However, the term "investigation" as such is not entirely clear. It is not expressly stated that there must be a "criminal investigation."[1432] Alternative

[1424] Part IV, B., III., 3., e), dd).

[1425] Wedgwood, *supra* note 423, 96–7; Stigen, *supra* note 205, 424–5; Hoffmeister/Knoke, *supra* note 169, 799; Razesberger, *supra* note 371, 159; Morel, *supra* note 1365, 230; Werle, *supra* note 1324, mn 215; Gropengießer/Meißner, *supra* note 679, 267; Seibert-Fohr, *supra* note 739, 561–2; Slye/van Schaack, *supra* note 534, 255–6; Mahnoush Arsanjani, "The International Criminal Court and amnesty laws" (1999) 93 ASIL Proceedings 65, 67; Gwen Young, "Amnesty and accountability" (2002) 35 U.C. Davis Law Review 427, 431–2.

[1426] Michael Scharf, "The amnesty exception to the jurisdiction of the International Criminal Court" (1999) 32 CILJ 507, 522; also Clark, *supra* note 1339, 406; Newman, *supra* note 774, 321–2; Naomi Roht-Arriaza, "Amnesty and the International Criminal Court" in Dinah Shelton (ed.), *International Crimes, peace, and human rights: The role of the International Criminal Court* (Transnational Publishers, Ardsley, New York 2000) 77, 79; Diba Majzub, "Peace and Justice? Amnesties and the International Criminal Court" (2002) 3 MJIL 247, 263–4; Djamchid Momtaz, "La compétence complémentaire de la Cour Pénale Internationale à l'épreuve des lois d'amnistie inconditionelle" (2003) 78 Friedenswarte 53, 53.

[1427] Wouters/Verhoeven, in Ankumah/Kwakwa, *supra* note 210, 152.

[1428] As an example, see Slye/van Schaack, *supra* note 534, 256.

[1429] Ssenyonjo, *supra* note 246, 369–70; Cárdenas, 2005, *supra* note 1387, 58–9.

[1430] Wouters/Verhoeven, in Ankumah/Kwakwa, *supra* note 210, 155.

[1431] Meißner, *supra* note 371, 76; Van der Wilt/Lyngdorf, *supra* note 1347, 47.

forms of accountability are not explicitly dealt with.[1433] The word "investigation" does therefore not enlighten us. On the other hand, the term "prosecution" used in article 17 (1) (a) and (b) creates a strong presumption in favor of genuine *criminal* proceedings.[1434] Furthermore, a contextual reading suggests a narrow approach. Preambular paragraph 10 and article 1 mention "complementary to national *criminal* jurisdictions," article 17 (2) (a) speaks of "shielding a person from *criminal* responsibility" and article 17 (2) (b) and (c) aims at bringing "the person to *justice* (emph. added)."[1435] Moreover, the ICC Statute adopted a complex procedural system that confirms a limitation to criminal proceedings under article 17.

From a teleological point of view, matters not of criminal law nature should be addressed as part of the "interests of justice" assessment. The Statute systematically divides legal issues of jurisdiction (article 53 (1) (a)), legal issues of admissibility (articles 53 (1) (b), 17), and issues of the "interests of justice" (article 53 (1) (c)). The object and purpose of the ICC Statute generally aims at criminal procedures. Preambular paragraph 5 aims at putting "an end to impunity for the perpetrators of these crimes," and the States Parties reaffirm in preambular paragraph 6 "that it is the duty of every State to exercise its *criminal* jurisdiction over those responsible for international crimes (emph. added)." On a systematic and teleological reading, article 17 (1) can only refer to criminal investigations.

On the other hand, a different interpretation is not ruled out *per se*. If the ICC's actors define the complementarity regime more widely, alternative mechanisms – if they are at least comparable to criminal proceedings – could be tolerated.[1436] In any event, there must then be some sort of inquiry into the crimes.[1437] It has, for instance, been argued that the more a TRC is aligned to the standards of criminal investigations the more is could fit under article 17.[1438] But the loophole for TRCs that substitute criminal pro-

---

1432 Stahn, *supra* note 726, 697; Scharf, *supra* note 1426, 525; Bartelt, *supra* note 677, 206; Majzub, *supra* note 1426, 267.

1433 Meyer, *supra* note 1153, 565.

1434 Kleffner, *supra* note 370, 268–9.

1435 Meißner, *supra* note 371, 76; Kleffner, *supra* note 370, 270–1. With regard to the last argument, the Spanish version is even clearer as it spells out "[…] hacer comparecer a la persona de que se trante ante la *justicia*" (emph. added); also Gropengießer/Meißner, *supra* note 679, 283 with fn. 87; contrary, Razesberger, *supra* note 371, 181.

1436 Cárdenas, 2005, *supra* note 1387, 175 et seq., whose broad approach has resulted in a legal survey, testing TRCs *vis-à-vis* article 17.

1437 Stahn, *supra* note 726, 710; Seibert-Fohr, *supra* note 739, 588; Stigen, *supra* note 205, 203.

1438 Razesberger, *supra* note 371, 181; similarly, Seibert-Fohr, *supra* note 739, 567 et seq.

ceedings is very small and they must at least be comparable to criminal law prosecutions.[1439] In such a case, the only feasible avenue would be article 17 (1) (b).[1440] The truth commission or other body must have "investigated" the matter, "decided" not to prosecute, and the decision must not have resulted from the unwillingness or inability of the State to genuinely prosecute.[1441] "Investigations" could be interpreted slightly broader than criminal proceedings as comprising "a diligent, methodical effort to gather the evidence and ascertain the facts relating to the conduct in question, in order to make an objective determination in accordance with pertinent criteria."[1442] Such an approach would allow for forms of investigation other than typical criminal prosecutions, and it would leave room for individualized truth and reconciliation formulas.[1443] In any event, if investigations are not limited to criminal ones, there must at least be the possibility of criminal proceedings at the end.[1444] The "decision not to prosecute" can only have the meaning that more than one option is available; as such, prosecution cannot be barred by legislation.[1445] Unwillingness and inability will be guided by articles 17 (2) and (3). In other words, this wide interpretation leaves room for TRC inquiries, but comes close to criminal proceedings and sees TRCs only as complements thereto.

In sum, the term "investigation" tends towards criminal law proceedings, but leaves a very small gateway for different approaches. One might have to conclude that "investigation" is an indefinite legal concept open for Court interpretation.[1446] The Judges will ultimately have to decide how far reaching article 17 is. If they decide to soften the scope of "investigations," the test has to be refined by setting the exact demarcation line between investigative commissions that meet the requirement of article 17 and, on the other hand, mechanisms that do not satisfy article 17. Criteria and a feasible test would have to be developed. As a starting point, one author gener-

---

1439 Bartelt, *supra* note 677, 210.

1440 Robinson, *supra* note 807, 499, who rejects article 17 (1) (a), that provides no durable solution, and article 17 (1) (c), 20, that requires a "trial by a Court;" also Bartelt, *supra* note 677, 204–5; Morel, *supra* note 1365, 242. Contrary, Cárdenas, 2005, *supra* note 1387, 175 et seq., who turns to article 17 (1) (b) and article 17 (1) (a).

1441 Robinson, *supra* note 807, 499; also Bartelt, *supra* note 677, 205.

1442 Robinson, *supra* note 807, 500.

1443 Stahn, *supra* note 726, 711; Young, *supra* note 1425, 468; Seibert-Fohr, *supra* note 739, 575.

1444 Robinson, in Kleffner/Kor, *supra* note 1416, 144; also Stigen, *supra* note 205, 429; Ambos, in Ambos/Large/Wierda, *supra* note 650, 75–6, para. 40.

1445 Robinson, *supra* note 807, 500; Stahn, *supra* note 726, 712; Bartelt, *supra* note 677, 208–9.

1446 Bartelt, *supra* note 677, 206.

ates a test of contextual proportionality.[1447] However, article 53 (1) (c) and (2) (c) provides a more solid basis for alternative mechanisms.[1448] A proportionality test could very well contribute to weighing the specific criteria under the "interests of justice" clause. For all these reasons, the Court is not entirely barred from considering alternatives to criminal investigations under article 17, but any transitional justice mechanism should be treated as an "interests of justice" matter.

In a nutshell, an investigation is a procedure to determine whether a crime within the jurisdiction of the Court has been or is being committed and aims at bringing the alleged perpetrator to justice.[1449] A prosecution is defined as the opening and undertaking of a judicial criminal process.[1450] Therefore, "prosecution" does not refer to the prosecution itself, but only to the "decision" to prosecute. The organ that takes this decision must have two options, namely to prosecute or not to prosecute.[1451] Both terms, investigations and prosecutions, have proven to be *generally* of a criminal law nature. Under certain circumstances, however, criminal proceedings might be unnecessary.[1452] Although a narrow gateway was identified that could allow for alternative mechanisms closely related to purely criminal proceedings (for instance TRCs), the broad notion of transitional justice instruments is an "interests of justice" matter, and, for this reason, is further discussed as part of article 53 (1) (c) and (2) (c). Article 17 does not provide much space for alternative forms of conflict resolution.[1453] There must always be a minimum threshold of accountability under article 17.[1454] In particular, the legal avenue of admissibility does not leave room for the exercise of prosecutorial discretion based on policy grounds.[1455]

1447 Meyer, *supra* note 1153, 573 et seq.

1448 Concurring, Roht-Arriaza, *supra* note 1426, 81 ("[...] third, and most likely, avenue for dealing with amnesty"); contrary, Seibert-Fohr, *supra* note 739, 582, who prefers the – from her point of view more precise – solution via article 17 which gives better guidance than article 53. Alike most authors, Michael Scharf, "Justice versus peace" in Sewall/Kaysen, *supra* note 784, 179, 186 et seq., identifies articles 16, 17, 20, and 53 as potential gateways, but leaves the matter undecided.

1449 Benzing, *supra* note 1349, 602.

1450 Cárdenas, in Kleffner/Kor, *supra* note 1387, 117.

1451 Ambos, in Ambos/Large/Wierda, *supra* note 650, 76, para. 41.

1452 Meyer, *supra* note 1153, 566.

1453 In the same vein, Bartelt, *supra* note 677, 211. If the Court favors a broader interpretation of "investigations" and takes into consideration TRCs and amnesties, the illustrative graphs by *Cárdenas* might provide a good starting point. She gives an overview of the different scenarios with regard to admissibility *vis-à-vis* amnesties and truth commission, see Cárdenas, in Kleffner/Kor, *supra* note 1387, 133 and 138.

1454 Slye/van Schaack, *supra* note 534, 260.

1455 Kleffner, *supra* note 370, 288.

cc) Exceptions to the ground of inadmissibility

Unwillingness and inability are the exceptions for the first two grounds of inadmissibility. They are further regulated in article 17 (2) and (3). If a State is unwilling or unable to genuinely investigate or prosecute, the situation or case becomes admissible. The main issues during the drafting process at the Preparatory Committee were indeed the definitions of "inability" and "unwillingness" as criteria to hold a situation and case admissible.[1456] Both concepts should nevertheless not be confused; they are regulated separately and should not be treated as one.[1457] They form the broad concepts setting out circumstances when the Court should proceed even where State action had occurred.[1458] The exception to the third ground of article 17 (1) (c) is regulated in article 20 (3) (c).

While one of the strengths of the complementarity regime is the relatively objective nature of the developed criteria, it was unavoidable that subjective elements were included as well.[1459] Moreover, the Court has taken an unexpected path of "uncontested admissibility" – or rather a concept of "inactivity"[1460] – as the over-reaching exception for rendering situations and cases admissible.

(1) Inactivity

The Prosecutor has developed a theory of "uncontested admissibility" according to which the complementarity test is satisfied by inactivity. According to this approach the Prosecutor has to distinguish between different scenarios: cases of inaction (which are admissible), or, only in a second step, cases of action in which the State nevertheless is unwilling or unable.[1461]

1456 Holmes, in Lee, *supra* note 581, 48; Benvenuti, in Lattanzi/Schabas, *supra* note 675, 43 et seq.

1457 Cárdenas, in Kleffner/Kor, *supra* note 1387, 121; Benzing, *supra* note 1349, 603 ("disjunctive"); *Prosecutor v. Katanga and Chui,* Motifs de la décision orale, *supra* note 459, para. 75 ("these criteria form the limbs of an alternative").

1458 Holmes, in Cassese/Gaeta/Jones, *supra* note 666, 673. On the classification of hybrid tribunals, suggesting a symbiotic relationship by regarding them as "domestic courts" for the purpose of article 17, see Erika de Wet, "The relationship between the International Criminal Court and *ad hoc* criminal tribunals: competition or symbiosis?" (2008) 83 Friedenswarte 33, 47 et seq., 49.

1459 Holmes, in Lee, *supra* note 581, 75.

1460 See El Zeidy, *supra* note 545, 214, who further differentiates the two terms. On inactivity see *Prosecutor v. Katanga and Chui,* Judgment on the appeal of Mr. Germain Katanga against the oral decision of Trial Chamber II of 12 June 2009 on the admissibility of the case, *supra* note 459, para. 2; Robinson, *supra* note 468, 67 et seq.

An informal expert group first enunciated this theory, which was later picked up and applied by the OTP:

> "Although it is common to emphasize the "unwilling or unable" test in article 17, the article in fact deals with three logically distinct circumstances.
>
> [...] First, the most straightforward scenario is where no State has initiated any investigation (the inaction scenario). In such a scenario, none of the alternatives of articles 17 (1) (a)–(c) are satisfied and there is no impediment to admissibility. Thus, there is no need to examine the factors of unwillingness or inability; the case is simply admissible under the clear terms of Article 17."[1462]

The OTP therefore states:

> "Where there have been no national proceedings, then the case is clearly admissible and there is no need to apply the "unwilling or unable" test (article 17 (1))."[1463]

In practice, the OTP heavily relies on uncontested admissibility.[1464] On the one hand, there is no reference to the term "inactivity" of the national justice system in article 17 (1).[1465] On the other hand, the wording implies a more-step test rather than a one-step test based on unwillingness/inability only.[1466] PTC I took the later approach based on an *e contrario* interpretation of article 17 (1) (a)–(c), and approved the inactivity criterion as part of the admissibility assessment when stating that "the case would be inadmis-

---

1461 ICTJ, Paul Seils/Marieke Wierda, "The International Criminal Court and conflict mediation," June 2005, 1, 6; Burke-White, *supra* note 1218, 78; similarly Kindt, *supra* note 650, 145; *Prosecutor v. Katanga and Chui,* Public redacted version of the 19th March 2009 Prosecution response to motion challenging the admissibility, *supra* note 459, para. 46; *Situation in Kenya*, Request for authorization, *supra* note 207, para. 52, 18–9; Robinson, *supra* note 468, 71.

1462 Informal expert paper: complementarity, *supra* note 572, paras. 17–8; Schabas, *supra* note 540, 7–8; El Zeidy, *supra* note 246, 106; see already *supra* notes 584 and 585 with corresponding text; most recently Williams/Schabas, in Triffterer, *supra* note 1347, article 17, mn 23; Stahn, *supra* note 540, 105–6.

1463 *Prosecutor v. Kony et al.,* Prosecution's observations regarding the admissibility, *supra* note 264, para. 9; *Prosecutor v. Kony et al.,* Prosecutor's Response to Observations submitted under Rule 103, 15.12.2008 (ICC-02/04-01/05-361) 3.

1464 See, for instance, Eight Report pursuant to UNSC 1593, *supra* note 290, para. 13: "All three Prosecution cases remain admissible. There are no proceedings in the Sudan against Ahmad Harun and Ali Kushayb, against Omar Al Bashir, or against the three rebel commanders of the Haskanita attack."; also Sheng, *supra* note 1347, 5.

1465 Williams/Schabas, in Triffterer, *supra* note 1347, article 17, mn 23; critically also Arsanjani/Reismann, in Sadat/Scharf, *supra* note 537, 336; *id., supra* note 533, 391.

1466 Robinson, *supra* note 468, 72 et seq. In Robinson's view, the test amounts to two steps. In my opinion, one should even speak of three prongs, cf. Part IV, B., III., 2., b), cc), (1).

sible only if those States with jurisdiction over it have remained inactive in relation to that case or are unwilling or unable."[1467] The Chamber therefore concluded that:

> "[c]oncerning the first part of the admissibility test, [...] no State with jurisdiction over the case against Mr. Thomas Lubanga Dyilo is acting, or has acted, in relation to such case. Accordingly, in the absence of any acting State, the Chamber need not make any analysis of unwillingness or inability."[1468]

In the earlier case of *Kony et al.,* PTC II did not even go into the merits but simply stated that the case "appears to be admissible."[1469] In contrast to PTC I in DRC, PTC II found it sufficient to make a *prima facie* finding of admissibility.[1470] In any event, if no State is acting in relation to a specific case, a further analysis of unwillingness or inability is not warranted by the Chambers.[1471] If inaction is demonstrated the case is automatically admissible, but there arguably needs to be *ne bis in idem* and gravity determinations in accordance with article 17 (1) (c) and (d).[1472] The inactivity concept as such was recently approved by the Appeals Chamber and can now be regarded as settled jurisprudence.[1473]

As part of the screening process for inactivity, if there are some kinds of national proceedings at all then these activities must correspond to the charges in the OTP's case. It must, however, be noted that *first* some na-

---

[1467] *Prosecutor v. Lubanga,* Decision on the Prosecutor's application for warrant of arrest, article 58, *supra* note 217, para. 29 with fn. 19; *Prosecutor v. Ntaganda,* Annex II, Decision on the Prosecutor's application for warrants of arrest, *supra* note 228, para. 29 with fn. 19; concurring *Prosecutor v. Al Bashir,* Decision on the Prosecutor's application for a warrant of arrest against Bashir, *supra* note 304, para. 48. On early confusions on the issues inability (in the technical sense) and inactivity by PTC I see El Zeidy, *supra* note 545, 230–1.

[1468] *Prosecutor v. Lubanga,* Decision on the Prosecutor's application for warrant of arrest, article 58, *supra* note 217, para. 40.

[1469] *Prosecutor v. Kony et al.,* Decision on the Prosecutor's application for warrants of arrest, *supra* note 1344, 2; *Prosecutor v. Kony et al.,* Decision on the admissibility of the case under article 19 (1), *supra* note 264, para. 16.

[1470] El Zeidy, *supra* note 545, 233. See already Part IV, B., III., 2., b), aa).

[1471] Ambos, in Bohlander, *supra* note 10, 448; Jurdi, *supra* note 99, 79; *Prosecutor v. Katanga and Chui,* Motion challenging the admissibility of the case by the Defence, *supra* note 459, para. 28 ("shared agreement"); *Prosecutor v. Katanga and Chui,* Judgment on the appeal of Mr. Germain Katanga against the oral decision of Trial Chamber II of 12 June 2009 on the admissibility of the case, *supra* note 459, paras. 1, 80 et seq.; 97; *Prosecutor v. Abu Garda,* Decision on the confirmation of charges, *supra* note 312, para. 30.

[1472] *Prosecutor v. Katanga and Chui,* Motifs de la décision orale, *supra* note 459, paras. 21, 81.

[1473] *Prosecutor v. Katanga and Chui,* Judgment on the appeal of Mr. Germain Katanga against the oral decision of Trial Chamber II of 12 June 2009 on the admissibility of the case, *supra* note 459, para. 2; thereto Akhavan, *supra* note 534, 108–9.

tional proceedings have to take place before testing the sufficiency of those proceedings. If there are no proceedings at all, the case is clearly admissible due to inactivity. If national proceedings take place and do not encompass *specifically* both the *person* and the *conduct,* the case is held to be admissible ("specificity" test).[1474] The developed "specificity" test thus consists of two decisive elements: (1) the same person, and (2) the same conduct.

Accordingly, the PTCs check whether the concerned person is being prosecuted at the national level for the conduct referred to in the Prosecutor's application.[1475] In *Lubanga* and *Ntaganda,* for instance, the PTC held that the DRC's proceedings did not encompass the conduct of the Prosecutor's application.[1476] It, however, based its decision on a doubtful comparison since the DRC had issued arrest warrants on considerably graver crimes (crimes against humanity with regard to *Ntaganda*).[1477] Arguably, the PTC wanted to bypass any analysis of unwillingness and inability because the DRC's justice system now could try these cases.[1478] It has therefore been argued that the inactivity requirement annuls the differentiated procedural system and diminishes the experiences of atrocity victims where authorities were genuinely unable or unwilling to investigate and prosecute.[1479] On the other hand, there are considerable practical implications of avoiding the time-consuming admissibility determination.[1480]

[1474] *Prosecutor v. Harun and Kushayb,* Decision on the Prosecution application under article 58 (7) of the Statute, *supra* note 292, para. 24; *Prosecutor v. Ntaganda,* Annex II, Decision on the Prosecutor's application for warrants of arrest, *supra* note 228, para. 31; *Prosecutor v. Chui,* Decision on the evidence and information, *supra* note 235, para. 21; also El Zeidy, *supra* note 545, 161; Burke-White/Kaplan, *supra* note 264, 267–8.

[1475] *Prosecutor v. Bemba,* Décision relative à la requête du procureur, *supra* note 465, para. 21; also Burke-White/Kaplan, *supra* note 264, 267; Schabas, *supra* note 13, 344.

[1476] *Prosecutor v. Ntaganda,* Annex II, Decision on the Prosecutor's application for warrants of arrest, *supra* note 228, para. 38.

[1477] *Prosecutor v. Ntaganda,* Annex II, Decision on the Prosecutor's application for warrants of arrest, *supra* note 228, para. 37; on the other hand, these crimes were allegedly committed before July 2002, cf. *ibid.,* para. 37 fn. 31.

[1478] Schabas, *supra* note 1151, 757. It is therefore submitted that the DRC situation would now rather qualify as being inadmissible. In contrast, the Uganda situation could hardly be based upon unwillingness or inability, cf. Wouters/Verhoeven, in Ankumah/Kwakwa, *supra* note 210, 144. On analysis of both referrals (DRC and Uganda) *vis-à-vis* complementarity see Jurdi, *supra* note 99, 79 et seq.

[1479] Schabas, *supra* note 1151, 757–8, who even calls the finding of the PTC a "polite arrangement proposed by the Prosecutor, accepted by the government of the DRC, blessed by the Pre-Trial Chamber and sanctified by the acquiescence of the accused." Contrary, Robinson, *supra* note 468, 80–1, who calls these "dire allegations" unproductive.

[1480] Stigen, *supra* note 205, 201.

Coming to the outlined "specificity" test in more detail, in the *Katanga and Chui* case the Defence challenged admissibility on the "same conduct" factor.[1481] While accepting the "same person" element, the Defence expressed its concerns about the "same conduct" element.[1482] The "same conduct" test allegedly amounts to primacy of the ICC instead of complementarity.[1483] As a refinement, the Defence therefore submits a combined "comprehensive conduct" and "comparative gravity" test.[1484] The Prosecution responded that the test adopted by PTC I ("same conduct test") is firmly grounded in law and that the tests proposed by the Defence have no legal basis in the ICC Statute or the RPE.[1485] In other words, while the Defence preferred a more flexible comparison of the OTP's case *vis-à-vis* national proceedings, the OTP demanded national criminal proceedings encompass the same person and *exactly* the same conduct. In the outcome, the Trial Chamber saw no need to rule on the "same conduct test" in the underlying case, since the admissibility test did not even reach the level of a conduct comparison.[1486] The DRC clearly expressed unwillingness to prosecute the case, which renders the case admissible before the Court.[1487] The Appeals Chamber followed Trial Chamber II and equally did not decide on the testing mechanism since there were no proceedings against Katanga in the DRC.[1488] As an intermediary result, testing inactivity is partly unsettled jurisprudence (is the specificity test correct?), while the concept as such has been approved by jurisprudence, and the inactivity test is presently conducted in a twofold manner:

1. Is the State totally *inactive* or has there been some State action?
2. If the State has initiated some kind of criminal proceedings, do the State's proceedings relate to the same *conduct* and *person* as the ICC's case?

[1481] *Prosecutor v. Katanga and Chui,* Motion challenging the admissibility of the case by the Defence, *supra* note 459, paras. 31 et seq.

[1482] *Prosecutor v. Katanga and Chui,* Motion challenging the admissibility of the case by the Defence, *supra* note 459, paras. 37 et seq.

[1483] *Prosecutor v. Katanga and Chui,* Motion challenging the admissibility of the case by the Defence, *supra* note 459, para. 39.

[1484] *Prosecutor v. Katanga and Chui,* Motion challenging the admissibility of the case by the Defence, *supra* note 459, paras. 47–8, 51; *Prosecutor v. Katanga and Chui,* Motifs de la décision orale, *supra* note 459, para. 13.

[1485] *Prosecutor v. Katanga and Chui,* Public redacted version of the 19th March 2009 Prosecution response to motion challenging the admissibility, *supra* note 459, paras. 51 et seq.

[1486] *Prosecutor v. Katanga and Chui,* Motifs de la décision orale, *supra* note 459, para. 95.

[1487] *Prosecutor v. Katanga and Chui,* Motifs de la décision orale, *supra* note 459, para. 95.

[1488] *Prosecutor v. Katanga and Chui,* Judgment on the appeal of Mr. Germain Katanga against the oral decision of Trial Chamber II of 12 June 2009 on the admissibility of the case, *supra* note 459, para. 81.

Thereby, Trial Chamber II inquired into the first prong above, yet it did not clearly distinguish unwillingness and inactivity. As just mentioned, inactivity is the first (unwritten and freestanding) criterion of complementarity and unwillingness forms the third criterion (besides inability) of complementarity. Unwillingness and inactivity nonetheless should not be merged, although the unwillingness of a State also suggests that the State is inactive. The Trial Chamber thus failed to address the elements of article 17 in the right order.[1489] In this respect, it has been clarified by the Appeals Chamber that *first* inactivity must be assessed before *second* matters of unwillingness and inability can be dealt with:

> "Therefore, in considering whether a case is inadmissible under article 17 (1) (a) and (b) of the Statute, the initial questions to ask are (1) whether there are ongoing investigations or prosecutions, or (2) whether there have been investigations in the past, and the State having jurisdiction has decided not to prosecute the person concerned. It is only when the answers to these questions are in the affirmative that one has to look to the second halves of sub-paragraphs (a) and (b) and to examine the question of unwillingness and inability. To do otherwise would be to put the cart before the horse. It follows that in case of inaction, the question of unwillingness or inability does not arise; inaction on the part of a State having jurisdiction (that is, the fact that a State is not investigating or prosecuting, or has not done so) renders a case admissible before the Court, subject to article 17 (1) (d) of the Statute."[1490]

Coming back to inactivity as such, the issue was raised before the Rome Conference, but was not answered in the final ICC Statute.[1491] It was the informal expert group that refined the concept in 2003. Several authors have noticed admissibility "without more" if the national system is absolutely inactive.[1492] In particular, systematic and teleological interpretation suggests that cases are, as a rule, admissible if the exceptions of article 17 (1) do not provide otherwise.[1493] And these provisions on complementarity

---

[1489] *Prosecutor v. Katanga and Chui,* Judgment on the appeal of Mr. Germain Katanga against the oral decision of Trial Chamber II of 12 June 2009 on the admissibility of the case, *supra* note 459, para. 73; also Robinson, *supra* note 468, 79; Schabas, *supra* note 13, 342.

[1490] *Prosecutor v. Katanga and Chui,* Judgment on the appeal of Mr. Germain Katanga against the oral decision of Trial Chamber II of 12 June 2009 on the admissibility of the case, *supra* note 459, para. 78; thereto Carsten Stahn, "Perspectives on *Katanga*: an introduction" (2010) 23 LJIL 311, 316.

[1491] Meißner, *supra* note 371, 73.

[1492] Ambos, in Ambos/Large/Wierda, *supra* note 650, 71 et seq., para. 37; Razesberger, *supra* note 371, 29; El Zeidy, *supra* note 246, 103; Kleffner, *supra* note 370, 105; Benzing, *supra* note 1349, 601; Van der Wilt/Lyngdorf, *supra* note 1347, 40; Burke-White, *supra* note 1218, 77–8.

[1493] Kleffner, *supra* note 370, 104–5. See further Robinson, *supra* note 468, 70 et seq.; 88 et seq.

only need to be applied if a State takes, at the minimum, initial investigative steps.[1494] With regard to self-referrals, the inactivity criterion seems coherent since it is difficult to classify such referrals as unwilling or unable,[1495] and, more importantly, the State did not undertake minimum investigative activities. Consequently, the Appeals Chamber recently approved the inactivity concept.[1496] Nonetheless, it is strongly recommended that the Court refines the approach through further case law. To some extent, PTC II has already done so in a noteworthy decision. It clarified the continuing nature of complementarity when it concluded that the admissibility scenario in Uganda remains the same due to total inaction of the State:

> "Considered as a whole, the corpus of these provisions delineates a system whereby the determination of admissibility is meant to be an ongoing process throughout the pre-trial phase, the outcome of which is subject to review depending on the evolution of the relevant factual scenario. Otherwise stated, the Statute as a whole enshrines the idea that a change in circumstances allows (or even, in some scenarios, compels) the Court to determine admissibility anew."[1497]

If new circumstances arise and the Chamber desires a new evaluation, admissibility can be checked again. The continuing nature of admissibility notwithstanding, the inactivity approach as such bears an inherent danger that the OTP has to pay careful attention to. If the Prosecutor, on the one hand, highlights his policy to focus on the ones bearing the greatest responsibility, but uses inactivity to pick up minor cases, the credibility of the Court as a whole is questionable.[1498] The OTP therefore needs to engage the diplomatic channel from the outset of proceedings. It must always examine whether national prosecutions would be possible and whether they are more fitting.[1499] In line with the principle of complementarity, national prosecutions come first, even if the State is *prima facie* inactive. It is the OTP's duty to alert the State of criminal activity before starting criminal proceedings.

[1494] Kleffner, *supra* note 370, 105.

[1495] Labelling self-referrals as a specific form of unwillingness see *Prosecutor v. Katanga and Chui,* Motifs de la décision orale, *supra* note 459, paras. 77 et seq.

[1496] *Prosecutor v. Katanga and Chui,* Judgment on the appeal of Mr. Germain Katanga against the oral decision of Trial Chamber II of 12 June 2009 on the admissibility of the case, *supra* note 459, paras. 1–2. See also *Situation in Kenya*, Decision pursuant to article 15, *supra* note 6, para. 53, 24–5.

[1497] *Prosecutor v. Kony et al.,* Decision on the admissibility of the case under article 19 (1), *supra* note 264, paras. 28, 52; see also *Prosecutor v. Katanga and Chui,* Judgment on the appeal of Mr. Germain Katanga against the oral decision of Trial Chamber II of 12 June 2009 on the admissibility of the case, *supra* note 459, para. 56.

[1498] In a similar vein, Jurdi, *supra* note 99, 89.

[1499] A shining example is the Lubanga case in DRC, see Jurdi, *supra* note 99, 90.

The Court should therefore encourage domestic proceedings, not in the sense of strict prioritization of domestic jurisdictions, but as a reminder to states of their obligations.[1500] The quoted PTC II decision heads in this direction as it recalls the primary duty of States to prosecute and the possibility of referring cases at a later stage if the relevant State has taken action in the meantime. Of course, the State would have to show a willingness and ability to genuinely take over the case. In conclusion, certain risks in too wide an application of inactivity have been identified, and the OTP should thoroughly undertake examinations first. In sum, the inactivity criterion leads to a three-pronged test in which complementarity is now analyzed:

- as a rule, situations and cases are admissible if the State remains inactive and does not take minimum investigative steps (admissibility due to inaction);
- articles 17 (1) (a)–(c), 20 (3) provide for exceptions that States must take to render a situation or case inadmissible before the ICC (inadmissibility due to one of the mentioned criteria);
- in turn, these exceptions can be rebutted by the exception to the exception, i.e. the formula of unwillingness and inability to genuinely carry out proceedings (admissibility due to one of the mentioned elements under article 17 (2), (3)).

(2) Unwillingness (article 17 (2))

While inactivity is an empirical question, the existence of national proceedings is essentially linked to the normative examinations of unwillingness and inability.[1501] This determination is politically and technically complex.[1502] Regarding unwillingness, the term is not further defined, but article 17 (2) spells out some of the elements that have to be considered:

> "In order to determine unwillingness in a particular case, the Court shall consider, having regard to the principles of due process recognized by international law, whether one or more of the following exist, as applicable:

[1500] Stahn, *supra* note 540, 108–9; also Burke-White, *supra* note 1218, 67 et seq.; Jurdi, *supra* note 99, 90 et seq. 95–6; similarly *Prosecutor v. Katanga and Chui,* Motion challenging the admissibility of the case by the Defence, *supra* note 459, paras. 48–9.

[1501] Ambos, in Ambos/Large/Wierda, *supra* note 650, 71 et seq., para. 37; Pichon, *supra* note 282, 191. For a table representing the nine combinations of willing and able (and its nuances), see Paolo De Stefani, "The ICC Prosecutor and the complementarity game," in Ulrich, *supra* note 1380, 39, 55.

[1502] Seils/Wierda, *supra* note 1461, 3; El Zeidy, *supra* note 545, 163.

(a) The proceedings were or are being undertaken or the national decision was made for the *purpose of shielding the person* concerned from criminal responsibility for crimes within the jurisdiction of the Court referred to in article 5;

(b) There has been an *unjustified delay* in the proceedings which in the circumstances is inconsistent with intent to bring the person concerned to justice;

(c) The proceedings were not or are not being conducted *independently or impartially*, and they were or are being conducted in a manner which, in the circumstances, is inconsistent with intent to bring the person concerned to justice (emph. added)."

The factors can be recapitulated as (1) the purpose of shielding, (2) undue delay, and (3) the lack of independence and impartiality. All three notions are relatively broad and raise questions about their proper meaning.[1503] The listing should be deemed exhaustive;[1504] the three factors as such should be applied alternatively ("one or more of the following").[1505] It has been suggested that unwillingness cannot be tested *vis-à-vis* a situation as a whole. Unwillingness must be assessed more specifically, such as looking to the State's willingness to investigate persons truly responsible.[1506] The discussion on how to apply complementarity and its sub-criteria *vis-à-vis* situations ("in a general manner") was already dealt with above. In the drafting process of the OTP policy paper, the unwillingness factor has been described as subjective while recognizing the need to develop a set of objective criteria.[1507] The drafters were well aware of the subjective potential of unwillingness, and some States argued strongly for the deletion of any perceived subjective criteria.[1508] Some subjectivity had to be retained, the least objectionable word being "genuinely."[1509] The resulting mix of objective and subjective standards in both unwillingness and inability leaves the Court vulnerable.[1510] Despite the indications given by article 17 (2) and (3), the terms

[1503] Holmes, in Cassese/Gaeta/Jones, *supra* note 666, 675; Benvenuti, in Lattanzi/Schabas, *supra* note 675, 45; Solera, *supra* note 1347, 159; Valiñas, in Stahn/van Herik, *supra* note 1423, 275.

[1504] Pichon, *supra* note 282, 191; Kindt, *supra* note 650, 150; Meißner, *supra* note 371, 73; Cárdenas, 2005, *supra* note 1387, 133; Stigen, *supra* note 205, 257–8; Kleffner, *supra* note 370, 104; contrary, Morel, *supra* note 1365, 117.

[1505] Morel, *supra* note 1365, 116.

[1506] Delmas-Marty, *supra* note 1048, 4–5.

[1507] Richard Dicker, HRW, Session 1: Transcript, First public hearing, of the OTP, 17.6.2003, 2–3. On the subjective-objective approach also Wei, *supra* note 156, 73.

[1508] Holmes, in Lee, *supra* note 581, 49; El Zeidy, *supra* note 651, 899.

[1509] Holmes, in Lee, *supra* note 581, 49–50; El Zeidy, *supra* note 651, 899; Bekou, in Ulrich, *supra* note 1380, 73; Kindt, *supra* note 650, 150–1; Schabas, *supra* note 13, 345.

[1510] Sheng, *supra* note 1347, 14; Kim, *supra* note 813, 143–4.

"unwillingness" and "inability" remain vague to a certain extent.[1511] Last but not least, it will be technically difficult and politically sensitive to demonstrate "unwillingness."[1512]

The first mentioned form of unwillingness is the purpose of shielding a person. This amounts to a State that engages in an investigation or prosecution, but in fact adheres only to the letters and not the spirit of the provision. The State here conducts sham proceedings to shield the person concerned from criminal responsibility under the ICC Statute.[1513] Proving intent to shield is a considerably high threshold (*dolus directus*) and indeed raises the question on how such intent can be proven.[1514] Surely, the initiation of national proceedings to prevent the ICC from acting does not constitute such intent, since this is allowed and even desired under the principle of complementarity.[1515] While the standards are undoubtedly high, the task is not impossible.[1516] The "shielding" factor will typically have to be inferred from objective circumstances (circumstantial evidence).[1517] Thus, indicia for shielding a person will have to be searched for.[1518] As an example, shielding could exist when the normal legal procedure is circumvented by appointing a special investigator politically aligned with the accused.[1519] Moreover, the decision to grant blanket amnesties and immunities could probably fulfill the requirement of shielding a person.[1520] It has been ar-

1511 Mark Ellis, "The International Criminal Court and its implication for domestic law and national capacity building" in Ellis/Goldstone, *supra* note 133, 85, 99; Slye/van Schaack, *supra* note 534, 59; Ambos, in Ambos/Large/Wierda, *supra* note 650, 76, para. 42 ("open to value judgment"); Melandri, *supra* note 1347, 538.

1512 Informal expert paper: complementarity, *supra* note 572, para. 44; Morel, *supra* note 1365, 112.

1513 Williams/Schabas, in Triffterer, *supra* note 1347, article 17, mn 30; Meißner, *supra* note 371, 83; Cárdenas, 2005, *supra* note 1387, 114; Kindt, *supra* note 650, 151; Enrique Gomez-Pardo, "The content of Colombian Justice and Peace Law accomplishes the International Criminal Court standards" (2009) 1 Revista Debate Interamericano 123, 148.

1514 Kleffner, *supra* note 370, 135; Benzing, *supra* note 1349, 609–10; Stigen, *supra* note 205, 261–2; Bekou, in Ulrich, *supra* note 1380, 73–4; Meißner, *supra* note 371, 84; Evans, *supra* note 1347, 2–3; Gavron, *supra* note 773, 111; Morel, *supra* note 1365, 120 ("[…] une des tâche les plus ardues du Procureur"); Michael Bothe, "Complementarity: ensuring compliance with international law though criminal prosecutions – whose responsibility?" (2008) 83 Friedenswarte 59, 65.

1515 Pichon, *supra* note 282, 195.

1516 Holmes, in Cassese/Gaeta/Jones, *supra* note 666, 675.

1517 Stigen, *supra* note 205, 259, 262; Kleffner, *supra* note 370, 136–7.

1518 Informal expert paper: complementarity, *supra* note 572, para. 47 with Annex 4 (at 28), where proposed indicia are listed; also El Zeidy, *supra* note 545, 175 et seq.; Morel, *supra* note 1365, 119; Stigen, *supra* note 205, 262, 263 et seq.

1519 Holmes, in Cassese/Gaeta/Jones, *supra* note 666, 675.

gued that article 17 (2) (a) seeks, in particular, to ban practices where amnesties exempt certain groups of perpetrators.[1521] In any event, there must be causality between the State's purpose and the inadequate procedural step.[1522] It has further been argued that unwillingness may come up years later if, for instance, the verdict is followed by lenient execution of the sentence.[1523] However, execution of sentence is not a matter of unwillingness; there appears to be a *lacuna* in the ICC Statute with regard to the execution of sentences.[1524]

The second exception mentioned requires an "unjustified delay" pursuant to article 17 (2) (b). "Unjustified delay" is supposedly a stricter criterion than "undue delay."[1525] Objective criteria must be assessed for establishing the delay criterion.[1526] The "unjustified delay" element can be subdivided into two pertinent questions: i) the existence of a delay, and ii) the unjustified nature thereof. It has been argued that proceedings must have taken longer than other similar proceedings in the particular State, the delay must be avoidable but State agents do not act with due diligence, and the State intent must be inconsistent with the intent to bring the person to justice.[1527] It still remains unclear how and against which standard delay is measured.[1528] Alternatives to the intra-State comparison could be an average of all domestic systems or an international standard.[1529] The Court could therefore assess the jurisprudence of Human Rights Bodies.[1530] In any event, it remains for the ICC's jurisprudence to refine the exact standard to measure a delay. It has to be noted though that the European Court of Human Rights (hereinafter ECtHR)

1520 Pichon, *supra* note 282, 194.

1521 Stahn, *supra* note 726, 714; Gropengießer/Meißner, *supra* note 679, 285.

1522 Stigen, *supra* note 205, 260.

1523 Klip, *supra* note 1380, 182.

1524 See further Part IV, B., III., 2., b), cc), (5).

1525 Benzing, *supra* note 1349, 610; Holmes, in Lee, *supra* note 581, 54; El Zeidy, *supra* note 651, 900; Razesberger, *supra* note 371, 45; Morel, *supra* note 1365, 121.

1526 Holmes, in Cassese/Gaeta/Jones, *supra* note 666, 676; El Zeidy, *supra* note 651, 901; Evans, *supra* note 1347, 3.

1527 Cárdenas, in Kleffner/Kor, *supra* note 1387, 123; Holmes, in Cassese/Gaeta/Jones, *supra* note 666, 676; Pichon, *supra* note 282, 195; Meißner, *supra* note 371, 84. On the term "justice" in this context Valiñas, in Stahn/van Herik, *supra* note 1423, 276–7.

1528 Benzing, *supra* note 1349, 611; Morel, *supra* note 1365, 123; El Zeidy, *supra* note 545, 182.

1529 Benzing, *supra* note 1349, 611; Razesberger, *supra* note 371, 45; Cárdenas, 2005, *supra* note 1387, 119, who favors an international comparison.

1530 Morel, *supra* note 1365, 122; Bekou, in Ulrich, *supra* note 1380, 74; Kleffner, *supra* note 370, 140; El Zeidy, *supra* note 545, 183 et seq.; Schabas, *supra* note 13, 345.

refrained from developing common criteria for State prosecution due to the complexity of each specific case, which renders it impossible to establish an average.[1531] Each case should rather be judged *in concreto*.[1532]

Independence or impartiality potentially leads to an overlap with shielding a person.[1533] In addition, the "or" between independence and impartiality indicates alternative application of either one of the two sub-elements. Proceedings should not be biased (impartial), and the entity in charge must not be subject to improper influence (independent).[1534] Article 17 (2) (c) builds its language on articles 10 (2) ICTY Statute and 9 (2) ICTR Statute, which use the terms in the context of *ne bis in idem*. The ICC Statute's provision must be interpreted in relation to admissibility.[1535] Keeping this in mind, the two terms can be defined by looking at human rights courts' jurisprudence, where they are well-known concepts,[1536] as well as by screening the *ad hoc* tribunals' jurisprudence. The chapeau of article 17 (2) should thereby be taken into account. For the notion of independence according to the ECtHR "regard must be had, *inter alia,* to the manner of appointment of the members and their term of office, the existence of guarantees against outside pressures and the question whether the body presents an appearance of independence."[1537] The ECtHR sets out the criteria for determining impartiality as follows: "As to the question of 'impartiality', there are two aspects to this requirement. First, the tribunal must be subjectively free of personal prejudice or bias. Secondly, it must also be impartial from an objective viewpoint; that is, it must offer sufficient guarantees to exclude any legitimate doubt in this respect. The ECtHR concludes by asserting that the concepts of impartiality and independence are closely linked."[1538] Impartiality has been addressed by the ICTY in the *Furundzija*

1531 Razesberger, *supra* note 371, 46; Kleffner, *supra* note 370, 140; El Zeidy, *supra* note 545, 187–8; Stigen, *supra* note 205, 292 ("there is no one-size-fits-all answer").

1532 Bekou, in Ulrich, *supra* note 1380, 75; Van der Wilt/Lyngdorf, *supra* note 1347, 60.

1533 Holmes, in Cassese/Gaeta/Jones, *supra* note 666, 676; also Stigen, *supra* note 205, 300, 305; Kindt, *supra* note 650, 154.

1534 Cárdenas, in Kleffner/Kor, *supra* note 1387, 123–4.

1535 Benzing, *supra* note 1349, 612.

1536 Benzing, *supra* note 1349, 612; Razesberger, *supra* note 371, 47; Stigen, *supra* note 205, 304, 306–7. Examining the jurisprudence in more detail, see Van der Wilt/Lyngdorf, *supra* note 1347, 51 et seq., Kleffner, *supra* note 370, 145 et seq., and El Zeidy, *supra* note 545, 196 et seq.

1537 *Langborger v. Sweden,* ECtHR judgment, 22.6.1989 (11179/84) para. 32; *Findlay v. United Kingdom,* ECtHR judgment, 25.2.1997 (22107/93) para. 73.

1538 *Findlay v. United Kingdom, supra* note 1537, para. 73; *Pullar v. United Kingdom,* ECtHR judgment, 10.6.1996 (22399/93) para. 30.

case in a similar manner, stating that "there is a general rule that a Judge should not only be subjectively free from bias, but also that there should be nothing in the surrounding circumstances which objectively gives rise to an appearance of bias."[1539] In sum, independence refers to objective criteria that focus on influence that can derive from sources from the outside of the Court, whereas impartiality is concerned with possible bias of the judicial personnel itself.[1540] Alike the unjustified delay criterion, it is left to the ICC's Judges if they adopt a similar definition, and only ICC jurisprudence can ultimately settle the issue. The Court may therefore directly apply the ECtHR or the ICTY standards or develop its own set of criteria.[1541]

In addition to the criteria of unjustified delay and independence or impartiality, the Court has to consider whether such circumstances are "inconsistent with [the] intent to bring the person concerned to justice."[1542] The inherent question is whether this phrasing simply means to face trial or whether it also refers to a proper judicial procedure (due process).[1543] A due process argument could be made by reference to independence and impartiality of article 17 (2) (c), the "principles of due process recognized by international law" pursuant to the chapeau of article 17 (2), inability under article 17 (3), and finally article 17 (1)'s genuineness language.[1544] At first sight, the wording seems to advocate adherence to due process on behalf of national States, otherwise rendering a case admissible before the ICC. Treaty interpretations by two different authors have yet resulted in exactly the opposite finding.[1545] The authors applied the basic principles of treaty interpretation: text, context, object and purpose, as well as its drafting history. A literal interpretation of article 17 (2) (b) and (c) has not proven to be decisive.[1546] Moreover, the phrasing "principles of due process recognized by international law" in the chapeau has to be read in conjunction with the three subparagraphs, thus both due process *and* one of the three conditions specified by article 17 (2) have to be violated to render a case

1539 *Prosecutor v. Furundžija,* Appeal's judgment, 21.7.2000 (IT-95-17/1) para. 189.

1540 Razesberger, *supra* note 371, 46.

1541 El Zeidy, *supra* note 545, 202.

1542 Enrique Carnero Rojo, "The role of fair trial considerations in the complementarity regime of the International Criminal Court: from 'no peace without justice' to 'no peace without victor's justice'?" (2005) 18 LJIL 829, 835; Kevin Jon Heller, "The shadow side of complementarity: the effect of article 17 of the Rome Statute on national due process" (2006) 17 CLF 255, 258.

1543 Carnero Rojo, *supra* note 1542, 835–6; Heller, *supra* note 1542, 257–8.

1544 Heller, *supra* note 1542, 258–9; also Kleffner, *supra* note 370, 127 et seq.; El Zeidy, *supra* note 545, 169.

1545 Carnero Rojo, *supra* note 1542, 852–3; Heller, *supra* note 1542, 273.

1546 Carnero Rojo, *supra* note 1542, 838.

admissible.[1547] Contextually nothing in the ICC Statute suggests that article 17 requires States to guarantee due process.[1548] The ICC clearly lacks the means to address human rights violations in the area of due process *as such*.[1549] The narrow object and purpose of the ICC Statute, i.e. to put an end to impunity, confirms the absence of a due process ground for admissibility.[1550] In addition, reference was made to the drafting history, which strongly indicates the absence of a due process ground. Proposals that would have included procedural fairness were rejected.[1551] In conclusion, it is not likely that the ICC protects the individual against possible due process abuses.[1552] The principle of complementarity only addresses situations where breaches of human rights standards work in favor of the accused.[1553] This urged one author to promote amending article 17 to recognize a due process ground for admissibility:

> "Most obviously, the criteria in article 17 (2) (c) should be made disjunctive instead of conjunctive, along the lines of Rule 9 of the ICTY Rules of Procedure. The subparagraph would then allow the Court to find unwillingness if '[t]he proceedings were not or are not being conducted independently or impartially, or they were or are being conducted in a manner which [...] is inconsistent with an intent to bring the person concerned to justice'."[1554]

The defendant should be given a right to refer his or her case pursuant to article 14, in other words, to include a referral power on the ground that national proceedings do not provide due process.[1555] While this recommendation is desirable from a human rights perspective, it appears unrealizable due to State concerns and budgetary dimensions. Including a right to refer due process violations would merely turn the ICC into a human rights court, potentially flooding the Court with complaints. The ICC is already working at full capacity and receives numerous article 15 communications every day. Adding an additional trigger for due process considerations must be rejected at present.

1547 Heller, *supra* note 1542, 262–3, who, moreover, rebuts the inability and genuineness arguments in a convincing manner (263 et seq.).

1548 Heller, *supra* note 1542, 266.

1549 Carnero Rojo, *supra* note 1542, 854; in the same vein recently *Prosecutor v. Katanga and Chui,* Motifs de la décision orale, *supra* note 459, paras. 83 et seq.

1550 Heller, *supra* note 1542, 270–1; undecided Carnero Rojo, *supra* note 1542, 840.

1551 Heller, *supra* note 1542, 272–3; Carnero Rojo, *supra* note 1542, 849; Pichon, *supra* note 282, 193.

1552 Carnero Rojo, *supra* note 1542, 869; Van der Wilt/Lyngdorf, *supra* note 1347, 64.

1553 Pichon, *supra* note 282, 194; Van der Wilt/Lyngdorf, *supra* note 1347, 63, 67 et seq.

1554 Heller, *supra* note 1542, 279.

1555 Heller, *supra* note 1542, 279.

All this having been said, it has to be noted that the threshold of article 17 (2) (a) is considerably higher than the other two scenarios according to article 17 (2) (b) and (c) and therefore arguably includes the latter two. It may be advisable for the Prosecutor to initially check articles 17 (2) (b) and (c) in a concrete case before considering article 17 (2) (a).[1556]

(3) Inability (article 17 (3))

Inability as such is not defined in the ICC Statute. It can be reasoned that article 17 (3) was inserted to focus attention on States lacking a central government (situation of a failed State such as Somalia or Rwanda after the genocide) or a State in chaos due to a civil war or national disaster.[1557] Inability is a more objective, fact-driven notion than unwillingness, and therefore was less contentious to negotiate.[1558] Nevertheless, the determination of inability is complex and sensitive, and its sub-criteria must be defined with the most possible specificity.[1559] Article 17 (3) sets out the elements to be considered for a determination of the inability criterion under article 17 (1):

> "In order to determine inability in a particular case, the Court shall consider whether, due to a total or substantial collapse or unavailability of its national judicial system, the State is unable to obtain the accused or the necessary evidence and testimony or otherwise unable to carry out its proceedings."

Thus, the inability of a State depends upon three disabling events: (1) a total collapse of the national judicial system, (2) a substantial collapse of the national judicial system, or (3) the unavailability of the national judicial system.[1560] Alike the list of factors for "unwillingness," the factors for "inability" are deemed exhaustive.[1561] It has to be further noted that all the elements for this determination are linked to the "national judicial system."[1562] Objective criteria, rather than subjective conditions, are to be con-

---

[1556] Pichon, *supra* note 282, 195–6.

[1557] Williams/Schabas, in Triffterer, *supra* note 1347, article 17, mn 33; Benzing, *supra* note 1349, 613; Klip, *supra* note 1380, 184; Meißner, *supra* note 371, 86; Stahn, *supra* note 540, 98; Razesberger, *supra* note 371, 47; Morel, *supra* note 1365, 131; Bekou, in Ulrich, *supra* note 1380, 76; El Zeidy, *supra* note 545, 222–3.

[1558] Holmes, in Cassese/Gaeta/Jones, *supra* note 666, 677; Wei, *supra* note 156, 74; Evans, *supra* note 1347, 4; Morel, *supra* note 1365, 129; Kleffner, *supra* note 370, 153.

[1559] Morel, *supra* note 1365, 129.

[1560] Arsanjani/Reismann, in Sadat/Scharf, *supra* note 537, 329; Informal expert paper: complementarity, *supra* note 572, para. 49; El Zeidy, *supra* note 651, 903; Philips, *supra* note 643, 79; Jurdi, *supra* note 99, 80, 83.

[1561] Stigen, *supra* note 205, 314, Cárdenas, 2005, *supra* note 1387, 133; contrary, Morel, *supra* note 1365, 130.

[1562] Arsanjani/Reismann, *supra* note 533, 387.

sidered.[1563] As additional factors, the drafters included the State being unable to obtain the accused or the necessary evidence and testimony. Their inclusion rendered a further definition of the collapse criterion unnecessary – in the view of the drafters – and to meet concerns that these additional criteria would limit the Court's ability to act, the phrase "or otherwise unable to carry out its proceedings" was included as a third inability scenario.[1564] Moreover, the term "partial" collapse was replaced by "substantial" collapse to reinforce the primacy of national courts while raising the admissibility threshold.[1565] Inability is further an on-going assessment: PTC I made this clear when it referred to the general statement of the Prosecutor on inability of the DRC's national judicial system as not corresponding to reality anymore.[1566]

Coming to the first criterion of a total collapse, the system of the State as a whole must not function anymore.[1567] Merely temporary or partial effects do not fulfill the requirements of inability.[1568] A total collapse can be assumed where State authorities have lost control over their territory to an extent that the administration of justice has broken down completely, or where the authorities, while exercising effective (military or police) control over the territory, do not perform such administration.[1569] In a nutshell, the total collapse may be defined as "a complete breakdown of the national administration of justice, either due to the State's loss of control over the ter-

---

[1563] Arsanjani/Reismann, in Sadat/Scharf, *supra* note 537, 329 et seq.; Kindt, *supra* note 650, 156; Holmes, in Lee, *supra* note 581, 48, who, however, regards "substantial" as being a subjective element.

[1564] Holmes, in Lee, *supra* note 581, 49. See further Jurdi, *supra* note 99, 86 et seq.

[1565] Arsanjani/Reismann, in Sadat/Scharf, *supra* note 537, 330–1; Hoffmeister/ Knoke, *supra* note 169, 798; Philips, *supra* note 643, 79; Morel, *supra* note 1365, 132; El Zeidy, *supra* note 545, 225.

[1566] *Prosecutor v. Lubanga,* Decision on the Prosecutor's application for warrant of arrest, article 58, *supra* note 217, para. 36. In 2005, Burke-White had, nevertheless, come to the opposite position, taking *inter alia* into account the following criteria for inability: availability of experienced and unbiased judicial personnel, the presence of viable legal infrastructure, the existence of adequate operative law, and a sufficient police capability to undertake arrest and investigation, cf. Burke-White, *supra* note 213, 576.

[1567] Cárdenas, in Kleffner/Kor, *supra* note 1387, 125; *id.,* 2005, *supra* note 1387, 126; Stigen, *supra* note 205, 314–5.

[1568] Cárdenas, in Kleffner/Kor, *supra* note 1387, 125; Kindt, *supra* note 650, 159; more flexible Stigen, *supra* note 205, 315 ("could arguably be temporary, albeit not to brief, [...]").

[1569] Benzing, *supra* note 1349, 614; Meißner, *supra* note 371, 86; Edoardo Greppi, "Inability to investigate and prosecute under article 17" in Politi/Gioia, *supra* note 517, 63, 64.

ritory or due to the national decision to efface the national administration of justice."[1570]

The following two elements "substantial" and "unavailability" are quite vague and could therefore include or exclude a number of categories.[1571] As to both criteria, it is disputable whether the provision embraces quantitative and/or qualitative assessment.

In the case of a substantial collapse State authorities are generally not capable of ensuring the investigation of the case and the prosecution of the individuals.[1572] It is argued that a localized collapse in a particular region should be sufficient to satisfy the criterion.[1573] A situation might emerge where a partial collapse might only affect some regions while the courts in the remaining regions would continue to function.[1574] Such a finding could be made with regard to the Ituri region in the DRC situation.[1575] However, it has to be taken into account that a substantial collapse constitutes something more thorough than a partial collapse, which was the original alternative before changing the wording to "substantial."[1576] Of course, what "substantial" means is again a matter of (Court) interpretation.[1577]

Unavailability also lacks clarity.[1578] Different interpretations are possible and have been argued for in the academic world. A wide linguistic interpretation can go one of three ways: unavailability as the non-existence of something, the non-accessibility of something, and the non-usefulness of a remedy irrespective of its existence and accessibility.[1579] A sufficiently broad reading of unavailability is underpinned by literal (English term most accurately captures the true meaning), systematic (article 88 uses the term "availability" in a broader sense than existence of legislation only), and teleologi-

---

1570 Pichon, *supra* note 282, 196; Razesberger, *supra* note 371, 48; Ellis, in Ellis/Goldstone, *supra* note 1511, 100.

1571 Informal expert paper: complementarity, *supra* note 572, para. 50; Ellis, in Ellis/Goldstone, *supra* note 1511, 101, who suggests four main areas of application: States entangled in conflict, States experiencing political unrest or economic crisis, States in transition, and States entirely lacking the type of judicial system that is representative of the international standard.

1572 Benzing, *supra* note 1349, 614.

1573 Hall, *supra* note 100, 17; El Zeidy, *supra* note 651, 904; differentiated Stigen, *supra* note 205, 315–6.

1574 El Zeidy, *supra* note 651, 903; Razesberger, *supra* note 371, 48–9.

1575 Wouters/Verhoeven, in Ankumah/Kwakwa, *supra* note 210, 138; Jurdi, *supra* note 99, 85 (for Uganda see *ibid.,* 83).

1576 Razesberger, *supra* note 371, 48–9.

1577 Greppi, in Politi/Gioia, *supra* note 1569, 65.

1578 Morel, *supra* note 1365, 133; Kindt, *supra* note 650, 159.

1579 Stigen, *supra* note 205, 316–7.

cal arguments ("unavailability" must be construed broad enough to reduce the number of situations the ICC must refer to national proceedings despite the State's actual inability to carry out proceedings).[1580] In contrast, one author argues – based on the authentic Spanish version of article 17 (3) – that a system is *only* unavailable when it is non-existent.[1581] A broader reading allows for a legal system and its authorities being generally in place and functioning, but the system is unable to deal with a specific case due to legal or factual reasons.[1582] Legal reasons for unavailability are closely intertwined with the implementation of the ICC Statute.[1583] The absence or inadequacies of substantive legislation could render a national system unavailable and therefore the case would be admissible before the ICC.[1584] A strong argument underlining this assumption can be made on the basis of an ICTR's decision in the case of *Prosecutor v. Bagaragaza*; though not in the context of the ICC Statute, the ICTR had to decide on a comparable issue when Norway requested a referral of the just mentioned case to its authorities based on rule 11*bis* ICTR RPE. Since Norway had not implemented the crime of genocide into its national criminal law, the ICTR's Trial Chamber came to the conclusion that Norway lacked jurisdiction *ratione materiae* over the crimes as charged in the indictment. Consequently "Michel Bagaragaza's alleged criminal acts cannot be given their full legal qualification under Norwegian criminal law, and the request for the referral to the Kingdom of Norway falls to be dismissed."[1585] One can therefore presume that – if the State has not properly implemented the ICC's Statute – the ICC would qualify the prosecution as "unavailable" in the sense of article 17 (3).

Others still rebut any inclusion of defects in the quality of justice into article 17 (3).[1586] For instance, an over-burdened national judicial system may not be appropriate as a consideration when assessing unavailability. Some

---

1580 Stigen, *supra* note 205, 317–8.

1581 Cárdenas, in Kleffner/Kor, *supra* note 1387, 124; *id.,* 2005, *supra* note 1387, 128; concurring Kindt, *supra* note 650, 160; Burke-White, *supra* note 1385, 74 ("lack of judicial infrastructure"); contrary, Hall, *supra* note 100, 17; El Zeidy, *supra* note 545, 226–7.

1582 Benzing, *supra* note 1349, 614; Informal expert paper: complementarity, *supra* note 572, para. 49; Meißner, *supra* note 371, 87; Razesberger, *supra* note 371, 49; for factual reasons in the CAR see *Prosecutor v. Bemba*, Decision on the admissibility, *supra* note 280, para. 245, 92.

1583 Federica Gioia, "Comments on chapter 3 of Jann Kleffner" in Kleffner/Kor, *supra* note 1415, 105, 107.

1584 Jann Kleffner, "The impact of complementarity on national implementation of substantive international criminal law" (2003) 1 JICJ 86, 89; *id., supra* note 608, 156–7. Bekou, in Ulrich, *supra* note 1380, 78, who also identifies the problematic lack of sufficient penal legislation.

1585 *Prosecutor v. Bagaragaza,* Decision on the Prosecution's motion for referral to the Kingdom of Norway, 19.5.2006 (ICTR-2005-86-R11) para. 16.

have noted that such an extensive interpretation is not possible.[1587] One should therefore exclude quality judgments and rather refer to the "necessity of some existent national infrastructure." The State thereby has to meet minimum international standards such as facilities to ensure the security for victims, witnesses, judges, and defendants.[1588] Without a minimum infrastructure, a State is yet "unable to otherwise carry out its proceedings."[1589]

Summing up, unavailability may either be interpreted narrowly or broadly. A too narrow scope would certainly render the element without any meaning beyond a "total or substantial collapse." An overly restrictive approach therefore must be rejected. If choosing a broad interpretation one must, however, bear in mind the limiting effect of "substantial collapse," which was deliberately favored over a "partial" collapse.[1590] A compromise formula could exclude any internal factual deficiencies within the judiciary itself.[1591] In principle, it is appropriate to adopt the above-mentioned definition that a legal system is unavailable if it is "generally in place and functioning, but unsuitable due to legal or factual obstacles," but (internal) factual quality judgments, such a capacity overload, must be excluded. In other words, the qualification of the justice system must be made from the outside by an external actor based on objective factors. This will be a difficult task for the OTP in any given case. In any event, "unavailability," just like the other elements of article 17 (2) and (3), is open to Court interpretation, and only the ICC's actors may ultimately settle the question through case law.[1592]

(4) Genuineness

"Genuineness" was inserted as the "least subjective concept" among other proposals, yet some degree of subjectivity on part of the Court was thought necessary despite the fact that many delegations took the position to delete all subjective criteria.[1593] The word is to a certain extent vague

---

1586 Arsanjani/Reismann, in Sadat/Scharf, *supra* note 537, 329 et seq.; Philips, *supra* note 643, 79; Holmes, in Lee, *supra* note 581, 48.

1587 Arsanjani/Reismann, in Sadat/Scharf, *supra* note 537, 331 et seq. (not possible because the drafting history did not consider this particular scenario, article 17 is envisaged as objective criteria, and States have considerable control over whether its judicial system is indeed over-burdened).

1588 Burke-White, *supra* note 213, 579.

1589 Burke-White, *supra* note 213, 579.

1590 Stigen, *supra* note 205, 323.

1591 Stigen, *supra* note 205, 323.

1592 Bassiouni, *supra* note 401, 138; Slye/van Schaack, *supra* note 534, 59; Melandri, *supra* note 1347, 540. For an alternative approach, replacing the problematic notions of "unwillingness" and "inability" through the term "effectiveness of national proceedings" as the decisive criterion, see Kleffner, *supra* note 370, 160–1.

and leads to uncertainty.[1594] The PTC will have to develop an interpretation of the term and its role in the application of article 17. Thereby, it is – to a certain extent – possible to envisage how the Court might interpret "genuinely."[1595] It is submitted that investigating and prosecuting, not unwillingness and inability, are conditioned by the adjective "genuinely."[1596] The authentic French version is much clearer in this respect: "[...] *à moins que cet État n'ait pas la volonté ou soit dans l'incapacité de mener véritablement à bien l'enquête ou les poursuites*."[1597] Moreover, practice seems to underline this reasoning since the Prosecutor refers to "genuine proceedings" in the national State.[1598] "Genuinely" thus sets a minimum standard (*bona fides*) to which States must adhere when carrying out investigations or prosecutions.[1599] Nevertheless, the term "genuinely" is not clearly defined. The exact standard, especially how high it is, will therefore remain open until the Court further defines the concept.

(5) Ne bis in idem *principle*

Articles 17 (1) (c) and 20 (3) provide for inadmissibility if a person has already been tried for the conduct which is the subject of the complaint before the ICC (*ne bis in idem* or double jeopardy principle[1600]). Article 20 (3)

1593 Benzing, *supra* note 1349, 604–5; Williams/Schabas, in Triffterer, *supra* note 1347, article 17, mn 25. On "genuineness" during the Rome Conference see Kindt, *supra* note 650, 165–6.

1594 El Zeidy, *supra* note 651, 900.

1595 Rod Jensen, "Complementarity, 'genuinely' and article 17: assessing the boundaries of an effective ICC," in Kleffner/Kor, *supra* note 1387, 147, 159.

1596 Kleffner, *supra* note 370, 115; Jensen, in Kleffner/Kor, *supra* note 1595, 160; Benzing, *supra* note 1349, 604–5; Informal expert paper: complementarity, *supra* note 572, para. 21; Morel, *supra* note 1365, 99–100; El Zeidy, *supra* note 545, 165 ("prevailing view"). Contrary, Williams/Schabas, in Triffterer, *supra* note 1347, article 17, mn 25; Holmes, in Cassese/Gaeta/Jones, *supra* note 666, 674; Razesberger, *supra* note 371, 52; Meyer, *supra* note 1153, 566.

1597 Morel, *supra* note 1365, 99–100; Kleffner, *supra* note 370, 115. The (not authentic) German version goes in the same direction as the French version, stating "[...], *die Ermittlungen oder die Strafverfolgung ernsthaft durchzuführen*."

1598 Remarks by Luis Moreno-Ocampo, *supra* note 1339, 3.

1599 Jensen, in Kleffner/Kor, *supra* note 1595, 168–9; El Zeidy, *supra* note 545, 164–5; Cárdenas, 2005, *supra* note 1387, 110–1. On possible standards also Stigen, *supra* note 205, 218 et seq.

1600 On the principle *as such*, which is translated as "not again about the same", see Tijana Surlan, "*Ne bis in idem* in conjunction with the principle of complementarity in the Rome Statute," "Agora" Papers presented at the 2005 Florence Founding Conference of the ESIL, 1 et seq.; El Zeidy, *supra* note 545, 283–4; Morel, *supra* note 1365, 102–3; Majzub, *supra* note 1426, 269–70; Christine van den Wyngaert/

(a) and (b) further contains two exceptions to this *ne bis in idem* principle: if i) the proceedings in the other Court were for the purpose of shielding the person or ii) were otherwise not conducted independently or impartially. Article 20 (3) thus sets out the standards for assessing whether a domestic adjudication makes a case inadmissible before the ICC (upwards *ne bis in idem* effect).[1601] It is the most controversial and complicated part of article 20.[1602] The first element mirrors the "shielding of a person" pursuant to article 17 (2) (a), and the second element of "impartiality and independence" is reflected in article 17 (2) (c). It should be noted, however, that the interpretation of the terms "has already been tried" and "proceedings in the other court" is unclear and the RPE are silent in this respect.[1603] Is the ICC limited to the trial stage or could it look at investigations and execution of sentences as well? A broad interpretation would allow for the latter, whereas a strict construction limits the phrasing to trial proceedings only. From an analytical standpoint, and according to the main purpose of the ICC, the term "proceedings" could embrace investigations, prosecutions, and trial.[1604] In this regard, it has to be noted that pre-trial proceedings are already subject to article 17 (1) (a) and (b). There is no need to vastly enlarge the term proceedings *vis-à-vis* investigations. As such, article 20 (3) must be limited to trial proceedings,[1605] but this does extend to internal remedies such as appeal and review.[1606] In consequence, the ICC is barred from screening the execution of sentences. It remains admittedly an inherent danger that States arrange for a criminal trial and do not execute in good faith. Indeed, article 20 (3) further allows for any termination of the proceedings, e. g. on procedural grounds, as long as the proceedings have been conducted *bona fide* – a final judgment on the merits is not necessary.[1607] This may be another illustration that the ICC Statute puts a greater trust in national systems.[1608] Ac-

---

Tom Ongena, "*Ne bis in idem* principle, including the issue of amnesty" in Cassese/Gaeta/Jones, *supra* note 133, 705, 705–6; Stigen, *supra* note 205, 207; Dawn Sedman, "Should the prosecution of ordinary crimes in domestic jurisdictions satisfy the complementarity principle?" in Stahn/van Herik, *supra* note 11, 259, 263 et seq.

[1601] El Zeidy, *supra* note 651, 931; Kleffner, *supra* note 370, 118–9; Meyer, *supra* note 1153, 554; Van den Wyngaert/Ongena, in Cassese/Gaeta/Jones, *supra* note 1600, 724 et seq.

[1602] El Zeidy, *supra* note 651, 931; Razesberger, *supra* note 371, 151.

[1603] Kleffner, *supra* note 370, 124; El Zeidy, *supra* note 651, 935.

[1604] El Zeidy, *supra* note 651, 937; *id., supra* note 545, 292 et seq.; Razesberger, *supra* note 371, 155–6.

[1605] In the same vein, Morel, *supra* note 1365, 105. Contrary, including the execution of sentences, Kindt, *supra* note 650, 145.

[1606] Kleffner, *supra* note 370, 124.

[1607] Benzing, *supra* note 1349, 618.

[1608] Benzing, *supra* note 1349, 618–9.

cordingly, a State that conducts a trial genuinely is expected to implement the sentence in the same vein. Nevertheless, States might not always proceed as expected (a common example cited is the pardon for William Calley less than 4 years after being convicted for the My Lai massacre), and therefore the Court should close the pardon *lacuna* to foreclose malpractice.[1609] The question of pardons is thus not covered by articles 17 or 20, and it is strongly recommended that a review conference tackles this issue.[1610]

c) *Legal gravity threshold – article 17 (1) (d)*

One basis for inadmissibility is that the situation is insufficiently grave according to articles 53 (1) (b), 17 (1) (d). This is a mandatory test not subject to derogation.[1611] Despite the important role of gravity in early OTP practice, the ICC Statute does not indicate how gravity should be applied. Early pronouncements did not address the issue and legal commentators did not pay attention to the gravity matter at the outset.[1612] It gained limited attention in the drafting history.[1613] Despite the rather modest attention at the beginning, gravity has turned into one of the central themes for selection of situations and cases.[1614] With respect to situation selection, once it is determined that the ICC has jurisdiction, the OTP then turns to the standard of gravity.[1615] All three situations the OTP addressed in its three years report – DRC, Northern Uganda, and Darfur – clearly met the gravity standard according to the Office.[1616] However, gravity as such is not defined in the ICC Statute or the later-adopted RPE. Many different interpretations of the term seem possible.[1617] Before turning to the interpreta-

---

[1609] Morel, *supra* note 1365, 252–3; Stigen, *supra* note 205, 334–5; Kleffner, *supra* note 370, 266.

[1610] Razesberger, *supra* note 371, 44–5; Evans, *supra* note 1347, 6; Van den Wyngaert/Ongena, in Cassese/Gaeta/Jones, *supra* note 1600, 726–7.

[1611] El Zeidy, *supra* note 269, 39.

[1612] Schabas, *supra* note 1151, 736; El Zeidy, *supra* note 269, 35.

[1613] Stahn, in Stahn/Sluiter, *supra* note 156, 267.

[1614] Stahn/Sluiter, in Stahn/Sluiter, *supra* note 5, 3; Susana Sá Couto/Katherine Cleary, "The gravity threshold of the International Criminal Court" (2008) 23 AUILR 807, 808. For a limited application to "cases" only see WCRO report "situation" and case selection, *supra* note 370, 3 et seq.

[1615] Outlining the Three-Year Report – Ms. Olivia Swaak-Goldman, *supra* note 473.

[1616] Outlining the Three-Year Report – Ms. Olivia Swaak-Goldman, *supra* note 473.

[1617] Schüller, *supra* note 1335, 73; Mark Osiel, "How should the ICC Office of the Prosecutor choose its cases? The multiple meanings of "situational gravity" (2009) The Hague Justice Portal 1, 1.

tion and application of the gravity threshold, the drafting history of article 17 (1) (d) will be briefly outlined below.

aa) Drafting history

Unlike a number of provisions that were included during the Rome Conference itself, article 17 (1) (d) appeared in nearly identical form in the ILC Draft Statute.[1618] The ILC focused on gravity for defining "crimes against the peace and security of mankind," but it did not attempt to place parameters for this concept.[1619] Nevertheless, a basic distinction between *existence* of jurisdiction and *exercise* of jurisdiction was made by the ILC: the Court should have discretion to decline jurisdiction in cases lacking sufficient gravity to ensure not only that the Court limits its focus to the most serious crimes but also that the Court is able to manage its case load.[1620]

It needs to be emphasized that the jurisdiction *ratione materiae* was not clear at this point and could potentially include treaty crimes.[1621] The gravity threshold seems to address a wider basis of crimes than under the current limitation of core crimes only and, for this reason, provides for an additional threshold in the case of a broad jurisdiction *ratione materiae.*[1622] *Ad Hoc* Committee meetings in 1995 returned to the idea of a few "core crimes"[1623] and the Preparatory Committee pointed out that it rather preferred "a more detailed definition of the crimes in article 20 Draft Statute" (nowadays article 5).[1624]

The gravity threshold, although initially formulated as an alternative to narrow down the prescriptive jurisdiction, received broad support during the negotiating process.[1625] Some delegations preferred to move or delete the

---

1618 ILC Draft Statute 1994, *supra* note 353, 105, article 35 (1) (c): "[...] is not of such gravity to justify further action by the Court"; also WCRO report gravity, *supra* note 1057, 12; Sá Couto/Cleary, *supra* note 1614, 817 et seq.

1619 McAuliffe deGuzman, *supra* note 1152, 12–3.

1620 WCRO report gravity, *supra* note 1057, 14–5; ILC Draft Statute 1994, *supra* note 353, 105.

1621 ILC Draft Statute 1994, *supra* note 353, 35–6; McAuliffe deGuzman, *supra* note 1152, 14–5.

1622 Yearbook of the International Law Commission 1994, Volume I, Summary records of the meetings on the forty-sixth session, 2 May–22 July 1994 (A/CN.4/SER.A/1994) para. 41, 25, para. 59, 27; ILC Draft Statute 1994, *supra* note 353, 32; WCRO report gravity, *supra* note 1057, 12 et seq.

1623 *Ad Hoc* Committee 1995, *supra* note 379, paras. 54 et seq., 11–2.

1624 Report of the Preparatory Committee 1996, Vol. 1, *supra* note 203, para. 169, 39.

1625 WCRO report gravity, *supra* note 1057, 16; Holmes, in Lee, *supra* note 581, 47; Williams/Schabas, in Triffterer, *supra* note 1347, article 17, mn 13.

provision, but they did not gain sufficient support.[1626] A common view arose that the Court should not be obliged to go ahead with every case within its jurisdiction. Instead, the Court should have discretion to decline jurisdiction, taking into account that the Court was intended for "the most serious crimes of concern to the international community" and was to complement national courts.[1627] The admissibility regime of article 17 was thought to consist of two components, complementarity and gravity, enabling the Prosecutor to defer to national jurisdictions in both cases. During the Rome Conference there was very little debate on the gravity issue, and the provision was left virtually unchanged from early drafts until the adoption of the ICC Statute.[1628] Only Mr. Salinas expressed concern on behalf of Chile, as he saw "a need to explain more clearly the vague reference in paragraph 1 (d) to sufficient gravity in regard to the justification of the Court's further action."[1629] On the other hand, the delegate of Sweden thought the lack of sufficient gravity should be a ground for inadmissibility.[1630] The Croatian delegate advised that there should be guarantees that cases dealt with are of significance and gravity in order to avoid burdening the Court with minor violations.[1631] It appears that most delegates, while not explicitly addressing the gravity issue in debates, felt that a gravity threshold was desirable given the undisputed gravity provision as it now stands.

bb) Interpretation of gravity

Gravity is at the heart of the statutory framework. It is an essential requirement for criminal offences falling within the jurisdiction of the ICC. The Preamble clearly stresses that "the serious crimes of concern to the international community as a whole must not go unpunished." Article 1 circumscribes that the Court "shall have the power to exercise its jurisdiction over persons for the most serious crimes of international concern," and article 5 equally limits jurisdiction to "the most serious crimes of concern to the international community as a whole," being genocide, crimes against

---

1626 Official Records, Vol. III, *supra* note 391, 27 with fn. 49; McAuliffe deGuzman, *supra* note 1152, 16; Stigen, *supra* note 205, 186.

1627 McAuliffe deGuzman, *supra* note 1152, 15–6; WCRO report gravity, *supra* note 1057, 16.

1628 McAuliffe deGuzman, *supra* note 1152, 17.

1629 Mr. Salinas (Chile) in Official Records, Vol. II, *supra* note 392, para. 29, 215.

1630 Mr. Saland (Sweden), in Official Records, Vol. II, *supra* note 392, para. 17, 205.

1631 Ms. Hodak (Croatia) in Official Records, Vol. II, *supra* note 392, para. 45, 94.

humanity, war crimes, and the crime of aggression. However, the wording of the ICC Statute and its auxiliary documents does not contribute to the definition of the gravity criterion. From my point of view, gravity has to be approached in a twofold systematic way. First and most important, what has to be analyzed is how gravity is applied at all. Is gravity a procedural, legal filter or a policy decision of the Prosecutor? In a second step, when this question is answered satisfactorily, the particular elements of gravity have to be considered.

It is my hypothesis that gravity has both, a legal and a policy dimension, which must be linked strictly to articles 53 (1) (b), 17 (d) and article 53 (1) (c) respectively. The latter involves discretionary evaluation contrary to the former which is a purely legal threshold. For substantiating this assumption, the subsequent analytical approach will turn to the OTP's view on gravity (1), the early practice by PTC I (2), the Appeal Chamber's judgment holding that PTC I erred in law when applying the gravity threshold (3), and the academic ideas on this matter (4). Last but not least, all theses views will be integrated into an interpretation of gravity.

(1) OTP approach

The OTP applies gravity twice, once with regard to situations and once when selecting cases inside the situation.[1632] Through this dual-use of gravity, the Prosecutor uses the concept at two distinct stages: in determining whether to initiate an investigation or proceed to a specific prosecution.[1633] In practice, the OTP has held that the situations of the DRC, Uganda, and Darfur were clearly admissible, though the Office did not further specify its gravity application:

> "The Office selected the DRC and Northern Uganda as the first situations because they were the gravest admissible situations under the Statute's jurisdiction, and, after the referral, the Office confirmed that the Darfur situation clearly met the gravity standard. The Office will continue to adhere to the rigorous standard of gravity established in the Statute."[1634]

In its early practice, the Prosecutor did not, in fact, mention the concept of gravity.[1635] Legal commentaries remained equally silent on the issue.[1636]

[1632] OTP Report on activities 2003–2006, *supra* note 23, 8; Ambos, in Ambos/Large/Wierda, *supra* note 650, 73–4, para. 38; El Zeidy, *supra* note 269, 39; for an application of gravity to cases only (and not to situations) see WCRO report "situation" and case selection, *supra* note 370, 3 et seq.

[1633] WCRO report gravity, *supra* note 1057, 7.

[1634] OTP Report on activities 2003–2006, *supra* note 23, 10.

[1635] Schabas, *supra* note 1151, 737.

In September 2003, a marginal reference in the newly drafted policy paper indicated the notion of gravity for the first time[1637] and the word then appears one additional time in the Annex to the policy paper.[1638] All-in-all, the Prosecutor did not pay attention to the gravity criterion during the first years of selecting cases and assessing their admissibility.[1639] This seemed to change by late 2005, when the Prosecutor made *inter alia* the following statement regarding the arrest warrants in Uganda:

> "The criteria [*sic*] for selection of the first case was gravity. We analyzed the gravity of all crimes in Northern Uganda committed by the LRA and Ugandan forces. Crimes committed by the LRA were much more numerous and of much higher gravity than alleged crimes committed by the UPDF. We therefore started with an investigation of the LRA."[1640]

The Prosecutor based his decision to select the LRA and not the UPDF on the gravity criterion, in other words, he used gravity as a prioritizing criterion for case selection. Since June 2006, the OTP has considered gravity to be its key situation and case selection criterion.[1641] Moreover, the Prosecutor states that the gravity threshold is very high and he considers "various factors" in his gravity analysis.[1642]

To date, the only publicly available profound determination of gravity *vis-à-vis* a whole situation has been in Iraq.[1643] In this response, the Prosecutor stated that, while in a general sense all crimes within the jurisdiction of the Court are valued as grave, an additional threshold of gravity is necessary because the Court is faced with multiple situations.[1644] The OTP identifies a specific gravity threshold in article 8 (1), which is not an ele-

---

1636 Schabas, *supra* note 1225, 20–1; *id.*, *supra* note 13, 348.

1637 Policy paper, *supra* note 99, 7; Schabas, *supra* note 1151, 737.

1638 Annex Paper, *supra* note 27, 3; Schabas, *supra* note 1151, 737.

1639 Schabas, *supra* note 1151, 737; *id.*, in Stahn/Sluiter, *supra* note 1152, 229–30.

1640 OTP-Press Release (Uganda), Press conference on the Uganda arrest warrants, Statement by Prosecutor Luis Moreno-Ocampo, 14.10.2005 (ICC-OTP-20051014-109); WCRO report gravity, *supra* note 1057, 26–7; Sá Couto/Cleary, *supra* note 1614, 830–1; Murphy, *supra* note 1048, 305; also Schabas, *supra* note 1151, 738, who reprints several similar follow-up statements; critical Phil Clark, "Law, politics and pragmatism: The ICC and case selection in the Democratic Republic of Congo and Uganda" in Waddell/Clark, *supra* note 246, 37, 42–3.

1641 Third Report pursuant to UNSC 1593, *supra* note 288, 2; Update on communications, *supra* note 316, 4; WCRO report gravity, *supra* note 1057, 19.

1642 Update on communications, *supra* note 316, 4.

1643 Iraq response, *supra* note 333, 8–9; Schüller, *supra* note 1335, 77; Ambos, in Bohlander, *supra* note 10, 438–9; WCRO report "situation" and case selection, *supra* note 370, 31 et seq.

1644 Iraq response, *supra* note 333, 8. This was named "gravest of the grave" by El Zeidy, *supra* note 269, 40.

ment of the crime ("particular"), but provides guidance on the gravity threshold: "[...] the Court shall have jurisdiction in respect of war crimes in particular when committed as part of a plan or policy or as part of a large-scale commission of such crimes."[1645] This specific threshold is confronted with the general gravity threshold of article 53 (1) (b).[1646] The OTP seems to apply the last-mentioned "large scale" general threshold when comparing the 4–12 victims in Iraq to the three situations of Northern Uganda, DRC, and Darfur: "even if one were to assume that article 8 (1) had been satisfied, it would then be necessary to consider the general gravity requirement under article 53 (1) (b)."[1647] This comparison of large-scale situations *vis-à-vis* the limited situation of Iraq has been harshly criticized ("[...] comparing apples and oranges").[1648] It has been regarded as a justification for refusing to pick up certain cases and not as a justification to select particular cases for prosecution over others.[1649]

Certainly, the OTP was only able to investigate crimes committed by British soldiers, as Iraq is not a member state, therefore depriving the OTP of jurisdiction over the whole territory. The basis was thus the nationality link of a member State pursuant to article 12 (2) (b), which could therefore only refer to British nationals.[1650] I believe that the Prosecutor could have avoided some criticism if he had applied gravity in a consistent manner from the outset. He supposedly used prosecutorial discretion, but did not carefully clarify this.[1651] His understanding of "specific," as opposed to "general" gravity points into this direction. In addition, the OTP did not clarify the exact factors its takes into consideration when assessing gravity.[1652] Overall, the OTP's early practice is not solid and lacks clarification whether gravity is applied as an admissibility criterion or as a matter of prosecutorial (discretionary) selection.[1653] For example, the Prosecutor found that the Darfur or DRC situations "clearly meet the gravity threshold," but gave no reasons for this determination. One shortcoming of the

1645 Iraq response, *supra* note 333, 8.

1646 Iraq response, *supra* note 333, 8.

1647 Iraq response, *supra* note 333, 8–9.

1648 Schabas, *supra* note 27, 190; *id., supra* note 1151, 741; El Zeidy, *supra* note 269, 40–1.

1649 Schabas, *supra* note 1151, 740. Critical on the analysis as such ("situational" gravity could inappropriately exclude cases) WCRO report "situation" and case selection, *supra* note 370, 33–4.

1650 Iraq response, *supra* note 333, 3; Moreno-Ocampo, in Stahn/Sluiter, *supra* note 99, 15; Murphy, *supra* note 1048, 309.

1651 In a similar vein, Schüller, *supra* note 1335, 78; McAuliffe deGuzman, *supra* note 1152, 32.

1652 Ambos, in Bohlander, *supra* note 10, 439.

1653 Schüller, *supra* note 1335, 78; McAuliffe deGuzman, *supra* note 1152, 30.

OTP's early practice is, therefore, not the application of the criterion gravity as such, but the lack of transparency when applying it.

(2) PTC I arrest warrants decision (Lubanga and Ntaganda)

Despite the fact that the following decision will be the subject of further interpretation by other Chambers of the Court,[1654] especially because it was partly reversed in appeal proceedings,[1655] I nevertheless turn to the PTC I 's decision that remains the only judicial treatment of gravity at the ICC. Earlier decisions did not go into the merits of gravity, and PTC I thus departed from the pattern established in the *Kony et al.* case to simply state that the case in question "appears to be admissible" without any detailed discussion.[1656] In the *Decision of the Prosecutor's application for a warrants of arrest* the PTC observed whether the case against *Lubanga* and *Ntaganda* met the gravity threshold under article 17 (1) (d) and applied a literal, contextual, and teleological interpretation to determine the content of the gravity threshold.[1657] The Chamber found that the gravity threshold was included in addition to the drafter's careful selection of the crimes in articles 6 to 8.[1658] A literal interpretation leads to a duty to assess gravity as an integral and mandatory part of the admissibility requirement, noting that the word "shall consider" in the chapeau of article 17 (1) leaves the Chamber no discretion.[1659] According to a contextual approach, the PTC ob-

---

[1654] Rastan, *supra* note 465, 447.

[1655] *Situation in DRC,* Judgment on the Prosecutor's appeal against the decision of Pre-Trial Chamber I, *supra* note 1360, paras. 1–3. The Appeals Chamber held *inter alia* that the Trial Chamber erred in its interpretation of "sufficient gravity." Thus, from a Chamber oriented point of view, gravity issues have to be readdressed *ab initio*. Recently, in the same vein, *Prosecutor v. Al Bashir,* Decision on the Prosecutor's application for a warrant of arrest against Bashir, *supra note* 304, para. 48 with fn. 51.

[1656] Smith, *supra* note 210, 335.

[1657] *Prosecutor v. Lubanga,* Decision on the Prosecutor's application for warrant of arrest, article 58, *supra* note 217, paras. 41 et seq.; *Prosecutor v. Ntaganda,* Annex II, Decision on the Prosecutor's application for warrants of arrest, *supra* note 228, paras. 29 et seq., 43 et seq. Further on the *Lubanga* arrest warrant decision, see WCRO report gravity, *supra* note 1057, 29 et seq.; Schüller, *supra* note 1335, 78; McAuliffe deGuzman, *supra* note 1152, 36; see also my earlier article Ignaz Stegmiller, "The gravity threshold under the ICC Statute: gravity back and forth in *Lubanga* and *Ntaganda*" (2009) 9 ICLR 547, 549 et seq.

[1658] *Prosecutor v. Lubanga,* Decision on the Prosecutor's application for warrant of arrest, article 58, *supra* note 217, para. 41; Ambos, in Bohlander, *supra* note 10, 448.

[1659] *Prosecutor v. Lubanga,* Decision on the Prosecutor's application for warrant of arrest, article 58, *supra* note 217, para. 43; *Prosecutor v. Ntaganda,* Annex II,

serves that the gravity threshold comes into play at two different procedural stages: at the stage of initiating an investigation and once a case arises from the investigation of a situation.[1660] In the same paragraph of the decision, the Chamber emphasizes that it only refers to gravity with regard to a specific case as opposed to a situation. Since the gravity threshold is an addition to the gravity-driven selection of crimes included within the subject-matter jurisdiction, there must be particular features for rendering the conduct specifically grave.[1661] The Chamber subsequently names two features, namely:

(1) the conduct which is the subject of the case must be either systematic (patterns of incidents) or large scale, and

(2) due consideration must be given to the social alarm such conduct may have caused in the international community.[1662]

The first sub-criterion is based upon the systematic argument that, if isolated acts were sufficient, the inclusion of an additional gravity threshold beyond the gravity-driven selection of crimes within the subject-matter jurisdiction was unnecessary.[1663] In contrast, the social alarm criterion seemingly arrives out of the blue; it is not further supported by interpretative arguments. PTC I continues with its teleological interpretation in analyzing the gravity threshold against the backdrop of the Preamble.[1664] Gravity is a key tool for maximizing the Court's deterrent effect and leads to the con-

---

Decision on the Prosecutor's application for warrants of arrest, *supra* note 228, para. 44.

1660 *Prosecutor v. Lubanga,* Decision on the Prosecutor's application for warrant of arrest, article 58, *supra* note 217, para. 44; *Prosecutor v. Ntaganda,* Annex II, Decision on the Prosecutor's application for warrants of arrest, *supra* note 228, para. 45.

1661 *Prosecutor v. Lubanga,* Decision on the Prosecutor's application for warrant of arrest, article 58, *supra* note 217, para. 45; *Prosecutor v. Ntaganda,* Annex II, Decision on the Prosecutor's application for warrants of arrest, *supra* note 228, para. 46; Smith, *supra* note 210, 336, who calls this "aggravated gravity."

1662 *Prosecutor v. Lubanga,* Decision on the Prosecutor's application for warrant of arrest, article 58, *supra* note 217, para. 46; thereto Wouters/Verhoeven/Demeyere, *supra* note 156, 296; El Zeidy, *supra* note 269, 45; Stahn, in Stahn/Sluiter, *supra* note 156, 274; Kindt, *supra* note 650, 146–7; Schabas, *supra* note 13, 348; Dov Jakobs, "Commentary, Arrest warrants and admissibility", in André Klip/Göran Sluiter (eds.), ALC, The International Criminal Court, 2005–2007, Vol. XXIII (Intersentia, Antwerp/Oxford/Portland 2010) 113, 118; also *Prosecutor v. Ntaganda,* Annex II, Decision on the Prosecutor's application for warrants of arrest, *supra* note 228, para. 46.

1663 *Prosecutor v. Lubanga,* Decision on the Prosecutor's application for warrant of arrest, article 58, *supra* note 217, para. 46.

1664 *Prosecutor v. Lubanga,* Decision on the Prosecutor's application for warrant of arrest, article 58, *supra* note 217, paras. 47 et seq.; *Prosecutor v. Ntaganda,* An-

clusion that other factors, in addition to the gravity of the relevant conduct, must be considered.[1665] The Chamber therefore establishes a gravity criterion of "the *most senior leaders* suspected of being the *most responsible* for the crimes within the jurisdiction of the Court (emph. added)."[1666] This additional criterion comprises three elements:

(1) the position of the person (most senior leaders);

(2) the roles such persons play, through acts or omissions, when the state entities, organizations or armed groups to which they belong commit systematic or large-scale crimes within the jurisdiction of the Court, and

(3) the role played by such state entities, organizations, or armed groups in the overall commission of crimes within the jurisdiction of the Court in the relevant situation (those suspected of being most responsible).[1667]

The Chamber legitimates its findings by making reference to the deterrent effects that can be maximized only by concentrating on this type of individuals.[1668] As already mentioned above, these factors were not discretionary according to the Chamber, but are rather core components of the gravity threshold.[1669] The outlined test was applied to the *Lubanga* and *Ntaganda* cases.[1670]

In sum, the Chamber sets the threshold very high, in particular through its focus on "senior leaders" only. If we divide the first criterion into its "scale" and "systematic" elements, the PTC's asks us to consider (1) the scale; (2) the manner of commission; (3) the social alarm caused; (4) and the senior leaders suspected of being the most responsible. Since the PTC

---

nex II, Decision on the Prosecutor's application for warrants of arrest, *supra* note 228, paras. 48 et seq.

[1665] *Prosecutor v. Lubanga,* Decision on the Prosecutor's application for warrant of arrest, article 58, *supra* note 217, paras. 48–9.

[1666] *Prosecutor v. Lubanga,* Decision on the Prosecutor's application for warrant of arrest, article 58, *supra* note 217, para. 50; HRW, A summary of the case law of the ICC, *supra* note 495, 2–3.

[1667] *Prosecutor v. Lubanga,* Decision on the Prosecutor's application for warrant of arrest, article 58, *supra* note 217, paras. 51 et seq., 63; *Prosecutor v. Ntaganda,* Annex II, Decision on the Prosecutor's application for warrants of arrest, *supra* note 228, paras. 52 et seq.

[1668] *Prosecutor v. Lubanga,* Decision on the Prosecutor's application for warrant of arrest, article 58, *supra* note 217, paras. 54, 60; Wouters/Verhoeven/Demeyere, *supra* note 156, 297.

[1669] *Prosecutor v. Lubanga,* Decision on the Prosecutor's application for warrant of arrest, article 58, *supra* note 217, para. 62; WCRO report gravity, *supra* note 1057, 33.

[1670] *Situation in DRC,* Judgment on the Prosecutor's appeal against the decision of Pre-Trial Chamber I, *supra* note 1360, para. 62.

focused only on the stage during which a case arises from a situation, the gravity threshold for a decision to initiate an investigation regarding a whole situation could, in any event, have lower criteria.[1671]

(3) Judgment on appeal against PTC I's arrest warrants decision

The aforementioned decision of PTC I was reversed on 13 July 2006 by the Appeals Chamber, yet remained under seal and was only reclassified as a public document on 23 September 2008.[1672] It is unclear why the judgment was kept confidential, but the non-disclosure appears to be closely related to the *Ntaganda* case and the Prosecutor's request to keep the warrant of arrest secret.[1673]

The Appeal's Judges decided to reverse the negative admissibility decision regarding *Ntaganda,* finding that the PTC erred in law when applying article 17 (1) (d).[1674] The Appeals Chamber addressed two major issues:

(1) Was the PTC correct in its finding that the admissibility of a case is a prerequisite to the issuance of an arrest warrant and under which circumstances could the PTC invoke its discretion to address admissibility in article 58 proceedings?

(2) Was the PTC correct in its interpretation of sufficient gravity under article 17 (1) (d)?[1675]

It is doubtful whether PTC I's approach to invoke article 19 (1) was congruent with the demarcation line between situations and cases.[1676] Article 58 proceedings lie somewhere between article 18 and 19; namely at a stage, which passes the phase of article 18, but does not quite yet reach article 19.[1677] The ICC Statute leaves open whether issues of admissibility may be or must be examined during arrest warrant proceedings.[1678] During article 58

1671 Schüller, *supra* note 1335, 81; El Zeidy, *supra* note 269, 47–8.

1672 *Situation in DRC,* Judgment on the Prosecutor's appeal against the decision of Pre-Trial Chamber I, *supra* note 1360 with corresponding text. Thereto Stegmiller, *supra* note 1657, 552 et seq; Jakobs, in Klip/Sluiter, *supra* note 1662, 118 et seq.

1673 See the critical comment by William Schabas, available at: <http://humanrightsdoctorate.blogspot.com/2008/11/laws-of-gravity-finally-revealed-by.html>.

1674 *Situation in DRC,* Judgment on the Prosecutor's appeal against the decision of Pre-Trial Chamber I, *supra* note 1360, para. 3.

1675 *Situation in DRC,* Judgment on the Prosecutor's appeal against the decision of Pre-Trial Chamber I, *supra* note 1360, para. 37.

1676 Part III, B., III., 3. and IV., 4.

1677 El Zeidy, *supra* note 598, 744, who later, however, concludes that it appears *legally* permissible to examine admissibility questions during the arrest warrant phase (at 746).

1678 Pichon, *supra* note 282, 198.

proceedings no case has yet been judicially determined, and as such a better approach would have been to only consider the factors expressly stipulated by article 58 (1).[1679] For this reason, as well as other gravity related reasons, various authors have stated that PTC I's gravity approach is too strict.[1680]

The Appeals Chamber equally held that an initial admissibility determination is not a prerequisite for the issuance of an arrest warrant;[1681] the Appeals Chamber found article 58 (1)'s requirements to be exhaustive in that circumstance.[1682] The impugned decision was found to be erroneous because PTC I did not give sufficient weight to the interests of *Ntaganda.*[1683] Moreover, the Appeals Chamber established three grounds for the exceptional exercise of discretion which would allow the Chamber to address admissibility issues at the arrest warrant stage: (1) instances where a case is based on the established jurisprudence of the Court; (2) where the case is based on uncontested facts that render a case clearly inadmissible; (3) or if an ostensible cause impels the exercise of *proprio motu* review.[1684] In the case at bar, the admissibility was not raised by the Prosecutor's *ex parte* application; the review was *ex parte* without participation of the suspect, victims or entities. Further, no ostensible cause or self evident factor was manifest that would compel the exercise of *proprio motu* review.[1685] In other words, where confidential and *ex parte* applications by the Prosecution do not address admissibility, there is a strong presumption against a discretionary admissibility check under article 19 (1) during early proceedings. Only in "exceptional circumstances," such as when an "ostensible cause" or a "self-evident factor" impels the exercise of discretion, may the Chamber test the admissibility on its own motion.[1686]

[1679] Rastan, *supra* note 465, 443.

[1680] El Zeidy, *supra* note 269, 49; Schüller, *supra* note 1335, 79; Smith, *supra* note 210, 350 ("[...] the Court should not apply the *Lubanga* aggravated gravity test in its future cases"); WCRO report gravity, *supra* note 1057, 37; Sá Couto/Cleary, *supra* note 1614, 811 et seq.; McAuliffe deGuzman, *supra* note 1152, 36 ("flawed in a number of respects").

[1681] *Situation in DRC,* Judgment on the Prosecutor's appeal against the decision of Pre-Trial Chamber I, *supra* note 1360, paras. 1, 41.

[1682] *Situation in DRC,* Judgment on the Prosecutor's appeal against the decision of Pre-Trial Chamber I, *supra* note 1360, paras. 42 et seq.

[1683] *Situation in DRC,* Judgment on the Prosecutor's appeal against the decision of Pre-Trial Chamber I, *supra* note 1360, paras. 48 et seq.

[1684] *Situation in DRC,* Judgment on the Prosecutor's appeal against the decision of Pre-Trial Chamber I, *supra* note 1360, para. 52.

[1685] *Situation in DRC,* Judgment on the Prosecutor's appeal against the decision of Pre-Trial Chamber I, *supra* note 1360, para. 53.

[1686] *Prosecutor v. Al Bashir,* Decision on the Prosecutor's application for a warrant of arrest against Bashir, *supra* note 304, paras. 47, 51.

The restrictive approach towards article 19 (1) has led to a more careful application of the admissibility test in follow-up cases, for instance, in the cases of *Harun and Kushayb, Bemba, Bashir,* and *Abu Garda.*[1687] However, recent case law in the *Kony et al.* case seems to put this restrictive application into perspective: the Judges limit the restrictive approach only to the arrest warrant stage and, by the same token, emphasize their broad discretionary powers under article 19 (1) in later procedural phases.[1688]

Turning to the interpretation of article 17 (1) (d), the Appeals Chamber considered it necessary to address the PTC's approach due to its possible impact on the Court as a whole.[1689] If not addressed, errors contained in the PTC's decision could lead to future cases being clearly inadmissible on grounds that are incorrect.[1690] The Appeals Chamber first summarized the PTC's main arguments, stressing that PTC I understood the application of "sufficient gravity" – based on a literal approach – as an obligatory test.[1691] As outlined above, the PTC developed a twofold prong (systematic or large scale; social alarm) from contextual interpretation, and two prongs (most senior leaders; most responsible) were derived through teleological interpretation.[1692]

The Prosecutor, however, neither agreed with the developed test nor with the application to the present case (*Ntaganda*).[1693] The rigid interpretation of the gravity threshold is, from his point of view, not justified.[1694] In relation to social alarm, the concept could not be found in the ICC Statute, and

---

1687 *Prosecutor v. Harun and Kushayb,* Decision on the Prosecution application under article 58 (7) of the Statute, *supra* note 292, para. 18; *Prosecutor v. Bemba,* Décision relative à la requête du procureur, *supra* note 465, paras. 20–1; *Prosecutor v. Al Bashir,* Decision on the Prosecutor's application for a warrant of arrest against Bashir, *supra* note 304, paras. 46 et seq.; *Prosecutor v. Abu Garda,* Decision under article 58, *supra* note 308, para. 4.

1688 See already Part IV, B., III., 2.

1689 *Situation in DRC,* Judgment on the Prosecutor's appeal against the decision of Pre-Trial Chamber I, *supra* note 1360, para. 54.

1690 *Situation in DRC,* Judgment on the Prosecutor's appeal against the decision of Pre-Trial Chamber I, *supra* note 1360, para. 54.

1691 *Situation in DRC,* Judgment on the Prosecutor's appeal against the decision of Pre-Trial Chamber I, *supra* note 1360, para. 58.

1692 *Situation in DRC,* Judgment on the Prosecutor's appeal against the decision of Pre-Trial Chamber I, *supra* note 1360, paras. 59–60; *Situation in DRC,* Judgment on the Prosecutor's appeal against the decision of Pre-Trial Chamber I, *supra* note 1360, Separate and partly dissenting opinion of Judge Georghios M. Pikis, paras. 11 et seq.

1693 *Situation in DRC,* Judgment on the Prosecutor's appeal against the decision of Pre-Trial Chamber I, *supra* note 1360, para. 66.

1694 *Situation in DRC,* Judgment on the Prosecutor's appeal against the decision of Pre-Trial Chamber I, *supra* note 1360, para. 66.

the Prosecutor mentions that the criterion relates to subjective rather than objective reactions.[1695] In addition, the OTP found flaws in the teleological interpretation; narrowing the gravity determination in the fashion foreseen by the PTC would not maximize the deterrent effect, but it would mean that most of the perpetrators would have nothing to fear from the ICC.[1696] Reference was made to article 8 (1) ("in particular"), which allows the Prosecutor to address the crime even if the plan or policy or large-scale element was not fulfilled; in the drafting history for genocide the inclusion of a "widespread or systematic" requirement was also rejected.[1697] The Prosecutor felt that the current test inappropriately limits his prosecutorial discretion and would make it impossible to investigate and prosecute perpetrators lower down the chain of command.[1698]

The Appeals Chamber equally arrived at the conclusion that the PTC's test was, in essence, incorrect.[1699] The requirement that conduct must be either systematic or large-scale was based on a flawed contextual interpretation. According to the Appeals Chamber the jurisdictional requirements for war crimes and crimes against humanity are otherwise blurred:

> "First, with regard to war crimes, the requirement of large-scale commission under the Statute is alternative to the requirement of commission as part of a policy. Second, the statutory requirement of either large-scale commission or part of a policy is not absolute but qualified by the expression "in particular." Third, the requirement of "systematic" commission of crime is not contained in article 8 but only article 7 on crimes against humanity." [1700]

As to the social alarm criterion, the Appeals Chamber noted that the PTC did not explain further why it had to be taken into account at all, and where it derived the criterion from.[1701] It is not mentioned in the Statute and depends upon subjective reactions to crimes rather than their objective gravity.[1702] Before the judgment was made publicly available, it had al-

---

1695 *Situation in DRC,* Judgment on the Prosecutor's appeal against the decision of Pre-Trial Chamber I, *supra* note 1360, para. 66.

1696 *Situation in DRC,* Judgment on the Prosecutor's appeal against the decision of Pre-Trial Chamber I, *supra* note 1360, para. 66; in the same vein, McAuliffe de-Guzman, *supra* note 1152, 36; Seils, in Bergsmo, *supra* note 99, 56.

1697 *Situation in DRC,* Judgment on the Prosecutor's appeal against the decision of Pre-Trial Chamber I, *supra* note 1360, para. 66.

1698 *Situation in DRC,* Judgment on the Prosecutor's appeal against the decision of Pre-Trial Chamber I, *supra* note 1360, para. 66.

1699 *Situation in DRC,* Judgment on the Prosecutor's appeal against the decision of Pre-Trial Chamber I, *supra* note 1360, paras. 68, 82.

1700 *Situation in DRC,* Judgment on the Prosecutor's appeal against the decision of Pre-Trial Chamber I, *supra* note 1360, para. 70.

1701 *Situation in DRC,* Judgment on the Prosecutor's appeal against the decision of Pre-Trial Chamber I, *supra* note 1360, paras. 59, 72.

ready been argued that "social alarm" appears so ill-defined and subjective a term as to be impossible to apply with any consistency.[1703]

Last but not least, the category of "most senior leaders suspected on being the most responsible" was based on defective interpretation. The Chamber found it difficult to follow the PTC's assumption that the deterrent effect is highest if all categories of perpetrators other than the most senior leaders cannot be brought before the Court.[1704] In fact, it seems more logical to assume that the deterrent effect is highest if no category or perpetrators is *per se* excluded from potentially being brought before the Court.[1705] An exclusion of many perpetrators would severely hamper the deterrent role of the Court.[1706] In addition, the teleological interpretation of the PTC conflicts with a systematic approach in that many provisions of the ICC Statute could relate to persons other than senior leaders (cf. articles 33, 27 (1)).[1707] The Appeal's Chamber then refers to the drafting history of article 17 (1) (d), which contradicts PTC I's approach: a strict proposal ("the matters of which complaint has been made were not of exceptional gravity as to justify further action by the Court") was made in 1996, but was never included.[1708]

Given the Appeals Chamber reversal of the PTC's gravity test gravity issues are – from a Court's perspective – open to new interpretation by the Chambers and the OTP. Regrettably, the Judges on Appeal only presented their reasoning to revoke the PTC's gravity assessment, but did not explain how the legal gravity threshold should be applied. Only Judge Pikis, in his separate and partly dissenting opinion, attempts to determine "gravity," but he does not develop a test. He remarks that "gravity" denotes weightiness, and is further qualified by "sufficient" meaning "enough, adequate."[1709]

1702 *Situation in DRC,* Judgment on the Prosecutor's appeal against the decision of Pre-Trial Chamber I, *supra* note 1360, para. 72.

1703 Murphy, *supra* note 1048, 289.

1704 *Situation in DRC,* Judgment on the Prosecutor's appeal against the decision of Pre-Trial Chamber I, *supra* note 1360, para. 73.

1705 *Situation in DRC,* Judgment on the Prosecutor's appeal against the decision of Pre-Trial Chamber I, *supra* note 1360, para. 73; thereto Schabas, *supra* note 13, 348-9.

1706 *Situation in DRC,* Judgment on the Prosecutor's appeal against the decision of Pre-Trial Chamber I, *supra* note 1360, para. 75.

1707 *Situation in DRC,* Judgment on the Prosecutor's appeal against the decision of Pre-Trial Chamber I, *supra* note 1360, para. 78.

1708 *Situation in DRC,* Judgment on the Prosecutor's appeal against the decision of Pre-Trial Chamber I, *supra* note 1360, para. 81.

1709 *Situation in DRC,* Judgment on the Prosecutor's appeal against the decision of Pre-Trial Chamber I, *supra* note 1360, Separate and partly dissenting opinion of Judge Georghios M. Pikis, para. 39.

"Sufficient" is an "adjective determinative of a given level, quality or quantity."[1710] After discussing the term "further action by the Court," Judge Pikis concludes that the case must be unworthy to qualify for consideration of the Court.[1711] Giving "unworthy" more substantive content, Pikis refers to "cases insignificant in themselves; where the criminality on the part of the culprit is wholly marginal; borderline cases" and holds a crime to be insignificant if "the acts constituting the crime are wholly peripheral to the objects of the law in criminalizing the conduct."[1712] Judge Pikis thus starts his own interpretation of gravity, but he does not develop it beyond some initial thoughts. In other words, he initiates an adequate interpretation of gravity, without proceeding to the second level.

What can be deduced from the early case law in *Lubanga* and *Ntaganda* and from the OTP's early approaches in the Iraq situation is that gravity was left undefined by the drafters and should, as an obligatory admissibility criterion, not be interpreted too narrowly. Similar to the OTP in its early practice, PTC I confused legal and discretionary considerations, and it introduced some concepts into the legal gravity threshold that are, if they are relevant criteria at all, aspects of relative gravity under article 53 (1) (c) and (2) (c). No congruent gravity approach exists, and it remains an open question when the OTP will present one. In other words, the OTP and PTC have generated more "heat than light" with respect to gravity.[1713] The remaining task for the ICC's actors is to generate a feasible testing mechanism for gravity under article 17 (1) (d). In this endeavor, two decisive questions must be answered sequentially:

- How is gravity basically interpreted, and what are the consequences, if any, of the twofold inclusion of the term "gravity" in articles 53 (1) (b) and 17 (1) (d) *vis-à-vis* article 53 (1) (c)?
- What are the exact gravity factors and how are they legally defined?

I will try to give initial answers on both questions, starting with a basic interpretation of gravity (4) and (5), before subsequently dealing with the criteria for the gravity threshold (cc) (1)–(4)).

1710 *Situation in DRC,* Judgment on the Prosecutor's appeal against the decision of Pre-Trial Chamber I, *supra* note 1360, Separate and partly dissenting opinion of Judge Georghios M. Pikis, para. 39.

1711 *Situation in DRC,* Judgment on the Prosecutor's appeal against the decision of Pre-Trial Chamber I, *supra* note 1360, Separate and partly dissenting opinion of Judge Georghios M. Pikis, para. 39.

1712 *Situation in DRC,* Judgment on the Prosecutor's appeal against the decision of Pre-Trial Chamber I, *supra* note 1360, Separate and partly dissenting opinion of Judge Georghios M. Pikis, para. 40.

1713 Schabas, in Stahn/Sluiter, *supra* note 1152, 246; very critical also Jakobs, in Klip/Sluiter, *supra* note 1662, 120 et seq.

(4) Academic approaches

As already mentioned, gravity is a central criterion for situation and case selection. It has been used for the purpose of determining prosecutorial priorities in early OTP practice. But gravity appears in article 17 (1) (d), inserted into article 53 via paragraph 1 (b), and is therefore closely related to purely legal determinations as opposed by prosecutorial policy decisions. Gravity was further included as one of the sub-criteria that have to be taken into account when determining the "interests of justice" under article 53 (1) (c). The need for repetition has been questioned,[1714] but this renders it possible to develop an own approach (5), based on the following ideas.

It has been argued that gravity has two dimensions: first, a relative (discretionary) gravity that allows the Prosecutor to prioritize cases and situations involving discretionary decisions, and second, a theoretically static concept of a (non-discretionary) gravity threshold that requires the Prosecutor and the Judges to reject inadmissible situations and cases that fall below this legal barrier.[1715] The Prosecutor performs a discretionary gravity prioritization in which he considers the most serious of all sufficiently serious situations. In light of the Court's limited resources and the proliferation of cases that meet the gravity threshold, this prosecutorial selection process will generally hinge on relative gravity.[1716] The distinction between relative gravity and the gravity threshold is often blurred, however.[1717] In the same vein, the WCRO has identified a dual-use of gravity.

The Prosecutor does not clearly distinguish between gravity "[...] for purposes of determining whether a situation or a case is *admissible* under Article 17 and considerations of gravity for purposes of determining which situations and cases will be investigated or prosecuted as a *matter of prosecutorial discretion* [...]."[1718] Similarly, it has been held that gravity is an admissibility criterion, thus a question of legality and not discretion, and is as such a procedural filter for determining situations and cases.[1719] Gravity is not a criterion upon which the Prosecutor could refuse to proceed or to start an investigation in the case of discretionary considerations such as limited resources.[1720]

1714 Bergsmo/Kruger, in Triffterer, *supra* note 906, article 53, mn 19; Razesberger, *supra* note 371, 39.

1715 McAuliffe deGuzman, *supra* note 1152, 5–6.

1716 McAuliffe deGuzman, *supra* note 1152, 9.

1717 McAuliffe deGuzman, *supra* note 1152, 6, 30 et seq.

1718 WCRO report gravity, *supra* note 1057, 7, 53.

1719 Schüller, *supra* note 1335, 81.

1720 Schüller, *supra* note 1335, 81.

(5) Interpretation of gravity: Linking gravity to articles 53 (1) (b), 17 (d) and 53 (1) (c)

First of all, it has to be clarified that the following deliberations deal with situational gravity only. The highly significant question of the relationship between article 53 (1) and (2) is further clarified below,[1721] and leads to four distinguishable gravity levels under article 53.

Article 53 (1) concerns the selection of situations for investigations. In paragraph 1 gravity appears twice: in articles 53 (1) (b), 17 (1) (d) and article 53 (1) (c). At first sight, an unnecessary repetition could be assumed. However, taking into account the legal nature of admissibility and the discretionary nature of the "interests of justice," it may be argued that gravity has two dimensions that have to be rooted in the particular subparagraphs of article 53. To substantiate this assumption, one might partly rely on the differentiation above of *relative* gravity and *legal* gravity.[1722] The former (relative) gravity is understood in a more policy fashion that allows for discretionary choices, whereas legal gravity must be regarded as a non-discretionary testing mechanism as part of (legal) admissibility determinations. These concepts need to be further refined by strictly linking the terms to the particular subparagraphs of article 53.

It has been argued that the discretion of the Prosecutor is broad for *proprio motu* situations, suggesting a relative gravity analysis via "seriousness of the information received" in article 15 (2). For SC and State referrals, an initiation of investigations is mandatory if admissibility – and thus legal gravity – is answered in the positive ("must initiate"), unless the "interests of justice" would not be served.[1723] This approach is innovative and tries to harmonize the practice of the OTP *vis-à-vis* statutory obligations. Moreover, it draws a line between legal gravity (for SC and State referrals), and an additional consideration of relative gravity for *proprio motu* situations.

Nonetheless, I prefer a different legal path by juxtaposing article 53 (1) (b) and 53 (1) (c), i. e. the double-mentioning of gravity in the norm. In my opinion, the differentiation between SC and State referrals as opposed to *proprio motu* is not entirely convincing, given the equal treatment of all triggering mechanisms under the ICC Statute and the RPE. While there is certainly a strong presumption in favor of SC referred situations, all have to pass the same threshold. As outlined in Part III of this study, the pre-investigation stage leads all situations to the criteria of articles 53 (1), 15 (3), and rule 48: jurisdiction, admissibility (including legal gravity), and the

[1721] Part IV, B., III., 2., c), dd).

[1722] See also my earlier deliberations: Stegmiller, *supra* note 1657, 562 et seq.

[1723] McAuliffe deGuzman, *supra* note 1152, 32–3.

"interests of justice." Equal treatment is necessary because it is ultimately an independent Prosecutor who must decide where to engage his efforts. If legal gravity is sufficient, it is again up to the Prosecutor to value the relative gravity in a second step, and he does so *vis-à-vis* all other situations no matter how they were triggered. Therefore, the gravity distinction between situations, which are referred by the SC or States, and *proprio motu* situations should not be upheld. Nonetheless, the question remains what legal and relative gravity exactly amount to, especially which factors these notions entail.

Having clarified that all situations are generally treated alike with regard to gravity, I will now turn to the different notions of the "gravity of a case" pursuant to articles 53 (1) (b), 17 (1) (d) and the "gravity of the crime" pursuant to article 53 (1) (c). A textual interpretation suggests a difference. The "gravity of the crime" could be limited to the severity of the offence, whereas the "gravity of the case" might be broader and include the circumstances of the individual. Such a finding stands against the envisaged approach: the first gravity notion (article 53 (1) (b)) would be wider than the second (article 53 (1) (c)). In turn, gravity under article 53 (1) (c) would be more limited than gravity under article 53 (1) (b). On the other hand, it has been argued – based on the drafting history of article 17 – that the terms "case" and "crime" basically refer to the same matter, and might even be used indistinctively.[1724] The latter view adopted a narrow interpretation of the term "case" for the purpose of the admissibility testing mechanism under article 17.[1725] It did not yet address the issue of article 53 and the double-inclusion of gravity. Moreover, instead of adopting one of these possible approaches, I must recall that literal interpretations have shown great defects with regard to the ICC Statute, particularly when the differentiation between situations and cases is involved. This distinction was not sufficiently incorporated into articles 53 and 17 (1) (d). It was left to the Court to harmonize the meaning of a "case" according to the different stages of the proceedings.[1726] In other words, the word "case" can have

---

[1724] *Prosecutor v. Katanga and Chui,* Public redacted version of the 19th March 2009 Prosecution response to motion challenging the admissibility, *supra* note 459, para. 84; *Situation in DRC,* Judgment on the Prosecutor's appeal against the decision of Pre-Trial Chamber I, *supra* note 1360, para. 81.

[1725] *Prosecutor v. Katanga and Chui,* Public redacted version of the 19th March 2009 Prosecution response to motion challenging the admissibility, *supra* note 459, paras. 68 et seq. If such a narrow interpretation is followed, admissibility (and in particular article 17 and the notion of gravity) could only be applied with regard to cases, cf. WCRO report "situation" and case selection, *supra* note 370, 35–6; Heller, in Stahn/van Herik, *supra* note 339, 229.

[1726] *Situation in Kenya*, Decision pursuant to article 15, *supra* note 6, para. 47, 21.

different meanings. One might therefore not base any results on the use of the terms gravity of a "crime" or "case," except that there might be a difference between the two subparagraphs. In accordance with the statutory wording, the gravity of the *case* can be distinguished from the gravity of the *crime* insofar as article 53 (1) (b) allows for a different notion of gravity than article 53 (1) (c).

Moreover, a systematic interpretation promotes different content of the gravity tests. Provisions of the ICC Statute must be interpreted in a manner which results in a coherent, rather than an internally inconsistent, system.[1727] Gravity under article 17 (1) (d) was inserted through article 53 (1) (b). Article 17 deals with admissibility. The "gravity of the case" is therefore a (narrow) legal threshold that involves the Prosecutor and ultimately the Judges.[1728] In contrast thereto, the "gravity of the crime" mentioned within article 53 (1) (c) must be a wider concept. It has to be seen in the light of the overarching concept of the "interests of justice." This time, gravity has to be taken into account when the "interests of justice" are determined and allows for policy considerations. Gravity under article 53 (1) (c) is one sub-criterion on the same level with the interest of victims, being both part of the discretionary "interests of justice."

A teleological view further prefers clear distinctions between relative, discretionary gravity and the legal gravity threshold. Some drafters were worried about the inclusion of the "interests of justice" phrase at all. The differentiated framework of article 53 clearly speaks in favor of discretion only as part of the "interests of justice." Otherwise, the careful procedural compromise, especially the review mechanism of article 53 (3), would be undermined. Distinctiveness equally favors this new, differentiated approach: discretionary policy decisions can be based upon article 53 (1) (c) and (2) (c), and the admissibility threshold can be carried out based on a

[1727] *Prosecutor v. Bemba,* Decision adjourning the hearing, *supra* note 276, paras. 34–6; *Prosecutor v. Katanga and Chui,* Public redacted version of the 19th March 2009 Prosecution response to motion challenging the admissibility, *supra* note 459, para. 69.

[1728] It is submitted that this approach refines the OTP's narrow interpretation of the term "case" in article 17 (cf. Part III, B., III, 2., and Part IV, B., III., 2., b), cc), (1)), and takes the OTP's approach to the next level, trying to harmonize articles 17 and 53 – which the OTP did not pay attention to in its motion. With regard to the case stage, the "specificity" test, which is based on a narrow concept of the term "case," can be applied pursuant to articles 53 (2) (b), 17. However, the OTP does not sufficiently address the matter of article 53 (1), which deals with situations as its objects. At this stage, article 53 (1) (b) is the *lex specialis,* and necessarily alters the narrow reading of article 17. In the later respect, article 17 can only be understood in a more general way and deals with situations, as previously acknowledged by the OTP, cf. Part IV, B., III., 2., b), aa).

set of legal criteria. All-in-all, legal and relative gravity should be clearly distinguished and linked to articles 53 (1) (b), 17 (1) (d) and article 53 (1) (c) respectively. For the sake of clarity, the terms "gravity of the case" and "gravity of the crime" should not be used, but the OTP should rather refer to "legal gravity" under article 17 (1) (d) or "relative gravity" under article 53 (1) (c) when it explains the basis for picking a particular situation in the future. It remains to be resolved which specific criteria should be part of the threshold test under article 17 (1) (d), how high the threshold is, and in what manner relative gravity under article 53 (1) (c) should be assessed.

cc) Criteria for the gravity threshold

The ICC Statute does not further define the sub-criteria to be taken into account under the gravity threshold. PTC I has developed criteria, but only for gravity *vis-à-vis* cases. Moreover, PTC I applied gravity too strictly, and most of its criteria are not helpful for the legal gravity analysis. The OTP has continuously refined its gravity approach, but the OTP's practice similarly shows that the Office does not have a congruent approach yet. For instance, the elements for legal and relative gravity are blurred. A former draft version of OTP Regulation 29 (2) promisingly mentioned "qualitative and quantitative factors,"[1729] but unfortunately the version adopted in April 2009 did away with these improvements and only refers to "various factors." Future developments will have to define the elements scale, nature, manner, and impact, and in particular the weighing process. Thereby, the OTP is well advised to continue its monitoring process to reconsider moving "impact" to gravity under article 53 (1) (c), and to take a mixed qualitative and quantitative approach in the way submitted below.[1730]

(1) PTC I arrest warrants decision (Lubanga and Ntaganda)

PTC I's approach to gravity has already been outlined as part of the interpretation of gravity, and the developed criteria can be recalled as follows:

(1) scale and (2) manner of commission (systematic);

(3) social alarm caused in the international community;

(4) most senior leaders suspected of being the most responsible.

[1729] In more detail on quantitative and qualitative assessment in practice see Agirre Aranburu, in Bergsmo, *supra* note 460, 151 et seq., 155 et seq. PTC II has recently adopted such a mixed quantitative-qualitative approach, cf. *Situation in Kenya*, Decision pursuant to article 15, *supra* note 6, para. 62, 27.

[1730] Part III, B., III., 2., c), dd).

The social alarm criterion, albeit not expressly endorsed by the OTP, is significantly analogous to the (former) impact criterion used by the Prosecutor.[1731] One might question the application thereof ("an assessment in the vacuum"), as the Chamber did *in casu* not even touch upon the subject of the social alarm caused by the invasion in Iraq.[1732] For the fourth criterion, the Chamber developed sub-elements, which will be critically evaluated.[1733] All mentioned criteria, as well as the PTC's decision *as such*, have caused extensive academic debate, and have therefore found their way into the subsequent critical analysis of gravity.

(2) OTP criteria

The OTP finds the following factors relevant to the gravity assessment:

(1) the scale of the crimes;

(2) the nature of the crimes;

(3) the manner of the commission of the crimes; and

(4) the impact of the crimes.[1734]

The Prosecutor mentioned that the gravity criterion is under on-going refinement.[1735] During this screening process, the Office referred *inter alia* to

---

[1731] Schabas, *supra* note 1151, 742; El Zeidy, *supra* note 269, 45. The impact criterion was later omitted, cf. Part IV, B., III., 2., c), cc), (2).

[1732] Schabas, *supra* note 1151, 743, who further states that "[u]nlike the Prosecutor, it [the Chamber] was not even comparing apples and oranges. It was comparing apples with nothing."

[1733] Part IV, C., IV., 4., b), aa).

[1734] OTP Regulation 29 (2); Prosecutorial Strategy 2009–2012, *supra* note 99, para. 20, 6. On these factors see Seils, in Bergsmo, *supra* note 99, 57; HRW selection policy paper, *supra* note 1215, 5; McAuliffe deGuzman, *supra* note 1152, 34 et seq.; Schüller, *supra* note 1335, 79; HRW Courting history report, *supra* note 126, 38; Stigen, *supra* note 205, 361; Unger/Wierda, in Ambos/Large/Wierda, *supra* note 678, 297; Stahn, in Stahn/Sluiter, *supra* note 156, 268; Sá Couto/Cleary, *supra* note 1614, 810, 824 et seq.; Stegmiller, *supra* note 1657, 560; El Zeidy, *supra* note 269, 44, further mentions the criteria "degree of participation" and other "aggravating factors."

PTC II has recently adopted the same criteria (with a slightly different wording), see *Situation in Kenya*, Decision pursuant to article 15, *supra* note 6, para. 62, 27:

(i) the scale of the alleged crimes (including assessment of geographical and temporal intensity);

(ii) the nature of the unlawful behaviour or of the crimes allegedly committed;

(iii) the employed means for the execution of the crimes (i.e. the manner of their commission);

(iv) the impact of the crimes and the harm caused to victims and their families.

[1735] Statement by Luis Moreno-Ocampo: Informal meeting, *supra* note 497, 6.

the following factors: number of persons killed; the number of victims; the severity of the crimes; the scale of the crimes; the systematicity of the crimes; the nature of the crimes; the manner in which those crimes were committed; and the impact of the crimes.[1736] Among the mentioned factors, the Prosecutor most notably referred several times to the impact of the crimes.[1737] This criterion was nevertheless questioned in an intermediary draft paper on selection criteria,[1738] but the Chief-Prosecutor reintroduced the factor in the final version of the OTP Regulations. It may be asked why the impact criterion was included in the final OTP Regulations. In a June 2006 draft document, the Prosecutor noted that he "will consider the broader impact of crimes on the community and on regional peace and security, including longer term social, economic and environmental damage."[1739] The definition of impact is largely analogous to PTC I's criterion of social alarm. Due to the policy and subjective nature of impact or social alarm caused, the Prosecutor is well advised to transfer the criterion from his legal gravity assessment to his discretionary gravity assessment under article 53 (1) (c) and (2) (c). Generally speaking, "impact" should no longer be categorized as being part of the legal gravity threshold. In my view, broader impact clearly belongs to other potential considerations under the "interests of justice" clause.

However, it must be noted that the OTP has referred to the "nature, manner and impact" in the Haskanita attack in the Darfur situation.[1740] If the Prosecutor thereby refers to the narrower impact on victims,[1741] an inclu-

---

1736 WCRO report gravity, *supra* note 1057, 19–20; Clark, in Waddell/Clark, *supra* note 1640, 38.

1737 Statement by Luis Moreno-Ocampo: Informal meeting, *supra* note 497, 6; Third Report pursuant to UNSC 1593, *supra* note 288, 2; also WCRO report gravity, *supra* note 1057, 2; Schabas, *supra* note 1151, 736.

1738 An alternative draft, omitting the factor "impact," is, for example, referenced by Senior App. Counsel Guariglia, in Stahn/Sluiter, *supra* note 1215, 214; critical also the former Head of the Situation and Analysis Section Seils, in Bergsmo, *supra* note 99, 59.

1739 Schabas, *supra* note 1151, 742; also Hall, *supra* note 100, 21; Benzing, *supra* note 1349, 619–20; Meißner, *supra* note 371, 79; McAuliffe deGuzman, *supra* note 1152, 35; Osiel, *supra* note 1617, 2. On the usage of impact by the OTP in the sense of preventive impact see – very sceptical – Seils, in Bergsmo, *supra* note 99, 59.

1740 Eight Report pursuant to UNSC 1593, *supra* note 290, para. 56. "Impact" is also mentioned by the OTP at: <www2.icc-cpi.int/Menus/ICC/Structure+of+the+Court/Office+of+the+Prosecutor/Investigations/>.

1741 See thereto *Prosecutor v. Abu Garda,* Decision on the confirmation of charges, *supra* note 312, para. 33. In a similar vein recently *Situation in Kenya*, Request for authorization, *supra* note 207, para. 59, 21 ([...] a devasting impact first and foremost on the victims."). In the very same paragraph (*ibid.*), the OTP refers

sion into the gravity criterion could be approved. The specific impact on victims – which could equally fall within the category circumstances of commission of the crime – could be taken into account, regardless of the broader impact on the community or regional peace. It is, however, speculative as to what the Prosecutor's final approach towards impact will be. Whether or not the word "impact" should be used for legal gravity ultimately depends on the OTP's understanding and legal interpretation of this vague term. Generally speaking, "impact" should no longer be categorized as being part of the legal gravity threshold, but should be moved to article 53 (1) (c) and (2) (c) determinations.

At the present stage, consistency on behalf of the OTP might be questioned and the Office should finally decide on the gravity elements to distinguish legal and policy matters more clearly. "Impact" appears to entail two layers: a narrow, victim-oriented notion, and a wider, community-related notion. If the factor is included for legal gravity at all, the two concepts must be clearly differentiated and linked to the gravity tests accordingly.

Coming to the other three sub-criteria one by one, the scale of the crimes has been deduced from articles 6, 7, and 8.[1742] The OTP added more substantive content to the scale of the crimes, permanently referring to the "numbers of persons killed" as the most reliable factor and main criterion for determining gravity.[1743] Geographic and temporal scope of crimes is also considered.[1744] Establishing such a killing rate has faced criticism, especially if only a quantitative test is used to determine gravity.[1745] It is debatable as to when numbers will be satisfactory and what happens when the numbers in the compared situations and cases converge.[1746] To acquire

---

to the "[...] impact on the local communities in terms of security, social structure, economy and persistence of impunity in the country."

1742 El Zeidy, *supra* note 651, 905.

1743 Statement by Luis Moreno-Ocampo: Informal meeting, *supra* note 497, 6; "Five minutes with Luis Moreno-Ocampo: An interview with the ICC Prosecutor," Adele Waugaman (2006) XV International Affairs Review 2; Hall, *supra* note 100, 21; further Agirre Aranburu, in Bergsmo, *supra* note 460, 151 et seq.; critical Heller, in Stahn/van Herik, *supra* note 339, 228. In favour of the OTP's focus Mark Osiel, "When law 'expresses' more than it cares to admit: comments on Heller" in Stahn/van Herik, *supra* note 11, 254, 254 et seq.

1744 McAuliffe deGuzman, *supra* note 1152, 35; Guariglia, in Stahn/Sluiter, *supra* note 1215, 214; *Situation in Kenya*, Request for authorization, *supra* note 207, para. 56, 20 ("Crimes have been committed in six out of eight Kenyan regions, and particularly in the country's most populated areas, [...]").

1745 Schabas, *supra* note 27, 190; *id., supra* note 1151, 741.

1746 Ambos, in Bohlander, *supra* note 10, 439; similarly Goldstone, *supra* note 1048, 401.

an authenticated data of the number of victims, in particular the number of deaths is a difficult but important task.[1747] In the Iraq situation, the number of potential victims within the jurisdiction of the Court was – in the words of the OTP – too "different" (4 to 12 victims of willful killing and a limited number of victims of inhuman treatment) from other situations under investigation or analysis.[1748] Establishing a "killing rate" was helpful for the OTP comparing country situations like Uganda and the DRC to one specific part of the entire Iraq situation (crimes committed by British forces only). Two similar situations with converging killing numbers might yet cause serious challenges for the OTP. Moreover, methodology of the comparison seems flawed. The Prosecutor did not compare the total number of deaths in Iraq with the total in the DRC or Uganda nor did he compare the total number of deaths resulting from the crimes attributed to specific perpetrators with those blamed on the British troops in Iraq.[1749] Genocide and aggression do not necessarily need large numbers of victims, and therefore the Court cannot rely only on the number of victims.[1750] Therefore, it has been suggested by several authors to include qualitative factors, for instance, the fact that crimes are committed by individuals acting on behalf of a State,[1751] whether the crimes are part of an aggressive war,[1752] the question whether the situations involves crimes that were committed systematically, as the result of a plan or policy,[1753] and/or whether the situation involves crimes that cause "social alarm" in the international community.[1754] Instead of advertising specific factors I have chosen a more principled approach based on a mixed qualitative-quantitative assessment.[1755]

The OTP itself has – in theory – considered adopting such a mixed *qualitative-quantitative* approach. The Prosecutor had already indicated earlier that no strict limitation to killing numbers would be applied, and that he

---

[1747] Helge Brunborg – Demographer, Session 3: Needs for demographic and statistical expertise at the International Criminal Court (paper), First public hearing OTP, 25.4.2003, 2.

[1748] Iraq response, *supra* note 333, 9; critical Kindt, *supra* note 650, 147–8.

[1749] Schabas, *supra* note 1151, 747.

[1750] Schüller, *supra* note 1335, 79.

[1751] Schabas, *supra* note 1151, 747–8; Heller, in Stahn/van Herik, *supra* note 339, 237 et seq.

[1752] Schabas, *supra* note 1151, 748; Kindt, *supra* note 650, 148.

[1753] Heller, in Stahn/van Herik, *supra* note 339, 229 et seq.

[1754] Heller, in Stahn/van Herik, *supra* note 339, 233 et seq. Critical Osiel, in Stahn/van Herik, *supra* note 1743, 257.

[1755] See Part IV, B., III., 2., c), cc), (3) and (4). A mixed approach that highlights the importance of the qualitative dimension has recently been adopted by PTC I, cf. *Prosecutor v. Abu Garda,* Decision on the confirmation of charges, *supra* note 312, para. 31.

would consider the number of victims of other crimes, especially crimes against physical integrity.[1756] However, the specific terminology "qualitative and quantitative factors" was unfortunately not included in the final OTP Regulation 29, while an earlier draft version entails the phrasing. In any event, the Prosecutor must further refine his gravity approach and specify the terms he uses.

With respect to the nature of the crimes, the OTP regards all of the crimes mentioned in the Statute as crimes of concern to the international community and, as such, grave in themselves. The OTP states that crimes resulting in death are the gravest and rape is "also at the level of highest gravity."[1757] It has recently been highlighted that some crimes of particular concern include killing, rape, and child conscription.[1758]

Regarding the manner of the commission of the crimes, the OTP gives some gravity guidance: elements of particular cruelty, crimes against particularly vulnerable victims, crimes involving discrimination, abuse of *de jure* or *de facto* power (e.g. the responsibility to protect), crimes involving the abuse of power or official capacity, and, under certain circumstances, and a so-called "added factor" – if, for example, it appears that crimes were committed with the aim or consequence of increasing the vulnerability of the civilian population at large (e.g. attacks on peacekeepers).[1759] Attacks on peacekeepers will not be tolerated and are inherently grave.[1760] All the mentioned criteria are standard factors that are equally applicable to situations and cases.[1761]

As already mentioned,[1762] the OTP did not – and still has not – carefully distinguished between legal and discretionary gravity. The factors discussed above – scale, nature, manner, and impact – are linked to legal gravity, but overlap with discretionary questions to some extent. In particular, the questionable impact criterion should be included as a matter of discretionary gravity, if used at all.

1756 Statement by Luis Moreno-Ocampo: Informal meeting, *supra* note 497, 6; Schüller, *supra* note 1335, 77.

1757 McAuliffe deGuzman, *supra* note 1152, 35.

1758 Guariglia, in Stahn/Sluiter, *supra* note 1215, 214; also Seils, in Bergsmo, *supra* note 99, 57–8; Selection paper, *supra* note 99, para. 17.

1759 McAuliffe deGuzman, *supra* note 1152, 35; Guariglia, in Stahn/Sluiter, *supra* note 1215, 214.

1760 Agirre Aranburu, in Bergsmo, *supra* note 460, 150.

1761 OTP Regulation 29 (5) clarifies this with regard to cases; also El Zeidy, *supra* note 269, 43; contrary WCRO report "situation" and case selection, *supra* note 370, 4.

1762 See Part IV, B., III., 2., c), bb), (1).

*(3) Gravity and sentencing (*ad hoc *tribunals, SCSL)*

Although the *ad hoc* tribunals conducted their gravity assessment in the different context of sentencing, it is nevertheless instructive to examine their approaches with regard to the gravity concept.[1763] Thereby, it has to be noted that only general guidelines on sentencing are provided by the ICTY Statute and ICTY RPE. Judges are thus given broad discretion,[1764] and there have been calls for (international) sentencing guidelines.[1765] Nonetheless, ICTY sentencing practice does provide for some predictable and consistent legal factors.[1766] The gravity of an offence has been called the primary consideration ("litmus test") when determining the sentence.[1767] Thereby, the ICTY has taken into account the inherent gravity of the crime and the criminal conduct of the convicted person.[1768] For determining gravity, the tribunal further held it necessary to consider the nature of the crime and "the particular circumstances of the case, as well as the form and degree of participation of the accused in the crime."[1769] The ICTR has also found that the gravity of the crime and individual circumstances are the two main categories for sentencing (besides taking into account former sentencing practice).[1770] As part of the themes *gravity* and *aggravating circum-*

[1763] In the following survey, I integrated previous ideas with regard to ICTY/ ICTR sentencing case law, which were presented by HRW, policy paper article 53, *supra* note 1263, 16; WCRO report gravity, *supra* note 1057, 41; Sá Couto/Cleary, *supra* note 1614, 841 et seq.; Murphy, *supra* note 1048, 296–7; McAuliffe deGuzman, *supra* note 1152, 40 et seq.; and Nemitz, *supra* note 109, 243 et seq. Another, systematic overview of ICTY aggravating circumstances can be found in *Prosecutor v. Martić,* Trial judgment, 12.6.2007 (IT-95-11-T) para. 495.

[1764] Nemitz, *supra* note 109, 246 et seq.

[1765] Barbora Holá/Alette Smeulers/Catrien Bijlevled, "Is ICTY sentencing predictable? An empirical analysis of ICTY sentencing practice" (2009) 22 LJIL 79, 80, 96–7.

[1766] Holá/Smeulers/Bijlevled, *supra* note 1765, 96.

[1767] *Prosecutor v. Milutinović et al.,* Trial judgment, Volume 3 of 4, 26.2.2009 (IT-05-87-T) para. 1147; *Prosecutor v. Simić,* Trial judgment, Sentence, 17.10.2002 (IT-95-9/2-S) para. 37; *Prosecutor v. Deronjić,* Trial judgment, Sentence, 30.3.2004 (IT-02-61-S) para. 184; Holá/Smeulers/Bijlevled, *supra* note 1765, 81.

[1768] *Prosecutor v. Kupreskic et al., supra* note 482, para. 852; *Prosecutor v. Milutinović et al., supra* note 1767, para. 1147; *Prosecutor v. Blagojević & Jokić,* Trial judgment, 17.1.2005 (IT-02-60-T) para. 826; *Prosecutor v. Brđanin,* Trial judgment, 1.9.2004 (IT-99-36-T) para. 1094; *Prosecutor v. Limaj et al.,* Trial judgment, 30.11.2005 (IT-03-66-T) para. 724; also Nemitz, *supra* note 109, 249.

[1769] *Prosecutor v. Kupreskic et al., supra* note 482, para. 852; *Prosecutor v. Banović,* Trial judgment, Sentence, 28.10.2003 (IT-02-65/1-S) para. 37; *Prosecutor v. Češić,* Trial judgment, Sentence, 11.3.2004 (IT-95-10/1-S) para. 32; *Prosecutor v. Nikolić,* Trial judgment, Sentence, 18.12.2003 (IT-94-2-S) para. 144.

stances – which largely overlap – the *ad hoc* tribunals have considered a variety of elements, such as:

- the gravity of the offence/conduct *as such,* also referred to as the crimes' "nature"[1771] (genocide as "crime of the crimes";[1772] crimes against humanity; murder; unlawful killing; rape; etc.);[1773]
- the scale (scope and extent) of the crimes, including the number of victims killed;[1774]

1770 *Prosecutor v. Kajelijeli,* Trial judgment, 1.12.2003 (ICTR-98-44A-T) para. 946; *Prosecutor v. Ntagerura et al.,* Trial judgment, 25.2.2004 (ICTR-99-46-T) para. 814; *Prosecutor v. Kamuhanda,* Trial judgment, 22.1.2004 (ICTR-95-54A-T) para. 755; *Prosecutor v. Karera,* Trial judgment, 7.12.2007 (ICTR-01-74-T) para. 571; *Prosecutor v. Muhimana,* Trial judgment, 28.4.2005 (ICTR-95-1B-T) para. 589; *Prosecutor v. Bagosora et al.,* Trial judgment, 18.12.2008 (ICTR-98-41-T) para. 2264 ("[...] from the number and type of crimes committed to the personal circumstances of the individual").

1771 *Prosecutor v. Rugambarara,* Trial judgment, Sentence, 16.11.2007 (ICTR-00-59-T) paras. 21 et seq.; *Prosecutor v. Bralo,* Trial judgment, Sentence, 7.12.2005 (IT-95-17-S) paras. 28 et seq.

1772 It must be noted that the *ad hoc* tribunal's jurisprudence generally states that there is no legal hierarchy between the core crimes of genocide, crimes against humanity, and war crimes, see *Prosecutor v. Kayishema et al.,* Appeal judgment, 1.6.2001 (ICTR-95-1-A) para. 367. However, this is only the case *a priori,* see *Prosecutor v. Tadić,* Appeal judgment, Sentence, Separate opinion of Judge Cassese, 26.1.2000 (IT-94-1-A and A*bis*) para. 7. Cassese further argues that crimes against humanity must be regarded as being inherently of greater gravity than if the same conduct is characterized as a war crime, *ibid.,* para. 16. It is therefore submitted that the ICC can go either way. While the ICC should not treat the crimes *in abstracto* differently, the OTP can base its gravity selection on the particular conduct and the specific crime it amounts to. In sum, the nature of the crime appears to be a legally possible consideration. See further on the hierarchy of gravity Agirre Aranburu, in Bergsmo, *supra* note 460, 150; Heller, in Stahn/van Herik, *supra* note 339, 230 et seq.; Nemitz, *supra* note 109, 259 et seq.

1773 *Prosecutor v. Rutaganda,* Trial judgment, 6.12.1999 (ICTR-96-3) para. 468; *Prosecutor v. Nahimana et al., supra* note 482, para. 1096; *Prosecutor v. Ruggiu,* Trial judgment, 1.6.2000 (ICTR-97-32-I) para. 48; *Prosecutor v. Gacumbtsi,* Trial judgment, 17.6.2004 (ICTR-2001-64-T) para. 339; *Prosecutor v. Kajelijeli, supra* note 1770, paras. 956, 962; *Prosecutor v. Kambanda,* Trial judgment, 4.9.1998 (ICTR-97-23-S) para. 33; *Prosecutor v. Muhimana, supra* note 1770, para. 603; *Prosecutor v. Musema,* Trial judgment, 27.1.2000 (ICTR-96-13-A) paras. 980, 1001; *Prosecutor v. Ndindabahizi,* Trial judgment, 15.7.2004 (ICTR-2001-71-I) para. 499; *Prosecutor v. Bikindi,* Trial judgment, 2.12.2008 (ICTR-01-72-T) para. 448; *Prosecutor v. Zigiranyirazo,* Trial judgment, 18.12.2008 (ICTR-01-73-T) paras. 452 et seq.; also Nemitz, *supra* note 109, 249–50.

1774 *Prosecutor v. Blaškić,* Trial judgment, 3.3.2000 (IT-95-14) para. 784; *Prosecutor v. Milutinović et al., supra* note 1767, para. 1147; *Prosecutor v. Blagojević & Jokić, supra* note 1768, para. 841; *Prosecutor v. Bisengimana,* Trial judgment, 13.4.2006 (ICTR-00-60-T) para. 202; *Prosecutor v. Zelenović,* Trial judgment, Sen-

- the sustainability and systematicity of the conduct;[1775]
- the repetitious and continuing nature of most crimes;[1776]
- the amount of premeditation or planning;[1777]
- the ramifications to (impact on) the victims (e.g. the extent of physical and psychological suffering; effect of the crimes of relatives and victims friends);[1778]
- the particular vulnerability of victims (civilians, women, children or handicapped);[1779]

---

tence, 4.4.2007 (IT-96-23/2-S) para. 38; *Prosecutor v. Deronjić, supra* note 1767, paras. 186, 222; *Prosecutor v. Plavšić,* Trial judgment, 27.2.2003 (IT-00-39&40/1) para. 52 (mentioning also "the grossly inhumane treatment of detainees" and "the scope of the wanton destruction of property and religious buildings"); *Prosecutor v. Semanza,* Trial judgment, 15.3.2003 (ICTR-97-20) para. 571 ("[...] the number of victims may be an aggravating factor in relation to genocide, a crime with no numeric minimum of victims"); *Prosecutor v. Karera, supra* note 1770, para. 575; *Prosecutor v. Krstić,* Trial judgment, 2.8.2001 (IT-98-33) para. 702; *Prosecutor v. Kordić,* Trial judgment, 26.2.2001 (IT-95-14/2-T) para. 852; *Prosecutor v. Janković,* Decision on referral of case under rule 11*bis,* 22.7.2005 (IT-96-23/2-PT) para. 19; *Prosecutor v. Hadžihasanović & Kubura,* Trial judgment, 15.3.2006 (IT-01-47-T) para. 2083; *Prosecutor v. Ljubičić,* Decision to refer the case to Bosnia & Herzegovina pursuant to rule 11*bis,* 12.4.2006 (IT-00-41-PT) para. 18 ("limited in geographic scope and temporal frame"); *Prosecutor v. Ademi & Norac,* Decision for referral to the authorities of the Republic of Croatia pursuant to rule 11*bis,* 14.9.2005 (IT-04-78-PT) paras. 19, 28.

1775 *Prosecutor v. Blaškić, supra* note 1774, para. 784; *Prosecutor v. Brđanin, supra* note 1768, para. 1112; *Prosecutor v. Akayesu,* Trial judgment, Sentence, 2.10.1998 (ICTR-96-4-T) 4. ("[h]is criminal conduct was sustained and systematic and lasted for almost three months becoming ever more intensive").

1776 *Prosecutor v. Kvočka et al.,* Trial judgment, 2.11.2001 (IT-98-30/1) para. 702.

1777 *Prosecutor v. Krstić, supra* note 1774, para. 711–2; *Prosecutor v. Milutinović et al., supra* note 1767, para. 1151; *Prosecutor v. Akayesu, supra* note 1775, 3; *Prosecutor v. Kvočka et al., supra* note 1776, para. 705; *Prosecutor v. Blaškić, supra* note 1774, para. 793.

1778 *Prosecutor v. Krstić, supra* note 1774, para. 703; *Prosecutor v. Deronjić, supra* note 1767, paras. 210 et seq.; *Prosecutor v. Simić, supra* note 1767, paras. 68 et seq.; *Prosecutor v. Bralo, supra* note 1771, paras. 36 et seq.; *Prosecutor v. Krnojelac,* Trial judgment, 15.3.2002 (IT-97-25) para. 512 ("physical, psychological and emotional suffering of the immediate victims"); *Prosecutor v. Kvočka et al., supra* note 1776, para. 702; *Prosecutor v. Blaškić, supra* note 1774, para. 787; *Prosecutor v. Milutinović et al., supra* note 1767, para. 1147; *Prosecutor v. Češić, supra* note 1769, paras. 38 et seq., 54.

1779 *Prosecutor v. Blaškić, supra* note 1774, para. 786; *Prosecutor v. Deronjić, supra* note 1767, paras. 207 et seq., *Prosecutor v. Plavšić, supra* note 1774, para. 58; *Prosecutor v. Krstić, supra* note 1774, para. 702; *Prosecutor v. Blagojević & Jokić, supra* note 1768, para. 844; *Prosecutor v. Brđanin, supra* note 1768, paras.

- sexual violence (rape);[1780]
- the discriminatory nature of the crime (persecution);[1781]
- manner in which the crime was carried out (torture; cruelty; heinous means and methods used to commit the crimes; humiliation; zealousness; premeditation);[1782]
- the superior position of the accused (level of authority; the abuse of his or her position);[1783]

1104 et seq.; *Prosecutor v. Zelenović, supra* note 1774, para. 39; *Prosecutor v. Kunarac et al.,* Trial judgment, 22.2.2001 (IT-96-23 & 23/1) para. 864 ("youthful age of certain of the victims"); *Prosecutor v. Muhimana, supra* note 1770, para. 607; *Prosecutor v. Niyitegeka,* Trial judgment, 16.5.2003 (ICTR-96-14-T) para. 499; *Prosecutor v. Rutaganira,* Trial judgment, 14.3.2005 (ICTR-95-1C-T) para. 143; *Prosecutor v. Obrenović,* Trial judgment, Sentence, 10.12.2003 (IT-02-60/2-S) paras. 102–3.

1780 *Prosecutor v. Kvočka et al., supra* note 1776, para. 702; *Prosecutor v. Blagojević & Jokić, supra* note 1768, para. 834; *Prosecutor v. Furundžija,* Trial judgment, 10.12.1998 (IT-95-17/1-T) paras. 282–3; *Prosecutor v. Gacumbtsi, supra* note 1773, para. 345; *Prosecutor v. Muhimana, supra* note 1770, para. 606; *Prosecutor v. Musema, supra* note 1773, para. 1008.

1781 *Prosecutor v. Kvočka et al., supra* note 1776, para. 702; *Prosecutor v. Blaškić, supra* note 1774, para. 784; *Prosecutor v. Milutinović et al., supra* note 1767, para. 1151; *Prosecutor v. Simić, supra* note 1767, para. 77; *Prosecutor v. Obrenović, supra* note 1779, para. 65; *Prosecutor v. Todorović,* Trial judgment, sentence, 31.7.2001 (IT-95-9/1-S) para. 32; *Prosecutor v. Vasiljević,* Trial judgment, 29.11.2002 (IT-98-32-T) para. 278.

1782 *Prosecutor v. Krstić, supra* note 1774, para. 703; *Prosecutor v. Nikolić, supra* note 1769, para. 186 et seq.; *Prosecutor v. Simić, supra* note 1767, paras. 60 et seq.; *Prosecutor v. Karera, supra* note 1770, para. 580 ("attacking a place of safe haven such as a church, constitutes a form of zeal"); *Prosecutor v. Muhimana, supra* note 1770, para. 613; *Prosecutor v. Kayishema et al.,* Trial judgment, Sentence, 21.5.1999 (ICTR-95-1-T) para. 18; *Prosecutor v. Kvočka et al., supra* note 1776, para. 702; *Prosecutor v. Blaškić, supra* note 1774, para. 783; *Prosecutor v. Milutinović et al., supra* note 1767, para. 1151; *Prosecutor v. Niyitegeka, supra* note 1779, paras. 486, 495, 499; *Prosecutor v. Ntakirutimana,* Trial judgment, 21.2.2003 (ICTR-96-10 & ICTR-96-17-T) para. 912; *Prosecutor v. Nchamihigo,* Trial judgment, 12.11.2008 (ICTR-01-63-T) para. 388; *Prosecutor v. Jelisić,* Trial judgment, 14.12.1999 (IT-95-10-T) para. 130: "The Trial Chamber points out the repugnant, bestial and sadistic nature of Goran Jelisić's behavior. His cold-blooded commission of murders and mistreatment of people attest to a profound contempt for mankind and the right to life."

1783 *Prosecutor v. Galić,* Trial judgment, 5.12.2003 (IT-98-29-T) para. 765; *Prosecutor v. Jokić,* Trial judgment, 18.3.2004 (IT-01-42/1-S) paras. 61–2; *Prosecutor v. Plavšić, supra* note 1774, para. 57; *Prosecutor v. Milutinović et al., supra* note 1767, paras. 1147, 1151; *Prosecutor v. Brđanin, supra* note 1768, para. 1099; *Prosecutor v. Blaškić, supra* note 1774, paras. 788–9; *Prosecutor v. Banović, supra* note 1769, para. 55; *Prosecutor v. Obrenović, supra* note 1779, para. 99; *Prosecutor v. Deronjić, supra* note 1767, paras. 187 et seq., 222; *Prosecutor v. Bagosora et al.,*

- the influence and relative importance of the accused in his or her community;[1784]
- the role of the accused in the commission of the offences;[1785]
- the motive of the crime (particularly flagrant; ethnic and religious persecution; desire for revenge; sadism);[1786]
- the form of participation (direct or secondary forms of participation; informed and voluntary); this criterion is related to the already mentioned "role of the accused" and partly overlaps.[1787]

---

supra note 1770, paras. 2265, 2272; *Prosecutor v. Karera, supra* note 1770, para. 577; *Prosecutor v. Serushago,* Trial judgment, Sentence, 5.2.1999 (ICTR-98-39) para. 29; *Prosecutor v. Bisengimana, supra* note 1774, para. 202; *Prosecutor v. Akayesu, supra* note 1775, 1. and 2; *Prosecutor v. Rutaganda, supra* note 1773, paras. 469–70; *Prosecutor v. Simba,* Trial judgment, 13.12.2005 (ICTR-01-76-T) paras. 435, 439; *Prosecutor v. Ndindabahizi, supra* note 1773, para. 508; *Prosecutor v. Niyitegeka, supra* note 1779, para. 499; *Prosecutor v. Serugendo,* Trial judgment, 12.6.2006 (ICTR-2005-84-I) paras. 48–9; *Prosecutor v. Mucić et al. (Čelebići Camp)*, Trial judgment, Sentence, 9.10.2001 (IT- 96-21-T*bis*-R117) para. 9; *Prosecutor v. Simić, supra* note 1767, para. 66; *Prosecutor v. Babić,* Trial judgment, Sentence, 29.6.2004 (IT-03-72-S) paras. 61–2; *Prosecutor v. Sikirica et al.*, Trial judgment, Sentence, 13.11.2001 (IT-95-8-S) para. 172; *Prosecutor v. Stakić,* Trial judgment, 31.7.2003 (IT-97-24-T) para. 912; *Prosecutor v. Aleksovski,* Trial judgment, 25.6.1999 (IT-95-14/1-T) para. 236 ("secondary role"). *Prosecutor v. Nchamihigo, supra* note 1782, para. 388 with fn. 235, further points out that life sentences have been imposed against senior government authorities such as *Ndindabahazi* (Minister of Finance), *Niyitegeka* (Minister of Information), *Kambanda* (Prime Minister), and *Kamuhanda* (Minister of Higher Education and Scientific Research), notwithstanding some life sentences for others without government positions as well.

1784 *Prosecutor v. Semanza, supra* note 1774, para. 573; *Prosecutor v. Nahimana et al., supra* note 482, paras. 1098 et seq.; *Prosecutor v. Serushago, supra* note 1779, para. 28; *Prosecutor v. Gacumbtsi, supra* note 1773, para. 345; *Prosecutor v. Kamuhanda, supra* note 1770, para. 764; *Prosecutor v. Karera, supra* note 1770, para. 578; *Prosecutor v. Ndindabahizi, supra* note 1773, para. 508; *Prosecutor v. Muhimana, supra* note 1770, para. 604; *Prosecutor v. Niyitegeka, supra* note 1779, para. 499; *Prosecutor v. Krstić, supra* note 1774, para. 709; *Prosecutor v. Ntakirutimana, supra* note 1782, paras. 900, 910; *Prosecutor v. Nzabirinda,* Trial judgment, 23.2.2007 (ICTR-2001-77-T) para. 107; *Prosecutor v. Seromba,* Trial judgment, 13.12.2006 (ICTR-2001-66-I) para. 390.

1785 *Prosecutor v. Ruggiu, supra* note 1773, paras. 49 et seq.; *Prosecutor v. Ljubičić, supra* note 1774, para. 15; *Prosecutor v. Simba, supra* note 1783, para. 435; *Prosecutor v. Mucić et al. (Čelebići Camp), supra* note 1783, para. 19.

1786 *Prosecutor v. Blaškić, supra* note 1774, para. 785; *Prosecutor v. Simba, supra* note 1783, para. 435.

1787 *Prosecutor v. Blaškić, supra* note 1774, para. 792; *Prosecutor v. Aleksovski, supra* note 1783, para. 236; *Prosecutor v. Simić, supra* note 1767, para. 61; *Prosecutor v. Strugar,* Trial judgment, 31.1.2005 (IT-01-42-T) para. 462; *Prosecutor v. Bisengimana, supra* note 1774, para. 199; *Prosecutor v. Gacumbtsi, supra* note 1773, para. 344–5; *Prosecutor v. Kajelijeli, supra* note 1770, paras. 953, 962.

According to an empirical study, the most frequent factors of the enumerated ones were (1) abuse of superior position/position of authority or trust (accepted in 35 cases); (2) special vulnerability of victims (accepted in 31 cases); (3) extreme suffering or harm inflicted on victims (accepted in 25 cases); (4) large number of victims (accepted in 15 cases); and (5) cruelty of the attack (accepted in 14 cases).[1788] Similar to the *ad hoc* tribunals, the SCSL takes into account factors such as the gravity of the offence ("litmus test") and the individual circumstances of the convicted person.[1789] In the *AFRC* sentencing judgment the gravity determination was designated as an individual assessment, which includes *inter alia*:

- the general nature of the underlying criminal conduct;
- the form and degree of participation of the accused or the specific role played by the accused in the commission of the crime;
- the degree of suffering, impact or consequences of the crime for the immediate victim in terms of physical, emotional and psychological effects;
- the effects of the crime on relatives of the immediate victims and/or the broader targeted group;
- the vulnerability of victims;
- the number of victims.[1790]

The *CDF* and *RUF* sentencing judgments mention the following factors for gravity of the offence:

- the scale and brutality of the offences committed;
- the role played by the accused in their commission (mode of liability; superior position[1791]);
- the degree of suffering or impact of the crime on the immediate victim as well as its effect on relatives;
- the vulnerability of victims;
- the number of victims.[1792]

1788 Holá/Smeulers/Bijlevled, *supra* note 1765, 86.

1789 *Prosecutor v. Brima, Kamara and Kanu (AFRC trial),* Sentencing judgment, 19.7.2007 (SCSL-04-16-T) para. 11; *Prosecutor v. Fofana and Kondawa (CDF trial),* Judgment on the sentencing of Moinina Fofana and Allieu Kondawa, 9.10.2007 (SCSL-04-14-T) para. 33; *Prosecutor v. Sesay, Kallon and Gbao (RUF trial),* Sentencing judgment, 8.4.2009 (SCSL-04-15-T) para. 17.

1790 *Prosecutor v. Brima, Kamara and Kanu (AFRC trial),* Sentencing judgment, *supra* note 1789, para. 19.

1791 *Prosecutor v. Sesay, Kallon and Gbao (RUF trial),* Sentencing judgment, *supra* note 1789, paras. 20–1.

It is worth noting that the recent *RUF* judgment specifically includes crimes against UN personnel and child soldiers as being inherently grave.[1793]

All in all, the SCSL's Trial Chambers relied heavily on ICTY and ICTR jurisprudence. The Chambers further state that gravity and aggravating factors may overlap and they have been considered together in the practice of some Trial Chambers. In any event, the various factors cannot be taken into account twice if gravity and aggravating factors are assessed separately.[1794] Aggravating circumstances – which are partly the same as the gravity criteria – were identified as:

- the leadership role of the accused;
- premeditation and motive;
- a willing and enthusiastic participation in the crime;
- the length of time during which the crime was committed.[1795]

In addition to these four factors, the Trial Chamber mentions in the *AFRC* case:

- the discriminatory intent of state of mind for crimes for which such a state of mind is not an element or ingredient of the crime;
- active and direct criminal participation, if linked to a high-rank position of command, the accused's role as fellow perpetrator, and the active participation of a superior in the criminal acts of subordinates;
- the sexual, violent, and humiliating nature of the acts and the vulnerability of the victims;
- the status of the victims, their youthful age and number, and the effect of the crime of them;
- the character of the accused;
- the circumstances of the offences generally.[1796]

[1792] *Prosecutor v. Fofana and Kondawa (CDF trial),* Judgment on the sentencing, *supra* note 1789, para. 33; *Prosecutor v. Sesay, Kallon and Gbao (RUF trial),* Sentencing judgment, *supra* note 1789, paras. 19, 107 et seq.

[1793] *Prosecutor v. Sesay, Kallon and Gbao (RUF trial),* Sentencing judgment, *supra* note 1789, paras. 179 et seq., 188 et seq., 204.

[1794] *Prosecutor v. Brima, Kamara and Kanu (AFRC trial),* Sentencing judgment, *supra* note 1789, para. 23; *Prosecutor v. Fofana and Kondawa (CDF trial),* Judgment on the sentencing, *supra* note 1789, para. 35; *Prosecutor v. Sesay, Kallon and Gbao (RUF trial),* Sentencing judgment, *supra* note 1789, paras. 23, 103; also *Prosecutor v. Krnojelac, supra* note 1778, para. 517.

[1795] *Prosecutor v. Fofana and Kondawa (CDF trial),* Judgment on the sentencing, *supra* note 1789, para. 37.

It is most interesting to note that the ICTY Chamber has stressed in the *Krstić* case that it

> "[...] must assess the seriousness of the crimes in the light of their *individual circumstances and consequences*. This presupposes taking into account *quantitatively* the number of victims and *qualitatively* the suffering inflicted on the victims. (emph. added)."[1797]

All mentioned factors are not exhaustive, but provide guidance. Rather than looking at all the – partly overlapping – factors that ICTY, ICTR and SCSL case law have generated, it is most important to summarize the main ideas. First and foremost, the *ad hoc* tribunals took a *case-specific approach* and considered *quantitative* and *qualitative* factors equally. No particular weight was given to the elements, and they varied quite noticeably from case to case. Moreover, there was apparently not one stringent approach with an all-embracing structure. It would therefore be important to group the various factors mentioned into main categories. In the *Blaškić* case the Chamber started a similar arrangement into groups. It arrived at the "scope of the crime" embracing the sub-categories "how the crime was committed" and "effects of the crimes upon victims," as well as the "degree of the accused's responsibility" embracing the sub-categories "command position," "form of participation," and "premeditation."[1798] *Mrđa et al.* even mentions four distinct groups for gravity similar to the ones the ICC-OTP uses in its categorization:

> "In determining the gravity of the crimes, the Trial Chamber will give consideration to the legal *nature* of the offences committed, their *scale*, the *role* Darko Mrđa played in their commission and the *impact* upon the victims and their families (emph. added)."[1799]

Orić refers to the nature, scale, brutality (manner of commission), and impact/extent, yet omits the role of the accused, which is an improved approach towards gravity since "role" comes very close to the separate notion of individual circumstances:

> "In determining the gravity of the subordinates' crimes, the Trial Chamber has reached the conclusion that the legal *nature* of these offences, their *scale* and *brutality*, their *impact* upon the victims and their families and the *extent* of the long-term physical, psychological, and emotional suffering of the survivors are to be considered as factors subsumed in the notion of gravity itself. In this exercise, the

---

1796 *Prosecutor v. Brima, Kamara and Kanu (AFRC trial),* Sentencing judgment, *supra* note 1789, para. 21. For the *RUF* case see *Prosecutor v. Sesay, Kallon and Gbao (RUF trial),* Sentencing judgment, *supra* note 1789, paras. 25–6.

1797 *Prosecutor v. Krstić, supra* note 1774, para. 701; also *Prosecutor v. Kvočka et al., supra* note 1776, para. 701.

1798 *Prosecutor v. Blaškić, supra* note 1774, paras. 783 et seq.

1799 *Prosecutor v. Mrđa et al.,* Trial judgment, 31.3.2004 (IT-02-59-S) para. 21; also *Prosecutor v. Rajić,* Trial judgment, 8.5.2006 (IT-95-12-S) paras. 82 et seq.

Trial Chamber has been mindful that factors taken into account as aspects of the gravity of the crime cannot additionally be considered as separate aggravating circumstances and *vice versa* (emph. added; fn. omitted)."[1800]

One might therefore distinguish two main areas at the outset: the gravity of the crimes, which involves some of the factors mentioned above (such as scale, systematicity, continuing nature, genocide and rape, discriminatory nature, vulnerability of victims, manner of commission, and effects on victims), and the individual circumstances of the accused (such as planning, form of participation, motive, and position and role).

In sum, the recent approach by the ICC-OTP is convincing insofar as it shows a systematic structure and names four sub-categories of gravity. The four notions of scale, nature, manner of commission, and impact embrace most of the mentioned factors by the ICTY, ICTR, and SCLS. The second category of individual circumstances is closely linked to the perpetrator; it involves far more subjective considerations in comparison to assessing a crime's gravity, although gravity of the crime and individual circumstances might overlap in practice. For instance, the manner of commission contains both, subjective and objective elements: How did the perpetrator subjectively execute the crime (brutal, humiliating, or zealous)? Were the crimes objectively brutal and did they involve vulnerable victims? Nevertheless, the particular circumstances of the accused are part of article 53 (2) (c), which explicitly mentions the role of the perpetrator in the alleged crime. Thus, subjective considerations must be left aside when legal gravity is looked at. Particular circumstances are clearly a matter of the "interests of justice," and are as such part of the weighing process under article 53 (2) (c).[1801] In this regard, one can learn from the *ad hoc* tribunals that have continuously struggled to distinguish gravity and aggravating circumstances.

(4) Recommendation regarding the legal gravity criteria

Gravity under article 17 (1) (d) has to be understood as a legal threshold and legal criteria should be used to give the standard more substance. The difficult task to develop such criteria was deliberately left to the ICC's actors. PTC I elaborated three criteria, which are not of great help to the determination of legal gravity.[1802] Correctly, the Appeals Chamber rejected the PTC's gravity test and revoked the application to the *Ntaganda* case. In

1800 *Prosecutor v. Orić,* Trial judgment, 30.6.2006 (IT-03-68-T) para. 729.

1801 See further Part IV, C., IV., 2. and 4.

1802 Coming to the same result, Schüller, *supra* note 1335, 80; Schabas, *supra* note 1151, 743; critical also the Defence in *Prosecutor v. Bemba*, Decision on the admissibility, *supra* note 280, para 98, 35 ("Court's jurisprudence has failed to establish criteria").

particular, the social alarm criterion is vague and does not provide any assistance.[1803] Moreover, focusing only on senior leaders as a legality criterion is not supported by statutory interpretation, and indeed brings about severe problems if strictly applied.[1804] Last but not least, "systematic" and "scale" fits better than the criteria "social alarm" or "senior leaders." However, the PTC goes too far in "requiring" systematic or large-scale commission in every case.[1805] On the large-scale commission, the Prosecutor turned to article 8 for guidance.[1806] But the ICC Statute rather gives thematic guidelines than absolute limitations.[1807] Thus, the criterion scale can be used as guidance for gravity, but it is not a *sine qua non* criterion. Otherwise, it would improperly modify the Court's carefully drafted subject-matter jurisdiction.[1808] In the past, both the PTC and the OTP have used gravity in inconsistent ways.[1809] Moreover, neither the ICC actors nor academics have found a suitable solution for the gravity issue because they did not lay the proper groundwork first. Before starting a debate on the numerous possible factors, a systematic approach towards the general application of gravity is necessary.

Most recently, OTP Regulation 29 (2) heads into the right direction by trying to strike a balance between the Office's practice and PTC I's approach. Taking into consideration various factors, including the scale, the nature, the manner of commission, and the impact of the crimes (the last factor is debatable), the Prosecutor found a useful general phrasing for the gravity test. In the context of Kenya, PTC II submitted a similar examination of gravity which involves an analysis of:

(i) whether the persons or groups of persons that are likely to be the object of an investigation include those *who may bear the greatest responsibility* for the alleged crimes committed; and

---

1803 Schüller, *supra* note 1335, 80–1; McAuliffe deGuzman, *supra* note 1152, 36; WCRO report gravity, *supra* note 1057, 5, 39; El Zeidy, *supra* note 269, 45 ("weird novelty"); *Situation in DRC,* Judgment on the Prosecutor's appeal against the decision of Pre-Trial Chamber I, *supra* note 1360, Separate and partly dissenting opinion of Judge Georghios M. Pikis, para. 34. Critical also Osiel, *supra* note 1617, 6. Contrary and in favor of "social alarm" Heller, in Stahn/van Herik, *supra* note 339, 233 et seq.

1804 Schüller, *supra* note 1335, 80; Smith, *supra* note 210, 340. Further Part IV, C., IV., 4., b).

1805 WCRO report gravity, *supra* note 1057, 5–6.

1806 Schüller, *supra* note 1335, 79.

1807 Galvin, *supra* note 1332, 18.

1808 McAuliffe deGuzman, *supra* note 1152, 36.

1809 William Schabas/Carsten Stahn/Mohamed El Zeidy, "The International Criminal Court and Complementarity: five years on" (2008) 19 CLF 1, 1; Clark, in Waddell/Clark, *supra* note 1640, 39.

(ii) the gravity of the crimes allegedly committed within the incidents, which are likely to be the object of an investigation. In relation to the latter, the Chamber stated earlier that it is guided by factors such as the *scale, nature, manner of commission, impact of crimes committed on victims and the existence of aggravating circumstances* (i.e. qualitative dimension).[1810]

What needs further fine-tuning is the difference between legal and relative (discretionary) gravity, which the OTP and PTC II again did not distinguish clearly. As a follow-up question, the exact content of the factors (scale, nature, manner of commission, and impact) has to be determined. Impact should be considered under the relative gravity assessment. The outlined ICTY, ICTR, and SCSL jurisprudence is meant to provide some categories that could be incorporated. Moreover, the ICC's own rules provide further guidance (equally with regard to sentencing) in rule 145 (1) (c) and (2) (b), which might very well be taken into account.[1811] If a qualitative and quantitative approach is adopted, another open question is the particular weight given to the factors. Any weighing of qualitative factors will be controversial.[1812] Once again, one must distinguish more precisely between legal and relative gravity. For the legal assessment, primarily quantitative factors should be included. Furthermore, the threshold for the legal test should not be very high. First of all, the drafting history supports this assumption. Legal gravity was originally conceived as an additional threshold for the exercise of jurisdiction. In contrast, the final Statute was limited to core crimes. Genocide and crimes against humanity already require a very high level of gravity. It has been correctly argued that the gravity threshold pertains mainly to war crimes.[1813] It could further play a role for crimes against humanity[1814] as well as for the crime of aggression. However, there is a strong presumption that genocide cases always satisfy the gravity threshold.[1815]

[1810] *Situation in Kenya*, Decision pursuant to article 15, *supra* note 6, para. 188, 73.

[1811] Stigen, *supra* note 205, 362–3; Agirre Aranburu, in Bergsmo, *supra* note 460, 155–6; most recently, *Prosecutor v. Abu Garda,* Decision on the confirmation of charges, *supra* note 312, para. 32; *Situation in Kenya*, Decision pursuant to article 15, *supra* note 6, para. 62, 27.

[1812] Osiel, *supra* note 1617, 4–5; *id.,* in Stahn/van Herik, *supra* note 1743, 256. A mechanical formula must be avoided, see *ibid,* at 256, since it introduces more rigidity into the case-selection process that anyone would want.

[1813] McAuliffe deGuzman, *supra* note 1152, 45. See also Part IV, B., III., 1., b).

[1814] Agirre Aranburu, in Bergsmo, *supra* note 460, 149 ("some crimes against humanity may be more 'widespread' than others").

[1815] In the same vein recently, see Kindt, *supra* note 650, 146.

To give examples for all four categories of crimes, and starting with war crimes, a very isolated war crime under article 8 (2) (iv), such as extensive destruction of property, that does not fulfill the requirement of "plan or policy or as part of a large-scale commission" would not pass legal gravity. With respect to crimes against humanity, one can hypothetically imagine the imprisonment (article 7 (1) (e)) of political opponents during a certain short period, during elections for instance, and their subsequent release. Compared to murder, torture, rape, etc., the inherent discrepancy of the acts enumerated in article 7 (1) becomes apparent. Thus, torture and rape, even if low in numbers, could possibly break the legal gravity barrier. Whether or not the ICC adopts such a hierarchy with regard to the core crimes and their defined acts is a matter of debate, but it remains legally possible.[1816]

Coming to the crime of aggression, the threshold of aggression could possibly be answered in the affirmative in the case of unauthorized humanitarian interventions. Gravity might provide an additional legal filter for borderline aggression cases, in particular those justified by self-defence under article 51 of the UN Charter.

Genocide cases will almost never fail the gravity threshold. I would even go as far as excluding them from the primarily quantitative assessment and allow for a qualitative assessment that excludes genocide cases from the legal gravity threshold. To take it to extremes, there could be an attempted genocide if State authorities already plan and arrange for its implementation, but UN forces intervene, for instance. In this (highly hypothetical) case, there would be very low numbers of killings, if any at all, but the envisaged crime is so grave that it would certainly fulfill the legal gravity threshold.

In sum, all given examples are speculative, and outline very uncommon events, but leave a certain ambit for the application of legal gravity. In particular, war crimes and aggression might require an additional gravity check. In any event, case law must further show which situations and cases fall below the legal gravity barrier.

With regard to relative gravity, quantitative and qualitative factors may be taken into account equally. The justification for a broader approach lies in article 53 (1) (c), namely the "interests of justice," and the wider margin of discretion on behalf of the Prosecutor. The OTP is further able to undertake a comparable gravity assessment under the "interests of justice" clause,[1817] and a proportionality test seems most operable for analyzing "relative" (discretionary) gravity.[1818]

[1816] See Part IV, B., III., 1., b) and Part IV, B., III., 2., c), cc), (3) with fn. 1772.

[1817] In more detail Part IV, B., III., 3., d), aa).

dd) Conclusion: Interpretation and criteria for legal and relative gravity

Gravity is a central criterion under the ICC Statute. It has been demonstrated that gravity involves different levels. Indeed, gravity can be summarized as embracing four distinct layers. First, gravity amounts to double gravity in the sense as being applied to situations and cases respectively. More important, there is a concept of a "gravity threshold" *versus* "relative gravity." As a refinement of the two standards, it has been submitted to link these two distinct gravity notions to articles 53 (1) (b), (2) (b), 17 (1) (d), and 53 (1) (c), (2) (c). Therefore, gravity has to be considered four times in a different manner:

- *legal* gravity with regard to *situations* pursuant to articles 53 (1) (b), 17 (1) (d);
- *relative* gravity with regard to *situations* under the "interests of justice" concept pursuant to article 53 (1) (c);
- *legal* gravity with regard to *cases* pursuant to articles 53 (2) (b), 17 (1) (d);
- *relative* gravity with regard to *cases* under the "interests of justice" concept pursuant to article 53 (2) (c).

It is therefore not the complementarity regime that governs (relative) situation and case selection, but the overarching "interests of justice" clause.[1819]

It remains to be clarified what the main difference between the four notions is and which factors and thresholds apply. Starting with situation-related gravity, the thresholds under articles 53 (1) (b), 17 (1) (d) and article 53 (1) (c) differ significantly. In contrast to the suggested low threshold with regard to legal gravity, the relative gravity threshold is conducted on a higher level of gravity.[1820] The same applies with regard to case-related gravity under articles 53 (2) (b), 17 (1) (d) and 53 (2) (c) respectively. The legal gravity threshold regarding cases should be low, whereas the relative case selection must operate on a high level of gravity given the enormous number of potential cases. In this regard, the Prosecutor's early policy conflated gravity as an admissibility threshold and as a relative discretionary consideration must be recalled, as well as the PTC's adoption of an overly rigid gravity threshold that amounts to an amendment of the ICC's personal and subject matter jurisdiction.[1821] For this reason, the Appeals Chamber

[1818] Further Part IV, B., III., 3., b).

[1819] Contrary, Clark, in Waddell/Clark, *supra* note 1640, 37.

[1820] McAuliffe deGuzman, *supra* note 1152, 45.

[1821] McAuliffe deGuzman, *supra* note 1152, 30.

nullified the PTC's test. The Prosecutor now has to clarify when he is rejecting a case based on gravity for admissibility reasons, and when he is prioritizing situations or cases based on relative gravity.[1822]

The remaining question is whether gravity for situations and cases is basically the same, or whether the criteria and the threshold must consequently be more specific for cases than for situations. With regard to legal, situation-related and case-related gravity the same minimum threshold should apply. Only the grounds are distinct: in the first scenario, the crimes of the overall situation are evaluated;[1823] in the second scenario, just the crimes within the specific case can be evaluated. The latter is thus narrower than the former, and therefore an additional gravity analysis must take place. With regard to relative, situation-related and case-related gravity the threshold supposedly ascends. The potential case numbers are so high that a stricter selection process is inevitable. Therefore, the relative case selection threshold and its criteria are most rigorous.

Nevertheless, the OTP should primarily look at quantitative factors – those being the most reliable parameters – as the starting point for all four gravity checks. All included quantitative elements must pertain to the crimes rather than the individual. It is submitted that, for the legal gravity assessment under articles 53 (1) (b) and 17 (1) (d), this quantitative approach, combined with a low threshold, would be sufficient and most appropriate for checking situations. In addition, certain (qualitative) exceptions that "jump" legal gravity could be developed by the Judges. In this regard, there is a strong presumption that genocide cases are so inherently grave that legal gravity can hardly be denied. As has been shown above, legal gravity is solely a preliminary filter, mainly for war crimes, some crimes against humanity, and potentially the crime of aggression.

Regarding the relative gravity of situations *vis-à-vis* its legal assessment, the important distinction is an additional inclusion of qualitative factors and a comparison to all – pending and potential – situations before the

---

[1822] McAuliffe deGuzman, *supra* note 1152, 34.

[1823] Contrary, *Situation in Kenya*, Decision pursuant to article 15, *supra* note 6, paras. 188–9, 73–4. PTC II states that the examination under articles 53 (1) (b), 17 (d) must be conducted against the backdrop of potential cases within a situation. This approach resembles the adopted complementarity assessment (cf. Part IV, B., III., 2., b), aa)). However, while an examination of complementarity of a whole situation is hardly feasible, the gravity of overall situations can be compared, cf. Part IV, B., III., 3., d), aa). In the alternative, if the Court follows PTC II's approach, my basic concept of four different gravity layers could equally be applied to a bundle of potential cases. More important is the differentiation article 53 (1) (b) – article 53 (1) (c) – article 53 (2) (b) – article 53 (2) (c), which PTC II did not take into consideration. It one adoptes PTC II 's approach, the "situational" gravity under article 53 (1) would refer to "potential cases" as its objects (instead of a "situation").

Court.[1824] This approach decisively alters the gravity test, which now amounts to a higher "situational" gravity threshold. Article 53 (1) (c) gives the Prosecutor this comparative tool for prosecutorial situation selection.

For cases, the procedure is even more complicated. Legal gravity – bearing once more in mind the case law in *Lubanga/Ntaganda* – cannot be limited to the senior leaders only. In addition, the question remains whether the circumstances of the accused should be looked at as a relative case selection criterion pursuant to article 53 (2) (c), or whether some individual circumstances should already be included in the legal gravity assessment pursuant to articles 53 (2) (b) and 17 (1) (d). The Appeals Chamber did not provide an answer in this respect, and the individualization process from article 53 (1) (b) to article 53 (2) (b) favors an inclusion of individual circumstances for legal gravity. On the other hand, article 53 (2) (c) explicitly refers to the individual circumstances (age or infirmity of the alleged perpetrator and role in the alleged crime) in the context of relative gravity. Furthermore, it has been stated that the legal gravity barrier should not be too high. The latter approach is therefore preferable, and the factors for legal, case-related gravity are primarily the crime related quantitative factors. These quantitative elements need to be applied to the limited case scenario under articles 53 (2) (b) and 17 (1) (d), which varies the test *vis-à-vis* legal situation selection. Last but not least, the elements for relative case selection combine four previously mentioned aspects: first, they include the quantitative criteria related to the crimes in question; second, they allow for qualitative considerations; third, they contain the individual circumstances of the perpetrator (such as the mentioned factors age, infirmity, or role[1825]); and fourth, they allow for an additional comparison to all pending and potential cases before the Court. In sum, the relative gravity for case selection gives the Prosecutor the broadest margin of discretion under the ICC Statute, yet only in the framework of article 53 (2) (c). In other words, the "interests of justice" significantly nuances the case-related gravity.

In conclusion, the legal gravity threshold is a low barrier to the ICC's exercise of jurisdiction that mainly precludes the Court from adjudicating situations and cases of isolated, small-scale war crimes. This test is limited to the objective gravity of the crimes and should primarily embrace quantitative factors. On the other hand, the Prosecutor's relative gravity policy aims

[1824] In more detail Part IV, B., III., 3., d), aa).

[1825] Presumably, the role in the alleged crime is a wide notion and could include the position of the accused, the relative importance of the accused in his or her community, the form of participation, premeditation or planning, the accused's motive, and the manner of commission.

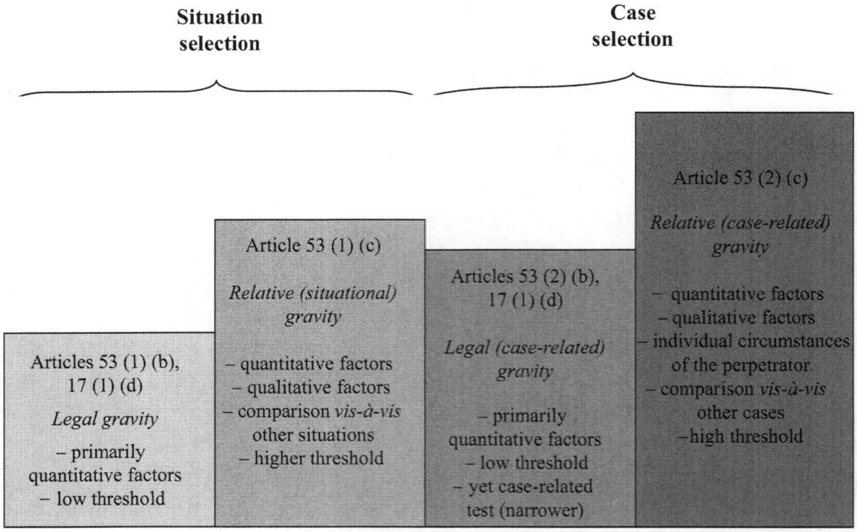

Source: Author.

Figure 7: Gravity in a nutshell

at focusing the Court's resources on the most serious available situations and, generally, on the most serious cases within each situation.[1826] Subjective qualitative factors may be taken into account, and the OTP may look at the responsibility of the offender for its relative case selection.

It is now left to the ICC's actors, especially the OTP and the Chambers, to arrive at a feasible categorization of the particular gravity sub-elements, and to arrive at a practical weighing procedure.

3. Subparagraph c – interests of justice

Article 53 (1) (c) deals with the initiation of an investigation with regard to the "interests of justice." The "interests of justice" is a very vague concept.[1827] If the Prosecutor considers that an investigation would "not serve

[1826] McAuliffe deGuzman, *supra* note 1152, 47.

[1827] McDonald/Haveman, *supra* note 1149, 5; El Zeidy, *supra* note 246, 117; Michael Kourabas, "A Vienna Convention interpretation of the 'Interests of justice' provision of the Rome Statute, the legality of domestic amnesty agreements, and the situation in Northern Uganda: a 'great qualitative step forward', or a normative retreat?" (2007) 14 U.C. Davis Journal of International Law and Policy 60, 61 ("curiously ambiguous provision"); Seils/Wierda, *supra* note 1461, 12; Goldstone, *supra* note 1048, 392 ("elastic").

the interests of justice," he may not proceed to an investigation. The "interests of justice" clause constitutes the third procedural step after jurisdiction and admissibility; the Prosecutor must determine whether "taking into account the gravity of the crime and the interests of the victims, there are nonetheless substantial reasons to believe that an investigation would not serve the interests of justice."

a) Interests of justice

The word justice is demanding, meaning different things to different people.[1828] It is a complex moral concept relating to human relationships in general, but is closely associated with the operation of legal institutions.[1829] There are all kinds of justice: retributive justice, deterrent justice, compensatory justice, rehabilitative justice, exonerative justice, and restorative justice.[1830] Black's Law dictionary primarily defines "justice" as the "fair and proper administration of laws," and enumerates no less than eleven different meanings under this general predefinition.[1831] Within the following survey the term "justice" is intertwined with the ICC Statute; reference is made to justice in the sense of criminal justice and not to a larger understanding of justice in the sense of moral theory and ethics.

Since the term "justice" under article 53 (1) (c) and (2) (c) has been left undefined by the drafters, an extensive interpretation allowing for all possibilities is deemed necessary. Thereby, I will mainly focus on two opposing views under article 53, trying to find a balance between the two: justice in

---

1828 Richard Goldstone/Nicole Fritz, "In the interests of justice and independent referral: The ICC prosecutor's unprecedented powers" (2000) 13 LJIL 655, 662; Henry Lovat, "Delineating the interests of justice: prosecutorial discretion and the Rome Statute of the International Criminal Court" (2006) 1435 bepress Legal Series 1, 3; Contag, *supra* note 426, 50. For a survey in the DRC, suggesting that justice is primarily viewed in relation to judicial mechanisms and the rule of law, see ICTJ DRC population-based survey, *supra* note 210, 44–5.

1829 The New Oxford Companion of Law, Peter Cane/Joanna Conaghan (eds.), (OUP, Oxford 2008) 660, "justice." On the origins of justice, including human rights, also John Manique, *The origins of justice* (University of Pennsylvania Press, Philadelphia 2003) 1 et seq. For institutional justice, see John Rawls, *A theory of justice, revised version,* Cambridge (MA): Harvard University Press 1999, 47 et seq. Most recently, Daniel Ntanda Nsereko, "The role of the international criminal tribunals in the promotion of peace and justice: the case of the International Criminal Court" (2008) 19 CLF 373 375.

1830 Yav Katshung, *supra* note 1892, 5.

1831 Black's Law Dictionary, *supra* note 1075, 869, "justice": "commutative justice, distributive justice, Jedburgh justice, justice *in personam,* justice *in rem,* natural justice, personal justice, popular justice, positive justice, social justice, and substantial justice."

the narrow sense of criminal (retributive) justice *vis-à-vis* justice in the broader sense of transitional (restorative) justice.

aa) Literal, contextual and teleological interpretations

The "interests of justice" clause of article 53 (1) (c), is very complex. Similar to the term "investigation" in article 17 (1), the expression "justice" is an indefinite legal concept open to Court interpretation.[1832] Neither the ICC Statute nor the RPE provide for a definition of "interests of justice."[1833] The standard test of article 31 VCLT must be applied, taking into consideration the literal, systematic, and teleological meaning of article 53 (1) (c). Several NGOs, the OTP itself, as well as various academic authors, have followed the VCLT interpretive guideline, but with opposing results. As already mentioned, the basic question revolves around two possible interpretations of the clause: "whether 'the interests of justice' standard denotes a retributive notion of 'justice', or whether additional, broader conceptions of 'justice' may also be taken into account."[1834] Subsequently, the most important inputs on the "interests of justice" will be delineated, differentiating between NGOs (1), the OTP (2), and academics (3), before I support a broader concept of justice (4), which embraces alternative conceptions rather than choosing the purely retributive approach.

(1) NGO input on the "interests of justice"

NGO involvement has been crucial to the ICC. However, NGOs pursue a range of objectives, and may even lobby for divergent views.[1835] Bearing this in mind, there have been diametrical input papers on the "interests of justice" submitted by NGOs upon request of the OTP between December 2004 and April 2005.[1836] HRW clearly favors a narrow reading of the "interests of justice" and states that the Prosecutor may not fail to initiate an investigation or prosecution "because of developments at the national level

[1832] Bartelt, *supra* note 677, 212. Yet, one must bear in mind that "investigation" contains a factual analysis while the "interests of justice" are largely normative.

[1833] Olásolo, *supra* note 368, 110; Roche, *supra* note 1423, 568; Morel, *supra* note 1365, 260; also *Situation in Darfur (Sudan),* Decision on application under rule 103, 4.2.2009 (ICC-02/05-185) para. 17.

[1834] Robinson, *supra* note 807, 488; Dukić, *supra* note 1256, 696–7; Refugee Law Project's position paper LRA investigations, *supra* note 554, 8 ("whose definition of justice?").

[1835] Schiff, *supra* note 128, 144.

[1836] Thereto Kourabas, *supra* note 1827, 61; Rodman, *supra* note 1249, 105 et seq.

such as truth commissions, national amnesties, or the implementation of traditional reconciliation methods, or because of concerns regarding an ongoing peace process."[1837] This assumption is based on the context of the ICC Statute, its object and purpose, and the requirements of international law. Moreover, HRW argues that policy reasons equally favor a strict construction.[1838]

HRW thereby adheres to the following interpretation, based on the VCLT. Literally, the ordinary meaning of "interests of justice" is unclear due to the fact that no consensus was reached at Rome.[1839] Teleologically, HRW emphasizes the preambular duty to put an end to impunity, followed by systematic arguments drawn from other provisions such as articles 55 (2) (c), 61, 65, and 67 that use the phrase "interests of justice" supposedly in a way that means "good administration of justice" opposed to any broader notion.[1840] In addition, the interface of international peace and security *vis-à-vis* justice is properly addressed by article 16; political decision-making power is only allocated to the SC, not the Prosecutor.[1841] The narrow meaning of the words "interests of justice" is further strengthened by the international law obligation to prosecute serious international crimes.[1842] Last but not least, there are considerable policy reasons that favor a narrow reading, i.e. the risk of being mired in making political judgments that would ultimately undermine the OTP's work and the risk of subjecting the Office to enormous political pressure and attempted manipulation by governments and rebel groups.[1843] In sum, HRW submits a preliminary draft for regulations, and it stresses the importance of new regulations for achieving objective standards.[1844]

A similarly restrictive view is taken by Amnesty International that emphasizes the limited scope of article 53.[1845] According to the AI approach, political decisions should be left to the SC under article 16.[1846] There should be a basic presumption that it is always in the "interests of justice"

[1837] HRW, policy paper article 53, *supra* note 1263, 2; HRW Courting history report, *supra* note 126, 34–5; critically Lovat, *supra* note 1828, 5 et seq.

[1838] HRW, policy paper article 53, *supra* note 1263, 2.

[1839] HRW, policy paper article 53, *supra* note 1263, 2–3.

[1840] HRW, policy paper article 53, *supra* note 1263, 4 et seq.

[1841] HRW, policy paper article 53, *supra* note 1263, 7 et seq.

[1842] HRW, policy paper article 53, *supra* note 1263, 9 et seq.

[1843] HRW, policy paper article 53, *supra* note 1263, 14.

[1844] HRW, policy paper article 53, *supra* note 1263, 23 et seq.

[1845] Amnesty International, "Open letter to the Chief Prosecutor of the International Criminal Court: Comments on the concept of the interests of justice" (hereinafter AI open letter) 17 June 2005, 1, 8.

[1846] AI open letter, *supra* note 1845, 2.

to prosecute, absent a compelling justification.[1847] Turning to national jurisdictions, in particular to the "public interest test," the importance of the seriousness of the offence might outweigh any public interest.[1848] Last but not least, comparison is drawn to other international prosecutors, who have repeatedly and firmly declared that they refuse to take into account any political considerations.[1849]

FIDH further advertises a strict interpretation in two papers on the subject. In the first paper, FIDH initially turns to a systematic approach, referring *inter alia* to rules 55, 65 (4), 67, 69, 73, 82, 100, 136, 165, and Court Regulations 21 (8), 29 (1), 55 (6), 66 (4), 76 (1), arriving at three possible meanings of the "interests of justice:" interests of judicial organs in the sense of good administration of justice; defence rights, meaning that the "interests of justice" can be invoked as an exception to prosecution if violated; and fair trial considerations.[1850] A survey of the jurisprudence of other international criminal tribunals – such as the ICTY, ICTR, and the SCSL – leads to the conclusion that the "interests of justice" were never used to suspend an investigation or prosecution for political motives.[1851] In September 2006, FIDH published a follow-up paper on the "interests of justice" which included specific comments on the draft paper of the since published OTP policy paper of 2007. First of all, FIDH welcomed the restrictive reading adopted by the OTP.[1852] Nevertheless, the NGO expresses its concern that article 53 might be used as some kind of political interference, yet only article 16 allows for such considerations.[1853] With regard to the case-by-case approach envisaged by the OTP, FIDH acknowledges the complex matter of article 53, but the NGO believes that some more guidance should be provided.[1854]

Coming to the remaining input papers, the *Action Sociale pour la Paix et le Développement* (ASPD), the *Corporación de Promoción y Defensa de los Derechos del Pueblo* (CODEPU), and the *Démocratie et Civisme pour le Développement Intégral* (DECIDI) add different nuances. ASPD states

1847 AI open letter, *supra* note 1845, 8.

1848 AI open letter, *supra* note 1845, 13.

1849 AI open letter, *supra* note 1845, 13.

1850 FIDH, "Réflexions sur la notion 'intérêts de la justice', au terme de l'article 53 du Statut de Rome," 1.6.2005, 2–3.

1851 FIDH, Réflexions sur la notion "intérêts de la justice," *supra* note 1850, 5.

1852 FIDH, Comments on the Office of the Prosecutor's draft policy paper on "The interests of Justice," 15.9.2006, 1.

1853 FIDH, Comments on the Office of the Prosecutor's draft policy paper on "The interests of Justice," *supra* note 1852, 2.

1854 FIDH, Comments on the Office of the Prosecutor's draft policy paper on "The interests of Justice," *supra* note 1852, 3.

that the discretionary power of the Prosecutor is, in principle, not restricted.[1855] It is interesting to note that ASPD departs from the narrow interpretation by HRW, Amnesty International, and FIDH, by stating: "Le concept d'intérêt de la justice ne se limite pas seulement à la justice punitive, car il inclut des considerations plus larges telle que: la justice répartitrice [...]."[1856] CODEPU places emphasis on the unique nature of the "interests of justice," which cannot be found in the ICTR/ICTY Statutes, and which is not defined in the ICC Statute itself.[1857] When it comes to questions of peace, reconciliation and justice, CODEPU takes a more flexible approach than HRW, Amnesty International, and FIDH. This NGO sees a complementarity role for TRCs in the ICC's system: "La existencia de comisiones de verdad y reconciliación pueden jugar un papel complementario al poder jurisdiccional [...]."[1858] Even though CODEPU generally favors the Court not being affected by international security reasons or a national reconciliation process, the NGO is aware of practical difficulties and therefore comes to the conclusion that security and stability must be taken into account when opening an investigation or prosecution: "Es por ello que consideramos a la situación de seguridad o estabilidad como una causal para no iniciar una investigación o enjuiciamiento, puesto que en vez de permitir la paz, se está engendrando situaciones que pueden llegar explosiones de violencias mayores que aquellas que se quieren evitar."[1859] Last but not least, DECIDI further understands the term "justice" in an open manner. Justice is not limited to punitive justice only: "Le concept d'intérêts de la justice n'est pas uniquement limité à la justice punitive, il inclut aussi des considérations plus larges: mesures de sûreté, condamnations civiles, amendes, [...]."[1860]

Although all NGO papers make valuable comments on the nature of the "interests of justice," some of these studies are partly flawed. Rather than addressing the "interests of justice" under article 53 in a general manner, they are misled by the pending "peace vs. justice" discussion, particularly having the Uganda situation in the back of their minds. Amnesty International, for instance, starts off with the suspension of investigations for political reasons.[1861] Later, when outlining the limited scope of article 53, Am-

---

1855 ASPD, "Commentaires sur l'intérêt de la justice," 1 May 2005, 1.

1856 ASPD, Commentaires sur l'intérêt de la justice, *supra* note 1855, 2.

1857 CODEPU and IMS, "El interés de la justicia como causal para no iniciar una investigación o enjuciamiento en el estatuto de rome de la corte penal internacional," 1 May 2005, 1.

1858 CODEPU and IMS, El interés de la justicia, *supra* note 1857, 6.

1859 CODEPU and IMS, El interés de la justicia, *supra* note 1857, 6.

1860 DECIDI, "Consultation sur les intérêts de la justice," 1 May 2005, 4.

1861 AI open letter, *supra* note 1845, 1–2.

nesty International emphasizes that the grounds under article 53 do "not include political factors such as the impact on negotiations to end armed conflict, and, so far, the Prosecutor has opened investigations in three situations, in two of which peace initiatives were underway."[1862] Alike, HRW quickly turns to article 16 and strongly emphasizes that only this article allows for political considerations against which the Prosecutor is a "judicial, non-political organ, with no political legitimation and liability [...]."[1863] The papers presented by DECIDI, ASPD, and CODEPU raise the open nature of "justice," potentially including broader ideas, but they regrettably do not put forward arguments that could convince the Prosecutor. Unfortunately, as will be demonstrated below, the OTP has *prima facie* followed a narrow interpretation of the "interests of justice" clause.

(2) OTP policy

In the past, the OTP itself has been quite reluctant to say anything publicly on the "interests of justice" issue. In September 2007, the OTP finally published a policy paper on "interests of justice," setting out how the Prosecutor understands article 53.[1864] In this paper, the OTP adopts a narrow interpretation; in other words, it stresses the very exceptional nature of the clause.[1865] The paper does not, however, enter into a detailed discussion on all possible factors. The OTP instead prefers a case-by-case approach that "[...] will necessarily have to depend on the facts and circumstances of the case or situation".[1866] A different method was applied in an earlier Memorandum of Law on the subject starting off with an interpretation of the "interests of justice," a second part enumerates all potentially relevant factors and clusters and briefly discusses the arguments for and against consideration of each factor.[1867] It is speculative as to why the OTP departed from this rudimentary approach. At this point, however, it must be re-emphasized that several authors demanded predefined prosecutorial guidelines.

[1862] AI open letter, *supra* note 1845, 8.

[1863] HRW, policy paper article 53, *supra* note 1263, 7; similarly, FIDH, Réflexions sur la notion "intérêts de la justice," *supra* note 1850, 5.

[1864] Interests of justice paper, *supra* note 99, 1; thereto Mallinder, *supra* note 1384, 287; Schabas, *supra* note 1151, 749; Ciampi, *supra* note 707, 893; Ohlin, in Stahn/Sluiter, *supra* note 428, 198. On the OTP policy also Goldstone, *supra* note 1048, 393 et seq.

[1865] Interests of justice paper, *supra* note 99, 1, 9. Thereto Valiñas, in Stahn/van Herik, *supra* note 1423, 278.

[1866] Interests of justice paper, *supra* note 99, 1.

[1867] Delmas-Marty, *supra* note 1048, 9, who outlines the MoL Interests of Justice, *supra* note 1288.

Before coming back to the case-by-case (and situation-by-situation) approach, three main ideas of the OTP need to be underlined: first, there is an exceptional nature of the clause and a general presumption in favor of investigations and prosecutions; second, that the criteria for the clause's exercise will be guided by the objects and purposes of the ICC Statute; and third, there is supposedly a difference between the "interests of justice" and the "interests of peace."[1868] It is further acknowledged that the PTC may choose to review a decision not to investigate or prosecute solely based on the "interests of justice."[1869]

The OTP further goes into details with regard to its own interpretation of the phrasing under article 53 (1) (c). The "interests of justice" is valued as "one of the most complex aspect[s] of the Treaty" in that it is defined nowhere and the preparatory works offer no significant elucidation.[1870] On the other hand, it is submitted that the text and purpose of the ICC Statute clearly favor the pursuit of investigations.[1871] While admissibility and jurisdiction are positive requirements, the "interests of justice" is not; the Prosecutor is not required to establish that an investigation or prosecution is in the "interests of justice."[1872] To substantiate the exceptional nature of the concept, the Prosecutor turns to the Preamble which

> "[...] provides a useful point of reference in this regard. Paragraph four of the Preamble underlines that the States Parties are determined to put an end to impunity for the perpetrators of the most serious crimes of concern to the international community and thus to contribute to their prevention. The last paragraph indicates their resolve 'to guarantee lasting respect for and the enforcement of international justice.' Thus, considerations of prevention of serious crimes and guaranteeing lasting respect for international justice may be significant touchstones in assessing the interests of justice."[1873]

In accordance with the structure of article 53 (1) and (2), the OTP enumerates the explicit factors of gravity, the interests of victims, and the particular circumstances of the accused before briefly addressing other potential considerations for the "interests of justice" test. The inclusion of unwritten factors does not, however, imply "that they are viewed as being

---

1868 Interests of justice paper, *supra* note 99, 1; Mallinder, *supra* note 1384, 287. Critically with regard to the third OTP statement, see Schabas, *supra* note 1151, 749, also further Part IV, B., III., 3., e), aa).

1869 Interests of justice paper, *supra* note 99, 1, 3, 9.

1870 Interests of justice paper, *supra* note 99, 2.

1871 Interests of justice paper, *supra* note 99, 2.

1872 Interests of justice paper, *supra* note 99, 3; also *Situation in Kenya*, Request for authorization, *supra* note 207, para. 60, 22; *Situation in Kenya*, Decision pursuant to article 15, *supra* note 6, para. 63, 27–8.

1873 Interests of justice paper, *supra* note 99, 4.

always necessarily relevant," and "will depend on the facts and circumstances of each case or situation."[1874] Other justice mechanisms and a potential peace process are also discussed in the paper. The Office reiterates that other justice mechanisms need to be integrated, and the OTP endorses a complementary role for them.[1875] However, it is explained nowhere how the Prosecutor conciliates the flexible approach towards alternative justice mechanisms with his narrow interpretation of the "interests of justice" clause as such. In any event, other alternative justice mechanisms will be readdressed in detail.[1876] For the moment, it suffices to welcome the OTP's departure from the overly restrictive interpretation advertised by some NGOs. Later, the OTP indirectly re-emphasizes its wider approach when stating that the "concept of the interests of justice established in the Statute, while necessarily broader than criminal justice in a narrow sense, must be interpreted in accordance with the objects and purposes of the Statute (fn. omitted)."[1877]

This statement is inspired by the discussion on peace processes, and the OTP further holds that not all issues related to peace and security fall within the ambit of the clause under article 53 (1) (c) and (2) (c). The broader matter of international peace and security clearly falls within the mandate of institutions other than the Prosecutor.[1878] While this result is persuasive, the path taken by the OTP is not. Instead of a narrow approach, the OTP should acknowledge its discretion – only! – under article 53 (1) (c) and (2) (c) and, in a second step, arrive at exceptions to the wider notion. The Office could thus discuss impact as a criterion under the "interests of justice," and further set limits on the specific factors in its guidelines. Such a limiting exception is "international peace and security," which embraces the issue of peace negotiations.[1879]

Recapitulating, the OTP has adopted a narrow – in my opinion overly restrictive – interpretation similar to the outlined input papers by HRW, Amnesty International, and FIDH. On the other hand, the Prosecutor tried to safeguard flexibility for alternative justice mechanism, which is desirable as a policy matter, but is hardly reconcilable with the taken legal approach. No prosecutorial guidelines have yet been published. As the sole provision

[1874] Interests of justice paper, *supra* note 99, 7 with fn. 9.

[1875] Interests of justice paper, *supra* note 99, 7–8.

[1876] See Part IV, B., III., 3., e), cc).

[1877] Interests of justice paper, *supra* note 99, 8.

[1878] Interests of justice paper, *supra* note 99, 9. On the limited mandate of the ICC further Burke-White, *supra* note 1218, 64–5.

[1879] See Part IV, B., III., 3., e), aa).

dealing specifically with the "interests of justice," the newly drafted OTP Regulation 31 spells out:

> "In acting pursuant to article 53, paragraphs 1 (c) and 2 (c), the Prosecutor shall base his or her decision on an internal report on the interests of justice submitted to ExCom for consideration and approval. If the decision not to proceed is based solely on article 53, paragraph 1 (c) or 2 (c), the Prosecutor shall promptly inform the Pre-Trial Chamber in accordance with rule 105, paragraphs 4 and 5, and rule 106."

No further guidance on the factors is provided in the OTP Regulations. Instead of pre-defining regulations or guidelines, the OTP has favored a purely situation- and case-related approach. Besides concerns regarding transparency, the Prosecutor risks leaving the matter to the Judges, who might introduce there very own understanding via PTC supervision.

(3) Academic approaches

The Prosecutor must consider the terms "gravity of the crime" and interest of victims" against the "interests of justice," on the one hand providing a wide degree of discretion due to the undefined nature of the term "interests of justice," on the other hand the discretion is held in check by the duty to inform the PTC if the determination was made solely on the "interests of justice" criterion.[1880] As it has been left undefined, several authors have approached the term "interests of justice," favoring either a narrow or broader meaning. The basic question is hence whether the concept of "interests of justice" should be interpreted narrowly, alike the NGOs' and OTP's approach, or in a wider sense that allows for restorative justice mechanisms. Some authors highlight a victim-centered interpretation of the term "interests of justice," which presupposes a narrow interpretation, ignoring wider issues of reconciliation and alternative justice mechanisms.[1881] One author equally adopts a very restrictive approach, seeing the object and purpose as the "strongest piece of evidence denying that amnesty can be read into article 53."[1882] However, the latter author mixes two

---

[1880] Brubacher, *supra* note 368, 80–1; also AMICC/John Washburn and Wasana Punyasena, "Interests of justice proposal," 1 May 2005, 1; Lovat, *supra* note 1828, 2.

[1881] Mr. Juan E Méndez, President International Center for Transitional Justice, *supra* note 409. On the victim centered approach see Chris Gallavin, "Article 53 of the Rome Statute of the International Criminal Court: in the interests of justice?" (2003) 14 KCLJ 179, 184; also favoring a narrow approach Slye/van Schaack, *supra* note 534, 259–60.

[1882] Kourabas, *supra* note 1827, 79.

things: a general interpretation of the "interests of justice" and its application to the Northern Ugandan situation, asking "whether the provision would permit the Prosecutor of the ICC to defer prosecution of LRA leaders on the basis of Uganda's amnesty law."[1883] While one might certainly agree with his finding *in casu,* one cannot infer that an interpretation favors a narrow approach in general. Amnesties are a specific question within the "interests of justice" design and will be readdressed below.[1884] In any event, the issue of amnesties is highly disputed. While one author states that careful political calculation should not necessarily be excluded as an option in the "interests of justice,"[1885] another author highlights that the "justice" element – if interpreted in a judicial sense – does not allow for amnesties, which are political acts.[1886]

Coming back to the "interests of justice" in more general terms, a broad approach has been taken by numerous authors.[1887] A wider consideration of "justice" appears to be the only supportable interpretation.[1888] Justice need not always be prosecution.[1889] There is a necessity of a broad interpretation of "justice" even broader than the narrow interpretation suggested by the OTP.[1890] The Prosecutor should, for instance, not be barred from considering non-prosecutorial mechanisms that provide for alternative forms of justice.[1891] A flexible concept must encompass restorative justice.[1892] Furthermore, a wide notion of justice can be derived from the broad justice element in transitional justice and can be defined as

---

1883 Kourabas, *supra* note 1827, 92.

1884 See Part IV, B., III., 3., e), dd).

1885 Takemura, *supra* note 1385, 13.

1886 Arsanjani, *supra* note 1425, 67.

1887 See, *inter alia,* Meyer, *supra* note 1153, 579; Robinson, *supra* note 807, 488; Stahn, *supra* note 726, 698; Gropengießer/Meißner, *supra* note 679, 296; Majzub, *supra* note 1426, 271; Allen, *supra* note 246, 129; Roche, *supra* note 1423, 568–9; Goldstone/Fritz, *supra* note 1828, 662; Rodman, *supra* note 1249, 99 et seq.; van Heeck, *supra* note 26, 190–1; Morel, *supra* note 1365, 260, 268; Louise Mallinder, "Can amnesties and international justice be reconciled?" (2007) 1 IJTJ 208, 218–9; Jean-Marie Eleylofede, "L'interprétation de l'article 53 des Statuts de Rome créant la cour penale internationale sur la notion intérêt de la justice," May 2005, 1, 10: "Il (le procureur) est libre de fixer sa décision dans le sens qui correspond à son sentiment personnel."

1888 Robinson, *supra* note 807, 488.

1889 Hanlon, *supra* note 256, 327.

1890 Stigen, *supra* note 205, 358–9.

1891 Stigen, *supra* note 205, 358.

1892 Joseph Yav Katshung, "The relationship between the International Criminal Court and truth commissions: some thoughts on how to build a bridge across retributive and restorative justice," May 2005, 23.

"[...] an ideal of accountability and fairness in the protection and vindication of rights and the prevention and punishment of wrongs. Justice implies regard for the rights of the accused, for the interests of victims and for the well-being of society at large. It is a concept rooted in all national cultures and traditions and, while its administration usually implies formal judicial mechanisms, traditional dispute resolution mechanisms are equally relevant."[1893]

(4) Own hypothesis: Broader concept of the "interests of justice"

The OTP, and ultimately the Judges, must devise a coherent and comprehensive approach as to how to assess mechanisms that fall short of criminal prosecution, but provide alternative forms of justice.[1894] It is supposedly the "interests of justice" clause that opens such a gateway. On the other hand, it has been shown that interpretations allow for argumentations either way. For this reason, there is no definite answer.[1895] The ordinary meaning is not clear at all. From a contextual perspective, it has to be noted that the term "interests of justice" appears several times in the ICC Statute, namely articles 53 (1) and (2) (c), 55 (2) (c), 61 (2), 65 (4), and 67 (1) (d). It further appears in rules 69, 73 (d), 82 (5), 100, 136 (1), and 165 (3), and Court Regulations 21 (8), 29 (1), 54, 60 (1), 66 (4), 76 (1), and 80 (1). Nonetheless, most of these provisions fall within the context of a good administration of justice. The use of the term with regard to prosecutorial selection is a novelty. From a contextual and teleological perspective, the OTP, HRW, Amnesty International, FIDH, and some academics have stressed the preambular duty to end impunity and therefore the exceptional nature of the "interests of justice" clause. A systematic argument is further drawn from article 16, which is supposedly the better gateway for political considerations. Despite these valid arguments, the demand for prosecutorial selection based on congruent practice prevails. If one does not link discretionary choices to one specific provision – article 53 (1) and (2) (c) – the notion has no clear legal foundation. Systematically, the statutory system favors a narrow interpretation of the legal admissibility test under articles 53 (1) (b) and 17, and, on the other hand, a broad approach towards the discretionary "interests of justice" test under article 53 (1) (c).

The object and purpose of the provision are a difficult métier. Interpretations either way are possible, and authors have vindicated their respective preferences. In sum, it has been shown that a literal, contextual, and teleological interpretation leaves the "interests of justice" open for divergent

1893 Ambos, in Ambos/Large/Wierda, *supra* note 650, para. 2, 22–3, and para. 53, 85–6.

1894 Meyer, *supra* note 1153, 581.

1895 Dukić, *supra* note 1256, 700.

views. It is, however, not at all mandatory to adopt a narrow reading. Quite the opposite, the very existence of the clause makes a limited reading difficult to reconcile with the rest of article 53.[1896] Therefore, the assumption that justice "encompasses alternative forms of justice and entails an overall assessment of the situation taking into account peace and reconciliation as the ultimate goals of every process of transition" is postulated as a first working hypothesis.[1897] This hypothesis will be substantiated by the drafting history, similar domestic notions, and other international contexts. A broad reading does not, however, mean that the Prosecutor can take any action in a legal vacuum. The elements of article 53 (gravity; interest of victims; etc.) constrain his choices, so that he cannot invoke the "interests of justice" clause if the reasons are purely political. The written – and potentially unwritten – factors thus form the decisive second part of this analysis.[1898]

bb) Drafting history

As already outlined above, article 53 was a compromise formula of two opposing views.[1899] The broad term "interests of justice" was maintained, yet additional factors were added and the judicial review power – confirmative decision in the case of "interests of justice" – was included into article 53 (3). This procedural compromise left the substantive interpretation wide open. As the meaning of "interests of justice" is not clear, a further recourse to the drafting history as supplementary means is necessary. This additional inquiry is thought to focus on the wording "interests of justice" as opposed to article 53 as a whole and searches for specifications that favor a broader or a more restrictive reading of the clause.

Articles 26 and 27 ILC Draft Statute of 1994 did not even refer to the "interests of justice." The terminology can first be found in the Report of the Preparatory Committee of 1996:

> "It was suggested that the Prosecutor should, for example, have broad discretion to decide not to initiate or to discontinue an investigation or prosecution in the *interests of justice* [...]."[1900]

The term was subsequently used in all drafting documents and finally found its way – though in brackets – into article 54 Draft Statute of April

---

[1896] Ambos, in Ambos/Large/Wierda, *supra* note 650, 82–3, para. 51.

[1897] Ambos, in Ambos/Large/Wierda, *supra* note 650, 85–6, para. 53.

[1898] See Part IV, B., III., 3., b)–e).

[1899] Part IV, B., I.

[1900] Cf. Part IV, B., I.

1998.[1901] The issue was apparently difficult to negotiate and a first paper of the Working Group of the Rome Conference still had all references to the "interests of justice" bracketed.[1902] The second report of 24 June 1998 referred to the debate as "*pending.*"[1903] Another proposal suggested the actual text of what is now article 53.[1904] During the Diplomatic Conference little reference to the issue can be found. In the third plenary meeting, Mr. Wako expressed on behalf of Kenya the "commitment to the establishment of an effective, impartial, credible and independent international criminal court, free from political manipulation, pursuing only the *interests of justice,* with due regard to the rights of the accused and the interests of the victims (emph. added)."[1905] Mr. Ojha (Nepal) believed that the "*interests of justice* would be served if victims could also be made parties to the trial and be given the opportunity to obtain restitution from the assets of the perpetrator (emph. added)."[1906]

The only explicit references to the term in the context of halting an investigation were made by Syria and Denmark. While Mr. Al-Sheikh (Syrian Arab Republic) expressed his "delegation's reservations regarding the provisions in article 54 allowing the Prosecutor to stop an investigation in the supposed *interests of justice* (emph. added),"[1907] the Danish position was the other way around, suggesting that one should not give suspension power to the SC, but rather the ICC "might itself consider that suspending a case would serve the *interests of justice,* or the Court and the Council might cooperate on the basis of nonbinding arrangements, but not through a dictate (emph. added)."[1908]

In conclusion, the drafting history shows that a procedural compromise formula through PTC supervision was agreed on, but the deliberations do not assist in determining the term's substantive content, which was not further discussed. Nonetheless, the history clearly reveals that wide prosecutorial discretion was built in the ICC Statute.

1901 Cf. Part IV, B., I.

1902 Working Paper on article 54, *supra* note 1172.

1903 Report of the Working Group on Procedural Matters, Committee of the Whole, United Nations Diplomatic Conference of Plenipotentiaries on the Establishment of an International Criminal Court, 15 June–17 July 1998, 23.6.1998 (A/CONF.183/C.1/WGPM/L.2).

1904 Working Paper on article 54, *supra* note 1175; imprinted at Part IV, B., I.

1905 Mr. Wako (Kenya), Official Records, Vol. II, *supra* note 392, para. 63, 77.

1906 Mr. Ojha (Nepal), Official Records, Vol. II, *supra* note 392, para. 47, 99.

1907 Mr. Al-Sheikh (Syrian Arab Republic), Official Records, Vol. II, *supra* note 392, para. 45, 359.

1908 Mr. Lehmann (Denmark), Official Records, Vol. II, *supra* note 392, para. 135, 302.

cc) Interests of justice in the law of domestic jurisdictions and legislation

A survey through various national criminal jurisdictions has revealed that prosecutorial discretion is basically known to all of the included countries.[1909] Generally speaking, all criminal justice systems, even those who follow the principle of mandatory prosecution, provide their competent authorities with a certain degree of leeway in deciding whether to investigate or prosecute a specific case.[1910] On the other hand, it needs to be clarified that a degree of generalization is necessary to compare the divergent systems. The possible actors, the degree of discretion, and procedures for checks and balances might vary quite largely.[1911] Therefore, every country was analyzed in respect of (1) the actor in charge of (pre-)investigations, (2) the point when a (pre-)investigation is triggered, (3) the entity that takes the formal decision to start investigations, (4) the level of discretion involved in initiating a formal investigation, (5) the circumstances under which investigations can be dismissed, and (6) the control of the decision by another body.[1912] Discretionary decisions are, generally speaking, controllable by another body. Even common law countries check the choice of discretion with regard to a clear abuse of process. In this regard, it is interesting to note the increasing case law in England and Wales that sets up factors allowing for the exceptional order of judicial review. However, in most countries the exact factors for discretion are unclear or left open. Nonetheless, some provide for prosecutorial guidelines to ensure a minimum standard. The terminology "interests of justice" was taken from the term "public interest" used in national jurisdictions (Canada, Colombia, Germany, The Netherlands, South Africa, Sudan, Uganda, England and Wales, and the United States).[1913]

However, international criminal justice requires a unique and tailor-made approach, and not every provision can be transferred to the international sphere easily.[1914] Nevertheless, it has been outlined that the term "interests of justice" derived from "public interest," leading to a strong presumption that the *core* of the "public interest" and the "interests of justice," namely the discretionary weighing process, is synonymous.[1915] In addition, the dis-

---

[1909] See Annex 2, C.

[1910] Kleffner, *supra* note 370, 254.

[1911] Kleffner, *supra* note 370, 254–5.

[1912] See Annex 2.

[1913] See further Annex 2, C., also Kleffner, *supra* note 370, 259; Gallavin, *supra* note 1881, 191 ("synonymous").

[1914] Gallavin, *supra* note 1881, 193.

[1915] Gallavin, *supra* note 1881, 194.

cretionary test is restricted to paragraphs 1 (c) and (2) (c) of article 53, and a judicial check was deemed necessary (article 53 (3)). Therefore, the formula of article 53 can truly be called an amalgam of different national concepts transposed to the international sphere. For this reason, analogy to the specific criteria used in one particular country quickly reaches its limits. Unfortunately, the country analysis is of limited relevance in this regard, and the exact content of the "interests of justice" criteria demands the ICC to adopt its own interpretation. That said, some guidance can be sought by a combined operation looking at national guidance factors and internatio-nal(ized) jurisdictions equally. In any event, the concept leaves the ICC with flexibility and must be interpreted in a broad, non-exhaustive manner. In conclusion, it has been shown that a wider concept of discretionary case selection is applied in several national criminal jurisdictions, be it common law or civil law.

dd) International(ized) jurisdictions

The expression "interests of justice" was not invented by the drafters of the ICC Statute, but has been used by other legal systems beforehand. For example, article 14 of the International Covenant on Civil and Political Rights and article 6 of the European Convention on Human Rights use the "interests of justice" standard in assessing whether to allow exceptions to the principle of a public trial and when to require funded counsel for a criminal defendant.[1916] It is, however, new that the "interests of justice" are used to eventually discontinue investigations or prosecutions. Since it has been concluded that the specific factors of the "public interest" phrase from national jurisdictions cannot be transferred to the international sphere easily,[1917] this chapter aims at giving the international "interests of justice" clause some meaning through existing international(ized) statutory and case law. The following analysis will focus on the ICTY, ICTR, SCSL, and ECCC. Two questions will be addressed for each of these international tribunals: first, investigation and prosecution proceedings will be outlined, focusing on preliminary investigations and the decisions to dismiss investigations or prosecutions; second, I will look for the term "interests of justice" and try to find the content of justice interests on the international community level.

Starting with the ICTY, article 16 (1) ICTY Statute assigns the duty to investigate or prosecute persons. The Prosecutor shall act "independently as a separate organ" (article 16 (2) ICTY Statute). According to article 18 (1) ICTY Statute, the Prosecutor decides whether there is a "sufficient basis"

1916 Schabas, *supra* note 1151, 748.

1917 See Part IV, B., III., 3., a), cc).

to proceed with an investigation. The term "sufficient basis" is basically left to the discretion of the Prosecutor.[1918] Some guidance is given by the "Final Report to the Prosecutor by the Committee established to review the NATO bombing campaign against the Federal Republic of Yugoslavia,"[1919] prepared at the Prosecutor's request. The Review Committee gave the following opinion as to the threshold test for the ICTY:

> "Are the prohibitions alleged sufficiently well-established as violations of international humanitarian law to form the basis of a prosecution, and does the application of the law to the particular facts reasonably suggest that a violation of these prohibitions may have occurred? And, upon the reasoned evaluation of the information by the committee, is the information credible and does it tend to show that crimes within the jurisdiction of the Tribunal may have been committed by individuals during the NATO bombing campaign?"

On the basis of the received information, the committee recommended

> "that neither an in-depth investigation related to the bombing campaign as a whole nor investigations related to specific incidents are justified. In all cases, either the law is not sufficiently clear or investigations are unlikely to result in the acquisition of sufficient evidence to substantiate charges against high level accused or against lower accused for particularly heinous offences."[1920]

The Prosecutor followed this recommendation and was heavily criticized concerning the non-investigation.[1921] Be that as it may, the Prosecutor can consult expert advice under article 18 (1) ICTY Statute, but in the end the decision to proceed or not is left to his wide discretion.

At the later stage when it comes to the decision to prosecute, the level of discretion is different. According to article 18 (4) ICTY Statute, the Prosecutor has limited discretion. This is in sharp contrast to national counterparts, particularly in the common-law countries.[1922] If the investigation conducted by the Prosecutor yields sufficient evidence that the Prosecutor can determine that a *prima facie* case exists, he shall prepare an indictment according to article 18 (4) ICTY Statute. Concerning the *prima facie* standard guidance is given by ICTY case law:

[1918] Nsereko, *supra* note 1204, 135; van Heeck, *supra* note 26, 183 et seq.; Dukić, *supra* note 1256, 710; Stigen, *supra* note 205, 348.

[1919] Final report to the Prosecutor by the Committee established to review the NATO bombing campaign against the Federal Republic of Yugoslavia, 13.6.2000; Côte, *supra* note 1190, 180 et seq.

[1920] Final report to the Prosecutor by the Committee, *supra* note 1919, para. 90.

[1921] Paolo Benevenuti, "The ICTY Prosecutor and the review of the NATO bombing campaign against the Federal Republic of Yugoslavia" (2001) 12 EJIL 503, 507; Dukić, *supra* note 1256, 713–4.

[1922] Nsereko, *supra* note 1204, 135.

"A *prima facie* case on any particular charge exists in the situation where the material facts pleaded in the indictment constitute a credible case which would (if not contradicted by the accused) be a sufficient basis to convict him of that charge."[1923]

Moreover, a Judge of the Trial Chamber shall review the indictment under article 19 (1) ICTY Statute and rules 28 and 47 of the ICTY RPE. The Chambers perform a supervisory function that restrains the discretion of the Prosecutor. It is mandatory that the Judge reviews and confirms the indictment (rule 47 (A)) ICTY RPE). If no *prima facie* case exists, the Judge further has the right to decline to confirm the case, to dismiss the matter, and to discharge the accused (rule 47 (F) ICTY RPE). Additionally, rule 28 (A) ICTY RPE requires that the Prosecutor has to concentrate "on one or more of the most senior leaders suspected of being most responsible for crimes within the jurisdiction of the Tribunal."

To conclude, the ICTY Prosecutor enjoys ample discretion under article 18 (1) ICTY Statute, but limited discretion under article 18 (4) ICTY Statute. In other words, his discretion is broad but not absolute.[1924]

The ICTR's legal framework is very similar to the ICTY's statutory standards. Article 15 ICTR Statute sets out the duty to investigate and prosecute (paragraph 1), and the Prosecutor shall do so as an independent organ of the Court (paragraph 2). Article 17 (1) ICTR Statute leaves it to the Prosecutor to determine if there is a "sufficient basis" to proceed. Again, a broad prosecutorial discretion to investigate is recognized.[1925] At the later stage of indicting a person, a similar review mechanism as known from the ICTY is introduced via article 18 (1) ICTR Statute, rules 28 and 47 ICTR RPE. Although the ICTR and ICTY both provide for the possibility of judicial scrutiny, Judges have declined to interfere with the Prosecutor's discretion on a number of occasions.[1926] In practice, the *ad hoc* tribunals' Prose-

[1923] *Prosecutor v Kordić,* Decision on the review of the indictment, 10.11.1995 (IT-95-14-4); Nsereko, *supra* note 1204, 136 with further references in fn. 44.

[1924] Dukić, *supra* note 1256, 710; Côte, *supra* note 1190, 167; Goldstone, *supra* note 1048, 390.

[1925] Côte, *supra* note 1190, 165; Jallow, *supra* note 1245, 147.

[1926] Côte, *supra* note 1190, 167; Jallow, *supra* note 1245, 148; Stigen, *supra* note 205, 404 et seq.; Alex Obote-Odora, "Case selection and prioritization criteria at the International Criminal Tribunal for Rwanda" in Bergsmo, *supra* note 99, 41, 41 et seq.; *Prosecutor v. Jelisić,* Appeal judgment, Partly dissenting opinion of Judge Wald, 5.7.2001 (IT-95-10-A) para. 4; *Prosecutor v. Akayesu,* Appeal judgment, 1.6.2001 (ICTR-96-4-A) para. 96; *Prosecutor v. Ntakirutimana, supra* note 1782, para. 871; *Prosecutor v. Ndindiliyimana,* Decision on urgent oral motion for stay of the indictment, or in the alternative a reference to the Security Council, 26.3.2004 (ICTR-2000-56-I) paras. 28–9.

cutors were therefore able to exercise large discretion with regard to investigations and the filing of indictments:

> "In the present context, indeed in many criminal justice systems, the entity responsible for prosecutions has finite financial and human resources and cannot realistically be expected to prosecute every offender which may fall within the strict terms of its jurisdiction. It must of necessity make decisions as to the nature of the crimes and the offenders to be prosecuted. It is beyond question that the Prosecutor has a broad discretion in relation to the initiation of investigations and in the preparation of indictments."[1927]

On the other hand, a number of limitations are self-evident. Article 21 (1) provides for a right to equality of law, which is a central principle of the due process of law.[1928] In *Mucić et al.,* however, the Judges approved the Prosecutor's suggestion that the burden of proof for discriminatory (selective) prosecution lies on the accused and the appellant (*Landžo*) failed to prove selectivity.[1929] The Akayesu Appeal's Chamber confirmed this high burden by holding that:

> "[...] the evidence of discriminatory intent must be coupled with the evidence that the Prosecutor's policy has a discriminatory effect, so that other similarly situated individuals of other ethnic or religious backgrounds were not prosecuted [...]."[1930]

A claim of selective prosecution is thus difficult to make, and prosecutorial selection at the *ad hoc* tribunals was basically the Prosecutor's domain. Judicial interference only takes place in the clearest cases of abuse.[1931] The following principles were therefore drawn from ICTY/ICTR jurisprudence with regard to prosecutorial discretion *vis-à-vis* judicial review:

(1) prosecutorial discretion is not absolute; it is in principle subject to judicial review;

(2) such judicial review can be undertaken where the discretion has been exercised for improper or impermissible motives or in contravention of principles of justice relating to equality, non-discrimination, fairness, etc.;

(3) there is, however, a presumption of regularity in favor of every exercise of prosecutorial discretion and a high burden of proof rests on those

---

1927 *Prosecutor v. Mucić et al. (Čelebići Camp)*, Appeal judgment, 20.2.2001 (IT-96-21A) para. 602.

1928 *Prosecutor v. Mucić et al. (Čelebići Camp), supra* note 1927, paras. 602 et seq.; Côte, *supra* note 1190, 174.

1929 *Prosecutor v. Mucić et al. (Čelebići Camp), supra* note 1927, paras. 607 et seq.

1930 *Prosecutor v. Akayesu, supra* note 1926, para. 96; also *Prosecutor v. Ndindiliyimana, supra* note 1926, para. 26.

1931 Jallow, *supra* note 1245, 155.

challenging it to establish that it was improperly or unlawfully exercised;

(4) in a challenge to prosecutorial discretion based on alleged selective prosecution, the applicant must pass a two-pronged test by establishing that:

(a) his own prosecution was for improper motives; and

(b) those other similarly situated persons were not so prosecuted.[1932]

With regard to the specific "interests of justice" factor, the tribunals are of limited importance. While the term is repeatedly used,[1933] the word never appears in the context of prosecutorial selection. Guidance *vis-à-vis* discretion and its limits are not given by the "interests of justice" inclusions of the *ad hoc* tribunals. Nevertheless, the ICTY has stated in the *Nikolić* case that there must be a correct balance "between the fundamental rights of the accused and the essential interests of the international community in the prosecution of persons charged with serious violations of international humanitarian law."[1934] It appears that "essential interests of the international community" might be an adequate rephrasing for the weighing of "interests of justice." Even more interesting are the mentioned guidance criteria by Jallow, the current Prosecutor of the ICTR, who names the following factors that influence his exercise of prosecutorial discretion:

- targeting the governmental, political and military *leadership* which planned the genocide;
- extent of *participation* of the accused suspect;
- the *nature and gravity* of the offences;
- the need for *geographic spread* with regard to targets and incidents;
- the *prospects* for dealing with the suspect or accused otherwise than by a prosecution at the ICTR (emph. added).[1935]

1932 Jallow, *supra* note 1245, 159–60; also Stigen, *supra* note 205, 407–8; Cryer, *supra* note 816, 193.

1933 ICTY Statute: article 21 (4) (d), article 28; ICTY RPE: rule 3 (D), rule 4, rule 15*bis* (A) (ii), B (ii), (B) (ii) (a), (D), (H), rule 15*ter* (A), rule 44 (A) (ii), (B), rule 45 (A), rule 45*ter,* rule 53 (A), (C), rule 62 (B), rule 70 (F), rule 71 (A), 73*bis* (F), rule 73*ter* (D), rule 79 (A) (iii), rule 81*bis,* rule 82 (B), rule 85 (A), rule 89 (F), rule 93 (A), rule 108*bis* (B), ICTR Statute: article 20 (4) (d), article 27; ICTR RPE: rule 3 (C), rule 4, rule 15*bis* (A) (ii), (B) (ii), (B) (ii) (a), (D), (F), rule 45*quater,* rule 46 (A), rule 53 (A), (C), rule 71 (A), 73*bis* (E), rule 73*ter* (E), rule 79 (A) (iii), rule 82 (A), rule 85 (A), rule 93 (A).

1934 *Prosecutor v. Nikolić,* Decision on interlocutory appeal concerning legality of arrest, 5.6.2003 (IT-94-2-AR73) para. 30.

1935 Jallow, *supra* note 1245, 152 et seq.

The first three elements of leadership, participation, and nature/gravity are akin to the sentencing practice of the tribunals.[1936] Some (stringent) conditions for case selection are, however, closely related to the completion strategies.[1937]

The above ICTY/ICTR criteria only evolved in the last time span of the tribunals. There has been great criticism regarding the disparity of the criteria used by the Prosecutor ("numerous, ill-assorted and sometimes hazy"), as well as the lack of transparency ("failed to adopt public regulations").[1938] At the outset, the ICTY's and ICTR's case-selection was not transparent, there were no public guidelines, and practice merely shows that criteria were not made and implemented in a consistent way. In this regard, the ICC has learned from the *ad hoc* tribunals and did initiate a process of consultation to develop a coherent selection process. Given the open nature of article 53, there is a practical necessity for the ICC to do so.

From the very outset, the SCSL's Prosecutor shall concentrate his efforts on "those who bear the greatest responsibility" pursuant to article 1 (1) SCSL Statute. The Prosecutor alone is responsible for investigations and prosecutions and he shall act independently as a separate organ of the Court (article 15 (1) SCSL Statute). With respect to juvenile offenders, appropriate alternative truth and reconciliation mechanisms may be taken into account in accordance with article 15 (5) SCSL Statute. If the Prosecutor is satisfied in the course of investigation that the suspect has committed crime(s), he shall prepare and submit an indictment (rule 47 (B) SCSL RPE). A Judge shall review and approve the indictment in accordance with rule 47 (A), (E)–(G) SCSL RPE. In comparison to the ICTY and ICTR, the basic procedure appears to be the same. Investigations are largely left to the discretion of the Prosecutor; he may further decide to file an indictment and only then can the Judges exercise some judicial scrutiny. However, one major difference is the inclusion of the term "those who bear the greatest responsibility" in the SCSL Statute. This criterion guides the SCSL Prosecutor in prosecutorial selection as the most important policy criterion.[1939] Regarding the "interests of justice," no further clarification can be found. The relevant provisions all refer to the administration of justice, and are not used in the context of prosecutorial selection.[1940] In conclusion, only the publicly announced

[1936] Part IV, B., III., 2., c), cc), (3).

[1937] Part IV, C., IV., 4., b), bb).

[1938] Côte, *supra* note 1190, 168 et seq., 171 et seq.

[1939] See Part IV, C., IV., 4., b), cc).

[1940] SCSL Statute: article 17 (4) (d), article 23; SCSL RPE: rule 16 (A), rule 42 (A) (i), rule 45 (B) (ii), rule 46 (A), rule 53 (A), (C), rule 71 (A), (B), rule 73*bis* (E), rule 73*ter* (E), rule 79 (A) (iii), rule 82 (B), rule 84, rule 85 (A), rule 86 (C), rule 93 (A), rule 124.

factor of the "persons who bear the greatest responsibility" is of relevance for the ICC. A similar notion has been introduced by the ICC Prosecutor through his statements and the application of his policy.[1941]

Last but not least, the Co-Prosecutors at the ECCC enjoy a large degree of discretion when initiating criminal proceedings. They have full discretion to initiate complaints according to the ECCC's internal rule 49 (1).[1942] Even complaints shall not automatically initiate proceedings, but the Co-Prosecutors – at their discretion – can reject the complaint, include the complaint in ongoing preliminary investigations, start new preliminary investigations, or forward it directly to the Co-Investigating Judges.[1943] Preliminary investigations at the ECCC aim at determining whether evidence indicates crimes within its jurisdiction, and they are conducted to identify suspects and potential witnesses, carried out by Judicial Police officers or by Investigators of the ECCC only at the request of the Co-Prosecutors.[1944] During investigation the Co-Prosecutors may only investigate facts set out in the introductory submission or a supplementary submission; it is left to the Co-Investigating Judges to charge any suspect.[1945] The Co-Investigating Judge may further take any investigative action conducive to ascertaining the truth.[1946] To end investigations the Co-Investigating Judge must write a closing order either indicting a charged person or dismissing the case. The Co-Investigating Judges are thereby not bound by the Co-Prosecutor's submission.[1947] Grounds for dismissal are as follows: the acts in question do not amount to crimes within the jurisdiction of the ECCC; the perpetrators of the acts have not been identified; or there is no sufficient evidence against the charged person or persons of the charges.[1948]

With respect to the term "interests of justice," the notion is scarcely used by the ECCC, and not at all in the context of dismissing or continuing investigations and/or prosecutions. It is used three times in connection with the good administration of justice: in the ECCC's internal rules 23 (8) (c), 72 (4) (b) (iv), and 77 (6).

Throughout the survey, it has been demonstrated that other internation-al(ized) Prosecutors enjoy large discretion when choosing their targets. Pro-

1941 See Part IV, B., II., 4., and C., IV., 4., b), ee).

1942 Extraordinary Chambers in the Courts of Cambodia, Internal Rules (Rev.5), 9.2.2010.

1943 ECCC's internal rule 49 (4), *supra* note 1942.

1944 ECCC's internal rule 50 (1), (2), *supra* note 1942.

1945 ECCC's internal rule 55 (2), (4), *supra* note 1942.

1946 ECCC's internal rule 55 (5), *supra* note 1942.

1947 ECCC's internal rule 67 (1), *supra* note 1942.

1948 ECCC's internal rule 67 (3), *supra* note 1942.

secutorial choices at the ICTY/ICTR were unguided and uncontrolled at the beginning of their emerging practice. Only subsequently, via practice and the completion strategies, has the selection process been refined and guided by some published criteria. The SCSL was different from the very beginning. Its principal criterion was to target the persons "bearing the greatest responsibility." The Co-Prosecutors at the ECCC have been struggling to arrange for an appropriate target selection, especially whom to charge.[1949]

Moreover, all these institutions cannot provide proper guidance for the "interests of justice" clause as such. It is a novelty that the ICC uses the phrasing in the context of starting investigations and prosecutions. Even more astonishing is the fact that article 53 (3) gives the PTC an explicit, far-reaching review power *vis-à-vis* prosecutorial selection. In this regard, it is submitted that the PTC should not interfere with the Prosecutor's choice of discretion, but must develop a principal oversight procedure. Like the *ad hoc* tribunals, the PTC should intervene in clear abuse cases. Nevertheless, it is worth noting one slight – but very important – difference: the PTC is authorized to scrutinize abuses during the early selection of situations for investigations. In contrast, the mentioned tribunals were only able to assess a case after the filing of an indictment. The very unique history of the ICC, in particular the common law and civil law voices that created it, led to the procedural compromise of article 53. This may explain why prosecutorial selection is not entirely left to the discretion of the Prosecutor. Guiding principles and proper judicial oversight was deemed necessary.

In sum, other international(ized) tribunals are of limited relevance to the specific "interests of justice" clause. The ICC might, nonetheless, benefit from the tribunals' experiences. In any event, it has been revealed that all international tribunals have used prosecutorial discretion when choosing their cases. Previous practice by international tribunals thus favors the need for wide prosecutorial discretion at the ICC.

ee) Conclusion and summary

The object and purpose of the ICC Statute suggest that a narrow interpretation of the admissibility criteria in article 17, combined with a broad interpretation of article 53 (1) (c), should be adopted.[1950] While a VCLT's interpretation was *prima facie* unclear, a survey into the ICC's drafting history, domestic jurisdictions, and international tribunals has favored the hypothesis that the "interests of justice" concept is a broad notion. The history

[1949] Statement of the Co-Prosecutors, 5.1.2009.

[1950] In the same vein, Stigen, *supra* note 205, 431.

of article 53 (1) (c) and (2) (c) did not add anything to the substantive content of the specific elements. On the other hand, it clearly revealed that the "interests of justice" clause was inserted as a broad, additional instrument for discretionary choices.[1951] In a similar vein, the survey into national and international(ized) jurisdictions could not specifically resolve the clause's content, which was never used before in the context of initiating investigations or prosecutions. However, domestic and international jurisdictions have exercised discretion when it comes to prosecutorial selection. They have initiated or denied further proceedings based on broad discretionary choices, which could be something for the ICC to follow in the "interests of justice" context.

Consequently, the term "justice" in article 53 must be understood in a broad sense, allowing for a variety of potential considerations. It is difficult to give a universal recipe as to how justice is achieved,[1952] and it remains, after all, a relative concept. Therefore, when adopting such a wide understanding, one must not forget the essential linkage to the criteria enumerated in article 53 (1) (c): gravity of the crime and interests of victims, which still require further definitions. Moreover, it is my hypothesis that alternative justice mechanisms and conditional amnesties must be arranged in a well-drafted legal corset that should be taken into account under article 53 (1) (c). On the contrary, considerations of *Realpolitik* (e.g. feasibility due to budgetary constraints) or the impact on peace negotiations are factors less reconcilable with the ICC Statute, even if a broader concept of interests of justice is adopted. The latter question of impact is not to be confused with the bigger picture of guidelines for peace negotiations within the framework of transition.[1953] The Prosecutor may certainly contribute to reconciliation by providing guidance as to how transitional mechanisms are in compliance with the ICC Statute. In contrast, it is presumed that the Prosecutor is not allowed to converge towards *being* a political actor himself; he must always "judicialize" the politics.[1954] Nevertheless, articles 53 (1) (c) and (2) (c) are the most explicit leeway to enable the Prosecutor not to investigate and/or prosecute based on policy decisions.

[1951] Ambos, in Ambos/Large/Wierda, *supra* note 650, 82–3, para. 51.

[1952] Stigen, *supra* note 205, 434.

[1953] Thereto Ambos, in Ambos/Large/Wierda, *supra* note 650, 19, abstract, para. 1.

[1954] Ambos, in Ambos/Large/Wierda, *supra* note 650, 19, abstract, para. 2; Gallavin, *supra* note 1881, 197.

b) Nonetheless substantial reasons: Proportionality test

Once the criteria for article 53 (1) (c) are identified, the Prosecutor must weigh them against each other ("nonetheless"). This balancing exercise constitutes the essential task for the OTP. One author carefully approaches this matter by weighing the interest of the parties to the case with those of the international community.[1955] Another author proposes a more specific, yet very complex and as such scarcely comprehensible, method of two axes: the axis of legitimacy/effectiveness for the initiation of an investigation, and the axis of universalism/relativism for the initiation of a prosecution.[1956] Methodologically, the preferred proportionality test consists of three layers: (1) is the measure appropriate?; (2) is the measure necessary/indispensable?; and (3) is the proportionality *stricto sensu* fulfilled?[1957] The latter approach tries to strike a fair balance. In particular, the third step of proportionality *stricto sensu* enables the OTP to look at all the different criteria and their elements. Certain limitations on the scope of available measures are further stressed: limitation *ratione materiae* with regard to international core crimes; limitation *ratione personae* with regard to the most responsible; the importance of the procedural stage at which the exemption takes place; some form of accountability and/or public procedure; and the overall political, social, and economic effects of the measure(s).[1958] In a similar vein, the available justice mechanisms have been linked to the OTP's Prosecutorial Strategy at hand,[1959] and the Prosecutor should therefore follow a differentiated approach when he checks the specific measure in a State.

To further explain the implementation of the testing mechanism, if the Prosecutor, for example, screens an amnesty law, the (simplified) process would be the following: first, the amnesty law must be appropriate to achieve the alleged object, i.e. peaceful transition. Second, the law must be indispensable, i.e. there cannot be other measures which would be less intrusive with regard to the "interests of justice." Third, the OTP would have to counterbalance gravity, the interests of the victims, and other relevant (unwritten) factors. The last step is most demanding; it urges the Prosecutor to pass a value judgment. He must thereby keep in mind the procedural

---

1955 Brubacher, *supra* note 368, 80.

1956 Delmas-Marty, *supra* note 1048, 10–1. In a similar vein, Hafner/Boon/Rübesame/Huston, *supra* note 695, 112–3.

1957 Ambos, in Ambos/Large/Wierda, *supra* note 650, 49 et seq., paras. 19 et seq. In the specific content of the English and Welsh public interest test, see Annex 2, England and Wales, with *infra* note 2847.

1958 Ambos, in Ambos/Large/Wierda, *supra* note 650, 50 et seq., para. 21.

1959 Part V, C.

check by the PTC pursuant to article 53 (3). On the other hand, the PTC may not simply set aside the actual weighing of the factors unless general principles of discretion have been violated; similar to the *ad hoc* tribunals, the PTC can only intervene in clear cases of abuse since prosecutorial discretion is the principal domain of the Prosecutor.[1960] The Chamber may thus control whether the proportionality testing by the OTP was in accordance with statutory and international law demands. It may, however, not replace the Prosecutor's balancing test through its own value judgment.

c) All the circumstances – open list of sub-criteria

The wording of article 53 (2) (c) suggests that the list of sub-criteria mentioned under the "interests of justice" clause is more illustrative than exhaustive. "Taking into account *all the circumstances,* including [...]" is a broad phrasing that embraces various factors. On the contrary, article 53 (1) is not phrased in such an open way, which has led to contextual conclusions that the listed criteria are exhaustive and not illustrative.[1961] This *e contrario* argumentation was identified by one author who, however, refutes an exhaustive reading by emphasizing the object and purpose of the provision and points to a broad understanding of the "interests of justice."[1962] "Taking into account" surely renders a narrow and broad understanding possible. In the study at hand, a broad interpretation of the "interests of justice" has been adopted.[1963] As such, discretionary considerations are rooted within article 53 (1) (c). Adopting a narrow construction and limiting the provision to an exhaustive reading would inappropriately touch upon the Prosecutor's wide discretion. As early as possible, he should be able to weigh relevant factors. Both lists under article 53 (1) (c) and (2) (c) seem illustrative, referring first to the gravity and interests of victims, and later adding the age or infirmity of the alleged perpetrator, as well as his or her role in the crime.[1964] The latter terms were included due to the individualizing process. For the allocation of resources the Prosecutor should be allowed to take factors into consideration to the extent known to him at an early stage.[1965] Accordingly, the list of article 53 (1) (c) should not be unnecessarily limited and a non-exhaustive reading is preferred.

[1960] Part IV, B., III., 3., a), dd). See further the potential guidance of judicial review by recent case law in England and Wales, Annex 2, B.

[1961] McDonald/Haveman, *supra* note 1149, 3.

[1962] Stigen, *supra* note 205, 360; also Meyer, *supra* note 1153, 579; Newman, *supra* note 774, 319; Morel, *supra* note 1365, 256.

[1963] Part IV, B., III., 3., a), ee).

[1964] In the same vein, *Situation in Darfur (Sudan),* Decision on application under rule 103, *supra* note 1833, 18.

d) *Explicit factors to be considered*

"Gravity of the crime" and the "interests of the victims" are specifically mentioned in article 53 (1) (c). Nonetheless, the list of factors is not strictly limited, and other potentially relevant factors can be taken into considerations. Earlier, the following four major clusters were identified as potential factors:

- Gravity of the situation (explicit factor);
- Interests of victims (explicit factor);
- Feasibility and effectiveness of an investigation (potentially relevant, unwritten factor);
- Impact of an investigation (potentially relevant, unwritten factor).[1966]

In line with the four main factors, gravity (aa), the interests of victims (bb), and unwritten factors (e), including feasibility and effectiveness, as well as impact, will be analyzed.

aa) Gravity of the crime – relative gravity under article 53 (1) (c)

First and most of all, the overlap between "gravity" in article 17 (1) (d) through reference of article 53 (1) (b) and the "gravity" element within the "interests of justice" clause in article 53 (1) (c) has not been entirely resolved. Since the "interests of justice" is discretionary in nature, it could be reasoned that article 53 (1) (c) is *lex specialis* because in the parameter before – under articles 53 (1) (b), 17 (1) (d) – "gravity" is only contemplated in a generic way.[1967] In accordance with this reasoning, "gravity" would be solely scrutinized as one part of the "interests of justice" assessment.[1968] On the other hand, significant differences can be observed between the two inclusions of "gravity" in article 53: articles 53 (1) (b) and 17 (1) (d) look at the fact whether "the case is not of sufficient gravity." If sufficient gravity exists, the Prosecutor may proceed; otherwise he has to discontinue further proceedings. The "gravity" test is essential for further proceedings and it is an important part of admissibility. In contrast, article 53 (1) (c) mentions "gravity of the crime" besides the "interests of the victims," which both have to be taken into account when looking at the "interests of

---

[1965] Stigen, *supra* note 205, 360.

[1966] Delmas-Marty, *supra* note 1048, 9, who takes these categories from the MoL Interests of Justice, *supra* note 1180.

[1967] Turone, in Cassese/Gaeta/Jones, *supra* note 26, 1154.

[1968] Wouters/Verhoeven/Demeyere, *supra* note 156, 297; Turone, in Cassese/Gaeta/Jones, *supra* note 26, 1154.

justice." The Prosecutor is supposed to balance gravity and the interest of victims *against* ("nonetheless") the "interests of justice."[1969] "Interests of justice" is the most relevant term of this parameter, but "gravity" is almost equally important as one prong under the over-all assessment and it is the decisive criterion for selecting the OTP's situations and cases. In practice, the Chamber determined gravity to be the second, inevitable part of the admissibility threshold;[1970] therefore, it cannot simply be ignored and must be taken into account under articles 53 (1) (b), 17 (d) *and* under 53 (1) (c).

Moreover, it has been submitted that the notion of gravity has two dimensions: a policy dimension, equally referred to as relative gravity, and a legal dimension, also called the gravity threshold.[1971] The latter is linked to articles 53 (1) (b) and 17 (1) (d), while the former amounts to the test under article 53 (1) (c). For their application, the model approach must be recalled: legal gravity, which has been discussed abundantly above, is a low barrier, primarily requiring a quantitative check; in sharp contrast, relative gravity deals with situation selection due to a comparison *vis-à-vis* other situations and qualitative factors should increasingly be taken into account.[1972] Only the latter (relative) gravity will now be readdressed in more detail.

Unlike legal gravity, the gravity threshold according to article 53 (1) (c) must be higher. Gravity is potentially the Prosecutor's most important factor when is comes to the "interests of justice" determination.[1973] Due to available resources and practical necessities to conduct selective prosecutions, the Prosecutor has developed focused investigations and prosecutions.[1974] The OTP bases its decisions on comparative gravity.[1975] Comparative gravity is an empirical and criminological analysis. A comparative flow-chart highlights situations and cases that are pending or are currently under analysis and tries to bring them into one comparable line.[1976] Crime

---

1969 The weighing against should be the general rule, however, the interest of the victims might – under certain circumstances – disfavor further investigations.

1970 *Prosecutor v. Lubanga,* Decision on the Prosecutor's application for warrant of arrest, article 58, *supra* note 217, para. 41.

1971 Cf. Part IV, B., III., 2., c), bb), (4) and (5).

1972 Part IV, B., III., 2., c), dd).

1973 Stigen, *supra* note 205, 187.

1974 Part IV, B., II., 4.

1975 McAuliffe deGuzman, *supra* note 1152, 24. For the comparative process at the ICTR, see Jallow, *supra* note 1245, 155. The Defence in the *Katanga and Chui* case submitted a "comparative-gravity test" for determining whether the national or international (ICC) level fits better for proceedings, cf. *Prosecutor v. Katanga and Chui,* Motion challenging the admissibility of the case by the Defence, *supra* note 459, para. 46.

mapping techniques help to identify the "hot spots" or areas with highest concentration of crimes.[1977] Thereby, the Prosecutor may base his decisions on a number of legal and policy criteria, but he must ensure consistency and objectivity as far as possible. So far, the Prosecutor has not carefully distinguished between considerations related to the gravity threshold and matters of prosecutorial discretion.[1978] It is strongly advised that the OTP must do so and the Prosecutor should indicate legal and policy considerations in its chart, as well as situation or case specific determinations. If the legal gravity threshold turns out to be "positive" and the situation is potentially admissible, there remains nevertheless a certain degree of discretion when applying relative gravity. However, the discretionary decision is not unfettered and the Prosecutor must indicate if he declines further proceedings on the basis of legal or policy determinations. For achieving a higher perception of legitimacy, the Prosecutor should continuously make his criteria public, apply them consistently, and – whenever circumstances allow – he should let us know the situations in which he declines further proceedings and his reasons for not choosing them.[1979]

bb) Interests of victims

With regard to the interest of the victims, the term "nonetheless" suggests that the factor favors an investigation or prosecution, and that it has to be weighed against the "interests of justice." In general, the interest of the victims weighs in favor of prosecution, but the Prosecutor acknowledges that "due consideration must be given to the sometimes divergent views of victims, their communities and the broader society."[1980] The Office will listen to all parties concerned.[1981] It is further essential to consult various sources, not confined to the victims themselves.[1982] In this respect, the OTP noted that:

> "It may be important to seek the views of respected intermediaries and representatives, or those who may be able to provide a comprehensive overview of a com-

---

1976 For such a chart with regard to DRC see Agirre Aranburu, in Bergsmo, *supra* note 460, 153.

1977 Agirre Aranburu, in Bergsmo, *supra* note 460, 154–5.

1978 WCRO report gravity, *supra* note 1057, 7.

1979 Similarly, McAuliffe deGuzman, *supra* note 1152, 45.

1980 Interests of justice paper, *supra* note 99, 5; ICTJ, Human Rights Center Berkely & Payson Center for International Development, "Research note on attitudes about peace and justice in Northern Uganda, New population-based data on attitude about peace and justice" (hereinafter ICTJ peace and justice research 2007), 13 August 2007, 7–8.

1981 Interests of justice paper, *supra* note 99, 5; Mallinder, *supra* note 1384, 289.

1982 Stigen, *supra* note 205, 364.

plex situation. This may include local leaders (religious, political, tribal), other states, local and international intergovernmental and nongovernmental organizations."[1983]

The OTP deemed it necessary to develop clear protocols and provide mechanisms: (1) to ensure that the views of the victims and local communities are systematically sought and (2) to allow for adequate outreach to enhance the understanding of the role and impact of the Office, without however (3) exposing victims and local communities to uncontrollable security risks due to a higher communication profile.[1984] The outreach programme of the ICC is a major step in this direction and makes the victims familiar with the existence and actions of the Court.[1985] *In situ* trials should, however, be considered as an valuable supplement given the surprising fact that the population in Ituri, as well as in North and South Kivu, is largely not familiar with neither the ICC nor its on-going *Lubanga* proceedings.[1986]

Any statement where the interests of victims speak against OTP proceedings would most likely be controversial and prompt considerable criticism.[1987] HRW has therefore favored a narrow interpretation that only takes into consideration certain interests of victims, namely interests that promote justice interests on the HRW interpretation of that term.[1988] The OTP has taken a different view.[1989] NGOs have argued that the interest of victims is in justice and justice alone.[1990] Since the criterion is technically listed in article 53 as a possible reason not to investigate or prosecute, it is part of the general weighing process under the "interests of justice" clause. As already noticed, it generally favors prosecution; however, protection issues could disfavor proceedings in the victims' views.[1991] On the other hand, if

---

[1983] Interests of justice paper, *supra* note 99, 6; Stigen, *supra* note 205, 364.

[1984] Outlining the Prosecutorial Strategy – Mr. Michel De Smedt, *supra* note 1226.

[1985] On the outreach programme see <www2.icc-cpi.int/Menus/ICC/Structure+of+the+Court/Outreach/>; ICC Outreach Report 2008, *supra* note 206; ICC Outreach Report 2009, 18.11.2009, *supra* note 206; also Nuremberg Declaration on Peace and Justice, in Ambos/Large/Wierda, *supra* note 2041, 544, IV., 2., 2.3: "Outreach and consultation are crucial elements of legitimacy and ownership of transitional justice measures. All those involved need to understand fully the potential and limitations of available options."

[1986] ICTJ DRC population-based survey, *supra* note 210, 47–8, 65; Borello, *supra* note 210, 32.

[1987] Stigen, *supra* note 205, 364.

[1988] HRW, policy paper article 53, *supra* note 1263, 19.

[1989] Interests of justice paper, *supra* note 99, 5–6.

[1990] Unger/Wierda, in Ambos/Large/Wierda, *supra* note 678, 275.

[1991] Interests of justice paper, *supra* note 99, 5; Mallinder, *supra* note 1384, 289; Stigen, *supra* note 205, 364.

the OTP takes into consideration security matters as part of its policy, potential perpetrators could destabilize the situation to avoid ICC intervention. Victims in on-going conflict situations also set different priorities than justice: they may not want to see a peace process jeopardized.[1992] Such statements must, however, be considered with caution as they might reflect short-term fears of the consequences and ignorance of the long-term consequences.[1993] Accountability and justice for grave crimes are equally important to most people, and many believe that these concepts are linked to peace.[1994] The remaining question is therefore who speaks on behalf of the victims,[1995] and how to identify the victims' needs.[1996] The principal rights of victims have been identified as truth, justice, and reparation.[1997] It has further been pointed out that their interests may vary, not only in distinct situations, but also within the same conflict.[1998] In this regard, the ICTJ has developed a promising research design through qualitative and quantitative assessment (survey work), nevertheless acknowledging certain limitations in light of the inherent challenges of doing population-based survey in conflict and post-conflict settings.[1999] It will be the OTP's task to further refine its own consultation process and develop a congruent strategy. The method of dialogue and consultation points into the right direction[2000] and should be supplemented by empirical survey work. It will remain a tremendous challenge to listen to all parties of the conflict and to weigh their diverging views against one another.

e) Other potential considerations

The idea of the "interests of justice" is an open concept, similar to the "public interest" test in some national jurisdictions and raises the question

---

1992 See for Northern Uganda ICTJ peace and justice research 2007, *supra* note 1980, 2, 4; already ICTJ & Human Rights Center Berkeley, "Forgotten voices: a population-based survey on attitudes about peace and justice in Northern Uganda," July 2005, 24 et seq.; for DRC see ICTJ DRC population-based survey, *supra* note 210, 23–4.

1993 Stigen, *supra* note 205, 366.

1994 ICTJ DRC population-based survey, *supra* note 210, 40.

1995 ICTJ peace and justice research 2007, *supra* note 1980, 8.

1996 Mallinder, *supra* note 1384, 358 et seq.

1997 Ambos, in Ambos/Large/Wierda, *supra* note 650, 33–4, para. 10.

1998 Morel, *supra* note 1365, 262–3.

1999 ICTJ DRC population-based survey, *supra* note 210, 15–6, 17. Further on the data collection methodology, see Phung Pham/Patrick Vinck, "Empirical research and the development and assessment of transitional justice mechanisms" (2007) 1 IJTJ 231, 234 et seq.; Unger/Wierda, in Ambos/Large/Wierda, *supra* note 678, 275.

2000 Unger/Wierda, in Ambos/Large/Wierda, *supra* note 678, 275.

whether circumstances not mentioned within the clause might be regarded as relevant.[2001] It has been argued above that the listing is open for unwritten factors. The same approach has been taken by the Prosecutor, who developed a rudimentary listing of potentially relevant factors. In a second step, the OTP breaks this non-exhaustive list down into component elements, highlighting arguments both for and against their consideration.[2002] Similarly, potential criteria not enumerated in article 53 will be identified and evaluated in the following survey.[2003] Due to the open nature of article 53, in particular article 53 (2) (c) – "taking into account all the circumstances, including" – but also the broad interpretative angle taken at hand with regard to the "interests of justice," it is submitted that a variety of elements could be included and it will be left to others authors and/or the Court to develop specific factors in a legally convincing manner.[2004] For the time being, I will deal with the impact of an investigation (aa), the feasibility and effectiveness of an investigation (bb), other alternative justice mechanisms *in general* (cc), and amnesties *in particular* (dd).

aa) Impact of an investigation (peace and security)

It has to be considered whether the OTP shall consider the impact of an investigation under article 53 (1) (c) and the impact of a prosecution under article 53 (2) (c). It has been argued that the Prosecutor may take the broader interests of the international community into consideration, including the potential political ramifications.[2005] The Prosecutor could be required "to balance his own interest in mounting prosecutions against any other interests which the victims may have, such as peace and stability."[2006] Such a determination could be similar to one made by the SC as to whether

2001 Seils/Wierda, *supra* note 1461, 12.

2002 Delmas-Marty, *supra* note 1048, 9.

2003 The analysis is, however, limited to a subjective selection, in other words, only a certain sample can be given.

2004 For a wider sample, see Stigen, *supra* note 205, 372 et seq.

2005 Brubacher, *supra* note 368, 81; concurring, Mallinder, *supra* note 1887, 219; Rodman, *supra* note 1249, 120 et seq.; *Situation in Darfur (Sudan),* Annexes to application on behalf of Citizen's Organisations of the Sudan in relation to the Prosecutor's applications for arrest warrants of 14 July 2008 and 20 November 2008, Annex 7, Alex de Waal, The public application by the Chief Prosecutor of the ICC for an arrest warrant against Sudanese President Omar al Bashir: A critique, 12.1.2009 (ICC-02/05-171-Anx7) para. 50; contrary, Dukić, *supra* note 1256, 715.

2006 Alex De Waal, "A critique of the public application by the Chief Prosecutor of the ICC for an arrest warrant against Sudanese President Omar al Bashir," SSRC blogs: Making sense of Darfur, 27.1.2009, para. 65; also Borello, *supra* note 210, 31.

a situation is a threat to peace and security.[2007] Thus, "impact" amounts to an unwritten element of article 53 (1) (c); it urges the OTP to take the stability and security of the concerned country into consideration[2008] if applied in such a manner. In particular, the question arose – theoretically, and also practically in the Northern Uganda situation – whether complications caused to a negotiation or reconciliation process through ICC investigations and prosecutions should be taken into account. This discussion has often been referred to as the "peace vs. justice" dilemma. It has to be noted that this issue presents a different question, namely whether the "interests of justice" allow the Prosecutor to consider alternative justice mechanisms and amnesties. This question will therefore be addressed separately.[2009]

The inclusion of peace and security concerns would require the Prosecutor to weigh the risk that an investigation or prosecution may have on a political situation against other interests that are likely to favor a prosecution such as the ones enumerated in article 53 (gravity, interest of victims, circumstances of the individual).[2010] The Prosecutor has stated that there can be no political compromise on legality and accountability.[2011] On the other hand, he has acknowledged various national and international efforts to achieve peace and security.[2012] The relationship between peace and justice has been addressed continuously and from different angles in international law literature. In his policy paper on the "interests of justice" of 2007 the Prosecutor has even distinguished between the "interests of peace" and the "interests of justice" by clearly saying "that there is a difference between the concepts of the 'interests of justice' and the 'interests of peace' and that the latter falls within the mandate of institutions other than the Office of the Prosecutor."[2013]

The Prosecutor could be reading too much into the term when literally differentiating peace and justice: the concept was deliberately left undefined for leaving the exercise of prosecutorial discretion unfettered.[2014] From my point of view, the narrow approach of the OTP is indeed questionable. Instead of contrasting peace and justice, the true question can be brought to

---

2007 Brubacher, *supra* note 368, 81.

2008 Delmas-Marty, *supra* note 1048, 9.

2009 Part IV, B., III., 3., e), cc) and dd).

2010 Brubacher, *supra* note 368, 82.

2011 "Building a Future on Peace and Justice," Address by Mr. Luis Moreno-Ocampo, *supra* note 258, 6–7; approvingly, E. Ronaldo Mota Sardenberg of Brazil, Session 3: Interested States, Second public hearing of the OTP, 17.10.2006.

2012 Address by the Prosecutor to the UN SC, *supra* note 672, 4.

2013 Interests of justice paper, *supra* note 99, 1.

2014 Schabas, *supra* note 1151, 749; *id.*, *supra* note 13, 663.

light by taking a step backwards: How far reaching are the "interests of justice"? The next question would be: Are the justice interests broad enough to allow for considerations of impact, as the case may be for political considerations that involve peace negotiations? At first sight, it appears therefore feasible to differentiate the terms peace and justice, yet not to juxtapose them against each other. The upcoming survey will further evaluate whether the OTP's narrow approach that excludes peace considerations from article 53 (1) (c) and (2) (c), has to be considered the best solution.

From a practical point of view, the matter arose in Northern Uganda when LRA leaders refused to sign a peace deal unless the ICC's arrest warrants were dropped.[2015] On the other hand, authors have stressed the positive impact the ICC had in pushing the LRA to the negotiating table in the first place.[2016] Rather than choosing one of the diametric options – prosecutions *vis-à-vis* blanket amnesties – it has been suggested to find a middle way according to the ICC's complementarity regime. If a rigorous and serious national plan for accountability was established, the warrants could be legitimately dropped without sacrificing either peace or justice.[2017] In the context of the Ugandan situation, it was difficult, if not unpromising, to define the two notions peace and justice in general terms. The words "peace" and "justice" should rather be seen in the context of a specific incident in order to clarify the interaction between the two concepts.[2018] In other words, the relationship between peace and justice should be empirically determined on a case-by-case basis rather than asserted as a matter of principle.[2019] In any event, the Ugandan matter has proven to be very delicate. The Prosecutor thus far has only rendered an ambiguous statement that he could suspend planned prosecutions to enable peace moves, but would not stop investigation and prosecution as such.[2020] The peace process and arrest warrants could, in the meantime, proceed simultaneously on "parallel tracks."[2021]

[2015] Schiff, *supra* note 128, 208; Rodman, *supra* note 1249, 111; HRW Courting history report, *supra* note 126, 34; Grono/O'Brien, in Waddell/Clark, *supra* note 246, 16; Chandra Lekha Sriram, "Conflict mediation and the ICC: challenges and options for pursuing peace with justice at the regional level" in Ambos/Large/Wierda, *supra* note 650, 303, 312–3; also Part III, B., I., 2.

[2016] Grono/O'Brien, in Waddell/Clark, *supra* note 246, 15; Otim/Wierda, in Waddell/Clark, *supra* note 260, 23; Stigen, *supra* note 205, 386–7; Unger/Wierda, in Ambos/Large/Wierda, *supra* note 678, 271; Jurdi, *supra* note 99, 93–4.

[2017] ICTJ, 2006/2007 annual report, 1, 3; Grono/O'Brien, in Waddell/Clark, *supra* note 246, 16 ("robust accountability").

[2018] RLP paper no. 17, *supra* note 246, 9.

[2019] De Waal, *supra* note 2006, para. 69.

[2020] Schiff, *supra* note 128, 204.

[2021] Unger/Wierda, in Ambos/Large/Wierda, *supra* note 678, 270–1.

In a similar vein, the issue of the peace v. justice "paradox" was raised in the Darfur situation in relation to the then pending arrest warrant decision against Omar Al Bashir.[2022] The African Union quickly requested a deferral by the SC under article 16 "to ensure that the ongoing peace efforts are not jeopardized."[2023] This request was noted by the SC, and the response was by no means clear in its language:

> "*Taking note* of the African Union (AU) communiqué of the 142nd Peace and Security Council (PSC) Meeting dated 21 July (S/2008/481, annex), *having in mind* concerns raised by members of the Council regarding potential developments subsequent to the application by the Prosecutor of the International Criminal Court of 14 July 2008, and *taking note* of their intention to consider these matters further, [...]."[2024]

The vague language even led the United States to abstain from the vote:

> "The United States abstained in the voting because the language added to the resolution would send the wrong signal to Sudanese President Al-Bashir and undermine efforts to bring him and others to justice."[2025]

However, other States, such as Russia, China, France, Libya, and Indonesia, lobbied for an article 16 deferral.[2026] Concern about the "possible negative impact of a potential indictment" was expressed by Vietnam.[2027] One may doubt Al Bashir portraying himself as the peacemaker and predictions about the impact are very difficult to make.[2028] Given the practice of the Prosecutor with respect to (political) peace consideration, it is unlikely that he will use his article 53 powers to discontinue proceedings. Article 16 would thus be the most direct gateway to halt proceedings. But deferral proceedings under this tool only allow for a renewable one year period and they set a high threshold.[2029] In other words, article 16 allows for tempor-

---

2022 Robert Cryer, "Prosecuting the leaders: promises, politics and practicalities" (2009) 1 GOJIL 45, 66–7; *Situation in Darfur (Sudan),* Application on behalf of Citizens' Organisations of The Sudan, *supra* note 303, para. 8; Ciampi, *supra* note 707, 885 et seq.; CICC, "Article 16 debated in Africa," Stephen Lamony, The Monitor, No. 37, Nov. 2008–April 2009, 14; Oette, *supra* note 633, 348.

2023 African Union Communiqué of the 142nd meeting of the Peace and Security Council, 21 July 2008, para. 11 i); in great detail Oette, *supra* note 633, 350 et seq.

2024 SC-Res. 1828 (2008), 31.7.2008; Cryer, *supra* note 2022, 67.

2025 Mr. Wolf, SC 5947th meeting, 31.7.2008 (S/PV.5947), 8; Ciampi, *supra* note 707, 887.

2026 See the Statements by Mr. Churkin (Russian Federation), Mr. Wang Guangya (China), Mr. De Rivière (France), Mr. Mubarak (Libyan Arab Jamahiriya), Mr. Kleib (Indonesia), SC 5947th meeting, *supra* note 2025.

2027 Mr. Le Luong Minh (Vietnam), SC 5947th meeting, *supra* note 2025, 11.

2028 Cryer, *supra* note 2022, 69–70; also Grono/O'Brien, in Waddell/Clark, *supra* note 246, 17 et seq.; contrary, *Situation in Darfur (Sudan),* Application on behalf of Citizens' Organisations of The Sudan, *supra* note 303, para. 10.

ary – not permanent – suspensions.[2030] In addition, it seems contradictory for the SC to refer the Darfur situation to the ICC and later, when the Court tries to hold the responsible persons accountable, to defer proceedings against them.[2031] This amounts to selective prosecution based on political motives. Prosecutorial selection is a matter for an independent Prosecutor and not a political organ like the SC.[2032] Nevertheless, an article 16 deferral remains legally possible even with respect to specific cases (Al Bashir) due to the clear wording ("investigations *and* prosecutions") of article 16.

A different path to prevent an arrest warrant was chosen by the Citizens' Organizations of The Sudan. They tried to influence the PTC's decision directly by submitting a filing as *amicus curiae* under rule 103 and requesting the Chamber to convene a hearing.[2033] Most notably, the Organization was neither asked to do so nor was it a party to the proceedings. The PTC clarified that any observations under rule 103 required leave by the competent Chamber, which was not granted in the case at bar.[2034] An appeal on the decision by the PTC was further denied on the grounds that the applicants are not a "party" to the Darfur proceedings in the meaning of article 82 (1) and rule 155.[2035] Nevertheless, a quick look at the arguments put forward by the Applicants will be taken. The Organization requested that no arrest warrants are issued by the PTC on the grounds that (1) issuing such warrants would have grave implications for peace building process in Sudan and deference must be given to considerations of national interest and security; (2) the "interests of justice" will not be served, particularly in light of the Prosecutor's conduct in bringing these applications; (3) such warrants could entrench the negative perceptions of the ICC and thus contribute to a deterioration of the situation in Sudan; and, (4) alternative means of transitional justice and resolution are being and will be pursued without need for any ICC involvement at this stage.[2036] While some points could at least

---

2029 Cryer, *supra* note 2022, 71.

2030 Slye/van Schaack, *supra* note 534, 261.

2031 The Applicants in *Situation in Darfur (Sudan),* Application on behalf of Citizens' Organisations of The Sudan, *supra* note 303, paras. 32–3, argue the converse. However, they do have a valid point with regard to double standards in international affairs and the three permanent (non ICC members) China, Russia, and the USA.

2032 Ciampi, *supra* note 707, 889–90; similarly Oette, *supra* note 633, 354.

2033 *Situation in Darfur (Sudan),* Application on behalf of Citizens' Organisations of The Sudan, *supra* note 303, paras. 46 et seq.

2034 *Situation in Darfur (Sudan),* Decision on application under rule 103, *supra* note 1833, paras. 6, 33. See further Part IV, E., I.

2035 *Situation in Darfur (Sudan),* Decision on the application for leave to appeal the decision on application under rule 103, 19.2.2009 (ICC-02/05-192) 5.

2036 *Situation in Darfur (Sudan),* Application on behalf of Citizens' Organisations of The Sudan, *supra* note 303, para. 8; *Situation in Darfur (Sudan),* Application for

theoretically speak against prosecution, it is not for the PTC to decide on these issues. The Chamber rightly stated that article 53 (3) is the only gateway for checking prosecutorial discretion and that this right is very limited to negative decisions by the Prosecutor under article 53 (2).[2037] In other words, the PTC can control a decision by the Prosecutor not to prosecute Al Bashir, but it is barred from inspecting the discretionary choices for doing so. In any event, the Prosecutor himself could consider implications on the peace process and alternative justice mechanisms under article 53 (2). Potential backlash against the ICC, on the other hand, can be left aside as prosecutorial motive as this concern is highly speculative and go well beyond the "interests of justice" clause. Grave implications for the peace building process in Sudan could be valid considerations, but it will be explained in more detail why these arguments lack merit. Last but not least, alternative justice mechanisms are the most likely tool to block ICC trials. Nevertheless, the filing by the Applicants has two significant *lacunae* in its argument: first, ICC involvement at some point is unavoidable, and it is the ICC that finally decides whether the transitional justice mechanism bars its proceedings or not. Second, the specific mechanisms must be in place and working; speculation that there will be sufficient means in the future is surely not enough. Last and foremost, it is strongly suggested that senior leaders such as Al Bashir cannot benefit from alternative (transitional) justice instruments.[2038] In conclusion, an "interests of justice" deferral by the Prosecutor is almost ruled out in the *Bashir* case. Since an arrest warrant against Al Bashir was issued on 4 March 2009 by the PTC, the article 16 discussions will certainly erupt again. The reactions were already by all means divided.[2039]

---

leave to appeal against decision on application under rule 103, 11.2.2009 (ICC-02/05-187) para. 5; also *Situation in Darfur (Sudan),* Annex 7, *supra* note 2005, paras. 50 et seq.

2037 *Situation in Darfur (Sudan),* Decision on application under rule 103, *supra* note 1833, para. 21; further Part IV, E., I.

2038 Cf. Part V, C.

2039 "Instant view – Reaction to warrant for Bashir's arrest," 4.3.2009, Reuters, quoting Sudan Presidential Advisor Mustafa Osman Ismail: "They do not want Sudan to become stable."; Senegal's President Abdoulaye Wade: "[…] That is what is blocking negotiations."; Abdel Wahed Mohamed Ahmed Al-Nur, Founder of the Darfur Rebel Sudan Liberation Movement (SLM): "[The ICC decision] is a great victory for justice in the world, a great victory for the people of Darfur, for the hundreds of thousands of people who have been killed, raped and tortured by this regime."; US State Department Spokesmen Robert Wood: "The United States believes those who have committed atrocities should be brought to justice."; Russian Special Envoy to Sudan, Mikhail Margelov: "The untimely fulfillment of the ICC decision to arrest the President of Sudan will create a dangerous precedent in the system of international relations and could negatively affect the situation both inside

Returning to the interpretation of article 53 as such, if a broad definition of "justice" is applied – as suggested in the study at hand – peace considerations could be, generally speaking, taken into consideration. But like "justice," the term "peace" is similarly broad and means different things to different people. From a legal perspective, Black's Law Dictionary simply refers to it as "a state of public tranquility; freedom of civil disturbance or hostility."[2040] In the Nuremberg Declaration on Peace and Justice, the term "peace" is understood as meaning sustainable peace.[2041] The term "peace" is not used in article 53 and it appears only once in the Statute within the general context of preambular paragraph 3 ("recognizing that such grave crimes threaten the peace, security and well-being of the world"). One author, even though not in the specific context of article 53, differentiates the (theoretical) concepts of positive and negative peace, and later concludes that – in general terms and theoretically speaking – the ICC enhances peace.[2042] But it remains difficult to inquire the meaning of peace and to reach a universally accepted definition.

It is submitted that, for the purpose of article 53, one must not necessarily reach a positive definition. In this respect, the whole "peace vs. justice" discussion is misleading to a certain extent. The two notions should not be juxtaposed, but should be recognized as a *peace and justice continuum* that works hand-in-hand.[2043] If properly pursued, peace and justice promote and sustain each other.[2044] One can therefore define "peace" in a negative way as not being reduced to the process of negotiating peace agreements only, and "justice" should not be treated as a synonym of prosecutions alone.[2045]

Sudan and the overall situation in the region."; International Center for Transitional Justice: "The reality about the peace process for Darfur is that no serious peace process exists. We know from history that silence in the face of atrocities does not prevent further crimes. The warrant could be an opportunity for the first real progress in Darfur."

2040 Black's Law Dictionary, *supra* note 1075, 1151, "peace."

2041 Nuremberg Declaration on Peace and Justice, Annex to the letter dated 13 June 2008 form the Permanent Representatives of Finland, Germany and Jordan to the United Nations addressed to the Secretary-General, in Ambos/Large/Wierda, *supra* note 650, 541, 542, II., 1.

2042 Nitsche, *supra* note 784, 53–4; also – on the difficult question what peace amounts to – see Nsereko, *supra* note 1829, 374; Contag, *supra* note 426, 32 et seq.

2043 Graeme Simpson, "One among many: The ICC as a tool of justice during transition" in Waddell/Clark, *supra* note 246, 73, 75; Chandra Lekha Sriram, *Confronting past human rights violations* (Frank Cass, London, New York 2004) 1, 203; Report on the major findings of the conference by Ambassador of Jordan to the USA HRH Prince Zeid Ra'ad Zeid Al-Hussein, in Ambos/Large/Wierda, *supra* note 650, 533, para. 1.

2044 Nuremberg Declaration on Peace and Justice, in Ambos/Large/Wierda, *supra* note 2041, 542, III., 1.

If such a broad approach towards justice and peace is adopted, this allows for a discussion on the different segments of peace under the "interests of justice" clause, rather than making a decision of general principle for or against peace. In particular, two aspects which have been blurred as part of the whole peace discussion must be distinguished: peace negotiations as such and alternative justice mechanisms as tools within peace agreements. To reach an intermediary conclusion, it is the overarching legal definition of the "interests of justice" that is highly disputed, and in place the exact scope of the term: Is it broad enough to involve questions of impact such as the spoiling of peace negotiations?

Exactly there the line must be drawn. Article 53 (1) (c) has to be given a working definition if the Prosecutor and the PTCs are supposed to apply the construct in a meaningful manner. The definition of "interests of justice" is already difficult, but at least the term is – to a certain extent – of legal nature and can be construed in accordance with the ICC Statute. But some aspects of the relationship between peace and justice certainly exceed the Prosecutor's domain. Not even a "case-by-case basis" approach alters the fact that impact (and peace negotiations as such) are political in nature, and, moreover, are highly speculative. Any argument will be based on predictions.[2046] Who can say if peace negotiations succeed or fail? The factors are often nebulous. Who can say if the involved actors act sincerely and wholeheartedly? Such a purely political decision rests upon the SC and article 16 is therefore the only – admittedly limited – tool:[2047]

> "If the judgment has to be made, on occasion, that the interests of peace should override those of justice, then that should be for the Security Council to decide, not the ICC, and the pressure and weight of expectations should be taken off the Prosecutor's shoulders in this respect."[2048]

In this regard, the OTP's policy paper comes to the same result. Broader matters of international peace and security fall outside the OTP's man-

---

2045 Simpson, in Waddell/Clark, *supra* note 2043, 75.

2046 Stigen, *supra* note 205, 386. With regard to Uganda see Burke-White/Kaplan, in Stahn/Sluiter, *supra* note 247, 101.

2047 Coming to the same result, see Interests of justice paper, *supra* note 99, 8–9; AI open letter, *supra* note 1845, 8; HRW, policy paper article 53, *supra* note 1263, 7; FIDH, Réflexions sur la notion "intérêts de la justice," *supra* note 1850, 5; Ssenyonjo, *supra* note 246, 378; Mr. Nick Grono – International Crisis Group, Session 2: NGOs and other experts, Second public hearing of the OTP, 26.9.2006; Heilmann, *supra* note 74, 155–6. On the limited scope of article 16 see Stahn, *supra* note 726, 716–7; Ambos, in Ambos/Large/Wierda, *supra* note 650, 82, para. 50; De Waal, *supra* note 2006, para. 78; differentiated, Stigen, *supra* note 205, 384.

2048 Mr. Gareth Evans of the International Crisis Group, *supra* note 414. The SC can though not exercise totally unfettered discretion, cf. Heilmann, *supra* note 74, 99–100.

date.[2049] However, the OTP could reach a similar result by taking a wide approach when considering the "interests of justice." Adopting such a wide approach would allow the OTP to exercise its flexibility where it belongs – under article 53 (1) (c) and (2) (c). If the Prosecutor follows this design, boundaries for the "interests of justice" must be set by self-restraint through prosecutorial guidelines and ICC case law. That said, "broader political matters of international peace and security" or "peace negotiations" should be excluded as relevant factors.

The Office must also pay careful attention to the security of its staff and witnesses.[2050] It is therefore submitted that the Prosecutor may take into consideration (narrow) security issues that affect the work on the ground. However, the Prosecutor should do so as an internal matter and might, for instance, use the tool of sealed indictments.[2051] By no means should the Office be open to blackmail;[2052] rough States would certainly increase victimization and instability if the Prosecutor openly states that security issues can lead to dropping an investigation.

In a nutshell, the relationship between peace and justice – abundantly addressed in legal and political literature[2053] – is not the decisive question to start with; it is instead the content and scope of the "interests of justice" element that has to be determined in the first place. Rightly so, it has been pointed out that the actual *result* of excluding political consideration from article 53 is unobjectionable. Some authors have nevertheless put the cart before the horse. A narrow interpretation of the "interests of justice" *per se* turns the carefully drafted compromise upside-down. Article 53 (1) entails legal considerations (jurisdiction and admissibility) and discretionary considerations (the "interests of justice"). The latter naturally involves broader ideas than the former. If construed too strictly, the Prosecutor starts searching for loopholes. With regard to the present Prosecutor's approach, as well as PTC I's findings in the arrest warrant decisions in Lubanga and Ntaganda, this can be designated the "slip-away towards gravity."

Broad discretion is preferable, but with the caveat that "broad" does not mean "unlimited."[2054] Of course, there must be boundaries, and these limits

---

2049 Interests of justice paper, *supra* note 99, 9; also Goldstone, *supra* note 1048, 398.

2050 Unger/Wierda, in Ambos/Large/Wierda, *supra* note 678, 298 et seq.

2051 Seils/Wierda, *supra* note 1461, 13; Unger/Wierda, in Ambos/Large/Wierda, *supra* note 678, 271 ("in a non-public manner"); Hall, in Stahn/Sluiter, *supra* note 206, 226.

2052 Stigen, *supra* note 205, 388.

2053 Côte, *supra* note 1190, 177.

2054 In the same vein, Ambos, in Ambos/Large/Wierda, *supra* note 650, 84–5, para. 52.

have to be set by the already mentioned OTP self-restraint and/or PTC control. Moreover, "discretion does not convert the clause to a mere policy instrument irrespective of the legal criteria provided by it (gravity of the crime, interests of victims, age or infirmity of the alleged offender, and the role of the perpetrator in the alleged crime)."[2055]

In conclusion, it is submitted that the "interests of justice" is a wide notion *as a general rule,* but purely political considerations (such as peace negotiations) fall outside its ambit. Otherwise the Prosecutor would be turned into a policy maker.[2056] Moreover, the OTP must be careful with using "impact" as a criterion, which is not a valuable factor of gravity, but is valuable for the "interests of justice." When the Prosecutor turns to "impact," he must be careful about the criterion's content and its application. As stated above, the spoiling of peace negotiations should not be taken into account, but, on the other hand, the Prosecutor must be aware of the significant effects his actions have. In any event, the Prosecutor can reconsider a decision to halt proceedings based on new facts or information in accordance with article 53 (4).

bb) Feasibility and effectiveness of an investigation

It has been argued that budgetary constraints force the Prosecutor to prioritize situations under the "interests of justice."[2057] Thereby, the prospects of success and whether the Prosecutor can manage to obtain the accused and evidence have been deemed essential.[2058] In a similar vein, the Prosecutor has stated in the context of the Darfur situation:

> "The selection and progress of these cases will be based on the best possible evidence available to the Office at the relevant time."[2059]

Feasibility touches upon obvious problems of *Realpolitik* such as resources and state cooperation.[2060] But both elements are not mentioned within article 53.[2061] Unwritten elements need further justification and need to be very precise. On the other hand, article 54 (1) (b) supports taking

---

[2055] Ambos, in Ambos/Large/Wierda, *supra* note 650, 19, abstract, para. 1.

[2056] Gallavin, *supra* note 1881, 197; Ohlin, in Stahn/Sluiter, *supra* note 428, 208; contrary, Rodman, *supra* note 1249, 120 et seq.

[2057] Morel, *supra* note 1365, 261.

[2058] Stigen, *supra* note 205, 374.

[2059] Third Report pursuant to UNSC 1593, *supra* note 288, 3.

[2060] On the ICC *vis-à-vis* Realpolitik, see Ambos, *supra* note 257, 15 et seq.; also Stigen, *supra* note 205, 374–5.

[2061] It has to be noted that these two elements, though initially discussed by the OTP, were not included in the final Interests of justice paper, *supra* note 99.

practical success into consideration as it allows the OTP to take "appropriate measures to ensure the effective investigation and prosecution of crimes within the jurisdiction of the Court." The "interests of justice" clause could be a potential gateway for ensuring effective investigation.

Evidentiary matters surely play a role in the decision of the Prosecutor, but the two mentioned elements of "scarcity of resources" and "cooperation" constitute a different matter. Resources are primarily an issue for the ASP to resolve, and for unanticipated financial resources a Contingency Fund was set up to ensure the independence of the OTP.[2062] While the operating range of the ICC is limited through resources if one considers the enormous number of world-wide conflicts, resources should not restrict the Prosecutor with respect to his specific selection choices. Otherwise the ASP would violate the OTP's independence and turn itself into the decision maker. Without effective support by States, the SC, and international organizations, the OTP is – to a certain degree – incapable of action. On the other hand, cooperation through self-referrals is, on some occasions, only *prima facie* support.[2063] In particular, many incidents involve criminality by the State government itself, which renders neutral cooperation difficult. The Prosecutor, if he accepts such self-referrals, is called "biased," giving a negative perception of the Court as a whole.[2064] In any event, States Parties' obligations are already covered by articles 86 et seq., and the OTP should not wait for cooperation in order to select a situation or case. Article 15 gives the Prosecutor the tool to start investigations without specific support by the SC or a State. In conclusion, the OTP should not be guided by cooperation and resource matters as a definite factor under the "interests of justice." Nevertheless, it has to be accepted that feasibility is a practical reality. In fact, without political support of key actors, the mandate of the Prosecutor can hardly be fulfilled.[2065]

cc) Other alternative justice mechanisms

The Prosecutor, when deciding what is in the "interests of justice," should consider the totality of justice mechanisms which are operating in a particular context (such as truth and reconciliation commissions, reparation programmes, and institutional reform).[2066] Alternative justice systems can

[2062] Part II, C.

[2063] Part III, B., IV., 3. See further Stigen, *supra* note 205, 396 et seq.

[2064] Part III, B., IV., 3.

[2065] Stigen, *supra* note 205, 376–7.

[2066] Marieke Wierda – ICTJ, Session 1: Transcript, 17.6.2003. On transitional justice mechanisms in general see ICTJ, 2004/2005 annual report, 1, 1; Ivan Šimo-

provide needed flexibility that criminal prosecution may not be able to offer.[2067] Most importantly, it has been pointed out that there is no hostility or contradiction between the objectives of the ICC and truth and reconciliation efforts *per se*.[2068] The idea of restorative approaches to justice has continuously gained in support.[2069] There have been attempts to build a bridge across prosecutions (retributive justice) and alternative mechanisms such as truth commission (restorative justice).[2070] Similarly, I have submitted that alternative justice mechanisms should be located within article 53 (1) (c) and (2) (c) rather than within article 17, based on a narrow interpretation of the term "investigation" in the sense of criminal investigations *stricto sensu*[2071] and a broader interpretation of "justice" not limited to criminal justice only.

It must further be evaluated whether alternative mechanisms could possibly satisfy the Prosecutor not to proceed with an investigation or prosecution. The first issue is whether alternative justice mechanisms are accepted at all, and if this question is answered in the affirmative, it must be clarified which particular mechanisms the Prosecutor might accept. Since the ICC Statute does not define the concept of "interests of justice," it has not taken an explicit position on transitional justice mechanisms.[2072] No expli-

---

ović, "Dealing with the legacy of past war crimes and human rights abuses" (2004) 2 JICJ 701, 702 et seq.; Neil Kritz, "Coming to terms with atrocities: a review of accountability mechanisms for mass violations of human right" (2006) 59 Law and Contemporary Problems 127, 128 et seq.; Kleffner, *supra* note 370, 268; Slye/van Schaack, *supra* note 534, 308 et seq.; Sriram, *supra* note 2043, 38 et seq. (including several case studies).

2067 Clark, *supra* note 1339, 405.

2068 John Dugard, "Possible conflicts of jurisdiction with truth commissions" in Cassese/Gaete/Jones, *supra* note 133, 693, 694; Robinson, *supra* note 807, 484; Nitsche, *supra* note 784, 299; Seibert-Fohr, *supra* note 739, 557; Clark, *supra* note 1339, 406–7; Roche, *supra* note 1423, 579 ("they could instead adopt a cooperative approach").

2069 Mallinder, *supra* note 1384, 184; Ambos, in Ambos/Large/Wierda, *supra* note 650, 40 et seq., paras. 12 et seq.; Razesberger, *supra* note 371, 105; Schiff, *supra* note 128, 33.

2070 Yav Katshung, *supra* note 1892, 1 et seq. To further define the two notions: "retributive justice" is most commonly associated with accountability and punishment, and focuses on forcing the perpetrator of a crime to "pay" for the actions he took in the commission of that crime. "Restorative justice," conversely, is a process of active participation in which the wider community deliberates over past crimes, giving centre stage to both victim and perpetrator in a process which seeks to bestow dignity and empowerment upon the victim, with special emphasis placed upon contextual factors, cf. RLP paper no. 17, *supra* note 246, 11; also Karen Brounéus, "Reconciliation and development" in Ambos/Large/Wierda, *supra* note 650, 203, 207–8.

2071 Part IV, B., III., 2., b), bb).

cit provision deals with the interrelationship of criminal prosecution *vis-à-vis* reconciliation through truth commissions.[2073] Neither does the drafting history reveal the matter.[2074] The question of substitutes for criminal prosecution was simply too contentious to be expressly dealt with.[2075] The OTP has endorsed the "complementary role that can be played by domestic prosecutions, truth seeking, reparations programs, institutional reform and traditional justice mechanisms" in its policy paper on the "interests of justice."[2076] A comprehensive approach thereto has, however, not been developed. The recognition of the possible alternative mechanisms has only stated the obvious, namely that a broad "interests of justice" concept allows the Prosecutor to consider different solutions than criminal law investigations and prosecutions. It seems that the OTP has not yet taken a congruent approach.[2077] If "interests of justice" is interpreted as narrowly as the Office suggests, then it is hardly reconcilable to admit alternative justice mechanisms which are not equivalent to criminal prosecution. For this reason, I support a broader interpretational approach that includes alternative mechanisms under article 53 (1) and (2) (c). In any event, the ICC will have to deal with the matter as the ultimate adjudicator when the question arises whether a peace agreement or any form of amnesty are compatible with the ICC Statute.[2078] Hence, the main question is to develop criteria for measures such as truth commissions, conditional amnesties, etc. It would have been helpful if the OTP had highlighted such specific requirements as "common standards" that are required to meet the Prosecutor's demands. In this regard, HRW suggests threefold substantial benchmarks for any domestic alternative to ICC proceedings: (1) credible, impartial and independent investigation and prosecution; (2) rigorous adherence to international fair trial standards; and (3), penalties that reflect the gravity of the crimes.[2079]

In the following, the three most discussed restorative options (TRCs, traditional justice, and amnesties) are introduced and tested *vis-à-vis* their per-

---

2072 Wouters/Verhoeven/Demeyere, *supra* note 156, 292. On the term "transitional justice" see Ambos, in Ambos/Large/Wierda, *supra* note 650, 21 et seq., paras. 1 et seq.

2073 Bartelt, *supra* note 677, 189; Roche, *supra* note 1423, 567; Dukić, *supra* note 1256, 694.

2074 Seils/Wierda, *supra* note 1461, 13; Priscilla Hayner, *Unspeakable truths* (Routledge, New York, London 2001) 206; Alison Bisset, "Rethinking the powers of truth commissions in light of the ICC Statute" (2009) 7 JICJ 963, 963–4.

2075 Kleffner, *supra* note 370, 261.

2076 Interests of justice paper, *supra* note 99, 8.

2077 The Prosecutor called this matter an "open question" according to Yav Katshung, *supra* note 1892, 1.

2078 Takemura, *supra* note 1385, 28; Klip, *supra* note 1380, 186.

2079 HRW, Alternative mechanisms, *supra* note 2129, 4 et seq.

missibility under the ICC Statute. In practice, transitional justice instruments are used selectively, simultaneously, or even chronologically, depending on the situation.[2080] Amnesties have enjoyed the most attention by authors, and need to be reconsidered as one sub-item,[2081] incorporating some (previous) thoughts on TRCs at hand. In the following deliberations, TRCs and traditional (non-western) justice will be dealt with. A survey of all possible alternative mechanisms, such as reparations, lustration, DDR (Disarmament, Demobilization and Reintegration), etc., would certainly exceed the study at hand.

Reparations focus more on the victim than the offender and result from victim's rights.[2082] The four main categories of reparations are restitution, indemnity, satisfaction, and declaratory judgment; they may be material or non-material.[2083] Lustration (meaning purification or illumination), vetting, and purges are administrative procedures aimed at the disqualification or removal of certain groups linked to the prior regime from certain public or private offices under the new regime.[2084] This approach, however, raises concerns of procedural fairness and due process, begging the question as to how far disqualification should extend.[2085] The international community has generally opposed lustration laws,[2086] but also acknowledged that "where such mechanisms exist and are seen to function fairly, effectively and in accordance with international human rights standards, they can play an important role in enhancing the legitimacy of official structures, restoring the confidence of the public and building the rule of law."[2087] DDR is "a collective process aimed at the reintegration of the former armed groups into the (new) society."[2088]

[2080] Pierre Hazan, "Measuring the impact of punishment and forgiveness: a framework for evaluating transitional justice" (2006) 861 IRRC 19, 23.

[2081] Part IV, B., III., 3., e), dd).

[2082] Olson, *supra* note 2089, 183; Ambos, in Ambos/Large/Wierda, *supra* note 650, 48–9, para. 17.

[2083] Olson, *supra* note 2089, 184.

[2084] Olson, *supra* note 2089, 181; Ambos, in Ambos/Large/Wierda, *supra* note 650, 48–9, para. 17; Schiff, *supra* note 128, 30. For an overview of lustration laws (in Czech Republic and Slovakia, Hungary, Albania, Bulgaria, Lithuania, Latvia, Estonia, Poland, Romania, Russia, Ukraine, Belarus, Kazakhstan, Kyrgyzstan, Tajikistan, and Uzbekistan), see Mark Ellis, "Purging the past: the current state of lustration laws in the former communist block" (2006) 59 Law and Contemporary Problems 181, 181 et seq.

[2085] Olson, *supra* note 2089, 182–3.

[2086] Ellis, *supra* note 2084, 181.

[2087] Report of the Secretary-General on the rule of law and transitional justice in conflict and post-conflict societies, 3.8.2004 (S/2004/616) paras. 52–3.

From the various alternatives discussed in international law, TRCs are most important. Several TRCs have been established to achieve peace and stability.[2089] A TRC is aimed at establishing a truth which goes beyond the judicial truth of the courtroom, but TRC truth also remains incomplete in that it only enables further inquiry and truth establishment.[2090] It is an official, temporary, non-judicial fact-finding body that investigates a pattern of abuses of human rights or humanitarian law, usually committed over a number of years, with a view to establishing a comprehensive and authoritive record of what happened.[2091] Nevertheless, each and every TRC must be analyzed on its own merits since their competence, powers and socio-political framework may vary widely.[2092] The following survey is therefore based on a simplified structural perspective, particularly designed for the relationship of TRCs *vis-à-vis* the ICC.

Truth commissions can supplement prosecutions as valuable means to give a voice to victims.[2093] Thereby, one has to distinguish two different situations: TRCs can either complement criminal proceedings (for instance dealing with lower-level criminality) or they aim at replacing all criminal prosecution.[2094] The first model can be better reconciled with the ICC Statute than the second option. If there is criminal prosecutions *stricto sensu,* either the ICC or States, in accordance with the complementarity principle, hold the most responsible perpetrators accountable. Low-level and mid-le-

---

2088 Ambos, in Ambos/Large/Wierda, *supra* note 650, 48–9, para. 17. In great detail on DDR, see Pablo De Greiff, "DDR and reparations: establishing links between peace and justice instruments" in Ambos/Large/Wierda, *supra* note 650, 321, 321 et seq.

2089 Ambos, in Ambos/Large/Wierda, *supra* note 650, 40 et seq., para. 13. For a list of truth commissions, constantly under development, see the digital collection of the United States Institute of Peace at <www.usip.org/library/truth.html>; also Hayner, *supra* note 2074, appendix 1, 291 et seq.; Mark Freeman, *Truth commissions and procedural fairness* (CUP, New York 2006) appendix 1, 317 et seq.; Laura Olson, "Mechanisms complementing prosecution" (2002) 84 IRRC 173, 176 with fn. 8.

2090 Ambos, in Ambos/Large/Wierda, *supra* note 650, 40 et seq., para. 13.

2091 International Council on Human Rights Policy, "Negotiating justice? Human rights and peace agreements," 2006, 80; Ambos, in Ambos/Large/Wierda, *supra* note 650, 40 et seq., para. 13. Further on the definition of TRCs Hayner, *supra* note 2074, 14; Freeman, *supra* note 2089, 12 et seq. (however, partly disagreeing with Hayner's approach).

2092 Ambos, in Ambos/Large/Wierda, *supra* note 650, 42 et seq., para. 14.

2093 Robinson, *supra* note 807, 484; Nitsche, *supra* note 784, 299; Brianne McGonigle, "Two for the price of one: attempts by the Extraordinary Chambers in the Courts of Cambodia to combine retributive and restorative justice principles" (2009) 22 LJIL 127, 133. In this respect, critically evaluating the South African TRCs, see Roche, *supra* note 1423, 572 et seq.

2094 Bartelt, *supra* note 677, 194 et seq.; Kritz, *supra* note 2066, 143.

vel perpetrators can be left to national truth commissions. A twofold set of norms is recommended for considering TRCs: first, the guiding principles have to be incorporated in new rules or at least OTP guidelines, and second, an explicit deferral procedure to national authorities is necessary.[2095]

The following guidelines (*Dugard principles*) have been consistently enumerated as minimum requirements for truth commissions if they are to serve as acceptable alternatives to prosecutions:

- the Commission should be established by the legislature or executive of a democratically elected regime;
- the Commission should be a representative and independent body;
- the Commission should have a broad mandate to enable it to make a thorough investigation. It should not, for example, be restricted to deaths and disappearances (as with Chile), but should be permitted instead to investigate all forms of gross human rights violations;
- the Commission should hold public hearings at which victims of human rights abuses are permitted to testify;
- the perpetrators of gross human rights violations should be named, provided adequate opportunity is given to them to challenge their accusers before the Commission;
- the Commission should be required to submit a comprehensive report and recommendations within a reasonable time;
- the Commission should be empowered to recommend reparations for victims of gross human rights violations; and
- amnesty should be denied to perpetrators of gross human rights abuses who refuse to cooperate with the Commission or who refuse to make a full disclosure of their crimes.[2096]

All these principles will need to be employed by the Prosecutor when exercising the prerogative not to initiate investigations or prosecutions.[2097] Arguably, article 17 could provide a narrow gateway for TRCs as well.[2098] In this regard, one author mentions almost identical characteristics for

---

[2095] On the latter, see Part IV, F.

[2096] John Dugard, "Dealing with crimes of a past regime. Is amnesty still an option?" (1999) 12 LJIL 1001, 1012; similarly, Goldstone/Fritz, *supra* note 1828, 664; further, on truth commission requirements, see Mallinder, *supra* note 1384, 168–9; Priscilla Hayner, "International guidelines for the creation and operation of truth commissions: a preliminary proposal" (2006) 59 Law and Contemporary Problems 173, 178 et seq.; Majzub, *supra* note 1426, 277–8; Borello, *supra* note 210, 39.

[2097] Goldstone/Fritz, *supra* note 1828, 665.

[2098] See Part IV, B., III., 2., b), bb).

TRCs that depart from the normal model of prosecution (quasi-judicial character, independence, effectiveness, the article 17 objective of "bringing to justice," and necessity to depart form classical prosecution).[2099] Guidelines have been adopted by various authors, either drafting a whole catalogue of ideas or addressing particular minimum requirements,[2100] and one author integrated the numerous proposals into eleven basic points (*Ambos principles*), taking into account the experience from various TRCs certain best practices can be deduced and guidelines developed:

- the TRC must be composed of recognized and independent personalities from all relevant social groups and sectors to be selected in a consultative and representative process;
- there must be serious efforts to assist victims (on the operational level, setting-up a contact point for victims and witnesses);
- a TRC must dispose adequate resources and sufficient independence; it must possess sufficient investigative powers and receive national and international support;
- the mandate of a TRC should not be limited to the establishment of individual responsibilities, but also shed light on the causes of the conflict in order to prevent the recurrence of future violations;
- the mandate should be time-bound (no more than two fully operational years), but eventually there should be a follow-up process;
- identification of victims and recommendation of reparations should be made to competent state organs by the TRC;
- there should be full cooperation with other state organs involved in transitional justice, including providing information to prosecution authorities;
- the suspected perpetrators should be brought before the TRC to publicly confess their crimes and give evidence on other crimes. Victims should be present; in cases where perpetrators are identified ("name names"), the accused's due process rights must be respected;

2099 Robinson, *supra* note 807, 501–2.

2100 Andreas O'Shea, *Amnesty for crime in international law and practice* (Kluwer Law International, The Hague et al. 2002) 326; Ivo Gross, "Die Vereinbarkeit von nationalen Amnestieregelungen mit dem Völkerstrafrecht am Beispiel Südafrika" (2001) 14 HuV-I 162, 168 et seq.; Bartelt, *supra* note 677, 207–8; Clark, *supra* note 1339, 408 et seq.; Olson, *supra* note 2089, 179–80; Roche, *supra* note 1423, 575 et seq.; Yav Katshung, *supra* note 1892, 19–20; OHCHR, Rule-of-law tools for post-conflict States, Truth commission, April 2006, 1, 8 et seq., 17 et seq.; Valiñas, in Stahn/van Herik, *supra* note 1423, 287.

- conditional granting of amnesties or pardons should depend on the nature and gravity of the crimes, the extent to which the suspects have cooperated in the discovery of the truth, and the necessary compensation of victims. The TRC must have the authority to reject the amnesty application and turn the applicant over to criminal justice system;
- there should be broad participation of the society, in particular victims and/or their representatives. There should be wide publication of the final report;
- all state organs are required to consider in good faith the recommendations of a TRC and implement them to the greatest extent possible; a monitoring body should be established for that purpose.[2101]

As an intermediary conclusion, truth commissions should be considered as valuable tools complementing – not substituting – criminal proceedings.[2102] It is submitted that these efforts should ideally take place at the national level.[2103] A TRC at the international level simply shifts the work load from one international institution to another. It will be practically impossible to deal with the large number of perpetrators; only setting up a national TRC system can do so.

A threefold course of action can improve TRC's relationship with the ICC. First, the ICC must find a feasible, yet demanding, set of rules that any national TRC must fulfill for qualifying as an adequate mechanisms under the ICC Statute (this involves the OTP and ultimately the Judges). Second, a watch-dog institution[2104] could be created to supervise and assist national authorities to implement a corresponding TRC framework. Third, the newly-created institution, as well as the OTP, have to monitor the TRCs' implementation.

The Northern Ugandan situation reveals an important debate: local restorative approaches *versus* international retributive approaches.[2105] Traditional (non-western) local justice means concepts such as *gacaca* in

---

[2101] Ambos, in Ambos/Large/Wierda, *supra* note 650, 45 et seq., para. 16; ICTJ, 2004/2005 annual report, *supra* note 2066, 6. For all-embracing recommendations how TRCs should be designed, see Freeman, *supra* note 2089, 301 et seq.

[2102] Yav Katshung, *supra* note 1892, 27; Cárdenas, 2005, *supra* note 1387, 172; Stigen, *supra* note 205, 465; Bisset, *supra* note 2074, 964.

[2103] Contrary, Nitsche, *supra* note 784, 299, who favors a TRC lead by the UN or in the form of an additional organ at the ICC itself.

[2104] Picking up Nitsche's idea, see above, this could be a UN or ICC related organ.

[2105] Baines, *supra* note 246, 96; RLP paper no. 17, *supra* note 246, 11–2; Tim Allen, "Ritual (ab)use? Problems with traditional justice in Northern Uganda" in Waddell/Clark, *supra* note 246, 47, 47; Kindt, *supra* note 650, 179 et seq.

Rwanda, *ubuntu* in South Africa or *mato oput* in Uganda. The Acholi, for instance, perform a traditional ritual called *mato oput* to reconcile parties formerly in conflict.[2106] The Acholi strongly lobbied for their traditional ways instead of ICC investigations when the Prosecutor announced ICC activities.[2107] *Mato oput,* however, lacks the basic characteristics of a system of criminal justice[2108] and any connection the ceremonies have to the LRA is doubtful.[2109]

The choice of forum shall further depend on the nature and gravity of the offending conduct and role of the alleged perpetrator in that conduct.[2110] Formal courts shall deal with individuals who are alleged to bear particular responsibility for the most serious crimes, especially crimes amounting to international crimes.[2111] Applied in the Uganda situation, it is not clear whether *Kony et al.* would benefit from alternative justice mechanisms or amnesties at all even if the peace agreement was implemented.[2112] In my opinion, the only choice would be between a genuine national criminal trial and a trial before the ICC.[2113] The actors have therefore tried to reach an appropriate legal framework that satisfies the ICC, stating that "a Special Division of the High Court of Uganda shall be established to try individuals who are alleged to have committed serious crimes during

---

2106 Agreement on accountability and reconciliation, *supra* note 261, 2, which further mentions alternative mechanisms of *ailuc* by the Iteso, *culo kwor* performed by the Acholi and Langi, *kayo cuk* by the Langi, and *toni ci koka* by the Madi. These traditional mechanisms shall be practiced in the affected communities pursuant to Sec.3.1 of the Agreement. On *mato oput* further Baines, *supra* note 246, 103 et seq.; Allen, *supra* note 246, 132 et seq.; *id.,* in Waddell/Clark, *supra* note 2105, 48; OHCHR, Making peace our own, *supra* note 246, 52 et seq.; Ssenyonjo, *supra* note 246, 373 et seq. On all the mentioned alternative justice mechanisms Apuuli (2004), *supra* note 246, 806 with fn. 25–29, and Mallinder, *supra* note 1384, 185 et seq. More general on traditional mechanisms, see RLP paper no. 17, *supra* note 246, 22 et seq.

2107 Baines, *supra* note 246, 96.

2108 Takemura, *supra* note 1385, 22; Ssenyonjo, *supra* note 246, 375.

2109 Allen, in Waddell/Clark, *supra* note 2105, 49.

2110 Sec.4.3 Agreement on accountability and reconciliation, *supra* note 261, 5.

2111 Sec.6.1 Agreement on accountability and reconciliation, *supra* note 261, 6; Allen, in Waddell/Clark, *supra* note 2105, 52.

2112 Unger/Wierda, in Ambos/Large/Wierda, *supra* note 678, 289; Burke-White/Kaplan, in Stahn/Sluiter, *supra* note 247, 108. On the Amnesty Act of 2000, see Hanlon, *supra* note 256, 304.

2113 Accordingly, the ICC Chief Prosecutor held the position that the warrants should be executed, "Uganda: ICC Prosecutor Louis Ocampo in his office at the Hague," 13.7.2007, Felix Osike, New Vision; Apuuli (2008), *supra* note 246, 811 arrives at the conclusion that "they can only face the traditional courts after being prosecuted."

the conflict."[2114] In response, the ICC asked Uganda to explain the impact of the Special Division of the High Court and the recourse to traditional justice mechanisms on the execution of the warrants against Kony and his commanders.[2115] It was though unclear if the government gave this explanation (or if it did so satisfactorily).[2116] While it is now known that the Ugandan Government responded to the ICC's inquiry continuously, the statements entailed ambiguities.[2117]

When PTC II – dealing with the *Kony et al.* case – initiated proceedings under article 19 to determine admissibility, it invited observations on the matter by the Republic of Uganda, the Prosecutor, the Counsel for the Defence and Victims,[2118] and it granted the Uganda Victims' Foundation and the Redress Trust to submit observations under rule 103 (1) as *amici curiae*. PTC II was particularly interested in the establishment of the Special Division of the High Court, its legal texts, and the experiences of victims of crimes seeking justice from Ugandan courts.[2119]

The *amici curiae* briefs highlight that, while the Annexure that relates to the Special Division was signed by the LRA and the Government of Uganda, the Peace Agreement to which it is annexed was not; thus, the Peace Agreement and its Annexure have not yet been approved by the Parliament.[2120] They further state that the Special Division's establishment has not been implemented and it is unclear when – supposedly after the (now doubtful) signing of a peace agreement – it will be set in place.[2121] Moreover, there is neither a formal legal text on the Special Division's establish-

---

2114 Quoted from Apuuli (2008), *supra* note 246, 807; also Burke-White/Kaplan, in Stahn/Sluiter, *supra* note 247, 102–3.

2115 "ICC writes to Uganda over Kony," 17.3.2008, Milton Olupot, New Vision.

2116 Apuuli (2008), *supra* note 246, 810.

2117 *Prosecutor v. Kony et al.,* Decision on the admissibility of the case under article 19 (1), *supra* note 264, paras. 43–4; also Otim/Wierda, in Waddell/Clark, *supra* note 260, 23: "[…] the government position has not always been consistent […]."

2118 *Prosecutor v. Kony et al.,* Decision initiating proceedings under article 19, *supra* note 264.

2119 *Prosecutor v. Kony et al.,* Decision on application for leave to submit observations under Rule 103, 5.11.2008 (ICC-02/04-01/05-333) 7.

2120 *Prosecutor v. Kony et al.,* Amicus Curiae dated 5 November 2008 (submitted by the Uganda Victims' Foundation and the Redress Trust), *supra* note 264, para. 9; also *Prosecutor v. Kony et al.,* Observations on behalf of victims pursuant to article 19 (1), *supra* note 264, paras. 22–3.

2121 *Prosecutor v. Kony et al.,* Amicus Curiae dated 5 November 2008 (submitted by the Uganda Victims' Foundation and the Redress Trust), *supra* note 264, paras. 12 et seq.; also *Prosecutor v. Kony et al.,* Observations on behalf of victims pursuant to article 19 (1), *supra* note 264, para. 25.

ment nor is there any accessible draft version.[2122] To the *amici's* knowledge, there have not been any investigations or prosecutions by other Ugandan courts; in fact: "impunity continues to be pervasive."[2123]

When going into the merits, PTC II identified some serious efforts to hold proceedings at the national level, but the Chamber did not want to further engage itself into hypothetical judicial decision-making given the preliminary and partial nature of the Peace Agreement and its Annexure.[2124] As confirmed by the *amici curiae*, and also by Uganda itself, the measures undertaken to implement the provisions of the Agreement and the Annexure are "in the initial stages" and "a lot is yet to be done."[2125] Therefore, the Chamber did not review its earlier positive determination of admissibility since the national authorities were still inactive, pending the adoption of all relevant legal texts and the implementation of all practical steps.[2126] In any event, a future "deferral" to Uganda by challenging admissibility remains possible[2127] given the fact that admissibility is an on-going assessment and might change. It would, however, require very specific steps to prosecute LRA leaders in order to satisfy the ICC's complementarity regime.[2128] These prosecutions must be in accordance with international legal standards.[2129] It would then be left to the ICC to examine admissibility again, this time with regard to the Annexure and the specific mechanisms that will be established for transitional justice in Uganda.[2130]

2122 *Prosecutor v. Kony et al.,* Amicus Curiae dated 5 November 2008 (submitted by the Uganda Victims' Foundation and the Redress Trust), *supra* note 264, para. 24.

2123 *Prosecutor v. Kony et al.,* Amicus Curiae dated 5 November 2008 (submitted by the Uganda Victims' Foundation and the Redress Trust), *supra* note 264, para. 32.

2124 *Prosecutor v. Kony et al.,* Decision on the admissibility of the case under article 19 (1), *supra* note 264, paras. 47 et seq.

2125 *Prosecutor v. Kony et al.,* Decision on the admissibility of the case under article 19 (1), *supra* note 264, para. 49.

2126 *Prosecutor v. Kony et al.,* Decision on the admissibility of the case under article 19 (1), *supra* note 264, para. 52.

2127 Cf. thereto already at *supra* note 1359; also Otim/Wierda, in Waddell/Clark, *supra* note 260, 26; Unger/Wierda, in Ambos/Large/Wierda, *supra* note 678, 273.

2128 Apuuli (2008), *supra* note 246, 811; Burke-White/Kaplan, in Stahn/Sluiter, *supra* note 247, 105 et seq.

2129 HRW, "Benchmarks for assessing possible national alternatives to International Criminal Court cases against LRA leaders" (hereinafter HRW, Alternative mechanisms), May 2007, 1, 2 et seq.; RLP paper no. 17, *supra* note 246, 40 et seq. For a discussion on the Colombian Justice and Peace Law *vis-à-vis* international standards, see Burbidge, *supra* note 335, 575 et seq; also Ambos, *supra* note 337, 3 et seq.

2130 Unger/Wierda, in Ambos/Large/Wierda, *supra* note 678, 272–3.

Coming back to traditional mechanisms in more general terms, these tools – unless accompanied by fair and credible investigations and prosecutions – would not meet the ICC Statute's criteria or other international standards.[2131] Turning once more to *mato oput* as a good example, this mechanisms in its current form would most certainly not satisfy international law for the following reasons: i) it does not adequately take into account the views of individual victims; ii) it does not require the perpetrators to be punished or pay adequate material compensation to the victims; and iii) it is a form of blanket amnesty reflecting a traditional attempt to shield perpetrators from justice.[2132] *Gacaca* has equally been criticized for several reasons: i) traditional forms of justice are no longer accepted by the entire population; ii) *gacaca* was never conceived to try serious crimes such as genocide; and iii) it lacks minimum judicial guarantees.[2133] In any event, *Gacaca* trials are not eligible for specifically zealous perpetrators.[2134]

In sum, traditional procedures may conflict with the (admittedly western) concept of due process.[2135] However, they should – if used at all – only complement criminal sanctions and not substitute them.[2136] It should thereby not be forgotten that some kind of efforts by the national system are necessary in order to supplement the (limited) ICC, which, even it works at full capacity, can only deal with a handful of individuals.[2137]

Any alternative (national) mechanisms cannot be applied to the most senior leaders. It remains possible, however, to consider the application of al-

---

2131 HRW, Alternative mechanisms, *supra* note 2129, 6; Unger/Wierda, in Ambos/Large/Wierda, *supra* note 678, 290. *Mato oput,* for example, is not generally regarded as a substitute for prosecution of even ordinary criminal offences in Uganda.

2132 Ssenyonjo, *supra* note 246, 375.

2133 Olson, *supra* note 2089, 187; critical also Susanne Buckley-Zistel, "The truth heals? *Gacaca* jurisdictions and the consolidation of peace in Rwanda" (2005) 80 Friedenswarte 113, 126; differentiated, Barbara Oomen, "Justice mechanisms and the question of legitimacy: the example of Rwanda's multi-layered justice mechanisms" in Ambos/Large/Wierda, *supra* note 650, 175, 192 et seq.

2134 Yale Human Rights Workshop, David Simon, "The role of *Gacaca* in politics and reconciliation in Rwanda," 16.4.2009; similarly Valiñas, in Stahn/van Herik, *supra* note 1423, 279 ("mid to low-level perpetrators").

2135 Ambos, in Ambos/Large/Wierda, *supra* note 650, 48–9, paras. 17–8. On the Ugandan African cultural background *vis-a-vis* Western justice concepts, see Hanlon, *supra* note 256, 311 et seq., 317.

2136 In the same vein, the delegates at Juba, see Otim/Wierda, in Waddell/Clark, *supra* note 260, 24; also Mallinder, *supra* note 1887, 221: "[…] amnesty accompanied by traditional community-based justice mechanisms can co-exist with international prosecutions for those who are 'most responsible'."

2137 Tenth Report pursuant to UNSC 1593, *supra* note 309, para. 56, 7–8. On this issue see further Part IV, C., IV., 4., b).

ternative forms of justice as a mitigating factor in criminal proceedings. For instance, a perpetrator's cooperation before a TRC would not sway the Prosecutor from prosecuting, but it could be a mitigating factor in sentencing.[2138] Moreover, it must be emphasized that cases that are approved for transitional justice mechanisms are not *de facto* inadmissible due to insufficient gravity under article 17 (1) (d),[2139] but can be left to national jurisdiction due to the "interests of justice" under article 53. This is an important distinction: the Prosecutor is not *per se* limited to the most senior leaders only and may put others down the chain of command on trial, but, based on comparative gravity as a *policy matter,* he may decide to leave those cases to transitional justice mechanisms.[2140]

dd) Amnesties (and truth commissions revisited)

Neither amnesties nor truth commissions are specifically regulated in the ICC Statute. The widely framed wording of article 53 appears to allow for amnesties.[2141] It has been argued that article 53 (1) (c) and (2) (c) is the most explicit gateway for the recognition of alternative processes of national reconciliation.[2142] If an amnesty exception exists at all, its primary embodiment is to be found in the "interests of justice" clause.[2143] Others have expressed doubt as to whether non-judicial efforts fall within the ambit of article 53, basically adopting a narrow interpretation that regards peace and reconciliation on the one hand and criminal justice on the other hand as contradictory objectives.[2144] Moreover, it has been highlighted by

---

2138 Roche, *supra* note 1423, 575; Ambos, in Ambos/Large/Wierda, *supra* note 650, 49, para. 18.

2139 Misleading, *Prosecutor v. Kony et al.,* Observations on behalf of victims pursuant to article 19 (1), *supra* note 264, para. 17.

2140 On the distinction legal vs. relative gravity see Part IV, B., III., 2., c), dd). Further, on comparative gravity, see Part IV, B., III., 3., d), aa).

2141 Cameron, in McGoldrick/Rowe/Donnelly, *supra* note 1318, 91; Arsanjani, *supra* note 1425, 67; Werle, *supra* note 1324, mn 215. On the definition of the term amnesty see Morel, *supra* note 1365, 215–6.

2142 Ambos, in Ambos/Large/Wierda, *supra* note 650, 82–3, para. 51; Dugard, *supra* note 2096, 1014; Bartelt, *supra* note 677, 213. Contrary, Stahn, *supra* note 726, 717–8, who argues that the concept of "interests of justice" is "individual and case-related" (*Einzelfallgerechtigkeit*). For this reason, he sees the more specific leeway in article 17. However, it needs to be emphasized that a broad interpretation of the "interests of justice" – as well as a careful distinction between article 53 (1) (c) and (2) (c) – suits better for general consideration of interests of national reconciliation.

2143 Majzub, *supra* note 1426, 271; Dugard, in Cassese/Gaeta/Jones, *supra* note 2068, 702–3.

one author that the purpose of an amnesty law is to create an atmosphere of reconciliation for the larger community, often at the expense of crime victims. Thereby, the question of "justice" in a judicial sense does not figure in and the whole issue is very difficult for the Prosecutor to address.[2145] In the end, it once more comes back to the interpretation of the term "justice." Since the narrow view is not convincing,[2146] article 53 gives indeed the only leeway for alternatives to criminal justice under the ICC Statute.

Touching specifically upon the amnesty issue, it is important to note that the concept of amnesties is not easy to define. Amnesties might vary to a certain degree in scope and conditions for their actual application. The term "amnesty" legally means foreclosing criminal prosecution for past offences.[2147] Although amnesties have been granted largely in domestic systems,[2148] it is clear that general amnesties are not legitimate accountability mechanisms under international law and the ICC Statute in particular.[2149] Blanket self-amnesties ("Chilean model") are not permissible.[2150] On the

---

[2144] Arsanjani, *supra* note 1425, 67; Seibert-Fohr, *supra* note 739, 579–80; AI open letter, *supra* note 1845, 11–2; FIDH, Réflexions sur la notion "intérêts de la justice," *supra* note 1850, 8.

[2145] Arsanjani, in Hebel/Lammers/Schukking, *supra* note 371, 76.

[2146] See already Part IV, B., III., 3., a), aa), (4).

[2147] Stigen, *supra* note 205, 418. On the definition of "amnesty" see Louise Mallinder, "Exploring the practice of States in introducing amnesties" in Ambos/Large/Wierda, *supra* note 650, 127, 132. Further on the legitimacy of amnesties Kindt, *supra* note 650, 177 et seq.

[2148] On an empirical research *vis-à-vis* state practice see Mallinder, *supra* note 1887, 209–210.

[2149] Meyer, *supra* note 1153, 557; Wouters/Verhoeven/Demeyere, *supra* note 156, 293; Kritz, *supra* note 2066, 134; differentiated, Garth Meintjes, "Domestic amnesties and international accountability," in Dinah, *supra* note 1426, 83, 86 et seq.

[2150] Mallinder, *supra* note 1384, 247–8, 266 et seq., 283; Seils/Wierda, *supra* note 1461, 14; Dugard, *supra* note 2096, 1005; Wouters/Verhoeven/Demeyere, *supra* note 156, 293; Ambos, in Ambos/Large/Wierda, *supra* note 650, 54 et seq., paras. 24 et seq., 45; Christine Bell, "The 'new law' on transitional justice" in Ambos/Large/Wierda, *supra* note 650, 105, 106 et seq.; Robinson, *supra* note 807, 484, 497, 501; Majzub, *supra* note 1426, 259, 278; Allen, *supra* note 246, 117–8; Roche, *supra* note 1423, 576; Takemura, *supra* note 1385, 13; Seibert-Fohr, *supra* note 739, 557–8; El Zeidy, *supra* note 651, 942; Werle, *supra* note 1324, mn 212; Bartelt, *supra* note 677, 201; Clark, *supra* note 1339, 413; Evans, *supra* note 1347, 5; Yav Katshung, *supra* note 1892, 24; International Council on Human Rights, Report negotiating justice, *supra* note 2091, 81–2; Burke-White, *supra* note 213, 582, who locates them within the inability assessment; also Kleffner, in Kleffner/Kor, *supra* note 1415, 93. Nsereko, *supra* note 1321, 119, considers blanket amnesties as *prima facie* evidence of unwillingness or inability; undecided, Razesberger, *supra* note 371, 176 et seq., who would, theoretically, accept them under article 53 (at 183).

other hand, several authors submit that a (highly) conditioned use of amnesties is not foreclosed by the ICC statutory framework.[2151] Conditional amnesties require the perpetrator to meet certain demands in order to benefit from an amnesty.[2152] It is suggested that the ICC should take a flexible stance since amnesties may be an integral component of peace and national reconciliation arrangements.[2153] So far, the Prosecutor has failed to highlight his demands on potential amnesty laws, such as the nature of an amnesty law, and whether the amnesty was preceded by a transparent decision-making process.[2154]

It is yet most important – and in the same way demanding – to set up criteria to decide on the lawfulness of amnesties under article 53 (1) (c) and (2) (c). Direct provisions must flesh out acceptable amnesties.[2155] Several authors have made proposals when considering the validity of an amnesty under the ICC Statute. They have tried to develop a framework for the acceptability of amnesties,[2156] and this framework will be reproduced as follows. They will hopefully provide a valuable basis for future studies, be it by the OTP, the Judges, or academics. An in-depth analysis of amnesties and the factors for being accepted under the ICC Statute goes beyond the study at hand; for this reason only preliminary thoughts will be sketched after the outline.

Scharf poses six questions: (1) Do the offences constitute grave breaches of the Geneva Conventions or genocide, for which there is an international obligation to prosecute?; (2) Would an end to the fighting or transition from repressive rule have occurred without some form of amnesty agreement?; (3) Has international community instituted a mechanism designed to discover the truth about victims and attribute individual responsibility to the perpetrators?; (4) Has the State provided victims with adequate repara-

---

2151 Ambos, in Ambos/Large/Wierda, *supra* note 650, 62 et seq., paras. 30 et seq.; Stahn, *supra* note 726, 708 et seq.; Wouters/Verhoeven/Demeyere, *supra* note 156, 292; Razesberger, *supra* note 371, 179.

2152 Morel, *supra* note 1365, 223; Ambos, in Ambos/Large/Wierda, *supra* note 650, 62–3, para. 30. On the possible conditions attached to amnesties see Mallinder, in Ambos/Large/Wierda, *supra* note 2147, 154 et seq.

2153 Nsereko, *supra* note 1321, 120; Ambos, in Ambos/Large/Wierda, *supra* note 650, 69–70, para. 35. For the frequent use of amnesties in peace agreements see Humanitarian Dialogue, Report on accountability and peace agreements, Mapping trends from 1980 to 2006, September 2007, 16 et seq.; also International Council on Human Rights, Report negotiating justice, *supra* note 2091, 83–4 (distinguishing between impermissible and permissible amnesties, as well as certain "grey areas").

2154 Mallinder, *supra* note 1384, 291.

2155 Young, *supra* note 1425, 470.

2156 Cf. Morel, *supra* note 1365, 271 et seq., Goldstone/Fritz, *supra* note 1828, 664–5, and Majzub, *supra* note 1426, 271 et seq., as good examples.

tion and/or compensation?; (5) Has the State implemented meaningful steps to ensure that violations of international humanitarian law and serious human rights abuses do no reoccur?; (6) Has the State taken steps to punish those guilty of committing violations of international humanitarian law through non-criminal sanctions, such as imposition of fines, removal from office, reduction of rank, and forfeiture of government or military pension and/or assets?[2157]

Arsanjani equally suggests six question to determine the amnesty option under the ICC Statute: (1) What crimes were the subject of the amnesty?; (2) What other remedies were provided for the victims in the absence of criminal prosecution?; (3) Did the amnesty have broad support among the population?; (4) Did the amnesty result in emplacement of a democratic system of government?; (5) Is that system being constructed in ways that would support human rights?; (6) What would the condition of human rights have been in the country in the absence of amnesties?[2158]

Young further names six relevant factors: (1) The process surrounding the grant of amnesty, paying specific attention to the actor granting the amnesty and to what domestic body has expressed approval; (2) Whether the crimes covered by the amnesty are referred to in article 5, 6, 7, or 8 of this Statue; (3) What proceedings the amnesty precludes and whether the amnesty allows investigation of crimes at issue in an administrative, judicial or official forum; (4) The stability of the judiciary in the state and whether prosecution of such acts by a national or international body, such as the ICC, would weaken the role of the judiciary; (5) Whether the amnesty allows official national recognition of the crimes and individual responsibility for such crimes, taking into account specific steps the state has taken to acknowledge the crimes and responsibility for those crimes; and (6) The ability of the victims to obtain redress and reparations for the atrocities suffered.[2159]

Razesberger brings up as many as ten different issues: (1) Who issued the amnesty? An independent body, a current government, a single politician?; (2) Is the granting of an amnesty self-satisfactory or is it a side-effect of a bigger process?; (3) Does the body granting the amnesty conduct genuine proceedings?; (4) Can the body granting an amnesty choose between amnesty and prosecution?; (5) Are these amnesties blanket or only in relation to specific crimes?; (6) What does the applicant have to do to obtain an amnesty?; (7) Is there a possibility for prosecution as a result to non-co-

---

2157 Scharf, *supra* note 1426, 526–7.

2158 Arsanjani, *supra* note 1425, 66–7.

2159 Young, *supra* note 1425, 476–7.

operation?; (8) What is the purpose of the body that is empowered to grant amnesties?; (9) Is there some form of compensation for the victims?; (10) Is there a necessity to follow that approach?[2160]

Robinson mentions nine pertinent criteria (in the context of TRCs): (1) Was the measure adopted by democratic will?; (2) Is the departure from the standard of criminal prosecution of all offenders based on necessity, i.e. irresistible social, economic or political realities?; (3) Is there a full and effective investigation into the facts; (4) Does the fact-finding inquiry "name names"?; (5) Is the relevant commission or body independent and suitably resourced?; (6) Is there at least some form of punishment of perpetrators (are they identified, required to come forward, required to do community service, subject to lustration)?; (7) Is some form of remedy or compensation provided to victims?; (8) Does the national approach provide a sense of closure or justice to victims?; (9) Is there a commitment to comply with other human rights obligations?[2161]

Most recently, Stigen suggests the following factors for the evaluation of national amnesties: (1) Where there compelling reasons to grant amnesty?; (2) Is the amnesty adopted and implemented democratically and in good faith?; (3) Has the amnesty-granting body proceeded in an effective manner?; (4) Does the mechanism provide some measure of accountability or compensation?; (5) Is amnesty granted to the most responsible perpetrators?; (6) Has the amnesty had positive effects and has it been internationally recognized?; (7) Do the involved parties perceive the amnesty as fair?[2162]

Last but not least, Mallinder has phrased the set of criteria in a positive manner, suggesting that in the domestic amnesty process:

(1) Amnesties must have democratic legitimacy;

(2) Amnesties must represent a genuine desire to promote peace and reconciliation;

(3) Amnesties must be limited in scope;

(4) Amnesties must be conditional; and

(5) Amnesties must be accompanied by reparations.[2163]

In sum, there is not yet one all-embracing approach towards amnesties (and TRCs). It will be a novelty for the ICC to develop a set of guidelines. Amnesties are practical realities, but so far the international community has

---

[2160] Razesberger, *supra* note 371, 174–5.
[2161] Robinson, *supra* note 807, 497–8.
[2162] Stigen, *supra* note 205, 451 et seq.
[2163] Mallinder, *supra* note 1887, 228 et seq.

failed to set a common standard. What can be drawn from the outlined academic ideas is a minimum standard: (1) transparent amnesty procedures issued by a (democratic) State and (2) that these procedures primarily incorporate victims' demands. It may very well be assumed that the OTP only accepts conditional amnesties. These kinds of amnesties are usually accompanied by a TRC.[2164] It is actually submitted that amnesty laws that do not go hand-in-hand with TRCs will not prevent ICC proceedings.[2165] A South African type of combination between a TRC and conditional amnesties might therefore constitute a feasible compromise model.[2166] In any event, if the Prosecutor adopts a flexible approach with regard to amnesties and truth commissions, criticism will certainly arise from some groups. To reduce the accusation of improper selectivity, the Court must enhance its legitimacy through transparent criteria.[2167] One author has therefore advertised the idea of a Protocol to the ICC Statute that should incorporate a set of guidelines, drafting a preliminary document.[2168] But the most sustainable solution of the amnesty issue would be the inclusion of a new rule in the RPE.[2169] This rule should contain a sample of the outlined guidelines, negotiated by the States Parties. The basic requirements can be phrased in the following draft rule that integrates a necessary minimum standard:[2170]

(1) Amnesties and TRCs are tools that can be taken into account by the Prosecutor as part of the "interests of justice" consideration.

(2) The State must have legitimate reasons for granting the amnesty.

(3) The amnesty must be granted in a manner consistent with international law.

(4) The amnesty must be granted by a Truth Commission process that meets certain basic standards (to be annexed in the style of the outlined TRC principles by Dugard, Ambos, et al.).

[2164] Ambos, in Ambos/Large/Wierda, *supra* note 650, 62–3, para. 30. On the fact that TRCs are rarely specified in peace agreements themselves see Humanitarian Dialogue, Report on accountability, *supra* note 2153, 26.

[2165] Olásolo, *supra* note 376, 139.

[2166] Human Rights, Report negotiating justice, *supra* note 2091, 85. In this respect, Cárdenas' survey (Cárdenas, 2005, *supra* note 1387, 183) does not sufficiently take into consideration the broader interests of peace and reconciliation when she states that the South African type of TRC was "for the purpose of shielding a person;" the South African TRC would therefore be admissible before the ICC. In any event, article 53 (1) (c) differs from article 17 exactly in this regard: While article 17 might apply in the way suggested by Cárdenas, article 53 also allows the Prosecutor to weigh a "shielding" against the broader "interests of justice" aspects in the sense of peace and reconciliation.

[2167] Roche, *supra* note 1423, 574–5.

[2168] O'Shea, *supra* note 2100, 319, 330 et seq.

[2169] Young, *supra* note 1425, 482.

[2170] Majzub, *supra* note 1426, 279.

(5) Victims' demands must be taken into account in proper form, providing them participatory rights and compensation.

However, given the fact that the drafters could not agree on a specific provision and that the law of amnesties is a very complex issue, a case by case analysis was deemed the only feasible solution.[2171] As such, it is more likely that the issue has to be resolved during the case selection phase. Therefore, the amnesty issue becomes a primary question once the Prosecutor applies article 53 (2) (c). In addition, taking into consideration the numerous questions open for discussion at the upcoming review conferences, it is more than doubtful that a delicate matter such as amnesties can be addressed in the next years. In the short-run, it appears more realistic that the OTP develops provisional policy guidelines on amnesties and other alternative justice mechanisms in general. The OTP's guidance must be made publicly available, mainly to provide guidance to affected States. Furthermore, the PTC should be consulted during the drafting process bearing in mind that decisions under article 53 (1) (c) and (2) (c) are subject to review by the named chamber. For the moment though, the amnesty question remains open.[2172]

The guidelines for alternative justice mechanisms, in particular amnesties and truth commissions, must yet be developed by the Court to allow for an operational framework.[2173] Thereby, the approaches outlined above, in particular the questionnaires on TRCs and on amnesties offer a solid basis for discussion and must be integrated. Most important, the ICC actors must bear in mind that amnesties cannot exclude the top leaders from prosecution.[2174] To conclude, it has been shown that article 53 (1) (c) and (2) (c) potentially allow for a holistic approach, taking into account criminal justice and alternative justice.[2175] A lot of work still lies ahead if the ICC wants to implement such a mixed transitional justice process. Given the complex, regional context of many on-going conflicts, a holistic process might be difficult to achieve.[2176]

[2171] Seibert-Fohr, *supra* note 739, 589–90.

[2172] Morel, *supra* note 1365, 270 ("la question reste ouverte").

[2173] Clark, *supra* note 1339, 406; Newman, *supra* note 774, 320; Kritz, *supra* note 2066, 141; Bisset, *supra* note 2074, 982.

[2174] Nuremberg Declaration on Peace and Justice, in Ambos/Large/Wierda, *supra* note 2041, 544, IV., 2., 2.6. In the context of the Ugandan situation see Newman, *supra* note 774, 336 et seq., 341. Nsereko, *supra* note 1829, 378, holds the view that violations committed on a large scale should also be dealt with by the courts of law.

[2175] On the integrated (holistic) approach in transitional justice *as such* see Report of the Secretary-General on the rule of law and transitional justice, *supra* note 2087, paras. 23 et seq.; Nuremberg Declaration on Peace and Justice, in Ambos/Large/Wierda, *supra* note 2041, 544, IV., 2., 2.4. For a holistic proposal of measures to be taken in the specific context of the DRC, see Borello, *supra* note 210, 49 et seq.

f) Conclusion

It can be concluded that two pertinent questions must be answered in order to give the "interests of justice" more substantive content: first, it has to be decided which elements are included and how they are specified. Secondly, it needs to be resolved how theses criteria are balanced. The core problem is how to weigh and combine the various factors.[2177] In other words: How are the different factors put into perspective and which criteria are actually taken into account?

It has to be noted that the OTP has not applied the "interests of justice" clause so far and understands it as a course of last resort. According to article 53 (3), the PTC may review a decision by the OTP not to proceed. If the OTP bases its decision solely on the "interests of justice," the Chamber has to confirm the finding (article 53 (3) (b)). The decision on the "interests of justice" in such a scenario leads to two considerations. First, the Prosecutor must be careful to use the "interests of justice" clause at present because the Pre-Trial Chamber has the review power. Second, whenever the OTP uses the clause in the future the PTC might provide us with some revealing case law on the "interests of justice." Sooner or later the matter will come before the Chambers, either *bona fide* or because the OTP allegedly violated the procedural check foreseen by article 53 (3). At that point, the weighing process will certainly be at dispute. In my view, the suggested proportionality test is most practicable.[2178] In particular, the proportionality *stricto sensu* appears to strike a fair balancing test that enables the Prosecutor to value all relevant criteria.

Currently, the issue remains unresolved. As a matter of fact, there have not been any article 53 (3) checks going into the merits. Coming to the specific elements, the written factors "gravity" and "interests of victims" are vague; even more unclear is which unwritten criteria might be taken into consideration. For gravity, a detailed scale has been outlined above.[2179] The "interests of victims" must be assessed through a qualitative and quantitative consultation process on the ground, and it will be the OTP's task to continuously work on its general approach and to screen each specific (pending and upcoming) situation. Coming to other potential factors not mentioned in article 53 (1), it has been submitted that – generally speaking – other factors can be taken into account. The main discussion has circled

2176 Sriram, in Ambos/Large/Wierda, *supra* note 2015, 316–7.

2177 Delmas-Marty, *supra* note 1048, 7, 9.

2178 Part IV, B., III., 3., b).

2179 Part IV, B., III., 2., c), dd).

around the so called restitutive vs. retributive justice debate, and I have favored a broad application of "interests of justice."

Moreover, the term "peace" must be understood in a broad manner and not be limited to peace negotiations. Further, the terms "peace" and justice" should not be juxtaposed. This wide notion of peace and justice has enabled me to distinguish between the different layers of peace and justice. For instance, the impact on peace negotiations is one aspect that is not appropriate to be taken into account under the "interests of justice" clause.

On the other hand, alternative justice mechanisms have been evaluated as a distinct layer of peace. Mainly screening through TRCs, amnesties, and national justice mechanisms, certain benefits and dangers have been identified. TRCs have been designated a valuable complement to prosecutions. Regarding amnesties, it has been argued that blanket amnesties are not permitted under the ICC Statute, but conditional amnesties remain possible under the "interests of justice." Restorative justice mechanisms need to be judged situation-specifically before one can consider whether they are satisfactory or not. Nonetheless, they cannot be applied to senior leaders.

The differentiation between peace negotiations as such and the tools used within the agreement (special courts, alternative justice mechanisms, etc.) seems to be in line with PTC II's recent approach in Uganda. While neither the Prosecutor nor the PTC intervened when the negotiations were ongoing, PTC II felt obliged to take a glance at the Ugandan Peace Agreement and the Annexure thereto with respect to its envisaged legal instruments. The PTC did not go further into the merits, mainly because implementation of these agreements had failed so far. It can be assumed that, if an agreement is put into effect in one of the situation countries, the Judges will test it *vis-à-vis* article 17. It remains possible that the Prosecutor will equally do so; his margin of appreciation is even broader as he may use the "interests of justice" clause to consider alternative justice mechanisms in peace agreements.

For all these reasons, it is most important that guidelines on the alternative justice mechanisms are developed by the OTP. A tool kit for peace negotiators is crucial if the ICC wants to enhance its effect. Only if the acting diplomats know where the ICC draws its line are they able to develop feasible agreements. Moreover, States must be able to consider whether, and under what conditions, they can opt for alternative mechanisms such as TRCs, amnesties, or traditional forms of justice. The ICC Statute reveals a *lacuna* in this respect and hopefully relevant factors will be identified in the future.[2180]

[2180] Kleffner, *supra* note 370, 308.

Within the framework of transitional justice, the current practice and debate suffers from a lack of clear rules and criteria.[2181] The international community as a whole is in great demand and authors have to change their approaches. Instead of calling for solutions by the OTP, more varied proposals are now necessary. There must be input on the international standards desired for TRCs, amnesties, and traditional justice mechanisms (as well as any other alternative solutions). To make an initial contribution, the following general outline is suggested for future regulatory guidance: the OTP should adopt a pyramidal structure of prosecution and link the specific alternative mechanisms thereto. In other words, the three general categories of senior leaders/those bearing the greatest responsibility, general perpetrators, and minor offenders should be treated alike – punitive sanctions (national or international) for the first category, TRCs and (conditional) amnesties complementary to prosecutions for the second category, and national justice mechanisms (only!) for minor offenders. Since the OTP has adopted a similar prosecution strategy, the pyramidical design is readdressed in more detail below.[2182]

C. Article 53 paragraph 2

Article 53 (2) refers to similar considerations for the case selection stage as article 53 (1) does for the situation selection phase: i) sufficient legal or factual basis to seek a warrant or summons under article 58, ii) admissibility (complementarity and gravity), and iii) considerations of the "interests of justice," taking into account all circumstances, including the gravity of the crime, the interests of the victims, the age or infirmity of the perpetrator, and his or her role in the perpetration of the crime. In a similar vein, OTP Regulation 33 states that in selecting potential cases within a situation, the Office shall analyze issues of jurisdiction, admissibility (including gravity), and "interests of justice." The information shall be reviewed by a joint team that determines a "provisional case hypothesis," and those hypotheses have to be approved by ExCom pursuant to OTP Regulation 34 (3). In addition, OTP Regulation 29 (5) clarifies that the situation selection process is applied *mutatis mutandis* to case selection under article 53 (2). In sum, article 53 (2) seems to pertain to cases, not situations,[2183] and its criteria govern the case selection phase.

However, if we take a look at the differentiation between situation and case,[2184] the object of article 53 (2) appears rather unclear. The PTC set

[2181] Ambos, in Ambos/Large/Wierda, *supra* note 650, 28, para. 6.

[2182] Part IV, C., IV., 4., b), ff) and Part V, C.

[2183] Stigen, *supra* note 205, 120.

the line between cases and situations at article 58 proceedings, but article 53 (2) proceedings lie well ahead of the issuance of a warrant or summons. In strict terms, article 53 (2) cannot deal with cases if this decision is upheld. It is thus debatable whether cases should legally begin only after article 58 proceedings have taken place or whether cases emerge somewhere during the investigation of a situation under article 53 (1) and article 53 (2). In my view, the latter scenario better corresponds to reality. There are two possible lines of argument that might be made in response to the problem: first, one departs from the strict demarcation line set by the PTC and acknowledges that cases evolve during the investigation of a situation. One major disadvantage, however, would be the difficulty of determining the exact point in time when the case was generated. A second, preferable approach would be to differentiate between two meanings of a "case" – a wider definition and a narrower definition. A narrow meaning of case *stricto sensu* is the legal cases that only come into being once a warrant of arrest or summons to appear is issued. Cases *lato sensu* – which might be referred to as "case hypotheses" – evolve very early during investigations and even during pre-investigations. As soon as the OTP bundles allegations against one or more specific individuals and possibly even generates a "case file" with their names, a case in the broader sense arises. On this view, article 53 (2) deals with cases in the broader sense and sets out the main criteria for case selection. An even more nuanced approach has recently been taken by one author who differentiates four possible objects of article 53 (2): a specific individual, a certain group of persons, certain crimes, and a situation.[2185] It remains an essential task for the Judges to exactly define the boundary of article 53 (2) when applying its review power under article 53 (3).

I. Chapeau

The chapeau of article 53 (2) mentions "sufficient basis for a prosecution" as the legitimate basis to proceed with a prosecution. This requires reliable and admissible evidence so that there is a realistic chance of securing a conviction.[2186] The standard under article 53 (2) is higher than under article 53 (1) as both paragraphs refer to different stages and have to apply different standards.[2187]

[2184] Part III, B., III.

[2185] Stahn, in Stahn/Sluiter, *supra* note 156, 270.

[2186] Hall, *supra* note 100, 28.

[2187] Razesberger, *supra* note 371, 105; recently also Schabas, *supra* note 13, 666-7.

II. Warrant or summons under article 58

Article 58 (1) states two substantive prerequisites for the issuance of a warrant of arrest: first, the Chamber must be satisfied that there "are reasonable grounds to believe that the person has committed a crime within the jurisdiction of the Court"; second, the arrest of the person must appear necessary for at least one of the three reasons enumerated in article 58 (1) (b).[2188] The PTC may only exceptionally look at admissibility requirements at the arrest warrant stage[2189] and "interests of justice" considerations are entirely barred at the arrest warrant stage when the Prosecutor reaches a positive decision to initiate a case.[2190] The review power of the PTC only covers negative decision by the Prosecutor *not* to proceed.[2191] In particular, articles 58 (1) and (7) provide that the Chamber "shall" issue a warrant of arrest or a summons to appear whenever it is satisfied that there are reasonable grounds to believe that the person subject to the Prosecution's request is criminally liable under the Statute.[2192] Article 58 (1) (b) arrest warrants exist (i) to ensure the person's appearance a trial, (ii) to ensure that the person does not obstruct or endanger the investigation or the Court proceedings, and (iii) to prevent the person from continuing with the commission of that crime or a related crime which is within the jurisdiction of the Court and which arise out of the same circumstances.[2193] In the alternative, the Prose-

---

2188 *Situation in DRC,* Judgment on the Prosecutor's appeal against the decision of Pre-Trial Chamber I, *supra* note 1360, para. 44; *Prosecutor v. Harun and Kushayb,* Decision on the Prosecution application under article 58 (7) of the Statute, *supra* note 292, para. 11; *Prosecutor v. Ntaganda,* Annex II, Decision on the Prosecutor's application for warrants of arrest, *supra* note 228, para. 9. On the conditions for the issuance of a warrant also Göran Sluiter, "The surrender of war criminals to the International Criminal Court" (2003) 25 Loyola of Los Angeles International and Comparative Law Review 605, 617–8; Kim, *supra* note 813, 204–5.

2189 *Situation in DRC,* Judgment on the Prosecutor's appeal against the decision of Pre-Trial Chamber I, *supra* note 1360, paras. 52–3; *Prosecutor v. Al Bashir,* Decision on the Prosecutor's application for a warrant of arrest against Bashir, *supra* note 304, para. 47; *Situation in Darfur (Sudan),* Decision on application under rule 103, 4.2.2009 (ICC-02/05-185) para. 25.

2190 *Situation in Darfur (Sudan),* Decision on application under rule 103, 4.2.2009 (ICC-02/05-185) paras. 19 et seq., 29. Contrary, and falsely questioning the entire structure of article 53, *Situation in Darfur (Sudan),* Application for leave to appeal against decision on application under rule 103, *supra* note 2036, paras. 20 et seq.

2191 Part IV, E.

2192 *Situation in Darfur (Sudan),* Decision on application under rule 103, 4.2.2009 (ICC-02/05-185) para. 23.

2193 *Prosecutor v. Harun and Kushayb,* Decision on the Prosecution application under article 58 (7) of the Statute, *supra* note 292, para. 126; *Prosecutor v. Katanga,* Decision on the evidence and information, *supra* note 398, para. 61; *Prose-*

cutor may request a summons to appear if this measure is sufficient to ensure that the person will appear before the Court pursuant to article 58 (7).[2194] The application of article 58 (7) is restricted to cases where the person appears voluntarily; the Prosecution must provide an application and sufficient supporting material that guarantees the person's appearance.[2195] In the case *Harun and Kushayb,* the Chamber concluded that the persons would not voluntarily appear and therefore issued an arrest warrant instead of a summons to appear.[2196] It is clear that the reasonable grounds are stricter than a reasonable basis to start investigations.[2197] In my view, the "reasonable grounds" test requires a higher level of specificity than the "reasonable basis to believe" test; it takes place at a later stage after having conducted a full investigation and must be seen in relation to seeking a warrant against a particular person. On the other hand, as we will see below, the standard under article 58 cannot be too high and must be seen in relation to later standards in the ICC Statute (confirmation hearing and trial stage).

First of all, the Prosecutor must fulfill the difficult task of construing the elements of the crimes and assessing the reliability of the evidence.[2198] When examining "reasonable grounds," PTC I saw itself guided by the "reasonable suspicion" standard under article 5 (l) (c) of the European Convention on Human Rights and the jurisprudence of the Inter-American Court of Human Rights on the fundamental right to personal liberty under article 7 of the American Convention on Human Rights.[2199] Moreover, the same Chamber interpreted the term "committed" as encompassing modes of liability other than the commission *stricto sensu* of a crime by a person un-

---

cutor v. Chui, Decision on the evidence and information, *supra* note 235, para. 62; *Prosecutor v. Bemba,* Décision relative à la requête du procureur, *supra* note 465, para. 85.

[2194] *Prosecutor v. Harun and Kushayb,* Decision on the Prosecution application under article 58 (7) of the Statute, *supra* note 292, para. 115; *Prosecutor v. Abu Garda,* Decision under article 58, *supra* note 308, para. 31; CICC, Factsheet, "Questions and answers, Issuance of a warrant of arrest or a summons by the ICC," 27.2.2007, 2.

[2195] *Prosecutor v. Harun and Kushayb,* Decision on the Prosecution application under article 58 (7) of the Statute, *supra* note 292, paras. 117–8.

[2196] *Prosecutor v. Harun and Kushayb,* Decision on the Prosecution application under article 58 (7) of the Statute, *supra* note 292, paras. 124–5; 134.

[2197] Wouters/Verhoeven/Demeyere, *supra* note 156, 312.

[2198] Danner, *supra* note 953, 542.

[2199] *Prosecutor v. Harun and Kushayb,* Decision on the Prosecution application under article 58 (7) of the Statute, *supra* note 292, para. 28; *Prosecutor v. Ntaganda,* Annex II, Decision on the Prosecutor's application for warrants of arrest, *supra* note 228, para. 12; *Prosecutor v. Bemba,* Décision relative à la requête du procureur, *supra* note 465, para. 24; *Prosecutor v. Al Bashir,* Decision on the Prosecutor's application for a warrant of arrest against Bashir, *supra* note 304, para. 32.

der Article 25 (3) (a) of the Statute.[2200] It therefore refined the "reasonable grounds" test for the issuance of an arrest warrant in the context of the *Lubanga* case as posing three questions that have to be answered in the affirmative:

> "(i) Are there reasonable grounds to believe that at least one crime within the jurisdiction of the Court has been committed?
>
> (ii) Are there reasonable grounds to believe that Mr. Thomas Lubanga Dyilo has incurred criminal liability for such crimes under any of the modes of liability provided for in the Statute?
>
> (iii) Does the arrest of Mr. Thomas Lubanga Dyilo appear to be necessary under article 58 (1) of the Statute?"[2201]

An arrest warrant must be issued when the three sub-questions are answered in the affirmative.[2202]

On the other hand, the question arises as to how high the "reasonable grounds" standard must be compared to later standards within the ICC Statute. There are three distinct stages to examine and review the evidence by the Judges: the issuance of an arrest warrant of summons under article 58, the confirmation of charges under article 61, and the conviction of a person under article 66.[2203] The Statute proscribes progressively higher standards

---

2200 *Prosecutor v. Ntaganda,* Annex II, Decision on the Prosecutor's application for warrants of arrest, *supra* note 228, paras. 91–2: "[...] the term "committed" in article 58 (1) of the Statute includes:

(i) the commission *stricto sensu* of a crime by a person "as an individual, jointly with another or through another person, regardless of whether that other person is criminally responsible;

(ii) any other forms of accessory, as opposed to principal, liability provided for in article 25 (3) (b) to (d) of the Statute;

(iii) an attempt to commit any of the crimes provided for in articles 6 to 8 of the Statute;

(iv) direct and public incitement to commit genocide (the only preparatory act punishable under the Statute); and

(v) the responsibility of commanders and other superiors under article 28 of the Statute"; concurring, *Prosecutor v. Katanga,* Decision on the evidence and information, *supra* note 398, para. 23; *Prosecutor v. Chui,* Decision on the evidence and information, *supra* note 235, para. 24.

2201 *Prosecutor v. Ntaganda,* Annex II, Decision on the Prosecutor's application for warrants of arrest, *supra* note 228, para. 93; concurring *Prosecutor v. Katanga,* Decision on the evidence and information, *supra* note 398, para. 24; *Prosecutor v. Chui,* Decision on the evidence and information, *supra* note 235, para. 25; *Prosecutor v. Al Bashir,* Decision on the Prosecutor's application for a warrant of arrest against Bashir, *supra* note 304, para. 28.

2202 Ambos, in Bohlander, *supra* note 10, 449.

2203 See already, in the context of "reasonable basis" under article 53 (1), Part IV, B., II., 3. Recently *Prosecutor v. Bemba,* Decision pursuant to article 61 (7) (a)

to be met at each mentioned stage.[2204] At the arrest warrant stage, the Prosecutor should not be required to meet an evidentiary threshold, which would be sufficient to support a conclusion beyond reasonable doubt, but only a lower "reasonable suspicion" threshold.[2205] In the *Bashir* case Judge Ušacka therefore issued a separate and dissenting opinion in which she argues that only evidence rendering an inference of genocidal intent reasonable must be presented.[2206] In my view, the dissenting opinion is persuasive, since the standard under article 58 is supposed to be lower than that applied at the later confirmation of charges hearing and still lower than that applied at the trial stage. Therefore, one cannot set too demanding a threshold at the arrest warrant stage, keeping in mind the role of the subsequent confirmation hearing. For a judicial settlement of this question leave to appeal was granted,[2207] and the Appeals Chamber came to the conclusion that PTC I applied an erroneous standard of proof (too high and demanding).[2208] It referred the matter back to PTC I for a new decision based on the correct standard of proof.[2209a] Accordingly, PTC I re-examined the matter, it applied a lower standard of proof, and the Judges decided to issue a second warrant of arrest against Al Bashir including genocide charges.[2209b]

III. Admissibility

In principle, the admissibility assessment under article 53 (2) (b) is the same as that under article 53 (1) (b). However, at the case level, admissibil-

---

and (b), *supra* note 279, para. 27; *Situation in Kenya*, Decision pursuant to article 15, *supra* note 6, para. 28, 14; Schabas, *supra* note 13, 707.

2204 *Prosecutor v. Al Bashir,* Separate and partly dissenting opinion of Judge Anita Ušacka, *supra* note 305, para. 8.

2205 *Prosecutor v. Al Bashir,* Separate and partly dissenting opinion of Judge Anita Ušacka, *supra* note 305, para. 9.

2206 *Prosecutor v. Al Bashir,* Separate and partly dissenting opinion of Judge Anita Ušacka, *supra* note 305, para. 34.

2207 Leave to appeal was granted regarding the issue "[w]hether the correct standard of proof in the context of article 58 requires that the *only* reasonable conclusion to be drawn from the evidence is the existence of reasonable grounds to believe that the person has committed a crime within the jurisdiction of the Court (the First Issue")," cf. *Prosecutor v. Al Bashir,* Decision on the Prosecutor's application for leave to appeal the "Decision on the Prosecution's application for an arrest warrant against Omar Hassan Ahmad Al Bashir," 24.6.2009 (ICC-02/05-01/09-21) 5, 10.

2208 *Prosecutor v. Al Bashir,* Judgment on the appeal of the Prosecutor, *supra* note 306, paras. 39, 41, 17–8.

2209a *Prosecutor v. Al Bashir,* Judgment on the appeal of the Prosecutor, *supra* note 306, para. 42, 18.

2209b *Prosecutor v. Al Bashir,* Second decision on the Prosecutor's application for a warrant of arrest, 12.7.2010 (ICC-02/05-01/09-94) paras. 1 et seq., 7, 28.

ity requires a more specific and detailed analysis involving the particular suspect.[2210] Accordingly, the OTP must first inquire if the State is investigating or prosecuting the same underlying facts.[2211] If not, then the case is admissible due to inactivity. On the other hand, if there are national proceedings, the Prosecutor must turn to the criteria set forth in article 17 (2) and (3). In sum, complementarity testing under articles 53 (2) (b) and 17 is more detailed and goes further into the merits than situational complementarity does.

For legal gravity, the considerations are similar. Once a situation is selected for investigation in accordance with article 53 (1), the Prosecutor must choose cases for prosecution. Those cases have to meet the legal gravity threshold of articles 53 (2) (b) and 17 (1) (d). If the Prosecutor finds many cases for potential prosecution, the ICC Statute is silent as to how he should decide which cases to prosecute.[2212] For this reason, legal gravity sets a minimum threshold for cases and relative gravity allows the Prosecutor to rank cases.[2213] Thus, when considering the legal gravity of a case, the OTP may consider primarily quantitative factors and the threshold is a very low one. Nonetheless, contrary to the legal gravity for situations, the test is narrower as it refers to specific cases as opposed to large-scale situations.

IV. Interests of Justice

The criterion under article 53 (2) (c) introduces a broad scope of discretion in the decision whether to proceed with a prosecution. First and foremost, a decisive question arises from the twofold investigation/prosecution nature of article 53's first two paragraphs: whether the application of the "interests of justice" clause is at core the same in both paragraphs. One author suggests an external interpretation of the "interests of justice" in the first paragraph, whereas the second paragraph should be seen as more limited through an internal interpretation.[2214] On the contrary, both paragraphs seem to introduce the idea of allowing the Prosecutor to consider broader considerations, and the "interests of justice" forms the overarching concept for both provisions. It should be regarded as the opening clause for various factors. On the other hand, the "interests of justice" clause is – with respect to both paragraphs – not a free-standing criterion, but rather is constrained

[2210] Burke-White/Kaplan, in Stahn/Sluiter, *supra* note 247, 88. On the differentiation situation – case see already Part III, B., III.

[2211] Burke-White/Kaplan, in Stahn/Sluiter, *supra* note 247, 88.

[2212] McAuliffe deGuzman, *supra* note 1152, 9.

[2213] Part IV, B., III., 2., c), dd).

[2214] Gallavin, *supra* note 1881, 185–6.

by the legal factors (gravity, interests of victims, age or infirmity, and role).[2215] The two paragraphs should thus be differentiated procedurally as paragraph 2 refers to the later stage of initiating a prosecution.

A very important distinction is that article 53 (1) has situations as its objects, whereas article 53 (2) (c) deals with cases. Due to the advanced individualization the sub-criteria are phrased in a broader and at the same time more particular manner. Article 53 (2) (c) is broader since the wording "taking into account all the circumstances" introduces an open list from the outset, and yet more specific since – besides gravity of the crime and interest of the victims – factors with regard to individuals can be found ("age and infirmity of the alleged perpetrator" and "his or her role in the alleged crime"). In any event, the dominating "interests of justice" standard is not clearly defined, as was already noticed under article 53 (1) (c). It has been suggested that the Prosecutor's margin of discretion is considerably higher when selecting "cases" within a given "situation."[2216] In any event, the notion of "interests of justice" is to a large extent analogous to the one under article 53 (1) (c).

1. Taking into account all the circumstances

The use of the terms "taking into account all the circumstances, including […]" has to be interpreted as an illustrative and non-exhaustive list.[2217] The Prosecutor is bound to take into consideration the four enumerated criteria, namely:

- the gravity of the crime;
- the interests of victims;
- the age of the alleged perpetrator or infirmity of the alleged perpetrator; and
- his or her role in the alleged crime.

2. Gravity of the crime – relative gravity under article 53 (2) (c)

Although any crime falling within the jurisdiction of the ICC is serious, gravity is central to the process of case selection. One key criterion for case selection should be the concept of relative gravity, which should be

[2215] Ambos, in Ambos/Large/Wierda, *supra* note 650, 84–5, para. 52.

[2216] Schabas, *supra* note 1225, 17; Stahn, in Stahn/Sluiter, *supra* note 156, 249.

[2217] Dukić, *supra* note 1256, 697; McDonald/Haveman, *supra* note 1149, 6. Contrary to McDonald/Haveman, article 53 (1) (c) should be interpreted in an open manner, cf. Part IV, B., III., 3., c).

considered when selecting cases in comparison to other cases the Court could prosecute and prioritizing cases accordingly.[2218] In connection with its completion strategy, the ICTY has similarly filtered cases and compared them with other pending cases:

> "In light of the positions of the Accused within the overall chain of responsible actors, and the *relative gravity* of their alleged crimes when *compared to other pending cases* before the Tribunal, it is apparent that neither Accused in the present case may be appropriately regarded as among the "most senior leaders suspected of being most responsible for crimes within the Tribunal's jurisdiction (emph. added)."[2219]

But the exact factors to be taken into account are unclear. It has been stated that the OTP looks at factors such as the scale and nature of the crimes (in particular, high numbers of killings), the systematic character of the crimes, as well as other aggravating factors.[2220] In addition, the OTP has analyzed crime patterns based on perpetrating groups, geographical location of alleged crimes, as well as the accessibility of evidence.[2221] OHCHR has named "seniority of the individuals concerned" or the "gravity of the crime they had committed" as two main criteria in determining accountability of parties.[2222] Rather than breaking down the numerous elements of gravity, the concept of relative gravity implies a high discretionary threshold that allows the Prosecutor to consider quantitative factors, qualitative factors, and the individual circumstances of the perpetrator.[2223] Thereby, a comparison *vis-à-vis* other pending cases becomes possible.[2224]

3. The interest of the victims

The interest of the victims is basically the same as under article 53 (1) (c). The notion is difficult to assess and it is a challenge to inquire as into victims' demands. As compared to 53 (1) (c), only the affected victims of the specific case may be taken into account under article 53 (2) (c). Alike any criteria under article 53 (2), the case assessment is narrower and more demanding than the situation assessment.

[2218] McAuliffe deGuzman, *supra* note 1152, 9.

[2219] *Prosecutor v. Todović & Rašević,* Decision on referral of case under rule 11*bis* with confidential annexes I and II, 8.7.2005 (IT-97-25/1-PT) para. 23.

[2220] Third Report pursuant to UNSC 1593, *supra* note 288, 2; Guariglia, in Stahn/Sluiter, *supra* note 1215, 214.

[2221] Third Report pursuant to UNSC 1593, *supra* note 288, 2.

[2222] OHCHR, Making peace our own, *supra* note 246, 26, 69.

[2223] PTC I recently mentioned the importance of the qualitative dimension to be taken into consideration, cf. *Prosecutor v. Abu Garda,* Decision on the confirmation of charges, *supra* note 312, para. 31.

[2224] Part IV, B., III., 2., c), dd).

4. Particular circumstances of the accused

In contrast to article 53 (1) (c), article 53 (2) (c) introduces two further explicit factors, which are closely related to the circumstances of the accused. An explanation might be the advanced stage under article 53 (2), and thus the fact that the individualization has progressed. The circumstances of the accused embrace: (1) the age or infirmity of the alleged perpetrator; and (2) his or her role in the alleged crime.

a) The age or infirmity of the alleged perpetrator

The criterion of age sets limits downwards and upwards. "Downwards" falls under article 26 and excludes any persons under 18 years of age from prosecution. In particular, child soldiers are thus exempted.[2225] The "upwards" is more difficult to define. If the suspect is too old, it is unlikely that he or she will live to the end of the trial and final judgment.[2226] For example, Augusto Pinochet was released from house arrest and allowed to fly to Chile because "his age and illness have rendered him mentally incapable of standing trial."[2227] But advanced age as such is no reason not to indict and attempt to prosecute the individual.[2228] Therefore, the Court will have to decide this matter after carefully considering the individual case. Infirmity means being unfit to stand trial and can be invoked only when all alternatives, including limits on the hours of the trial have been considered and rejected.[2229] Although it elaborates the concept in the context of sentencing, one might turn to ICTY/ICTR jurisprudence to find guidance on the age or infirmity requirement,[2230] naming the following factors:

- the young age of the accused;[2231]
- the poor health of the accused (in exceptional or rare cases);[2232]
- the advanced age of the accused.[2233]

[2225] Morel, *supra* note 1365, 264.

[2226] Hall, *supra* note 100, 28.

[2227] Kim, *supra* note 813, 198.

[2228] HRW, policy paper article 53, *supra* note 1263, 17.

[2229] Hall, *supra* note 100, 28; Stigen, *supra* note 205, 368.

[2230] HRW, policy paper article 53, *supra* note 1263, 17.

[2231] *Prosecutor v. Serushago, supra* note 1779, para. 39; *Prosecutor v. Erdemović,* Trial judgment, Sentence, 5.3.1998 (IT-96-22T*bis*), para. 16; *Prosecutor v. Furundžija, supra* note 1780, para. 284; *Prosecutor v. Blaškić, supra* note 1774, para. 778; *Prosecutor v. Simić, supra* note 1767, para. 41; *Prosecutor v. Kordić, supra* note 1774, para. 848; *Prosecutor v. Seromba, supra* note 1784, para. 399; also *Prosecutor v. Milutinović et al., supra* note 1767, para. 1152, where an exhaustive enumeration of all mitigating factors is given.

b) Role in the alleged crime – those bearing the greatest responsibility

As we will see below, international criminal jurisdictions have all focused their efforts on the top perpetrators.[2234] The ICC Statute though uses the term "role in the alleged crime," and no references to "those bearing the greatest responsibility" can be found. It has been concluded from the ICTY and ICTR's sentencing practices that the role in the alleged crime is a wide notion and could include i) the position of the accused, ii) the relative importance of the accused in his or her community, iii) the form of participation, premeditation or planning, iv) the accused's motive, and v) the manner of commission.[2235]

aa) Big fish v. small fish debate: Focused investigations on those "bearing the greatest responsibility"

Given the large number of perpetrators in the international crime context, it is clear that the question is how widely the net should be cast.[2236] One author roughly distinguishes three classifications out of which only the first two require actual trials (from his point of view, it will already be difficult to prosecute everyone in the second category): (1) the leaders who gave the orders to commit war crimes and those who actually carried out the worst offences; (2) those who perpetrated abuses not rising to the first category; and (3) those whose offences were minimal.[2237] The underlying philosophical question is thus whether prosecutions at the international level should focus on those at the top or include individuals in lower positions.[2238]

In early practice at the International Military Tribunal and the International Military Tribunal for the Far East, trials were limited to the "major

---

2232 *Prosecutor v. Zelenović, supra* note 1774, paras. 55–6; *Prosecutor v. Milutinović et al., supra* note 1767, para. 1152; *Prosecutor v. Rutaganira, supra* note 1779, paras. 135–6; *Prosecutor v. Rutaganda, supra* note 1773, para. 472; *Prosecutor v. Ntakirutimana, supra* note 1782, para. 898; *Prosecutor v. Kordić, supra* note 1774, para. 848; *Prosecutor v. Simić, supra* note 1767, para. 98.

2233 *Prosecutor v. Plavšić, supra* note 1774, paras. 95 et seq., 106; *Prosecutor v. Krnojelac, supra* note 1778, para. 533; *Prosecutor v. Ntakirutimana, supra* note 1782, para. 898; *Prosecutor v. Rutaganira, supra* note 1779, para. 134.

2234 In the same vein, Stigen, *supra* note 205, 369.

2235 Part IV, B., III., 2., c), dd).

2236 Kritz, *supra* note 2066, 134. Further on selectivity in international criminal law see Cryer, *supra* note 816, 191 et seq.; Agirre Aranburu, in Bergsmo, *supra* note 460, 156 et seq.

2237 Kritz, *supra* note 2066, 134.

2238 Guariglia, in Stahn/Sluiter, *supra* note 1215, 210.

war criminals."[2239] Other than that, these tribunals failed to list specific criteria for case selection.[2240] In recent years there has been a tendency to limit international criminal law prosecutions to "those bearing the greatest responsibility" or "those most responsible."[2241] Some prefer the latter, more general term "most responsible" because it embraces political or military leadership on the one hand, but could equally include others down the chain of command.[2242] Others prefer the terminology "those bearing the greatest responsibility" with regard to the ICC for the following reasons:

> "First, it locates responsibility with the people who actually make the decisions. Second, it is the best chance for deterrence, as the planning of these crimes occurs at the highest level of decision-making, where the likelihood of criminal prosecution can be a deterrent factor. Third, it is the best chance of reaching the greatest number of victims, as these people are responsible for multiple crimes, not just for individual atrocities."[2243]

By targeting the main leaders and criminals, the Prosecutor confirms that the ICC's aim is to target so-called "big fish."[2244] Transitional societies may be faced with extraordinary situations were the prosecution of all offenders is simply not possible or desirable.[2245] Representative or symbolic prosecutions are thus a necessity. It remains to be seen how much the Prosecutor goes after "small fish" in order to build up a case against the major leaders on some occasions.[2246] There has been criticism in the past that rather than those most responsible, it is those most "available" that are tried.[2247] One advantage of the *ad hoc* tribunals was considered to be

---

2239 Article 1 Charter of the International Military Tribunal, 8 August 1945; Article 1 Charter of the International Military Tribunal for the Far East, 19 January 1946.

2240 Stigen, *supra* note 205, 347.

2241 NPWJ, "Prosecuting violations of International Criminal Law: Who should be tried?," NPWJ International Criminal Justice Policy Series No. 1, November 2004, 5. On the extent to which international tribunals managed to focus on the "most responsible" see Agirre Aranburu, in Bergsmo, *supra* note 460, 159 et seq.

2242 Report of the Secretary-General on the establishment of a Special Court for Sierra Leone, 4.10.2000 (S/2000/915) para. 30; contrary, Letter dated 22 December 2000 from the President of the Security Council Addressed to the Secretary-General, UN Doc. S/2000/1234, 1.

2243 Ms. Alison Smith – No Peace Without Justice, Session 2: NGOs and other experts, Second public hearing of the OTP, 26.9.2006.

2244 Wouters/Verhoeven/Demeyere, *supra* note 156, 291; Hitomi Takemura, "Big fish and small fish debate – an examination of the prosecutorial discretion" (2007) 7 ICLR 677, 677 et seq.

2245 Robinson, *supra* note 807, 493.

2246 Wouters/Verhoeven/Demeyere, *supra* note 156, 291; Takemura, *supra* note 2244, 678; Ms. Géraldine Mattioli, HRW, *supra* note 473, who names the Janjaweed leaders in the Darfur situation.

"the freedom to indict people who were called "small fish" by the media. This was not inconsistent with giving priority to the leaders who were the guiltiest. But it did enable us to get out quick indictments and so provide the Court with work, and so build its credibility. The *Tadić* trial is the most important illustration of this. It helped lay an important foundation for the jurisprudence that has come from the ICTY. As I understand the position, this is not open to the Prosecutor of the ICC."[2248]

Indeed, the ICC Prosecutor made early statements to focus *only* on those "who bear the greatest responsibility for the most serious crimes."[2249] But this is merely a policy question, not one of strict admissibility.[2250] In contrast, the SCSL and the ECCC have been given limited competence from the outset by restricting their mandates to the "persons bearing the greatest responsibility" in articles 1, 15 SCSCL Statute and the "senior leaders of Democratic Kampuchea and those who were most responsible" in articles 1 and 2 ECCC Law.[2251]

It has to be noted that the term "those who bear the greatest responsibility" is not introduced by the ICC Statute and bringing low-level cases to trial is therefore not ruled out *per se*. The open nature of article 53 (2) (c) ("all the circumstances"), the considerations of age and infirmity, and the role in the alleged crime favor the prioritization of top-level officials.[2252] Nevertheless, as already mentioned, this is a policy matter and not a jurisdictional or admissibility problem.[2253] Moreover, since the term "bearing the greatest responsibility" was only introduced by the Prosecutor, the notion of "role" is the most valid link. By taking a look at ICTY/ICTR approaches (bb), the SCSL and ECCC (cc), PTC I's arrest warrant decision in Lubanga and Ntaganda (dd), as well as the OTP's policy (ee), the exact content of "those bearing the greatest responsibility" will be determined.

2247 Yav Katshung, *supra* note 1892, 3.

2248 Mr. Richard Goldstone, Session 4: NGOs and other experts, Second public hearing of the OTP, 18.10.2006.

2249 WCRO report gravity, *supra* note 1057, 43. See the references in *supra* note 1222.

2250 Policy: Policy paper, *supra* note 99, 7; Outlining the Three-Year Report – Ms. Olivia Swaak-Goldman, *supra* note 473; further Part IV, C., IV., 4., b), ff).

2251 Articles 1, 15 SCSL Statute, *supra* notes 434, and articles 1, 2 ECCC Law, *supra* note 435.

2252 Brubacher, *supra* note 368, 81.

2253 For the policy nature of "most responsible" under the Special Court for Sierra Leone, see Report of the Secretary-General, *supra* note 2242, para. 30.

bb) ICTY and ICTR completion strategies (and sentencing decisions)

The ICTY and ICTR have developed a strategy of focusing on those who bear the greatest responsibility, perhaps caused by the pressure placed upon them by completion strategies. At the outset, no provision specifically limited the admissibility in such a way.[2254] Carla del Ponte emphasized that, while the first case of *Duško Tadić* was not among the most responsible, in general the ICTY concentrated its investigations and prosecution on the category of the ones bearing the greatest responsibility.[2255] However, a review of years of ICTY practice suggests that those "lesser responsible" make up about 45 percent of all defendants and that they were selected due to a number of reasons: (1) arrest opportunities; (2) notorious perpetrators; (3) expectations of national authorities, victims, and NGOs; (4) investigative value to build the higher case; (5) need to address particularly grave types of offences; and (6) because the officer in charge had the evidence and nobody restricted their discretion.[2256]

In SC-Res. 1503 (2003) the SC urged the ICTY and ICTR to review their caseloads to determine which cases to proceed with and which to transfer to competent national jurisdictions, and to complete all work in 2010.[2257] The SC called upon the tribunals "to ensure that any such indictments concentrate on the most senior leaders suspected of being most responsible for crimes within the jurisdiction of the relevant Tribunal as set out in resolution 1503 (2003)."[2258] When presenting its course of action for the completion strategy, the ICTR explained that it would be guided by the need to focus on those who are alleged to have been in positions of leadership and those who, according to the Prosecutor, bear the greatest responsibility for genocide. The criteria taken into consideration when making this determination are:

- the alleged status and extent of participation of the individual during the genocide;

[2254] Takemura, *supra* note 2244, 680; Claudia Angermeier, "Case selection and prioritization criteria in the work of the International Criminal Tribunal for the Former Yugoslavia" in Bergsmo, *supra* note 99, 29, 29.

[2255] Carla Del Ponte, "Prosecuting the individuals bearing the highest level of responsibility" (2004) 2 JICJ 516, 516 et seq.

[2256] Agirre Aranburu, in Bergsmo, *supra* note 460, 161–2.

[2257] SC-Res. 1503 (2003), 28.8.2003; further SC-Res. 1543 (2004), 26.3.2004; Smith, *supra* note 210, 339; Takemura, *supra* note 2244, 680 et seq.; Dominic Raab, "Evaluating the ICTY and its completion strategy" (2005) 3 JICJ 82, 88 et seq.; Mallinder, *supra* note 1887, 222; Angermeier, in Bergsmo, *supra* note 2254, 33 et seq.

[2258] SC-Res. 1543 (2004), 26.3.2004, § 5.

- the alleged connection an individual may have with other cases;
- the need to cover the major geographical areas of Rwanda in which the crimes were allegedly committed;
- the availability of evidence with regard to the individual concerned;
- the concrete possibility of arresting the individual concerned;
- the availability of investigative material for transmission to a State for national prosecution.[2259]

The ICTY even introduced a new rule 28 (A) ICTY RPE to review "whether the indictment, *prima facie,* concentrates on one or more of the most senior leaders suspected of being most responsible for crimes within the jurisdiction of the Tribunal."[2260] Moreover, rule 11*bis* (c) ICTY RPE provides that: "[...] the Referral Bench shall, in accordance with Security Council resolution 1534 (2004), consider the gravity of the crimes charged and the level of responsibility of the accused."[2261] At first sight, it seems that the completion strategy focuses only on the "most senior leaders" who, in addition, have to be the "most responsible." In this regard, the SC President specified the SC's understanding of leaders as focusing on "[...] civilian, military and paramilitary leaders suspected of being responsible for serious violations of international humanitarian law committed in the territory of the former Yugoslavia since 1991, rather than on minor actors."[2262] Rule 28 (A) ICTY RPE yet adopts a wider approach by the inclusion of the word "*prima facie*." According to the former Prosecutor of the ICTY, it is

---

2259 Completion strategy of the International Criminal Tribunal for Rwanda, Annex to the Letter dated 30 April 2004 from the President of the ICTR addressed to the President of the Security Council, 3.5.2004 (S/2004/341) para. 14; Côte, *supra* note 1190, 185; further on ICTR selection criteria Obote-Odora, in Bergsmo, *supra* note 1926, 47 et seq.

2260 Enclosure I to the Letter dated 21 May 2004 from the President of the ICTY addressed to the President of the Security Council, 24.5.2004 (S/2004/420) paras. 32–4; Takemura, *supra* note 2244, 681–2; Angermeier, in Bergsmo, *supra* note 2254, 37.

2261 In contrast, rule 11*bis* ICTR RPE does not follow this approach. In lit. (C) it contains the requirements of a fair trial for the accused and that no death penalty will be imposed; the same phrasing can be found in rule 11*bis* (B) ICTY RPE. Yet, the ICTR did not include the terms "gravity" and "level of responsibility." It remains a mystery why the rules were drafted differently, given the similar completion strategies of both tribunals. It is strongly suggested that the ICTR should explicitly refer to both factors. For the ICTR's practice, see *Prosecutor v. Munyeshyaka,* Decision on the Prosecutor's request for the referral of Wenceslas Munyeshyaka's indictment to France, 20.11.2007 (ICTR-2005-87-I) paras. 18 et seq.; also, denying a 11*bis* referral to Norway, *Prosecutor v. Bagaragaza, supra* note 1585.

2262 Statement by the President of the SC, 23.7.2002 (S/PRST/2002/21).

possible to differentiate two main categories of people among those possibly bearing the highest level of responsibility: first, functional responsibility; and second, those who had no particular functional role but played a great role in setting examples and encouraging, by their acts, speech and behavior, the commission of other gruesome crimes.[2263] Thus, the ICTY focused its efforts on persons in leadership position and the class of notorious offenders ("example setters").

In conclusion, the *ad hoc* tribunals did not have a mandatory prosecutorial limitation in their statutory provisions; however, they developed a procedural focus due to their completion strategies. The terminology of leaders has to be regarded as a broader concept rather than as a strict limitation. The SC urged the ICTY and ICTR to focus its activities on senior leaders who are *prima facie* the most desirable targets as a policy matter. The tribunals are, in any event, not barred from investigating and prosecuting mid-level and minor offenders under exceptional circumstances. For example, it has been reasoned that extraordinarily cruel behavior might qualify as "bearing the greatest responsibility," even if the accused is not a senior leader.[2264] In addition, it might be helpful to take a glance at ICTY/ICTR sentencing decisions and 11*bis* ICTY RPE referral decisions which suggest the following factors for the "role in the alleged crimes:"[2265]

- How important a role the accused played regarding the crimes (position of authority: is he or she one of the most senior leaders who were most responsible for the crimes?);[2266]
- Whether the individual actually participated in the crimes directly, or is otherwise responsible for the crimes, for example by having planned or ordered others to carry them out;[2267]

[2263] Del Ponte, *supra* note 2255, 517; also Smith, *supra* note 210, 348.

[2264] See Smith, *supra* note 210, 347 et seq., who calls this the *Jelisić* problem.

[2265] The following analysis is an extended version of the sentencing jurisprudence given by HRW, policy paper article 53, *supra* note 1263, 18; recently also David Tolbert/Aleksandar Kontic, "The International Criminal Tribunal for the former Yugoslavia: transitional justice, the transfer of cases to national courts, and lessons for the ICC," in Stahn/Sluiter, *supra* note 5, 135, 152 et seq.

[2266] *Prosecutor v. Kovačević,* Decision on referral of case pursuant to rule 11*bis* with confidential and partly ex parte annexes, 17.11.2006 (IT-01-42/2-I) para. 20; *Prosecutor v. Mejakić et al.,* Decision of Prosecutor's motion for referral of case pursuant to rule 11*bis,* 20.7.2005 (IT-02-65-PT) para. 26; *Prosecutor v. Janković, supra* note 1774, para. 19; *Prosecutor v. Todović & Rašević, supra* note 2219, para. 23; *Prosecutor v. Ljubičić, supra* note 1774, para. 19; *Prosecutor v. Naletilić and Martinović,* Trial judgment, 31.3.2003 (IT-98-34) para. 744; *Prosecutor v. Ruggiu, supra* note 1773, paras. 49, 75; see further the jurisprudence in *supra* notes 1782 and 1783.

- The informed, voluntary, willing or enthusiastic participation in the crime.[2268]

In other words, for the role of the accused the ICTY/ICTR looks at two main factors: the *rank* of the accused and the *actual role* the person played in the commission of the crimes.[2269] When the ICTY filters its cases in this way it applies a relative gravity assessment in light of other pending cases.[2270] In sum, while the ICTY and ICTR were keen to pick up a wide range of cases at the beginning, a completion strategy was implemented that now confines case selection.

cc) SCSL and ECCC

The SCSL and the ECCC have been given limited competence from the outset. Articles 1 and 15 SCSL Statute limit the SCSL's jurisdiction to the "persons who bear the greatest responsibility." This terminology has been understood as an "indication of a limitation on the number of accused by reference to their command authority and the gravity and scale of the crime."[2271] However, as mentioned above, the Secretary-General preferred the term "most responsible" for two reasons: first, the term is broader in nature and could possibly include others down the chain of command; and second, because it is not a test criterion, but rather provides guidance for the Prosecutor when adopting a prosecution strategy.[2272] While the "most responsible" would include 300–400 individuals, the "greatest responsibil-

---

2267 *Prosecutor v. Ljubičić, supra* note 1774, para. 19; *Prosecutor v. Ruggiu, supra* note 1773, paras. 77 et seq.; *Prosecutor v. Kvočka et al., supra* note 1776, para. 705; *Prosecutor v. Krnojelac, supra* note 1778, para. 77; *Prosecutor v. Blaškić, supra* note 1774, para. 790.

2268 *Prosecutor v. Blaškić, supra* note 1774, para. 792; *Prosecutor v. Tadić,* Trial judgment, Sentence, 11.11.1999 (IT-94-1) para. 20.

2269 *Prosecutor v. Ademi & Norac, supra* note 1774, para. 29.

2270 *Prosecutor v. Todović & Rašević, supra* note 2219, para. 23. See already Part IV, C., IV., 2. Further on the ICTY's set of case selection criteria Angermeier, in Bergsmo, *supra* note 2254, 31 et seq.

2271 Report of the Secretary-General on the establishment of a SCSL, *supra* note 2242, para. 29.

2272 Report of the Secretary-General on the establishment of a SCSL, *supra* note 2242, para. 30: "[...] 'Most responsible', therefore, denotes both a leadership and authority position of the accused, and a sense of the gravity, seriousness or massive scale of the crime. It must be seen, however, not as a test criterion or a distinct jurisdictional threshold, but as guidance to the Prosecutor in the adoption of a prosecution strategy and in making decisions to prosecute in individual cases." Further Mallinder, *supra* note 1887, 222, who stresses that, due to limited resources, it is unlikely that the SCSL will indict lower-level offenders.

ity" was understood as including less than two dozen individuals.[2273] The phrase "those who bear the greatest responsibility" has therefore been interpreted as a deliberate decision to limit the SCSL's jurisdiction to a small group of people in leadership positions.[2274]

The Trial Chamber of the CDF case (with regard to Fofana) had to address the issue whether the phrasing was indeed a jurisdictional requirement or merely an articulation of prosecutorial discretion.[2275] After careful discussions the Chamber arrived at the conclusion that the matter is a jurisdictional requirement, mainly because otherwise the agreed text was unduly modified.[2276] As a second question, the Judges approached at what stage of the proceedings the personal jurisdiction should be determined. During the review procedure of an indictment the Judge must take into account personal, temporal, and subject matter jurisdictional requirements.[2277] The ultimate analysis is an evidentiary matter to be determined at the trial stage.[2278]

The Appeals Chamber addressed the issue differently in the AFRC case on 22 February 2008. The accused Kanu argued that the Trial Chamber erred in law by finding that the words "those bearing the greatest responsibility" is not a jurisdictional requirement and further erred in law when convicting him without first establishing whether it has jurisdiction over him.[2279] He thereby relied on the Trial Chamber's finding in the CDF trial as outlined above.[2280] The assessment should accordingly be based on the accused's leadership position and Kanu submitted that he is not one of those "bearing the greatest responsibility."[2281] On the other hand, the Prosecution regards the criterion as a guide to its Prosecutorial Strategy rather

2273 Murphy, *supra* note 1048, 300.

2274 Murphy, *supra* note 1048, 301.

2275 *Prosecutor v. Fofana and Kondawa (CDF trial),* Decision on the preliminary Defence motion on the lack of personal jurisdiction filed on behalf of the accused Fofana, 3.3.2004 (SCSL-04-16-PT-026) para. 21.

2276 *Prosecutor v. Fofana and Kondawa (CDF trial),* Decision on the preliminary Defence motion on the lack of personal jurisdiction, *supra* note 2275, paras. 26–7.

2277 *Prosecutor v. Fofana and Kondawa (CDF trial),* Decision on the preliminary Defence motion on the lack of personal jurisdiction, *supra* note 2275, para. 31.

2278 *Prosecutor v. Fofana and Kondawa (CDF trial),* Decision on the preliminary Defence motion on the lack of personal jurisdiction, *supra* note 2275, para. 44.

2279 *Prosecutor v. Brima, Kamara and Kanu (AFRC trial),* Appeals judgment, 22.2.2008 (SCSL-04-16-A-675) para. 272; Cryer, *supra* note 2022, 49–50.

2280 *Prosecutor v. Brima, Kamara and Kanu (AFRC trial),* Appeals judgment, 22.2.2008 (SCSL-04-16-A-675) para. 273.

2281 *Prosecutor v. Brima, Kamara and Kanu (AFRC trial),* Appeals judgment, 22.2.2008 (SCSL-04-16-A-675) para. 273.

than as a jurisdictional requirement.[2282] The Appeals Chamber agreed with the Prosecutor's interpretation in that article 1 guides prosecutorial discretion rather than setting up a jurisdictional barrier, therefore dismissing the ground of appeal on the merits.[2283]

Article 1 and article 2 new of the ECCC Law limits the ECCC's competence to the "senior leaders of Democratic Kampuchea and those who were most responsible."[2284] In 1999 an expert group brought up the preliminary question how many persons should be prosecuted given the thousands of individuals that committed crimes across the country.[2285] A great majority of persons, whom the group met, suggested that "leaders" of the Khmer Rouge and not low-level cadre should form the targets.[2286] On the meaning of the term "leaders" there was a wide disparity.[2287] The experts arrived at the conclusion that the term should not be interpreted too narrowly:

> "[...] the Group recommends that any tribunal focus upon those persons most responsible for the most serious violations of human rights during the reign of Democratic Kampuchea. This would include senior leaders with responsibility over the abuses as well as those at lower levels who are directly implicated in the most serious atrocities. We do not wish to offer a numerical limit on the number of such persons who could be targets of investigation. It is, nonetheless, the sense of the Group from its consultations and research that the number of persons to be tried might well be in the range of some 20 to 30. While the decisions on whom and when to indict would be solely within the discretion of a prosecutor, the Group believes that the strategy undertaken by the prosecutor of any tribunal should fully take into account the twin goals of individual accountability and national reconciliation."[2288]

Moreover, the experts recommended that the leadership limitation should be no more than a guide for the Prosecutor and not an element of the jurisdiction. In general, "any legal instrument related to a court should give it personal jurisdiction over any persons whose acts fall within its subject matter jurisdiction, and the decision on whom to indict should rest solely with the prosecutor, bearing the above guidance in mind. *A fortiori,* the

[2282] *Prosecutor v. Brima, Kamara and Kanu (AFRC trial),* Appeals judgment, 22.2.2008 (SCSL-04-16-A-675) para. 274.

[2283] *Prosecutor v. Brima, Kamara and Kanu (AFRC trial),* Appeals judgment, 22.2.2008 (SCSL-04-16-A-675) paras. 282 et seq.

[2284] Articles 1 and 2 (new) ECCC Law, *supra* note 435; Anees Ahmed/Margaux Day, "Prosecution criteria at the Khmer Rouge Tribunal" in Bergsmo, *supra* note 99, 79, 79 et seq.

[2285] Report of the group of experts for Cambodia established pursuant to GA resolution 52/135, 18.2.1999, para. 102.

[2286] Report of the group of experts for Cambodia, *supra* note 2285, para. 103.

[2287] Report of the group of experts for Cambodia, *supra* note 2285, para. 103.

[2288] Report of the group of experts for Cambodia, *supra* note 2285, para. 110.

Group opposes the creation of a tribunal that would explicitly be limited in advance to the prosecution of named individuals."[2289]

On the other hand, it has been argued that the phrasing of articles 1 and 2 of the ECCC Law limits the ECCC to 5–12 cases in practice and excludes any lower-level cases.[2290] Negotiators never limited the pool of suspects to be charged and brought to trial to a fixed number of individuals, although some Cambodian officials desired an even smaller number.[2291] Moreover, the drafters did not attempt to find a literal definition of "senior leaders and those most responsible," but a choice had to be made between the terms "those responsible," the high threshold "those most responsible," and the even higher threshold "those bearing the greatest responsibility."[2292] In the end, the middle way was chosen, which embraces "senior leaders" – to my understanding a very limited phrasing – and the "most responsible" – a broader wording. The decisive question of who will be prosecuted thus amounts to the sub-elements "senior leaders" and "most responsible."[2293] The case of *Kaing Guek Eav* apparently strengthens this argument as the accused was "not a senior leader of Democratic Kampuchea, he may be considered in the category of most responsible for crimes and serious violations [...]."[2294] In late 2008, the ECCC's Co-Prosecutors disagreed concerning the appropriateness of opening new judicial investigations against certain additional perpetrators.[2295] The International Prosecutor proposed filing two new Introductory Submissions, believing that (1) the crimes described in those submissions were comitted, (2) these crimes are within the jurisdiction of the Court, and (3) they should be investigated by the Co-Investigating Judges.[2296] On the other hand, the National Prosecutor

---

2289 Report of the group of experts for Cambodia, *supra* note 2285, para. 111.

2290 Jürgen Assmann, Speech: The Cambodian Situation, International Conference "The Genocide Convention," Commemorating its 60th anniversary, Marburg, ICWC, 4.–6.12.2008.

2291 David Scheffer, "How many are too many defendants at the KRT?," Opinion, 8.1.2009, 1, 2.

2292 Scheffer, *supra* note 2291, 2–3.

2293 Jürgen Assmann, Speech: The Cambodian Situation, International Conference "The Genocide Convention," Commemorating its 60th anniversary, Marburg, ICWC, 4.–6.12.2008; also Ahmed/Day, in Bergsmo, *supra* note 2284, 80 et seq., 84.

2294 Closing Order indicting Kaing Guek Eav alias Duch, 8.8.2008 (002/14-08-2006), para. 129; also Sá Couto/Cleary, *supra* note 1614, 813, 846.

2295 Statement of the Co-Prosecutors, 5.1.2009, *supra* note 1949; ECCC, The Court Report, January 2009, 3; also Statement regarding prosecutorial disagreement, Annex I: Public Reducted Version, Considerations of the Pre-Trial Chamber regarding the disagreement between Co-prosecutors pursuant to internal rule 71, PTC ECCC, 18.8.2009 (001/18-11-2008-ECCC/PTC) paras. 1–2, 18.

2296 Statement of the Co-Prosecutors, 5.1.2009, *supra* note 1949.

argued that these investigations should not proceed due to (1) a lack of jurisdiction ("not senior leaders or those most responsible"), (2) considerations of peace, stability and national reconciliation, and (3) the limited duration and budget of the ECCC.[2297a] As the PTC did not reach a super-majority of votes on a decision concerning this dispute, it proceeded in accordance with rule 74 ECCC RPE, meaning that the International Co-Prosecutor was able to forward his new Introductory Submissions to the Co-Investigating Judges to open judicial investigations.[2297b]

In a nutshell, the legal instruments of the SCSL and ECCC have been phrased in a way that suggests a limited personal jurisdiction. It has, nevertheless, been argued that such jurisdictional restrictions should not be too stringent. The Prosecutors should rather focus on senior leaders as a policy matter. In any event, the wording varies insofar as it refers to the "ones bearing the greatest responsibility" (SCSL) or the "senior leaders" *and* the "most responsible" (ECCC). Only case law can further clarify how the SCSL and ECCC interpret these terms and if they adhere to them as jurisdictional barriers or policy choices. In this regard, the SCSL has not followed a stringent line of argument in its early jurisprudence. On the one hand, the Trial Chamber followed a jurisdictional approach in the CDF trial, while the Appeals Chamber preferred to locate "those bearing the greatest responsibility" within prosecutorial discretion in the AFRC trial. The ECCC has not yet addressed the core of the disputed issue; however, the future decision of the Co-Investigating Judges thereon will be interesting to watch.

dd) PTC I arrest warrants decision (Lubanga and Ntaganda)

At the ICC, the PTC in the *Lubanga* and *Ntaganda* cases approached the category of "those most senior officials responsible for the most serious crimes" and identified three elements:

(1) the position of the person (most senior leaders);

(2) the roles such persons play, trough acts or omissions, when the State entities, organizations or armed groups to which they belong commit systematic or large-scale crimes within the jurisdiction of the Court; and

(3) the role played by such State entities, organizations or armed groups in the overall commission of crimes within the jurisdiction of the Court in the relevant situation (those suspected of being most responsible).[2298]

[2297a] Statement of the Co-Prosecutors, 5.1.2009 supra *note* 1949; in more detail Annex I, PTC ECCC, *supra* note 2295, paras. 32 et seq.

[2297b] Annex I, PTC ECCCC, *supra* note 2295, paras. 44–5.

PTC I justifies its emphasis on senior leaders by deterrent effects of the Court, and it further refers to the current practice of the ICTY and ICTR. The Chamber relies upon SC-Res. 1534 (2004), as well as rules 28 (A) and 11*bis* ICTY RPE.[2299] Unlike other tribunals, the ICC's mandate is not explicitly limited; the ICC Statute's Preamble simply refers to the "perpetrators" of "the most serious crimes of concern to the international community as a whole,"[2300] PTC I used an overly narrow interpretation, especially when limiting the admissibility *only* to senior leaders at *all times*.[2301] A requirement to bring cases only against the "most senior leaders suspected of being the most responsible" may be desirable as a matter of policy, but it is not as an issue of admissibility.[2302]

Be that as it may, PTC I applied this restrictive interpretation to the *Ntaganda* case, and it did not consider the accused to be among "the most senior leaders within the DRC situation."[2303] Unlike Lubanga, Ntaganda did not have *de jure* or *de facto* authority and only occupied the third level of the command structure of the military wing of the broader UPC/FPLC movement.[2304] As a result, the Chamber arrived at the conclusion that the case against him did not meet the gravity threshold provided for in article 17 (1) (d) and found the case to be inadmissible.[2305] This finding was revoked by the Appeals Chamber who, *inter alia,* held the limited category of "senior leaders most responsible" as being too rigid.[2306] The Trial Cham-

2298 *Prosecutor v. Lubanga,* Decision on the Prosecutor's application for warrant of arrest, article 58, *supra* note 217, paras. 51 et seq., 63; *Prosecutor v. Ntaganda,* Annex II, Decision on the Prosecutor's application for warrants of arrest, *supra* note 228, paras. 52 et seq.; El Zeidy, *supra* note 269, 46. See already Part IV, B., III., 2., c), bb), (2) and cc) (1).

2299 *Prosecutor v. Lubanga,* Decision on the Prosecutor's application for warrant of arrest, article 58, *supra* note 217, paras. 54 et seq.; *Prosecutor v. Ntaganda,* Annex II, Decision on the Prosecutor's application for warrants of arrest, *supra* note 228, paras. 56 et seq.; Smith, *supra* note 210, 339.

2300 Ms. Géraldine Mattioli, HRW, *supra* note 473.

2301 El Zeidy, *supra* note 269, 49; WCRO report gravity, *supra* note 1057, 44–5.

2302 WCRO report gravity, *supra* note 1057, 44; Stahn, *supra* note 726, 707, however, suggests taking into account the assessment of "most responsible" as an admissibility matter.

2303 *Prosecutor v. Ntaganda,* Annex II, Decision on the Prosecutor's application for warrants of arrest, *supra* note 228, para. 85.

2304 *Prosecutor v. Ntaganda,* Annex II, Decision on the Prosecutor's application for warrants of arrest, *supra* note 228, paras. 86 et seq.

2305 *Prosecutor v. Ntaganda,* Annex II, Decision on the Prosecutor's application for warrants of arrest, *supra* note 228, para. 89.

2306 *Situation in DRC,* Judgment on the Prosecutor's appeal against the decision of Pre-Trial Chamber I, *supra* note 1360, paras. 73 et seq.; Cryer, *supra* note 2022, 52. See already Part IV, B., III., 2., c), bb), (3).

ber's holding could easily lead to the automatic exclusion of perpetrators of many serious crimes.[2307] In addition, the Preamble mentions "most serious crimes," but not "most serious perpetrators;" if the drafters intended to limit the Statute's application to only the most senior leaders they could have done so expressly.[2308]

The reliance on procedural law and practice of the ICTY and ICTR respectively was, moreover, flawed in the present case.[2309] Those tribunals adopted the "senior leaders" criterion in the context of their completion strategies; the ICC, by contrast, is only just beginning its activities. In addition, the *ad hoc* tribunals did, prior to the adoption of rules 28 (A) and 11*bis* ICTY RPE, conduct proceedings against individuals of various ranks over a number of years without being restricted to the most senior leaders.[2310]

In his separate and partly dissenting opinion, Judge Pikis further points out that the PTC's approach confines the Court's jurisdiction to try only a small class or group of persons that might under certain circumstances dwindle down to one.[2311] But the jurisdiction under article 5 is not dependant on any gravity requirement or threshold.[2312]

In sum, the leadership requirement improperly limits the Court's personal jurisdiction, as applied by PTC I.[2313] For all these reasons, the leadership element can neither be admitted as a jurisdictional nor as an admissibility criterion.[2314] Rather, what will be discussed below, a constraint to "those bearing the greatest responsibility" is part of prosecutorial discretion, and as such is only applicable as an "interests of justice" matter.

[2307] *Situation in DRC,* Judgment on the Prosecutor's appeal against the decision of Pre-Trial Chamber I, *supra* note 1360, para. 77.

[2308] *Situation in DRC,* Judgment on the Prosecutor's appeal against the decision of Pre-Trial Chamber I, *supra* note 1360, para. 79.

[2309] *Situation in DRC,* Judgment on the Prosecutor's appeal against the decision of Pre-Trial Chamber I, *supra* note 1360, para. 80.

[2310] *Situation in DRC,* Judgment on the Prosecutor's appeal against the decision of Pre-Trial Chamber I, *supra* note 1360, para. 80.

[2311] *Situation in DRC,* Judgment on the Prosecutor's appeal against the decision of Pre-Trial Chamber I, *supra* note 1360, Separate and partly dissenting opinion of Judge Georghios M. Pikis, para. 18.

[2312] *Situation in DRC,* Judgment on the Prosecutor's appeal against the decision of Pre-Trial Chamber I, *supra* note 1360, Separate and partly dissenting opinion of Judge Georghios M. Pikis, para. 33.

[2313] McAuliffe deGuzman, *supra* note 1152, 36; *Situation in DRC,* Judgment on the Prosecutor's appeal against the decision of Pre-Trial Chamber I, *supra* note 1360, Separate and partly dissenting opinion of Judge Georghios M. Pikis, para. 35.

[2314] Similarly, Seils, in Bergsmo, *supra* note 99, 56 ("not a legal requirement").

ee) OTP policy

In its early policy statements the OTP stated that it would focus activities on those individuals who bear the greatest responsibility for the most serious crimes.[2315] The Prosecutor has further acknowledged that the focus of an investigation may go wider than high-ranking officers.[2316] The investigation and prosecution of low and mid-level perpetrators may sometimes be necessary to generate evidence and build a case against the perpetrators on the highest level.[2317] Unlike the PTC, it does not associate the greatest responsibility requirement strictly with the gravity threshold (as part of the admissibility assessment), but rather as one of the general case selection criteria.[2318] It is unfortunate that the OTP is very reluctant to link senior leadership to the legal criteria of article 53.[2319] This reluctance might very well arise from concerns that defendants can bring admissibility challenges demanding evidence that they are not only guilty but most guilty.[2320] The Office specifies three categories of perpetrators that this policy threshold may comprise:

(1) civilian or military authorities if the systems under their responsibility have been instrumental to the crime and their effective subordinates are involved in the crimes;

(2) those playing a major causal role in the crimes that does not necessarily require a hierarchical status over the direct perpetrators; and

(3) notorious perpetrators who distinguish themselves by their direct responsibility for particularly serious crimes.[2321]

2315 Agirre Aranburu, in Bergsmo, *supra* note 460, 159; Prosecutorial Strategy 2009–2012, *supra* note 99, para. 19, 5–6; Takemura, *supra* note 1385, 6; Mallinder, *supra* note 1887, 223; El Zeidy, *supra* note 269, 42; Unger/Wierda, in Ambos/Large/Wierda, *supra* note 678, 296. See further the references in *supra* note 1222.

2316 WCRO report gravity, *supra* note 1057, 44.

2317 *Situation in DRC,* Judgment on the Prosecutor's appeal against the decision of Pre-Trial Chamber I, *supra* note 1360, para. 66.

2318 Schabas, supra note 1151, 745; Burke-White, *supra* note 1385, 82 with fn. 58 ("policy choice, more than a legal requirement, [...]").

2319 However, the Interests of justice paper, *supra* note 99, 7, seems to point into the right direction as it mentions "those bearing the greatest responsibility" under the "particular circumstances of the accused" of article 53 (2) (c), and, moreover, states: "The OTP has clearly stated its *policy* of focusing its investigations on those bearing the greatest degree of responsibility. Factors to be taken into account include the alleged status or hierarchical level of the accused or implication in particularly serious or notorious crimes. That is, the significance of the role of the accused in the overall commission of crimes and the degree of the accused's involvement (actual commission, ordering, indirect participation). It is possible, however, that even an individual deemed by the OTP to be among the "most responsible" *would not be prosecuted in the "interests of justice"* [...] (emph. added)."

2320 Schabas, supra note 1151, 745.

By including the second and third categories, the OTP adopts a broad interpretation of "those bearing the greatest responsibility." The Office does not confine the term to the persons on the top only, but incorporated others down the formal chain of command.[2322] The OTP implemented the approach taken by the *ad hoc* tribunals towards notorious offenders, and it considered the fears of jurisdictional confinement that were expressed regarding the ICTY, ICTR, SCSL, and ECCC. It further emphasized that the term "senior leaders" should not be applied excessively narrow, exempting top commanders from prosecution.[2323]

ff) Conclusion

Neither a policy nor an admissibility requirement that focuses on a particular category of persons ("most responsible; those bearing the greatest responsibility; most senior leaders") is explicitly reflected in the ICC Statute. The negotiators indeed rejected the notion to limit the competence to a handful at the top from the outset.[2324] The term "those bearing the greatest responsibility" was only introduced by the OTP and mentioned by the Chief Prosecutor on several occasions.[2325] PTC I even seemed to limit the personal jurisdiction of the Court to the "most senior leaders."[2326] Other tribunals have formulated this idea as "persons who bear the greatest responsibility" (SCSL) or "those who were most responsible" (ECCC). Therefore, a terminological distinction of the three mentioned categories of persons is necessary and will be analyzed one by one *vis-à-vis* the ICC Statute.

Starting with the "most senior leaders," the term preferred by PTC I, it is submitted that a limitation in such a manner is not in line with the ICC Statute and is overly restrictive. Article 1 refers to the "jurisdiction over *persons* for the *most serious crimes* of international concern (emph. added)." However, the persons are not further classified and the only statutory limitation is specifying a focus on the most serious crimes. The term "senior leaders" is used by the ECCC, but, in the alternative, the ECCC's Statute allows for a prosecution of the "most responsible." For this reason, the ECCC can prosecute someone like "Comrade Duch," in contrast to PTC I's strict interpreta-

---

2321 HRW Courting history report, *supra* note 126, 59.

2322 HRW Courting history report, *supra* note 126, 59.

2323 *Situation in DRC,* Judgment on the Prosecutor's appeal against the decision of Pre-Trial Chamber I, *supra* note 1360, para. 67.

2324 Arsanjani/Reismann, *supra* note 533, 399.

2325 "Building a Future on Peace and Justice," Address by Mr. Luis Moreno-Ocampo, *supra* note 258, 8. See numerous other references in *supra* note 1222.

2326 WCRO report gravity, *supra* note 1057, 45.

tion of gravity.[2327] Moreover, neither the *ad hoc* tribunals nor the SCSL and ECCC applied a jurisdictional confinement to "senior leaders" only.

In addition, there are crimes in which mid-level commanders can play a disproportionate role, in particular in the case of crimes of sexual violence.[2328] HRW suggests a more flexible criterion of "persons most responsible," also comprising others down the chain of command.[2329] Moreover, a distinction must be drawn between focusing efforts on senior leaders as a policy matter and a permanent statute-driven imposition of such a limitation.[2330] An application of strict inadmissibility with respect to lower cases would create an even greater impunity gap.[2331] And, moreover, the OTP could not close this gap even if it wanted to, since a legal gravity threshold of senior leaders would bar the Office to consider any low-level cases. An unwilling State could assume that all low-level perpetrators are beyond the reach of the ICC and these kinds of persons would thus benefit from impunity.[2332] One should further treat the restriction to senior leaders with caution due to complications of effectively prosecuting gender crimes. If, for instance, the ICTY and ICTR had not adopted a "pyramidal strategy," they would not have been able to gain any convictions for gender crimes (such as the now-infamous names of "nobodies" Akayesu, Furundžija, Kunarac, Kovač, and Vuković).[2333] For all these reasons, a general focus as a policy matter on the "most senior leaders" may be welcomed, but the ICC Statute must safeguard its flexibility so as to preserve the possibility of prosecuting lower-level perpetrators where appropriate. Thereby, one has to bear in mind the potential criticism if the OTP focuses on too many low-level perpetrators and minor charges.[2334]

This last statement brings about the differentiation "those bearing the greatest responsibility" and the "most responsible." Both terms have been contrasted with each other, the former being more restrictive as potentially focusing on senior leaders only. However, it is doubtful to what extent the two terms can be differentiated as in practice they might overlap. A strict demarcation line between the two ideas cannot be established, and therefore the terms should not be juxtaposed strictly. Yet, this survey has shown that

---

[2327] WCRO report gravity, *supra* note 1057, 46.

[2328] Bruce Broomhall – Open Society Justice Initiative, Session 2: Transcript, 17.6.2003, 1.

[2329] HRW selection policy paper, *supra* note 1215, 12.

[2330] Smith, *supra* note 210, 340.

[2331] Smith, *supra* note 210, 340–1.

[2332] Kleffner, in Kleffner/Kor, *supra* note 1415, 94–5.

[2333] Smith, *supra* note 210, 343–4; also Takemura, *supra* note 2244, 678.

[2334] In this regard, and on the practice of the Special Panels for Serious Crimes of East Timor, see Takemura, *supra* note 2244, 683.

their scope is different to some extent: "most responsible" is a wider phrasing than "those bearing the greatest responsibility." The ICC and other international tribunals thus have to make policy choices and must decide which term they prefer. Arguably, a selection criterion of "those bearing the greatest responsibility" could then be more limited and narrower than a factor referring to those "most responsible." The ICC Statute does not use either term. However, it can be argued that articles 1, 5 ("most serious crimes"), and 53 (2) (c) ("role in the alleged crime"), favor a confinement of some sort.

Indeed, the OTP has consistently referred to limiting its efforts to "those bearing the greatest responsibility." Contrary to PTC I, it has thereby preferred a broad interpretation, which embraces others down the chain of command, especially notorious perpetrators. If such an interpretation is adopted, the differentiation "most responsible" and "those bearing the greatest responsibility" collapses, which has to be welcomed. In my opinion, an obligatory jurisdictional limitation is too rigid. On the other hand, a focused approach as a policy matter – as taken by the OTP – appears necessary. If the Prosecutor targets senior leaders in general, but safeguards the possibility to prosecute others down the chain of command under exceptional circumstances, he strikes a viable balance.

Nevertheless, the OTP should pay attention to the concepts of gravity and "those bearing the greatest responsibility." It must carefully distinguish the two, especially with regard to legal gravity as an admissibility criterion under articles 53 (1), (2) (b), and 17 (1) (d). As a policy matter, the concept of "greatest responsibility" has to be applied under article 53 (2) (c).[2335] It gives guidance in the phase of selecting cases out of situations, thereby targeting specific perpetrators. Such a selective strategy requires value judgments and equal treatment. For this reason, there is an urgent need that the Prosecutor publishes more precise guidelines concerning "those bearing the greatest responsibility" and its sub-elements. Moreover, the term must be included in the RPE or even in the ICC Statute as part of article 53 (2) (c), and future ICC case law will have to give the term some more substance.

Cases that do not reach the threshold of gravity have to be left to the national authorities.[2336] This division of labor needs an adequate framework. The complementarity provisions only deal with the *substantive* obligation to withdraw from action if States are able and willing to act. How-

---

2335 Benzing, *supra* note 1349, 620, who posed the question where an additional restriction of the degree of participation (substantial role in the commission of the crime) could be located – article 17 (1) (d) or rather article 53 (1) (c) and (2) (c).

2336 Burke-White, *supra* note 1385, 82; Wei, *supra* note 156, 174.

ever, the exact procedure to refer situations and cases back to national actors is not specified in the ICC Statute. It is submitted that a rule similar to rule 11*bis* ICTY RPE (a new rule 106*bis*) should be drafted that addresses the referral *procedure* of situations and cases back to national authorities, complementing the complementarity regime.[2337]

Recapitulating, for the present factor of "those who bear the greatest responsibility," the following pyramidal prosecution strategy is suggested for ICC-OTP purposes:

Source: Author.

Figure 8: Pyramid: Prosecutorial Strategy

D. Duty to notify of a decision not to investigate

If the Prosecutor decides not to investigate or prosecute, he is under an obligation to notify certain parties. The ICC Statute itself stipulates a duty to notify the PTC if "the Prosecutor determines that there is no reasonable basis to proceed and his or her determination is based solely on subpara-

[2337] Further on this idea Part IV, F.

graph (c) above (article 53 (1) *in fine*)."[2338] With regard to a decision not to prosecute based solely upon the "interests of justice" clause, "the Prosecutor shall inform the Pre-Trial Chamber and the State making a referral under article 14 or the Security Council in a case under article 13, paragraph (b) [...] (article 53 (2) (c) *in fine*)." This amounts to inconsistent drafting, as there seems to be no justification for excluding the State and SC under article 53 (1).[2339] The RPE fortunately fill in the gaps.[2340] Rule 105 (1) obligates the Prosecutor to promptly inform the SC or State that referred the situation if he decides not to start an investigation.[2341] In fact, the duty under rule 105 (1) exists with regard to any of the grounds named in article 53 (1), and not only for "interests of justice" considerations. Rule 105 (2) then makes reference to rule 49, thus re-emphasizing the Prosecutor's duty to inform information providers under article 15 (6) in the case of *proprio motu* proceedings. Rule 105 (4) further recalls the duty to promptly notify the PTC if the Prosecutor decides not to proceed solely on the basis of the "interests of justice." With regard to an insufficient basis for a prosecution, rule 106 (1) states that the same three actors – PTC, State, and SC – need to be notified if a prosecution is denied.[2342] All notifications shall contain the conclusion of the Prosecutor and the reasons for the conclusion (rules 105 (6), 106 (2)).

In sum, it is, from a procedural perspective, interesting that the PTC has a *proprio motu* right to review a negative decision if based solely on the "interests of justice." An inherent danger is, however, that the Prosecutor might try to escape from this review power by referring merely to article 53 (1) (a) and (b) rather than article 53 (1) (c). In other words, the OTP will base its decisions rather on jurisdictional or admissibility aspects than on an "interests of justice" finding. In fact, the OTP's early gravity approach heads into this direction. As part of the gravity assessment, a getaway from prosecutorial discretion under article 53 (1) (c) to "legal" findings under articles 53 (1) (b) and 17 (1) (d) has been identified. Authors have, in consequence, advertised the idea that the notification duty under article 53 (1) *in fine* equally applies to a decision based on article 17 (1) (d). The latter decision

2338 Also Stigen, *supra* note 205, 109 et seq.

2339 Razesberger, *supra* note 371, 106.

2340 Razesberger, *supra* note 371, 106.

2341 *Situation in CAR,* Prosecution's report pursuant to Pre-Trial Chamber III's 30 November 2006 decision requesting information on the status of the preliminary examination, *supra* note 172, para. 10.

2342 *Prosecutor v. Kony et al.,* Decision to convene a status conference on the investigation in the situation in Uganda, *supra* note 248, para. 12; *Prosecutor v. Kony et al.,* Decision on the Prosecutor's application for unsealing of the warrants of arrest, 13.10.2005 (ICC-02/04-01/05-52) para. 32.

substantially overlaps with a decision under article 53 (1) (c) where gravity is considered as an essential part of the "interests of justice."[2343]

A different way is desirable: the Prosecutor must carefully distinguish relative gravity under article 53 (1) (c) and legal gravity under articles 53 (1) (b) and 17 (1) (d). Moreover, the OTP must clearly label its decision either way and shall not blur the line. If this proves not being feasible, it is strongly submitted that the PTC gains a right to screen gravity dismissals.

E. Article 53 paragraph 3

Pursuant to article 53 (3), a decision by the Prosecutor not to proceed under article 53 (1) or (2) may be reviewed by the PTC. The State making the referral or the SC may request such a judicial check according to article 53 (3) (a), but the Chamber may, in such a case, only "request the Prosecutor to reconsider that decision." In the event that the decision not to proceed is based upon the "interests of justice," the PTC can review *proprio motu*. A persistent objection by the PTC can even obligate the Prosecutor to investigate (article 53 (3) (b)). From a purely common-law perspective, this might represent significant interference with prosecutorial independence,[2344] but the procedural system of the ICC cannot be categorized common law or civil law. It is a truly mixed system and the drafters developed a complex compromise.[2345]

On its own motion, the PTC can review the decision not to investigate or prosecute if based solely on the "interests of justice" pursuant to articles 53 (1) (c), (2) (c) and (3) (b). In this case, if the Prosecutor reaches a negative decision on the reasonable basis to proceed or sees no sufficient basis for a prosecution, the PTC has to confirm the decision of the OTP in order to render it effective.[2346] In contrast, a review based on article 53 (3) (a), thus on grounds other than the "interests of justice" clause and upon request by the referring State or the SC, is not binding. In accordance with article 53

[2343] Wouters/Verhoeven/Demeyere, *supra* note 156, 301.

[2344] In this vein, Brubacher, *supra* note 368, 87.

[2345] Part IV, B., I.

[2346] *Prosecutor v. Kony et al.,* Decision to convene a status conference on the investigation in the situation in Uganda, *supra* note 248, para. 13; *Situation in DRC,* Decision on the requests of the Legal Representative for victims VPRS1 to VPRS 6 regarding "Prosecutor's information on further investigation," 26.9.2007 (ICC-01/04-399) 5; El Zeidy, *supra* note 269, 51; Seils/Wierda, *supra* note 1461, 5. Overstretching article 53 (3), Heller, in Stahn/van Herik, *supra* note 339, 249 et seq., suggests that the PTC can review any decision based on gravity considerations and may order the OTP to investigate a situation.

(3) (a), the PTC may only request the Prosecutor to reconsider the decision. The fundamental difference is therefore the power of the PTC if the OTP bases its decision solely on "interests of justice." The PTC then has first a review power on its own initiative and second the authority to decide on the validity of the Prosecutor's decision. Hence, if the Chamber does not confirm the OTP's findings, the Prosecutor is nevertheless obligated to proceed with an investigation or prosecution.[2347]

It has not been settled whether the PTC must indeed review every decision of the Prosecutor not to proceed based on the "interests of justice." It has been argued that any decision under article 53 (1) (c) is not effective *per se* and needs to be validated through a PTC check, which in turn leads to necessarily reviewing all decisions since otherwise the Court would risk being paralyzed.[2348] However, there is no need to confirm every decision.[2349] The wording is clear in this respect as it provides that the Chamber *may* review on its own initiative. Moreover, the argument of a potential paralysis can be rebutted: only decisions, which are in fact reviewed, require confirmation, i.e. only the ones that the Chamber actually chooses need a positive recognition. The wording of article 53 (3) (b) states that confirmation of the PTC is obligatory "in such a case," meaning the PTC actually decides to pick an "interests of justice" determination for review.

Returning to the review upon request pursuant to article 53 (3) (a), the procedure is further spelled out by rules 107 and 108. Pursuant to rule 107 (1), the SC and the referring State can address the PTC in writing within 90 days and request a review under article 53 (3) (a). According to rule 107 (2) the Chamber can ask the Prosecutor to transmit information or documents that the PTC considers necessary. The Chamber is obliged to protect the information and documents received for the safety of witnesses and victims and members of their families pursuant to rule 107 (3). Further observations may be requested from the State or SC if they made a request for review according to rule 107 (4). The requesting party, as well as victims and their representatives, must be notified and heard in accordance with rules 107 (5) and 59 when jurisdictional and admissibility matters are addressed.

It is not directly stated what the Chamber should take into consideration for a review under article 53 (3) (a). Rule 108 (1) refers to a majority of judges who shall make the decision and stipulates that "it shall contain rea-

[2347] Rule 110 (2); Wouters/Verhoeven/Demeyere, *supra* note 156, 302.

[2348] Bergsmo/Kruger, in Triffterer, *supra* note 906, article 53, mn 38.

[2349] In favor of such an interpretation see Turone, in Cassese/Gaeta/Jones, *supra* note 26, 1157–8; Wouters/Verhoeven/Demeyere, *supra* note 156, 302–3; Gropengießer/Meißner, *supra* note 679, 297–8.

sons." The Prosecutor is obliged to reconsider his decision as soon as possible (rule 108 (2)), and the final decisions shall be communicated to the PTC and those who participated in the review (rule 108 (3)). It can be reasoned that the Chamber takes into consideration the same criteria of article 53 (1) and (2) when conducting its review.[2350] Systematically, article 53 (3) (b) refers exclusively to the "interests of justice," which, in turn, seems to imply all criteria of article 53 (1) and (2) for the review pursuant to article 53 (3) (a). In addition, rule 107 (5) explicitly mentions jurisdictional and admissibility issues that might be raised. On the other hand, the Chamber can only give guidance on these criteria; the ultimate decision rests upon the Prosecutor. The Prosecutor must reconsider his decision, but he is not obliged to adhere to the PTC's suggestions. Thus, the review under article 53 (3) (a) is not binding upon the Prosecutor.

As already outlined above, only the review of "interests of justice" decisions might be repealed. For this review power, the process is further delineated in rules 109 and 110. Within 180 days following a notification under rule 105 or 106, the Chamber may decide to review a negative decision of the Prosecutor pursuant to rule 109 (1). The Prosecutor has to be informed thereof, and the Chamber shall set a time limit within which the Prosecutor may submit observations and other material in accordance with rule 109 (1) and Court Regulation 48. Court Regulation 48 (2) closes a gap by introducing the same safety demands of rule 107 (3) into the review procedure of article 53 (3) (b). Pursuant to rule 93, the Chamber can seek views of victims and their legal representatives. If the review was submitted by a State or the SC, they shall be informed and may submit observations pursuant to rule 109 (2). Like rule 108 (1), rule 110 (1) indicates that the majority of judges have to concur with the decision and that the decision shall be accompanied by reasons. In contrast, rule 110 (2) lays down the main distinction between the two review mechanisms as it states:

> "When the Pre-Trial Chamber does not confirm the decision by the Prosecutor referred to in sub-rule 1, he or she shall proceed with the investigation or prosecution."

The Prosecutor can thus be forced to continue an investigation or prosecution if the Chamber does not agree with the OTP's findings on the "interests of justice." The PTC should thereby not set aside the actual weighing of the factors, unless general principles of discretion have been violated.[2351] However, if this is the case, the Chamber might issue a particular form of judicial order forcing the OTP to investigate or prosecute.[2352] On the other

---

2350 Bergsmo/Kruger, in Triffterer, *supra* note 906, article 53, mn 34.

2351 Stigen, *supra* note 205, 404.

2352 Turone, in Cassese/Gaeta/Jones, *supra* note 26, 1176.

hand, since it was submitted above that the Chamber must only approve the decisions which it actually chooses as being worth reviewing, silence on the matter equals a confirmation of the OTP's decision not to proceed.[2353]

Last but not least, it has to be emphasized that the judicial check only covers a negative decision ("*not* to proceed").[2354] A positive decision to proceed with investigations pursuant to article 53 (1) cannot be reviewed by the PTC; in fact, this question is reviewed at later stages (confirmation hearing or arrest warrant stage). For *proprio motu* investigations, the initial position is reversed. The Chamber has to authorize positive decisions pursuant to article 15 (4),[2355] and negative decision on *proprio motu* situations can presently not be screened.[2356] Once again, one must therefore distinguish the particular trigger mechanism, but one must pay attention to the situation stage and the later case stage. With regard to the investigation of situations, the PTC may review negative decisions on SC and State referrals, either on its own initiative if they are based on the "interests of justice" (article 53 (3) (b)), or upon the request of the SC or the referring State (article 53 (3) (a)). The Chamber can never check positive decisions. Regarding *proprio motu* situations, the PTC has to confirm any positive decision to investigate, but it cannot check negative decisions. Even if the OTP declines to investigate *proprio motu* situations based on the "interests of justice," no review similar to article 53 (3) (b) is available.[2357] Moreover, this complicated differentiation applies only for selecting situations. With respect to the scope of the review power, PTC I designated it an open question whether this power is only applicable "in relation to the Prosecution's decision to put an end to the investigation of a given situation, or whether it is also applicable in relation to each Prosecution's decision not to prosecute a specific individual."[2358] However, article 53 (2) (c) deals with cases (or at least a case hypothesis that concerns individuals), and a reference to paragraph 2 (c) explicitly appears in article 53 (3) (b). At the

---

2353 Turone, in Cassese/Gaeta/Jones, *supra* note 26, 1177.

2354 *Situation in Darfur (Sudan),* Decision on application under rule 103, *supra* note 1833, para. 21; *Situation in CAR,* Prosecution's report pursuant to Pre-Trial Chamber III's 30 November 2006 decision requesting information on the status of the preliminary examination, *supra* note 172, para. 1; contrary *Situation in Darfur (Sudan),* Application on behalf of Citizens' Organisations of The Sudan, *supra* note 303, paras. 52–3.

2355 See Part III, B., VI., 6.; also Gropengießer/Meißner, *supra* note 679, 298–9.

2356 Part III, D.

2357 Part III, C., II. Contrary, *Situation in Kenya*, Decision pursuant to article 15, *supra* note 6, para. 24 with fn.35, 12–3; para. 63, 27–8. PTC II does not differentiate the three trigger mechanisms with regard to article 53 (3) (b).

2358 *Situation in Darfur (Sudan),* Decision on application under rule 103, *supra* note 1833, para. 21.

stage of article 53 (2), all cases arising from *proprio motu,* SC, or State triggering are subject to the same criteria. In this regard, the review mechanism equals exactly the outlined review procedure under article 53 (3) (a) or (b). Therefore, it is submitted that the Chamber may review *any* decision not to prosecute individuals. However, the Chamber must wait for a negative decision on behalf of the Prosecutor; it cannot exercise judicial scrutiny when an article 53 (2) (c) decision is non-existent.[2359]

F. Concluding observations Part IV: Prosecutorial guidelines approach and referrals to national jurisdictions

The selection of situations and cases is governed by article 53's criteria. For the future, the most important questions are: How are situations, cases, and charges selected?[2360] Credibility rests upon these choices, and a permanent court cannot afford to be viewed as a one-sided institution. On the other hand, it has been stated that the OTP is faced with a number of dilemmas and will be forced to make difficult, unpopular, but unavoidable decisions.[2361] The survey has shown that jurisdiction and complementarity involve tough choices, but the more difficult issue to deal with are the undefined terms "gravity" and "interests of justice." The appropriate role of "gravity" at the ICC remains a matter of debate,[2362] as does the exact content of the "interests of justice." Surely, further research must dig deeper into international and national jurisprudence with regard to the two notions. Future case law of the ICC itself might also solve some of the questions posed. For the time being, I have defended a basic interpretation of article 53 that distinguishes clearly between a legal gravity threshold (article 53 (1) (b), 17 (1) (d)) and a discretionary "interests of justice" (including relative gravity) threshold (article 53 (1) (c)). The same essential differentiation applies to cases: legal gravity is entailed in articles 53 (2) (b) and 17 (1) (d), and the relative "interests of justice" clause can be found in article 53 (2) (c). In addition, a threefold approach clarifies these matters:

2359 *Situation in DRC,* Decision on the request submitted pursuant to rule 103 (1) of the Rules of Procedure and Evidence, 17.8.2007 (ICC-01/04-373) para. 5; *Situation in DRC,* Decision on the requests of the Legal Representative for victims, *supra* note 2346, 5; Guariglia, in Stahn/Sluiter, *supra* note 1215, 216; Stahn, in Stahn/Sluiter, *supra* note 156, 276–7.

2360 On the charging practice see Informal expert paper: Fact-finding and investigative functions of the Office of the Prosecutor, including international co-operation, ICC-OTP 2003, paras. 44 et seq.

2361 Guariglia, in Stahn/Sluiter, *supra* note 1215, 216.

2362 WCRO report gravity, *supra* note 1057, 10.

(1) the OTP must refine its prosecutorial policy, clearly differentiating legal and policy arguments;

(2) in consultation with the Judges and external experts, the Office must design prosecutorial guidelines (as an official, publicly available document);

(3) the ASP should discuss a new draft rule 104*bis* addressing some core questions, such as the basic elements of gravity and "interests of justice" (including a short but exhaustive list of precise, binding criteria).[2363] In particular, the term "those bearing the greatest responsibility" must find statutory recognition.

For ASP discussions, the following drafting of rule 104*bis* establishes a basis:

Rule 104bis

Gravity and interests of justice elements

(1) Gravity entails two different notions, legal gravity of articles 53 (1) (b), (2) (b), 17 (1) (d) and relative gravity of article 53 (1) (c), (2) (c).

(2) Legal gravity involves primarily quantitative factors.

(3) Relative gravity involves quantitative and qualitative factors equally. Case-related gravity also allows for considering the individual circumstances of the perpetrator.

(4) The interests of justice embrace the written factors of article 53 (1) (c) and (2) (c), as well as a non-exhaustive list of unwritten factors. The concept is of an open nature, allowing for broader, discretionary choices on behalf of the Prosecutor.

(5) As a general rule, the Prosecutor should focus efforts on those bearing the greatest responsibility.

After all, the selection criteria lead to a major policy decision for the Prosecutor and the Court as a whole. A formal set of elements would certainly ensure that selected situations and cases reflect the policy of the OTP and that – should its decision in selecting a specific case for prosecution be challenged – the Office can defend such a decision on the basis of rational criteria that have statutory support. Such a framework should encourage the OTP to use its *proprio motu* tool more often and thus strengthens its independence. From my point of view, no other trigger mechanism enables the Prosecutor to use similar discretion as situations and case may be defined *a priori* by the Office itself.[2364] Even if one takes into consideration the

---

2363 In the same vein, Olásolo, *supra* note 29, 190; see already above Part IV, B., II., 5. and 6.

2364 Most recently, Moreno-Ocampo, in Stahn/Sluiter, *supra* note 99, 13–4.

PTC's authorization requirement, the Prosecutor has the power of first action. Within a given set of rules, he has the power to define situations and cases in accordance with his policy from the very outset. Contrastingly, State referrals and SC referrals can have a negative impact on the OTP's public image, even if they are carefully redefined. The Ugandan self-referral has clearly demonstrated such possible negative implications.

Another core problem that has been identified is the possibility of referring cases back to national criminal jurisdictions. No provision expressly contains the possibility of referring cases to States. Nevertheless, the statutory framework allows for some procedural avenues: not picking up cases and thus "referring" them to States or "dropping" them due to (changed) admissibility considerations. Most of these mechanisms have been addressed above, mainly as part of the transitional justice considerations. There are potentially three gateways for non-interference with State action:

(1) the Prosecutor may decline to investigate or prosecute on the grounds of the interests of justice pursuant to article 53 (1) (c) and (2) (c);

(2) deferrals might exceptionally be possible under article 17 (1) (a) or (b);

(3) the SC may require the ICC to suspend action if it determines that investigations or prosecutions would interfere with efforts to maintain or restore international peace and security (article 16).[2365]

I have argued that the most suitable gateway for non-interference is through the "interests of justice" clause. This finding is based on a broad interpretation of "justice," opposed by more narrow retributive justice interpretations of "investigation" and "prosecution" under article 17. Article 17 opens a very small gateway for proceedings similar to criminal ones, such as certain TRCs that perform investigations in the strict sense and supplement criminal proceedings.

In my view, an article 16 deferral would not be the most desirable solution. Article 16 is meant to exceptionally allow for a SC intervention and only temporarily allows suspension of ICC activities.[2366] For transitional justice mechanisms it is the third "best" option, subsidiary to articles 53 and 17.

Foremost, a guideline based approach must construe a demarcation line for alternative justice mechanisms. Proceedings below the predefined line can then be rejected and retributive alternatives above the line must be scrutinized against the backdrop of the developed criteria. In any event, the Prosecutor lacks a deferral tool if he desires to work hand-in-hand with na-

---

[2365] Robinson, *supra* note 807, 486.

[2366] Stahn, *supra* note 726, 717; Gavron, *supra* note 773, 109.

tional authorities. If cases have been declared admissible and circumstances have changed, article 19 provides the most likely avenue: article 19 (1) allows the Court to revisit a previous admissibility finding and article 19 (3) allows the Prosecutor to seek a ruling on admissibility more than once.[2367] In addition, the OTP may reconsider a decision to investigate or prosecute based on new facts or information pursuant to article 53 (4).[2368]

However, all these procedural avenues are not designed for a referral to a national jurisdiction *stricto sensu*. If complementarity is to be taken seriously, it requires the Court to refer inadmissible cases back to national actors. There should be conditions on which case referrals are based. An express procedural mechanism, similar to ICTY rule 11*bis,* appears warranted.[2369] If (legal) admissibility determinations change, a case could simply be referred back to the State that originally self-referred to the ICC. In Uganda, for instance, if the Agreement and Annexure was implemented and was in accordance with the ICC Statute (in particular with the principle of complementarity), a referral backwards would be possible.[2370] But referrals to national criminal jurisdictions are also desirable as a matter of positive complementarity.

The ICC has so far not, at least intentionally, engaged in a policy of positive (sending back) complementarity.[2371] In practice, the ICC and States should work hand-in-hand. It is therefore submitted that the ICC should be given an *active tool* to send persons to *any* national courts, especially mid- or low level perpetrators that fall within the gap of legal and relative gravity. Minor cases, for example cases that are sorted out by the OTP due to a lack of relative gravity or other discretionary choices, could be referred to national actors under the new deferral rule. That way, the Prosecutor would be able to focus his resources and bring the "ones bearing the greatest responsibility" to justice before the ICC. Moreover, a monitoring obligation should be included in the new rule. Under a new rule 106*bis* (similar to ICTY rule 11*bis*) the following scenarios should then be referred to national criminal jurisdiction:

(1) cases that were held to be admissible, but where circumstances have considerably changed (cases that would now be inadmissible);

(2) situations that falls short of relative gravity (those in-between legal and relative gravity);

[2367] Part IV, B., III., 2.; also Kleffner, *supra* note 370, 192–3.

[2368] Kleffner, *supra* note 370, 193.

[2369] Cf. already Part IV, C., IV., 4., b), ff). In the same vein, Razesberger, *supra* note 371, 140; Kleffner, *supra* note 370, 193–4.

[2370] Kleffner, *supra* note 370, 191 et seq.

[2371] Burke-White, *supra* note 1218, 55.

(3) cases that fall within the same gravity gap (in-between legal and relative gravity);

(4) general information already gathered about situations and possible cases that fall within the gap of potentially prosecuting all (core) crimes and legal gravity;

(5) situations and cases that are not selected by the OTP based on other discretionary choices ("interests of justice").

A positive referral (or deferral) tool allows the ICC to interact with national authorities and enhances positive complementarity. Statutory demands are best implemented by such a flexible mechanism. The ICC would truly help making national systems stronger and, in the long run, close the impunity gap. The foregoing discussion urges me to draw three concluding assumptions:

(1) relative gravity saves the ICC from being overloaded, and a deferral tool to national jurisdictions of minor cases/situations appears urgently necessary;

(2) the potential of the ICC is not only to prosecute perpetrators, but to make national criminal justice systems stronger;

(3) in accordance with positive complementarity and a new positive deferral rule, the OTP might not simply lean back if the gravity threshold is not reached. Inactivity is not allowed by the ICC Statute, and the new rule procedurally closes the impunity gap.

Part V

Concluding remarks

The interplay between the PTC and the Prosecutor at the early stages of the proceedings constitutes the most striking example of the uniqueness of the ICC's procedural law.[2372] One norm dealing with this interplay is article 53. The article 53 procedure has not been tested in ICC practice to date. Accordingly, article 53, and most notably "gravity" and the "interests of justice," have been at the heart of the study at hand. An all-embracing answer was not obsessively intended due to the complexity of the two terms that require studies on their own. My aim was rather to outline the pre-investigation stage in its entirety, to comment on the most important facets that came up during the research, and to reach a common basis for further analysis.

A. Summary of Parts I and II

Part I gives a general introduction to the problem of pre-investigations. Pre-investigations essentially deal with the selection of situations for investigation. The basic structure of the research resulted from the two most striking questions with regard to this selection process: What is its course of action? According to which criteria are situations selected?

Accordingly, Part III deals with the first matter, while Part IV addresses the second issue. Coming back to Part I, it was deemed necessary to apply a congruent methodology before commencing the actual analysis. Article 21 was used as a starting point. Using the ICC's proper law soon came to its limits due to several *lacunas* or deliberate ambiguities in the Statute. This survey thus relied to a large extent on literal, systematic, and teleological interpretation (article 32 VCLT). Supplementary to this analysis, the *travaux préparatoires* were consulted. Thereby, OTP documents and statements provided the most important source. Academic opinions and early ICC jurisprudence supplied additional material. It was particularly case law that ascended increasingly during the realization of this study. It is an easy guess to assume that jurisprudence will solve – sooner or later – some of the questions posed.

[2372] Kress, *supra* note 11, 606.

Briefly summarizing Part II, an overview of the ICC's structure was deemed necessary. Particularly with regard to the OTP, certain terms had to be introduced before commencing the in-depth survey. The description of the OTP structure is inevitable for understanding how potential situations are analyzed. Three functional divisions – JCCD, ID, and PD – correspond to the three major areas of activity of the OTP: pre-investigations, investigations, and prosecutions. An organization chart of the OTP was included (Part II, B.). JCCD constitutes the pertinent operational division for pre-investigations and thus this study: it is the JCCD section that provides analysis and legal advice on issues pertaining to jurisdiction, complementarity, and cooperation. The unit is subdivided into the International Cooperation Section and the Situation Analysis Section. The latter provides objective and systematic analysis of situations of interest, conducts the initial review of incoming communications (in conjunction with IEU), and prepares reports and recommendations for ExCom. The requirements under articles 15 and 53 are hence dealt with by JCCD, which gives legal advice on these matters to ExCom. It is, in conclusion, this division that heavily influences policy decisions and the Prosecutor's selective choices originate from here.

B. Summary of Part III

First of all, I would like to recall the six basic stages that were identified with regard to the ICC's procedure: pre-investigation stage, investigation stage, intermediate stage, trial stage, appeal stage, and enforcement stage. Given the particular importance and novelty of pre-investigations at the ICC, this phase led to the framework of this study. Its course of action and the involved criteria provided for the main parts to be addressed. In Part III, the three trigger mechanisms (State referrals, SC referrals, and the *proprio motu* mechanism) were illustrated and it was further explained what kind of preliminary inquiries the ICC Statute foresees. With regard to the latter issue, statutory demands and OTP practice were analyzed. The OTP's model process for preliminary inquiries (three phases model) is within statutory demands. On the other hand, several difficult issues were identified and some policy decisions can be questioned.

For the initiation of an investigation, all three triggers are essential tools of the Prosecutor, and legally no hierarchy exists. Due to the Prosecutor's policy a practical hierarchy has evolved over the last several years. SC referrals are apparently on the top, given the backup by the SC. Then State referrals have risen to the second level on the basis of *Realpolitik*. In the DRC, Uganda, and the CAR, self-referrals were either preferred or lobbied for by the OTP; even in Kenya the Prosecutor strongly negotiated for a self-referral before making use of his *proprio motu* trigger mechanism. All this leaves *proprio motu* action on the lowest level of the Prosecutor's agenda. Fortunately, the Statute provides safeguards. The notion of "situations" only allows States (and the SC) to refer predefined situations, and not individualized cases. Since referrals are treated as *notitia criminis* and may be altered by the Prosecutor for achieving objectivity, self-referral's inherent dangers are minimized.

A referral does not automatically trigger the powers of the Prosecutor; the decision lies ultimately in the hands of the Prosecutor whether to initiate investigations or decline proceedings. It is the OTP that groups and selects situations and at a later stage chooses cases for prosecution. In sum, self-referrals have been regarded as legally possible, but with the addition that the OTP should use its *proprio motu* power instead on some occasions. The Prosecutor should not underestimate the political echoes of his decisions, though he should not take political voices into consideration when starting his action. He should carefully weigh his policy choices, such as the present policy of preferring self-referral over *proprio motu*. Particularly in the Ugandan situation one must be aware of the negative effects by Museveni's potential misuse of the Court.[2373] If the Court is called Museveni's tool, or a "new mechanism of neo-colonialism" in the Sudan situation,[2374] negative associations are spread throughout the countries. These voices cannot be prevented, but they can be fought and revealed as false. To win this battle on the media, the OTP must provide solid reasoning, always showing its independence and impartiality. It is my view that the *proprio motu* tool can have a great share in that.

In addition to the particular triggers, the third part explains the preliminary examination process as a whole. Most important, the criteria for selection are the same for all three triggering mechanisms according to articles 53 (1), 15 (3), and rule 48. Moreover, the preliminary examination has proven to be quite complex. From a purely terminological perspective, the terms "preliminary examinations" and "pre-investigations" may be used interchangeably. In any event, the former term is preferable for the three-phased process applied by the OTP, whereas the latter term more precisely covers the procedural stage in its entirety. Pre-investigations start with one of the triggers, followed by the analysis process as laid down in article 15 (2), rules 46, 47, and 104, and culminate in the decision whether there is a reasonable basis to initiate an investigation. The last step formally ends pre-investigation and transfers the process into investigations *stricto sensu*.

2373 "Uganda: West angered by Museveni's call for ICC to pardon Kony group," 17.3.2008, Paul Redfern, The East African.

2374 "Warrant issued for Sudan's leader," 4.3.2009, BBC News.

In any event, pre-investigations can be called an own procedural stage for several reasons, all of which are included in Chapter III, and the survey has resulted in two graphs which can be found in Annex 1 (A. & B.).

C. Summary of Part IV

The Prosecutor must exercise prosecutorial selection due to his limited capacity. I have argued that article 53 provides a complicated framework that has to be applied in a consistent manner. Thereby, the Prosecutor is vested with discretion. However, this discretion is neither unlimited nor unchecked. Article 53 (1) and (2) rest upon the principle of legality due to the general gravity of crimes included under the ICC Statute. The mandatory language is softened in the very same chapeau through an exception ("unless he or she determines that there is no reasonable basis to proceed"). Discretionary choices are therefore introduced through the "back door," which is less troublesome than it seems at first. If one limits the discretion to the "interests of justice" clause, the procedural checks through article 53 (3) apply.

Further, I have argued that the Judges should only control cases of clear abuses, and they cannot replace the Prosecutor's discretion *per se*. On the other hand, if the Prosecutor adopts an unlawful policy or does not adhere to its own settled policy, a claim of review could be made.[2375] It remains for the Judges to develop the exact scope and factors for issuing an order of review under article 53 (3). It is submitted that the review power must be handled with caution, but the Judges must engage more actively in the process of setting up criteria for reconsideration. The framework by the law presumably provides for a check and balance system of discretionary choices. In practice, the interrelationship between the Prosecutor *vis-à-vis* accountability has so far enjoyed limited prominence. In the study at hand, the necessity to request authorization in the case of *proprio motu* triggering, the duty to notify of a decision not to investigate, and the PTC's review power pursuant to article 53 (3) have all been mentioned and analyzed in detail. Nonetheless, these classic review mechanisms have largely remained dead letters in first practices.[2376] Defining the interplay between the scope of discretion and the standard of review is the crucial challenge for the Court.[2377]

As a matter of fact, the Prosecutor has avoided any judicial check under articles 15 and 53, as has the PTC. Instead of opening the "Pandora's box,"

[2375] In this regard see the jurisprudence in England and Wales, Annex 2, B.

[2376] Stahn, in Stahn/Sluiter, *supra* note 156, 251.

[2377] Stahn, in Stahn/Sluiter, *supra* note 156, 257.

the OTP has essentially focused on scrutiny through political control (reports to the ASP and SC) and informal accountability (consultation with States Parties, NGOs, and external experts).[2378] This open policy on behalf of the Prosecutor has to be welcomed; nevertheless, the balance between the institutional independence of the Prosecutor and his accountability as an agent of justice has not yet been addressed in a satisfactory manner at the international level.[2379] The imbalance between statutory regulation and practice can be described as follows:

> "The introductory wording of Article 53 (1) [...] appears to suggest that the Prosecutor, is in principle, bound to initiate an investigation. The criteria of Articles 17 and 53 (1) (a) to (c), however, and the corresponding ambiguities and gaps of the Statute, have in fact left leeway for a rather wide degree of discretion in practice. Many of the key factors guiding the selection of situations and cases were developed outside the box of legality requirements and thus moved from the domain of review to the area of prosecutorial policy (fn. omitted)."[2380]

The drafters intended to find a balance between the PTC and the Prosecutor. In reality this "checks and balances" has not worked properly. Both the Prosecutor and the PTC are the ones who suffer. Since the operating scheme is unclear, the Prosecutor tries to hide discretionary choices behind legality and performs overly restrictive self-regulation (narrow "interests of justice" approach), while the PTC does not want to illegitimately invade the Prosecutor's domain (reluctance to exercise any article 53 (3) check at all). Most notably, the OTP has used grey zones due to the vagueness of the law in the area of situation and case selection. To enhance accountability and transparency, I have proposed a threefold approach:

- a more transparent, well arranged prosecutorial policy;
- a set of prosecutorial guidelines; and
- a new draft rule 104*bis*.[2381]

In particular, guidelines and limitations to discretion are well known for regulating the exercise of discretion.[2382] One might further depart from the common law vs. civil law differentiation as both have been considerably merged in the ICC Statute. The country analysis included in Annex 2

2378 Stahn, in Stahn/Sluiter, *supra* note 156, 251.

2379 Stahn, in Stahn/Sluiter, *supra* note 156, 258. For more information on the four models of accountability: political accountability, process-based checks and balances, (self-) regulation and judicial review, *ibid.*, 259.

2380 Stahn, in Stahn/Sluiter, *supra* note 156, 270.

2381 See, in more detail, Part IV, F.

2382 Pattenden, *supra* note 1243, 11 et seq.; Stahn, in Stahn/Sluiter, *supra* note 156, 261 et seq.

clearly shows that prosecutorial discretion is known to all countries included in the survey; only the procedural superstructures vary. Guidelines for the Prosecutor are quite common in most countries, and so is judicial oversight. The setting of article 53 is well designed as a hypothetical framework. On the other hand, the substantive criteria require further clarification as to allow for a feasible judicial review implementation. It is thus the ultimate task for the ICC's actors to develop guidelines that concretize the various factors, in particular the ones under the "interests of justice" clause. In addition, the ICC's Judges must develop factors when the review power comes into play; the survey of English and Welsh jurisprudence might reveal a starting point. The latter countries' Judges have engaged more actively in judicial review recently, developing a catalogue of factors that allow for an order of reconsideration.[2383]

From here, I will now summarize the principle recommendations with regard to the article 53 analysis. Article 53 entails three principal criteria: jurisdiction (subdivided into the questions "reasonable basis that a crime exists" and "jurisdiction *stricto sensu*"), admissibility (complementarity and gravity), and, last but not least, the "interests of justice." If all these parameters exist the Prosecutor shall initiate an investigation/prosecution. Starting with the first criterion, the Prosecutor must examine whether:

- the event in question occurred;
- the event constitutes criminal activity under article 5;
- the crime falls within the temporal jurisdiction of the Court (article 11);
- the crime falls within the personal or territorial jurisdiction of the Court (article 12).

As regards admissibility, the two notions of complementarity and gravity can be distinguished. Bearing in mind the inactivity criterion, complementarity is basically analyzed in a threefold manner:

(1) as a rule, situations and cases are admissible if the State remains inactive (admissibility due to inaction);

(2) exceptions can be found in articles 17 (1) (a)–(c), 20 (3), requiring some kind of activity on behalf of the State (inadmissibility due to State action);

(3) these exceptions can be rebutted by the exception to the exception, i.e. the formula of unwillingness and inability to genuinely carry out proceedings (admissibility due to one of the mentioned factors of article 17 (2), (3)).

[2383] See Annex 2, B., XVII., England and Wales.

The notion of gravity is very complex. At the outset, legal and relative gravity should be clearly differentiated, and they must be linked to article 53 (1) (b) and article 53 (1) (c) respectively. Legal gravity refers to the non-discretionary inquiry under article 17 (1) (d), whereas relative gravity is a wider concept connected to the "interests of justice" clause. Moreover, gravity comes into play at two different procedural stages, namely during situation and case selection. Gravity thus involves four different layers:

(1) legal gravity with regard to situations pursuant to articles 53 (1) (b), 17 (1) (d);

(2) relative gravity with regard to situations under the interests of justice concept pursuant to article 53 (1) (c);

(3) legal gravity with regard to cases pursuant to articles 53 (2) (b), 17 (1) (d);

(4) relative gravity with regard to cases under the interests of justice concept pursuant to article 53 (2) (c).

Furthermore, I have indicated that the legal gravity threshold is a reasonably low barrier to the ICC's exercise of jurisdiction. It mainly precludes the Court from adjudicating situations and cases of isolated, small-scale war crimes. In contrast, the OTP's relative gravity policy focuses the Court's resources on the most serious situations and, generally, on the most serious cases within each situation. To sum up, the four notions' factors can be circumscribed in the following manner:

(1) legal gravity (situations): primarily quantitative factors, low threshold;

(2) relative gravity (situations): quantitative factors, qualitative factors, comparison *vis-à-vis* other situations possible, higher threshold;

(3) legal gravity (cases): primarily quantitative factors, low threshold, yet narrower, case-related test;

(4) relative gravity (cases): quantitative factors, qualitative factors, individual circumstances of the perpetrator, comparison *vis-à-vis* other cases possible, high threshold.

For the "interests of justice" clause, a broad application of the term has been preferred. Only a wide approach allows the Prosecutor to apply his discretion in a meaningful manner. He can then consider a variety of factors under the opening clause, yet within the procedural setting of article 53 (1) (c) and (2) (c), in other words, under the abuse control by the PTC pursuant to article 53 (3). With regard to the restorative vs. retributive justice debate, a wide interpretation allows the OTP to operate with necessary flexibility.

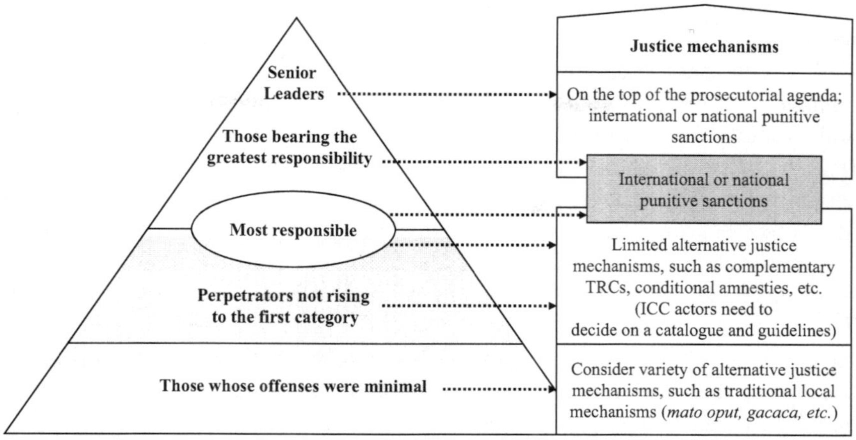

Source: Author.

Figure 9: Justice Mechanisms linked to the Prosecutorial Strategy

In my opinion, "peace" and "justice" should not be juxtaposed, but all involved actors should try to develop an integrated approach that satisfies both. For the notion of peace, two main aspects have been discussed: first, the impact upon peace negotiations, and second, the variety of alternative justice mechanisms used to foster peace. From my point of view, impact is awkward as a factor. It entails more risks than benefits, and peace negotiations *stricto sensu* should not be taken into account.

Subsequently, I have looked at alternative mechanisms to prosecution, which are – generally speaking – valuable options under the "interests of justice." In particular, TRCs might prove to be useful complements to purely criminal proceedings. However, a feasible framework for transitional justice in relation to the ICC Statute remains to be drafted. As a preliminary recommendation, I would like to suggest a threefold prosecutorial hierarchy to alternative justice mechanisms. The presented approach picks up some ideas from other studies that suggested putting up a credible prosecution mechanism for leaders, as well as alternative (national) forms of accountability for those lower down the chain of command.[2384] To substantiate these preliminary thoughts, it is suggested to link the available justice mechanisms to the ICC-OTP's Prosecutorial Strategy, as illustrated above.

[2384] International Council on Human Rights Policy, "Negotiating justice? Human rights and peace agreements," 2006, 88; Ambos, in Ambos/Large/Wierda, *supra* note 650, 40 et seq.; Burbidge, *supra* note 335, 577–8; Robinson, *supra* note 807, 493 et seq.; Mallinder, *supra* note 1887, 223.

It is now left to the ICC's actors, and the International Community as a whole, to flesh out how a particular mechanism is in accordance with the ICC Statute and international obligations. It is, however, strongly recommended to limit the category "senior leaders" to punitive sanctions only and to allow for traditional local justice solely for the third category of offenders. With respect to the fluctuating second category – fluctuating in the sense that there are exceptions when second category perpetrators rise to the "ones bearing the greatest responsibility" (those otherwise playing a major role, notorious offenders, but also persons needed to build up a case) – the OTP holds more discretion. In general, a model for complementary TRCs combined with conditional amnesties appears advisable. Although I have been skeptical *vis-à-vis* the OTP's case-by-case approaches on some occasions, the case specific realities need to be taken into account. This does not mean that *ex-ante* guidelines are useless. The OTP has to draft a set of requirements in order to set up a common standard. What I am referring to is the fact that a specific measure in a specific case lies to a certain degree within the Prosecutor's evaluation. It is his choice whether he needs one particular suspect to build up his case. The Prosecutor ultimately determines whether he values a perpetrator as "one who bears the greatest responsibility." Moreover, it is his choice where to draw the line for alternative justice mechanisms: Should they be limited to the persons not rising to the first category of offenders or might they be available for higher level perpetrators under certain circumstances?

In this respect, it is submitted that for the senior leaders there must be international or national criminal law trials, for those "bearing the greatest responsibility" the only option should equally be national or international punitive sanctions, and only the category "most responsible" (perpetrators floating in between category one and two) is debatable. It is the Prosecutor's discretionary choice whether he deems punitive or alternative mechanisms appropriate for them. In any event, the accountability tool ICC can be just one part of a broader integrated programme in each particular conflict.

It might not be expected that the Court does away with all problems overnight and international and national actors need to implement an individual solution for a conflict area. The ICC can be part of that, but transitional justice involves a lot more than holding some people criminally accountable.

Part VI

Zusammenfassung

Das Verfahrensrecht des IStGH ist in seiner Rechtsnatur einzigartig. Es verbindet Elemente aus verschiedenen Rechtskreisen und zwar des anglo-amerikanischen und des romanisch-germanischen. Diese Mischnatur tritt in zahlreichen Normen des IStGH-Statuts deutlich hervor. Artikel 53, welcher die Einleitung von Ermittlungen sowie die Anklageerhebung betrifft, kann hierfür als gutes Beispiel angeführt werden. Obwohl diese Vorschrift in der Gerichtspraxis des IStGH eine zentrale Rolle spielt, ist es bis dato nicht gelungen, den Kriterien „Schwere der Tat/des Verbrechens" sowie „Interesse der Gerechtigkeit" hinreichend klare Inhalte zu geben. Offensichtlich war es von Anfang an im Sinne einiger Vertragsstaaten, den Chefankläger mit einem weiten Entschließungsermessen auszustatten und die Vorverfahrenskammer als Kontrollinstanz dienen zu lassen. Dieses ausdifferenzierte System erfährt seine Umsetzung in Artikel 53 Abs. 1–4: Absatz 1 regelt die Einleitung von (formellen) Ermittlungen. Die Vorschrift setzt dabei am Legalitätsprinzip an („leitet [...] Ermittlungen ein"), um dann aber sogleich – teilweise am Opportunitätsgedanken ausgerichtete – Ausnahmen festzulegen („[...] sofern er nicht feststellt, dass es für die Verfahrenseinleitung nach diesem Statut keine hinreichende Grundlage gibt"). Das Statut nennt vier maßgebliche Kriterien für die Einleitung von Ermittlungen:

(1) hinreichende Verdachtsgründe, dass ein Verbrechen begangen wurde;

(2) Zuständigkeit des IStGH;

(3) Zulässigkeit (Komplementarität und Schwere der Tat);

(4) Interesse der Gerechtigkeit (unter Berücksichtigung der Schwere des Verbrechens und von Opferinteressen).

Absatz 2 regelt das spätere Verfahrensstadium der Anklageerhebung. Demnach muss eine „hinreichende Grundlage" zur Strafverfolgung vorliegen. Es sei an dieser Stelle darauf aufmerksam gemacht, dass die deutsche Textfassung nicht hinreichend differenziert: Die englische Version des IStGH-Statuts unterscheidet „reasonable basis" (Abs. 1) und „sufficient basis" (Abs. 2).[2385] Offensichtlich handelt es sich um zwei unterschiedlich

[2385] Ebenso die französische und spanische Fassung: „base raisonnable" und „base suffisante," bzw. „fundamento razonable" und „fundamento suficiente".

hohe Standards, doch kommt diese Unterscheidung in der deutschen Fassung nicht zum Ausdruck. Die „reasonable basis“ in Abs. 1 sollte daher mit „angemessen“ oder „zumutbar“ übersetzt werden. Weiterhin nimmt Absatz 2 Bezug auf die bereits bekannten Kriterien der Zulässigkeit und des Interesses der Gerechtigkeit. An die Stelle der ersten beiden Elemente tritt eine „hinreichende rechtliche oder sachliche Grundlage für die Beantragung eines Haftbefehls oder einer Ladung“. Im Rahmen des Interesses der Gerechtigkeit werden zusätzlich Faktoren im Zusammenhang mit den individuellen Eigenschaften des Täters angeführt: Alter oder Gebrechlichkeit des angeblichen Täters sowie seine Rolle bei dem angeblichen Verbrechen.

Absatz 3 regelt die sog. „checks and balances“, also die (gerichtliche) Kontrolle der Anklagebehörde durch die Vorverfahrenskammer. Sollte der Ankläger ein Verfahren nach Absatz 1 oder Absatz 2 einstellen, so ist er der Kammer zur Rechenschaft verpflichtet (Artikel 53 Abs. 3 (a)). Jedoch können die Richter lediglich um eine erneute Prüfung „ersuchen“; allein im Falle eines Einstellungsbeschlusses nach Artikel 53 Abs. 1 (c) oder Abs. 2 (c) bedarf der Ankläger einer positiven Bestätigung seines Beschlusses durch die Kammer (Artikel 53 Abs. 3 (b)). Gemäß Absatz 4 hat der Ankläger selbst jederzeit die Möglichkeit seine Entscheidung zu überprüfen, sofern ihm neue Tatsachen oder Informationen vorliegen.

Stark verkürzt gesprochen besteht Artikel 53 aus einem anglo-amerikanischen sowie einem romanisch-germanischen Block: Die Absätze 1 (c) und (2) (c) sind primär dem angloamerikanischen Rechtskreis entnommen („public interest“), und legen eine weitreichende Ermessensausübung durch den Ankläger zugrunde. Demgegenüber wurde in Artikel 53 Abs. 3 ein Kontrollmechanismus integriert, welcher auf Forderungen der romanisch-germanischen Interessenvertreter zurückgeht. Allerdings ergibt sich unter rechtsvergleichender Betrachtung (Annex 2), dass die Unterschiede zwischen beiden Systemen zunehmend schwinden: Ermessen und Rechtsaufsicht im Zusammenhang mit Strafverfahren sind beiden Rechtskreisen nicht fremd.

Ausgehend von der umstrittenen Norm des Artikels 53 Abs. 1 ergeben sich die zwei wesentlichen Teile der vorliegenden Arbeit: Teil III befasst sich mit dem *Ablauf* von Vorermittlungen, die in der Entscheidung nach Artikel 53 Abs. 1 kumulieren; Teil IV beschäftigt sich mit den *Kriterien*, welche für die Auswahl einer Situation maßgeblich sind. Ziel der Studie ist es, die Silhouette des Vorermittlungsverfahrens mit Leben zu füllen, also einerseits das Verfahren in seiner Gesamtheit zu erfassen, und andererseits die wichtigsten Auswahlkriterien zu definieren.

Während des Vorermittlungsverfahrens sieht sich die Anklagebehörde vor die Aufgabe gestellt, aus einer Vielzahl von Situationen diejenigen auszuwählen, in denen ein formelles Ermittlungsverfahren erforderlich ist. Innerhalb der Anklagebehörde ist die „Jurisdiktions-, Komplementaritäts-, und Kooperationsabteilung" (JCCD) dafür zuständig, erste Empfehlungen abzugeben. Die endgültige Entscheidung wird durch den Chefankläger im Zusammenwirken mit dem Exekutivkomitee (ExCom) getroffen.

Sodann stellte sich die Frage, auf welcher Basis der Gerichtshof überhaupt tätig werden kann. Hierbei ist der sog. „Trigger-Mechanismus" ausschlaggebend, der im Wesentlichen drei Auslösungsmöglichkeiten vorsieht:

- Staatenüberweisungen nach Artikeln 13 (a), 14;
- Verweise des UN Sicherheitsrates nach Artikel 13 (b);
- das sog. *proprio motu* Verfahren nach Artikeln 13 (c), 15.

Um politischem Missbrauch vorzubeugen, wurde in Zusammenhang mit den Auslösungsmechanismen der Begriff der „Situation" eingeführt. Im Gegensatz zu konkreten, individualisierten Fällen sollten Staaten und der Sicherheitsrat nur generalisierte Konflikte, derartige „Situationen" eben, an den IStGH verweisen dürfen.

Dieses im Statut angelegte Konzept wurde durch den IStGH inzwischen in einer fragwürdigen Weise mit der Folge ausgeweitet, dass die formelle Trennlinie zwischen Situationen und Fällen nun beim Erlass eines Haftbefehls nach Artikel 58 verläuft. Im Lubanga Fall legte die Vorverfahrenskammer beide Rechtsbegriffe zugrunde, und schlussfolgerte, dass ein Fall im streng juristischen Sinne erst nach dem Erlass eines Haftbefehls anzunehmen sei. Zuvor handle es sich stets um Situationen. In der praktischen Anwendung drohen sich die Begriffe des Falles und der Situation jedoch zu überlagern, denn es lässt sich kaum eine randscharfe Abgrenzung finden. Zudem war eine weite Ausdehnung des Begriffs „Situation" ins (formelle) Ermittlungsverfahren nicht zwingend notwendig. Die Gefahr der Politisierung leuchtet im Moment des Verweises durch Dritte ein; wogegen der Ankläger nach Kenntnisnahme auch die Herrschaft über den weiteren Verfahrensablauf übernimmt. Sobald er die *notitia criminis* empfangen hat, erscheint die weitere Unterscheidung zwischen „Situationen" und „Fällen" verzichtbar, zumal sich der Vorgang der sich an die Kenntniserlangung durch die Anklagebehörde anschließenden Konkretisierung (Individualisierungsprozess) bei jedem nationalen und internationalen Strafverfahren in ähnlicher Form wiederfindet.

Nichtsdestotrotz setzt die formelle Einleitung eines Ermittlungsverfahrens nach Artikel 53 Abs. 1 das Vorliegen einer Situation im Rechtssinne voraus. Gegenwärtig sind fünf Situationen anhängig, welche die Demokratische Republik Kongo, die Zentralafrikanische Republik, Uganda, die Republik Kenia und Darfur (Sudan) betreffen. Die Behandlung letzterer beruht auf einem Verweis des Sicherheitsrates, wohingegen die drei ersten Situationen auf sog. Staateneigenüberweisungen („self-referrals") zurückgehen. Überweisungen durch den Vertragsstaat selbst wurden ursprünglich nicht in Erwägung gezogen, allerdings auch nicht explizit ausgeschlossen. Diese Lücke im Statut ermöglichte es dem Chefankläger, durch eine recht weite Auslegung den – an sich vorzugswürdigen – *proprio motu* Mechanismus zu umgehen. *Proprio motu* Ermittlungen würden einen weniger angreifbaren, direkten Weg zur Verfügung stellen. Daher muss der Frage nachgegangen werden, warum der Chefankläger Staateneigenüberweisungen bevorzugt. Im Verfahren nach den Artikeln 13 (c) und 15 kann die Anklagebehörde Ermittlungen von sich aus beginnen, ohne dass eine Überweisung von dritter Seite vorliegt. Normalerweise beruhen derartige Vorermittlungen im Rahmen von Artikel 15 auf Informationen von Individuen und Nichtregierungsorganisationen. Diese haben in der Praxis bereits umfangreich von ihrem Eingaberecht Gebrauch gemacht. Derartige Informationen (oder „Kommunikationen") werden in der Anklagebehörde zusammengetragen und nach potentiellen Situationen gruppiert. Zum jetzigen Zeitpunkt wurde erst eine formelle Ermittlung (Kenia) auf der Grundlage dieser „Kommunikationen" eröffnet, jedoch erst nachdem eine Staateneigenüberweisung oder nationale Strafverfolgungsmechanismen scheiterten. Zudem wurden lediglich informelle Vorermittlungen u.a. im Irak und in Venezuela erfolglos abgeschlossen, und werden zur Zeit in Afghanistan, im Tschad, in Kolumbien, in Guinea, in Georgien, in Palästina, und in der Elfenbeinküste durchgeführt. Nur dann, wenn die „Kommunikationen" den Voraussetzungen der Artikel 15 Abs. 3, 53 Abs. 1, und IStGH-Regel 48 gerecht werden, wenn also eine „angemessene Grundlage" vorliegt, müsste die Vorverfahrenskammer der formellen Ermittlungseinleitung zustimmen (Artikel 15 Abs. 4). Es ist offenbar diese erhebliche prozessrechtliche Hürde sowie die *prima facie* Kooperationsbereitschaft von betroffenen Staaten, welche den Ankläger veranlasst haben, zu einer Strategie der Eigenüberweisungen überzugehen. Diese Strategie mag zwar mit den Buchstaben des Statuts vereinbar sein. Gleichwohl stellt sie eine fragwürdige Entwicklung dar, die überdacht werden sollte. Zu groß sind nämlich die Gefahren, dass sich der IStGH dem Vorwurf der Befangenheit aussetzt. Zwar hat der Chefankläger versucht, Manipulationsversuchen durch weite Auslegung der Überweisungserklärungen entgegenzuwirken – so wurden in der Uganda Erklärung Verbrechen beider Konfliktparteien nachträglich einbezogen. Nichtsdestotrotz wäre eine unabhängige Verfahrenseinleitung *a priori* vorzugswürdig. Stattdessen hat die Anklagebehörde momentan eine faktische Hierarchie, die von politischen Gegebenheiten beeinflusst wird, begründet, obgleich derartige Abstufungen im Statut nicht vorgesehen sind. Im Ergebnis sollte die Möglichkeit einer *proprio motu* Verfahrenseinleitung verstärkt genutzt werden, wenn Regierungs- und Rebellengruppen gleichermaßen an den Verbrechen beteiligt sind.

Über die drei Auslösemechanismen hinaus wird im Teil III das Gesamtverfahren der Vorermittlungen dargestellt. Die Selektionskriterien für Situationen sind dabei identisch, es kommt durch IStGH-Regeln 48 und 104 zu einer (teilweisen) Tatbestandsüberlagerung der maßgeblichen Normen von Artikel 15 und Artikel 53. Gerade aufgrund dieser Tatbestandsüberlagerung stellen IStGH-Vorermittlungen eine überaus komplexe Materie dar, sind doch die relevanten Regelungen über zahlreiche Normen des IStGH-Statuts und der IStGH-Regeln verstreut. So findet man beispielsweise keine spezifische Normierung von Vorermittlungen („pre-investigations"); stattdessen wird – eher beiläufig – lediglich der Terminus Voruntersuchungen („preliminary examinations") in Artikel 15 Abs. 6 erwähnt. Nichtsdestotrotz hat die vorliegende Untersuchung ergeben, dass die Anklagebehörde umfangreiche Vorermittlungen durchführt. Diese beginnen mit einem der drei Auslösungsmechanismen, folgen sodann einem Analyseprozess nach Artikel 15 (2), IStGH-Regeln 46, 47 und 107, bevor eine Entscheidung hinsichtlich der „angemessenen Grundlage" notwendig wird. Die letztgenannte Hürde basiert auf den Kriterien des Artikels 53 Abs. 1 und eröffnet zugleich das Ermittlungsverfahren *stricto sensu*. Zur Veranschaulichung der Vorermittlungen finden sich insbesondere zwei Übersichtsgrafiken in Annex 1 (A. & B.).

Die Betrachtung der Vorermittlungen lässt erneut sehr deutlich hervortreten, dass der IStGH nicht alle in seine Jurisdiktion fallende Verbrechen aufklären kann und dass die Aufgabe des Anklägers nicht zuletzt darin besteht, diesbezüglich die Weichen zu stellen. Zwangsläufig muss dem Chefankläger bei seinen Auswahlentscheidungen ein gewisser rechtlicher Spielraum gegeben werden, sollen seine Entscheidungen einer Überlastung des Gerichtshofs effektiv vorbeugen können. Wie erwähnt wurde durch Artikel 53 ein mehrstufiger Filtermechanismus eingeführt. Dabei sollten die rechtlichen Faktoren Zuständigkeit und Zulässigkeit klar von den Opportunitätserwägungen des „Interesses der Gerechtigkeit" abgegrenzt werden. Insoweit hat der amtierende Chefankläger bisher keine klare Trennlinie gezogen, sondern vielmehr die Kriterien „Schwere der Tat/des Verbrechens" und „Interesse der Gerechtigkeit" in einer zweideutigen Weise verwendet ohne klar zu differenzieren. Zunächst wurde das „Interesse der Gerechtigkeit" zu eng ausgelegt, was wiederum zu einer extensiven Auslegung des Begriffs „Schwere" führte. Darüber hinaus wurden die „Schwere des Tat" im Sinne der Artikel 53 Abs. 1 (b) und 17 Abs. 1 (d) und die „Schwere des Verbrechens" in dem hiervon abweichenden Sinne, in dem Artikel 53 Abs. 1 (c) diesen Begriff gebraucht, miteinander vermengt.

Vieles spricht – wie unter Teil 4 im Einzelnen entfaltet – für ein hiervon deutlich abweichendes Verständnis, wonach Ermessenserwägungen allein eine Frage der Anwendung des Artikels 53 Abs. 1 (c) darstellen, also der

Abwägung des „Interesses der Gerechtigkeit“ und der „Schwere des Verbrechens“ (sowie unter Einbeziehung von Opferinteressen und ungeschriebenen Faktoren). Dagegen sollten die Merkmale in Artikel 53 Abs. 1 (a) und (b) – und damit auch dasjenige der „Schwere der Tat“ (vgl. Art. 53 Abs. 1 (b) und 17 Abs. 1 (d)) – nach rechtlichen Kriterien bemessen werden, ohne Opportunitätserwägungen, allenfalls mit einem gewissen Beurteilungsspielraum. In diesem Sinne wurde dann in Teil IV der vorliegenden Untersuchung zwischen den einzelnen Absätzen des Artikels 1 wie folgt unterschieden:

- rechtliches Kriterium der Zuständigkeit;
- rechtliches Kriterium der Zulässigkeit;
- Ermessenskriterium des „Interesses der Gerechtigkeit“.

Sofern alle Parameter vorliegen leitet der Ankläger Ermittlungen ein. Bezüglich des ersten Kriteriums lassen sich die weiteren vier Bestandteile differenzieren:

(1) das fragliche Ereignis hat tatsächlich stattgefunden;

(2) es handelt sich dabei um einen Tatbestand, der nach Artikel 5 unter Strafe gestellt ist (Jurisdiktion *ratione materiae*);

(3) der Tatbestand fällt unter die Jurisdiktion *ratione temporis* (Artikel 11);

(4) der Tatbestand fällt unter die Jurisdiktion *ratione personae* und unter die formelle Zuständigkeit (Artikel 12).

Die Zulässigkeit setzt zwei wichtige Elemente voraus: die Komplementarität und die Schwere des Verbrechens. In der Praxis des Gerichtshofs wurde zur näheren Ausfüllung des Komplementaritätserfordernisses insbesondere ein Kriterium der Ausganglage der sog. Inaktivität („inactivity“ oder „uncontested admissibility“) entwickelt; dies hat zu einer dreistufigen Ausprägung des Komplementaritätssatzes geführt:

(1) Grds. ist Zulässigkeit bezüglich aller Situationen und Fälle, in denen der jeweilige Staat nicht tätig wird, anzunehmen (*Inaktivitätskriterium*).

(2) Artikel 17 (1) (a)–(c), 20 (3) listet Ausnahmen von der grds. gegebenen Zulässigkeit; diese setzen jedoch irgendein Handeln des Staates voraus, d.h., dass ein Handeln des Staates erkennbar sein muss, um überhaupt in die Prüfung eines Ausnahmetatbestands einzusteigen.

(3) Zudem können Gegenausnahmen wiederum zur Zulässigkeit führen, sofern der Staat, der zwar irgendwie tätig wird, gleichwohl nicht willens oder fähig ist, ein völkerrechtliches Kernverbrechen ordnungsgemäß („genuinely“) zu verfolgen.

Ein mangelnder Wille soll etwa dann vorliegen, wenn (1) Scheinverfahren eingeleitet werden, wenn (2) ein Verfahren verzögert wird, oder wenn (3) kein unabhängiges oder unparteiisches Verfahren durchgeführt wird (Artikel 17 Abs. 2 (a)–(c)). Zur Feststellung der Gegenausnahme der Unfähigkeit ist zu fragen, ob der Staat wegen eines völligen oder weitgehenden Zusammenbruchs oder mangelnder Verfügbarkeit seines Justizsystems nicht in der Lage ist, des Beschuldigten habhaft zu werden oder die notwendigen Beweismittel zu erlangen (Artikel 17 Abs. 3)).

Das Merkmal der „Schwere" wird unter zwei verschiedenen Gesichtspunkten relevant: zum einen formuliert Artikel 17 Abs. 1 (d) ein gleichsam rechtliches Schwereerfordernis, während der Feststellung der Schwere im Sinne des Artikels 53 Abs. 1 (c) eine spezifische Ermessensausübung vorausgeht. Wie bereits erwähnt wurden beide Sichtweisen in der Gerichtspraxis sowohl vom Chefankläger wie auch von der Vorverfahrenskammer I nicht klar unterschieden. Zum Teil lässt sich dies auf die unglückliche Wortwahl („gravity of the case" und „gravity of the crime") zurückführen. Hinzu tritt, dass bei der Einführung des IStGH-Statuts insbesondere die Artikel 17 und 53 nicht an die Einführung der Begrifflichkeit „Situation" und an den Auslösungsmechanismus angepasst worden sind. Daraus resultierte eine Mehrdeutigkeit entscheidender Normenpassagen, mit der Folge dass der (ähnliche) Wortlaut der termini „Schwere der Tat" und „Schwere des Verbrechens" nur in geringem Maße Rückschlüsse auf ihren Inhalt ermöglicht. Systematisch und teleologisch spricht nämlich einiges dafür, die „Schwere der Tat" und die „Schwere des Verbrechens" deutlich voneinander zu unterscheiden. Denn Artikel 17 war als rechtliche Zulässigkeitsschranke gedacht, wogegen Artikel 53 Abs. 1 (c) dem Ankläger einen gewissen Opportunitätsspielraum geben sollte. Zudem sollte durch die Schwere in Artikel 17 Abs. 1 (d) eine (zusätzliche) Minimalhürde aufgestellt werden, als im Entwurfsstadium des IStGH-Statuts die genaue Jurisdiktion *ratione materiae* noch unklar ist. Es lässt sich daher schlussfolgern, dass Artikel 17 Abs. 1 (d) lediglich eine Mindestschwelle – insbesondere für isolierte Kriegsverbrechen – etabliert. Im Gegensatz dazu stellt die „Schwere" im Rahmen des Artikels 53 Abs. 1 (c) einen Teil einer umfassenden Gesamtabwägung dar, welche es dem Ankläger gestattet, zur Entscheidungsfindung alle anhängigen und potentiellen Situationen in Relation zu setzen. Im Ergebnis finden sich damit vier verschiedene Ebenen von „Schwere" im IStGH-Statut:

(1) die rechtliche Schwere bzgl. einer Situation gem. Artikel 53 Abs. 1 (b) und Artikel 17 Abs. 1 (d);

(2) die relative Schwere bzgl. einer Situation (Interessenabwägung) gem. Artikel 53 Abs. 1 (c);

(3) die rechtliche Schwere bzgl. eines Falles gem. Artikel 53 Abs. 2 (b) und Artikel 17 Abs. 1 (d);

(4) die relative Schwere bzgl. eines Falles (Interessenabwägung) gem. Artikel 53 Abs. 2 (c).

Veranlasst war damit eine eingehende Analyse der Sachgesichtspunkte, die für die Feststellung der (unterschiedlichen) Schwerekriterien maßgeblich sind. Die Anklagebehörde nennt diesbezüglich das „Ausmaß der Verbrechen" („scale"), die „Verbrechensnatur" („nature"), sowie die „Art und Umstände der Verbrechensbegehung" („manner and circumstances"). Auf dieser Grundlage wurde die Rechtssprechung der *ad hoc* Tribunale sowie des Gerichtshofs für Sierra Leone analysiert, um hiervon ausgehend die zahlreich hervortretenden Aspekte in die drei Oberkategorien qualitativer und quantitativer Faktoren sowie die individuellen Umstände des Täters einzugliedern. Abschließend lassen sich die unterschiedlichen „Schwere"-Kriterien wie folgt systematisieren:

(1) Rechtliche Schwere (Situationen): Primär quantitative Faktoren, niedrige Anforderungen;

(2) relative Schwere (Situationen): Quantitative und qualitative Faktoren, Vergleich mit anderen Situationen möglich, erhöhte Anforderungen;

(3) rechtliche Schwere (Fall): Primär quantitative Faktoren, niedrige Anforderungen, allerdings engere Anwendung (individualisiert);

(4) relative Schwere (Fall): Quantitative und qualitative Faktoren, individuelle Umstände des Täters, Vergleich mit anderen Fällen möglich, hohe Anforderungen.

Abschließend wurde Artikel 53 Abs. 1 (c), mithin das Erfordernis des Gerechtigkeitsinteresses, betrachtet. Das „Interesse der Gerechtigkeit" bildet den Lackmustest des IStGH-Statuts. Nur eine weite Auslegung erlaubt dem Chefankläger eine Ermessensausübung, die im Einklang mit dem IStGH-Statut steht. Ansonsten ergibt sich die Gefahr einer Ermessensauslagerung ähnlich derjenigen, die sich in Form der „Flucht" unter den Begriff „Schwere" bereits vollzogen hat. Zudem kann der Ankläger nur auf der Grundlage eines umfassenden Begriffsverständnisses sämtliche sachgerechterweise heranzuziehenden Gesichtspunkte berücksichtigen; dies aber scheint u. a. deswegen geboten, um den Einsatz alternativer Justizmechanismen anstelle rein strafrechtlicher Sanktionen (Wahrheitskommissionen, bedingte Amnestien, traditionelle Justiz, etc.) nicht von vornherein zu verunmöglichen. Insbesondere sollten vor diesem Hintergrund die Begriffe „Frieden" und „Gerechtigkeit" nicht nebeneinander gestellt bzw. in einen Gegensatz gebracht werden; stattdessen erscheint ein ganzheitlicher Auslegungsprozess vorzugswürdig, der sich sämtlichen Aspekten öffnet. In diesem Zusammenhang wurden zwei grundlegende Aspekte unterschieden: Erstens die Auswirkungen auf Friedensverhandlungen an sich, zweitens die Vielzahl an alternativen Gerechtigkeitsmechanismen, um einen Friedensprozess zu fördern. Das Kriterium der „Auswirkungen" erwies sich als spekulativ. Es sollte daher hinsichtlich des Merkmals des Interesses der Gerechtigkeit nicht als ausschlaggebend behandelt werden, sondern allenfalls als internes Abwägungskriterium im engeren Sinne. Der Chefankläger kann also zwar Auswirkungen auf die Sicherheit von Ermittlern und Zeugen (intern) einbeziehen, Friedensverhandlungen als solche bzw. die positiven Entwicklungen, die „Auswirkungen" also, die man sich von solchen verspricht, können jedoch nicht berücksichtigt werden.

Alternative Justizmechanismen sind grundsätzlich nützliche Optionen und sollten daher in die vorzunehmende umfassende Interessenabwägung einbezogen werden. Vor allem Wahrheitskommissionen könnten, sofern sich für diese allgemein gültige Standards von der Internationalen Gemeinschaft entwickeln ließen, rein strafrechtliche Verfahren sinnvoll ergänzen. Wie dem auch sei, die Rahmenbedingungen für eine Übergangsjustiz in Bezug auf das IStGH-Statut müssen noch konzipiert werden. Es wurden diesbezüglich von mir folgende einleitende Thesen entwickelt:

1. Alternativen zur Strafverfolgung sollten mit der dreistufigen Verfolgungsstrategie der Anklagebehörde koordiniert werden, d.h., dass für Straftäter der Kategorie 1 nur – nationale oder internationale – Strafverfahren in Betracht kommen, während für Straftäter der Kategorie 2 (in begrenztem Maße) alternative Wege (Wahrheitskommissionen, bedingte Amnestien, etc.) in Frage kommen können. Lediglich für Straftäter der Kategorie 3 sollten alternative Justizmechanismen ohne Einschränkung (z.B. traditionelle Bewältigung) in Betracht gezogen werden.

2. Straftäter der Kategorie 1 sind insbesondere die ranghöchsten Personen („senior leaders"). Darüber hinaus können zur Kategorie 1 solche Personen zählen, welche „Hauptverantwortung" tragen („those persons bearing the greatest responsibility"). Letztere Gruppe umfasst Personen, die „anderweitig eine wichtige Rolle gespielt haben", zudem „berühmt-berüchtigte" (z.B. besonders grausame) Täter („notorious offenders"), aber auch solche Personen, die vom Ankläger benötigt werden, um Beweismaterial zusammenzutragen. Mithin ist zwischen Kategorie 1 (a) und (b) zu differenzieren: „Senior leaders" der Kategorie 1 (a) müssen strafrechtlich behandelt werden, d.h. ein Staat kann nur durch nationale Strafverfahren im engeren Sinne bewirken, dass ein Verfahren vor dem IStGH unzulässig wird. Dagegen kommt der Anklagebehörde bei Tätern der Kategorie 1 (b), welche sich indessen mit der Kategorie 2 überschneiden kann, ein gewisses Ermessen zu. Hier scheinen solche alternativen Justizmechanismen denkbar, die Straf-

verfahren ähneln. Beispielsweise könnten u. U. Wahrheitskommissionen oder bedingte Amnestien in Betracht gezogen werden. Festzuhalten bleibt, dass es der Anklagebehörde überlassen ist, wo genau sie die Trennlinie zwischen Kategorie 1 (b) und Kategorie 2 zieht, bzw. für welche Täter sie alternative Modelle zulässt. Straftäter der Kategorie 3 haben vergleichsweise weniger schwerwiegende Taten begangen. In Anbetracht der enormen Anzahl solcher Straftäter, die, wie im Fall Ruanda, in die Millionen gehen können, sind strafrechtliche Verfahren für alle Täter utopisch. Hier muss in Zusammenarbeit von IStGH, dem betroffenen Staat und der UN ein – konfliktbezogenes – alternatives System entwickelt werden. Es darf dabei aber nicht vergessen werden, dass die Opfer naturgemäß vor allem den Täter von nebenan im Sinn haben und es für sie unerträglich sein kann, wenn genau diese Personen straffrei bleiben.[2386]

3. In der Verfahrenswirklichkeit ist die im Statut vorgesehene Balance zwischen Ankläger und Vorverfahrenskammer keineswegs umgesetzt. Beispielsweise hat der Chefankläger Ermessensausübung und juristische Subsumtion (ohne Ermessensspielraum) nicht klar voneinander abgegrenzt; zudem hat die Vorverfahrenskammer Artikel 53 Abs. 3 sehr zurückhaltend interpretiert, um nicht in unzulässiger Art und Weise in die Ermessensausübung des Anklägers einzugreifen. Im Ergebnis agiert die Anklagebehörde bei der Situations- und Fallauswahl damit in einer Grauzone, ohne dass eine effektive Kontrolle durch die Vorverfahrenskammer gewährleistet wäre. Um mehr Transparenz zu erzielen, sollte daher folgender Ansatz gewählt werden:

(1) Eine eindeutige, einheitlich normierte Anklagestrategie;

(2) Richtlinien zur Ermessensausübung;

(3) zwei neue IStGH Regeln 104*bis* und 106*bis* (vgl. dazu ferner Part IV, F.).

4. Die neue Regel 106*bis* soll dem Gerichtshof die Möglichkeit geben, Verfahren an Staaten (zurück-)zu überweisen. Ein solcher *aktiver* Verweis ist im bisherigen System nicht vorgesehen. Vergleichbar ICTY-Regel 11*bis* sollte der IStGH jedoch Verfahren an nationale Rechtssysteme abgeben können. Zwar gibt es einige prozessuale Möglichkeiten im jetzigen Regelwerk (u. a. Artikel 19), allerdings legt die positive Komplementarität insoweit eine weniger zurückhaltende Praxis des IStGH nahe. Staaten und Gerichtshof sollten zusammenarbeiten, und ein wichtiger Aspekt wäre ein Mechanismus, welcher Überweisungen in Eigeninitiative zulässt. Nur so ließe sich die sog. Straflosigkeitslücke verengen und weniger schwerwiegende

[2386] Zu Kambodia vgl. Haing Ngor/Roger Warner, *Survival of the killing fields* (Robinson, London 1987) 500–1.

Fälle – solche also, die beispielsweise mangels relativer Schwere abgeschichtet wurden – könnten nationalen Behörden überlassen werden. Zudem sollte Regel 106*bis* eine diesbezügliche Überwachungspflicht schaffen. Der im Rahmen der vorgelegten Arbeit entwickelte Vorschlag sei durch drei abschließende Bemerkungen charakterisiert:

(1) Das Kriterium der relativen Schwere würde den IStGH vor Überlastung schützen; ein flankierender (Rück-)Überweisungsmechanismus erscheint unabdingbar.

(2) Der IStGH sollte potentiell nicht nur Personen aburteilen, sondern vor allem die nationalen Strafrechtssysteme stärken.

(3) Durch die Einführung einer neuen, aktiven Verweisungsregelung wird der Grundsatz der positiven Komplementarität gestärkt: die Anklagebehörde könnte sich nicht aufgrund mangelnder „Schwere“ zurückziehen und vom Verfahren Abstand nehmen, sondern müsste – was wünschenswert ist – eine eventuelle Überweisung an nationale Jurisdiktionen prüfen.

5. Von hergebrachten Unterscheidungen des „Common Law“ und des „Civil Law“ sollte in der Verfahrenspraxis des IStGH zunehmend Abstand genommen werden. Beide Systeme sind im Statut nämlich ohnehin verschmolzen, ohne dass eines dem anderen vorgehen würde, oder dass durch eine schroffe Gegenüberstellung der Systeme dem Statut klarere Konturen gegeben werden könnten. Zwar lässt sich – wie bei Artikel 53 – der Ursprung einiger Rechtsbegriffe klären, jedoch sind dadurch kaum Rückschlüsse auf die jeweilige Auslegung möglich. Jedenfalls sind durch einseitige Bezugnahme auf Common oder Civil Law geprägte Ansätze nicht angebracht. Es sollten stattdessen Leitlinien, welche die Merkmale des Artikels 53 konkretisieren, entwickelt werden. Dies sollte mittel- bzw. langfristig auf internationaler Ebene geschehen. Letztlich sind es aber die IStGH-Akteure, d.h. Anklagebehörde und Kammern, die zeitnah einen praktikablen Ansatz entwickeln müssen.

Annex 1

Graphs of the Pre-Investigation Stage

A. Graph of the distinction situations and cases (Part III, B., III.)

Situation – Case

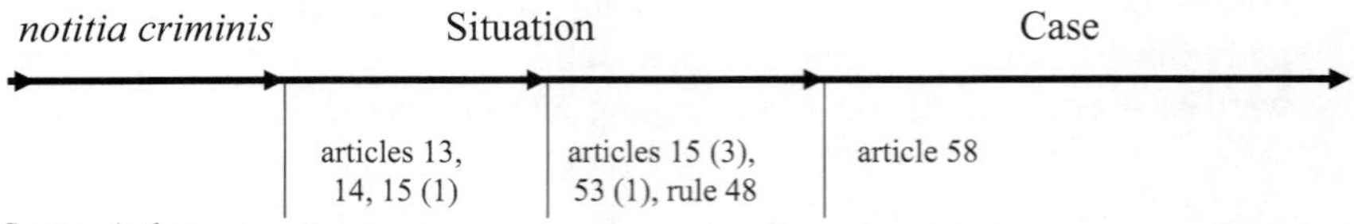

Source: Author.

Figure A1: Demarcation Line Situation – Case

B. Pre-Investigation Stage as conducted by the OTP (Situation Selection)

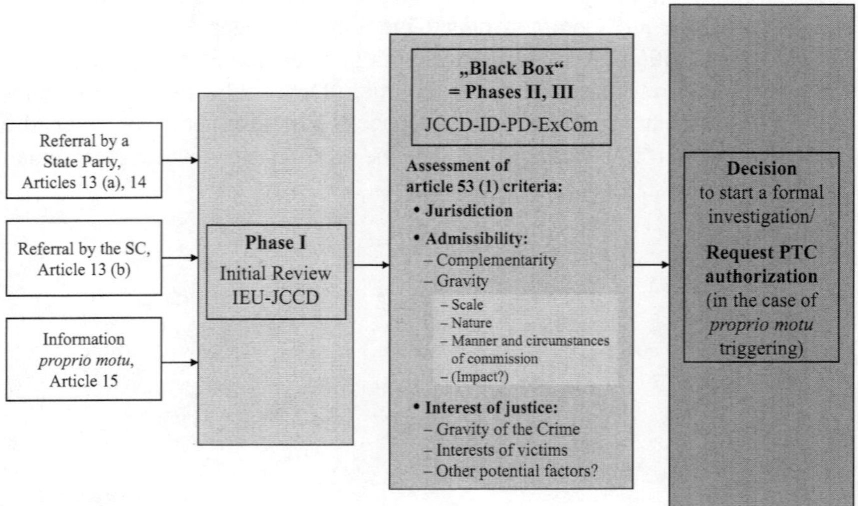

Source: Author.

Figure A2: Pre-Investigation Stage before the ICC

C. OTP Analysis Phase I–III (in detail)

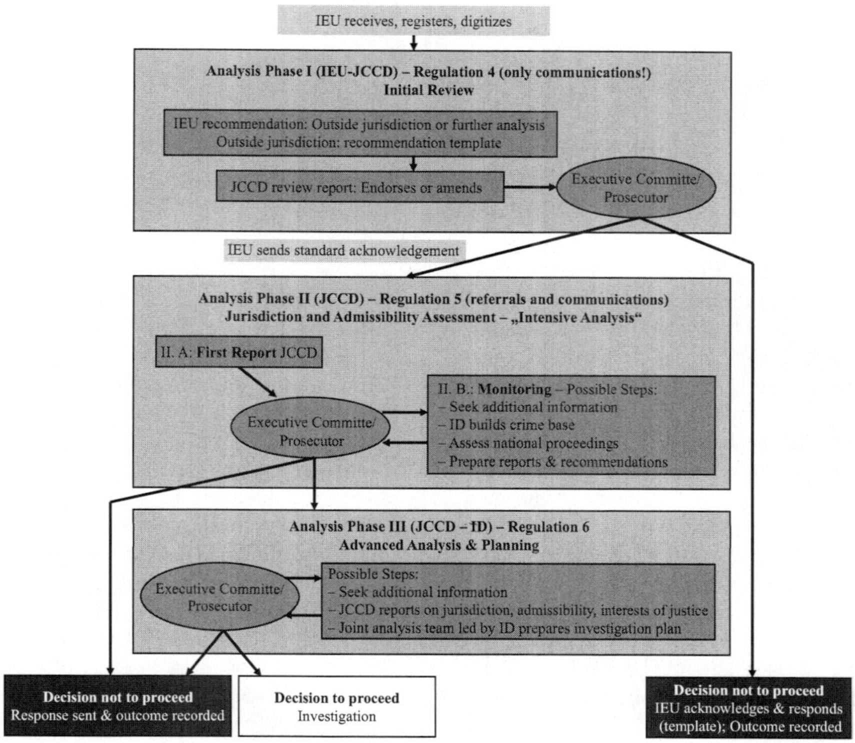

Sources: Author – Draft Regulations, Annex to the Policy Paper (Regulations regarding analysis of referrals and communications).

Figure A3: OTP Analysis of Communications and Referrals

Annex 2

Country analysis

A. Working hypothesis

According to the functional method the point of comparison must be phrased in functional terms, meaning that the *tertium comparationis* is not a legal term or institution but a pertinent question. The analysis can be divided into two key stages, the pre-investigation phase and the actual start of a full investigation. In order to distinguish clearly between the two different procedural stages, the terms pre-investigation ("preliminary examination") and formal investigation were introduced with regard to the ICC.[2387] It should, however, be noted that each national system has its own specific rationale and that a comparison on certain key aspects may render only an incomplete picture of the interplay between the different actors. The stages of criminal procedure vary in each country, and the terms "pre-investigation" and "formal investigation" might not be found in most countries. It is not always entirely clear when an investigation is actually commenced or ended; the process is often fluid. Some preliminary steps are taken by the police, at some point of time the Prosecutor/*Judge d'instruction* becomes involved, and ultimately the Judge(s) might take action. The pertinent question is thus to track down the process of preliminary inquiries until the start of an investigation and to identify the actors involved. As a guiding framework,[2388] the following seven questions, which may overlap in part, will be referenced and answered if feasible:

1. Who is in charge of (pre-)investigations?
2. What triggers the initiation of a (pre-)investigation? (What is the standard of proof – if any – to start (pre-)investigations?)
3. Who takes the decision to start a formal investigation?
4. Is a discretionary evaluation performed before initiating a formal investigation/prosecution, and if so, how is it conducted (level of discretion)?

[2387] See Part. I, A. All mentioned sections and articles within each country report are those of the relative country's codes (for instance, "Criminal Code" in the context of Canada refers to the Canadian Criminal Code, whereas "Criminal Code" in the context of India refers to the Indian Criminal Code, etc.).

[2388] For another comparative survey inquiring the role of the Prosecutor and the corresponding questionnaire see Louise Arbour/Albin Eser/Kai Ambos/Andrew Sanders (eds.), *The Prosecutor of a Permanent International Criminal Court* (edition iuscrim, Freiburg 2000) 1, 193 et seq.; Jörg-Martin Jehle/Marianne Wade, *Copying with overloaded criminal justice systems* (Springer, Berlin 2006).

5. Under which circumstances can investigations (preliminary and/or full investigation) be dismissed? Are there criteria for dismissal or is the decision fully discretionary? If there are criteria, which are those and how are they defined?
6. Is the decision to start/drop an investigation/prosecution subject to control by another body?

For the choice of countries, the basic distinction between civil law and common law is taken as a basis, while other additional factors are also taken into consideration to achieve a wider representation (Romanistic, Germanic, and Nordic family; Chinese, Hindu, and Islamic law; African law; current situations pending before the ICC).[2389] However, the ideal choice for a survey is factually limited due to languages spoken by each particular author and logistical problems. It is difficult to make some legal sources accessible (for example, the African law), and, moreover, the texts might only be found in its original language. Secondary law sources (textbooks and commentaries) will play a major role; moreover, translations of criminal procedural codes into English, French, and German will form the epicenter. For all mentioned reasons, the survey will necessarily remain on the surface, only brief outlines of the countries' relevant criminal procedure will be given, and the study of each country does not claim to be complete. Authors with in-depth knowledge on the specific country might therefore find inaccuracies, especially because many secondary and not always brand-new sources had to be used, and therefore the country analysis was included in Annex 2 instead of being an integral part of the ICC's pre-investigation analysis as such. Further, the analysis was based on the written law, so practical realities might depart in some of the survey countries.

Taking into account the various additional factors, the following countries were selected:

1. Austria (Civil law, Germanic family);
2. Canada (Common law and Civil law);
3. Cameroon (Civil law and Common law influence; African family);
4. China (Chinese law);
5. Colombia (Civil law, Romanistic family, potential situation country);
6. Côte d'Ivoire (Civil law, Romanistic family, African family, situation country);
7. Democratic Republic of Congo (Civil law, Romanistic family, African family, situation country);
8. France (Civil law, Romanistic family);
9. Germany (Civil law, Germanic family);
10. India (Hindu law);
11. Kenya (Common law, African family, situation country);
12. The Netherlands (Civil law);
13. Norway (Civil law, Nordic family);

[2389] See Part I, C., III.

14. South Africa (Common law);
15. Sudan (Common law, Sharia law);
16. Uganda (Common law, African family, situation country);
17. United Kingdom (England and Wales) (Common law);
18. United States (Common law).

B. Country analysis

I. Austria (Civil law, Germanic family)

Austrian criminal law has significant similarities to German criminal law as it is divided into the *Strafgesetzbuch* (StGB; Austrian Penal Code) and the new *Strafprozessordnung* (StPO; Austrian Code of Criminal Procedure, hereinafter ACCP).[2390]

Who is in charge of (pre-)investigations?

Investigation proceedings are conducted by the police, the Prosecution, and even judges under certain circumstances.[2391] On the other hand, it is the Prosecution Service that decides whether to prosecute, to drop the charges, or to discontinue investigations.[2392]

In general, police and Prosecution shall investigate by mutual consent, but it is ultimately the Prosecution who is in charge.[2393] The Prosecution Service directs any investigation.[2394] In accordance with sections 98 (2) and 104 et seq. ACCP, judges have the authority to take investigative steps in rare occasions. Coercive measures and evidence gathering is further regulated in sections 109–166 ACCP.

What triggers the initiation of a (pre-)investigation? (What is the standard of proof – if any – to start (pre-)investigations?)

The police may initiate investigations *ex officio* or upon a complaint.[2395] Upon specific decrees by the Prosecutor or the judges, however, the police are obliged to take action.[2396]

[2390] Strafgesetzbuch (Austrian Penal Code) 1974, 1.5.2004; Strafprozessordnung (Austrian Code of Criminal Procedure) 1.1.2009. On the Austrian criminal procedure before the reform, see Otto Triffterer, "Austria" in Arbour/Eser/Ambos/Sanders, *supra* note 2388, 207, 207 et seq.

[2391] Sec.104 Strafprozessordnung, *supra* note 2390.

[2392] Sec.20 (1) Strafprozessordnung, *supra* note 2390.

[2393] Secs.98 (1) and 99 (1) Strafprozessordnung, *supra* note 2390.

[2394] Sec.101 (1) Strafprozessordnung, *supra* note 2390.

[2395] Sec.99 (1) Strafprozessordnung, *supra* note 2390.

[2396] Secs.99 (1) and 105 (2) Strafprozessordnung, *supra* note 2390.

Who takes the decision to start a formal investigation?

In principle, the police start formal investigations. It is, however, the Prosecution that decides whether or not to initiate proceedings; against the Prosecution's declared intention no investigations can be initiated or preceded.[2397] Furthermore, the Prosecution Service controls any police reports and makes dispositions accordingly.[2398]

Is a discretionary evaluation performed before initiating a formal investigation/prosecution, and if so, how is it conducted (level of discretion)?

The Prosecutor decides upon investigations whether to proceed directly with a prosecution, whether to ask for further investigations or, alternatively, whether to drop the case.[2399]

Under which circumstances can investigations (preliminary and/or full investigation) be dismissed? Are there criteria for dismissal or is the decision fully discretionary? If there are criteria, which are those and how are they defined?

Proceedings may be discontinued if there are not sufficient legal or factual grounds to prosecute.[2400] Sections 191 and 192 ACCP foresee further causes that might allow for discontinuance (for instance, minor violations). Alternative procedures are regulated in sections 198–209 ACCP.

Is the decision to start/end an investigation/prosecution subject to control by another body?

If the Prosecution Service stops proceedings on the basis of sections 190–192 ACCP, victims and other persons, who have a legitimate interest, can request continuation.[2401] The petition has to be communicated to the Higher Regional Court if the Prosecution decides not to resume its previous investigation activities.[2402] The final decision is then settled by the Higher Regional Court, and against its decision there are no further legal remedies available.[2403]

Conclusion

The police commonly conduct investigations in Austria. It is, on the other hand, the Prosecution Service that rules on the decisive matters. The decision to initiate investigations and prosecutions, as well as the determination to discontinue any proceedings, is left to the evaluation of the Prosecutors.

2397 Sec.101 (1) Strafprozessordnung, *supra* note 2390.

2398 Sec.101 (4) Strafprozessordnung, *supra* note 2390.

2399 Secs.20 (1) and 101 Strafprozessordnung, *supra* note 2390.

2400 Sec.190 Strafprozessordnung, *supra* note 2390.

2401 Sec.195 (1) Strafprozessordnung, *supra* note 2390.

2402 Sec.195 (3) Strafprozessordnung, *supra* note 2390.

2403 Sec.196 (1) Strafprozessordnung, *supra* note 2390.

II. Canada (Common law and Civil law)

The majority part of Canadian criminal procedural and substantive law is established by the Criminal Code (a federal statute).[2404] Canadian Criminal Law has its roots in British Common Law, but since the introduction of the Criminal Code in 1892 is has been largely codified.[2405]

Gaps in statutory criminal procedure are filled in by jurisprudence interpreting the Canadian Charter of Rights and Freedoms and common law.[2406] There are three types of offences in Canada: summary conviction offences, hybrid offences, and the most serious ones, which are the indictable offences. Indictable offences include only the most serious crimes, which are punishable by at least 2 years imprisonment, such as murder, rape, and robbery.

Who is in charge of (pre-)investigations?

Canadian Criminal Law foresees a preliminary inquiry.[2407] However, this phase is not to be confused with the ICC's type of preliminary inquiry or pre-investigation. It is rather a special procedure to determine whether there is sufficient evidence to put an accused on trial.[2408]

The police are generally in charge of (pre-)investigations.[2409] During the course of investigations police officers will attempt to obtain evidence for bringing charges. Police forces are generally divided into provincial, municipal, and federal units.

When may activation be triggered? (What is the standard of proof – if any – to start (pre-)investigations?)

Anyone can report incidents involving criminal behavior to the police. Through complaints from citizens or the actual detection of offences, the police usually learn that an offence might have been committed.[2410]

Who takes the decision to start a formal investigation?

The process of moving towards a prosecution lies within the discretion of the police.[2411] The prosecutorial authority is given to the Attorney General (provincial Attorney General for provincial offences, and Attorney General of Canada for other

---

2404 Criminal Code, 1985 (c. C-46), 25.6.2008.

2405 Quigley, *supra* note 1248, 2–8; Kent Roach, "Canada" in Craig Bradely (ed.) *Criminal procedure: a worldwide study,* 2nd edition (Carolina Academic Press, Durham 2007) 57.

2406 Roach, in Bradely, *supra* note 2405, 57.

2407 Part XVIII (Sec.535 et seq.) Criminal Code.

2408 Quigley, *supra* note 1248, 14–1.

2409 Quigley, *supra* note 1248, 1–3.

2410 Quigley, *supra* note 1248, 1–3.

2411 Bureau of Justice Statistics, US Department of Justice, State University of New York at Albany, World factbook of criminal justice systems, Canada, Debra Cohen/Sandra Longtin, "Prosecutorial and judicial process, 2. Procedures."

offences enacted by the Parliament of Canada).[2412] However, the Prosecutors do not initiate or participate in the investigation of crimes. The police further remain independent of the Prosecutor who does not direct the police.[2413]

Is a discretionary evaluation performed before initiating a formal investigation/prosecution, and if so, how is it conducted (level of discretion)?

Both the police and the Prosecution have a great deal of discretion. For instance, the manner in which an investigation is pursued and whether to lay a charge is left to the police, and the decision whether to proceed at all and on what charge is an issue for the Prosecution to determine.[2414] In *R. v. Campell* the Supreme Court acknowledged the independence of the police from the executive to lay charges.[2415] The name for the charges itself is called the "information."[2416] If the police investigate and develop "reasonable grounds," an allegation may be brought to a judge or justice in peace in form of a document ("information"). Section 504 of the Criminal Code states that "*any one* who, on reasonable grounds, believes that a person has committed an indictable offence may lay information in writing and under oath before a justice, and the justice shall receive the information (emph. added)." But in most cases the person, who swears on the information presented to the justice, will be a police officer.[2417] Nevertheless, ordinary citizens could swear in information and launch a prosecution against individuals.[2418] There are situations were little or no guidance for the exercise of discretion is given by legislation or common law.[2419]

The Canadian Prosecutors have wide discretion concerning the commencement of a prosecution and its continuation.[2420]

Under which circumstances can investigations (preliminary and/or full investigation) be dismissed? Are there criteria for dismissal or is the decision fully discretionary? If there are criteria, which are those and how are they defined?

During preliminary and full investigations the police enjoy a large degree of discretion. Generally, the Prosecutor does not have the responsibility for decisions to stop an investigation, although police officers often consult with prosecutors.[2421]

Prosecutions require the consent of the Prosecutor; they are generally within the power of the Crown who underlies no constraint except that it is not within its

---

2412 Patrick Healy, "Canada" in Arbour/Eser/Ambos/Sanders, *supra* note 2388, 245, 245.

2413 Healy, in Arbour/Eser/Ambos/Sanders, *supra* note 2412, 248.

2414 Quigley, *supra* note 1248, 2–11.

2415 Roach, in Bradely, *supra* note 2405, 80; *R. v. Campell* [1999], 22.4.1999 (1 S.C.R. 565) 3.

2416 Quigley, *supra* note 1248, 9–8.

2417 Bureau of Justice Statistics, *supra* note 2411, "Prosecutorial and judicial process, 2. Procedures."

2418 Quigley, *supra* note 1248, 16–4.

2419 Quigley, *supra* note 1248, 16–3.

2420 Healy, in Arbour/Eser/Ambos/Sanders, *supra* note 2412, 247.

2421 Healy, in Arbour/Eser/Ambos/Sanders, *supra* note 2412, 247.

power to grant blanket dispensation.[2422] In other words, the Crown may exercise its discretion and not lay charges in a given case.[2423]

The criterion for dismissal or continuation appears to be fully discretionary. The Supreme Court has not indicated that it might find the Crown guilty of selective prosecutions and order a stay of proceedings. Where the Crown prosecutes some persons, but not others, who have allegedly committed the same offences, injustice might be claimed.[2424] However, the Ontario Court of Appeal held in *R. v. Magder Furs Ltd.*:

> "The mere fact of discrimination in the prosecution of some cases and some defendants is not itself improper. For the selectivity to be constitutionally impermissible, it must fail on both of two standards. First, there must be a showing that others in the same or similar position, or bearing the same or similar characteristics, have not been prosecuted in the same or similar manner. Second, the standard upon which the discrimination is based must itself be impermissible. Discriminations based on race or political affiliation, for example, have been ruled impermissible, but the examples in which the courts have found standards of unfair discrimination are few."[2425]

So far, there has been little litigation under this test, and the only case (*R. v. St. Jean*) that has been successful – and actually stayed the charges based on discrimination – was reversed by the Supreme Court of British Columbia in 1995.[2426] These decisions largely affirm the discretion of the Crown to charge or not to charge and appropriate considerations are *inter alia*:

- sufficient evidence to warrant proceedings;
- whether it is in the public interest to prosecute;
- whether it is necessary to grant immunity to one person in order to obtain his evidence against another.[2427]

Most notably, the terms "sufficient evidence" and "public interest" are used. Both tests are particularly used in common law jurisdictions, and the tests will be outlined in more detail with regard to the report on the United Kingdom (England and Wales).

Is the decision to start/end an investigation/prosecution subject to control by another body?

There are no mechanisms in Canadian law by which a prosecutor could be compelled to initiate a prosecution.[2428] The Supreme Court of Canada has recognized

2422 Quigley, *supra* note 1248, 16–2 with fn. 4, 16–3.

2423 Quigley, *supra* note 1248, 16–4.

2424 Quigley, *supra* note 1248, 16–5.

2425 *R. v. Magder Furs Ltd.* [1989], 4.10.1989 (49 C.C.C. (3d) 267) 282, quoted from *R. v. St. Jean* [1995], 9.11.1995, 1995 CannLII 1427 (BC S.C.) 8.

2426 *R. v. St. Jean* [1995], *supra* note 2425, 12. Thereto Quigley, *supra* note 1248, 16–5.

2427 Quigley, *supra* note 1248, 16–6.

2428 Healy, in Arbour/Eser/Ambos/Sanders, *supra* note 2412, 247.

the independence of prosecutors and the Attorney General in terms of exercise of non-abusive forms of prosecutorial discretion, and denied all-embracing judicial review of discretionary decisions.[2429] Judge L'Heureux-Dubé held:

> "In our system, a judge does not have the authority to tell prosecutors which crimes to prosecute or when to prosecute them."[2430]

Nevertheless, the exercise of discretion is subject to review regarding the Canadian Charter of Rights and Freedoms and the common law doctrine of abuse of process.[2431] Either party may appeal a decision on these grounds; but relatively few complaints have been successful.[2432] Theoretically, however, the Supreme Court has the opportunity to decide – based on an inquiry into the public interest – whether to proceed with prosecutions.[2433] In addition, there exists pre-charge review by the prosecutors *vis-à-vis* the police in some Canadian provinces.[2434]

Conclusion

Prosecutorial discretion is the guiding principle in Canadian criminal law, a typically common law feature. In general, the police enjoy considerable influence of the course of proceedings. The Crown is involved only at a later stage. It is, however, left to the Crown to decide whether to bring charges. Thereby, the criteria "public interest" and "sufficient evidence" play a vital role. Canadian Courts have been very reluctant to get involved into discretionary determinations. It is, though, submitted that judges could intervene if the actors' decisions are based on arbitrary grounds, and if the "public interest" so requires.

III. Cameroon (civil law and common law influence; African family)

Cameroon enacted a new Criminal Procedure Code (*Code de Procédure Pénale*) in July 2005,[2435] and its Penal Code (*Code Penal*) dates back to 1965.[2436]

In Cameroon, similar to French criminal proceedings, there are two procedural phases that could be translated as preliminary inquiries: (1) a preliminary police inquiry (*l'enquête préliminaire*),[2437] and (2) judicial investigations preceding the trial *stricto sensu* (*l'information judiciaire*).[2438] The latter are obligatory in the case of

---

[2429] *R. v. Power* [1994], 14.4.1994 (1 S.C.R. 601).

[2430] *R. v. Power* [1994], *supra* note 2429, 31.

[2431] Roach, in Bradely, *supra* note 2405, 80.

[2432] For an overview see Quigley, *supra* note 1248, 16–15 et seq.

[2433] *R. v. Campell* [1999], *supra* note 2415, 16–7; *R. v. Mack* [1988], 15.12.1988 (2 S.C.R. 903) 6.

[2434] Roach, in Bradely, *supra* note 2405, 80 with fn. 205.

[2435] Code de Procédure Pénale 2005 (loi no. 2005/007), imprinted in loi no. 2005/007 du 27 Juillet 2005 portant code de procedure penale (Sedif, Douala 2005).

[2436] Code Penal de la Republique du Cameroun 1965/1967 (loi no. 65-LF-24 et loi no. 67-LF-1), les editions de l'imprimerie nationale 2001.

[2437] Secs.116 et seq. Code de Procédure Pénale, *supra* note 2435.

[2438] Secs.142 et seq. Code de Procédure Pénale, *supra* note 2435.

felonies and discretionary in the case of misdemeanors.[2439] In any event, solely the police inquiry comes close to a pre-investigation in the strict sense.

Who is in charge of (pre-)investigations?

The judicial police (*police judiciaire*) acts under supervision of the district prosecutor (*procureur de la République*).[2440] It is in charge of investigating offences, collecting evidence, identifying possible other persons involved, and bringing the case before the Legal Department.[2441] Moreover, the police conduct preliminary inquiries.[2442] Only in the case of a felony committed *flagrante delicto* the district prosecutor has the right to carry out the investigation when he arrives at the scene of commission of the offence.[2443]

What triggers the initiation of a (pre-)investigation? (What is the standard of proof – if any – to start (pre-)investigations?)

The mandate of the judicial police embraces receiving complaints and reports against persons (*plainte et dénonciations*).[2444] Any person, who has gained knowledge of an offence classified as a felony or misdemeanor, shall directly and immediately inform either the district prosecutor or the police.[2445] Matters brought to the attention of the public prosecutor can be in writing or oral.[2446]

Who takes the decision to start a formal investigation?

Investigations are carried out on their own by the judicial police officers and agents, or on the institutions of the district prosecutor.[2447] It is, however, the district prosecutor who directs and controls the operations of the police.[2448] At the closure of the investigation the police officer shall inform the district prosecutor of the offences he gained knowledge of.[2449]

Is a discretionary evaluation performed before initiating a formal investigation/prosecution, and if so, how is it conducted (level of discretion)?

During investigations the district prosecutor takes all major decisions. He may refer information and complaints to the police, return a case file for further investigation, decide to close a matter, or decide to initiate criminal proceedings.[2450]

2439 Sec.142 (1), (2) Code de Procédure Pénale, *supra* note 2435.

2440 Sec.78 (1) Code de Procédure Pénale, *supra* note 2435. It needs to be clarified that throughout the survey the French term *procureur de la République* is translated as district prosecutor, whereas the term *procureur général* is translated as chief public prosecutor.

2441 Sec.82 a) Code de Procédure Pénale, *supra* note 2435.

2442 Secs.83 (1), 116 et seq. Code de Procédure Pénale, *supra* note 2435.

2443 Sec.111 Code de Procédure Pénale, *supra* note 2435.

2444 Sec.83 (1) Code de Procédure Pénale, *supra* note 2435.

2445 Sec.135 (2) Code de Procédure Pénale, *supra* note 2435.

2446 Sec.135 (1) Code de Procédure Pénale, *supra* note 2435.

2447 Sec.116 (1) Code de Procédure Pénale, *supra* note 2435.

2448 Sec.137 (1) Code de Procédure Pénale, *supra* note 2435.

2449 Sec.89 (1) Code de Procédure Pénale, *supra* note 2435.

Under section 134 (1) of the *Code de Procédure Pénale* the public prosecutor has the authority to intervene and instruct prosecutors within his department. He can order his subordinates to investigate offences, halt activities, or institute proceedings. The code does not clarify the basis on which district and public prosecutors reach their decisions, and it appears that these decisions are within their discretion. For prosecutions the issue depends on the severity of the offence. In the case of a felony committed *flagrante delicto* a judicial investigation required prior to bringing charges.[2451] The investigating judge (*Judge d'instruction*) then decides whether to bring the case to trial or to give a no case ruling, based on an evaluation of the facts.[2452]

Under which circumstances can investigations (preliminary and/or full investigation) be dismissed? Are there criteria for dismissal or is the decision fully discretionary? If there are criteria, which are those and how are they defined?

Exceptionally, the district prosecutor may stop a police officer from continuing the investigation, and shall inform the officer's immediate superior of the reasons for doing so.[2453] Moreover, the district prosecutor may decide to close the matter upon investigation and inform the complainant of his decision. In the latter scenario the decision closing the file must be forwarded to the chief public prosecutor (*procureur général*).[2454]

Section 62 of the *Code de Procédure Pénale* further enumerates common circumstances under which criminal proceedings shall be discontinued, for example, the death of the suspect, the defendant or of the accused, prescription, amnesty, repeal of law, an agreement between the parties if allowed for, or the withdrawal of a complaint.[2455] Moreover, the public prosecutor of a Court of Appeal can intervene and stop proceedings at any stage before the judgment if the social interest or public order (*l'intérêt social ou la paix publique*) so requires.[2456] In the special case of a judicial investigation it is left to the investigating judge to dismiss a case if he is not satisfied of the facts underlying the alleged offence.

Is the decision to start/end an investigation/prosecution subject to control by another body?

The public prosecutor shall supervise the police and prosecutors within the department of his jurisdiction.[2457] He can therefore check the activities performed by them, including decisions to start investigations or to halt proceedings. Judicial investigations can be re-opened if new evidence or facts come to light, or they can be appealed before the *Chambre de Contrôle de l'Instruction*.[2458]

[2450] Sec.141 Code de Procédure Pénale, *supra* note 2435.

[2451] Sec.112 Code de Procédure Pénale, *supra* note 2435.

[2452] Sec.256 Code de Procédure Pénale, *supra* note 2435.

[2453] Sec.83 (5) Code de Procédure Pénale, *supra* note 2435.

[2454] Sec.141 (c) Code de Procédure Pénale, *supra* note 2435.

[2455] See in more detail sec.62 Code de Procédure Pénale, *supra* note 2435.

[2456] Sec.65 (1) Code de Procédure Pénale, *supra* note 2435.

[2457] Secs.133 and 134 Code de Procédure Pénale, *supra* note 2435.

Conclusion

Cameroon has a relatively new procedural code, based largely on French criminal procedural law. Pre-investigations and investigations are conducted by the police. But it is the district prosecutor who is in charge of any important decision. The public prosecutor apparently enjoys the largest margin of discretion; he may even intervene at any stage before the judgment, flanked by the broad notions of social interest and public order.

IV. China (Chinese law)

Chinese criminal law is codified in the Criminal Law and the Criminal Procedure Law of the People's Republic of China.[2459] The actors in China are the police, procuratorates, courts, and correctional institutions.[2460]

Who is in charge of (pre-)investigations?

The public security organs (equivalent to the police in most countries) are primarily responsible for preliminary inquiries (*yushen*) and investigations (*zhencha*).[2461] Moreover, there is a prosecution service that is divided into four levels: the Supreme People's Procuratorate; the people's procuratorates of provinces, autonomous regions, and municipalities; the branches of the people's procuratorates, and people's autonomous prefecture cities; and the people's procuratorates of counties, cities, autonomous counties, and municipal districts.[2462] At a later stage, the people's courts are responsible for adjudication.[2463]

When may activation be triggered? (What is the standard of proof – if any – to start (pre-)investigations?)

Any unit or individual has the right and the duty to make a report to a public security organ, a People's Procuratorate, or a People's Court.[2464] A victim has the right to report if his personal or property rights are infringed upon.[2465] All reports, complaints, and information shall be accepted and filed in writing or orally.[2466] All

[2458] Secs.265 and 267 Code de Procédure Pénale, *supra* note 2435.

[2459] Criminal Law of the People's Republic of China, 14.3.1997; Criminal Procedure Law of the People's Republic of China, 1.1.1997.

[2460] Bureau of Justice Statistics, US Department of Justice, State University of New York at Albany, World factbook of criminal justice systems, China, Jianan Guo/Guo Xiang/Wu Zongxian/et al., "General overview, 1. Political system."

[2461] Articles 3, 18 (1), and 89 Criminal Procedure Law, *supra* note 2459.

[2462] Feng Ye, "People's Republic of China" in Arbour/Eser/Ambos/Sanders, *supra* note 2388, 257, 257.

[2463] World factbook, China, *supra* note 2460, "General overview. 2. Legal system."

[2464] Article 84 (1) Criminal Procedure Law, *supra* note 2459.

[2465] Article 84 (2) Criminal Procedure Law, *supra* note 2459.

[2466] Article 84 (3), (5) Criminal Procedure Law, *supra* note 2459.

three entities (security organ, Procuratorate, and People's Court) shall file a case if they believe that there are "facts of a crime and criminal responsibility should be investigated."[2467] If they decide the other way around, the complainant needs to be notified of the reason, and he or she may ask for reconsideration.[2468]

Who takes the decision to start a formal investigation?

In general, the police carry out investigations and enjoy a large deal of discretion for initial action.[2469] Upon discovery of facts, cases can further be filed for investigations by the public security organs or the People's Procurator.[2470]

Is a discretionary evaluation performed before initiating a formal investigation/prosecution, and if so, how is it conducted (level of discretion)?

Article 86 (1) of the Chinese Criminal Procedure Law obliges the police to start investigations if a crime has presumably been committed. After investigating a crime the police draft a report, either recommending prosecution or exemption from prosecution. The draft, any case file materials and the evidence are then transferred to a procuratorate at the same level for review who makes a decision on whether to prosecute.[2471] The newly introduced articles 141 and 142 Chinese Criminal Procedure Law strengthen the principle of legality, while doing away with the former article 101 Chinese Criminal Procedure Law that allowed the prosecution division to abstain from bringing charges (*mianyu qisu*).[2472] Moreover, the Prosecution is under an obligation to initiate public prosecution in a People's Court if "the facts of a criminal suspect's crime have been ascertained" and the evidence is "reliable and sufficient."[2473]

Under which circumstances can investigations (preliminary and/or full investigation) be dismissed? Are there criteria for dismissal or is the decision fully discretionary? If there are criteria, which are those and how are they defined?

First of all, article 15 (1) Chinese Criminal Procedure Law concerns circumstances under which no investigation shall be performed, mainly because the act in question is not considered a crime. Article 142 (1) Chinese Criminal Procedure Law provides that in such cases a decision not to initiate a prosecution shall be made by the Prosecution. Article 142 (2) Chinese Criminal Procedure Law further gives the Prosecution a large deal of discretion ("may decide not to initiate") regarding minor offences.

[2467] Article 86 Criminal Procedure Law, *supra* note 2459.

[2468] Article 86 Criminal Procedure Law, *supra* note 2459.

[2469] World factbook, China, *supra* note 2460, "Police. 5. Discretion."

[2470] Article 83 Criminal Procedure Law, *supra* note 2459.

[2471] World factbook, China, *supra* note 2460, "Prosecutorial and judicial process. 2. Procedures."

[2472] Heuser/Weigend, *supra* note 10, 24–5. On the old article 101 see Ye, in Arbour/Eser/Ambos/Sanders, *supra* note 2462, 259.

[2473] Article 141 Criminal Procedure Law, *supra* note 2459; also Heuser/Weigend, *supra* note 10, 58.

Is the decision to start/end an investigation/prosecution subject to control by another body?

The Prosecution can request the security organ to state the reasons for not filing a case, and if the reasons are untenable it can notify the organ to bring the case.[2474] On the other hand, the security organ can – if it transferred a case to the Procurator and a prosecution was not initiated – demand reconsideration and may submit the case to the next higher level.[2475]

Conclusion

In China the police organs generally control pre- and full investigations. The Prosecution, however, is in charge of the decision to initiate a public prosecution. While the reform of 1996 introduced a shift towards the principle of legality through articles 141 and 142 Chinese Criminal Procedure Law, it left untouched the Prosecution's discretion regarding minor offences.

V. Colombia (Civil law, Romanistic family, potential situation country)

Colombian law goes back to civil law tradition and the Romanistic family. Moreover, the country's situation is under pre-investigation by the ICC. Colombia's penal law was redrafted in 2000, leading to the New Penal Code (*Nuevo Código Penal*),[2476] and the New Criminal Procedure Code (*Nuevo Código de Procedimiento Penal*) was adopted in 2004.[2477] Most important, some accusatorial elements were included through the reforms, for example, the principle of opportunity is now specifically mentioned in the Constitution and the New Criminal Procedure Code.[2478]

Who is in charge of (pre-)investigations?

The Chief Prosecutor's Office (*Fiscalía General de la Nación*) is in charge of investigative activities. The Chief Prosecutor directs, coordinates, and supervises the judicial police.[2479] The Prosecutor's Office is responsible to investigate and to charge perpetrators.[2480] The judicial police (*policía judicial*) thereby assist the Chief Prosecutor and support any investigative activity.[2481]

2474 Article 87 Criminal Procedure Law, *supra* note 2459.

2475 Article 144 Criminal Procedure Law, *supra* note 2459.

2476 Nuevo Código Penal, 24.7.2000, ley no. 599 de 2000, in Alejandro Bañol Betancur, Nuevos código penal y código de procedimiento penal (Libreria juridica, Medellín 2003).

2477 Nuevo Código de Procedimiento Penal, 31.8.2004, ley no. 906 de 2004.

2478 Article 250 (1) Constitución Política de Colombia 1991, edición agosto, 2005; articles 321 et seq. Nuevo Código de Procedimiento Penal, *supra* note 2477.

2479 Articles 117, 200 (2) Nuevo Código de Procedimiento Penal, *supra* note 2477.

2480 Article 114 No. 1 Nuevo Código de Procedimiento Penal, *supra* note 2477.

2481 Article 200 (3) Nuevo Código de Procedimiento Penal, *supra* note 2477.

What triggers the initiation of a (pre-)investigation? (What is the standard of proof – if any – to start (pre-)investigations?)

The Chief Prosecutor may start investigations based on his power *ex officio* (*de oficio*), or upon reports (*denuncia*), special petitions (*petición especial*), complaints (*querella*), or any other adequate medium (*cualquier otro medio idóneo*).[2482] Reports, complaints, or other information may also be presented to the judicial police that can arrange for preliminary inquiries.[2483]

In general, crimes must be reported by all natural persons, but some exceptions are regulated by the strict duty to give notice.[2484] Complaints, on the other hand, can only be filed by a limited group of people, and the Chief Prosecutor himself may do so only in the case of affairs of public interest.[2485] Some crimes even require a mandatory filing of a complaint in order to be admitted for criminal proceedings at all.[2486] Special petitions can be brought solely by the Chief Prosecutor as they concern crimes committed abroad.[2487] Furthermore, reports, complaints, and petitions must be made in writing, orally, or by any other technical medium that allows for identification of the author.[2488]

Who takes the decision to start a formal investigation?

The Chief Prosecutor's Office (*Fiscalía General de la Nación*) is under a general obligation to investigate crimes.[2489] If the judicial police initiate proceedings, it must inform the competent prosecutor of their results.[2490] The Prosecutor must evaluate whether the facts that are brought to his knowledge amount to a crime.[2491] He decides whether or not to approve the investigative acts and he coordinates further investigations.[2492] For the latter purpose the Prosecutor develops an investigation plan that he presents to the judicial police.[2493]

Is a discretionary evaluation performed before initiating a formal investigation/prosecution, and if so, how is it conducted (level of discretion)?

The Chief Prosecutor is under a duty to prosecute (principle of legality), unless one of the specifically regulated statutory grounds of opportunity apply.[2494] The

---

2482 Articles 66, 200 (1) Nuevo Código de Procedimiento Penal, *supra* note 2477; article 250 (1) Constitución Política de Colombia 1991, *supra* note 2478.

2483 Article 205 (1) Nuevo Código de Procedimiento Penal, *supra* note 2477.

2484 Articles 67 and 68 Nuevo Código de Procedimiento Penal, *supra* note 2477.

2485 Article 71 Nuevo Código de Procedimiento Penal, *supra* note 2477.

2486 Article 74 Nuevo Código de Procedimiento Penal, *supra* note 2477.

2487 Article 75 Nuevo Código de Procedimiento Penal, *supra* note 2477.

2488 Article 69 (1) Nuevo Código de Procedimiento Penal, *supra* note 2477.

2489 Article 66 Nuevo Código de Procedimiento Penal, *supra* note 2477.

2490 Article 205 (4) Nuevo Código de Procedimiento Penal, *supra* note 2477.

2491 Article 79 Nuevo Código de Procedimiento Penal, *supra* note 2477.

2492 Article 207 (1) Nuevo Código de Procedimiento Penal, *supra* note 2477.

2493 Article 207 (2), (3) Nuevo Código de Procedimiento Penal, *supra* note 2477.

2494 Article 322 Nuevo Código de Procedimiento Penal, *supra* note 2477.

Chief Prosecutor may suspend, interrupt, or abstain from prosecution (*suspender, interrumpir o renunciar a la persecución penal*) based on certain opportunity grounds regulated in the New Criminal Procedure Code.[2495] Given the mentioned general duty to investigate and prosecute, there is a strong presumption that at least some action on behalf of the prosecutor must be taken before discontinuation based on opportunity grounds can be applied.

Under which circumstances can investigations (preliminary and/or full investigation) be dismissed? Are there criteria for dismissal or is the decision fully discretionary? If there are criteria, which are those and how are they defined?

The Prosecutor is responsible for bringing a person on trial. Within 30 days after formulating the allegations the Prosecutor must bring an indictment (*formular la acusación*), request closure of proceedings (*solicitar la preclusión*), or apply opportunity grounds (*aplicar el principio de oportunidad*).[2496] A request for closure (*la preclusion*) must be submitted for approval by a judge. Such a request is submitted by the Prosecution in cases where only insufficient evidence supporting the allegations was found.[2497]

Coming to the opportunity principle, articles 321–330 of the New Criminal Procedure Code spell out the exact procedure. In particular, article 324 of the New Criminal Procedure Code mentions several grounds for discontinuation:

(1) if the penalty for the crime does not exceed six years, the victim has obtained reparations, and there are no interests of the State in pursuing an investigation;

(2) if the person has been extradited for the same conduct;

(3) if the person has been extradited to the ICC for the same conduct;

[...]

(8) in the case of suspension due to restorative justice, and if the perpetrator complied with the imposed conditions;

(9) if the external security of the State is at risk;

[...]

(15) if the prosecution of a crime brings about significant social troubles, and if there are adequate alternative resolutions for victims;

(16) if the prosecution is very difficult and entails many obstacles, and if there are other crimes for investigation which are of more relevance to society;

[...].[2498]

2495 Articles 114 No. 2 and 323 Nuevo Código de Procedimiento Penal, *supra* note 2477.

2496 Article 175 (1) Nuevo Código de Procedimiento Penal, *supra* note 2477.

2497 Article 331 Nuevo Código de Procedimiento Penal, *supra* note 2477. For the specific grounds see further article 332 *ibid.*

2498 Article 324 Nuevo Código de Procedimiento Penal, *supra* note 2477.

Most important, paragraphs 1–3 regulate clear cases when the opportunity principle cannot be applied. First of all, grounds 15 and 16 (mentioned above) cannot be used to exempt superiors from criminal liability (*los jefes, organizadores o promotores, o a quienes hayan suministrado elementos para su realización*).[2499] Second, crimes exceeding a penalty of six years must be left to the decision of the Chief Prosecutor or a specifically appointed chairman.[2500] Third, opportunity deliberations cannot be taken into account at all if the facts amount to grave violations of international humanitarian law, crimes against humanity, or genocide as spelled out in the ICC Statute, as well as with regard to crimes of drug-trafficking and terrorism (*violaciones graves al derecho internacional humanitario, crímenes de lesa humanidad o genocidio de acuerdo con lo dispuesto en el Estatuto de Roma, y delitos de narcotráfico y terrorismo*).[2501]

A suspension of proceedings can further be conditional and temporary, thus depends on the adherence to imposed conditions.[2502] Moreover, the Prosecutor is obliged to take into account the interests of victims for any decision based on the opportunity principle.[2503]

Is the decision to start/end an investigation/prosecution subject to control by another body?

If the Prosecutor does not make a decision in accordance with article 175 (1) of the New Criminal Procedure Code, the superior must assign the case to a new prosecutor who must decide within a new period of 30 days; if again no decision is taken, the suspect must be released and the proceedings will be closed.[2504]

Regarding the opportunity principle, judicial control is introduced through a special judge (*juez de control de garantías*), who may approve the Prosecutor's opportunity decisions and thereby end all criminal proceedings.[2505] There can be a special hearing on the issue with the victims and the Public Ministry, but any final negative decision by the judge cannot be appealed (*El juez resolverá de plano y contra esta determinación no procede recurso alguno*).[2506]

Conclusion

Colombian criminal procedure has experienced several reforms in the last years (in particular in 2000 and 2004). Most noticeable, the opportunity principle was included and specific grounds for its application were drafted. The basic methodology is similar to the ICC Statute: first, mandatory investigation and prosecution is pre-

---

2499 Article 324 (1) Nuevo Código de Procedimiento Penal, *supra* note 2477.

2500 Article 324 (2) Nuevo Código de Procedimiento Penal, *supra* note 2477.

2501 Article 324 (3) Nuevo Código de Procedimiento Penal, *supra* note 2477.

2502 Articles 325 and 326 Nuevo Código de Procedimiento Penal, *supra* note 2477.

2503 Article 328 Nuevo Código de Procedimiento Penal, *supra* note 2477.

2504 Article 294 Nuevo Código de Procedimiento Penal, *supra* note 2477.

2505 Article 327 (1) Nuevo Código de Procedimiento Penal, *supra* note 2477.

2506 Article 327 (2) Nuevo Código de Procedimiento Penal, *supra* note 2477.

sumed; second, reasons that allow for discontinuation are incorporated. Colombia's system further foresees that victims have to be heard, and a special judge (*juez de control de garantías*) controls the prosecutor's decisions to a certain extent. Practice will show if the balance between prosecutorial independence and opportunity *vis-à-vis* judicial control is well arranged.

VI. Côte d'Ivoire (Civil law, Romanistic family, African family, situation country)

Côte d'Ivoire's legal system is based on French civil law and customary law. Its criminal law is codified in the *Code Pénal* (Penal Code)[2507] and the *Code de Procédure Pénale* (Code of Criminal Procedure).[2508] The upcoming survey is solely based on the version of 1962 of the latter *Code de Procédure Pénale,* and therefore has limited value only.

Who is in charge of (pre-)investigations?

The judicial police (*police judiciaire*) investigate alleged crimes.[2509] Police officers and police agents generally carry out the functions of the judicial police.[2510] On the one hand, pre-investigations (*enquêtes préliminaires*) are executed by the police officers.[2511] On the other hand, the district prosecutor (*procureuer de la République*) gives instructions for any activities.[2512] Moreover, the police are under supervision of the Minister of Justice (*garde de Sceaux*), the Chief Public Prosecutor (*procureuer général*), and the accusation chamber (*chambre d'accusation*).[2513]

What triggers the initiation of a (pre-)investigation? (What is the standard of proof – if any – to start (pre-)investigations?)

Police officers may receive complaints and denunciations (*plaintes et dénonciations*).[2514] Based on these allegations they start pre-investigations, yet they must inform the disctrict prosecutor (*procureur de la République*) of all potential crimes they gain knowledge of.[2515] The district prosecutors may further evaluate notice themselves, received directly through complaints and denunciations.[2516]

2507 Code Pénal (Penal Code), 31.7.1981 (loi no. 1981-640), modifiée par la loi no. 1995-522 du 6 juillet 1995.

2508 Code de Procédure Pénale, 14.11.1960 (loi no. 60–366), modifiée par la loi no. 62–231 du 29 juin 1962, in: Jean-Bernard Blaise/Jacques Mourgeon (eds.), *Lois er décrets de Côte-d'Ivoire* (Librairies techniques, Paris 1970).

2509 Article 14 Code de Procédure Pénale, *supra* note 2508.

2510 Article 15 Code de Procédure Pénale, *supra* note 2508.

2511 Articles 17, 74–76 Code de Procédure Pénale, *supra* note 2508.

2512 Article 74 Code de Procédure Pénale, *supra* note 2508.

2513 Articles 13 and 74 Code de Procédure Pénale, *supra* note 2508.

2514 Articles 17, 74–76 Code de Procédure Pénale, *supra* note 2508.

2515 Article 19 Code de Procédure Pénale, *supra* note 2508.

2516 Article 40 Code de Procédure Pénale, *supra* note 2508.

Different investigations take place if someone is caught in the act *(enquête de flagrance)*.[2517]

Who takes the decision to start a formal investigation?

The Chief Public Prosecutor (*procureur général*) has the competence with regard to penal law on the territory of the Côte d'Ivoire, and assigns budgets to the district prosecutors (*procureurs de la République*).[2518] Each district prosecutor holds the power to discover alleged crimes and to continue proceedings in his department.[2519]

Similar to French law the Criminal Procedural Law in Côte d'Ivoire distinguishes between *contraventions* (petty offences), *délits* (misdemeanors), and *crimes* (felonies). For the latter (*crimes*) proceedings by an investigative judge (*juge d'instruction*) are obligatory.[2520]

Is a discretionary evaluation performed before initiating a formal investigation/ prosecution, and if so, how is it conducted (level of discretion)?

It appears that the decision to start investigations is vested with the judicial police and the district prosecutor. District prosecutors can continue with any action they deem necessary, and may direct the officers and agents of the police in their department.[2521]

With regard to commencing prosecutions the investigative judge and the Chief Public Prosecutor have important roles. After investigation has been terminated, the investigative judge asks the Chief Public Prosecutor for his requisition.[2522] The judge must then decide if there are sufficiently proven charges against the accused to continue criminal proceedings.[2523]

Under which circumstances can investigations (preliminary and/or full investigation) be dismissed? Are there criteria for dismissal or is the decision fully discretionary? If there are criteria, which are those and how are they defined?

The investigative judge must examine whether there are grounds to bring charges against the accused: if the facts do not constitute a felony, misdemeanor, or petty offence, or the perpetrator remains unknown, or there are not sufficient charges against the accused, then the judge orders to discontinue proceedings.[2524] On the other hand, if the judge comes to the conclusion that the facts amount to a felony, he orders the handover of the dossier from the district prosecutor to the Chief Pub-

---

2517 Articles 53 et seq. Code de Procédure Pénale, *supra* note 2508.

2518 Article 38 Code de Procédure Pénale, *supra* note 2508.

2519 Article 46 Code de Procédure Pénale, *supra* note 2508.

2520 Article 77 Code de Procédure Pénale, *supra* note 2508.

2521 Article 41 Code de Procédure Pénale, *supra* note 2508.

2522 Article 175 Code de Procédure Pénale, *supra* note 2508.

2523 Articles 176 et seq. Code de Procédure Pénale, *supra* note 2508.

2524 Articles 176 and 177 Code de Procédure Pénale, *supra* note 2508. For the later stage before the accusation chamber (*d'instruction du second degré*) see article 212 *ibid.*

lic Prosecutor for further proceedings before the Higher Courts (*chambre d'accusation*).[2525] Lower courts deal with petty offences (*tribunal de simple police*) and misdemeanors (*tribunal correctionnel*).[2526]

Is the decision to start/end an investigation/prosecution subject to control by another body?

The Chief Public Prosecutor (*procureuer général*) exercises oversight regarding the judicial police.[2527] In turn, the accusation chamber (*chambre d'accusation*) may exercise judicial control over the police and the Chief Public Prosecutor (*procureuer général*).[2528]

Against any order by the investigative judge an appeal by the district prosecutors is possible.[2529]

Conclusion

The old Criminal Procedure Code of the Côte d'Ivoire resembles the French Code in many aspects. Especially, the disparity between felonies, misdemeanors, and petty offences governs further proceedings. No specific discretionary rule could be found that gives the Prosecutor or the investigative judge a right to discontinue based on expediency deliberations. Therefore, Côte d'Ivoire's legal system follows the principle of mandatory prosecution. It remains to be seen what influence the ICC and on-going pre-investigations with regard to Côte d'Ivoire have on potential reforms on the criminal justice system in the country.

VII. Democratic Republic of Congo (Civil law, Romanistic family, African family, situation country)

The DRC constitutes one of the pending situations before the ICC. It is a civil law country, its codes are primarily based on Belgian law, but some customary law found its way into the current legal system.[2530] Congolese substantive criminal law is basically set out in the *Code Pénal Congolais* of 1940.[2531] However, unlike Belgian and French law, Congolese criminal law does not differentiate between felonies (*crimes*), misdemeanors (*délits*), and contraventions (*contraventions*).[2532] The crim-

2525 Article 181 Code de Procédure Pénale, *supra* note 2508.

2526 Articles 178, 179, 213, 370 et seq., and 514 et seq. Code de Procédure Pénale, *supra* note 2508.

2527 Articles 224–230 Code de Procédure Pénale, *supra* note 2508.

2528 Articles 224–230 Code de Procédure Pénale, *supra* note 2508.

2529 Article 185 Code de Procédure Pénale, *supra* note 2508.

2530 NYU School of Law, GlobaLex, "The legal system and research of the Democratic Republic of Congo (DRC): an overview," Dunia Zongwe/Francois Butedi/Clement Phebe, December 2007, 2.

2531 Code Pénal Congolais (Penal Code), 30.1.1940. See further the Code pénal militaire (Penal Code for the Military), 18.11.2002, loi no. 023–2002 du 18 novembre 2002 portant Code judiciaire militaire.

2532 NYU School of Law, GlobaLex, DRC, *supra* note 2530, 2.4.1.

inal procedural law of the DRC is laid down in the *Code de Procédure Pénal* (Code of Criminal Procedure),[2533] and the follow-up analysis in based on the cited version of 1999 only.

Who is in charge of (pre-)investigations?

The judicial police (*police judiciaire*) are competent to investigate alleged crimes.[2534] They act under supervision of the Secretary of Justice[2535] and the Public Prosecution Service (*ministère public*).[2536] The Chief Public Prosecutor (*Procureur général de le République*) acts on behalf of the Secretary of Justice and the Public Prosecution Service.[2537]

Moreover, the judicial police are composed of police officers (*les officiers de police judiciaire*) and police agents (*les agents de police judiciaire*).[2538]

What triggers the initiation of a (pre-)investigation? (What is the standard of proof – if any – to start (pre-)investigations?)

A preliminary investigation is triggered through denunciations (*dénonciations*), complaints (*plaintes*), and reports (*rapports*).[2539] Preliminary inquiries are carried out by the police officers, either upon instruction of the Public Prosecution Service (*ministère public*), or on its own initiative, or upon complaints and denunciations (*plaint ou dénonciation d'un justiciable*).

A different type of investigation takes place if a crime is about to be committed or has just been committed *(enquête de flagrance)*. The police officer has more competences in such a scenario and he is able to react in a speedy manner.[2540]

Who takes the decision to start a formal investigation?

Investigations are generally carried out by the judicial police and aim at discovering the nature of the crime, the circumstances and manner in which it was com-

---

2533 Code de Procédure Pénale, 6.8.1959, in Jean Jacques Yoka Mampunga (ed.), *Codes Congolais de Procédure Pénale* (Editions Yoka, Kinshasa 1999).

2534 Article 2 Code de Procédure Pénale, *supra* note 2533.

2535 Article 1 Police Judiciaire, 3.7.1978, in Jean Jacques Yoka Mampunga (ed.), *Codes Congolais de Procédure Pénale* (Editions Yoka, Kinsahasa 1999).

2536 Article 6 Code de l'organisation et de la compétence judiciaires, 1.4.1982, in Jean Jacques Yoka Mampunga (ed.), *Codes Congolais de Procédure Pénale* (Editions Yoka, Kinshasa 1999).

2537 Article 12 Code de l'organisation et de la compétence judiciaires, *supra* note 2536. On the organization of the Congolese Prosecution Service see further articles 73 et seq. of the Règlement Intérieur des Cours, Tribunaux et Parquets, 20.8.1979, in Jean Jacques Yoka Mampunga (ed.), *Codes Congolais de Procédure Pénale* (Editions Yoka, Kinshasa 1999).

2538 Article 4 Police Judiciaire, *supra* note 2535.

2539 Article 2 Code de Procédure Pénale, *supra* note 2533.

2540 Articles 5 et seq. Code de Procédure Pénale, *supra* note 2533; articles 82 et seq. Police Judiciaire, *supra* note 2535.

mitted, the time and location it took place, and the identity of the perpetrators.[2541] The Prosecutors of the Public Prosecution Service can take over any activities from the judicial police if necessary.[2542]

Is a discretionary evaluation performed before initiating a formal investigation/prosecution, and if so, how is it conducted (level of discretion)?

With regard to court proceedings the Code of Criminal Procedure only states that the Public Prosecutor decides whether or not to bring charges ([...] *le ministère public décide d'exercer l'action publique,* [...]).[2543] However, it does not specify the relevant criteria. Internal regulations mention that any decision whether to prosecute or not is the sole domain of the Public Prosecution Service.[2544] As a matter of principle, the Public Prosecutor presents his perceptions and applies a notation to end evidence gathering.[2545] On the other hand, an investigative judge (*magistrate-instructeur*) plays a role at the very end of the inquiry as he also attaches a note with his classification to the dossier.[2546]

Under which circumstances can investigations (preliminary and/or full investigation) be dismissed? Are there criteria for dismissal or is the decision fully discretionary? If there are criteria, which are those and how are they defined?

No specific regulatory norms could be found referring to the dismissal of investigations and/or prosecutions. There is a strong presumption that such decisions are left to the discretion of the Public Prosecution Service, depending on the position within the hierarchical structure of the agency.

Is the decision to start/end an investigation/prosecution subject to control by another body?

As mentioned above, the judicial police are under the supervision of the Public Prosecution Service (*le ministère public*).[2547] Moreover, the Public Prosecution Service has internal checks to reveal any inconsistencies.[2548] No particular norm regarding judicial checks and balances could be found in the procedural codes.

[2541] Article 34 Police Judiciaire, *supra* note 2535.

[2542] Article 11 Code de Procédure Pénale, *supra* note 2533.

[2543] Article 53 Code de Procédure Pénale, *supra* note 2533.

[2544] Article 142 Règlement Intérieur des Cours, Tribunaux et Parquets, *supra* note 2537.

[2545] Article 143 Règlement Intérieur des Cours, Tribunaux et Parquets, *supra* note 2537.

[2546] Article 146 Règlement Intérieur des Cours, Tribunaux et Parquets, *supra* note 2537.

[2547] Article 6 Code de l'organisation et de la compétence judiciaires, *supra* note 2536.

[2548] See, for example, articles 81 and 122 of the Règlement Intérieur des Cours, Tribunaux et Parquets, *supra* note 2537.

Conclusion

Criminal procedure in the DRC resembles Belgian and French law in some aspects, but also shows specific characteristics. The DRC provides for a complex, hierarchical Public Prosecution Service, which would require more in-depth research to understand its practical functioning. For reforms of the current criminal justice system it appears advisable to include specific norms in the *Code de Procédure Pénale* dealing with the commencement and dismissal of prosecutions. Explicit criteria for the latter decisions should be included. For the sake of clarity it is even recommended to draft one provision that covers the decision whether or not to start prosecutions, integrating a judicial control mechanism, similar to article 53 ICC Statute.

VIII. France (Civil law, Romanistic family)

Two texts generate French Criminal law: the *Code Pénal* (Penal Code) and the *Code de Procédure Pénale* (Code of Criminal Procedure).[2549] The *Code Pénal* is the third criminal codification in French history.[2550] Further, there has been a major reform on the *Code de Procédure Pénale* in 2000.[2551] In France there are two procedural phases preceding trial: (1) a preliminary police inquiry (*l'enquête préliminaire*),[2552] and (2) a judicial investigations (*l'instruction*).[2553] The French penal system distinguishes *contraventions* (petty offences), *délits* (misdemeanors), and *crimes* (felonies).

Who is in charge of (pre-)investigations?

The judicial police are in charge with the task of discovering violations of the criminal law, of gathering evidence of such violations, and of identifying their perpetrators until a full investigation is opened (*constater les infractions à la loi pénale, d'en rassembler les preuves et d'en rechercher les auteurs tant qu'une information n'est pas ouverte*).[2554] They proceed with preliminary inquiries either upon

---

2549 Code Pénal (Penal Code), 30.7.2008; for the current French version see Code Pénal, Yves Mayaud/Emanuelle Allain/Carole Gayet (eds.), 105th edition (Édition Dalloz, Paris 2008); Code de Procédure Pénale (Code of Criminal Procedure), 12.12.2005; for the current French version see Code de Procédure Pénale, Jean-François Renucci/Emanuelle Allain/Carole Gayet (eds.), 49th edition (Édition Dalloz, Paris 2008).

2550 On the history of French Criminal Law see Sophie Clavier, *Perspectives on French Criminal Law,* July 1997, 4 et seq.; Zweigert/Kötz, *supra* note 112, 74 et seq.

2551 See Jean Cédras, "France" in Arbour/Eser/Ambos/Sanders, *supra* note 2388, 323, 323 et seq., who outlines the old procedure and already incorporates the new proposals.

2552 Secs.75–78 Code de Procédure Pénale, *supra* note 2549.

2553 Chapter I, Sec.11 et seq., Chapter III, Secs.79 et seq. Code de Procédure Pénale, *supra* note 2549.

2554 Sec.14 Code de Procédure Pénale, *supra* note 2549.

the instructions of the District Prosecutor (*procureur de la République*), or on their own initiative, but under the supervision of the Chief Public Prosecutor (*procureur général*).[2555] The judicial police embrace (1) the judicial police officers, (2) the judicial police agents and assistant judicial police agents, and (3) the civil servants and agents to whom the law assigns certain judicial police functions.[2556] The District Prosecutor has overall responsibility for the formal investigation.[2557]

What triggers the initiation of a (pre-)investigation? (What is the standard of proof – if any – to start (pre-)investigations?)

A preliminary investigation by the judicial police takes place either upon the instructions of the District Prosecutor, or on their own initiative.[2558] Complaints (*plainte*) by victims of an offence trigger action of the judicial police.[2559] Moreover, the District Prosecutor (*procureur de la République*) receives complaints and denunciations and decides how to deal with them.[2560] It is also the District Prosecutor who sets a time-table for the inquiry. In the case of an inquiry on the initiative of the judicial police, the police officer must report to the District Prosecutor after six months.[2561] Another type of investigation *(enquête de flagrance)* takes place if a felony or misdemeanor is in the course of being committed or has just been committed. Police officers can investigate flagrant offences up to eight days.[2562]

Who takes the decision to start a formal investigation?

The District Prosecutor (*procureur de la République*) directs the activities during investigations,[2563] and he decides the course of action on the basis of the principle of opportunity (*décide s'il est opportune*).[2564] Under certain circumstances the Investigative Judge *(juge d'instruction)* or the indictment division (*chambre de l'instruction)* may take action.[2565] The Investigative Judge can begin investigating if a submission is made by the District Prosecutor or he receives a complaint with a petition to become a civil party.[2566]

2555 Secs.75, 12, 13 Code de Procédure Pénale, *supra* note 2549; also Bureau of Justice Statistics, US Department of Justice, State University of New York at Albany, World factbook of criminal justice systems, France, Jacques Borricand, "Prosecutorial and judicial process. 2. Procedures."

2556 Sec.15 Code de Procédure Pénale, *supra* note 2549.

2557 Secs.40 and 41 Code de Procédure Pénale, *supra* note 2549.

2558 Sec.75 Code de Procédure Pénale, *supra* note 2549.

2559 Sec.15 (3) Code de Procédure Pénale, *supra* note 2549.

2560 Sec.40 Code de Procédure Pénale, *supra* note 2549.

2561 Sec.75 (1) Code de Procédure Pénale, *supra* note 2549.

2562 Sec.53 Code de Procédure Pénale, *supra* note 2549.

2563 Sec.41 Code de Procédure Pénale, *supra* note 2549.

2564 Sec.40 (1) Code de Procédure Pénale, *supra* note 2549.

2565 Title III, Chapter I and II, Secs.79–190, 191–229 Code de Procédure Pénale, *supra* note 2549.

2566 Sec.51 Code de Procédure Pénale, *supra* note 2549.

Is a discretionary evaluation performed before initiating a formal investigation/prosecution, and if so, how is it conducted (level of discretion)?

According to article 40 (1) *Code de Procédure Pénale* the District Prosecutor (*procureur de la République*) (1) initiates a prosecution, or (2) implements alternative proceedings, or (3) closes the case without taking further action, if it is appropriate *(s'il est opportune)*; thus it is the District Prosecutor that may exercise discretion based on the principle of opportunity.[2567]

But this discretion is restricted if the offence is a *crime* (felony). For a felony the District Prosecutor is under an obligation to refer the case to the Investigative Judge for judicial investigation (*réquisitoire introductif*).[2568] With regard to less serious offences (petty offences), however, the Prosecutor does have discretion whether to request an investigation or not.[2569] In the case of a petition to become a civil party, the District Prosecutor (*procureur de la République*) may only send the Investigating Judge submissions not to investigate where the facts of the case cannot lead to a lawful prosecution for reasons relating to the right to prosecute, or where, if the facts were shown to exist, they would not amount to any criminal offence.[2570]

Under which circumstances can investigations (preliminary and/or full investigation) be dismissed? Are there criteria for dismissal or is the decision fully discretionary? If there are criteria, which are those and how are they defined?

The District Prosecutor (*procureur de la République*) can decide to close a case (article 40 *Code de Procédure Pénale*) and has to inform the complainants and the victims thereof.[2571]

Similarly, the Investigating Judge may consider "that the facts do not constitute a crime, a misdemeanor, or a petty offence, or if the perpetrator has remained unidentified, or if there are no sufficient charges against the person under judicial examination, he makes an order ruling that there is no case to prosecute."[2572] In the same vein, the Investigating Chamber can consider "that the facts of the case do not constitute a felony, a misdemeanor, or a petty offence or if the perpetrator remains unidentified, or where there are no sufficient charges against the person under judicial examination, it declares there is no case to prosecute."[2573]

Is the decision to start/end an investigation/prosecution subject to control by another body?

The Chief Public Prosecutor can decide to close a case and has to inform the complainants and the victims thereof.[2574] Any person who has reported an offence to

---

[2567] Fabian Pfefferkorn, *Einführung in das französische Strafverfahren,* Hamburg 2006, 95 et seq.

[2568] Sec.79 Code de Procédure Pénale, *supra* note 2549; see further Pfefferkorn, *supra* note 2567, 102 et seq.

[2569] Sec.44 Code de Procédure Pénale, *supra* note 2549.

[2570] Sec.86 Code de Procédure Pénale, *supra* note 2549.

[2571] Sec.40 (2) Code de Procédure Pénale, *supra* note 2549.

[2572] Sec.177 Code de Procédure Pénale, *supra* note 2549.

[2573] Sec.212 Code de Procédure Pénale, *supra* note 2549.

the District Prosecutor may lodge an appeal with the Public Prosecutor (*procureur de la République*), who may, under the conditions provided for by article 36 *Code de Procédure Pénale,* instruct the District Prosecutor to initiate a prosecution.[2575] Article 36 *Code de Procédure Pénale* states: "The Prosecutor General may, by written instructions which are attached to the file of the case, direct District Prosecutors to initiate prosecutions, or to cause them to be initiated, or to refer to the competent court such written submissions as the prosecutor general considers appropriate."

Conclusion

In France pre-investigations are conducted by the police. Nevertheless, it is the District Prosecutor who is in charge of any major decisions during investigations. It has to be noted that his discretion ends where serious offences begin, thus judicial control is introduced via the Chief Public Prosecutor. Moreover, the investigation judge is involved in any important determinations regarding felonies, and, under certain circumstances, victims may force the Public Prosecutor to take action.[2576]

IX. Germany (Civil law, Germanic family)

German criminal law is basically regulated in two codes, the *Strafgesetzbuch* (StGB; German Penal Code)[2577] and the *Strafprozessordnung* (StPO; German Code of Criminal Procedure, hereinafter GCCP).[2578] It is worth noting that Germany has enacted a specific codification with regard to the crimes of international criminal law, namely the *Völkerstrafgesetzbuch* (VStGB; German Code of International Criminal Law, hereinafter GCICL).[2579]

Generally speaking, criminal proceedings can be subdivided into three phases: investigation phase (*Ermittlungsverfahren oder Vorverfahren*), interim proceedings (*Zwischenverfahren*), and trial stage (*Hauptverfahren*). Moreover, German criminal law distinguishes the procedure leading to a judgment (*Erkenntnisverfahren*) and the enforcement process (*Vollstreckungsverfahren*).

Who is in charge of (pre-)investigations?

The main responsibility during investigation is vested with the Prosecutor.[2580] The Prosecution is therefore called the "master of investigations" (*Herrin des Ermittlungsverfahrens*).[2581] On the other hand, general practice leaves investigative steps

2574 Sec.40 (2) Code de Procédure Pénale, *supra* note 2549.

2575 Sec.40 (3) Code de Procédure Pénale, *supra* note 2549.

2576 World factbook of criminal justice systems, France, *supra* note 2555, "Prosecutorial and judicial process. 2. Procedures."

2577 Strafgesetzbuch 1871, 31.10.2008.

2578 Strafprozessordnung 1877, 31.10.2008.

2579 Völkerstrafgesetzbuch, 26.6.2002. Further on the German legal system see Bureau of Justice Statistics, US Department of Justice, State University of New York at Albany, World factbook of criminal justice systems, Germany, Alexis Aronowitz.

2580 Secs.152 (1), (2), and 160 Strafprozessordnung, *supra* note 2578.

largely to the police.[2582] The police are even under a duty to ensure the preservation of evidence under certain circumstances.[2583] Moreover, German law distinguishes between regular police forces and public servants, which are equally police forces, supporting the Prosecutor (*sog. Ermittlungspersonen der Staatsanwaltschaft*).[2584] In any event, the result of a preliminary investigation must be transmitted to the Prosecutor without delay, and the Prosecutor is at all times in charge of investigations.[2585] The investigative judge (*Ermittlungsrichter*) may act on behalf of the Prosecutor only in urgent matters, and he must afterwards leave further investigations entirely to the directive of the Prosecutor.[2586]

What triggers the initiation of a (pre-)investigation? (What is the standard of proof – if any – to start (pre-)investigations?)

Complaints may be lodged – orally or in writing – with the Prosecution, the police, and the district courts.[2587] The Prosecution service is under an obligation to inquire the circumstances of any allegation.[2588] In principle, both the Prosecution and the police are subjected to the principle of mandatory prosecution (*Legalitätsprinzip*),[2589] meaning that they are under an obligation to conduct preliminary and full investigations. Inaction is thus not permitted at the outset, but it will be outlined later that there are possibilities to abstain from prosecuting (sections 153–154e GCCP). German criminal law further rests on the principle of the *Amtsermittlungsgrundsatz,* which means that State authorities are under a general obligation to inquire any alleged crimes.[2590] The Prosecutor is under an obligation to inquire incriminating and exonerating circumstances equally.[2591]

An investigation can be started based on a report (*Strafanzeige*) or a complaint to investigate (*Strafantrag*).[2592] Reports and complaints can be filed by anyone, citi-

---

2581 Jens Dallmeyer/Matthias Jahn, "Einleitung und Einstellung des Ermittlungsverfahrens" in Michael Heghmanns/Uwe Scheffler (eds.), *Handbuch zum Strafverfahren* (C.H. Beck, München 2008) 1, 17, mn 37; Werner Beulke, *Strafprozessrecht,* 8. Aufl. (C.F. Müller Verlag, Heidelberg 2005) 48, § 5 mn 79.

2582 Beulke, *supra* note 2581, 60–1, § 6 mn 101.

2583 Sec.163 (1) Strafprozessordnung, *supra* note 2578.

2584 Sec.152 Gerichtsverfassungsgesetz 1877, 17.12.2008; Beulke, *supra* note 2581, 61, § 6 mn 102.

2585 Sec.163 (2) Strafprozessordnung, *supra* note 2578; Dallmeyer/Jahn, in Heghmanns/Jahn, *supra* note 2581, 19, mn 40 ("kein staatsanwaltsfreier Raum").

2586 Secs.165 and 167 Strafprozessordnung, *supra* note 2578.

2587 Sec.158 (1) Strafprozessordnung, *supra* note 2578.

2588 Sec.160 (1) Strafprozessordnung, *supra* note 2578.

2589 Secs.152 (2) and 170 (1) Strafprozessordnung, *supra* note 2578; Gerd Pfeiffer/Rolf Hannich, "Einleitung" in Rolf Hannich (ed.), *Karlsruher Kommentar zur Strafprozessordnung,* 6th edition (C.H. Beck, München 2008) Einleitung, mn 5; Beulke, *supra* note 2581, 19, § 2 mn 17; Julia Fionda, *Public prosecutors and discretion* (Clarendon Press, Oxford 1995) 135.

2590 Secs.155 (2), 160 (2), and 244 (2) Strafprozessordnung, *supra* note 2578.

2591 Sec.160 (2) Strafprozessordnung, *supra* note 2578.

2592 Sec.158 (1) Strafprozessordnung, *supra* note 2578.

zens and legal entities.[2593] In addition, the police and the Prosecution conduct observations on their own and in the context of their official capacity.[2594] The standard of proof to start investigations is one of simple suspicion (*Anfangsverdacht*), which means that according to factual circumstances, and taking into account criminalistic experience, a participation of the person concerned in the alleged criminal offence(s) seems possible.[2595] The police and the Prosecutor often carry out preliminary investigations (*Vorermittlungen*) for reaching a determination of simple suspicion. Some kind of preliminary measures are a *condicio sine qua non* to evaluate the simple suspicion.[2596] On the other hand, preliminary investigations are not regulated in the GCCP.[2597] The law in action yet shows that preliminary steps are conducted, and the majority view acknowledges their existence.[2598] However, preliminary investigations are not within the ambit of statutory investigations, and can only be applied within a limited framework.[2599] They must be constrained to section 160 (1) GCCP, thus the circumstances of the specific case under pre-investigation. Any further inquiries can be conducted solely after the initiation of a formal investigation; in particular, coercive measures that touch upon basic liberty rights can only be taken at the formal investigation stage.[2600]

Who takes the decision to start a formal investigation?

The Prosecutor is the competent authority to decide whether or not to investigate.[2601]

Is a discretionary evaluation performed before initiating a formal investigation/prosecution, and if so, how is it conducted (level of discretion)?

In accordance with the principle of mandatory prosecution the Prosecutor must commence investigations if there is sufficiently factual evidence to support an initia-

---

2593 Dallmeyer/Jahn, in Heghmanns/Jahn, *supra* note 2581, 10, mn 8; Beulke, *supra* note 2581, 177, § 15 mn 309.

2594 Secs.160 (1) and 163 (1) Strafprozessordnung, *supra* note 2578; Beulke, *supra* note 2581, 48, § 5 mn 79, 62, § 6, mn 104, 178, § 15 mn 310.

2595 Dallmeyer/Jahn, in Heghmanns/Jahn, *supra* note 2581, 21, mn 48; Beulke, *supra* note 2581, 178, § 15 mn 311; also Pfeiffer/Hannich, in Hannich, *supra* note 2589, Einleitung, mn 33; Mark Deiters, *Legalitätsprinzip und Normengeltung* (Mohr Siebeck, Tübingen 2006) 115 et seq.

2596 Deiters, *supra* note 2595, 137.

2597 Dallmeyer/Jahn, in Heghmanns/Jahn, *supra* note 2581, 29, mn 77; Beulke, *supra* note 2581, 179, § 15 mn 311; Pfeiffer/Hannich, in Hannich, *supra* note 2589, Einleitung, mn 33; Martin Böse, "Aufsichtsrechtliche Vorermittlungen in der Grauzone zwischen Strafverfolgung und Gefahrenabwehr" (2007) 119 ZStW 848, 851 et seq.

2598 Pfeiffer/Hannich, in Hannich, *supra* note 2589, Einleitung, mn 33.

2599 Differentiated Dallmeyer/Jahn, in Heghmanns/Jahn, *supra* note 2581, 29–30, mn 78 et seq.

2600 Deiters, *supra* note 2595, 138; Dallmeyer/Jahn, in Heghmanns/Jahn, *supra* note 2581, 29–30, mn 78–9.

2601 Sec.152 (1) Strafprozessordnung, *supra* note 2578.

tion.[2602] The standard to initiate investigations is, as mentioned above, one of simple suspicion, which entails a certain scope of judgment evaluation (*Beurteilungsspielraum*).[2603] On the other hand, there is no discretion at this stage.[2604]

Investigations end with a decision by the Prosecutor to press charges or to discontinue further proceedings. Pursuant to section 170 (1) GCCP, the Prosecutor must be satisfied that there are "sufficient reasons" to bring the case to trial. The threshold is one of "probable cause."[2605] Otherwise, all proceedings are terminated and the suspect is informed thereof.[2606] Moreover, the Prosecutor is exempted from mandatory prosecution under certain expediency conditions (sections 153 et seq. GCCP), which are explained below.

Under which circumstances can investigations (preliminary and/or full investigation) be dismissed? Are there criteria for dismissal or is the decision fully discretionary? If there are criteria, which are those and how are they defined?

The general duty of mandatory prosecution is put into perspective via regulations that allow for discretionary discontinuation (sections 153–154c and 376 GCCP).[2607] Section 153 GCCP names two prerequisites for a decision to stop any prosecutorial activities: minor guilt and lack of public interests.[2608] "Minor guilt" amounts to the expected range of punishment, which, in turn, is closely linked to the seriousness of the offence.[2609] Criteria for the public interest can be found in complementary regulations for criminal and summary proceedings.[2610] The factors mentioned to determine the public interest are not exhaustive, and the following ones are specifically named: severity of the wrongdoing (*Ausmaß der Rechtsverletzung*), brutality or hazardousness of the offence (*Rohheit und Gefährlichkeit der Tat*), base motives of the perpetrator (*niedrige Beweggründe des Täters*), or the position of the victim in public life (*Stellung des Verletzten im öffentlichen Leben*).[2611] In any event, the concepts of "minor guilt" and "public interest" are left wide open to interpretation.[2612]

2602 Sec.152 (2) Strafprozessordnung, *supra* note 2578.

2603 BGHSt 38, 214 [1992], 27.2.1992 (5 StR 190/91) para. 30.

2604 Dallmeyer/Jahn, in Heghmanns/Jahn, *supra* note 2581, 21, mn 48.

2605 Secs.170 (2) and 203 Strafprozessordnung; Dallmeyer/Jahn, in Heghmanns/Jahn, *supra* note 2581, 40–1, mn 119; Beulke, *supra* note 2581, 182, § 15 mn 319; Pfeiffer/Hannich, in Hannich, *supra* note 2589, Einleitung, mn 41; Michael Heghmanns, "Anklageentscheidung" in Heghmanns/Jahn, *supra* note 2581, 409, 413, mn 6 et seq.

2606 Sec.170 (2) Strafprozessordnung, *supra* note 2578.

2607 Heghmanns, in Heghmanns/Jahn, *supra* note 2581, 417, mn 22; Peter Morré, "Germany," in Arbour/Eser/Ambos/Sanders, *supra* note 2388, 341, 343.

2608 Sec.153 (1) Strafprozessordnung, *supra* note 2578.

2609 Heghmanns, in Heghmanns/Jahn, *supra* note 2581, 420–1, mn 32 et seq.

2610 Heghmanns, in Heghmanns/Jahn, *supra* note 2581, 421, mn 38, 418–9, mn 29; Fionda, *supra* note 2589, 140.

2611 No. 86 (2) Richtlinien für das Strafverfahren und das Bußgeldverfahren, 1.1.2008.

2612 Fionda, *supra* note 2589, 140.

In principle, the Prosecutor carries out the evaluation; yet, the judges undertake any such determination after the formal indictment has been filed.[2613]

Further, section 153a GCCP gives the Prosecutor a tool to impose alternative sanctions (attaching conditions to a waiver of prosecution) rather than penalties (such as compensation).[2614] Last but not least, sections 153c and 153f GCCP require specific attention. Sections 153c (1) and (2) GCCP allow for discontinuation if the crime was committed abroad or on a foreign vessel or aircraft. Section 153f GCCP regulates a very complicated system for dropping cases that involve crimes under the GCICL. Section 1 of the GCICL establishes the principle of universal jurisdiction with regard to core crimes "even when the offence was committed abroad and bears no relation to Germany." For limiting those cases the Prosecutor was given the exceptions of section 153f GCCP, which structures his discretion in two directions: first, in cases of crimes committed abroad with a domestic link (i.e. the accused is present in Germany and/or is of German nationality), there is an obligation to prosecute, unless the offence is being prosecuted before an international court or by the territorial or victim State; second, the Prosecutor may abstain from prosecutions if there is no domestic link and a German citizen is neither involved as a victim or perpetrator, or if the suspect of the offence is not residing in Germany and a stay of the suspect in Germany is unlikely.[2615] Arguably, the second ground also presumes – as a mandatory requirement – the prosecution by an international court or the territorial/suspect/victim State.[2616]

Further, an exception applies where a foreigner, who is suspected of having committed an offence abroad, is residing in Germany, but there are no German victims, and a transfer of the suspect to an international court, or an extradition to the prosecuting State, is permissible and intended.[2617] As a matter of fact, section 153f GCCP has been used in almost all petitions under the GCICL to abstain from prosecutions.[2618]

2613 Sec.153 (1), (2) Strafprozessordnung, *supra* note 2578.

2614 Fionda, *supra* note 2589, 136–7. On other dismissal options (sections 153b et seq. Strafprozessordnung) see further Heghmanns, in Heghmanns/Jahn, *supra* note 2581, 431 et seq., mn 79 et seq.

2615 Kai Ambos, "International core crimes, universal jurisdiction and § 153f of the German Criminal Procedure Code: a commentary on the decisions of the Federal Prosecutor General and the Stuttgart Higher Regional Court in the Abu Ghraib/Rumsfeld case" (2007) 18 CLF 43, 47–8.

2616 Ambos, *supra* note 2615, 48, 57.

2617 Ambos, *supra* note 2615, 48.

2618 Ambos, *supra* note 2615, 43. See, for example, OLG Stuttgart, Beschluss vom 13.9.2005 (5 Ws 109/05); critically evaluating the former decision Ambos, *ibid.,* 50 et seq; Tobias Singelnstein/Peer Stolle, "Völkerstrafrecht und Legalitätsprinzip – Klageerzwingungsverfahren bei Opportunitätseinstellung und Auslegung des § 153f StPO" (2006) 3 ZIS 118, 118 et seq.; also Michael Kurth, "Zum Verfolgungsermessen des Generalbundesanwalts nach § 153f StPO" (2006) 2 ZIS 82, 86.

Is the decision to start/end an investigation/prosecution subject to control by another body?

The decision to initiate an investigation is subject to minimum judicial control. It is yet controversial to which extent the standard of "simple suspicion" can be checked.[2619] While in the past judicial control at this stage has been neglected, it appears that three factors for judicial control, which have emerged in the jurisprudence of the German Federal Constitutional Court, could be accepted for controlling the decisions of the Prosecutor to discontinue after pre-investigations: an imperative to base the decision on correct facts; a ban of arbitrary considerations (*Verbot sachfremder Erwägungen*); and no violation of generally accepted standards of evaluation, as well as adherence to any essential process regulations.[2620]

In any event, if there has been a formal request to start investigations and proceedings are discontinued, the person who filed the request must be informed.[2621] A person, who is further a victim of the crime, may then file an administrative complaint to the superior of the prosecution service.[2622] Against a refusal on behalf of the superior the victim may demand a court order (*Klageerzwingungsverfahren*).[2623] It has to be noted that the success rate of petitions pursuant to section 172 (2) GCCP is very low.[2624] Moreover, the control proceedings of sections 172 et seq. GCCP are not permissible with regard to decisions by the Prosecutor based on the expediency principle (sections 153 et seq. GCCP).[2625] The *Klageerzwingungsverfahren* is only meant to ensure the general principle of mandatory prosecution,[2626] and thus mainly applies to mistakes of law, and it is not convenient for sections 153 et seq. GCCP.

However, even if discretionary decisions are subjected to limited control only, the substantive elements of the specific regulation have to be fulfilled, i.e. with regard to section 153f GCCP, two elements can be scrutinized by the judges: the "stay in Germany" and the matter whether a "transfer of the suspect to an international court, or an extradition to the prosecuting State, is permissible and intended."[2627] It has further been submitted that section 153f GCCP entails a *lacuna* to the extent that it does not require judicial consent, and therefore one should ensure the international duty to prosecute either by analogous proceedings to section 172 GCCP or

---

2619 Dallmeyer/Jahn, in Heghmanns/Jahn, *supra* note 2581, 23–4, mn 54 et seq.

2620 Dallmeyer/Jahn, in Heghmanns/Jahn, *supra* note 2581, 24–5, mn 58 et seq.

2621 Sec.171 Strafprozessordnung, *supra* note 2578; Dallmeyer/Jahn, in Heghmanns/Jahn, *supra* note 2581, 46–7, mn 143 et seq.

2622 Sec.172 (1) Strafprozessordnung, *supra* note 2578.

2623 Sec.172 (2)–(4) Strafprozessordnung, *supra* note 2578.

2624 Dallmeyer/Jahn, in Heghmanns/Jahn, *supra* note 2581, 55, mn 166; Peter Rackow, "Die Darstellung der Verletzteneigenschaft durch den Anwalt im Antrag auf gerichtliche Entscheidung im Klageerzwingungsverfahren" (2001) 148 Goltdammer's Archiv 482, 482 et seq.

2625 Dallmeyer/Jahn, in Heghmanns/Jahn, *supra* note 2581, 56, mn 168.

2626 Lutz Meyer-Goßner, *Strafprozessordnung, Kommentar,* 51st edition (C.H. Beck, München 2008) § 172, 778, mn 3.

2627 Singelnstein/Stolle, *supra* note 2618, 120 et seq.

through the additional requirement of a (high) court consent for a dismissal decision under section 153f GCCP (which needs to be inserted by way of legal reform).[2628]

Conclusion

As a matter of principle the German Prosecutors must adhere to the principle of mandatory prosecution. On the other hand, many exceptions allow for discretionary considerations, be that through written law (section 153f GCCP) and the provision's large scope of judgment evaluation, or by using grey areas through the police and the Prosecutor. Especially with regard to universal, international core crimes in the ambit of section 1 GCICL, the dismissal based on section 153f GCCP has been used abundantly. So far, judicial review could not refine findings by the Prosecutor and was exercised very reluctantly. Checks on the federal level in Germany are currently inadequate.[2629] In sum, the German system shows similarities to article 53 ICC Statute. In a similar vein, mandatory prosecution is presumed to be the principle idea, but several discretionary provisions soften its implementation. It remains most important to strike a feasible balance between (necessary) self-restraint through expediency criteria *vis-à-vis* the international duty to prosecute core crimes. At present, Germany and the ICC have struggled to find such a balance; in particular the judicial review mechanisms of both systems require refinement.

X. India (Common law, Hindu law)

Indian court procedure in civil and criminal matters basically follows common law.[2630] A Criminal Code of 1860 and an Ordinance relating to Criminal Procedure of 1861 were drafted based on English criminal law, but also paid attention to other European models such as the French Code Pénal.[2631] Nowadays, criminal law is still embodied in two principal statutes: the Indian Penal Code and the Code of Criminal Procedure of 1973.[2632] In sum, the criminal system is merely a legacy of the British system, albeit Indian law in general incorporates Hindu, Islamic, common and customary laws, and is a mix of adversarial and accusatorial systems.[2633]

Who is in charge of (pre-)investigations?

Information is generally given to the police that can start investigating a cognizable case, but shall refer the informant to the Magistrate for non-cognizable cases.[2634] No police officer shall investigate a non-cognizable case without the or-

2628 Ambos, *supra* note 2615, 55 et seq., 58.

2629 Fionda, *supra* note 2589, 161.

2630 Zweigert/Kötz, *supra* note 112, 228.

2631 Zweigert/Kötz, *supra* note 112, 227.

2632 Indian Penal Code 1860, 6.10.1860; Indian Code of Criminal Procedure 1973, 25.1.1974.

2633 Bureau of Justice Statistics, US Department of Justice, State University of New York at Albany, World factbook of criminal justice systems, India, R. K. Rakhavan, "General overview. 1. Political system."

der of a Magistrate.[2635] For cognizable cases, the police officer shall report to the Magistrate and proceed in person, or delegate the matter to subordinate officers. He may then investigate the facts and circumstances of the case, and, if necessary, take measures for the discovery and arrest of the offender.[2636] In sum, the police are in charge of pre-investigations under supervision of the Magistrate.

What triggers the initiation of a (pre-)investigation? (What is the standard of proof – if any – to start (pre-)investigations?)

Any information can be submitted to the police. The substance of the information must be kept in a book, and, in the case of refusal, the informant may send it to the next level of authority in writing and by post. The so-called Superintendent of the Police must then either investigate the case of complaint himself or direct an investigation.[2637]

Who takes the decision to start a formal investigation?

With regard to cognizable cases, if it appears to the officer in charge of a police station that there is no sufficient ground for entering on an investigation, he shall not investigate the case.[2638] In addition, when information as to the commission of any such offence is given against any person by name, and the case is not of a serious nature, the police officer need not proceed in person.[2639]

Is a discretionary evaluation performed before initiating a formal investigation/prosecution, and if so, how is it conducted (level of discretion)?

With regard to cognizable cases the police officer must evaluate the "sufficient ground for entering on an investigation," and either proceed or deny action. In any event, the police officer must send a report to the Magistrate in charge, stating reasons, and he must further notify the informant, if any, that he will not investigate the case or not cause it to be investigated.[2640] After the investigation is completed and upon obtaining legal opinion from the prosecuting personnel, the police officer can either establish a charge-sheet before the competent Magistrate, or, in the event of insufficient evidence, file a report to drop any further action.[2641]

2634 Secs.154–156 Code of Criminal Procedure, *supra* note 2632. "Cognizable offence" means an offence for which, and "cognizable case" means a case in which, a police officer may, in accordance with the First Schedule or under any other law for the time being in force, arrest without warrant; "non-cognizable offence" means an offence for which, and "non-cognizable case" means a case in which, a police officer has no authority to arrest without warrant, cf. sec.2 (c) and (l) Code of Criminal Procedure. See also World factbook of criminal justice systems, India, *supra* note 2633, "Police. 5. Discretion."

2635 Sec.155 (2) Code of Criminal Procedure, *supra* note 2632.

2636 Sec.157 Code of Criminal Procedure, *supra* note 2632.

2637 Secs.154 (1), (3), and 155 (1) Code of Criminal Procedure, *supra* note 2632.

2638 Sec.157 (1) (b) Code of Criminal Procedure, *supra* note 2632.

2639 Sec.157 (1) (a) Code of Criminal Procedure, *supra* note 2632.

2640 Sec.157 (2) Code of Criminal Procedure, *supra* note 2632.

Under which circumstances can investigations (preliminary and/or full investigation) be dismissed? Are there criteria for dismissal or is the decision fully discretionary? If there are criteria, which are those and how are they defined?

Preliminary examinations can be dismissed if there is "no sufficient ground for entering on an investigation." Upon full investigation, the officer in charge has to evaluate if there is "sufficient evidence or reasonable ground of suspicion" to justify the forwarding of the accused to a Magistrate.[2642] If the officer decides in the affirmative, he must forward the accused under custody to a Magistrate.[2643] The Magistrate issues a summons or warrant if he believes that there are sufficient grounds for prosecution based on the available record.[2644]

Is the decision to start/end an investigation/prosecution subject to control by another body?

The Magistrate, on receiving a negative report under section 157 (1) Code of Criminal Procedure, i. e. denying further proceedings, may hold an investigation or preliminary inquiry "if he thinks fit."[2645] Moreover, a report of any completed investigation must be sent to the Magistrate.[2646] The Magistrate can take cognizance of any offence upon receiving a complaint of facts which constitute such an offence, upon a police report of such facts, upon information received from any person other than a police officer, or upon his own knowledge, that such an offence has been committed.[2647]

Conclusion

Pre-investigations in India are conducted by the police under certain supervision of the Magistrates. With regard to minor offences a certain degree of discretion is given to the police officer in charge of preliminary investigations ("sufficient ground for entering on an investigation"), as well as upon full investigations ("sufficient evidence or reasonable ground of suspicion"). The exact definition and criteria involved are not further explained in the Code of Criminal Procedure, however, the Magistrate is the decision maker on the substance since he can exercise broad judicial control.

2641 World factbook of criminal justice systems, India, *supra* note 2633, "Police. 5. Discretion."

2642 Sec.169 Code of Criminal Procedure, *supra* note 2632.

2643 Sec.170 Code of Criminal Procedure, *supra* note 2632.

2644 World factbook of criminal justice systems, India, *supra* note 2633, "Prosecutorial and judical process. 2. Procedures."

2645 Sec.159 Code of Criminal Procedure, *supra* note 2632.

2646 Sec.173 (2) Code of Criminal Procedure, *supra* note 2632.

2647 Sec.190 Code of Criminal Procedure, *supra* note 2632.

XI. Kenya (Common law, African family, situation country)

Kenya is a Commonwealth country with a common law system. Courts adhere to the principle of *stare decisis* and the legal system is deemed adversarial.[2648] Nonetheless, its criminal law is regulated in statutes: the Kenyan Penal Code of 1985[2649] and the Kenyan Criminal Procedure Code of 1987.[2650] It has to be noted that Kenya also has an informal, customary criminal justice system, but the types of criminal cases these local chiefs and councils of elders can deal with have been limited.[2651]

Who is in charge of (pre-)investigations?

The officers in charge of a police station shall make investigations and shall give information to the nearest magistrate if they receive information that a person (a) has committed suicide, (b) has been killed, (c) has died under circumstances raising a reasonable suspicion, or (d) is missing and believed to be dead.[2652] The police officer must draw up a report, which is, in the case of (a)–(c), forwarded to the nearest magistrate, and in the case of (d) send to the Attorney General.[2653] Arrest proceedings are generally a police matter, yet under certain supervision by the magistrates.[2654] At later stages in the proceedings, the power of controlling prosecutions is vested with the Attorney General.[2655]

What triggers the initiation of a (pre-)investigation? (What is the standard of proof – if any – to start (pre-)investigations?)

Proceedings can be initiated by a complaint, or by bringing a person, who has been arrested without a warrant, before a magistrate.[2656] Any person, who believes from a "reasonable and probable cause" that an offence has been committed by another person, can bring a complaint to the attention of a magistrate.[2657] Such an

---

[2648] Bureau of Justice Statistics, US Department of Justice, State University of New York at Albany, World factbook of criminal justice systems, Kenya, Obi Ebbe, "General overview. 2. Legal system."

[2649] Kenyan Penal Code 1985, revised edition 2007, chapter 63, Gladys Boss Shollei (ed.), The laws of Kenya, Grey book (Kenya Law Reports, Nairobi 2007).

[2650] Kenyan Criminal Procedure Code 1987, revised edition 2007, chapter 75, in Shollei, *supra* note 2649.

[2651] World factbook of criminal justice systems, Kenya, *supra* note 2648, "General overview. 2. Legal system."

[2652] Sec.386 (1) Criminal Procedure Code, *supra* note 2650.

[2653] Sec.386 (1) Criminal Procedure Code, *supra* note 2650.

[2654] Secs.21 et seq. Criminal Procedure Code, *supra* note 2650.

[2655] Sec.26 (3) of the Constitution of Kenya 2001, revised edition 2008, in Shollei, *supra* note 2649; also PLO Lumumba, *A handbook on criminal procedure in Kenya* (Law Africa Publishing, Nairobi 2005) 8.

[2656] Sec.89 (1) Criminal Procedure Code, *supra* note 2650.

[2657] Sec.89 (2) Criminal Procedure Code, *supra* note 2650.

allegation must be made orally or in writing.[2658] Nonetheless, citizens are permitted to arrest offenders and bring them to the nearest police station.[2659]

Who takes the decision to start a formal investigation?

The Kenyan police have broad discretion to arrest a suspect with or without a warrant, albeit the law requires "probable cause."[2660] The offender is brought to the nearest police station for questioning.[2661]

Is a discretionary evaluation performed before initiating a formal investigation/prosecution, and if so, how is it conducted (level of discretion)?

For starting an investigation by arresting a suspect, the requirement of "probable cause" states that there must be some facts and circumstances that justify the action; i.e. there must be solid grounds to believe that the suspect committed the crime.[2662]

The starting point of almost all criminal cases is the District's Magistrate Court.[2663] The Prosecutor studies the case and designs his presentation before a preliminary hearing takes place during which Prosecution and Defence present their case.[2664] Thereby, the Prosecutor is usually a senior police officer; more serious cases are handled by the Director of Public Prosecution.[2665] The magistrate can make an order refusing to admit a complaint if he is of the opinion that the complaint or formal charge does not disclose an offence.[2666]

The broadest control power for controlling prosecutions is, however, given to the Attorney General. His instruments are *nolle prosequi* and withdrawal.[2667] He can take over any criminal proceedings and continue or discontinue at any stage.[2668]

2658 Sec.89 (3) Criminal Procedure Code, *supra* note 2650.

2659 World factbook of criminal justice systems, Kenya, *supra* note 2648, "Police. 5. Discretion."

2660 World factbook of criminal justice systems, Kenya, *supra* note 2648, "Police. 5. Discretion."

2661 World factbook of criminal justice systems, Kenya, *supra* note 2648, "Prosecutorial and judical process. 2. Procedures."

2662 World factbook of criminal justice systems, Kenya, *supra* note 2648, "Police. 5. Discretion."

2663 World factbook of criminal justice systems, Kenya, *supra* note 2648, "Prosecutorial and judicial process. 2. Procedures."

2664 World factbook of criminal justice systems, Kenya, *supra* note 2648, "Prosecutorial and judicial process. 2. Procedures."

2665 World factbook of criminal justice systems, Kenya, *supra* note 2648, "Prosecutorial and judicial process. 2. Procedures."

2666 Sec.89 (5) Criminal Procedure Code, *supra* note 2650.

2667 Lumumba, *supra* note 2655, 8 et seq.

2668 Sec.26 (3) of the Constitution of Kenya, further Secs.82–3 Criminal Procedure Code, *supra* note 2650.

Under which circumstances can investigations (preliminary and/or full investigation) be dismissed? Are there criteria for dismissal or is the decision fully discretionary? If there are criteria, which are those and how are they defined?

In any criminal case and at any stage before reaching a verdict or judgment, the Attorney General, as already mentioned, may decide to discontinue proceedings (*nolle prosequi*).[2669] He shall either make a statement in Court or inform the Court in writing that the Republic intends not to continue its activities, and thereupon the accused shall be discharged.[2670] This power can be delegated from the Attorney General to the Solicitor General, the Deputy Public Prosecutor, the Assistant Deputy Public Prosecutor, or a state counsel.[2671] It has to be noted that neither the Constitution nor the Criminal Code attach any preconditions to this power.[2672]

Furthermore, a public prosecutor may, with the consent of the Court and instructions from the Attorney General, withdraw from prosecution.[2673] Before a final order is passed, a complainant may equally ask for withdrawal, and the Court may permit so if it is satisfied that there are "sufficient grounds."[2674]

Is the decision to start/end an investigation/prosecution subject to control by another body?

The police are supervised by the Public Service Commission, who is supposed to discipline corrupt officers. Since it is, however, a political institution, disciplinary action is rarely taken.[2675]

For discontinuance of prosecutions, the difference between withdrawals and *nolle prosequi* is important. While the former is subject to consent of the Court, the latter is not, and therefore overrides – generally speaking – any judicial control.[2676] Nonetheless, the High Court of Kenya, sitting as the Constitutional Court, has set limits if the Attorney General's exercise of *nolle prosequi* was capricious and oppressive, and amounts to an abuse of Court process.[2677] It stated:

> "Thus, rightly contended, this court is the sole constitutional entity vested with the responsibilities rather than the Attorney General of ensuring that criminal justice system is not abused or used oppressively. [...] Where, therefore, the exercise of the discretion to enter *nolle prosequi* does not meet the test of constitutionality by virtue of section 123 (8) of the Constitution then the *nolle prosequi* so entered will be deemed and declared unconstitutional."[2678]

2669 Sec.82 (1) Criminal Procedure Code, *supra* note 2650.

2670 Sec.82 (1) Criminal Procedure Code, *supra* note 2650.

2671 Sec.83 Criminal Procedure Code, *supra* note 2650.

2672 Lumumba, *supra* note 2655, 9.

2673 Sec.87 Criminal Procedure Code, *supra* note 2650.

2674 Sec.204 Criminal Procedure Code, *supra* note 2650.

2675 World factbook of criminal justice systems, Kenya, *supra* note 2648, "Police. 6. Accountability."

2676 Lumumba, *supra* note 2655, 9.

2677 *Crispus Karanja Njogu v. The Attorney-General & others* [2005], Civil suit 574 of 2002, 4.

In sum, the High Court strengthened the Constitution and limited the scope of *nolle prosequi*. In other words, the discretion of the Attorney General ends where the Constitution is otherwise violated, and the Court further revealed that it has the power to check the Attorney General's acts against this background.

Conclusion

During early proceedings the police enjoy large discretion. For bringing a case to trial, the supervision by the magistrate is significant. At any stage, the Attorney General may intervene and halt prosecution. Little, however, could be found with respect to the criteria that guide the discretionary choices by the police and the Attorney General. On the other hand, the Kenyan High Court set limits to the unfettered discretion of the Attorney General by looking at constitutional standards. An abuse of process can therefore be examined by the High Court, but by the High Court only, since subordinate courts cannot question the discretion of the Attorney General.[2679]

XII. The Netherlands (Civil law)

The Netherlands generally follows civil law, and its criminal law is embedded in the *Wetboek van Strafrecht* of 1881/1886 (Penal Code), the *Wetboek van Strafvordering* of 1926 (Code of Criminal Procedure), and special acts.[2680] The Code of Criminal Procedure has been characterized as "being moderately accusatorial."[2681]

It must be noted that procedural law reforms have been discussed and partly adopted in recent years, based upon four expert reports on issues such as, for example, report two on the pre-trial investigation phase.[2682] Nonetheless, the upcoming survey will focus on a German translation of the Dutch Code of Criminal Procedure of 2002,[2683] yet carefully checking the translation *vis-à-vis* the recent Dutch version's numbering.

Who is in charge of (pre-)investigations?

Some specific departments within the police force concentrate on investigations.[2684] There are further two kinds of pre-trial investigations:

2678 *Crispus Karanja Njogu v. The Attorney-General* [2000], Criminal application no. 39 (unreported), quoted from Lumumba, *supra* note 2655, 9–10.

2679 Lumumba, *supra* note 2655, 10.

2680 Bureau of Justice Statistics, US Department of Justice, State University of New York at Albany, World factbook of criminal justice systems, The Netherlands, Alex Aronowitz, "General overview. 1. Political system."; Peter Tak, *The Dutch criminal justice system* (Wolf legal publishers, Nijmegen 2008) 25 et seq., 29 et seq.

2681 Tak, *supra* note 2680, 29.

2682 Tak, *supra* note 2680, 31 et seq.

2683 Wetboek van Strafvordering/Strafprozeßordnung der Niederlande, 31.10. 2002, Hans-Joseph Scholten (edition iuscrim, Freiburg 2003).

2684 Tak, *supra* note 2680, 39.

– the investigation by the police under the direction of the Prosecutor;

– the preliminary judicial investigation led by an investigative judge.[2685]

In any event, the Prosecution Service is ultimately responsible for all aspects of criminal investigations.[2686]

What triggers the initiation of a (pre-)investigation? (What is the standard of proof – if any – to start (pre-)investigations?)

For certain serious crimes there is a duty to report to investigative authorities.[2687] Moreover, every person that gains knowledge of a criminal offence may file a report or complaint thereof.[2688] Notice must be given orally or in writing.[2689]

Who takes the decision to start a formal investigation?

The Public Prosecutor is formally in charge of investigative activities and supervises the police.[2690] On the other hand, it is the police that deal with most cases in practice even before consulting the Public Prosecutor.[2691]

In cases of a more complicated nature or a serious crime, the Public Prosecutor may request the Investigative Judge to carry out a preliminary judicial investigation.[2692] Moreover, some measures can only be authorized by a judge.[2693]

Is a discretionary evaluation performed before initiating a formal investigation/prosecution, and if so, how is it conducted (level of discretion)?

To start a formal investigation there must be a reasonable suspicion that a criminal offence has been committed.[2694]

On the one hand, the power to prosecute is vested with the Prosecution Service which may employ the expediency principle.[2695] On the other hand, it must be noted that the expediency principle is limited with regard to international core crimes as it only applies to the extent allowed by international law.[2696]

2685 Tak, *supra* note 2680, 82.

2686 Tak, *supra* note 2680, 43. On the organization of the Prosecution Service see *ibid.*, 49 et seq.

2687 Article 160 Wetboek van Strafvordering, *supra* note 2683.

2688 Article 161 Wetboek van Strafvordering, *supra* note 2683.

2689 Article 163 Wetboek van Strafvordering, *supra* note 2683.

2690 Article 148 (1)–(3) Wetboek van Strafvordering, *supra* note 2683.

2691 Tak, *supra* note 2680, 43.

2692 Article 181 (1) Wetboek van Strafvordering, *supra* note 2683; Tak, *supra* note 2680, 47.

2693 Tak, *supra* note 2680, 47, 83–4.

2694 Tak, *supra* note 2680, 82.

2695 Tak, *supra* note 2680, 47.

2696 Directives for the Public Prosecution Service re international crimes: Aanwijzing afdoening aangiften m.b.t. de strafbaarstellingen in de Wet internationale misdrijven, extended until 31.12.2011, Staatscourant 22.12.2003, no. 24; further Hans Bevers/Olivia Swaak/Jaap Roording, "The Dutch International Crimes Act

Generally speaking, the Prosecutor is not obliged to bring all sufficiently strong cases.[2697] Moreover, even in the case of investigations by the Judge, if the investigation is completed, the ultimate decision whether or not to prosecute is left to the Prosecution Service.[2698] The discretionary power based on policy decisions was restricted earlier, but its exercise increased gradually.[2699] The Board of Prosecutors General issues national guidelines for a more harmonized application of this discretionary prosecution decision.[2700] Nonetheless, the amount of discretion in the hands of the Prosecutor and its vast application is remarkable,[2701] yet limited with regard to international core crimes.

Under which circumstances can investigations (preliminary and/or full investigation) be dismissed? Are there criteria for dismissal or is the decision fully discretionary? If there are criteria, which are those and how are they defined?

First, the Prosecutor can decide not to prosecute in cases where sufficient evidence is lacking or for technical considerations (technical or procedural waiver).[2702] Second, the Prosecutor can abstain from further proceedings for reasons of public interest (*algemeen belang*).[2703] The latter policy waiver allows the Prosecution to drop any case, despite sufficient evidence for its prosecution.[2704] With regard to this expediency principle the main reasons for its application are:

- measures other than penal sanctions are preferable; and
- prosecution will be disproportionate, unjust or ineffective because:
- the crime is of a minor nature;
- the suspect's contribution to the crime was minor;
- the crime has a low degree of punishability; or
- the crime is old;
- the suspect is too young or too old;
- the suspect has recently been sentenced for another crime;
- the crime has negatively affected the suspect himself (victim of his own crimes);
- the health conditions of the suspect;
- rehabilitation prospects of the suspect;
- change of circumstances in the life of the suspect;

(Bill)" in Matthias Neuner (ed.), *National legislation implementing international crimes* (BWV, Berlin 2003) 179, 179 et seq.

2697 Nico Keijzer, "The Netherlands," in Arbour/Eser/Ambos/Sanders, *supra* note 2388, 418.

2698 Articles 238, 242 and 244 Wetboek van Strafvordering, *supra* note 2683.

2699 Fionda, *supra* note 2589, 99.

2700 Tak, *supra* note 2680, 85.

2701 Fionda, *supra* note 2589, 96.

2702 Fionda, *supra* note 2589, 97–8; Tak, *supra* note 2680, 84.

2703 Article 167 (2) Wetboek van Strafvordering, *supra* note 2683.

2704 Fionda, *supra* note 2589, 98.

- suspect cannot be traced;
- corporate criminal liability;
- the person in control of the unlawful behavior is prosecuted, not the perpetrator;
- the suspect has paid compensation;
- the victim has contributed to the crime; and
- a close relation between the victim and the suspect, and prosecution would be contrary to the interest of the victim.[2705]

However, the contained criteria were taken from secondary sources as the public interest list is unpublished in the Netherlands.[2706] In any event, the list and the enumerated factors above are not binding or complete for the Prosecutor, but offer merely guidance.[2707]

Is the decision to start/end an investigation/prosecution subject to control by another body?

If an alleged offence is not investigated or proceedings are discontinued, any person concerned can file a complaint with the competent Court of Appeal.[2708] The Court must decide on the permissibility of the challenge and, if the case may be, on the merits.[2709] It can order a continuation of criminal prosecutions or decline to do so in the public interest (*op gronden aan het algemeen belang*).

Furthermore, the accused can lodge a written notice of objection against a decision to prosecute (*dagvaarding*) with the district court.[2710] However, the judicial review is fairly limited.[2711] The grounds on which prosecutions can be dismissed are the following four:

- where the case is to be dismissed because the prosecutor no longer has the right to prosecute, e.g. due to the statute of limitations;
- where the evidence against the accused is manifestly insufficient;
- where the act does not constitute a criminal offence; and
- where the accused is not liable, e.g. due to self-defence.[2712]

Conclusion

The discretion relating to public interest considerations is significantly high in the Netherlands. There is clear evidence that the expediency principle (*opportuniteitsbeginsel*) is an integral part of prosecution decision-making.[2713] It must, however, be

[2705] Tak, *supra* note 2680, 85–6.
[2706] Fionda, *supra* note 2589, 98.
[2707] Fionda, *supra* note 2589, 98.
[2708] Article 12 (1) Wetboek van Strafvordering, *supra* note 2683.
[2709] Article 12i (1) Wetboek van Strafvordering, *supra* note 2683.
[2710] Article 250 Wetboek van Strafvordering, *supra* note 2683.
[2711] Tak, *supra* note 2680, 48.
[2712] Tak, *supra* note 2680, 48.

noted that the application of expediency is very limited in the case of international core crimes.

Judicial checks of the Prosecution's discretion are limited only, and guiding principles are existent but mainly unpublished.

XIII. Norway (Civil law, Nordic family)

The Norwegian system is difficult to classify. It is most similar to other Nordic countries, such as Denmark and Sweden.[2714] Norway's criminal law is codified in the Criminal Code of the Kingdom of Norway[2715] and the Criminal Procedure Code of the Kingdom of Norway.[2716] The upcoming survey is very limited as it is solely based on the Norwegian Criminal Procedure Code and aims at giving a very basic overview of the procedural law.

Who is in charge of (pre-)investigations?

The police may investigate and bring charges.[2717] In principle, police authorities are thus in charge of investigative activities in Norway.

What triggers the initiation of a (pre-)investigation? (What is the standard of proof – if any – to start (pre-)investigations?)

Criminal acts shall be reported to the police, they may be given orally or in writing, and they can alternatively be reported to any prosecuting authorities.[2718]

Who takes the decision to start a formal investigation?

The police enjoy discretion whether or not to investigate ("may").[2719] A prosecuting authority is established for dealing with decisions to prosecute and the later court procedure. This authority consists of (1) the Director General of Public Prosecutions and the Assistant Director; (2) public prosecutors, deputy public prosecutors,

---

2713 Fionda, *supra* note 2589, 99.

2714 Bureau of Justice Statistics, US Department of Justice, State University of New York at Albany, World factbook of criminal justice systems, Norway, Lee Bygrave, "General overview. 2. Legal system."

2715 Criminal Code of the Kingdom of Norway, 22.5.1902, Act No. 10 amended by Act No. 50 of 1.7.1994.

2716 Criminal Procedure Code of the Kingdom of Norway, 22.5.1981, Act No. 25 amended by Act No. 56 of 17.7.1998.

2717 Secs.67 (1) and 225 (1) Criminal Procedure Code of the Kingdom of Norway, *supra* note 2716.

2718 Sec.223 Criminal Procedure Code of the Kingdom of Norway, *supra* note 2716.

2719 Sec.67 (1) Criminal Procedure Code of the Kingdom of Norway, *supra* note 2716; also World factbook of criminal justice systems, Norway, *supra* note 2714,"Police. 5. Discretion."

and assistant public prosecutors; (3) the chiefs of police, the deputy chiefs of police, the head of the security service, the assistant chiefs of police, police prosecutors, and police intendants; and (4) district sheriffs.[2720] The Director General and public prosecutors may order an investigation to be instituted and supervise how it is carried out.[2721] In sum, the police take the decision on investigations, but the police might be directed by higher prosecuting authorities on some occasions. Furthermore, the Prosecuting Authority can apply for a judicial inquiry.[2722]

Is a discretionary evaluation performed before initiating a formal investigation/prosecution, and if so, how is it conducted (level of discretion)?

As mentioned above, the police decide whether or not to investigate. The decision whether or not to prosecute is also vested with the police for misdemeanors.[2723] On the other hand, the Public Prosecutor shall generally decide whether to prosecute in cases of felonies.[2724] For most serious crimes the decision rests on the Director General of Public Prosecutions or the King in Council.[2725] Therefore, the Prosecuting Authority controls the most important discretionary evaluations, whereas the police decide on minor cases during early proceedings.

Under which circumstances can investigations (preliminary and/or full investigation) be dismissed? Are there criteria for dismissal or is the decision fully discretionary? If there are criteria, which are those and how are they defined?

The standard to commence investigations is one of "reasonable grounds" to inquire whether any criminal matter requires prosecution by public authorities.[2726]

A prosecution may be waived even though there is sufficient evidence if the Prosecuting Authority finds that there are "weighty reasons" for not prosecuting the act.[2727] Before a judgment is issued a prosecution may be discontinued at any time.[2728]

[2720] Sec.55 Criminal Procedure Code of the Kingdom of Norway, *supra* note 2716.

[2721] Secs.225 and 75 Criminal Procedure Code of the Kingdom of Norway, *supra* note 2716.

[2722] Sec.237 (1) Criminal Procedure Code of the Kingdom of Norway, *supra* note 2716.

[2723] Sec.67 (2) Criminal Procedure Code of the Kingdom of Norway, *supra* note 2716.

[2724] Sec.66 Criminal Procedure Code of the Kingdom of Norway, *supra* note 2716.

[2725] Secs.64 and 65 Criminal Procedure Code of the Kingdom of Norway, *supra* note 2716.

[2726] Sec.224 (1) Criminal Procedure Code of the Kingdom of Norway, *supra* note 2716.

[2727] Sec.69 (1) Criminal Procedure Code of the Kingdom of Norway, *supra* note 2716.

[2728] Sec.72 (1) Criminal Procedure Code of the Kingdom of Norway, *supra* note 2716.

Is the decision to start/end an investigation/prosecution subject to control by another body?

A decision not to prosecute or to waive prosecution by the Prosecuting Authority can be appealed by way of complaint to the immediately superior prosecuting authority.[2729]

A superior prosecuting authority may drop any prosecution commenced by lower authorities and it may reverse a decision to waive prosecution by another authority within three months.[2730]

Conclusion

Norwegian criminal procedure leaves (pre-)investigations mainly to the police, yet introduces a hierarchical Prosecution Authority that decides whether or not to continue with prosecutions. Prosecutors further exercise control over the police, especially with regard to serious crimes. The decisions to initiate investigations and prosecutions provide for discretionary choices through the terms "reasonable grounds" and "weighty reasons." No factors for discretion could be found in the Criminal Procedure Code of Norway. Apparently, the "weighty reasons" are left undefined and allow for very broad considerations.

XIV. South Africa (Common law)

South Africa's legal system was strongly influenced by common law, but there was also considerable impact of Roman-Dutch law. Moreover, its criminal procedure can be found in statutory law: the South African Constitution,[2731] the Criminal Procedure Act,[2732] and the National Prosecuting Authority Act.[2733]

Who is in charge of (pre-)investigations?

It must be noted that South African criminal law distinguishes between the police, who are generally in charge of investigations, and a single National Prosecuting Authority – including the National Director of Public Prosecution (hereinafter NDPP), the Director(s) of Public Prosecutions (hereinafter DPP), and prosecutors – which is in charge of prosecutions.[2734] Thus, the responsibility for investigations is

---

[2729] Sec.59 Criminal Procedure Code of the Kingdom of Norway, *supra* note 2716.

[2730] Sec.75 (1) and (2) Criminal Procedure Code of the Kingdom of Norway, *supra* note 2716.

[2731] Constitution of the Republic of South Africa, Act No. 108 of 1996, 8.5.1996.

[2732] Criminal Procedure Act, Act No. 51 of 1977, 22.7.1977, in Etienne Du Toit et al. (eds.), Commentary on the Criminal Procedure Act, revision service 40 (Juta, Cape Town 2008).

[2733] National Prosecuting Authority Act, Act No. 32 of 1998, 3.7.1998.

[2734] Article 179 (1) Constitution of the Republic of South Africa, *supra* note 2731; secs.2 et seq. National Prosecuting Authority Act, *supra* note 2733; sec.1 NDPP prosecution policy, 1.12.2005; Commentary on the Criminal Procedure Act,

given to the police and not the Prosecutor.[2735] However, for specific offences or specified categories of offences, Investigating Directorates can be established in the NDPP.[2736] The later power to institute and conduct criminal prosecutions, as well as to discontinue such proceedings, is given to the Prosecuting Authority.[2737]

What triggers the initiation of a (pre-)investigation? (What is the standard of proof – if any – to start (pre-)investigations?)

No legal duty to report crimes exists in South Africa.[2738] The initial investigation is yet conducted upon a complaint received by the police or upon their own initiative.[2739]

Any person may further lay an affidavit or affirmed declaration before the Investigating Director who may hold an inquiry on the matter in question.[2740]

Who takes the decision to start a formal investigation?

There exists a formal separation of powers between the police and the Prosecuting Authority. Therefore, the police operate under their own statute and prosecutors cannot compel the police to carry out investigations.[2741] Nonetheless, there is cooperation between the police and prosecutors.[2742]

Is a discretionary evaluation performed before initiating a formal investigation/prosecution, and if so, how is it conducted (level of discretion)?

South Africa does not follow a system of compulsory prosecution.[2743] With regard to investigation practice the police do exercise discretion of their own and often refrain from bringing trivial matters and allegations, which are not adequately supported by evidence.[2744]

Whereas the initial investigation is conducted by the police, a docket (file, dossier) is prepared later and submitted to the Prosecutor who takes the decision to

---

supra note 2732, 1–4 et seq.; J. Joubert (ed.), *Criminal procedure handbook,* 7th edition (Juta, Cape Town 2005) 43 et seq.

2735 Jan De Olivera, "South Africa" in Arbour/Eser/Ambos/Sanders, *supra* note 2388, 469, 476.

2736 Secs.7 (1) (a), 13 (1) National Prosecuting Authority Act, *supra* note 2733.

2737 Article 179 (2) Constitution of the Republic of South Africa, *supra* note 2731; sec.20 (1) National Prosecuting Authority Act, *supra* note 2733.

2738 Joubert, *supra* note 2734, 57; Commentary on the Criminal Procedure Act, *supra* note 2732, 1-4L-1.

2739 Joubert, *supra* note 2734, 56.

2740 Secs.27 and 28 (1) (a) National Prosecuting Authority Act, *supra* note 2733.

2741 De Olivera, in Arbour/Eser/Ambos/Sanders, *supra* note 2735, 477.

2742 Sec.8 NDPP prosecution policy, *supra* note 2734; Commentary on the Criminal Procedure Act, *supra* note 2732, 1-4K; Joubert, *supra* note 2734, 56.

2743 Commentary on the Criminal Procedure Act, *supra* note 2732, 1-4M; Joubert, *supra* note 2734, 59.

2744 Commentary on the Criminal Procedure Act, *supra* note 2732, 1-4K; Joubert, *supra* note 2734, 56.

prosecute or not.[2745] The Prosecutors thus have the final say whether a prosecution should be instituted, and not the police.[2746] Even if there is sufficient evidence in a specific case for further proceedings, the Prosecutor is not obliged to bring prosecutions. In other words, the Prosecutor has discretion to continue proceedings.[2747] On the other hand, all prosecutors must act within the ambit of the NDPP's prosecution policy and policy directives.[2748]

Under which circumstances can investigations (preliminary and/or full investigation) be dismissed? Are there criteria for dismissal or is the decision fully discretionary? If there are criteria, which are those and how are they defined?

The identified discretion to bring prosecutions notwithstanding, if there is a *prima facie* case and no compelling reason for a refusal to prosecute, the Prosecutor should – in general – proceed with a case to trial.[2749] Grounds for refusing to prosecute despite a *prima facie* case are:

- triviality of the offence;
- advanced age or very young age of an accused;
- plea bargain between the Prosecution and the Defence;
- antiquated nature of the offence; or
- tragic personal circumstances of the accused.[2750]

When evaluating the evidence the Prosecutor must take into account the following factors: (1) How strong is the case for the State?; (2) Will the evidence be admissible?; (3) Will the state witness be credible?; (4) Will the evidence be reliable?; (5) Is the evidence available?; and (6) How strong is the case for the defence?[2751] If the Prosecutor is satisfied that there is enough evidence to provide a reasonable prospect of conviction, a prosecution must follow, unless public interest demands otherwise.[2752] For the public interest test the NDPP prosecution policy lists:

"*The nature and seriousness of the offence*:

- The seriousness of the offence, taking into account the effect of the crime on the victim, the manner in which it was committed, the motivation for the act and the relationship between the accused and the victim.
- The nature of the offence, its prevalence and recurrence, and its effect on public order and morale.

2745 Commentary on the Criminal Procedure Act, *supra* note 2732, 1-4K; Joubert, *supra* note 2734, 56.

2746 Commentary on the Criminal Procedure Act, *supra* note 2732, 1-4K.

2747 De Olivera, in Arbour/Eser/Ambos/Sanders, *supra* note 2735, 474.

2748 Article 179 (5) (a) and (b) Constitution of the Republic of South Africa, *supra* note 2731; secs.21 and 22 (2) (a) National Prosecuting Authority Act, *supra* note 2733; Joubert, *supra* note 2734, 49.

2749 Joubert, *supra* note 2734, 59.

2750 Joubert, *supra* note 2734, 60.

2751 Sec.4 (b) NDPP prosecution policy, *supra* note 2734.

2752 Sec.4 (c) NDPP prosecution policy, *supra* note 2734.

- The economic impact of the offence on the community, its threat to people or damage to public property, and its effect on the peace of mind and sense of security of the public.
- The likely outcome in the event of a conviction, having regard to sentencing options available to the court.

The interests of the victim and the broader community:

- The attitude of the victim of the offence towards a prosecution and the potential effects of discontinuing it. Care should be taken when considering this factor, since public interest may demand that certain crimes should be prosecuted – regardless of a complainant's wish not to proceed.
- The need for individual and general deterrence, and the necessity of maintaining public confidence in the criminal justice system.
- Prosecution priorities as determined from time to time, the likely length and expense of a trial and whether or not a prosecution would be deemed counterproductive.

The circumstances of the offender:

- The previous convictions of the accused, his or her criminal history, background, culpability and personal circumstances, as well as other mitigating or aggravating factors.
- Whether the accused has admitted guilt, shown repentance, made restitution or expressed a willingness to cooperate with the authorities in the investigation or prosecution of others. (In this regard the degree of culpability of the accused and the extent, to which reliable evidence from the said accused is considered necessary to secure a conviction against others, will be crucial).
- Whether the objectives of criminal justice would be better served by implementing non-criminal alternatives to prosecution, particularly in the case of juvenile offenders and less serious matters.
- Whether there has been an unreasonably long delay between the date when the crime was committed, the date on which the prosecution was instituted and the trial date, taking into account the complexity of the offence and the role of the accused in the delay."[2753]

The weight to be given to the particular elements depends on the particular circumstances of the case.[2754] For concluding the discretionary observations, it is further interesting to note the different procedural levels at which the Prosecutor can exercise his discretion, namely at:

– the decision whether or not to institute criminal proceedings against an accused;

– the decision whether or not to withdraw charges or stop the prosecution;

[2753] Sec.4 (c) NDPP prosecution policy, *supra* note 2734; Joubert, *supra* note 2734, 60–1; Commentary on the Criminal Procedure Act, *supra* note 2732, 1-4N and 1-4O.

[2754] Sec.4 (c) NDPP prosecution policy, *supra* note 2734.

- the decision whether or not to oppose an application for bail or release by an accused who is in custody following arrest;
- the decision about which crimes to charge an accused with and in which court the trial should proceed;
- the decision whether or not to accept a plea of guilty tendered by an accused;
- the decision about which evidence to present during the trial;
- the decision about which evidence to present during sentence proceedings, in the event of a conviction; and
- the decision whether or not to appeal to a higher court in connection with a question of law, an inappropriate sentence or the improper granting of bail, or to seek review of proceedings.[2755]

Is the decision to start/end an investigation/prosecution subject to control by another body?

If the police decide not to investigate, no judicial control mechanism is available.

Regarding decisions to prosecute or not to prosecute, the NDPP may exercise review.[2756] The NDPP may further intervene if policy directives are not complied with.[2757] In addition, the National Prosecuting Authority is accountable to Parliament.[2758] On the other hand, judicial control over the Prosecuting Authority is very limited. In principle, courts cannot interfere with a *bona fides* decision to prosecute or not to prosecute, and only reviews based on ordinary administrative law grounds are possible.[2759]

Conclusion

South Africa follows the expediency principle and ensures a margin of discretion for the police and the Prosecuting Authority. On the other hand, the choice not to prosecute must follow a specific legal procedure. First, evidence is evaluated, and might lead to a *prima facie* case. Second, the mentioned *prima facie* cases must – generally speaking – proceed to trial, *unless* there are profound grounds that stand against prosecution. The structure of exceptions ("unless") is similar to the design of article 53 (1) and (2) ICC Statute. "Public interest" is then the main criterion, and three standard factors are mentioned for public interest consideration: the nature and seriousness of the offence, the interests of the victim and the broader community, and the circumstances of the offender. In sum, essential parts of the decision whether or not to prosecute show methodical similarities to article 53 ICC Statute.

2755 Sec.3 NDPP prosecution policy, *supra* note 2734.

2756 Article 179 (5) (d) Constitution of the Republic of South Africa, *supra* note 2731; sec.22 (2) (c) National Prosecuting Authority Act, *supra* note 2733.

2757 Sec.22 (2) (b) National Prosecuting Authority Act, *supra* note 2733.

2758 Sec.35 National Prosecuting Authority Act, *supra* note 2733; Commentary on the Criminal Procedure Act, *supra* note 2732, 1-4D.

2759 Commentary on the Criminal Procedure Act, *supra* note 2732, 1-4G et seq., citing abundant case law.

Only the judicial review mechanism falls short in South African criminal procedure, yet it requires more profound analysis of the abundant case law to reach a precise appraisal.

XV. Sudan (Common law, Sharia law)

Sudan's legal system is based on English common law and Islamic law. The upcoming survey is solely based upon an English translation of the Sudanese Code of Criminal Procedure of 1994,[2760] and for this reason must be given limited value.

Who is in charge of (pre-)investigations?

Investigations are generally carried out by the police. On the other hand, a chief may carry out certain (pre-)investigative duties.[2761] In conducting the investigation he shall then forward the report to the nearest police station.[2762]

What triggers the initiation of a (pre-)investigation? (What is the standard of proof – if any – to start (pre-)investigations?)

Every person shall give information to the nearest judge, a policeman, or a chief, if there is reason to believe that a suicide or a killing took place, if a dead body has been discovered, or if any offence under the New Sudan Penal Code of 1994 has been committed.[2763] In addition, the Attorney-General may undertake investigations or authorize any other person to do so if he is satisfied on his own knowledge or upon information received that there is a "reason to believe or suspect" that an offence has been committed.[2764] Furthermore, judges can examine complaints, and a judge may proceed with a further inquiry or a trial "if he thinks fit."[2765] In the case of frivolous or vexatious complaints compensation can be awarded.[2766]

Who takes the decision to start a formal investigation?

A chief may carry out preliminary investigations, but the police officer who is in charge can take the lead, notify the chief thereof, and the latter must terminate any further investigations.[2767] The police officer has to draft a "first information report," which is sent to the appropriate judge. The officer shall then proceed to the crime scene for investigating if the offender is not already in custody.[2768] Upon

---

2760 The Code of Criminal Procedure, 1994, Laws of the new Sudan, Secretariat for Legal Affairs.

2761 Sec.90 Code of Criminal Procedure, *supra* note 2760.

2762 Sec.90 (5) Code of Criminal Procedure, *supra* note 2760.

2763 Sec.89 Code of Criminal Procedure, *supra* note 2760.

2764 Sec.109 (1) Code of Criminal Procedure, *supra* note 2760.

2765 Sec.118 Code of Criminal Procedure, *supra* note 2760.

2766 Sec.138 Code of Criminal Procedure, *supra* note 2760.

2767 Sec.90 (1) Code of Criminal Procedure, *supra* note 2760.

2768 Secs.91, 92 (1) and (2) Code of Criminal Procedure, *supra* note 2760.

receiving the first report the judge may direct the police as to the conduct of the investigation, or, if he thinks fit, assign a judge subordinate for inquiries.[2769]

Is a discretionary evaluation performed before initiating a formal investigation/prosecution, and if so, how is it conducted (level of discretion)?

If it appears to the police officer that investigations should be terminated before any further actions are taken, he must summarize the case and submit it to the judge, who may order to terminate or to continue proceedings.[2770] However, if the officer finds "reasonable grounds of suspicion" against a person of having committed an offence, and he believes that an inquiry or trial should begin, a submission must be filed with the judge.[2771] The judge can either begin an inquiry or trial if the documents appear sufficient, or, otherwise, shall give directions that further investigation is necessary.[2772] On the other hand, a judge can refuse to proceed with any given case if there is no "sufficient ground" for proceeding.[2773] When the "sufficient ground" is affirmed, he must either continue with an inquiry or a trial.[2774]

Under which circumstances can investigations (preliminary and/or full investigation) be dismissed? Are there criteria for dismissal or is the decision fully discretionary? If there are criteria, which are those and how are they defined?

For the dropping of a case in early proceedings the judge can give a termination order "if he thinks fit,"[2775] implying large discretion on behalf of the judge in charge. In the case of an investigation that is commenced under section 109, thus by the Attorney General, the Attorney General or his representative can terminate their activities if it appears that the "public interest" is not served.[2776] As already mentioned, the judge applies "sufficient grounds" for testing if prosecutorial action should proceed. All these terms ("thinks fit," "public interest," and "sufficient ground") imply discretion. However, criteria for their application are not explicitly mentioned in the code.

Is the decision to start/end an investigation/prosecution subject to control by another body?

In the course of investigations judges and Attorney Generals can demand the submission of a case diary.[2777] In addition, judges can intervene in investigations quite largely: if a judge is not satisfied that the offence was committed, or if he deems it

[2769] Sec.94 Code of Criminal Procedure, *supra* note 2760.
[2770] Sec.103 Code of Criminal Procedure, *supra* note 2760.
[2771] Sec.104 (1) Sudanese Code of Criminal Procedure, *supra* note 2760.
[2772] Sec.104 (3) and (4) Sudanese Code of Criminal Procedure, *supra* note 2760.
[2773] Sec.121 Code of Criminal Procedure, *supra* note 2760.
[2774] Sec.122 Code of Criminal Procedure, *supra* note 2760.
[2775] Sec.103 Code of Criminal Procedure, *supra* note 2760.
[2776] Sec.110 Code of Criminal Procedure, *supra* note 2760.
[2777] Sec.106 Code of Criminal Procedure, *supra* note 2760.

expedient for any other reasons to do so, he may either make investigations himself or direct any subordinate judge. If the police have already investigated the case, the additional investigation shall be deemed a continuation of that investigation.[2778]

Conclusion

Sudanese criminal procedure foresees differentiated procedures. Dynamic interaction between the chiefs, police officers, Attorney General, and judges occurs. Police officers are in charge of (pre-)investigations. On the other hand, it ultimately rests upon the Attorney General and the Judge which cases reach the further inquiry or trial level. Their discretion is considerably high ("thinks fit" and "public interest"). In sum, the judge plays a more proactive role in Sudan compared to other countries. In this respect, the system shows, albeit generally drafted under English influence, large influence from the French model (*juge d'instruction*).

XVI. Uganda (Common law, African family, situation country)

Uganda's legal system is based on English Common Law and African customary law. Uganda also constitutes one of the pending situations before the ICC. Its criminal law sources can be found in various statutes, most important the Penal Code Act regarding substantive criminal law.[2779] Previously, all rules governing criminal procedure were contained in the Criminal Procedure Code Act,[2780] but in 1970 a decision was made to make two comprehensive laws on governing procedure, the Magistrates' Court Act 1970 and the Trial on Indictments Decree 1971.[2781] In consequence, relevant norms were divided for lower court proceedings (Magistrate Courts) and the Ugandan High Court.

Who is in charge of (pre-)investigations?

Various law enforcement agencies can conduct investigations, among them the Uganda Police Force, the Local Administration Police Forces, the Chiefs, etc.; in any event, the main responsibility lies with the Uganda Police Force to commence investigations.[2782]

[2778] Sec.120 Code of Criminal Procedure, *supra* note 2760.

[2779] Penal Code Act 1950, 15.6.1950 (Chapter 120).

[2780] Criminal Procedure Code Act 1950 (Chapter 116).

[2781] B. J. Odoki, *Criminal procedure in Uganda,* 2nd edition (The Law Development Centre, Kampala 1990) 1; see further The Trial on Indictments Decree 1971, 1.8.1995 (22/71), reprint authorized and approved by the Attorney General as per S.I 107/95 under powers conferred upon him by S. 14 of the Acts of Parliament Act Cap. 15 (Kampala Law Reports, Kampala 1995); The Magistrates' Courts Act 1971, 1.8.1995 (13/70), reprint authorized and approved by the Attorney General as per S.I 107/95 under powers conferred upon him by S. 14 of the Acts of Parliament Act Cap. 15 (Kampala Law Reports, Kampala 1995).

[2782] Odoki, *supra* note 2781, 13.

What triggers the initiation of a (pre-)investigation? (What is the standard of proof – if any – to start (pre-)investigations?)

The process is brought in motion through a complaint or report of a crime to the police. Any complainant, victim, his relative, the Chief, or even another person totally unconnected with the offence, may bring alleged crimes to the attention of the police.[2783]

Criminal proceedings can be commenced at the Magistrate's Courts level as well. There are three ways by which proceedings can be instituted: first, by a police officer bringing a person arrested; second, by a public prosecutor or a police officer laying a charge; and third, by any other person making a complaint.[2784] The person filing a complaint must have reasonable and probable cause to believe that an offence has been committed and shall submit its allegations orally or in writing.[2785]

Who takes the decision to start a formal investigation?

The officer in charge of the Criminal Investigation Department decides whether or not a case file should be opened and on what charge.[2786] His decision is passed on to one of the senior members of his staff who carry out further investigations.[2787] If a complaint is filed with the Magistrate Court, the magistrate can proceed only if he is satisfied that *prima facie* the commission of an offence has been disclosed and that the complaint is neither frivolous nor vexatious.[2788] Depending on their gravity and complexity cases may require involvement by the Director of Public Prosecutions (hereinafter DPP).[2789] A number of statutes provide that no prosecution can be instituted without the consent of the DPP.[2790]

Is a discretionary evaluation performed before initiating a formal investigation/prosecution, and if so, how is it conducted (level of discretion)?

The overall conduct and supervision of criminal prosecutions is the responsibility of the DPP.[2791] Article 120 (3) of the Ugandan Constitution states:

"The functions of the Director of Public Prosecutions are the following:

(a) to direct the police to investigate any information of a criminal nature and to report to him or her expeditiously;

(b) to institute criminal proceedings against any person or authority in any court with competent jurisdiction other than a court martial;

2783 Odoki, *supra* note 2781, 14.

2784 Sec.41 (1) Magistrates' Courts Act 1971, *supra* note 2781.

2785 Sec.41 (3) Magistrates' Courts Act 1971, *supra* note 2781.

2786 Odoki, *supra* note 2781, 14.

2787 Odoki, *supra* note 2781, 14.

2788 Ayume, *supra* note 2789, 3.

2789 Odoki, *supra* note 2781, 16; Francis Ayume, *Criminal procedure and law in Uganda* (Longman, Nairobi 1986) 9 et seq.

2790 Odoki, *supra* note 2781, 61–2; Ayume, *supra* note 2789, 12 et seq.

2791 Ayume, *supra* note 2789, 5.

(c) to take over and continue any criminal proceedings instituted by any other person or authority;

(d) to discontinue at any stage before judgment is delivered, any such criminal proceedings to which this article relates, instituted by himself or herself or any other person or authority; except that the Director of Public Prosecutions shall not discontinue any proceedings commenced by another person or authority except with the consent of the court."[2792]

The DPP enjoy ample discretion in any decision to prosecute or not to prosecute.[2793]

Under which circumstances can investigations (preliminary and/or full investigation) be dismissed? Are there criteria for dismissal or is the decision fully discretionary? If there are criteria, which are those and how are they defined?

For the different Court levels (magistrate courts and High Court) similar provisions to article 120 of the Ugandan Constitution flesh out the DPP's control of prosecutions. Section 119 of the Magistrates' Court Act states that "[i]n any proceedings before a magistrate's court the prosecutor may, with the consent of the court or on the instructions of the Director of Public Prosecutions, at any time before judgment is pronounced, withdraw from the prosecution of any person [...]."[2794] There are two limbs to this section. The first gives only a right to withdraw with the consent of the court, thus giving the court the discretion to permit or refuse withdrawal, while the second gives the DPP unfettered discretion to terminate proceedings.[2795]

With respect to the High Court, similar powers are vested with the DPP to discontinue proceedings. Section 133 of the Trial on Indictments Decree provides for the right to enter a *nolle prosequi* at any stage before verdict.[2796] Any decision of the DPP to discontinue proceedings appears to be discretionary, and no further criteria could be identified.

In the different context of sentencing it is interesting to note that the term "gravity of the offence," well-known from the ICC's procedure, can be found. When the Court is faced with gravity, it takes into considerations other factors outside the statute to determine the relative gravity of the offence under consideration.[2797] Factors are the nature of the offence, the circumstances of the offence, and the circumstances of the offender. For the nature of the offence matters are taken into account such as (a) whether the offence passes special social danger or menace to society; (b) whether it causes more alarm to the public, e. g. by being too prevalent; (c)

[2792] Article 120 (3) of the Constitution of the Republic of Uganda, 22.9.1995. For the former article 71 (2) of the Constitution see Ayume, *supra* note 2789, 10; Odoki, *supra* note 2781, 79.

[2793] Odoki, *supra* note 2781, 81.

[2794] Sec.119 Magistrates' Courts Act 1971, *supra* note 2781.

[2795] Ayume, *supra* note 2789, 10–11.

[2796] Article 133 (1) The Trial on Indictments Decree 1971, *supra* note 2781; further Odoki, *supra* note 2781, 125–6.

[2797] Odoki, *supra* note 2781, 150.

whether it causes great social disapproval; and (d) the degree of wickedness involved in the commission of the offence.[2798]

Is the decision to start/end an investigation/prosecution subject to control by another body?

The DPP is vested with the power of control over criminal prosecutions and may, for example, intervene with regard to activities by subordinates if the public interest so requires.[2799] On the other hand, it is worth noting that the newly drafted version of article 120 (3) of the Ugandan Constitution foresees consent of the court for discontinuance. Therefore, although discretionary decisions are in principle vested with the DPP, there is a shift towards more judicial control. It remains a matter for future analysis to inquire the exact scope of judicial control in Uganda.

Conclusion

Preliminary investigations are a matter for the Ugandan police. The DPP and its subordinate prosecutors play the decisive role with regard to directing prosecutions. It is further the DPP that exercises control over the police, and, in turn, the courts that have to consent to certain withdrawal decisions of the DPP.

In the context of sentencing the term "gravity" was found. It is worthwhile to note that the factors in Ugandan law appear to be very similar to the ones identified by PTC I in its arrest warrant decision in Lubanga and Ntaganda (social danger or menace to society; alarm to the public; social disapproval; and degree of wickedness). On the other hand, Ugandan law mentions them for relative, discretionary gravity, which is in line with the approach taken in the study at hand.

XVII. United Kingdom (England and Wales) (Common law)

The English and Welsh legal system adopts common law and is adversarial in all courts.[2800] Its criminal law derives from the common law and from various statutes. The process of criminal investigations is regulated in numerous principal sources, most important the Police and Criminal Evidence Act 1984 (Police Reform Act 2002) and the Regulations of Investigatory.[2801] The majority of prosecutions in England and Wales are dealt with by the Prosecution of Offences Act of 1985 (hereinafter POA) establishing the Crown Prosecution Service (hereinafter CPS) headed by the Director of Public Prosecutions (hereinafter DPP).[2802]

[2798] Odoki, *supra* note 2781, 150.

[2799] Odoki, *supra* note 2781, 80–1.

[2800] Bureau of Justice Statistics, US Department of Justice, State University of New York at Albany, World factbook of criminal justice systems, England & Wales, Corretta Phillips/Gemma Cox/Ken Pease, "General overview. 2 Legal system."

[2801] Denis Clark, *Bevan & Lidstone's, The investigation of crime,* 3rd edition (Lexis Nexis, UK 2004) 7.

[2802] Prosecution of Offences Act 1985; Andrew Sanders, "England and Wales (United Kingdom)" in Arbour/Eser/Ambos/Sanders, *supra* note 2388, 297, 297;

Who is in charge of (pre-)investigations?

A number of diverse organizations are empowered to conduct investigations, the most important one being the police.[2803] In principle, criminal offences are investigated by the police.

When may activation be triggered? (What is the standard of proof – if any – to start (pre-)investigations?)

There are two broad forms of investigations: reactive and proactive investigations. The traditional style of reactive investigations consists of a search for evidence, following an allegation of or discovery of circumstances which amount to a crime.[2804] The overwhelming majority of offences are reported by members of the public.[2805] However, only a low proportion results in formal proceedings.[2806]

Who takes the decision to start a formal investigation?

There is a clear demarcation line of roles between the police and the CPS: the police investigate and take the initial decisions to prosecute or not; only after this initial determination does the CPS become involved.[2807] Although, as a general rule, the CPS does not intervene, the police may consult the CPS.[2808] The Police and Criminal Evidence Act 1984 (hereinafter PACE) codifies the investigative powers of the police,[2809] and the Code for Crown Prosecutors assists prosecutors in the exercise of their duties.[2810]

Is a discretionary evaluation performed before initiating a formal investigation/prosecution, and if so, how is it conducted (level of discretion)?

With regard to opening formal investigations the police enjoy vast powers.[2811] However, the police officer in charge must pursue all reasonable lines of inquiry, whether these point towards or away from the suspect, and the officer may not make speculative inquiries.[2812] In any event, the officers at the lowest level, i.e.

Gallavin, *supra* note 1881, 187; Fionda, *supra* note 2589, 14. Further on the CPS, see S. H. Bailey/J. P. L. Ching/N. W. Taylor, *Smith, Bailey and Gunn on the modern English legal system* (Sweet & Maxwell, London 2007)843 et seq.

2803 Bailey/Ching/Taylor, *supra* note 2802, 785.

2804 Clark, *supra* note 2801, 6.

2805 Bailey/Ching/Taylor, *supra* note 2802, 786.

2806 Andrew Ashworth, *The criminal process, an evaluative study* (OUP, Oxford 1998) 140; Bailey/Ching/Taylor, *supra* note 2802, 786.

2807 Sanders, in Arbour/Eser/Ambos/Sanders, *supra* note 2802, 301.

2808 Sec.3 (2) (e) Prosecution of Offences Act 1985, *supra* note 2802; Sanders, in Arbour/Eser/Ambos/Sanders, *supra* note 2802, 301–2.

2809 Police and Criminal Evidence Act 1984.

2810 The Code for Crown Prosecutors; thereto Gallavin, *supra* note 1881, 188 et seq.

2811 Sec.2 Code of Practice, Criminal Procedure and Investigations Act 1996 (s.23(1)).

those dealing with the suspects, have a great amount of discretion whether or not to start an investigation.[2813] Investigative bodies in England and Wales operate under the expediency system, meaning that they have large discretion to actively pursue inquiries and to prosecute or not.[2814] The police exercises selectivity and have at least five alternative forms of formal response to a case: (1) no further action; (2) informal warning; (3) formal police cautions; (4) reparations or mediation scheme; and (5) prosecutions.[2815] At or near the starting point of an investigation the "reasonable suspicion" standard arises. It is a low threshold that "presupposes the existence of facts or information which would satisfy an objective observer that the person concerned may have committed a criminal offence."[2816]

Furthermore, the police take the initial decision as to whether or not to proceed to a prosecution.[2817] However, it is worth noting that reforms in 2003 have introduced statutory charging: whilst the custody officer still makes a decision whether or not the case is appropriate for prosecution, the case is then passed on to the Prosecutor who takes the final decision.[2818] The CPS was introduced to establish consistent application of charging, in other words, to ensure a more congruent exercise of discretion.[2819] When ultimately deciding to prosecute (decision of charging),[2820] the CPS has to conduct a two stage test: section 5 of the Code for Crown Prosecutors establishes an "evidentiary test" and a "public interests test." Currently, 26 percent of all cases are discontinued on the basis of insufficient evidence or public interest.[2821]

Under which circumstances can investigations (preliminary and/or full investigation) be dismissed? Are there criteria for dismissal or is the decision fully discretionary? If there are criteria, which are those and how are they defined?

The police officer, when initiating investigations, most likely takes into account the following considerations: the gravity of the offence; the evidence likely to be available in a prosecution; the degree of certainty that the crime has been committed; the attitude of the victim; the personal circumstances of the offender; and the efficacy of a prosecution compared with other ways of dealing with the problem.[2822] These factors are similar to the considerations of the CPS's decision whether to continue a prosecution, but will need to be taken quickly and often with-

---

2812 Secs.3.5 and 3.6 Code of Practice, Criminal Procedure and Investigations Act, *supra* note 2811.

2813 Bailey/Ching/Taylor, *supra* note 2802, 790, 852.

2814 Sanders, in Arbour/Eser/Ambos/Sanders, *supra* note 2802, 298; Asworth, *supra* note 2806, 146 et seq.

2815 Asworth, *supra* note 2806, 147 et seq., 152.

2816 Bailey/Ching/Taylor, *supra* note 2802, 790–1.

2817 Bailey/Ching/Taylor, *supra* note 2802, 852–3.

2818 Bailey/Ching/Taylor, *supra* note 2802, 854.

2819 Bailey/Ching/Taylor, *supra* note 2802, 845 et seq.

2820 Sec.3 Code for Crown Prosecutors, *supra* note 2810.

2821 World factbook of criminal justice systems, England & Wales, *supra* note 2800, "Prosecutorial and judicial process. 1. Procedures."

2822 Bailey/Ching/Taylor, *supra* note 2802, 853.

out help from colleagues.[2823] As already mentioned, the police officers enjoy large discretion, both when initiating investigations and prosecutions, and its principles are rather informal than clearly codified factors.

To some extent, the prosecutorial selection is guided by the CPS, particularly the evidentiary and the public interests tests. At the evidentiary stage, the Crown Prosecutor must be satisfied that there is a "realistic prospect" of conviction.[2824] It is an objective test, and Crown Prosecutors must consider whether the evidence can be used and is reliable.[2825] This depends *inter alia* on the exclusionary rules, and reliability primarily rests upon the credibility of the defendant and witnesses.[2826] In any event, the threshold cannot be too high:

> "The Crown Prosecution Service should not look for the same standard of proof that a jury or bench of magistrates would need to find before it could convict, which would set too high a standard and tend to usurp the role of the court. The test based on "more likely than not" meant just that."[2827]

At the public interest stage, the Crown Prosecutors must "*balance* factors for and against prosecution carefully and fairly. Public interest factors that can affect the decision to prosecute usually depend on the *seriousness of the offence* or the *circumstances of the suspect* (emph. added)."[2828] Albeit the Code for Crown Prosecutors acknowledges the uniqueness of each case, it holds that there are general principles that apply to every case.[2829] A non-exhaustive list of factors enumerates factors in favor of prosecution in section 5.9, stating that

> "[t]he more serious the offence, the more likely it is that a prosecution will be needed in the public interest. A prosecution is likely to be needed if:
>
> (a) a conviction is likely to result in a significant sentence;
>
> (b) a conviction is likely to result in a confiscation or any other order;
>
> (c) a weapon was used or violence was threatened during the commission of the offence;
>
> (d) the offence was committed against a person serving the public (for example, a police or prison officer, or a nurse);
>
> (e) the defendant was in a position of authority or trust;
>
> (f) the evidence shows that the defendant was a ringleader or an organizer of the offence;
>
> (g) there is evidence that the offence was premeditated;

[2823] Bailey/Ching/Taylor, *supra* note 2802, 853.

[2824] Sec.5.2 Code for Crown Prosecutors, *supra* note 2810. In more detail on this test, see Asworth, *supra* note 2806, 181 et seq.

[2825] Secs.5.3 and 5.4 Code for Crown Prosecutors, *supra* note 2810.

[2826] Sec.5.4 Code for Crown Prosecutors, *supra* note 2810.

[2827] *R v. DPP, ex p. Manning* [2001], 17.5.2000 (Q.B. 330) para. 22.

[2828] Sec.5.8 Code for Crown Prosecutors, *supra* note 2810. In more detail on this test, see Asworth, *supra* note 2806, 184 et seq.; Fionda, *supra* note 2589, 22 et seq.

[2829] Sec.2.1 Code for Crown Prosecutors, *supra* note 2810.

(h) there is evidence that the offence was carried out by a group;

(i) the victim of the offence was vulnerable, has been put in considerable fear, or suffered personal attack, damage or disturbance;

(j) the offence was committed in the presence of, or in close proximity to, a child;

(k) the offence was motivated by any form of discrimination against the victim's ethnic or national origin, disability, sex, religious beliefs, political views or sexual orientation, or the suspect demonstrated hostility towards the victim based on any of those characteristics;

(l) there is a marked difference between the actual or mental ages of the defendant and the victim, or if there is any element of corruption;

(m) the defendant's previous convictions or cautions are relevant to the present offence;

(n) the defendant is alleged to have committed the offence while under an order of the court;

(o) there are grounds for believing that the offence is likely to be continued or repeated, for example, by a history of recurring conduct;

(p) the offence, although not serious in itself, is widespread in the area where it was committed; or

(q) a prosecution would have a significant positive impact on maintaining community confidence."

Section 5.10 names the following factors against prosecution:

"(a) the court is likely to impose a nominal penalty;

(b) the defendant has already been made the subject of a sentence and any further conviction would be unlikely to result in the imposition of an additional sentence or order, unless the nature of the particular offence requires a prosecution or the defendant withdraws consent to have an offence taken into consideration during sentencing;

(c) the offence was committed as a result of a genuine mistake or misunderstanding (these factors must be balanced against the seriousness of the offence);

(d) the loss or harm can be described as minor and was the result of a single incident, particularly if it was caused by a misjudgment;

(e) there has been a long delay between the offence taking place and the date of the trial, unless:

- the offence is serious;
- the delay has been caused in part by the defendant;
- the offence has only recently come to light; or
- the complexity of the offence has meant that there has been a long investigation;

(f) a prosecution is likely to have a bad effect on the victim's physical or mental health, always bearing in mind the seriousness of the offence;

(g) the defendant is elderly or is, or was at the time of the offence, suffering from significant mental or physical ill health, unless the offence is serious or there is real possibility that it may be repeated. The Crown Prosecution Service, where necessary, applies Home Office guidelines about how to deal with mentally disordered offenders. Crown Prosecutors must balance the desirability of diverting a defendant who is suffering from significant mental or physical ill health with the need to safeguard the general public;

(h) the defendant has put right the loss or harm that was caused (but defendants must not avoid prosecution or diversion solely because they pay compensation); or

(i) details may be made public that could harm sources of information, international relations or national security."

As to the weight of each factor, the Prosecutors may decide on the circumstances of each case.[2830] The police and CPS have more detailed, internal guidelines, which are, however, not published.[2831]

Is the decision to start/end an investigation/prosecution subject to control by another body?

Prosecutors have no control over decisions by the police whether or not to initiate investigations or over any prior decisions.[2832]

In turn, the CPS and its decision whether or not to prosecute do underlie certain accountability mechanisms: accountability to Parliament and accountability to the Courts.[2833] The primary basis for judicial review is that either the policy or the individual decision was unreasonable, i.e. no reasonable prosecuting authority would have adopted the policy or taken the decision (*Wednesbury* unreasonableness).[2834] It has further been argued that judicial review could be based on the failure to follow a declared policy, or on failure to take account of a relevant consideration in reaching the decision, as well as abuse of process.[2835] According to *R v. DPP, ex p. C*, the DPP cannot adopt an unlawful policy, and it must act in accordance with its own settled policy: "[p]rimarily however I base my decision on what seems to have been a patent failure to act in accordance with the settled policy as set out in the Code."[2836]

2830 Sec.5.11 Code for Crown Prosecutors, *supra* note 2810.

2831 Sanders, in Arbour/Eser/Ambos/Sanders, *supra* note 2802, Appendix A, 304.

2832 Sanders, in Arbour/Eser/Ambos/Sanders, *supra* note 2802, 302.

2833 Asworth, *supra* note 2806, 200–1.

2834 *Associated Provincial Pictures Houses v. Wednesbury* [1948], 10.11.1947 (1 K.B. 223); Asworth, *supra* note 2806, 201.

2835 Asworth, *supra* note 2806, 202 et seq.

2836 *R v. DPP, ex p. C* [1995], 15.2.1994 (1 Cr. App. R. 136), further emphasizing the exceptional nature of its review power: "The Divisional Court has power to review a decision of the Director of Public Prosecutions not to prosecute but the power is one to be sparingly exercised."

There is abundant case law on judicial review of decisions not to prosecute, and applications have been successful in some of these cases.[2837] On the other hand, *R v. DPP, ex p. Manning* states that:

> "[a]uthority makes clear that a decision by the Director not to prosecute is susceptible to judicial review [...]. But, as the decided cases also make clear, the power of review is one to be sparingly exercised. The reasons for this are clear. The primary decision to prosecute or not to prosecute is entrusted by Parliament to the Director as head of an independent, professional prosecuting service, answerable to the Attorney General in his role as guardian of the public interest, and to no one else."[2838]

However, the mentioned case resulted in a review, *inter alia* because the DPP did not give reasons for its decision not to prosecute: whilst there is "no absolute and unqualified obligation" for the Prosecutor to give reasons for his decision not to prosecute, in the rare circumstances, where an individual has died in the custody of the State, and if the death resulted from violence inflicted by agents of the state, reasons must be given.[2839] Integrating all the above authorities, Lord Justice Waller (*The Queen on the application of Peter Dennis v. DPP*) arrived at four reasons to order reconsideration:

> "First, if it can be demonstrated on an objective appraisal of the case that a serious point or serious points supporting a prosecution have not been considered, that will give a ground for ordering reconsideration of the decision. Second, if it can be demonstrated that in a significant area a conclusion as to what the evidence is to support a prosecution is irrational, that will provide a ground. Third, the points have to be such as to make it seriously arguable that the decision would otherwise be different, but the decision is one for the prosecutor and not for this court. Indeed it is important to bear that fact in mind at all stages. Fourth, where an inquest jury has found unlawful killing the reasons why a prosecution should not follow need to be clearly expressed."[2840]

Despite the fact that some applications were indeed successful, the sparing exercise may not be forgotten, and review has also been refused on a number of occasions.[2841] With regard to positive decisions to prosecute, review is even more limited: "in the absence of evidence of fraud, corruption or *mala fides*, judicial review will not be allowed to probe a decision to charge individuals in criminal proceedings."[2842] In a similar vein, the House of Lords denied judicial review "in the ab-

---

2837 *R v. DPP, ex p. Jones (Timothy)* [2000], 23.3.2000 (Crim. L.R. 858); *R (on the application of Joseph) v. DPP* [2001], 21.12.2000 (Crim. L.R. 489).

2838 *R v. DPP, ex p. Manning, supra* note 2827, para. 23.

2839 *R v. DPP, ex p. Manning, supra* note 2827, para. 33.

2840 *The Queen on the application of Peter Dennis v. DPP* [2006], 29.12.2006 (EWHC 3211) para. 30.

2841 *Patrick John Lewin v. CPS* [2002], 24.5.2002 (EWHC 1049); *R (on the application of Da Silva) v. DPP* [2006], 14.12.2006 (EWHC 3204); *Marshall v. DPP* [2007], 24.1.2007 (WL 2866).

2842 *R v. Panel on Takeovers and Mergers, ex p. Fayed* [1992], 3.4.1992 (B.C.C. 524), *obiter dictum* by Judge Steyn, 536.

sence of any claim of dishonesty, bad faith or other exceptional circumstances."[2843] On the other hand, the House of Lords stressed the narrow gateway via an abuse of process claim: "if this is indeed as blatant and obvious a case as counsel for the applicants contends, it may arguably be open to the applicants to submit that the prosecution is an abuse of process inasmuch as it is so unfair and wrong that the court should not allow a prosecutor to proceed with it."[2844]

Conclusion

The decisions to investigate and prosecute are the principal domain of the police, albeit the CPS decides whether to charge or not. However, unlike public prosecutors in other jurisdictions, the CPS was not given the power to direct the police to investigate a matter.[2845] It is interesting to note that the CPS has a statutory duty to publish its guidelines (Code for Crown Prosecutors).[2846] Moreover, the CPS applies a twofold testing mechanism: an evidentiary test and a public interest test. With regard to the public interest, several factors for and against prosecution are included in the listing of section 5.9 of the Code for Crown Prosecutors. Many of the factors show similarities to sentencing and seem to be related to the notion of proportionality.[2847] Judicial review with regard to the decision to prosecute or not to prosecute is possible, but only under rare circumstances. On the other hand, the field of judicial review is developing, from a very reluctant to a more frequent allowance of orders for judicial review. Furthermore, the factors for the review power (unreasonableness; unlawful policy; non-compliance with settled policy; evidence of fraud, corruption, or *mala fides*) are starting to take shape. Nonetheless, the CPS has a degree of (uncontrollable) discretion under the applied tests and can even reinstate a prosecution.[2848]

XVIII. United States (Common law)

The criminal system of the United States is based on common law tradition; nonetheless criminal procedure is largely regulated through codification. In addition to the federal court system, the United States has 50 separate state court systems.[2849] Besides criminal procedural codes, the procedural system has its roots in the US Constitution and in the constitutions of the fifty states.[2850] There is thus no single American criminal justice process,[2851] which renders an exhaustive analysis not feasible for the study at hand and requires generalization. Therefore, I focus on

---

2843 *R v. DPP, ex p. Kebilene and others* [2000], 28.10.1999 (2 A.C. 326) 327, 376.

2844 *R v. DPP, ex p. Kebilene and others, supra* note 2843, 371.

2845 Asworth, *supra* note 2806, 178.

2846 Asworth, *supra* note 2806, 179.

2847 Asworth, *supra* note 2806, 185–6.

2848 *R v. DPP, ex p. Burke* [1997], 12.12.1996 (C.O.D. 169).

2849 John Michelich, "United States of America" in Arbour/Eser/Ambos/Sanders, *supra* note 2388, 481, 481.

2850 Stephen Saltzburg/Daniel Capra, *American criminal procedure,* 8th edition (Thomson/West, St.Paul 2007) 7–8.

the Federal system. However, it must be noted that state procedures in any of the fifty states may not be inconsistent with US constitutional due process rights.

Who is in charge of (pre-)investigations?

Three basic groups of investigations can be distinguished: police procedures that are aimed at solving specific past crimes known to the police ("reactive" investigations); police procedures that are aimed at unknown but anticipated ongoing and future criminal activity ("proactive" investigations); and prosecutorial and other non-police investigations conducted primarily through the use of subpoena authority.[2852] The latter subpoena investigation is a specific form of investigation conducted by the Prosecutor and the grand jury.[2853]

When may activation be triggered? (What is the standard of proof – if any – to start (pre-)investigations?)

The police typically receive a citizen report of a crime, or they discover physical evidence that a crime has been committed.[2854]

Who takes the decision to start a formal investigation?

Investigations are ordinarily left to the police.[2855] The Prosecutor usually acts as an advisor, and sometimes supervisor, of the police or other investigative agencies.[2856] In general, the police must thus decide whether to arrest or investigate, and the Prosecutors must decide whether to initiate cases, what charges to file, and whether to plea bargain.[2857]

Is a discretionary evaluation performed before initiating a formal investigation/prosecution, and if so, how is it conducted (level of discretion)?

The first level of screening is carried out by the police who may decide whom to arrest.[2858] Some states, however, have enacted mandatory arrest laws when there is probable cause to believe that a domestic violence assault has occurred.[2859] Furthermore, the types of interaction between the police and prosecution during the screen-

---

2851 Yale Kamisar/Wayne La Fave/Jerold Israel/Nancy King, *Modern criminal procedure,* 11th edition (Thomson/West, St. Paul 2005) 1.

2852 Kamisar/La Fave/Israel/King, *supra* note 2851, 4.

2853 Kamisar/La Fave/Israel/King, *supra* note 2851, 7–8; further Marc Miller/Ronald Wright, *Criminal procedures,* 3rd edition (Wolters Kluwer, Austin, Boston 2007) 725 et seq.

2854 Kamisar/La Fave/Israel/King, *supra* note 2851, 4.

2855 Saltzburg/Capra, *supra* note 2850, 868.

2856 James Haddad/Elizabeth Marsh et al., *Criminal procedure,* 7th edition (Thomson Reuters/Foundation press, New York 2008) 902.

2857 Saltzburg/Capra, *supra* note 2850, 865.

2858 Saltzburg/Capra, *supra* note 2850, 868; Miller/Wright, *supra* note 2853, 886; Kamisar/La Fave/Israel/King, *supra* note 2851, 9–10.

2859 Kamisar/La Fave/Israel/King, *supra* note 2851, 989.

ing of cases can vary a great deal, thus the independence of the police in reaching decisions is diverse.[2860]

For initiating prosecutions there are 93 US Attorneys in the federal criminal justice system and numerous assistant US Attorneys who are given considerable autonomy in their exercise of prosecutorial discretion.[2861] In the decision whether or not to charge the Prosecutor's discretion is immensely broad and important.[2862] A rejection of proceedings can even be based on the "interest of justice."[2863] It is most important to note that declinations are the rule, not the exception.[2864]

At the post-filing procedures a dismissal can be obtained through a *nolle prosequi* if the Prosecutor determines that the charge is not justified.[2865]

Under which circumstances can investigations (preliminary and/or full investigation) be dismissed? Are there criteria for dismissal or is the decision fully discretionary? If there are criteria, which are those and how are they defined?

The decision whether to charge depends on the following considerations: (1) the suspect is guilty; (2) the evidence is sufficient to secure conviction; and (3) it is in the community's best interest to prosecute the suspect.[2866] With regard to the specific factors, which may enter the Prosecutor's decision, the following criteria have been mentioned: the Prosecutor's reasonable belief that the accused is in fact guilty; the extent of harm caused by the offence; the disproportion of the authorized punishment in relation to the particular offence or the offender; possible improper motives of a complaint; reluctance of the victim to testify; cooperation of the accused; and availability and likelihood of prosecution by another jurisdiction.[2867] Others even refer to more policy based factors, such as: whether the case fits within the prosecution priorities; the defendant's background; the quality of the prosecution's case; the age of a case; the "winability" of a case; the defendant's cooperation; and how the case will be perceived by the press and public.[2868] The latter factors show a very wide, common-law type understanding of the Prosecutor's discretion. On the other hand, it must be noted that there are guidelines for the exercise of discretion.[2869] However, these guidelines are so general and leave room for subjective judgment that a defendant will rarely be able to claim that the standards have been violated.[2870]

2860 Miller/Wright, *supra* note 2853, 886.

2861 Kamisar/La Fave/Israel/King, *supra* note 2851, 975. On the US Attorneys see <www.usdoj.gov/usao/>.

2862 Saltzburg/Capra, *supra* note 2850, 871; Miller/Wright, *supra* note 2853, 890.

2863 Kamisar/La Fave/Israel/King, *supra* note 2851, 10.

2864 Miller/Wright, *supra* note 2853, 899.

2865 Miller/Wright, *supra* note 2853, 909; Kamisar/La Fave/Israel/King, *supra* note 2851, 11.

2866 Saltzburg/Capra, *supra* note 2850, 873.

2867 Kamisar/La Fave/Israel/King, *supra* note 2851, 985.

2868 Haddad/Marsh et al., *supra* note 2856, 907 et seq.

2869 Miller/Wright, *supra* note 2853, 897 et seq.

2870 Haddad/Marsh et al., *supra* note 2856, 911.

Is the decision to start/end an investigation/prosecution subject to control by another body?

The arrest decision by the police is essentially unreviewable.[2871] At the later stage of initiating cases, all US Attorneys and their assistants are supervised by the Attorney General who has set forth a series of departmental guidelines.[2872] Other than that, the US Prosecutors are almost completely free from review by third persons or agencies.[2873] Although the statutory language makes prosecution of all violations mandatory, the courts have been very reluctant to demand prosecution where the Prosecutor has decided against it.[2874] The authority of a court to compel prosecution is barred by the separation of powers.[2875] For a decision in favor of prosecution there is equally limited leeway for judicial check. In particular, a claim of selective (discriminatory) prosecution is very difficult to prove.[2876]

Conclusion

Prosecutors in the United States occupy the most powerful position and make the decision whether or not to prosecute a particular individual. In early proceedings the discretion of the police is the controlling factor that filters cases. With regard to discretionary choices, prosecutors seem to enjoy the broadest scope. In the United States, the term "community interest" or "interests of justice" is frequently applied. So far, case law on judicial control of a decision whether or not to prosecute is very limited. There is virtually no judicial review of a decision not to prosecute. But the decision to prosecute receives checks by the Judiciary in the form of the exclusionary rule, the Court's ability to dismiss charges due to prosecutorial misconduct, etc., and prosecutors are *de facto* regulated by the weighty due process protections of the accused. In any event, US prosecutors enjoy large flexibility in their charging decision.

C. Conclusion regarding the country analysis

The survey of eighteen national criminal jurisdictions has revealed that some kind of prosecutorial discretion is known to all included systems. With regard to (pre-)investigations the primary actor is typically the police, yet often under the supervision of prosecuting authorities. The decisions whether or not to prosecute are mainly left to the Prosecutors. Only in some countries (Cameroon, Côte d'Ivoire, DRC, France,

---

2871 Saltzburg/Capra, *supra* note 2850, 868.

2872 Kamisar/La Fave/Israel/King, *supra* note 2851, 975, 997; Michelin, in Arbour/Eser/Ambos/Sanders, *supra* note 2849, 482.

2873 Haddad/Marsh et al., *supra* note 2856, 903.

2874 Saltzburg/Capra, *supra* note 2850, 876–7.

2875 *Attica v. Rockefeller* [1973], 18.4.1973 (477 F.2d 375); further Haddad/Marsh et al., *supra* note 2856, 918–9; Kamisar/La Fave/Israel/King, *supra* note 2851, 992 et seq.

2876 *United States v. Armstrong* [1996], 13.5.1996 (517 U.S. 456) 465; also Kamisar/La Fave/Israel/King, *supra* note 2851, 998 et seq.; Miller/Wright, *supra* note 2853, 955 et seq., 961.

and Sudan; to some extent Germany and the United States) an investigative judge/grand jury pursues investigations with regard to the most serious offences and/or upon request.

It is most interesting to note that one principal difference has been identified regarding the commencement of investigations *vis-à-vis* the continuation of prosecutions. Whereas both entail discretionary decisions, the factors for not proceeding with prosecutions are more often than not given by the legislator or by the actor in charge. On the other hand, the criteria for dropping investigations very often remain in a legal grey area.

Moreover, the distinction between the adversarial and inquisitorial systems has proven to be greater in theory than in practice. It is not a very accurate labeling. The starting point might be different, since Anglo-American systems foresee discretion for the prosecuting authority at the outset, contrary to the Romano-Germanic systems, which assume mandatory prosecution for all crimes. However, both systems take similar approaches in practical reality.[2877] They differentiate minor and serious cases and allow for broader discretion with regard to the former. Furthermore, both systems regulate exceptions under which prosecution can be discontinued. Moreover, it is not only the civil law countries that introduce judicial checks and balances, but also the common law countries through judicial scrutiny and enforcement of due process protections of the accused. In particular, the author identified increasing case law on this issue in England and Wales.

It was further revealed that the term "public interest" is known to several countries included in the analysis (Canada, Colombia, Germany, The Netherlands, South Africa, Sudan, Uganda, England and Wales, and the United States). A closer look at the countries criteria can be helpful for the ICC to shape its own factors and to learn from national experiences. The OTP should pursue an in-depth survey into international(ized) and national jurisdictions with a specific focus on the criteria used for discretion. While the OTP has done so to a certain extent, it must concentrate on the (internal) policy documents of national authorities. It should be feasible for the OTP to gain better access to those than any academic request could ever get. In any event, it can be concluded that a wide concept of discretionary case selection is applied in several national criminal jurisdictions, be it common law or civil law. The factors for these choices are sometimes published in transparent statutes, regulations and policies, and in other countries they remain vague and unclear.

[2877] Similarly Miller/Wright, *supra* note 2853, 896.

Annex 3

SC-Res. 1593 (2005)

The Security Council,

Taking note of the report of the International Commission of Inquiry on violations of international humanitarian law and human rights law in Darfur (S/2005/60),

Recalling article 16 of the Rome Statute under which no investigation or prosecution may be commenced or proceeded with by the International Criminal Court for a period of 12 months after a Security Council request to that effect,

Also recalling articles 75 and 79 of the Rome Statute and encouraging States to contribute to the ICC Trust Fund for Victims,

Taking note of the existence of agreements referred to in Article 98-2 of the Rome Statute,

Determining that the situation in Sudan continues to constitute a threat to international peace and security,

Acting under Chapter VII of the Charter of the United Nations,

1. *Decides* to refer the situation in Darfur since 1 July 2002 to the Prosecutor of the International Criminal Court;

2. *Decides* that the Government of Sudan and all other parties to the conflict in Darfur, shall cooperate fully with and provide any necessary assistance to the Court and the Prosecutor pursuant to this resolution and, while recognizing that States not party to the Rome Statute have no obligation under the Statute, urges all States and concerned regional and other international organizations to cooperate fully;

3. *Invites* the Court and the African Union to discuss practical arrangements that will facilitate the work of the Prosecutor and of the Court, including the possibility of conducting proceedings in the region, which would contribute to regional efforts in the fight against impunity;

4. *Also encourages* the Court, as appropriate and in accordance with the Rome Statute, to support international cooperation with domestic efforts to promote the rule of law, protect human rights and combat impunity in Darfur;

5. *Also emphasizes* the need to promote healing and reconciliation and encourages in this respect the creation of institutions, involving all sectors of Sudanese society, such as truth and/or reconciliation commissions, in order to complement judicial processes and thereby reinforce the efforts to restore long-lasting peace, with African Union and international support as necessary;

6. *Decides* that nationals, current or former officials or personnel from a contributing State outside Sudan which is not a party to the Rome Statute of the International Criminal Court shall be subject to the exclusive jurisdiction of that contributing State for all alleged acts or omissions arising out of or related to operations in Sudan established or authorized by the Council or the African Union, unless such exclusive jurisdiction has been expressly waived by that contributing State;
7. *Recognizes* that none of the expenses incurred in connection with the referral including expenses related to investigations or prosecutions in connection with that referral, shall be borne by the United Nations and that such costs shall be borne by the parties to the Rome Statute and those States that wish to contribute voluntarily;
8. *Invites* the Prosecutor to address the Council within three months of the date of adoption of this resolution and every six months thereafter on actions taken pursuant to this resolution;
9. *Decides* to remain seized of the matter.

Bibliography*

1. Books and monographs

Allen, Tim: Trial justice, The International Criminal Court and the Lord's Resistance Army, London/New York 2006

Ambos, Kai: The Colombian Peace Process and the principle of complementarity of the International Criminal Court, Heidelberg 2010

– Internationales Strafrecht, 2nd edition, München 2008

– Der Allgemeine Teil des Völkerstrafrechts, 2. Aufl., Berlin 2004

Arnold, Pascal: Der UNO-Sicherheitsrat und die strafrechtliche Verfolgung von Individuen, Basel/Genf/München 1999

Ashworth, Andrew: The criminal process, an evaluative study, Oxford 1998

Aust, Anthony: Modern treaty law and practice, Cambridge 2000

Ayume, Francis: Criminal procedure and law in Uganda, Nairobi 1986

Bailey, S. H./*Ching,* J. P. L./*Taylor,* N. W.: Smith, Bailey and Gunn on the modern English legal system, London 2007

Bassiouni, Cherif: The legislative history of the International Criminal Court: Introduction, analysis and integrated text, Vol. 1, Ardsley/New York 2005

– The legislative history of the International Criminal Court: An article-by-article evolution, Vol. 2, Ardsley/New York 2005

Beulke, Werner: Strafprozessrecht, 8. Aufl., Heidelberg 2005

Bevers, Hans/*Joubert,* Chantal: Schengen investigated, The Hague/London/Boston 1996

Brownlie, Ian: Principles of Public International Law, 6th edition, Oxford 2003

Calvo-Goller, Karin: The trial proceedings of the International Criminal Court, Leiden/Boston 2006

Cárdenas, Claudia: Die Zulässigkeitsprüfung vor dem Internationalen Strafgerichtshof, Berlin 2005

Cassese, Antonio: International Criminal Law, 2nd edition, Oxford 2008

Clark, Denis: Bevan & Lidstone's, The investigation of crime, 3rd edition, UK 2004

Contag, Corinna: Der Internationale Strafgerichtshof im System kollektiver Sicherheit, Baden-Baden 2009

* All websites in this bibliography last visited 1.9.2010.

Cryer, Robert: Prosecuting international crime: selectivity and the international criminal law regime, Cambridge 2005

Cryer, Robert/*Friman,* Håkan/*Robinson,* Darryl/*Wilmshurst,* Elizabeth: An introduction to International Criminal Law and Procedure, Cambridge 2007

Deiters, Mark: Legalitätsprinzip und Normengeltung, Tübingen 2006

Düker, Arnd: Die Strafverfolgung von Angehörigen einer Friedenstruppe der Vereinten Nationen, Hamburg 2008

El Zeidy, Mohamed: The principle of complementarity in international criminal law, Leiden/Boston 2008

Fionda, Julia: Public prosecutors and discretion, Oxford 1995

Fraas, Michael: Sicherheitsrat der Vereinten Nationen und Internationaler Gerichtshof, Frankfurt a.M. 1998

Freeman, Mark: Truth commissions and procedural fairness, New York 2006

Haddad, James/*Marsh,* Elizabeth et al.: Criminal procedure, 7th edition, New York 2008

Hayner, Priscilla: Unspeakable truths, New York/London 2001

Heilmann, Daniel: Die Effektivität des Internationalen Strafgerichtshofs, Frankfurt a.M. 2006

Heuser, Robert/*Weigend,* Thomas: Das Strafprozessgesetz der Volksrepublik China in vergleichender Perspektive, Hamburg 1997

Jehle, Jörg-Martin/*Wade,* Marianne: Copying with overloaded criminal justice systems, Berlin 2006

Joubert, J. J. (ed.): Criminal procedure handbook, 7th edition, Cape Town 2005

Junck, Christoph: Die Gerichtsbarkeit des Internationalen Strafgerichtshofs, Frankfurt a.M. 2006

Kadelbach, Stefan: Zwingendes Völkerrecht, Berlin 1992

Kamisar, Yale/*La Fave,* Wayne/*Israel,* Jerold/*King,* Nancy: Modern criminal procedure, 11th edition, St. Paul 2005

Kim, Young Sok: The law of the International Criminal Court, Buffalo/New York 2007

Kindt, Anne: Menschenrechte und Souveränität, Beiträge zum Internationalen und Europäischen Strafrecht, Bd. 3, Berlin 2009

Kleffner, Jann: Complementarity in the Rome Statute and national criminal jurisdictions, Oxford/New York 2008

Kurth, Michael: Das Verhältnis des Internationalen Strafgerichthofes zum UN-Sicherheitsrat, Frankfurt a.M. 2006

Laucci, Cyril: The annotated digest of the International Criminal Court, 2004–2006, Leiden 2007

Lumumba, PLO: A handbook on criminal procedure in Kenya, Nairobi 2005

Mallinder, Louise: Amnesty, human rights and political transition, Oxford/Portland 2008

Manique, John: The origins of justice, Philadelphia 2003

Meißner, Jörg: Die Zusammenarbeit mit dem Internationalen Strafgerichtshof nach dem Römischen Statut, München 2003

Meißner, Philipp: The International Criminal Court controversy, Münster 2005

Melloh, Florian: Einheitliche Strafzumessung in den Rechtsquellen des ICC-Statuts, Berlin 2010

Meyer-Goßner: Lutz, Strafprozessordnung, Kommentar, 51st edition, München 2008

Miller, Marc/*Wright,* Ronald: Criminal procedures, 3rd edition, Austin/Boston 2007

Morel, Sophie, La mise en œuvre du principe de complémentarité par la cour pénale internationale le case particulier des amnisties, Lausanne 2005

Nemitz, Jan-Christoph: Strafzumessung im Völkerstrafrecht, Freiburg i. Brsg. 2002

Ngor, Haing/*Warner,* Roger: Survival of the killing fields, London 1987

Nitsche, Dennis: Der Internationale Strafgerichtshof ICC und der Frieden, Baden-Baden 2007

O'Shea, Andreas: Amnesty for crime in international law and practice, The Hague et al. 2002

Odoki, B. J.: Criminal procedure in Uganda, 2nd edition, Kampala 1990

Olásolo, Héctor: The triggering procedure of the International Criminal Court, Leiden 2005 (For the earlier Spanish version see: *Olásolo,* Héctor, Corte Penal International ¿Dónde investigar?, Valencia 2003)

Orakhelashvili, Alexander: Peremptory norms in international law, Oxford 2006

Örücü, Esin: The enigma of comparative law, Leiden/Boston 2004

Pattenden, Rosemary: The Judge, discretion, and the criminal trial, Oxford 1982

Pfefferkorn, Fabian: Einführung in das französische Strafverfahren, Hamburg 2006

Quigley, Tim: Procedure in Canadian criminal law, 2nd edition, Toronto 2005

Raimondo, Fabián: General principles of law in the decisions of International Criminal Courts and Tribunals, Leiden 2008

Rawls, John: A theory of justice, revised version, Cambridge (MA) 1999

Razesberger, Florian: The ICC, the principle of complementarity, Frankfurt a. M. 2006

Safferling, Christoph: Towards an international criminal procedure, Oxford 2001

Saltzburg, Stephen/*Capra,* Daniel: American criminal procedure, 8th edition, St. Paul 2007

Schabas, William: An introduction to the International Criminal Court, 3rd edition, Cambridge 2007

– The international Criminal Court: a commentary on the Rome Statute, Oxford 2010

Schiff, Benjamin: Building the International Criminal Court, Cambridge 2008

Slye, Ronald/*Schaack,* Beth van: International criminal law, Austin 2009

Sriram, Chandra Lekha: Confronting past human rights violations, London/New York 2004

Stagel, Daniela: Sicherheitsrat und Internationaler Strafgerichtshof: Zur Abgrenzung ihrer Kompetenzen nach der Charta der Vereinten Nationen und dem Römischen Statut, Hamburg 2008

Steinberger-Fraunhofer, Theresa: Internationaler Strafgerichtshof und Drittstaaten, Berlin 2008

Stigen, Jo: The relationship between the International Criminal Court and national jurisdictions, Leiden/Boston 2008

Stuckenberg, Carl-Friedrich: Vorstudien zu Vorsatz und Irrtum im Völkerstrafrecht, Berlin 2007

Tak, Peter: The Dutch criminal justice system, Nijmegen 2008

Van Heeck, Stefan: Die Weiterentwicklung des formellen Völkerstrafrechts, Berlin 2006

Vogler, Richard: A worldview of criminal justice, Aldershot 2005

Wei, Wu: Die Rolle des Anklägers eines internationalen Strafgerichthofs, Frankfurt a. M. 2007

Werle, Gerhard: Völkerstrafrecht, 2. Aufl., Tübingen 2007

Zweigert, Konrad/*Kötz,* Hein: Introduction to comparative law, 3rd edition, Oxford 1998

Legal dictionaries

Black's Law Dictionary, Garner, Bryan (ed.), 7th edition, St. Paul 1999

Free Online Dictionary by Farlex, <www.thefreedictionary.com>

Oxford English Dictionary, <www.oed.com>

Oxford Thesaurus of English, 2nd revised edition, Oxford 2006

The New Oxford Companion of Law, Cane, Peter/Conaghan, Joanna (eds.), Oxford 2008

2. Articles (journals, yearbooks and posted on the internet)

Abass, Ademola: "The competence of the Security Council to terminate the jurisdiction of the International Criminal Court," Texas International Law Journal, Vol. 40 (2005) 263–299

Akhavan, Payam: "Developments at the ICC: the Lord's Resistance Army case: Uganda's submission of the first state referral to the ICC," American Journal of International Law, Vol. 99 (2005) 403–421

– "Self-referrals before the International Criminal Court: Are States the villains or the victims of actrocities," Criminal Law Forum, Vol. 21 (2010) 103–210

Ambos, Kai: "Critical issues in the Bemba confirmation decision," Leiden Journal of International Law, Vol. 22 (2009) 715–726

– "International core crimes, universal jurisdiction and § 153f of the German Criminal Procedure Code: a commentary on the decisions of the Federal Prosecutor General and the Stuttgart Higher Regional Court in the Abu Ghraib/Rumsfeld case," Criminal Law Forum, Vol. 18 (2007) 43–58

– "Die Rolle des Internationalen Strafgerichtshofs," Aus Politik und Zeitgeschichte, Vol. 41 (2006) 10–17

– "International criminal procedure: 'adversarial', 'inquisitorial' or mixed," International Criminal Law Review, Vol. 3 (2003) 1–37

– "International criminal law has lost its innocence," The original German version of this article was published in the German newspaper "Süddeutsche Zeitung" 16 July 2002, 13, translated by Frank Schorkopf, German Law Journal, Vol. 3 (2002) paras. 1–8

– "Zur Rechtsgrundlage des Internationalen Strafgerichtshofs," Zeitschrift für die gesamte Strafrechtswissenschaft, Vol. 111 (1999) 175–211

– "Der neue Internationale Strafgerichtshof – Ein Überblick," Neue Juristische Wochenschrift, Vol. 51 (1998) 3743–3746

Ambos, Kai/*Miller,* Dennis: "Structure and function of the confirmation procedure before the ICC from a comparative perspective," International Criminal Law Review, Vol. 7 (2007) 335–360

Apuuli, Kasaija Phillip: "The ICC's possible deferral of the LRA case to Uganda," Journal of International Criminal Justice, Vol. 6 (2008) 801–813

– "The ICC arrest warrants for the Lord's Resistance Army leaders and peace prospects for Northern Uganda," Journal of International Criminal Justice, Vol. 4 (2006) 179–187

– "The International Criminal Court (ICC) and the Lord's Resistance Army (LRA) insurgency in Northern Uganda," Criminal Law Forum, Vol. 15 (2004) 391–409

Arnaut, Damir: "When in Rome …? The International Criminal Court and avenues for U.S.," Virginia Journal of International Law, Vol. 43 (2003) 525–587

Arsanjani, Mahnoush: "The Rome Statute of the International Criminal Court," American Journal of International Law, Vol. 93 (1999) 22–43

– "The International Criminal Court and amnesty laws," American Society of International Law Proceedings, Vol. 93 (1999) 65–68

Arsanjani, Mahnoush/*Reismann,* Michael: "Developments at the International Criminal Court: The law-in-action of the ICC," American Journal of International Law, Vol. 99 (2005) 385–403

Baines, Erin: "The haunting of Alice: local approaches to justice and reconciliation in Northern Uganda," The International Journal of Transitional Justice, Vol. 1 (2007) 91–114

Bartelt, Sandra: "Die Zulässigkeit von Wahrheitskommissionen im Lichte des neuen Internationalen Strafgerichtshofs," Archiv des Völkerrechts, Vol. 43 (2005) 187–217

Bassiouni, Cherif: "The ICC – Quo vadis?," Journal of International Criminal Justice, Vol. 4 (2006) 421–427

– "Note explicative sur le Statut de la Cour Pénale Internationale (CPI)," Revue Internationale de Droit Pénal, Vol. 70 (2000) 1–41

Batros, Ben: "The *Katanga* admissibility appeal: judicial restraint at the ICC," Leiden Journal of International Law, Vol. 23 (2010) 343–362

Behrens, Hans-Jörg: "Das Verfahren des Internationalen Strafgerichtshofes nach dem Statut von Rom" Humanitäres Völkerrecht Informationsschriften, Vol. 11 (1998) 144–151

– "Investigation, trial and appeal in the International Criminal Court Statute," European Journal of Crime, Criminal Law and Criminal Justice, Vol. 6 (1998) 113–125

Bekou, Olympia: "Pre-Trial procedures before the International Criminal Court," 20th International Conference of the International Society for the Reform of Criminal Law, Brisbane, 2 July–6 July 2006, <www.isrcl.org>, 1–6

Benevenuti, Paolo: "The ICTY Prosecutor and the review of the NATO bombing campaign against the Federal Republic of Yugoslavia," European Journal of International Law, Vol. 12 (2001) 503–530

Benzing, Markus: "The complementarity regime of the International Criminal Court: international criminal justice between State sovereignty and the fight against impunity," Max Planck Yearbook of the United Nations Law, Vol. 7 (2003) 591–632

Bergsmo, Morten: "Occasional remarks on certain state concerns about the jurisdictional reach of the ICC, and their possible implications for the relationship between the Court and the Security Council," Nordic Journal of International Law, Vol. 69 (2000) 87–113

– "The jurisdictional regime of the International Criminal Court," European Journal of Crime, Criminal Law and Criminal Justice, Vol. 6 (1998) 29–47

Bisset, Alison: "Rethinking the powers of truth commissions in light of the ICC Statute," Journal of International Criminal Justice, Vol. 7 (2009) 963–982

Bitti, Gilbert/*El Zeidy,* Mohamed: "The *Katanga* Trial Chamber Decision: selected issues," Leiden Journal of International Law, Vol. 23 (2010) 319–329

Böse, Martin: "Aufsichtsrechtliche Vorermittlungen in der Grauzone zwischen Strafverfolgung und Gefahrenabwehr," Zeitschrift für die gesamte Strafrechtswissenschaft, Vol. 119 (2007) 848–886

Boshoff, Henri/*Vircoulon,* Thierry: "Update on Ituri," African Security Review, Vol. 13 (2004) 65–68

Bothe, Michael: "Complementarity: ensuring compliance with international law though criminal prosecutions – whose responsibility?," Friedenswarte, Vol. 83 (2008) 59–72

Brubacher, Matthew: "Prosecutorial discretion within the International Criminal Court," Journal of International Criminal Justice, Vol. 2 (2004) 71–95

Buckley-Zistel, Susanne: "The truth heals? Gacaca jurisdictions and the consolidation of peace in Rwanda," Friedenswarte, Vol. 80 (2005) 113–129

Burbidge, Peter: "Justice and peace? – The role of law in resolving Colombia's civil conflict," International Criminal Law Review, Vol. 8 (2008) 557–587

Burke-White, William: "Proactive complementarity: The International Criminal Court and national courts in the Rome system of international justice," Harvard International Law Journal, Vol. 49 (2008) 53–108

– "Implementing a policy of positive complementarity in the Rome system of justice," Criminal Law Forum, Vol. 19 (2008) 59–85

– "Complementarity in practice: The International Criminal Court as part of a system of multi-level global governance in the Democratic Republic of Congo," Leiden Journal of International Law, Vol. 18 (2005) 557–590

Burke-White, William/*Kaplan,* Scott: "Shaping the contours of domestic justice," Journal of International Criminal Justice, Vol. 9 (2009) 257–279

Carnero Rojo, Enrique: "The role of fair trial considerations in the complementarity regime of the International Criminal Court: from 'no peace without justice' to 'no peace without victor's justice'?" Leiden Journal of International Law, Vol. 18 (2005) 829–869

Cassese, Antonio: "Is the ICC still having teething problems?," Journal of International Criminal Justice, Vol. 4 (2006) 434–441

– "The Statute of the International Criminal Court: some preliminary reflections," European Journal of International Law, Vol. 10 (1999) 144–171

Cerone, John: "Dynamic equilibrium: The evolution of US attitudes toward International Criminal Courts and Tribunals," European Journal of International Law, Vol. 18 (2007) 277–315

Chaitidou, Eleni: "Rechtssprechungsübersicht: Aktuelle Entwicklung am Internationalen Strafgerichtshof," Zeitschrift für Internationale Strafrechtsdogmatik, Vol. 14 (2008) 371–375

Ciampi, Annalisa: "The proceedings against President Al Bashir and the prospects of their suspension under article 16 ICC Statute," Journal of International Criminal Justice, Vol. 6 (2008) 885–897

Clark, Thomas Hethe: "The Prosecutor of the International Criminal Court, amnesties, and the 'interests of justice': striking a delicate balance," Washington University Global Studies Law Review, Vol. 4 (2005) 389–414

Clavier, Sophie: Perspectives on French Criminal Law, July 1997, available at: <http://userwww.sfsu.edu/~sclavier/research/frenchpenalsystem.pdf>

Condorelli, Luigi/*Ciampi,* Annalisa: "Comments of the Security Council referral of the situation in Darfur to the ICC," Journal of International Criminal Justice, Vol. 3 (2005) 590–599

Conso, Giovanni: "The basic reasons for US hostility to the ICC in light of the negotiating history of the Rome Statute," Journal of International Criminal Justice, Vol. 3 (2005) 314–322

Côte, Luc: "Reflections on the exercise of prosecutorial discretion in international criminal law," Journal of International Criminal Justice, Vol. 3 (2005) 162–186

Cryer, Robert: "Prosecuting the leaders: promises, politics and practicalities," Göttingen Journal of International Law, Vol. 1 (2009) 45–75

– "Sudan, Resolution 1593 and international criminal justice," Leiden Journal of International Law, Vol. 19 (2006) 195–222

Danner, Alison Marston: "Enhancing the legitimacy and accountability of prosecutorial discretion at the International Criminal Court," American Journal of International Law, Vol. 97 (2003) 510–552

– "Navigating law and politics: The Prosecutor of the International Criminal Court and the independent counsel," Stanford Law Review, Vol. 55 (2003) 1633–1665

De Beco, Gauthier: "The confirmation of charges before the International Criminal Court: evaluation and first application," International Criminal Law Review, Vol. 7 (2007) 469–481

De Hemptinne, Jérôme: "The creation of investigating chambers at the ICC: an option worth pursuing?," Journal of International Criminal Justice, Vol. 5 (2007) 402–418

De Hemptinne, Jérôme/*Rindi,* Francesco: "ICC Pre-Trial Chamber allows victims to participate in the investigation phase of proceedings," Journal of International Criminal Justice, Vol. 4 (2006) 342–350

De Waal, Alex: "A critique of the public application by the Chief Prosecutor of the ICC for an arrest warrant against Sudanese President Omar al Bashir," SSRC blogs: Making sense of Darfur, 27.1.2009, 1–24, available at: <http://blogs.ssrc.org/sudan/wp-content/uploads/2009/01/bashir-public-application-critique-d6-250109.pdf>

De Wet, Erika: "The relationship between the International Criminal Court and *ad hoc* criminal tribunals: competition or symbiosis?," Friedenswarte, Vol. 83 (2008) 33–57

Deen-Racsmány, Zsuzsanna: "The ICC, peacekeepers and Resolution 1422: will the Court defer to the Council?," Netherlands International Law Review, Vol. XLIX (2002) 353–388

Del Ponte, Carla: "Prosecuting the individuals bearing the highest level of responsibility," Journal of International Criminal Justice, Vol. 2 (2004) 516–519

Delmas-Marty, Mireille: "Interactions between national and international criminal law in the preliminary phase of trial at the ICC," Journal of International Criminal Justice, Vol. 4 (2006) 2–11

– "La CPI et les interactions entre droit international pénal et droit pénal interne à la phase d'ouverture du procès pénal," Revue de science criminelle et de droit pénal comparé (2005) 473–481

– "The contribution of comparative law to a pluralist conception of international law," Journal of International Criminal Justice, Vol. 1 (2003) 13–25

Dugard, John: "Dealing with crimes of a past regime. Is amnesty still an option?" Leiden Journal of International Law, Vol. 12 (1999) 1001–1015

Dukić, Dražan: "Transitional Justice and the International Criminal Court: in the 'interests of justice'?" International Review of the Red Cross, Vol. 89 (2007) 691–718

El Zeidy, Mohamed: "The gravity threshold under the Statute of the International Criminal Court," Criminal Law Forum, Vol. 19 (2008) 35–57

– "Some remarks on the question of the admissibility of a case during arrest warrant proceedings before the International Criminal Court," Leiden Journal of International Law, Vol. 19 (2006) 741–751

– "The Ugandan government triggers the first test of the complementarity principle: as assessment of first State Party's referral to the ICC," International Criminal Law Review, Vol. 5 (2005) 83–119

– "The principle of complementarity: a new machinery to implement international criminal law," Michigan Journal of International Law, Vol. 23 (2002) 869–975

– "The United States dropped the atomic bomb of article 16 of the ICC Statute: Security Council power of deferrals and resolution 1422," Vanderbilt Journal of Transitional Law, Vol. 35 (2002) 1503–1544

Eleylofede, Jean-Marie: "L'interprétation de l'article 53 des Statuts de Rome créant la cour penale internationale sur la notion intérêt de la justice," May 2005, 1–28, available at: <www.iccnow.org/?mod=browserdoc&type=1>

Ellis, Mark: "Purging the past: the current state of lustration laws in the former communist block," Law and Contemporary Problems, Vol. 59 (2006) 181–196

Evans, Rhys David: "Amnesties, pardons and complementarity: does the International Criminal Court have the tools to end impunity?," Human Rights Law Commentary, Vol. 1 (2005) 1–10, available at: <www.nottingham.ac.uk/shared/shared_hrlcpub/HRLC_Commentary_2005/EVANS.pdf>

Fairlie, Megan: "Establishing admissibility at the International Criminal Court: does the buck stop with the prosecutor, full stop?," International Lawyer, Vol. 39 (2005) 817–842

– "The marriage of common and continental law at the ICTY and its progeny, due process deficit," International Criminal Law Review, Vol. 4 (2004) 243–319

Fastenrath, Ulrich: "Der Internationale Strafgerichtshof," Juristische Schulung, Vol. 39 (1999) 632–635

Fletcher, George/*Ohlin,* Jens David: "The ICC – two courts in one?," Journal of International Criminal Justice, Vol. 4 (2006) 428–433

Fronza, Emanuela/*Malarino,* Ezequiel: "Die Auslegung von multilingualen strafrechtlichen Texten am Beispiel des Statuts für den Internationalen Strafgerichtshof," Zeitschrift für die gesamte Strafrechtswissenschaft, Vol. 118 (2006) 927–952

Gaeta, Paola: "Is the practice of 'self-referrals' a sound start for the ICC?," Journal of International Criminal Law, Vol. 2 (2004) 949–952

Gallant, Kenneth: "The International Criminal Court in the system of States and International Organizations," Leiden Journal of International Law, Vol. 16 (2003) 553–591

Gallavin, Chris: "Prosecutorial discretion within the ICC: under the pressure," Criminal Law Forum, Vol. 17 (2006) 43–58

– "Article 53 of the Rome Statute of the International Criminal Court: in the interests of justice?," King's College Law Journal, Vol. 14 (2003) 179–197

Galvin, Richard John: "The ICC Prosecutor, collateral damage and NGOs: evaluating the risk of politicized prosecution," University of Miami International and Comparative Law Review, Vol. 13 (2005) 1–103

Gavron, Jessica: "Amnesties in the light of developments in international law and the establishment of the International Criminal Court," International and Comparative Law Quaterly, Vol. 51 (2002) 91–117

Goldmann, Matthias/*Schneider,* Cornelia: "ICC case simulation exercise: Prosecutor v Five Pilots from Blueland and Whiteland," German Law Journal, Vol. 4 (2003) 815–825

Goldstone, James: "More candour about criteria," Journal of International Criminal Justice, Vol. 8 (2010) 383–406

Goldstone, Richard/*Fritz,* Nicole: "In the interests of justice and independent referral: The ICC prosecutor's unprecedented powers," Leiden Journal of International Law, Vol. 13 (2000) 655–667

Gomez-Pardo, Enrique: "The content of Colombian Justice and Peace Law accomplishes the International Criminal Court standards," Revista Debate Interamericano, Vol. 1 (2009), 123–154, available at: <www.cancilleria.gov.co>

Greenawalt, Alexander: "Justice without politics? Prosecutorial discretion and the International Criminal Court," NYU Journal of International Law and Politics, Vol. 39 (2007) 583–673

Gropengießer, Helmut/*Meißner,* Jörg: "Amnesties and the Rome Statute of the ICC," International Criminal Law Review, Vol. 5 (2005) 267–300

Gross, Ivo: "Die Vereinbarkeit von nationalen Amnestieregelungen mit dem Völkerstrafrecht am Beispiel Südafrika," Humanitäres Völkerrecht Informationsschriften, Vol. 14 (2001) 162–172

Guhr, A. H.: "Victim participation during the pre-trial stage at the International Criminal Court," International Criminal Law Review, Vol. 8 (2008) 109–140

Hafner, Gerhard: "An attempt to explain the position of the USA towards the ICC," Journal of International Criminal Justice, Vol. 3 (2005) 323–332

Hafner, Gerhard/*Boon,* Kristen/*Rübesame,* Anne/*Huston,* Jonathan: "A response to the American view as presented by Ruth Wedgwood," European Journal of International Law, Vol. 10 (1999) 108–123

Hall, Christopher Keith: "The third and fourth sessions of the UN Preparatory Committee on the Establishment of the International Criminal Court," American Journal of International Law, Vol. 92 (1998) 124–133

Hamann, Hartmut: "Internationaler Strafgerichtshof und Vereinte Nationen in der Demokratischen Republik Kongo," Zeitschrift für die gesamte Strafrechtswissenschaft, Vol. 118 (2006) 799–822

Hanlon, Kimberly: "Now that peace is being negotiated in Uganda, will the ICC still pursue justice?," Tulsa Journal of Comparative & International Law, Vol. 14 (2007) 295–337

Happold, Matthew: "The ICC and the LRA," Melbourne Journal of International Law, Vol. 8 (2007) 1–26, available at: <www.mjil.law.unimelb.edu.au/go/issues/issue-archive/volume-8-1>

Hayner, Priscilla: "International guidelines for the creation and operation of truth commissions: a preliminary proposal," Law and Contemporary Problems, Vol. 59 (2006) 173–180

Hazan, Pierre: "Measuring the impact of punishment and forgiveness: a framework for evaluating transitional justice," International Review of the Red Cross No. 861 (2006) 19–47

Heiss, Helmut: "Hierarchische Rechtskreiseinteilung," Zeitschrift für Vergleichende Rechtswissenschaft, Vol. 100 (2001) 396–424

Heller, Kevin Jon: "The shadow side of complementarity: the effect of article 17 of the Rome Statute on national due process," Criminal Law Forum, Vol. 17 (2006) 255–280

Herbst, Jochen: "Immunität für Angehörige der U.S.-Streitkräfte vor der Strafverfolgung durch den IStGH?," Europäische Grundrechte Zeitschrift, Vol. 29 (2002) 581–588

Heselhaus, Sebastian: "Resolution 1422 (2002) des Sicherheitsrates zur Begrenzung der Tätigkeit des Internationalen Strafgerichtshofs," Zeitschrift für ausländisches öffentliches Recht und Völkerrecht, Vol. 62 (2002) 907–940

Hoffmeister, Frank/*Knoke,* Sebastian: "Das Vorermittlungsverfahren vor dem Internationalen Strafgerichtshof – Prüfstein für die Effektivität der neuen Gerichtsbarkeit im Völkerstrafrecht," Zeitschrift für ausländisches öffentliches Recht und Völkerrecht, Vol. 59 (1999) 785–807

Holá, Barbora/*Smeulers,* Alette/*Bijlevled,* Catrien: "Is ICTY sentencing predictable? An empirical analysis of ICTY sentencing practice," Leiden Journal of International Law, Vol. 22 (2009) 79–97

Hunt, David: "The International Criminal Court. High hopes, 'creative ambiguity' and an unfortunate mistrust in international judges," Journal of International Criminal Justice, Vol. 2 (2004) 56–70

Jackson, John: "Finding the best epistemic fit for international criminal tribunals," Journal of International Criminal Justice, Vol. 7 (2009) 17–39

Jain, Neha: "A separate law for peacekeepers: The clash between the Security Council and the International Criminal Court" European Journal of International Law, Vol. 16 (2005) 239–254

Jakobs, Dov: "The importance of being earnest: the timeliness of the challenge to admissibility in *Katanga*," Leiden Journal of International Law, Vol. 23 (2010) 331–342

Jalloh, Charles Chernor: "Regionalizing International Criminal Law," International Criminal Law Review, Vol. 9 (2009) 445–499

Jallow, Hassan: "Prosecutorial discretion and international criminal justice," Journal of International Criminal Justice, Vol. 3 (2005) 145–161

Jarasch, Frank: "Errichtung, Organisation und Finanzierung des Internationalen Strafgerichtshofs und die Schlußbestimmungen des Statuts," Humanitäres Völkerrecht Informationsschriften, Vol. 12 (1999) 10–22

Jescheck, Hans-Heinrich: "The general principles of International Criminal Law set out in Nuremberg, as mirrored in the ICC Statute," Journal of International Criminal Justice, Vol. 2 (2004) 38–55

Joakim, Jennifer: "The Singapore plan: maximising the power of the ICC," New England International and Comparative Law Annual, Vol. 4 (1998) 211–220

Jurdi, Nidal Nabil: "The prosecutorial interpretation of the complementarity principle: does it really contribute to ending impunity on the national level?," International Criminal Law Review, Vol. 10 (2010) 73–96

Kaul, Hans-Peter/*Kreß,* Claus: "Jurisdiction and cooperation in the Statute of the International Criminal Court: principles and compromises," Yearbook of International Humanitarian Law, Vol. 2 (1999) 143–175

Kirsch, Phillipe/*Holmes,* John T.: "The Rome conference on an ICC: the negotiating process," American Journal of International Law, Vol. 93 (1999) 2–12

Kirsch, Stefan: "The trial proceedings before the ICC," International Criminal Law Review, Vol. 6 (2006) 275–292

Kleffner, Jann: "The impact of complementarity on national implementation of substantive international criminal law," Journal of International Criminal Justice, Vol. 1 (2003) 86–113

Klip, André: "Complementarity and concurrent juridiction," Nouvelles études pénal, Vol. 19 (2004) 173–197

Knoops, Geert-Jan Alexander, "Challenging the legitimacy of initiating contemporary international criminal proceedings: rethinking prosecutorial discretionary powers from a legal, ethical and political perspective," Criminal Law Forum, Vol. 15 (2004) 365–390

Kourabas, Michael: "A Vienna Convention interpretation of the 'Interests of Justice' provision of the Rome Statute, the legality of domestic amnesty agreements, and the situation in Northern Uganda: a 'great qualitative step forward', or a normative retreat?," U.C. Davis Journal of International Law and Policy, Vol. 14 (2007) 60–94

Kress, Claus: "The crime of genocide and contextual elements," Journal of International Criminal Justice, Vol. 7 (2009) 297–306

– "The procedural texts of the International Criminal Court," Journal of International Criminal Justice, Vol. 5 (2007) 537–543

– "'Self referrals' and 'waivers of complementarity'," Journal of International Criminal Justice, Vol. 2 (2004) 944–948

– "The procedural law of the International Criminal Court in outline: anatomy of a unique compromise," Journal of International Criminal Justice, Vol. 1 (2003) 596–602

– "The International Criminal Court and the United States. Reflections on Resolution 1422 of the UN Security Council," Art & Thought, Vol. 77 (2003) 56–60, available at: <www.qantara.de/webcom/show_download.php/_c-496/i.html>

Kritz, Neil: "Coming to terms with atrocities: a review of accountability mechanisms for mass violations of human right," Law and Contemporary Problems, Vol. 59 (2006) 127–152

Kurth, Michael: "Zum Verfolgungsermessen des Generalbundesanwalts nach § 153f StPO," Zeitschrift für Internationale Strafrechtsdogmatik, Vol. 2 (2006) 82–86

Lavalle, Roberto: "A vicious storm in a teacup: the action by the United Nations Security Council to narrow the jurisdiction of the International Criminal Court," Criminal Law Forum, Vol. 14 (2003) 195–220

Lovat, Henry: "Delineating the interests of justice: prosecutorial discretion and the Rome Statute of the International Criminal Court," bepress Legal Series Working Paper 1435 (2006) 1–9, available at: <http://law.bepress.com/expresso/eps/>

MacPherson, Brian: "Authority of the Security Council to exempt peacekeepers from International Criminal Court proceedings," ASIL Insights July 2002, available at: <www.asil.org/insigh89.cfm>

Maged, Adel: "Withdrawal of referrals – a serious challenge to the function of the ICC," International Criminal Law Review, Vol. 6 (2006) 419–446

Majzub, Diba: "Peace and Justice? Amnesties and the International Criminal Court," Melbourne Journal of International Law, Vol. 3 (2002) 247–279

Mallinder, Louise: "Can amnesties and international justice be reconciled?," The International Journal of Transitional Justice, Vol. 1 (2007) 208–230

Martenczuk, Bernd: "The Security Council, the International Court and judicial review: What lessons from Lockerbie?" European Journal of International Law, Vol. 10 (1999), 517–547

McAuliffe deGuzman, Margaret: "Gravity and the Legitimacy of the International Criminal Court," Yale Law School Student Scholarship Series, paper 69, 25.8.2008, 1–48, available at: <http://lsr.nellco.org/yale/student/papers/69>; see also Fordham International Law Journal, Vol. 32 (2009) 1400–1465

McDonald, Avril/*Haveman,* Roelof: "Prosecutorial discretion – some thoughts on objectifying the exercise of prosecutorial discretion by the Prosecutor of the ICC," Contribution to an expert consultation process on general issues relevant to the ICC OTP, 15 April 2003, 1–10 (copy on file with the author)

McGoldrick, Dominic: "The Permanent International Criminal Court: An end to the culture of impunity?," Criminal Law Review (1999) 627–655

McGonigle, Brianne: "Two for the price of one: attempts by the Extraordinary Chambers in the Courts of Cambodia to combine retributive and restorative justice principles," Leiden Journal of International Law, Vol. 22 (2009) 127–149

Melandri, Manuela: "The relationship between State sovereignty and the enforcement of international criminal law under the Rome Statute (1998): a complex interplay," International Criminal Law Review, Vol. 9 (2009) 531–545

Meyer, Frank: "Complementing complementarity," International Criminal Law Review, Vol. 6 (2006) 549–583

Miraglia, Michela: "The first decision of the ICC Pre-Trial Chamber," Journal of International Criminal Justice, Vol. 4 (2006) 188–195

Mokhtar, Aly: "The fine art of arm twisting: The US, Resolution 1422 and the Security Council deferral power under the Rome Statute," International Criminal Law Review, Vol. 3 (2003) 295–344

Momtaz, Djamchid: "La compétence complémentaire de la Cour Pénale Internationale à l'épreuve des lois d'amnistie inconditionelle," Friedenswarte, Vol. 78 (2003) 53–62

Moy, H. Abigail: "The ICC's arrest warrants and Uganda's LRA: renewing the debate over amnesty and complementarity," Harvard's Human Rights Journal, Vol. 19 (2006) 267–273

Mundis, Daryl: "The United States of America and International Justice," Journal of International Criminal Justice, Vol. 2 (2004) 2–10

Murphy, Ray: "Gravity issues and the International Criminal Court," Criminal Law Forum, Vol. 16 (2006) 281–315

Naqvi, Yasmin: "Amnesty for war crimes: defining the limits of international recognition," International Review of the Red Cross No. 851 (2003) 583–625

Neuer, Matthias: "The Darfur referral of the Security Council and the scope of jurisdiction of the International Criminal Court," Yearbook of International Humanitarian Law, Vol. 8 (2005) 320–343

Newman, Dwight: "The Rome Statute, some reservations concerning amnesties, and a distributive problem," American University International Law Review, Vol. 20 (2005) 293–356

Nsereko, Daniel Ntanda: "The role of the international criminal tribunals in the promotion of peace and justice: the case of the International Criminal Court," Criminal Law Forum, Vol. 19 (2008) 373–393

– "The relationship between the International Criminal Court and the United Nations Security Council," Zeitschrift für Internationale Strafrechtsdogmatik 13 (2007) 500–506

– "Prosecutorial discretion before the national courts and international tribunals," Journal of International Criminal Justice, Vol. 3 (2005) 124–144

– "The International Criminal Court: Jurisdictional and related issues," Criminal Law Forum, Vol. 10 (1999) 87–120

Obembe, Jean-Pascal: "The International Criminal Court – a work in progress in the Democratic Republic of Congo," Humanitäres Völkerrecht – Informationsschriften, Vol. 18 (2005) 11–23

Oette, Lutz: "Peace and justice, or neither?," Journal of International Criminal Justice, Vol. 8 (2010) 345–364

Okuta, Antonina: "National legislation for prosecution of international crimes in Kenya," Journal of International Criminal Justice, Vol. 7 (2009) 1063–1076

Olàsolo, Héctor: "The lack of attention to the distinction between situation and cases in national laws on co-operation with the International Criminal Court with particular reference to the Spanish case," Leiden Journal of International Law, Vol. 20 (2007) 193–205

– "Reflections on the International Criminal Court's jurisdictional reach," Criminal Law Forum, Vol. 16 (2005) 279–301

– "The triggering procedure of the International Criminal Court, procedural treatment of complementarity and the role of the Office of the Prosecutor," International Criminal Law Review, Vol. 5 (2005) 121–146

– "The prosecutor of the ICC before the initiation of investigations: a quasi-judicial or a political body?," International Criminal Law Review, Vol. 3 (2003) 87–150

Olson, Laura: "Mechanisms complementing prosecution," International Review of the Red Cross, Vol. 84 (2002) 173–189

Oosthuizen, Gabriël: "Some preliminary remarks on the relationship between the envisaged International Criminal Court and the UN Security Council," Netherlands International Law Review, Vol. XLVI (1999) 313–342

Orentlicher, Diane: "Settling accounts: The duty to prosecute human rights violations of a prior regime," Yale Law Journal, Vol. 100 (1991) 2537–2615

Osiel, Mark: "How should the ICC Office of the Prosecutor choose its cases? The multiple meanings of 'situational gravity'," The Hague Justice Portal, 5.3.2009, 1–7, available at: <www.haguejusticeportal.net/eCache/DEF/10/344.html>

Paulus, Andreas: "Legalist groundwork for the International Criminal Court," European Journal of International Law, Vol. 14 (2003), 843–860

Payandeh, Mehrdad: "Rechtskontrolle des UN-Sicherheitsrates durch staatliche und überstaatliche Gerichte," Zeitschrift für ausländisches öffentliches Recht und Völkerrecht, Vol. 66 (2006) 41–71

Peteculescu, Ioana: "The review of the United Nations Security Council decisions by the International Court of Justice," Netherlands International Law Review, Vol. LII (2005) 167–195

Pham, Phuong/*Vinck,* Patrick: "Empirical research and the development and assessment of transitional justice mechanisms," The International Journal of Transitional Justice, Vol. 1 (2007) 231–248

Pham, Phuong/*Vinck,* Patrick/*Stover,* Eric: "The LRA and forced conscription in Northern Uganda," Human Rights Quarterly, Vol. 30 (2008) 404–411

Philips, Ruth: "Jurisdiction and admissibility," Criminal Law Forum, Vol. 10 (1999) 61–85

Pichon, Jakob: "The principle of complementarity in the cases of the Sudanese nationals Ahmad Harun and Ali Kushayb before the International Criminal Court," International Criminal Law Review, Vol. 8 (2008) 185–228

Politi, Mauro: "Le Statut de Rome de la Cour pénale internationale. Le point de vue d'un négociateur," Revue Générale de Droit International Public, Vol. 103 (1999) 817–850

Quénivet, Noëlle: "Who changed the road rules? The ICC and the Security Council hammering in conflict road signs," Friedenswarte, Vol. 78 (2003) 29–51

Raab, Dominic: "Evaluating the ICTY and its completion strategy," Journal of International Criminal Justice, Vol. 3 (2005) 82–102

Rackow, Peter: "Die Darstellung der Verletzteneigenschaft durch den Anwalt im Antrag auf gerichtliche Entscheidung im Klageerzwingungsverfahren," Goltdammer's Archiv, Vol. 148 (2001) 482–491

Rastan, Rod: "What is a 'case' for the purpose of the Rome Statute?," Criminal Law Forum, Vol. 19 (2008) 435–448

– "The power of the Prosecutor in initiating investigations," International Centre for Criminal Law Reform and Criminal Justice Policy, A paper prepared for the symposium on the International Criminal Court, 3.–4.2.2007, Bejing, 1–8, available at: <www.icclr.law.ubc.ca/Site%20Map/Publications%20Page/International.htm>

Reismann, Michael: "On paying the piper: financial responsibility for Security Council referrals to the International Criminal Court," American Journal of International Law, Vol. 99 (2005) 615–618

– "Learning to deal with rejection: The International Criminal Court and the United States," Journal of International Criminal Justice, Vol. 2 (2004) 17–18

Röben, Volker: "The procedure of the ICC: Status and functions of the Prosecutor," Max Planck UNYB, Vol. 7 (2003) 513–552

Robinson, Darryl: "The mysterious mysteriousness of complementarity," Criminal Law Forum, Vol. 21 (2010) 67–102

– "Serving the interests of justice: amnesties, truth commissions and the International Criminal Court," European Journal of International Law, Vol. 14 (2003) 481–505

Roche, Declan: "Truth Commission, amnesties and the International Criminal Court," British Journal of Criminology, Vol. 45 (2005) 565–581

Rodman, Kenneth: "Is peace in the interests of justice? The case of broad prosecutorial discretion at the International Criminal Court," Leiden Journal of International Law, Vol. 22 (2009) 99–126

Ronan, Yaël: "ICC jurisdiction over acts committed in the Gaza strip," Journal of International Criminal Justice, Vol. 8 (2010) 3–27

Rubin, Alfred: "The International Criminal Court: possibilities for prosecutorial abuse," Law & Contemporary Problems, Vol. 64 (2001) 153–165, available at: <www.law.duke.edu/journals/64LCPRubin>

Sá Couto, Susana/*Cleary,* Katherine: "The gravity threshold of the International Criminal Court," American University International Law Review, Vol. 23 (2008) 807–854

– "The *Katanga* complementarity decisions: Sound law but flawed policy," Leiden Journal of International Law, Vol. 23 (2010) 363–374

Sarooshi, Dan: "Prosecutorial policy and the ICC: Prosecutor's *proprio motu* action or self-denial?," Journal of International Criminal Justice, Vol. 2 (2004) 940–943

Schabas, William: "Prosecutorial discretion v. judicial activism at the International Criminal Court," Journal of International Criminal Justice, Vol. 6 (2008) 731–761

– "Complementarity in practice: some uncomplimentary thoughts," Criminal Law Forum, Vol. 19 (2008) 5–33

– "The role of the Prosecutor of the International Criminal Court," Friedenswarte, Vol. 83 (2008) 11–31

– "First prosecutions at the International Criminal Court," Human Rights Law Journal, Vol. 27 (2006) 25–40

– "United States hostility towards the International Criminal Court: it's all about the Security Council," European Journal of International Law, Vol. 15 (2004) 701–720

Schabas, William/*Stahn,* Carsten/*El Zeidy,* Mohamed: "The International Criminal Court and Complementarity: five years on," Criminal Law Forum, Vol. 19 (2008) 1–3

Scharf, Michael: "The amnesty exception to the jurisdiction of the International Criminal Court," Cornell International Law Journal, Vol. 32 (1999) 507–527

Scheffer, David: "How many are too many defendants at the KRT?," Opinion, 8.1.2009, 1–4, available at: <www.cambodiatribunal.org/index.php?option=com_content&view=article&id=20&Itemid=21>

– "How to turn the tide using the Rome Statute's temporal jurisdiction," Journal of International Criminal Justice, Vol. 2 (2004) 26–34

– "Article 98 (2) of the Rome Statute: America's original intent," Journal of International Criminal Justice, Vol. 3 (2005) 333–353

Schüller, Andreas: "Gravity under the Rome Statute: Procedural filter or instrument of shaping criminal policy?," Humanitäres Völkerrecht Informationsschriften, Vol. 21 (2008) 73–81

Seibert-Fohr, Anja: "The relevance of the Rome Statute of the International Criminal Court for amnesties and truth commissions," Max Planck Yearbook of the United Nations, Vol. 7 (2003) 553–590

Seidel, Gerd/*Stahn,* Carsten: "Das Statut des Weltstrafgerichtshofs. Ein Überblick über Entstehung, Inhalt und Bedeutung," Jura, Vol. 21 (1999) 14–21

Sendel, Björn: "Bilaterale Nichtüberstellungsabkommen der Vereinigten Staaten und Art. 98 Abs. 2 des Römischen Statuts zur Errichtung eines ständigen Internationalen Strafgerichtshofs", Zeitschrift für Internationale Strafrechtsdogmatik, Vol. 3 (2007) 118–128

Sheng, Ada: "Analysing the International Criminal Court complementarity principle through a Federal Courts lens," bepress Legal Series Working Paper 1249 (2006) 1–30, available at: <http://law.bepress.com/expresso/eps/1249/>

Sheppard, Daniel: "The International Criminal Court and 'internationally recognized human rights': understanding article 21 (3) of the Rome Statute," International Criminal Law Review, Vol. 10 (2010) 43–71

Šimonović, Ivan: "Dealing with the legacy of past war crimes and human rights abuses," Journal of International Criminal Justice, Vol. 2 (2004) 701–710

Singelnstein, Tobias/*Stolle,* Peer: "Völkerstrafrecht und Legalitätsprinzip – Klageerzwingungsverfahren bei Opportunitätseinstellung und Auslegung des § 153f StPO," Zeitschrift für Internationale Strafrechtsdogmatik, Vol. 3 (2006) 118–122

Sluiter, Göran: "The surrender of war criminals to the International Criminal Court," Loyola of Los Angeles International and Comparative Law Review, Vol. 25 (2003) 605–651

Smith, Stephen Eliot: "Inventing the laws of gravity: the ICC's initial Lubanga decision and its regressive consequences," International Criminal Law Review, Vol. 8 (2008) 331–352

Solera, Oscar: "Complementary jurisdiction and international criminal justice," International Review of the Red Cross, Vol. 84 (2002) 145–171

Sriram, Chandra Lekha/*Ross,* Amy: "Geographies of crime and justice: contemporary transitional justice and the creation of 'zones of impunity'," The International Journal of Transitional Justice, Vol. 1 (2007) 45–65

Ssenyonjo, Manisuli: "The International Criminal Court and the Lord's Resistance Army Leaders: prosecution or amnesty?," International Criminal Law Review, Vol. 7 (2007) 361–389 (also published in Netherlands International Law Review, Vol. LIV (2007) 51–80)

Stahn, Carsten: "Complementarity: a tale of two notions," Criminal Law Forum, Vol. 19 (2008) 87–113

– "Perspectives on *Katanga*: an introduction," Leiden Journal of International Law, Vol. 23 (2010) 311–318

– "Complementarity, amnesties and alternative forms of justice: some interpretative guidelines for the International Criminal Court," Journal of International Criminal Justice, Vol. 3 (2005) 695–720

– "The ambiguities of Security Council Resolution 1422," European Journal of International Law, Vol. 14 (2003) 85–104

Stahn, Carsten/*El Zeidy,* Mohamed/*Olásolo,* Héctor: "Developments at the International Criminal Court: The International Criminal Court's *ad hoc* jurisdiction revisited," American Journal of International Law, Vol. 99 (2005) 421–431

Stahn, Carsten/*Olásolo,* Héctor/*Gibson,* Kate: "Participation of victims in pre-trial proceedings of the ICC," Journal of International Criminal Justice, Vol. 4 (2006) 219–238

Stegmiller, Ignaz: "The gravity threshold under the ICC Statute: gravity back and forth in Lubanga and Ntaganda," International Criminal Law Review, Vol. 9 (2009) 547–565

Surlan, Tijana: "Ne bis in idem in conjunction with the principle of complementarity in the Rome Statute," "Agora" Papers presented at the 2005 Florence Founding Conference of the ESIL, 1–8, available at: <www.esil-sedi.eu/english/papers.html>

Takemura, Hitomi: "Big fish and small fish debate – an examination of the prosecutorial discretion," International Criminal Law Review, Vol. 7 (2007) 677–685

– "A critical analysis of positive complementarity," XVth International Congress of Social Defense, Toledo, 20.–22.9.2007, 1–29, available at: <www.defensesociale.org/warandpiece/HITOMI TAKEMURA.pdf>

Tomuschat, Christian: "Das Statut von Rom für den Internationalen Strafgerichtshof," Friedenswarte, Vol. 73 (1998) 335–347

Van der Wilt, Harmen: "Bilateral agreements between the United States and States Parties to the Rome Statute: are they compatible with the object and purpose of the Statute?," Leiden Journal of International Law, Vol. 18 (2005) 93–111

Van der Wilt, Harmen/*Lyngdorf,* Sandra: "Procedural obligations under the European Convention of Human Rights: useful guidelines for assessment of 'unwillingness' and 'inability' in the context of the complementarity principle," International Criminal Law Review, Vol. 9 (2009) 39–75

Wald, Patricia: "Is the United States' opposition to the ICC intractable?," Journal of International Criminal Justice, Vol. 2 (2004) 19–25

Wedgwood, Ruth: "The International Criminal Court: an American view," European Journal of International Law, Vol. 10 (1999), 93–107

– "The United States and the ICC: achieving a wider consensus through the Ithaca Package," Cornell Journal of International Law, Vol. 32 (1999) 535–541

Werle, Gehard/*Jessberger,* Florian: "Unless otherwise provided," Journal of International Criminal Justice, Vol. 3 (2005) 35–55

Wilhelmi, Theresa: "Die Verfahrensordnung des Internationalen Strafgerichtshofs – Modell eines universalen Strafverfahrens?," Institut für Rechtspolitik – Rechtspolitisches Forum Nr. 24, 2004, <www.irp.uni-trier.de/typo3/fileadmin/tem plate/pdf/24_wilhelmi.pdf>

Wouters, Jan/*Verhoeven,* Sten/*Demeyere,* Bruno: "The International Criminal Court's Office of the Prosecutor: navigating between independence and accountability?," International Criminal Law Review, Vol. 8 (2008) 273–318

– "The International Criminal Court's Office of the Prosecutor: navigating between independence and accountability?" Institute for International Law, Working paper No. 97, July 2006, available at: <http://law.kuleuven.be/iir/nl/onderzoek/wp/WP97e.pdf>

Yav Katshung, Joseph: "The relationship between the International Criminal Court and truth commissions: some thoughts on how to build a bridge across retributive and restorative justice," May 2005, 1–28, available at: <www.iccnow.org/?mod=browserdoc&type=1>

Young, Gwen: "Amnesty and accountability," U.C. Davis Law Review, Vol. 35 (2002) 427–482

Zappalà, Salvatore: "The reaction of the US to the entry into force of the ICC Statute: comments on UN SC Resolution 1422 (2002) and article 98 agreements," Journal of International Criminal Justice, Vol. 1 (2003) 114–134

– "Are some peacekeepers better than others? UN Security Council Resolution 1497 (2003) and the ICC," Journal of International Criminal Justice, Vol. 1 (2003) 671–678

– "Il procuratore della Corte Penal Internazionale: luci e ombre" Rivista de diritto internazionale, Vol. 82 (1999) 39–85

Zimmermann, Andreas: "Die Schaffung eines ständigen Internationalen Strafgerichtshofs," Zeitschrift für ausländisches öffentliches Recht und Völkerrecht, Vol. 58 (1998) 47–108

Zimmermann, Andreas/*Scheel,* Holger: "Zwischen Konfrontation und Kooperation. Die Vereinigten Staaten und der Internationale Strafgerichtshof," Vereinte Nationen, Vol. 50 (2002) 137–144

Zwanenburg, Marten: "The Statute of the International Criminal Court and the United States: peacekeepers under fire?," European Journal of International Law, Vol. 10, 124–143

3. Contributions to collected work

Abtahi, Hirad: "The Judges of the International Criminal Court and the organization of their work," in: Doria, José/Gasser, Hans-Peter/Bassiouni, Cherif (eds.), The legal regime of the International Criminal Court, Essays in Honour of Professor Igor Blishchenko, Leiden/Boston 2009, 331–344

Agirre Aranburu, Xabier: "Gravity of crimes and responsibility of the suspect," in: Bergsmo, Morten (ed.), Criteria for prioritizing and selecting core international crimes cases, Forum for International Criminal and Humanitarian Law (FICHL), Oslo 2009, 147–166

Ahmed, Anees/*Day,* Margaux: "Prosecution criteria at the Khmer Rouge Tribunal," in: Bergsmo, Morten (ed.), Criteria for prioritizing and selecting core international crimes cases, Forum for International Criminal and Humanitarian Law (FICHL), Oslo 2009, 79–85

Allen, Tim: "Ritual (ab)use? Problems with traditional justice in Northern Uganda," in: Waddell, Nicholas/Clark, Phil (eds.), Courting conflict? Justice, peace and the ICC in Africa, London 2008, 47–54

Ambos, Kai: "International Criminal Law at the crossroads: from *ad hoc* imposition to a treaty-based universal system," in: Stahn, Carsten/van Herik, Larissa (eds.), Future Perspectives on International Criminal Justice, The Hague 2010, 161–177

– " 'Witness proofing' before the ICC: neither legally admissible nor necessary," in: Stahn, Carsten/Sluiter, Göran (eds.), The Emerging Practice of the International Criminal Court, Leiden/Boston 2009, 599–614

– "The legal framework of transitional justice. A systematic study with a special focus on the role of the ICC," in: Ambos, Kai/Large, Judith/Wierda, Marieke (eds.), Building a future on peace and justice. Studies on Transitional Justice, Conflict Resolution and Development, Berlin et al. 2009, 19–103 (For an earlier version see: *Ambos,* Kai, "The legal framework of transitional justice," Study Workshop 4 – The legal framework, International conference building a future on peace and justice, Nuremberg 25.–27. June 2007, 1–95, available at: <www.peace-justice-conference.info/documents.asp>)

– "The structure of international criminal procedure: adversarial, inquisitorial or mixed?," in: Bohlander, Michael (ed.), International criminal justice: a critical analysis of institutions and procedures, London 2007, 429–503

– "Prosecuting international crimes at the national and international level: between justice and Realpolitik," in: Kaleck, Wolfgang/Ratner, Michael/Singelnstein, Tobias/Weiss, Peter (eds.), International prosecution of human rights crimes, Berlin/Heidelberg/New York 2007, 55–68

Angermeier, Claudia: "Case selection and prioritization criteria in the work of the International Criminal Tribunal for the Former Yugoslavia," in: Bergsmo, Morten (ed.), Criteria for prioritizing and selecting core international crimes cases, Forum for International Criminal and Humanitarian Law (FICHL), Oslo 2009, 29–39

Arsanjani, Mahnoush: "ICC and trigger mechanism by a State," in: Perakis, S. (ed.), International Criminal Court, A new dimension in international justice. Questions and prospects for a new humanitarian order, Colloqium, Santorini 14–16 September 2000, Athens 2002, 147–150

– "Reflections on the jurisdiction and trigger mechanism of the International Criminal Court," in: Hebel, Herman/Lammers, Johan/Schukking, Jolien (eds.), Reflections on the International Criminal Court, Essays in honour of Adriaan Bos, The Hague 1999, 57–76

Arsanjani, Mahnoush/*Reismann,* Michael: "The International Criminal Court and the Congo: from theory to reality," in: Sadat, Leila/Scharf, Michael (eds.), The theory and practice of International Criminal Law, Essays in honor of M. Cherif Bassiouni, Leiden 2008, 325–345

Behrens, Hans-Jörg: "The trial proceedings," in: Lee, Roy (ed.), The International Criminal Court, the making of the Rome Statute, issues, negotiations, results, The Hague 1999, 238–246

Behrens, Hans-Jörg/*Staker,* Christopher: "Article 52," in: Triffterer, Otto (ed.), Commentary on the Rome Statute of the International Criminal Court, 2nd edition, München/Oxford/Baden-Baden 2008

Bekou, Olympia: "Complementarity and the ICC: a dangerous gamble?," in: Ulrich, George (ed.), The International Criminal Court: challenges and prospects, Proceedings of an international conference organised by the European Inter-University Centre for Human Rights and Democratisation (EIUC), Venice 2005, 61–81

Bell, Christine: "The 'new law' on transitional justice," in: Ambos, Kai/Large, Judith/Wierda, Marieke (eds.), Building a future on peace and justice. Studies on Transitional Justice, Conflict Resolution and Development, Berlin et al. 2009, 105–126

Benvenuti, Paolo: "Complementarity of the International Criminal Court to national jurisdictions," in: Lattanzi, Flavia/Schabas, William (eds.), Essays on the Rome Statute of the International Criminal Court, Vol. 1, Ripa Fagnano Alto 1999

Bergsmo, Morten: "The theme of selection and prioritization criteria and why it is relevant," in: Bergsmo, Morten (ed.), Criteria for prioritizing and selecting core international crimes cases, Forum for International Criminal and Humanitarian Law (FICHL), Oslo 2009, 15–19

Bergsmo, Morten/*Kruger,* Pieter: "Article 53," in: Triffterer, Otto (ed.), Commentary on the Rome Statute of the International Criminal Court, 2nd edition, München/Oxford/Baden-Baden 2008

– "Article 54," in: Triffterer, Otto (ed.), Commentary on the Rome Statute of the International Criminal Court, 2nd edition, München/Oxford/Baden-Baden 2008

Bergsmo, Morten/*Pjeić,* Jelena: "Article 15," in: Triffterer, Otto (ed.), Commentary on the Rome Statute of the International Criminal Court, 2nd edition, München/Oxford/Baden-Baden 2008

– "Article 16," in: Triffterer, Otto (ed.), Commentary on the Rome Statute of the International Criminal Court, 2nd edition, München/Oxford/Baden-Baden 2008

Berman, Franklin: "The relationship between the International Criminal Court and the Security Council," in: Hebel, Herman/Lammers, Johan/Schukking, Jolien (eds.), Reflections on the International Criminal Court, Essays in honour of Adriaan Bos, The Hague 1999, 173–180

Bevers, Hans/*Swaak,* Olivia/*Roording,* Jaap: "The Dutch International Crimes Act (Bill)," in: Neuner, Matthias (ed.), National legislation implementing international crimes, Berlin 2003, 179–197

Bitti, Gilbert: "Article 21 of the Statute of the International Criminal Court and the treatment of sources of law in the jurisprudence of the ICC," in: Stahn, Carsten/Sluiter, Göran (eds.), The Emerging Practice of the International Criminal Court, Leiden/Boston 2009, 285–304

– "Two bones of contention between civil and common law: the record of the proceedings and the treatment of concursus delictorum," in: Fischer, Horst/Kreß, Claus/Lüder, Sascha (eds.), International and national prosecution of crimes under international law, Berlin 2001, 273–288

Blewitt, Graham: "Exercising independence: the ICTY and ICC prosecutors," in: Perrakis, Stelios (ed.), International Criminal Court, A new dimension in international justice. Questions and prospects for a new humanitarian order, Colloqium, Santorini 14–16 September 2000, Athens 2002, 155–161

Bos, Adriaan: "Assembly of States Parties," in: Cassese, Antonio/Gaeta, Paola/Jones, John (eds.), The Rome Statute of the ICC: a commentary, Vol. I, Oxford 2002, 297–314

Bourgon, Stéphan: "Jurisdiction ratione temporis," in: Cassese, Antonio/Gaeta, Paola/Jones, John (eds.), The Rome Statute of the ICC: a commentary, Vol. I, Oxford 2002, 543–558

– "Jurisdiction ratione loci," in: Cassese, Antonio/Gaeta, Paola/Jones, John (eds.), The Rome Statute of the ICC: a commentary, Vol. I, Oxford 2002, 559–569

Brady, Helen/*Jennings,* Mark: "Appeal and revision," in: Lee, Roy (ed.), The International Criminal Court, the making of the Rome Statute, issues, negotiations, results, The Hague 1999, 294–304

Brounéus, Karen: "Reconciliation and development," in: Ambos, Kai/Large, Judith/Wierda, Marieke (eds.), Building a future on peace and justice. Studies on Transitional Justice, Conflict Resolution and Development, Berlin et al. 2009, 203–216

Bryde, Brun Otto/*Reinisch,* August: "Article 48," in: Simma, Bruno (ed.), The Charter of the United Nations: a commentary, Vol. 1, Oxford 2002

Burke-White, William/*Kaplan,* Scott: "Shaping the contours of domestic justice: The International Criminal Court and an admissibility challenge in the Ugandan situation," in: Stahn, Carsten/Sluiter, Göran (eds.), The Emerging Practice of the International Criminal Court, Leiden/Boston 2009, 79–114

Cameron, Iain: "Jurisdiction and admissibility under the ICC Statute," in: McGoldrick, Dominic/*Rowe,* Peter/*Donnelly,* Eric (eds.): The Permanent International Criminal Court, Oxford 2004, 65–94

Cárdenas, Claudia: "The admissibility test before the International Criminal Court under special consideration of amnesties and truth commissions," in: Kleffner, Jan/Kor, Gerben (eds.), Complementary views on complementarity, The Hague 2006, 115–139

Cassese, Antonio: "Genocide," in: Cassese, Antonio/Gaeta, Paola/Jones, John (eds.), The Rome Statute of the ICC: a commentary, Vol. I, Oxford 2002, 335–351

– "Crimes against humanity," in: Cassese, Antonio/Gaeta, Paola/Jones, John (eds.), The Rome Statute of the ICC: a commentary, Vol. I, Oxford 2002, 353–378

Cédras, Jean: "France," in: Arbour, Louise/Eser, Albin/Ambos, Kai/Sanders, Andrew (eds.), The Prosecutor of a Permanent International Criminal Court, Freiburg 2000, 324–332

Chimimba, Trevor Pascal: "Establishing an enforcement regime," in: Lee, Roy (ed.), The International Criminal Court, the making of the Rome Statute, issues, negotiations, results, The Hague 1999, 345–356

Clark, Phil: "Law, politics and pragmatism: The ICC and case selection in the Democratic Republic of Congo and Uganda," in: Waddell, Nicholas/Clark, Phil (eds.), Courting conflict? Justice, peace and the ICC in Africa, London 2008, 37–46

Condorelli, Luigi/*Villalpando,* Santiago: "Can the Security Council extend the ICC's jurisdiction?," in: Cassese, Antonio/Gaeta, Paola/Jones, John (eds.), The Rome Statute of the ICC: a commentary, Vol. I, Oxford 2002, 571–582

– "Referral and deferral by the Security Council," in: Cassese, Antonio/Gaeta, Paola/Jones, John (eds.), The Rome Statute of the ICC: a commentary, Vol. I, Oxford 2002, 627–655

Cottier, Michael: "Article 8, para. 1," in: Triffterer, Otto (ed.), Commentary on the Rome Statute of the International Criminal Court, 2nd edition, München/Oxford/Baden-Baden 2008

Dallmeyer, Jens/*Jahn,* Matthias: "Einleitung und Einstellung des Ermittlungsverfahrens," in: Heghmanns, Michael/Scheffler, Uwe (eds.), Handbuch zum Strafverfahren, München 2008, 1–63

Dascalopoulou-Livada, Phani: "The principle of complementarity and security council referrals," in: Politi, Mauro/Gioia, Federica (eds.), The International Criminal Court and national jurisdictions, Hampshire 2008, 57–62

Däubler-Gmelin, Herta: "Die Stärke des Rechts im Zeitalter der Globalisierung – Beginn der Arbeit des Internationalen Strafgerichtshofs," in: Arnold, Jörg (ed.), Menschengerechtes Strafrecht, Festschrift für Albin Eser, München 2005, 717–738

Daws, Sam: "The origins and developments of UN electoral groups," in: Thakur, Ramesh (ed.), What is equitable geographic representation in the twenty-first century, New York 1999, 11–29, available at: <www.unu.edu/unupress/equitable.pdf>

De Greiff, Pablo: "DDR and reparations: establishing links between peace and justice instruments," in: Ambos, Kai/Large, Judith/Wierda, Marieke (eds.), Building a future on peace and justice. Studies on Transitional Justice, Conflict Resolution and Development, Berlin et al. 2009, 321–355

De Olivera, Jan: "South Africa," in: Arbour, Louise/Eser, Albin/Ambos, Kai/Sanders, Andrew (eds.), The Prosecutor of a Permanent International Criminal Court, Freiburg 2000, 469–480

De Smet, Simon: "A structural analysis of the role of the Pre-Trial Chamber in the fact-finding process of the ICC," in: Stahn, Carsten/Sluiter, Göran (eds.), The Emerging Practice of the International Criminal Court, Leiden/Boston 2009, 405–440

De Stefani, Paolo: "The ICC Prosecutor and the complementarity game," in: Ulrich, George (ed.), The International Criminal Court: challenges and prospects, Proceedings of an international conference organised by the European Inter-University Centre for Human Rights and Democratisation (EIUC), Venice 2005, 39–60

De Waal, Alex: "Darfur, the Court and Khartoum: The politics of State non-cooperation," in: Waddell, Nicholas/Clark, Phil (eds.), Courting conflict? Justice, peace and the ICC in Africa, London 2008, 29–36

Dicker, Richard: "Making justice meaningful for victims," in: Bergsmo, Morten (ed.), Criteria for prioritizing and selecting core international crimes cases, Forum for International Criminal and Humanitarian Law (FICHL), Oslo 2009, 187–190

Dubber, Markus Dirk: "Comparative criminal law," in: Reiman, Mathias/Zimmermann, Reinhard (eds.), The Oxford handbook of comparative law, Oxford 2006, 1287–1326

Dugard, John: "Possible conflicts of jurisdiction with truth commissions," in: Cassese, Antonio/Gaeta, Paola/Jones, John (eds.), The Rome Statute of the ICC: a commentary, Vol. I, Oxford 2002, 693–704

Dupuy, Pierre-Marie: "Principe de complémentarité et droit international général," in: Politi, Mauro/Gioia, Federica (eds.), The International Criminal Court and national jurisdictions, Hampshire 2008, 17–24

Durham, Ralf Michaels: "The functional method of comparative law," in: Reiman, Mathias/Zimmermann, Reinhard (eds.), The Oxford handbook of comparative law, Oxford 2006, 339–382

Eckelmans, Franziska: "The first jurisprudence of the Appeals Chamber of the ICC," in: Stahn, Carsten/Sluiter, Göran (eds.), The Emerging Practice of the International Criminal Court, Leiden/Boston 2009, 527–552

El Zeidy, Mohamed: "The legitimacy of withdrawing State Party referrals and *ad hoc* declarations under the Statute of the International Criminal Court," in: Stahn, Carsten/Sluiter, Göran (eds.), The Emerging Practice of the International Criminal Court, Leiden/Boston 2009, 55–78

Elaraby, Nabil: "The role of the Security Council and the independence of the International Criminal Court: some reflections," in: Politi, Mauro/Nesi, Giuseppe (eds.), The Rome Statute of the International Criminal Court – A challenge to impunity, Aldershot 2001, 43–47

Ellis, Mark: "The International Criminal Court and its implication for domestic law and national capacity building," in: Ellis, Mark/Goldstone, Richard (eds.), The

International Criminal Court: Challenges to achieving justice and accountability in the 21st century, New York 2008, 85–114

Fernández de Gurmendi, Silvia: "The role of the international prosecutor," in: Lee, Roy (ed.), The International Criminal Court, the making of the Rome Statute, issues, negotiations, results, The Hague 1999, 175–188

Fixon, Oliver: "Der IStGH: Seine Entstehung und seine Stellung im Völkerrecht," in: Kirsch, Stefan (ed.), Internationale Strafgerichtshöfe, Baden-Baden 2005, 207–229

Fourmy, Olivier: "Powers of the Pre-Trial Chamber," in: Cassese, Antonio/Gaeta, Paola/Jones, John (eds.), The Rome Statute of the ICC: a commentary, Vol. II, Oxford 2002, 1207–1230

Friman, Håkan: "Interlocutory appeals in the early practice of the International Criminal Court," in: Stahn, Carsten/Sluiter, Göran (eds.), The Emerging Practice of the International Criminal Court, Leiden/Boston 2009, 553–561

– "Investigation and prosecution," in: Lee, Roy (ed.) The International Criminal Court: Elements of Crimes and Rules of Procedure and Evidence, Ardsley 2001, 493–538

– "The Rules of Procedure and Evidence in the investigative stage," in: Fischer, Horst/Kreß, Claus/Lüder, Sascha Rolf (eds.), International and national prosecution of crimes under international law, Berlin 2001, 191–217

Fritsche, Claudia: "Security Council Resolution 1422: peacekeeping and the International Criminal Court," in: Frowein, Jochen et al. (eds.), Verhandeln für den Frieden – Negotiating for peace, Liber Amicorum Tono Eitel, Berlin 2003, 107–120

Fronza, Emanuela/*Malarino,* Ezequiel: "Problemas de determinación de la norma penal y soluciones de interpretación en textos penales plurilingües en el ejemplo del Estatuto de Roma," in: Ambos, Kai/Malarino, Ezequiel/Woischnik, Jan (eds.), Temas actuales del derecho penal internacional: contribuciones de América latina, Alemania y Espana, Berlin 2005, 61–95

Frowein, Jochen: "Issues of legitimacy around the United Nations Security Council," in: Frowein, Jochen et al. (eds.) Verhandeln für den Frieden – Negotiating for peace, Liber Amicorum Tono Eitel, Berlin 2003, 121–139

Frowein, Jochen/*Krisch,* Nico: "Article 39," in: Simma, Bruno (ed.), The Charter of the United Nations: a commentary, Vol. 1, Oxford 2002

Gaja, Giorgio: "Issues of admissibility in case of self-referrals," in: Politi, Mauro/Gioia, Federica (eds.), The International Criminal Court and national jurisdictions, Hampshire 2008, 49–52

Gallmetzer, Reinhold: "The Trial Chamber's discretionary power to devise the proceedings before it and its exercise in the trial of Thomas Lubanga Dyilo," in: Stahn, Carsten/Sluiter, Göran (eds.), The Emerging Practice of the International Criminal Court, Leiden/Boston 2009, 501–524

Gargiulo, Pietro: "The controversial relationship between the International Criminal Court and the Security Council," in: Lattanzi, Flavia/Schabas, William (eds.), Essays on the Rome Statute of the International Criminal Court, Vol. 1, Ripa Fagnano Alto 1999, 67–103

Gioia, Federica: "The complementarity role of the International Criminal Court: Are there any time-limits?," in: Politi, Mauro/Gioia, Federica (eds.), The International Criminal Court and national jurisdictions, Hampshire 2008, 71–80

– "Comments on chapter 3 of Jann Kleffner," in: Kleffner, Jan/Kor, Gerben (eds.), Complementary views on complementarity, The Hague 2006, 105–113

Goetz, Mariana: "The International Criminal Court and its relevance to affected communities," in: Waddell, Nicholas/Clark, Phil (eds.), Courting conflict? Justice, peace and the ICC in Africa, London 2008, 65–72

Gowlland-Debbas, Vera: "The relationship between political and judicial organs of international organisations: the role of the Security Council in the new International Criminal Court," in: de Chazournes, Laurence Boisson/Romano, Cesare/Mackenzie, Ruth (eds.), International organisations and international dispute settlement: trends and prospects, Ardsley/New York 2002, 195–218 (For an earlier version see: *Gowlland-Debbas,* Vera "The role of the Security Council in the new International Criminal Court from a systemic perspective," in de Chazournes, Laurence Boisson/Gowlland-Debbas, Vera (eds.), The international legal system in quest of equity and universality, Liber Amicorum Georges Abi-Saab, The Hague/London/Boston 2001, 629–650)

Greppi, Edoardo: "Inability to investigate and prosecute under article 17," in: Politi, Mauro/Gioia, Federica (eds.), The International Criminal Court and national jurisdictions, Hampshire 2008, 63–70

Grono, Nick/*O'Brien,* Adam: "Justice in conflict? The ICC and peace processes," in: Waddell, Nicholas/Clark, Phil (eds.), Courting conflict? Justice, peace and the ICC in Africa, London 2008, 13–20

Guariglia, Fabricio: "The selection of cases by the Office of the Prosecutor of the International Criminal Court," in: Stahn, Carsten/Sluiter, Göran (eds.), The Emerging Practice of the International Criminal Court, Leiden/Boston 2009, 209–217

– "The rules of procedure and evidence of the International Criminal Court: a new development in international adjudication of individual criminal responsibility," in: Cassese, Antonio/Gaeta, Paola/Jones, John (eds.), The Rome Statute of the International Criminal Court: A Commentary, Vol. II, Oxford 2002, 1111–1133

– "Investigation and prosecution," in: Lee, Roy (ed.), The International Criminal Court, the making of the Rome Statute, issues, negotiations, results, The Hague 1999, 227–238

Hall, Christopher: "Developing and implementing an effective positive complementarity prosecution strategy," in: Stahn, Carsten/Sluiter, Göran (eds.), The Emerging Practice of the International Criminal Court, Leiden/Boston 2009, 219–228

– "Article 19," in: Triffterer, Otto (ed.), Commentary on the Rome Statute of the International Criminal Court, 2nd edition, München/Oxford/Baden-Baden 2008

Healy, Patrick: "Canada," in: Arbour, Louise/Eser, Albin/Ambos, Kai/Sanders, Andrew (eds.), The Prosecutor of a Permanent International Criminal Court, Freiburg 2000, 245–250

Heghmanns, Michael: "Anklageentscheidung," in: Heghmanns, Michael/Scheffler, Uwe (eds.), Handbuch zum Strafverfahren, München 2008, 409–482

Heinsch, Robert: "How to achieve fair and expeditious trail proceedings before the ICC: is it time for a more judge-dominated approach?," in: Stahn, Carsten/Sluiter, Göran (eds.), The Emerging Practice of the International Criminal Court, Leiden/Boston 2009, 479–499

Heller, Kevin Jon: "Situational gravity under the Rome Statute," in: Stahn, Carsten/van Herik, Larissa (eds.), Future directions in international criminal justice, The Hague 2010, 227–253

Holmes, John: "Complementarity: national courts versus the ICC," in: Cassese, Antonio/Gaeta, Paola/Jones, John (eds.), The Rome Statute of the ICC: a commentary, Vol. I, Oxford 2002, 667–686

– "Jurisdiction and admissibility," in: Lee, Roy (ed.) The International Criminal Court: Elements of Crimes and Rules of Procedure and Evidence, Ardsley 2001, 321–348

– "The principle of complementarity," in: Lee, Roy (ed.), The International Criminal Court, the making of the Rome Statute, issues, negotiations, results, The Hague 1999, 41–78

Jakobs, Dov: "Commentary, Arrest warrants and admissibility," in: Klip, André/Sluiter, Göran (eds.), Annotated Leading Cases of International Criminal Tribunals, The International Criminal Court, 2005–2007, Vol. XXIII, Antwerp/Oxford/Portland 2010, 113-122

Jensen, Rod: "Complementarity, 'genuinely' and article 17: assessing the boundaries of an effective ICC," in: Kleffner, Jan/Kor, Gerben (eds.), Complementary views on complementarity, The Hague 2006, 147–170

Kaul, Hans-Peter: "Preconditions of the exercise of jurisdiction," in: Cassese, Antonio/Gaeta, Paola/Jones, John (eds.), The Rome Statute of the ICC: a commentary, Vol. I, Oxford 2002, 583–616

Keijzer, Nico: "The Netherlands," in: Arbour, Louise/Eser, Albin/Ambos, Kai/Sanders, Andrew (eds.), The Prosecutor of a Permanent International Criminal Court, Freiburg 2000, 413–423

Kirsch, Phillipe/*Robinson,* Darryl: "Referral by States Parties," in: Cassese, Antonio/Gaeta, Paola/Jones, John (eds.), The Rome Statute of the ICC: a commentary, Vol. I, Oxford 2002, 619–625

– "Initiation of proceedings by the Prosecutor," in: Cassese, Antonio/Gaeta, Paola/Jones, John (eds.), The Rome Statute of the ICC: a commentary, Vol. I, Oxford 2002, 657–664

Kleffner, Jann: "Auto-referrals and the complementarity nature of the ICC," in: Stahn, Carsten/Sluiter, Göran (eds.), The Emerging Practice of the International Criminal Court, Leiden/Boston 2009, 41–53

– "Complementarity as a catalyst for compliance," in: Kleffner, Jan/Kor, Gerben (eds.), Complementary views on complementarity, The Hague 2006, 79–104

Kress, Claus: "Der Internationale Strafgerichtshof und der Sicherheitsrat der Vereinten Nationen," in: Kempf, Eberhard/Jansen, Gabriele/Müller, Egon (eds.), Verstehen und Widerstehen, Festschrift für Christian Richter II, Baden-Baden 2006, 319–330

Kress, Claus/*Prost,* Kimberly: "Article 86," in: Triffterer, Otto (ed.), Commentary on the Rome Statute of the International Criminal Court, 2nd edition, München/Oxford/Baden-Baden 2008

– "Article 98," in: Triffterer, Otto (ed.), Commentary on the Rome Statute of the International Criminal Court, 2nd edition, München/Oxford/Baden-Baden 2008

Kress, Claus/*Sluiter,* Göran: "Section 8, Enforcement," in: Cassese, Antonio/Gaeta, Paola/Jones, John (eds.), The Rome Statute of the ICC: a commentary, Vol. II, Oxford 2002, 1751–1838

Lattanzi, Flavia: "The Rome Statute and State sovereignty. ICC competence, jurisdictional links, trigger mechanism," in: Lattanzi, Flavia/Schabas, William (eds.), Essays on the Rome Statute of the International Criminal Court, Vol. 1, Ripa Fagnano Alto 1999, 51–66

Mallinder, Louise: "Exploring the practice of States in introducing amnesties," in: Ambos, Kai/Large, Judith/Wierda, Marieke (eds.), Building a future on peace and justice. Studies on Transitional Justice, Conflict Resolution and Development, Berlin et al. 2009, 127–171

Marchesi, Antonio: "Article 14," in: Triffterer, Otto (ed.), Commentary on the Rome Statute of the International Criminal Court, 2nd edition, München/Oxford/Baden-Baden 2008

Marchesiello, Michele: "Proceedings before the Pre-Trial Chambers," in: Cassese, Antonio/Gaeta, Paola/Jones, John (eds.), The Rome Statute of the ICC: a commentary, Vol. II, Oxford 2002, 1231–1246

Massidda, Paolina/*Pellet,* Sarah: "Role and practice of the Office Counsel for Victims," in: Stahn, Carsten/Sluiter, Göran (eds.), The Emerging Practice of the International Criminal Court, Leiden/Boston 2009, 691–706

Mattioli, Géraldine/*Van Woudenberg,* Anneke: "Global catalyst for national prosecutions? The ICC in the Democratic Republic of Congo," in: Waddell, Nicholas/Clark, Phil (eds.), Courting conflict? Justice, peace and the ICC in Africa, London 2008, 55–64

McAuliffe deGuzman, Margaret: "Article 21," in: Triffterer, Otto (ed.), Commentary on the Rome Statute of the International Criminal Court, 2nd edition, München/Oxford/Baden-Baden 2008

McGoldrick, Dominic: "Political and legal responses to the ICC," in: McGoldrick, Dominic/Rowe, Peter/Donnelly, Eric (eds.), The Permanent International Criminal Court, Oxford 2004, 389–449

Meintjes, Garth: "Domestic amnesties and international accountability," in: Shelton, Dinah (ed.), International Crimes, peace, and human rights: The role of the International Criminal Court, Ardsley/New York 2000, 83–91

Michelich, John: "United States of America," in: Arbour, Louise/Eser, Albin/Ambos, Kai/Sanders, Andrew (eds.), The Prosecutor of a Permanent International Criminal Court, Freiburg 2000, 481–485

Mochochoko, Phakiso: "International cooperation and judicial assistance," in: Lee, Roy (ed.), The International Criminal Court, the making of the Rome Statute, issues, negotiations, results, The Hague 1999, 305–317

Moreno-Ocampo, Luis: "The International Criminal Court in motion," in: Stahn, Carsten/Sluiter, Göran (eds.), The Emerging Practice of the International Criminal Court, Leiden/Boston 2009, 13–19

Morré, Peter: "Germany," in: Arbour, Louise/Eser, Albin/Ambos, Kai/Sanders, Andrew (eds.), The Prosecutor of a Permanent International Criminal Court, Freiburg 2000, 341–348

Nerlich, Volker: "The status of ICTY and ICTR precedent in proceedings before the ICC," in: Stahn, Carsten/Sluiter, Göran (eds.), The Emerging Practice of the International Criminal Court, Leiden/Boston 2009, 305–325

Nsereko, Daniel Ntanda: "Article 18," in: Triffterer, Otto (ed.), Commentary on the Rome Statute of the International Criminal Court, 2nd edition, München/Oxford/Baden-Baden 2008

Obote-Odora, Alex: "Case selection and prioritization criteria at the International Criminal Tribunal for Rwanda," in: Bergsmo, Morten (ed.), Criteria for prioritizing and selecting core international crimes cases, Forum for International Criminal and Humanitarian Law (FICHL), Oslo 2009, 41–54

Ohlin, Jens David: "Peace, security, and prosecutorial discretion," in: Stahn, Carsten/Sluiter, Göran (eds.), The Emerging Practice of the International Criminal Court, Leiden/Boston 2009, 185–208

Oomen, Barbara: "Justice mechanisms and the question of legitimacy: the example of Rwanda's multi-layered justice mechanisms," in: Ambos, Kai/Large, Judith/Wierda, Marieke (eds.), Building a future on peace and justice. Studies on Transitional Justice, Conflict Resolution and Development, Berlin et al. 2009, 175–202

Orie, Alphons: "Accusatorial versus inquisitorial approach in international criminal proceedings," in: Cassese, Antonio/Gaeta, Paola/Jones, John (eds.), The Rome Statute of the ICC: a commentary, Vol. II, Oxford 2002, 1439–1495

Osiel, Mark: "When law 'expresses' more than it cares to admit: comments on Heller," in: Stahn, Carsten/van Herik, Larissa (eds.), Future directions in international criminal justice, The Hague 2010, 254–258

Otim, Michael/*Wierda,* Marieke: "Justice at Juba: international obligations and local demands in Northern Uganda," in: Waddell, Nicholas/Clark, Phil (eds.), Courting conflict? Justice, peace and the ICC in Africa, London 2008, 21–28

Palmisano, Giuseppe: "The ICC and third States," in: Lattanzi, Flavia/Schabas, William (eds.), Essays on the Rome Statute of the International Criminal Court, Vol. 1, Ripa Fagnano Alto 1999, 391–425

Pellet, Allain: "Applicable law," in: Cassese, Antonio/Gaeta, Paola/Jones, John (eds.), The Rome Statute of the ICC: a commentary, Vol. II, Oxford 2002, 1051–1084

Pfeiffer, Gerd/*Hannich,* Rolf: "Einleitung," in: Hannich, Rolf (ed.), Karlsruher Kommentar zur Strafprozessordnung, 6th edition, München 2008

Piragoff, Donald: "Article 69," in: Triffterer, Otto (ed.), Commentary on the Rome Statute of the International Criminal Court, 2nd edition, München/Oxford/Baden-Baden 2008

Rastan, Rod: "The responsibility to enforce – connecting justice with unity," in: Stahn, Carsten/Sluiter, Göran (eds.), The Emerging Practice of the International Criminal Court, Leiden/Boston 2009, 163–182

Roach, Kent: "Canada," in: Bradely, Craig (ed.) Criminal procedure: a worldwide study, 2nd edition, Durham 2007, 57–90

Robinson, Darryl: "Comments on chapter 4 of Claudia Cárdenas," in: Kleffner, Jan/Kor, Gerben (eds.), Complementary views on complementarity, The Hague 2006, 141–146

Roht-Arriaza, Naomi: "Amnesty and the International Criminal Court," in: Shelton, Dinah (ed.), International Crimes, peace, and human rights: The role of the International Criminal Court, Ardsley/New York 2000, 77–82

Roth, Robert/*Henzelin,* Marc: "The appeal procedure of the ICC," in: Cassese, Antonio/Gaeta, Paola/Jones, John (eds.), The Rome Statute of the ICC: a commentary, Vol. II, Oxford 2002, 1535–1558

Rwelamira, Medard: "Composition and administration of the Court," in: Lee, Roy (ed.), The International Criminal Court, the making of the Rome Statute, issues, negotiations, results, The Hague 1999, 153–173

Sanders, Andrew: "England and Wales (United Kingdom)," in: Arbour, Louise/Eser, Albin/Ambos, Kai/Sanders, Andrew (eds.), The Prosecutor of a Permanent International Criminal Court, Freiburg 2000, 297–306

Sarooshi, Dan: "The peace and justice paradox: The International Criminal Court and the Security Council," in: McGoldrick, Dominic/Rowe, Peter/Donnelly, Eric (eds.), The Permanent International Criminal Court, Oxford 2004, 95–120

Schabas, William: "Prosecutorial discretion and gravity," in: Stahn, Carsten/Sluiter, Göran (eds.), The Emerging Practice of the International Criminal Court, Leiden/Boston 2009, 229–246

– "Structure and administration of the Court," in: Ellis, Mark/Goldstone, Richard (eds.), The International Criminal Court: Challenges to achieving justice and accountability in the 21st century, New York 2008, 35–46

– "Complementarity in practice: creative solutions or a trap for the Court?," in: Politi, Mauro/Gioia, Federica (eds.), The International Criminal Court and national jurisdictions, Hampshire 2008, 25–48

– "Crimes against humanity: The State plan or policy element," in: Sadat, Leila/Scharf, Michael (eds.), The theory and practice of International Criminal Law, Essays in honor of M. Cherif Bassiouni, Leiden 2008, 347–364

Scharf, Michael: "Justice versus peace," in: Sewall, Sarah/Kaysen, Carl (eds.), The United States and the International Criminal Court, Oxford 2000, 179–193

Scheffer, David: "The U.S. perspective on the ICC," in: Sewall, Sarah/Kaysen, Carl (eds.), The United States and the International Criminal Court, Oxford 2000, 115–118

Sedman, Dawn: "Should the prosecution of ordinary crimes in domestic jurisdictions satisfy the complementarity principle?," in: Stahn, Carsten/van Herik, Larissa (eds.), Future directions in international criminal justice, The Hague 2010, 259–266

Seils, Paul: "The selection and prioritization of cases by the Office of the Prosecutor of the International Criminal Court," in: Bergsmo, Morten (ed.), Criteria for prioritizing and selecting core international crimes cases, Forum for International Criminal and Humanitarian Law (FICHL), Oslo 2009, 55–60

Sewall, Sarah/*Kaysen,* Carl (eds.): The United States and the International Criminal Court, Oxford 2000, 1–27

Sewall, Sarah/*Kaysen,* Carl/*Scharf,* Michael: "The United States of America and the International Criminal Court: An overview," in: Sewall, Sarah/Kaysen, Carl (eds.), The United States and the International Criminal Court, Oxford 2000, 1–27

Simpson, Graeme: "One among many: The ICC as a tool of justice during transition," in: Waddell, Nicholas/Clark, Phil (eds.), Courting conflict? Justice, peace and the ICC in Africa, London 2008, 73–80

Sluiter, Göran: "Human rights protection on the ICC pre-trial phase," in: Stahn, Carsten/Sluiter, Göran (eds.), The Emerging Practice of the International Criminal Court, Leiden/Boston 2009, 459–475

Sriram, Chandra Lekha: "Conflict mediation and the ICC: challenges and options for pursuing peace with justice at the regional level," in: Ambos, Kai/Large, Judith/Wierda, Marieke (eds.), Building a future on peace and justice. Studies on Transitional Justice, Conflict Resolution and Development, Berlin et al. 2009, 303–319

Stahn, Carsten: "Judicial review of prosecutorial discretion: five years on," in: Stahn, Carsten/Sluiter, Göran (eds.), The Emerging Practice of the International Criminal Court, Leiden/Boston 2009, 247–279

Stahn, Carsten/*Sluiter,* Göran: "From 'infancy' to emancipation? – A review of the Court's first practice," in: Stahn, Carsten/Sluiter, Göran (eds.), The Emerging Practice of the International Criminal Court, Leiden/Boston 2009, 1–7

Stegmiller, Ignaz: "The pre-investigation stage of the ICTY and ICC compared," in: Kruessmann, Thomas (ed.), ICTY: towards a fair trial?, Wien/Graz 2008, 311–339

Terrier, Frank: "Powers of the Trial Chamber," in: Cassese, Antonio/Gaeta, Paola/Jones, John (eds.), The Rome Statute of the ICC: a commentary, Vol. II, Oxford 2002, 1259–1276

– "The Procedure before the Trial Chamber," in: Cassese, Antonio/Gaeta, Paola/Jones, John (eds.), The Rome Statute of the ICC: a commentary, Vol. II, Oxford 2002, 1277–1318

Tochilovsky, Vladimir: "Legal systems and cultures in the ICC: the experience from the ICTY," in: Fischer, Horst/Kreß, Claus/Lüder, Sascha (eds.), International and national prosecution of crimes under International Law, Berlin 2001, 627–644

Tolbert, David/*Kontic,* Aleksandar: "The International Criminal Tribunal for the former Yugoslavia: transitional justice, the transfer of cases to national courts, and lessons for the ICC," in: Stahn, Carsten/Sluiter, Göran (eds.), The Emerging Practice of the International Criminal Court, Leiden/Boston 2009, 135–162

Trendafilova, Ekaterina: "Fairness and expeditiousness in the International Criminal Court's pre-trial proceedings," in: Stahn, Carsten/Sluiter, Göran (eds.), The Emerging Practice of the International Criminal Court, Leiden/Boston 2009, 441–457

Triffterer, Otto: "Can the 'elements of crimes' narrow or broaden the responsibility for criminal behaviour defined in the Rome Statute," in: Stahn, Carsten/Sluiter, Göran (eds.), The Emerging Practice of the International Criminal Court, Leiden/Boston 2009, 381–400

– "Austria," in: Arbour, Louise/Eser, Albin/Ambos, Kai/Sanders, Andrew (eds.), The Prosecutor of a Permanent International Criminal Court, Freiburg 2000, 207–225

Tsereteli, Nino: "Victim participation in ICC proceedings," in: Stahn, Carsten/van Herik, Larissa (eds.), Future directions in international criminal justice, The Hague 2010, 625–658

Turone, Giuliano: "Powers and duties of the Prosecutor," in: Cassese, Antonio/Gaeta, Paola/Jones, John (eds.), The Rome Statute of the ICC: a commentary, Vol. II, Oxford 2002, 1137–1180

Unger, Thomas/*Wierda,* Marieke: "Pursuing justice in ongoing conflict: a discussion of current practice," in: Ambos, Kai/Large, Judith/Wierda, Marieke (eds.), Building a future on peace and justice. Studies on Transitional Justice, Conflict Resolution and Development, Berlin et al. 2009, 263–302 (For an earlier version see: International Centre for Transitional Justice, "Pursuing justice in ongoing conflict: a discussion of current practice," Study Workshop 7 – The impact of the International Criminal Court, International conference building a future on peace and justice, Nuremberg, 25–27 June 2007, 1–26, available at: <www.peace-justice-conference.info/documents.asp>)

Valiñas, Marta: "Interpreting complementarity and interests of justice in the presence of restorative-based alternative forms of justice," in: Stahn, Carsten/van Herik, Larissa (eds.), Future directions in international criminal justice, The Hague 2010, 267–288

Van den Wyngaert, Christine/*Ongena,* Tom: "Ne bis in idem principle, including the issue of amnesty," in: Cassese, Antonio/Gaeta, Paola/Jones, John (eds.), The Rome Statute of the ICC: a commentary, Vol. I, Oxford 2002, 705–729

Vasiliev, Sergey: "Article 68 (3) and personal interest of victims in the emerging practice of the ICC," in: Stahn, Carsten/Sluiter, Göran (eds.), The Emerging Practice of the International Criminal Court, Leiden/Boston 2009, 635–690

Vogenauer, Stefan: "Sources of law and legal method in comparative law," in: Reiman, Mathias/Zimmermann, Reinhard (eds.), The Oxford handbook of comparative law, Oxford 2006, 870–898

Weschler, Lawrence: "Exceptional cases in Rome: The United States and the struggle for an ICC," in: Sewall, Sarah/Kaysen, Carl (eds.), The United States and the International Criminal Court, Oxford 2000, 85–111

White, Nigel/*Cryer,* Robert: "The ICC and the Security Council: an uncomfortable relationship," in: Doria, José/Gasser, Hans-Peter/Bassiouni, Cherif (eds.), The legal regime of the International Criminal Court, Essays in Honour of Professor Igor Blishchenko, Leiden/Boston 2009, 455–484

Williams, Sharon: "Article 11," in: Triffterer, Otto (ed.), Commentary on the Rome Statute of the International Criminal Court, 2nd edition, München/Oxford/Baden-Baden 2008

Williams, Sharon/*Schabas,* William: "Article 12," in: Triffterer, Otto (ed.), Commentary on the Rome Statute of the International Criminal Court, 2nd edition, München/Oxford/Baden-Baden 2008

– "Article 13," in: Triffterer, Otto (ed.), Commentary on the Rome Statute of the International Criminal Court, 2nd edition, München/Oxford/Baden-Baden 2008

– "Article 17," in: Triffterer, Otto (ed.), Commentary on the Rome Statute of the International Criminal Court, 2nd edition, München/Oxford/Baden-Baden 2008

Wilmshurst, Elizabeth: "The International Criminal Court: The role of the Security Council," in: Politi, Mauro/Nesi, Giuseppe (eds.), The Rome Statute of the International Criminal Court – A challenge to impunity, Aldershot 2001, 39–41

– "Jurisdiction of the Court," in: Lee, Roy (ed.), The International Criminal Court, the making of the Rome Statute, issues, negotiations, results, The Hague 1999, 127–141

Wouters, Jan/*Verhoeven,* Sten: "Cases identified for investigation and prosecution by the International Criminal Court," in: Ankumah, Evelyn/Kwakwa, Edward (eds.), African Perspectives on International Criminal Justice, African Legal Aid Special Series, Vol. 3, Accra/Maastricht/Pretoria 2005, 133–160

Ye, Feng: "People's Republic of China," in: Arbour, Louise/Eser, Albin/Ambos, Kai/Sanders, Andrew (eds.), The Prosecutor of a Permanent International Criminal Court, Freiburg 2000, 257–265

Yee, Lionel: "The International Criminal Court and the Security Council: articles 13 (b) and 16," in: Lee, Roy (ed.), The International Criminal Court, the making of the Rome Statute, issues, negotiations, results, The Hague 1999, 143–152

Zimmermann, Andreas: "'Acting under Chapter VII (...)' – Resolution 1422 and possible limits of the powers of the Security Council," in: Frowein, Jochen et al. (eds.) Verhandeln für den Frieden – Negotiating for peace, Liber Amicorum Tono Eitel, Berlin 2003, 253–278

– "The exercise of universal jurisdiction in criminal matters," in: Tomuschat, Christian/Thouvenin, Jean-Marc (eds.), The fundamental rules of the international legal order, Leiden/Boston 2006, 335–353

4. International documents and reports

If not otherwise indicated cited documents are searchable on the ICC's official website, <www.icc-cpi.int/Menus/ICC/Home>, mainly under the following sections:

- Office of the Prosecutor;
- Press and Media, Press Releases;
- Reports on Activities;
- Legal texts and tools;
- Assembly of States Parties.

Geneva Conventions and Additional Protocols
(all available at <www.icrc.org/ihl>)

Geneva Convention (I) for the Amelioration of the Condition of the Wounded and Sick in Armed Forces in the Field, 12.8.1949

Geneva Convention (II) for the Amelioration of the Condition of Wounded, Sick and Shipwrecked Members of Armed Forces at Sea, 12.8.1949

Geneva Convention (III) relative to the Treatment of Prisoners of War, 12.8.1949

Geneva Convention (IV) relative to the Protection of Civilian Persons in Time of War, 12.8.1949

Protocol Additional (I) to the Geneva Conventions of 12 August 1949, and relating to the Protection of Victims of International Armed Conflicts, 8.1.1977

Reports (to and from) the United Nations and other UN related documents

African Union Communiqué of the 142nd meeting of the Peace and Security Council, 21.7.2008, available at: <www.africa-union.org/root/au.organs142-communique-eng.pdf>

Convention against Torture and Other Cruel, Inhuman or Degrading Treatment or Punishment, 26.6.1987, available at: <www.ohchr.org>

Draft Articles on the Law of Treaties with commentaries, ILC 18th session, Yearbook of the ILC, Vol. II (1966)

Draft Model Status of Forces Agreement for Peacekeeping Operations, Annex Report of the Secretary General, 9.10.1990 (A/45/594), available at: <http://unbisnet.un.org>

OHCHR, Making peace our own, Victims' perceptions of accountability, reconciliation and transitional justice in Northern Uganda, 14.8.2007, 1–74, available at: <www.unhcr.org/refworld/docid/46cc4a690.html>

OHCHR, Rule-of-law tools for post-conflict States, Truth commission, April 2006, 1–36, available at: <www.ohchr.org/Documents/Publications/RuleoflawTruthCommissionsen.pdf>

Report of the International Criminal Court for 2004, GA sixtieth session, 1.8.2005 (A/60/177)

Report of the International Criminal Court to the United Nations for 2006/2007, GA sixty-second session, 31.8.2007 (A/62/314)

Report of the International Criminal Court to the United Nations for 2007/2008, GA sixty-third session, 22.8.2008 (A/63/323)

Report of the International Criminal Court to the United Nations for 2008/2009, GA sixty-fourth session, 17.9.2009 (A/64/356)

Report of the Secretary-General on the rule of law and transitional justice in conflict and post-conflict societies, 3.8.2004 (S/2004/616), available at: <www.un.org/Docs/sc/sgrep04.html>

Reports of the Secretary General on the Sudan, Security Council, 5158th meeting, 31.3.2005 (S/PV.5158), available at: <www.un.org/depts/dhl/resguide/scact.htm>

SC, 5947th meeting, 31.7.2008 (S/PV.5947), available at: <www.ppl.nl/blogs/documents/N0844474.pdf>

Statement by the President of the SC, 23.7.2002 (S/PRST/2002/21), available at: <www.un.org/Docs/sc/statements/2002/prst2002.htm>

The situation in Bosnia and Herzegovina, Security Council, 4563rd meeting, 30.6.2002 (S/PV.4563), available at: <www.un.org/depts/dhl/resguide/scact.htm>

The situation in Bosnia and Herzegovina, Security Council, 4568th meeting, 10.7.2002 (S/PV.4568), available at: <www.un.org/depts/dhl/resguide/scact.htm>

The situation in Liberia, Security Council, 4803rd meeting, 1.8.2003 (S/PV.4803), available at: <www.un.org/depts/dhl/resguide/scact.htm>

UN Secretary-General Kofi Annan, Statement at the Inaugural Meeting of the Judges of the International Criminal Court, 11.3.2003, The Hague, The Netherlands, available at: <www.iccnow.org/documents/Annan03112003.pdf>

United Nations Peacekeeping, Security Council, 4772nd meeting, 12.6.2003 (S/PV.4772), available at: <www.un.org/depts/dhl/resguide/scact.htm>

Vienna Convention of the Law of Treaties, adoption 23.5.1969/entry into force 27.1.1980, UN Treaty Series, Vol. 1155, 331, available at: <http://treaties.un.org/Pages/Home.aspx?lang=en>

Security Council Resolutions

SC-Res. 808 (1993), 22.2.1993

SC-Res. 955 (1994), 8.11.1994

SC-Res. 1421 (2002), 3.7.2002

SC-Res. 1422 (2002), 12.7.2002

SC-Res. 1423 (2002), 12.7.2002

SC-Res. 1487 (2003), 12.6.2003

SC-Res. 1497 (2003), 1.8.2003

SC-Res. 1503 (2003), 28.8.2003

SC-Res. 1543 (2004), 26.3.2004

SC-Res.1593 (2005), 31.3.2005

SC-Res. 1828 (2008), 31.7.2008

Darfur Reports

First Report of the Prosecutor of the International Criminal Court, Mr. Luis Moreno-Ocampo, to the Security Council pursuant to UNSC 1593 (2005), 29.6.2005

Second Report of the Prosecutor of the International Criminal Court, Mr. Luis Moreno-Ocampo, to the Security Council pursuant to UNSC 1593 (2005), 13.12.2005

Third Report of the Prosecutor of the International Criminal Court, to the Security Council pursuant to UNSC 1593 (2005), 14.6.2006

Fourth Report of the Prosecutor of the International Criminal Court, to the Security Council pursuant to UNSC 1593 (2005), 14.12.2006

Fifth Report of the Prosecutor of the International Criminal Court, to the Security Council pursuant to UNSC 1593 (2005), 7.6.2007

Sixth Report of the Prosecutor of the International Criminal Court, to the Security Council pursuant to UNSC 1593 (2005), 5.12.2007

Seventh Report of the Prosecutor of the International Criminal Court, to the Security Council pursuant to UNSC 1593 (2005), 5.6.2008

Eighth Report of the Prosecutor of the International Criminal Court, to the Security Council pursuant to UNSC 1593 (2005), 3.12.2008

Ninth Report of the Prosecutor of the International Criminal Court, to the Security Council pursuant to UNSC 1593 (2005), 5.6.2009

Tenth Report of the Prosecutor of the International Criminal Court, to the Security Council pursuant to UNSC 1593 (2005), 7.12.2009

Eleventh Report of the Prosecutor of the International Criminal Court, to the Security Council pursuant to UNSC 1593 (2005), 17.6.2010

Report of the International Commission of Inquiry on Darfur to the United Nations Secretary-General, Pursuant to Security Council Resolution 1564 of 18 September 2004, 25.1.2005

Other international law conventions (EU etc.)

American Convention on Human Rights, 18.7.1978, available at: <www.oas.org/juridico/english/sigs/b-32.html>

European Convention for the Protection of Human Rights and Fundamental Freedoms, 3.9.1953, CETS No. 005, available at: <http://conventions.coe.int>

IMT, IMTFE, ICTY, ICTR, SCSL and ECCC documents

IMT/IMTFE

Charter of the International Military Tribunal, 8.8.1945, available at: <http://avalon.-law.yale.edu/imt/imtconst.asp>

International Military Tribunal for the Far East, 19.1.1946, available at: <www.icwc.de/index.php?id=42>

ICTR/ICTY

Completion strategy of the International Criminal Tribunal for Rwanda, Annex to the Letter dated 30 April 2004 from the President of the ICTR addressed to the President of the Security Council, 3.5.2004 (S/2004/341), available at: <http://69.94.11.53/default.htm>

Enclosure I to the Letter dated 21 May 2004 from the President of the ICTY addressed to the President of the Security Council, 24.5.2004 (S/2004/420), available at: <www.icty.org/tabs/14/2>

Final report to the Prosecutor by the Committee established to review the NATO bombing campaign against the Federal Republic of Yugoslavia, 13.6.2000, available at: <www.icty.org/x/file/About/OTP/otp_report_nato_bombing_en.pdf>

ICTR Rules of Procedure and Evidence, 14.3.2008, available at: <http://69.94.11.53/default.htm>

ICTR Statute, adopted 8.11.1994 by SC-Res. 955/last amended 13.10.2006 by SC-Res.1717, available at: <http://69.94.11.53/default.htm>

ICTY Rules of Procedure and Evidence, 10.12.2009 (IT/32/Rev.44), available at: <www.icty.org/sections/LegalLibrary>

ICTY Statute, adopted 25.5.1993 by SC-Res. 827/last amended 29.6.2009 by SC-Res.1931, available at: <www.icty.org/sections/LegalLibrary>

ECCC

ECCC, The Court Report, January 2009, available at: <www.eccc.gov.kh/english/cabinet/fileUpload/99/2009-01-Court-Report.pdf>

Extraordinary Chambers in the Courts of Cambodia, Internal Rules (Rev.5), 9.2.2010, available at: <www.eccc.gov.kh/english/internal_rules.aspx>

Law on the Establishment of the Extraordinary Chambers in the Courts of Cambodia for the prosecution of crimes committed during the period of Democratic Kampuchea, with inclusion of amendments as promulgated on 27.10.2004, available at: <www.eccc.gov.kh/english/law.list.aspx>

Report of the group of experts for Cambodia established pursuant to GA resolution 52/135, 18.2.1999, available at: <www.unakrt-online.org/04_documents.htm>

Statement of the Co-Prosecutors, 5.1.2009, available at: <www.eccc.gov.kh/english/cabinet/press/84/Statement_OCP_05-01-09_EN.pdf>

SCSL

Letter dated 22 December 2000 from the President of the Security Council Addressed to the Secretary-General, UN Doc. S/2000/1234, available at: <www.un.org/Depts/dhl/index.html>

Report of the Secretary-General on the establishment of a Special Court for Sierra Leone, 4.10.2000 (S/2000/915), available at: <www.un.org/Docs/sc/reports/2000/sgrep00.htm>

SCSL Rules of Procedure and Evidence, 28.5.2010, available at: <www.sc-sl.org>

SCSL Statute, 16.1.2002, annexed to the Agreement between the United Nations and the Government of Sierra Leone on the Establishment of the Special Court for Sierra Leone, signed on 16.1.2002, available at: <www.sc-sl.org>

ICC drafting history documents (including ILC, Preparatory Committee, Preparatory Commission and Diplomatic Conference documents)

Bureau Discussion Paper, Part 2. Jurisdiction, Admissibility and Applicable Law, United Nations Diplomatic Conference of Plenipotentiaries on the Establishment of an International Criminal Court, 15 June–17 July 1998, 6.7.1998 (A/CONF.183/C.1/L.53)

Bureau Proposal, Part 2. Jurisdiction, Admissibility and Applicable Law, United Nations Diplomatic Conference of Plenipotentiaries on the Establishment of an International Criminal Court, 15 June–17 July 1998, 10.7.1998 (A/CONF.183/C.1/L.59)

Committee of the Whole, Summary records of the 29th meeting, United Nations Diplomatic Conference of Plenipotentiaries on the Establishment of an International Criminal Court, 15 June–17 July 1998, 20.11.1998 (A/CONF.183/C.1/SR.29)

Committee of the Whole, Summary records of the 30th meeting, United Nations Diplomatic Conference of Plenipotentiaries on the Establishment of an International Criminal Court, 15 June–17 July 1998, 20.11.1998 (A/CONF.183/C.1/SR.30)

Committee of the Whole, Summary records of the 31st meeting, United Nations Diplomatic Conference of Plenipotentiaries on the Establishment of an International Criminal Court, 15 June–17 July 1998, 20.11.1998 (A/CONF.183/C.1/SR.31)

Decision taken by the Preparatory Committee at its session held from 4 to 15 August 1997, 14.8.1997 (A/AC.249/1997/L.8/Rev.1)

Draft Statute for the International Criminal Court, United Nations Diplomatic Conference of Plenipotentiaries on the Establishment of an International Criminal Court, 15 June–17 July 1998, 16.7.1998 (A/CONF.183/C.l/L.76/Add.1-Add.14)

Draft Statute for an International Criminal Court 1994, Report of the International Law Commission on the work of its forty-sixth session, 2 May–22 July 1994, GA forty-ninth session, 1.9.1994 (A/49/10(Supp.)) 43–141

Draft Statute of the ICC, Working paper submitted by France, 6.8.1996 (A/AC.249/L.3)

Official Records, Vol. II, Summary records of the plenary meetings and of the meetings of the Committee of the Whole, United Nations Diplomatic Conference of Plenipotentiaries on the Establishment of an International Criminal Court, 15 June–17 July 1998, UN, New York 2002 (A/CONF.183/13 (Vol. II))

Official Records, Vol. III, Reports and other documents, United Nations Diplomatic Conference of Plenipotentiaries on the Establishment of an International Criminal Court, 15 June–17 July 1998, UN, New York 2002 (A/CONF.183/13 (Vol. III))

Proceedings of the Preparatory Committee during the period 25 March–12 April 1996, Draft Summary, Trigger Mechanism, 8.4.1996 (A/AC.249/CRP.5)

Proposal by France, General outline of the RPE, 1.2.1999 (PCNICC/1999/DP.2, DP.3, DP.6, DP.7 and Add.1, DP.8 and Add.1 and 2, and DP.10 and Add.1)

Proposal by Singapore on article 23, Preparatory Committee on the Establishment of the International Criminal Court, 8.8.1997 (Non-Paper/WG.3/No.16)

Proposal by the United Kingdom of Great Britain and Northern Ireland – Trigger mechanism, Preparatory Committee on the Establishment of the International Criminal Court, 25.3.1998, Working group on complementarity and trigger mechanism, 16 March–3 April 1998 (A/AC.249/1998/WG.3/DP.1)

Proposal for article 10 submitted by Spain, Committee of the Whole, United Nations Diplomatic Conference of Plenipotentiaries on the Establishment of an International Criminal Court, 15 June–17 July 1998, 25.6.1998 (A/CONF.183/C.1/L.20)

Proposal submitted by Argentina and Germany, article 46, Information submitted to the Prosecutor, 25.3.1998, Preparatory Committee on the Establishment of the International Criminal Court, 25.3.1998, Working group on procedural matters, 16 March–3 April 1998 (A/AC.249/1998/WG.4/DP.35)

Proposal submitted by Australia, Draft Rules of RPE of the ICC, 26.1.1999 (PCNICC/1999/DP.1)

Proposal submitted by Belgium, Committee of the Whole, United Nations Diplomatic Conference of Plenipotentiaries on the Establishment of an International Criminal Court, 15 June–17 July 1998, 19.6.1998 (A/CONF.183/C.1/L.7)

Proposal submitted by Canada for article 23, Preparatory Committee on the Establishment of the International Criminal Court, 18.8.1997 (Non-Paper/WG.3/No.18)

Proposal submitted by France concerning part 2 of the Rome Statute of the International Criminal Court, jurisdiction, admissibility and applicable law, 23.11.1999 (PCNICC/1999/WGRPE/DP.43)

Report of the *Ad Hoc* Committee on the Establishment of an International Criminal Court, GA fiftieth session, Supplement No. 22, 6.9.1995 (A/50/22)

Report of the Committee of the Whole, 17.7.1998 (A/CONF.183/8) in Official Records, Vol. III, Reports and other documents, United Nations Diplomatic Conference of Plenipotentiaries on the Establishment of an International Criminal Court, 15 June–17 July 1998, UN, New York 2002 (A/CONF.183/13 (Vol. III)) 93–147

Report of the ILC on its work of its forty-sixth session, 2.5.1994–22.7.1994, GA forty-ninth session, Supplement No. 10 (A/49/10)

Report of the inter-sessional meeting from 19 to 30 January 1998 in Zutphen, the Netherlands, Preparatory Committee on the Establishment of an International Criminal Court, 4.2.1998 (A/AC.249/1998/L.13)

Report of the Preparatory Commission for the International Criminal Court, Addendum Part I, Finalized Draft Text of the Rules of Procedure and Evidence, 2.11.2000 (PCNICC/2000/1/Add.1)

Report of the Preparatory Commission for the International Criminal Court, Addendum Part II, Finalized Draft Text of the Elements of Crimes, 2.11.2000 (PCNICC/2000/1/Add.2)

Report of the Preparatory Committee on the Establishment of the International Criminal Court, Vol. 1, Proceedings of the Preparatory Committee during March–April and August 1996, GA fifty-first session, Supplement No. 22, 13.9.1996 (A/51/22)

Report of the Preparatory Committee on the Establishment of the International Criminal Court, Vol. 2, Compilation of Proposals, GA fifty-first session, Supplement No. 22A, 13.9.1996 (A/51/22)

Report of the Preparatory Committee on the Establishment of an International Criminal Court, United Nations Diplomatic Conference of Plenipotentiaries on the Establishment of an International Criminal Court, 14.4.1998 (A/CONF.183/2/Add.1)

Report of the Working Group on Procedural Matters, Committee of the Whole, United Nations Diplomatic Conference of Plenipotentiaries on the Establishment of an International Criminal Court, 15 June–17 July 1998, 13.7.1998 (A/CONF.183/C.1/WGPM/L.2/Add.7)

Report of the Working Group on Procedural Matters, Committee of the Whole, United Nations Diplomatic Conference of Plenipotentiaries on the Establishment of an International Criminal Court, 15 June–17 July 1998, 23.6.1998 (A/CONF.183/C.1/WGPM/L.2)

United States Delegation, Preparatory Committee on ICC, Proposed amendments pertaining to the trigger mechanism ILC Draft Statute for International Criminal Court, 1.4.1996

United States Delegation, Preparatory Committee on ICC, "Trigger Mechanism," Second question, The role of the Security Council and of complaints by States articles 23 and 25, 1.4.1996

Working Paper on article 54, paragraphs 1 (c) and 3 (c), submitted by the informal working group composed of the delegations of Argentina, Belgium, Canada, Finland, France, Germany, Israel, Italy, Japan, Malawi, Mexico, New Zealand, Poland, Portugal, Sweden, Switzerland, The United Kingdom of Great Britain and Northern Ireland and the United States of America, Working Group on Procedural Matters, Committee of the Whole, United Nations Diplomatic Conference of Plenipotentiaries on the Establishment of an International Criminal Court, 15 June–17 July 1998, 25.6.1998 (A/CONF.183/C.1/WGPM/L.18)

Working Paper on article 54, Working Group on Procedural Matters, Committee of the Whole, United Nations Diplomatic Conference of Plenipotentiaries on the Establishment of an International Criminal Court, 15 June–17 July 1998, 18.6.1998 (A/CONF.183/C.1/WGPM/L.1)

Yearbook of the International Law Commission 1994, Volume I, Summary records of the meetings on the forty-sixth session, 2 May–22 July 1994 (A/CN.4/SER.A/1994), available at: <http://untreaty.un.org/ilc/publications/yearbooks/1994.htm>

ICC documents (including ICC press releases)

Address by the Prosecutor to the United Nations Security Council, 13.12.2005

Address to the Assembly of States Parties, Mr. Luis Moreno-Ocampo, Prosecutor of the International Criminal Court, 14.11.2008

Address to the Assembly of States Parties, Mr. Luis Moreno-Ocampo, Prosecutor of the International Criminal Court, 30.11.2007

Address to the United Nations General Assembly, Judge Philippe Kirsch, President of the International Criminal Court, 1.11.2007

Agreed Minutes of the meeting between Prosecutor Moreno-Ocampo and the delegation of the Kenyan government, The Hague, 3.7.2009

Agreement between the ICC and the European Union on Cooperation and Assistance, adoption 10.4.2006/entry into force 1.5.2006 (ICC-PRES/01-01-06)

Agreement between the ICC and the Federal Government of Austria on the enforcement of sentences of the International Criminal Court, adoption 27.10.2005/entry into force 26.11.2005 (ICC-PRES/01-01-05)

Agreement between the ICC and the International Committee of the Red Cross on Visits to Persons deprived of Liberty Pursuant to the Jurisdiction of the ICC, adoption 29.3.2006/entry into force 13.4.2006 (ICC-PRES/02-01-06)

Agreement of Privileges and Immunity, adoption 9.9.2002/entry into force 22.7.2004 (ICC-ASP/1/3)

Annex to the "Paper on some policy issues before the Office of the Prosecutor:" referrals and communications, September 2003 (ICC-OTP 2003)

Annex to the Three Year Report and the Report on the prosecutorial strategy, 20.9.2006

Background note on the opening by the Prosecutor of an investigation in CAR, 22.5.2007 (ICC-OTP-BN-20070522-220-A)

Building a Future on Peace and Justice, Address by Mr. Luis Moreno-Ocampo, Prosecutor of the ICC, Nuremberg, 24.–25.6.2007

Code of Judicial Ethics, adoption/entry into force 9.3.2005 (ICC-BD/02-01-05)

Code of Professional Conduct for Counsel, Adoption 2.12.2005/entry into force 1.1.2006 (ICC-ASP/4/3/Res.1)

Communications received by the Prosecutor since 2002, 24.7.2003 (ICC-OTP-20030724-28)

Criteria for selection of situations and cases, Draft for discussion, 2006 (ICC-OTP) *(copy on file with the author)*

Discussion paper on the crime of aggression proposed by the Chairman (revision June 2008), ASP resumed sixth session, 2.–6.6.2008, 14.5.2008 (ICC-ASP/6/SWGCA/2)

Draft Regulations of the OTP, 3.6.2003 (ICC-OTP 2003)

Elements of Crimes, 9.9.2002 (ICC-ASP/1/3)

Financial Regulations and Rules, adoption/entry into force 9.9.2002 (ICC-ASP/1/3)

Hall, Christopher Keith, "Suggestions concerning International Criminal Court prosecutorial policy and strategy and external relations," Contribution to an expert consultation process on general issues relevant to the ICC Office of the Prosecutor, 28.3.2003

Headquarter Agreement between the International Criminal Court and the Host State, adoption 7.6.2007/entry into force 1.3.2008 (ICC-BD/04-01-08)

ICC Outreach Report 2008, 20.11.2008

ICC Outreach Report 2009, 18.11.2009

Informal expert paper: Fact-finding and investigative functions of the Office of the Prosecutor, including international co-operation, ICC-OTP 2003

Informal expert paper: Measures available to the International Criminal Court to reduce the length of proceedings, ICC-OTP 2003

Informal expert paper: The principle of complementarity in practice, ICC-OTP 2003

Iraq response, Annex to the update on communications received by the office of the prosecutor of the ICC, 10.2.2006

Memorandum of Law, Interpretation and scope of "interests of justice" in article 53 of the Rome Statute, 7.5.2004 (MoL 19-040507-1) *(copy on file with the author)*

Memorandum of Understanding between the International Criminal Court and the Asian-African Legal Consultative Organization, adoption 5.2.2008/entry into force 5.2.2008 (ICC-PRES/05-01-08)

Memorandum of Understanding regarding Administrative Arrangements between the ICC and the Special Court for Sierra Leone, adoption/entry into force 13.4.2006 (ICC-PRES/03-01-06)

Negotiated Relationship Agreement between the ICC and the UN, adoption/entry into force 4.10.2004 (ICC-ASP/3/Res.1)

OTP, Kenyan authorities committed to cooperate as ICC Prosecutor informs them that in December he will request ICC Judges to open an investigation into post-election violence, 6.11.2009

OTP-Press Release (CAR), Confirmation of charges hearing in the case of the Prosecutor v. Jean-Pierre Bemba Gombo – Opening remarks by Fatou Bensouda, Deputy Prosecutor of the ICC, 12.1.2009

OTP-Press Release (CAR), Prosecutor opens investigation in the Central African Republic, 22.5.2007 (ICC-OTP-PR-20070522-220)

OTP-Press Release (CAR), Prosecutor receives referral concerning Central African Republic, 7.1.2005 (ICC-OTP-20050107-86)

OTP-Press-Release (Darfur), Abu Garda arrived at the premises of the Court, 17.5.2009 (ICC-CPI-20090517-PR413)

OTP-Press-Release (Darfur), "Attacks on peacekeepers will not be tolerated," ICC Prosecutor presents evidence in third case in Darfur, 20.11.2008 (ICC-OTP-20081120-PR373)

OTP-Press-Release (Darfur), ICC Prosecutor presents case against Sudanese President, Hassan Ahmad Al Bashir, for genocide, crimes against humanity and war crimes in Darfur, 14.7.2008 (ICC-OTP-20080714-PR341)

OTP-Press-Release (Darfur), List of Names of Suspects in Darfur opened by the ICC OTP, 14.4.2005 (ICC-OTP-20050411-98)

OTP-Press-Release (Darfur), Prosecutor receives list prepared by Commission of Inquiry on Darfur, 5.4.2005 (ICC-OTP-20050405-97)

OTP-Press-Release (Darfur), Prosecutor: "The attack on African Union peacekeepers in Haskanita was an attack on millions of civilians they had come to protect; we will prosecute those allegedly responsible," 17.5.2009 (ICC-OTP-20090517-PR412)

OTP-Press-Release (Darfur), Security Council refers situation in Darfur to ICC Prosecutor, 1.4.2005 (ICC-OTP-20050401-96)

OTP-Press-Release (Darfur), The Prosecutor of the ICC opens investigation in Darfur, 6.6.2005 (ICC-OTP-0606-104)

OTP-Press Release (DRC), DRC: ICC Warrant of Arrest unsealed against Bosco Ntaganda, 29.4.2008 (ICC-OTP-20080429-PR311)

OTP-Press Release (DRC), ICC Prosecutor recalls ICC has jurisdiction over crimes against the civilian population in the Kivus, 4.11.2008 (ICC-OTP-20081104-PR369)

OTP-Press Release (DRC), Press Conference of the Prosecutor – Communications, 24.7.2003 (ICC-OTP-20030724-28)

OTP-Press Release (DRC), Prosecutor receives referral of the situation in the Democratic Republic of Congo, 19.4.2004 (ICC-OTP-20040419-50)

OTP-Press Release (DRC), The Office of the Prosecutor of the International Criminal Court opens its first investigation, 23.6.2004 (ICC-OTP-20040623-59)

OTP-Press Release (Georgia), ICC Prosecutor confirms situation in Georgia under analysis, 20.8.2008 (ICC-OTP-20080820-PR346)

OTP-Press Release (Guinea), ICC Prosecutor confirms situation in Guinea under analysis, 14.10.2009 (ICC-OTP-20091014-PR464)

OTP-Press Release (Kenya), Prosecutor reaffirms that the situation in Kenya is monitored, 11.2.2009

OTP-Press Release (Kenya), Prosecutor's statement at the press conference in Kenya, 26.11.2009, Nairobi and The Hague

OTP-Press Release (Uganda), Press conference on the Uganda arrest warrants, Statement by Prosecutor Luis Moreno-Ocampo, 14.10.2005 (ICC-OTP-20051014-109)

OTP-Press Release (Uganda), Prosecutor calls for renewed efforts to arrest LRA leader Kony in wake of new attacks, 6.10.2008 (ICC-OTP-20081006-PR359)

OTP-Press Release (Uganda), Prosecutor of the International Criminal Court opens an investigation into Northern Uganda, 29.7.2004 (ICC-OTP-20040729-65)

OTP-Press Release (Uganda), Statements by ICC Chief Prosecutor and the visiting Delegation of Acholi leaders from Northern Uganda, 18.3.2005 (ICC-OTP-20050318-95)

OTP-Press Release (Uganda), Statement by Prosecutor Luis Moreno-Ocampo, 6.7.2006 (ICC-OTP-20060706-146)

OTP-Press Release (Uganda), Statement by the Chief Prosecutor Luis Moreno-Ocampo, 12.7.2006 (ICC-OTP-20060712-149)

OTP public notice: victims of post-election violence in Kenya have 30 days to make representations to ICC in the Hague, 23.11.2009

OTP Report on prosecutorial strategy, 14.9.2006

OTP Report on the activities performed during the first three years (June 2003–June 2006), 12.9.2006

OTP-Statement (Uganda), OTP statement in relation to events in Uganda, 4.3.2008

OTP statement in relation to events in Kenya, 5.2.2008

OTP weekly briefing, 4.–9. August 2010, Issue # 49, 11.8.2010

OTP weekly briefing, 15.–21. December 2009, Issue # 18, 21.12.2009

OTP weekly briefing, 8.–14. December 2009, Issue # 17, 16.12.2009

OTP weekly briefing, 24.–30. November 2009, Issue # 15, 2.12.2009

OTP weekly briefing, 17.–23. November 2009, Issue # 14, 25.11.2009

OTP weekly briefing, 10.–16. November 2009, Issue # 13, 18.11.2009

OTP weekly briefing, 15.–22. September 2009, 23.09.2009

Paper on some policy issues before the Office of the Prosecutor, September 2003 (ICC-OTP 2003)

Policy paper on the interests of justice, September 2007 (ICC-OTP-2007)

Policy paper on victim participation under article 68 (3) of the ICC Statute, OTP Draft December 2009, 7.12.2009

Press Release (CAR), Commencement of the trial of Jean-Pierre Bemba postponed until 5 July 2010, 8.3.2010 (ICC-CPI- 20100308-PR503)

Press Release (CAR), Jean-Pierre Bemba Gombo arrested for crimes allegedly committed in the Central African Republic, 24.5.2008 (ICC-CPI-20080524-PR315)

Press Release (CAR), Surrender of Jean-Pierre Bemba to the International Criminal Court, 3.7.2008 (ICC-CPI-20080703-PR335)

Press Release (CAR), The commencement of the trial in the case The Prosecutor v. Jean-Pierre Bemba Gombo is postponed, 7.7.2010 (ICC-CPI-20100707-PR 554)

Press Release (CAR), The confirmation of charges hearing in the case of The Prosecutor v. Jean-Pierre Bemba Gombo is postponed, 2.12.2008 (ICC-CPI-20081202-PR378)

Press Release (Côte d'Ivoire), Registrar confirms that the Republic of Côte d'Ivoire has accepted the jurisdiction of the Court, 15.2.2005 (ICC-20050215-91)

Press Release (Darfur), New suspects in the situation in Darfur, Sudan arrive voluntarily at the ICC: First appearance scheduled for tomorrow, 16.6.2010 (ICC-CPI-20100616-PR 547)

Press Release (Darfur), Confirmation of charges hearing in the case of The Prosecutor v. Bahr Idriss Abu Garda scheduled to start on Monday, 12 October 2009, 19.5.2009 (ICC-CPI-20090519-PR414)

Press Release (Darfur), ICC issues a warrant of arrest for Omar Al Bashir, President of Sudan, 4.3.2009 (ICC-CPI-20090304-PR394)

Press Release (DRC), Callixte Mbarushimana arrested in France for crimes against humanity and war crimes allegedly committed in the Kivus (Democratic Republic of Congo), 11.10.2010 (ICC-CPI-20101011-PR581)

Press Release (DRC), Decision on the confirmation of charges in the case of The Prosecutor v. Germain Katanga and Mathieu Ngudjolo Chui, 26.9.2008 (ICC-CPI-20080926-PR357)

Press Release (DRC), First appearance of Mathieu Ngudjolo Chui before Pre-Trial Chamber I, 11.2.2008 (ICC-CPI-20080211-PR286)

Press Release (DRC), First appearance of Mr. Germain Katanga before the Pre-Trial Chamber I, 22.10.2007 (ICC-20071022-260)

Press Release (DRC), Opening of the confirmation hearing against Germain Katanga and Mathieu Ngudjolo Chui, 27.6.2008 (ICC-CPI-20080627-PR333)

Press Release (DRC), Second arrest: Germain Katanga transferred into the custody of the ICC, 18.10.2007 (ICC-20071018-250)

Press Release (DRC), Third detainee for the International Criminal Court: Mathieu Ngudjolo Chui, 7.2.2008 (ICC-CPI-20080207-PR284)

Press Release (DRC), Trial of Germain Katanga and Mathieu Ngudjolo Chui to commence Thursday, 24 September 2009, 27.3.2009 (ICC-CPI-20090327-PR402)

Press Release (DRC), Warrant of arrest against Bosco Ntaganda unsealed, 29.4.2008 (ICC-CPI-20080429-PR310)

Press Release (Kenya), The situation of the Republic of Kenya assigned to Pre-Trial Chamber II, 6.11.2009 (ICC-CPI-20091106-PR473)

Press Release (Uganda), President of Uganda refers situation concerning the Lord's Resistance Army (LRA) to the ICC, 29.1.2004 (ICC-20040129–44)

Proposed Programme Budget for 2006 of the International Criminal Court, ASP fourth session, 24.8.2005 (ICC-ASP/4/5)

Proposed Programme Budget for 2008 of the International Criminal Court, ASP sixth session, 25.7.2008 (ICC-ASP/6/8)

Proposed Programme Budget for 2009 of the International Criminal Court, ASP seventh session, 29.7.2008 (ICC-ASP/7/9)

Proposed Programme Budget for 2011 of the International Criminal Court, ASP ninth session, 2.8.2010 (ICC-ASP/9/10 (MPII))

Prosecutor's speech to the Eighth Session of the Assembly of States Parties, 18.11.2009

Prosecutor's statement at the ISS Symposium on "The ICC that Africa wants," 14.12.2009, Cape Winlands 9.11.2009

Prosecutor's statement on the Prosecutor's application for a warrant of arrest under article 58 against Omar Hassan Ahmad Al Bashir, 14.7.2008

Prosecutorial Strategy 2009-2012, OTP, The Hague, 1.2.2010

Refugee Law Project's position paper on the announcement of formal investigations of the LRA by the Chief Prosecutor of the ICC and its implications on the search for peaceful solutions to the war in Northern Uganda, 28.7.2004

Regulations of the Court, 26.5.2004 (ICC-BD/01-01-04)

Regulations of the OTP, 23.4.2009 (ICC-BD/05-01-09)

Regulations of the Registry, 3.3.2006 (ICC-BD/03-01-06), amended 25.9.2006 (ICC-BD/03-01-06-Rev1)

Regulations of the Trust Fund for Victims, adoption/entry into force 3.12.2005 (ICC-ASP/4/3/Res.3)

Remarks by ICC Prosecutor Luis Moreno-Ocampo at the 27th meeting of the Committee of Legal Advisers on Public International Law – CADHI (Strasbourg, France), 18.3.2004, available at: <www.iccnow.org/documents/ICCProsecutor-CADHI18Mar04.pdf>

Remarks by Luis Moreno-Ocampo, Prosecutor of the ICC, Conference on "Justice in post armed conflicts and the ICC: Reduction of impunity and a support to international justice," 15.1.2009

Report on the activities of the Court, ASP sixth session, 18.10.2007 (ICC-ASP/6/18)

Report on the activities of the Court, ASP fifth session, 17.10.2006 (ICC-ASP/5/15)

Report on the activities of the Court, ASP fourth session, 16.9.2005 (ICC-ASP/4/16)

Report of the Bureau on geographical representation and gender balance in the recruitment of staff of the International Criminal Court, ASP sixth session, 24.10.2007 (ICC-ASP/6/22)

Report of the Committee on Budget and Finance on the work of its eighth session, ASP sixth session, 29.5.2007 (ICC-ASP/6/2)

Report of the First Session (Official Records of the Assembly of States Parties to the Rome Statute of the International Criminal Court), ASP first session, 3.–10.9.2002 (ICC-ASP/1/3), available at: <http://treaties.un.org/Pages/Home.aspx?lang=en>

Resolution ICC-ASP/3/Res.4, Programme budget for 2005, Contingency Fund, Working Capital Fund for 2005, scale of assessments for the apportionment of expenses of the International Criminal Court and financing of appropriations for the year 2005, 10.9.2004 (ICC-ASP/3/25)

Resolution RC/Res.6, The Crime of Aggression, ASP Review Conference 13th plenary metting, 11.6.2010

Rome Statute of the International Criminal Court, adoption 17.7.1998/entry into force 1.7.2000 (A/CONF.183/9)

Rules of Procedure of Evidence, 9.9.2002 (ICC-ASP/1/3)

Rules of Procedure of the Assembly of States Parties, ASP first session, 3.–10.9.2002 (ICC-ASP/1/3)

Security arrangements between the EU Council General Secretariat Security Office (GSCSO) and The European Commission Security Directorate (ECSD) and the International Criminal Court Security and Safety Section (ICC-SSS) for the protection of classified information exchanged between the EU and the ICC, entry into force 1.3.2008 (ICC/GSCSO/ECSD)

Staff Regulations, adoption/entry into force 12.9.2003 (ICC-ASP/2/Res.2)

Staff Rules of the ICC (Annex to ICC/AI/2005/03), adoption 3.12.2005/entry into force 21.4.2005 (ICC-ASP/4/3)

Statement by Fatou Bensouda, Deputy Prosecutor of the International Criminal Court, Report on the conference held in Turin from 14.–18.5.2007, ASP sixth session, 30.11.–14.12.2007 (ICC-ASP/6/INF.2)

Statement by Luis Moreno-Ocampo: Commemoration of the 10th anniversary of the adoption of the Rome Statute of the International Criminal Court, 17.7.2008

Statement by Luis Moreno-Ocampo: Fifth session of the Assembly of States Parties, 24.11.2006

Statement by Luis Moreno-Ocampo: Informal meeting of Legal Advisors of Ministries of Foreign Affairs, 24.10.2005

Statement by the Prosecutor of the International Criminal Court, Mr. Luis Moreno-Ocampo, made at the first meeting of the Assembly of its second session, 8.9.2003

Statement of the Prosecutor, ICC Prosecutor: Harun is a fugitive, 25.4.2008

Statement of the Prosecutor of the International Criminal Court, Mr. Luis Moreno-Ocampo to the Security Council on 29 June 2005 pursuant to UNSCR 1593 (2005), 29.6.2005

Summary of the case: Prosecutor's application for warrant of arrest under article 58 against Omar Hassan Ahmad Al Bashir, 14.7.2008

Turin report, ASP sixth session, 19.10.2007 (ICC-ASP/6/INF.2)

Update on communications received by the office of the prosecutor of the ICC, 10.2.2006

Venezuela response, Annex to the update on communications received by the office of the prosecutor of the ICC, 10.2.2006

Visit of the Minister of Justice of the Palestinian National Authority, 22.1.2009

Visit of the Palestinian National Authority Minister of Foreign Affairs and Minister of Justice, 13.2.2009

Transcripts of the Public hearing of the Office of the Prosecutor

All available at: <www2.icc-cpi.int/Menus/ICC/Structure+of+the+Court/Office+of+the+Prosecutor/Network+with+Partners/Public+Hearings/>

First public hearing

Broomhall, Bruce: Open Society Justice Initiative, Session 2: Transcript, 17.6.2003

Brunborg, Helge: Demographer, Session 3: Needs for demographic and statistical expertise at the International Criminal Court (paper), 25.4.2003

Dicker, Richard: Human Rights Watch, Session 1: Transcript, 17.6.2003

Friman, Håkan: Session 3: Transcript, 17.6.2003

Guariglia, Fabricio: Session 3: Transcript, 17.6.2003

Hamilton, James: Session 3: General input on ICC-OTP questions (paper), 19.3.2003

Leanza, Umberto: Professor of International Law at the Rome University, Session 1: Transcript, 17.6.2003

Othman, Mohamed: Former Chief of Prosecutions of the ICTR and the UN administration in East Timor, Session 1: Briefing Note (paper), 3.2.2003

Schense, Jennifer: Session 5: Transcript, 17.6.2003

Schrag, Minna: Session 4: Lessons learned form ICTY experience: Notes for the ICC Prosecutor (paper), 20.3.2003

Tochilovsky, Vladimir: Session 3: Transcript, 17.6.2003

Triffterer, Otto: Session 2: Transcript, 17.6.2003

Vámos-Goldman, András: Institute of Global Issues at the University of British Columbia, Session 5: Transcript, 17.6.2003

Wierda, Marieke: International Centre for Transitional Justice, Session 1: Transcript, 17.6.2003

Wilmshurst, Elizabeth: Session 5: Transcript, 17.6.2003

Yanez-Barnuevo, Juan: Session 3: Transcript, 17.6.2003

Second public hearing

Bernard, Antoine: International Federation for Human Rights (FIDH), Session 2: NGOs and other experts, 26.9.2006

De Smedt, Michel: Session 1: Interested States, 25.9.2006 – Outlining the Prosecutorial Strategy

Dicker, Richard: Human Rights Watch, Session 4: NGOs and other experts, 18.10.2006

Evans, Gareth: International Crisis Group, Session 1: Interested States, 25.9.2006

Getz, Mariana: Redress, Session 2: NGOs and other experts, 26.9.2006

Goldstone, Richard: Session 4: NGOs and other experts, 18.10.2006

Grono, Nick: International Crisis Group, Session 2: NGOs and other experts, 26.9.2006

Keith Hall, Christopher: Amnesty International, Session 2: NGOs and other experts, 26.9.2006

Maqungo, Sivu: South Africa, Session 3: Interested States, 17.10.2006

Mattioli, Géraldine: Human Rights Watch, Session 2: NGOs and other experts, 26.9.2006

Méndez, Juan E.: President of the International Center for Transitional Justice, Session 4: NGOs and other experts, 18.10.2006

Mota Sardenberg, Ronaldo, H. E. of Brazil: Session 3: Interested States, 17.10.2006

Smith, Alison: No Peace Without Justice, Session 2: NGOs and other experts, 26.9.2006

Sulzer, Jeanne: Coordination of the FIDH Legal Action Group, Session 4: NGOs and other experts, 18.10.2006

Swaak-Goldman, Olivia: Session 1: Interested States, 25.9.2006 – Outlining the Three-Year Report

Wellenstein, Edmond H. Dr., Director-General: Task Force ICC, Session 1: Interested States, 25.9.2006

Internet resources

Press

"BBC News: Q&A International Criminal Court," 20.3.2006, available at: <http://news.bbc.co.uk/2/hi/americas/3834237.stm>

"Bellinger says International Court flawed but deserving of help in some cases," 10.7.2007, Interview with John Bellinger, Legal Adviser to the Secretary of State, Council of Foreign Relations, available at: <www.cfr.org/publication/by_type/interview.html>

"Central African Republic: ICC Opens Investigation," 22.5.2007, Human Rights News, available at: <http://hrw.org/doc/?t=africa&c=carepu>

"Comment: Bemba is ICC's biggest fish," 18.6.2008, Eugène Bakama Bope, ICC – Africa Update 175, Institute for war & peace reporting, available at: <www.iwpr.net/?p=acr&s=p&o=-&apc_state=henpacr200804>

"Five minutes with Luis Moreno-Ocampo: An interview with the ICC Prosecutor," Adele Waugaman, International Affairs Review, Vol. XV, Spring/Summer 2006, available at: <www.iar-gwu.org/>

"ICC May Drop LRA Charges," 15.11.2004, New Vision, available at: <http://allafrica.com>

"ICC prosecutor to inform UNSC of Sudan's non-cooperation," 9.10.2007, Sudan Tribune, available at: <www.iccnow.org/?mod=newsdetail&news=2186>

"ICC takes decisive step for justice in Uganda," 14.10.2005, Human Rights Watch, available at: <www.hrw.org/node/70189>

"ICC writes to Uganda over Kony," 17.3.2008, Milton Olupot, New Vision, available at: <www.newvision.co.ug/D/8/13/617185>

"Instant view – Reaction to warrant for Bashir's arrest," 4.3.2009, Reuters, available at: <www.alertnet.org/thenews/newsdesk/L4607332.htm>

"Interview with Daniel Nsereko," 16.10.2007, Phone Interview, 10:30–11 AM NY time, CICC, available at: <www.iccnow.org/documents/Daniel_Nsereko-_Judicial_Candidate_Interview_Notes.pdf>

"Kenya: Spokesman – ICC analyses country's situation," 22.4.2008, Hirondelle News Agency (Lausanne), available at: <http://allafrica.com/stories/200804230021.html>

"LRA prepares for war, not peace," 24.4.2008, Katy Glassborow/Peter Eichstaedt/Emma Mutaizibwa, ICC – Africa Update 168, Institute for war & peace reporting, available at: <www.iwpr.net/?p=acr&s=p&o=-&apc_state=henpacr>

"LRA's murky negotiators," 17.4.2008, Emma Mutaizibwa, ICC – Africa Update 167, Institute for war & peace reporting, available at: <www.iwpr.net/?p=acr&s=p&o=-&apc_state=henpacr>

"Murder in the name of war – My Lai," 20.7.1998, BBC News, available at: <http://news.bbc.co.uk/2/hi/special_report/1998/03/98/mylai/64344.stm>

"Northerners weigh up Odhiambo killing," 15.4.2008, Joe Wacha, ICC – Africa Update 167, Institute for war & peace reporting, available at: <www.iwpr.net/?p=acr&s=p&o=-&apc_state=henpacr>

"Press Statement Richard Boucher, Spokesman," 6.5.2002, Washington DC, International Criminal Court: Letter to UN Secretary General Kofi Annan from Under Secretary of State for Arms Control and International Security John R. Bolton, available at: <http://archives.cnn.com/2002/US/05/06/court.letter.text/index.html>

"Prosecutor calls on citizens to push for arrest of Darfur war crimes suspect," 13.10.2007, The Canadian Press, available at: <www.iccnow.org/?mod=newsdetail&news=2186>

"Tribunal bill debate halted over quorum," 18.11.2009, Daily Nation, available at <www.nation.co.ke/News/-/1056/687796/-/uopcqm/-/index.html>

"Uganda: First ever arrest warrants by International Criminal Court – a first step towards addressing impunity," 14.10.2005, Amnesty International (AFR 59/008/2005), available at: <www.amnesty.org/en/library/info/AFR59/008/2005/en>

"Uganda: ICC Prosecutor Louis Ocampo in his office at the Hague," 13.7.2007, Felix Osike, New Vision, available at: <http://allafrica.com/stories/200707160105.html>

"Uganda Insists Peace Not at Odds With ICC," 14.4.2008, Katy Glassborow, ICC – Africa Update 167, Institute for war & peace reporting, available at: <www.iwpr.net/?p=acr&s=p&o=-&apc_state=henpacr>

"Ugandan Rebels to appeal ICC warrants," 12.3.2008, Katy Glassborow/Peter Eichstaedt, ICC – Africa Update 160, Institute for war & peace reporting, available at: <www.iwpr.net/?p=acr&s=p&o=-&apc_state=henpacr>

"Uganda: West angered by Museveni's call for ICC to pardon Kony group," 17.3.2008, Paul Redfern, The East African, available at: <http://allafrica.com/stories/200803171480.html>

"Warrant issued for Sudan's leader," 4.3.2009, BBC News, available at: <http://news.bbc.co.uk/2/hi/africa/7923102.stm>

"Why the International Criminal Court must withdraw indictments against the top LRA leaders: a legal perspective," 20.8.2006, Zachary Lomo, The Sunday Monitor, available at: <www.refugeelawproject.org/press_releases.php>

Other documents
(e.g. by International Organisations, Conferences, etc.)

AMICC/John Washburn and Wasana Punyasena, "Interests of justice proposal," 1.5.2005, 1–2, available at.: <www.iccnow.org/?mod=interestofjustice&idudctp=21&show=all#21>

Amnesty International, "International Criminal Court: The unlawful attempt by the Security Council to give US citizens permanent impunity from international justice," 1.5.2003, 1–77, available at: <www.amnesty.org/en/library/info/IOR40/006/2003>

Amnesty International, "Open letter to the Chief Prosecutor of the International Criminal Court: Comments on the concept of the interests of justice," 17.6.2005, 1–14, available at: <www.amnesty.org/en/library/info/IOR40/023/2005>

ASPD, "Commentaires sur l'intérêt de la justice," 1.5.2005, 1–2, available at.: <www.iccnow.org/?mod=interestofjustice&idudctp=21&show=all#21>

Bureau of Justice Statistics, US Department of Justice, State University of New York at Albany, World factbook of criminal justice systems, Canada, Cohen, Debra/Longtin, Sandra, available at: <www.ojp.usdoj.gov/bjs/pub/ascii/wfbcjcan.txt>

Bureau of Justice Statistics, US Department of Justice, State University of New York at Albany, World factbook of criminal justice systems, China, Guo, Jianan/Xiang, Guo/Zongxian, Wu/et al., available at: <http://bjs.ojp.usdoj.gov/content/pub/ascii/wfbcjchi.txt>

Bureau of Justice Statistics, US Department of Justice, State University of New York at Albany, World factbook of criminal justice systems, England & Wales, Phillips, Corretta/Cox, Gemma/Pease, Ken, available at: <http://bjs.ojp.usdoj.gov/content/pub/ascii/wfbcjeng.txt>

Bureau of Justice Statistics, US Department of Justice, State University of New York at Albany, World factbook of criminal justice systems, France, Borricand, Jacques, available at: <http://bjs.ojp.usdoj.gov/content/pub/ascii/wfbcjfra.txt>

Bureau of Justice Statistics, US Department of Justice, State University of New York at Albany, World factbook of criminal justice systems, Germany, Aronowitz, Alexis, available at: <http://bjs.ojp.usdoj.gov/content/pub/ascii/wfbcjger.txt>

Bureau of Justice Statistics, US Department of Justice, State University of New York at Albany, World factbook of criminal justice systems, India, Rakhavan, R. K., available at: <http://bjs.ojp.usdoj.gov/content/pub/ascii/wfbcjind.txt>

Bureau of Justice Statistics, US Department of Justice, State University of New York at Albany, World factbook of criminal justice systems, Kenya, Ebbe, Obi, available at: <http://bjs.ojp.usdoj.gov/content/pub/ascii/wfbcjken.txt>

Bureau of Justice Statistics, US Department of Justice, State University of New York at Albany, World factbook of criminal justice systems, Norway, Bygrave, Lee, available at: <http://bjs.ojp.usdoj.gov/content/pub/ascii/wfbcjnor.txt>

Bureau of Justice Statistics, US Department of Justice, State University of New York at Albany, World factbook of criminal justice systems, The Netherlands, Aronowitz, Alex, available at: <http://bjs.ojp.usdoj.gov/content/pub/ascii/wfbcjnet.txt>

Candidate Questionnaire Response, Citizens of Global Solutions, 2004, available at: <http://globalsolutions.org/politics/elections_and_candidates/questionnaire>

CICC, "Article 16 debated in Africa," Lamony, Stephen, The Monitor, Journal of the CICC, Issue No. 37, Nov. 2008 – April 2009, 14, available at: <www.iccnow.org/?mod=monitor>

CICC, "ASP Highlights," The Monitor, Journal of the CICC, Issue No. 38, May – October 2009, 4, available at: <www.iccnow.org/?mod=monitor>

CICC, "Comments by US Officials on Situations before the ICC and Cooperation with ICC Investigations," 1.12.2006, available at: <www.iccnow.org/?mod=usaicc>

CICC, Factsheet, "Questions and answers, Issuance of a warrant of arrest or a summons by the ICC," 27.2.2007, 1–3, available at: <www.iccnow.org/documents/CICC-FS_QA_ArrestWarrants_27feb07.pdf>

CICC, Factsheet, "Status of U.S. Bilateral Immunity Agreements by region," 14.12.2006, available at: <www.iccnow.org/?mod=bia>

CICC, Government responses to US – proposed Security Council Resolution on ICC and peacekeeping, Special Plenary Session, Preparatory Commission for the ICC, 3.7.2002, 1–5, available at: <www.iccnow.org/documents/countrychart 20020703.pdf>

CICC, "History and analysis of UN Security Council Resolutions 1422/1487," August 2004, available at: <www.iccnow.org/?mod=tools>

CICC, "Obama administration on the record: show of support for Darfur investigation significant, but full engagement still lacking," The Monitor, Journal of the CICC, Issue No. 38, May – October 2009, 20, available at: <www.iccnow.org/?mod=monitor>

CICC, "Prosecutor request opening of ICC investigation in Kenya," 26.11.2009, Media advisory, available at <www.iccnow.org/documents/KenyaOTP26Nov09_en.pdf>

CICC, "Situations," The Monitor, Journal of the CICC, Issue No. 37, Nov. 2008 – April 2009, 8–9, available at: <www.iccnow.org/?mod=monitor>

CICC, "The numbers, NGO coalition special report on country positions," The Monitor, Journal of the CICC, Issue No. 36, May–October 2008, 11, available at: <www.iccnow.org/?mod=monitor>

CODEPU and IMS, "El interés de la justicia como causal para no iniciar una investigación o enjuciamiento en el estatuto de rome de la corte penal internacional," 1.5.2005, 1–7, available at.: <www.iccnow.org/?mod=interestofjustice&idudctp=21&show=all#21>

DECIDI, "Consultation sur les intérêts de la justice," 1.5.2005, 1–5, available at.: <www.iccnow.org/?mod=interestofjustice&idudctp=21&show=all#21>

FIDH, "Comments on the Office of the Prosecutor's draft policy paper on 'Criteria for selection of situations and cases'," 15.9.2006, 1–4, available at: <www.fidh.org/spip.php?article3988>

FIDH, "Comments on the Office of the Prosecutor's draft policy paper on 'The interests of Justice'," 15.9.2006, 1-6, available at: <www.fidh.org/spip.php?article 3987>

FIDH, "FIDH statement on the prosecutorial strategy of the OTP of the ICC," Ms. Jeanne Sulzer, 18.10.2006, available at: <www.fidh.org/IMG/pdf/FIDH_Strategy_OTP_NY.pdf>

FIDH, "Réflexions sur la notion 'intérêts de la justice', au terme de l'article 53 du Statut de Rome," 1.6.2005, 1–8, available at.: <www.iccnow.org/?mod=interesto fjustice&idudctp=21&show=all#21>

FIDH, “Victims’ rights before the ICC,” 23.4.2007, available at: <www.fidh.org/spip.php?article4208>

Freiburg Declaration on the position of the prosecutor of a Permanent International Criminal Court, European Journal of Crime, Criminal Law and Criminal Justice, Vol. 6 (1998) 301–303

Human Rights Watch, “A summary of the case law of the International Criminal Court,” March 2007, 1–11, available at: <www.hrw.org/legacy/backgrounder/ij/icc0307/icc0307web.pdf >

Human Rights Watch, “Benchmarks for assessing possible national alternatives to International Criminal Court cases against LRA leaders,” May 2007, 1–10, available at: <www.iccnow.org/documents/icc0507web[1].pdf>

Human Rights Watch, “Courting history. The landmark International Criminal Court’s first years,” July 2008, 1–244, available at: <http://hrw.org/reports/2008/icc0708>

Human Rights Watch, “Policy paper: the meaning of the “interests of justice” in article 53 of the Rome Statute,” June 2005, 1–25, available at: <www.iccnow.org/documents/HRWInterestsOfJusticeJun2005.pdf>

Human Rights Watch, “The adoption of Security Council Resolution 1497: A setback for international justice,” 1.9.2003, 1–3, available at: <www.iccnow.org/documents/HRWPaperSCRes1497.pdf>

Human Rights Watch, “The selection of situations and cases for trial before the International Criminal Court. A Human Rights Watch Policy Paper,” October 2006, 1–15, available at: <www.hrw.org/backgrounder/ij/ij1006/ij1006web.pdf>

Human Rights Watch, World Report 2008, Events of 2007, 88–93, available at: <http://hrw.org/wr2k8/pdfs/wr2k8_web.pdf>

Humanitarian Dialogue, Report on accountability and peace agreements, Mapping trends from 1980 to 2006, September 2007, 1–56, available at: <www.hdcentre.org/publications>

International Bar Association, “Balancing rights: The ICC at a procedural crossroads,” May 2008, 1–75, available at: <www.ibanet.org/Article/Detail.aspx?ArticleUid=152711BA-7EE9-4861-9996-8C43E8CFE420>

International Centre for Transitional Justice, Borello, Federico “A first few steps,” October 2004, 1–56, available at: <www.ictj.org/images/content/1/1/115.pdf>

International Centre for Transitional Justice, 2006/2007 annual report, 1–40, available at: <www.ictj.org/en/news/reports/2298.html>

International Centre for Transitional Justice, 2004/2005 annual report, 1–40, available at: <www.ictj.org/en/news/reports/977.html>

International Centre for Transitional Justice, Human Rights Center Berkeley & Payson Center for International Development, “Living with fear, a population-based survey on attitudes about peace, justice, and social reconstruction in Eastern Democratic Republic on Congo,” August 2008, 1-66, available at: <www.ictj.org/en/news/pubs/index.html>

International Centre for Transitional Justice, Human Rights Center Berkeley & Payson Center for International Development, "Research note on attitudes about peace and justice in Northern Uganda, New population-based data on attitude about peace and justice," 13.8.2007, 1–16, available at: <www.ictj.org/images/content/7/3/737.pdf>

International Centre for Transitional Justice & Human Rights Center Berkeley, "Forgotten voices: a population-based survey on attitudes about peace and justice in Northern Uganda," July 2005, 1-60, available at: <www.ictj.org/images/content/1/2/127.pdf>

International Centre for Transitional Justice, Seils, Paul/Wierda, Marieke, "The International Criminal Court and conflict mediation," June 2005, 1–20, available at: <www.ictj.org/images/content/1/1/119.pdf>

International Council on Human Rights Policy, "Negotiating justice? Human rights and peace agreements," 2006, available at: <www.iue.it/LAW/WGHumanRights-ReportSummary.pdf>

NPWJ, "Prosecuting violations of International Criminal Law: Who should be tried?," NPWJ International Criminal Justice Policy Series No. 1, November 2004, 1–7, available at: <www.npwj.org/Newsroom/List-publications.html>

Nuremberg Declaration on Peace and Justice, Annex to the letter dated 13 June 2008 form the Permanent Representatives of Finland, Germany and Jordan to the United Nations addressed to the Secretary-General, in Ambos, Kai/Large, Judith/Wierda, Marieke (eds.), Building a future on peace and justice. Studies on Transitional Justice, Conflict Resolution and Development, Berlin et al. 2009, 541–545

NYU School of Law, GlobaLex, "The legal system and research of the Democratic Republic of Congo (DRC): an overview," Zongwe, Dunia/Butedi, Francois/Phebe, Clement, December 2007, available at: <www.nyulawglobal.org/globalex/democratic_republic_congo.htm>

Refugee Law Project, Working Paper No. 17, Peace first, justice later: traditional justice in Northern Uganda, Lucy Hovil/Joanna Quinn, July 2005, 1–59, available at: <www.refugeelawproject.org/working_papers/RLP.WP17.pdf>

Report on the major findings of the conference by Ambassador of Jordan to the USA HRH Prince Zeid Ra'ad Zeid Al-Hussein, in Ambos, Kai/Large, Judith/Wierda, Marieke (eds.), Building a future on peace and justice. Studies on Transitional Justice, Conflict Resolution and Development, Berlin et al. 2009, 533–535

War Crimes Research Office, "The confirmation of charges process at the International Criminal Court," International Criminal Court Legal Analysis and Education Project, American University Washington College of Law, United States of America: October 2008, 1–86, available at: <www.wcl.american.edu/warcrimes/icc/icc_reports.cfm>

War Crimes Research Office, "The gravity threshold of the International Criminal Court," International Criminal Court Legal Analysis and Education Project, American University Washington College of Law, United States of America:

March 2008, 1-65, available at: <www.wcl.american.edu/warcrimes/icc/icc_reports.cfm>

War Crimes Research Office, "The relevance of 'a situation' to the admissibility and selection of cases before the International Criminal Court" International Criminal Court Legal Analysis and Education Project, American University Washington College of Law, United States of America: October 2009, 1–36, available at: <www.wcl.american.edu/warcrimes/icc/icc_reports.cfm>

War Crimes Research Office, "Victim participation before the International Criminal Court," International Criminal Court Legal Analysis and Education Project, American University Washington College of Law, United States of America: November 2007, 1–84, available at: <www.wcl.american.edu/warcrimes/icc/icc_reports.cfm>

5. Domestic legislation

Austria

Strafgesetzbuch (Penal Code) 1974, 1.5.2004, available at: <www.sbg.ac.at/ssk/docs/stgb/stgb_index.htm> (German version)

Strafprozeßordnung (Code of Criminal Procedure) 1.1.2009, available at: <www.jusline.at/Strafprozessordnung_(StPO).html> (German version)

Canada

Criminal Code, 1985 (c. C-46), 25.6.2008, available at: <http://laws.justice.gc.ca/en/C-46/index.html>

Cameroon

Code de Procédure Pénale 2005 (loi no. 2005/007), imprinted in loi no. 2005/007 du 27 Juillet 2005 portant code de procedure penale, Douala 2005

Code Penal de la Republique du Cameroun 1965/1967 (loi no. 65-LF-24 et loi no. 67-LF-1), 2001

China

Criminal Law of the People's Republic of China, 14.3.1997, available at: <www.cecc.gov/pages/newLaws/criminalLawENG.php>

Criminal Procedure Law of the People's Republic of China, 1.1.1997, available at: <http://en.chinacourt.org/public/detail.php?id=2693>

Colombia

Constitución Política de Colombia 1991, edición agosto, 2005, available at: <www.assetrecovery.org/kc/node/60eca2a0-46a2-11dd-a84e-155588dfe3d4.2>

Nuevo código de procedimiento penal, 31.8.2004, ley no. 906 de 2004, available at: <www.unhcr.org/refworld/country,,,LEGISLATION,COL,4562d94e2,46d688082,0.html>

Nuevo Código Penal, 24.7.2000, ley no. 599 de 2000, in: Betancur, Alejandro Bañol, Nuevos código penal y código de procedimiento penal, Medellín 2003

Côte d'Ivoire

Code de Procédure Pénale, 14.11.1960 (loi no. 60–366), modifiée par la loi no. 62–231 du 29 juin 1962, in: Blaise, Jean-Bernard/Mourgeon, Jacques (eds.), Lois er décrets de Côte-d'Ivoire, Paris 1970

Code Pénal (Penal Code), 31.7.1981 (loi no. 1981-640), modifiée par la loi no. 1995-522 du 6 juillet 1995, available at: <www.unhcr.org/refworld/docid/3ae6b5860.html>

Democratic Republic of Congo

Code de l'organisation et de la compétence judiciaires, 1.4.1982, in Mampunga, Jean Jacques Yoka (ed.), Codes Congolais de Procédure Pénale, Kinshasa 1999

Code de Procédure Pénale, 6.8.1959, in Mampunga, Jean Jacques Yoka (ed.), Codes Congolais de Procédure Pénale, Kinshasa 1999

Code Pénal Congolais (Penal Code), 30.1.1940, available at: <www.unhcr.org/refworld/country,,NATLEGBOD,,COD,456d621e2,47303b9e2,0.html>

Code pénal militaire (Penal Code for the Military), 18.11.2002, loi no. 023-2002 du 18 novembre 2002 portant Code judiciaire militaire, available at: <www.lexadin.nl/wlg/legis/nofr/oeur/lxwerdc.htm>

Police Judiciaire, 3.7.1978, in Mampunga, Jean Jacques Yoka (ed.), Codes Congolais de Procédure Pénale, Kinshasa 1999

Règlement intérieur des cours, tribunaux et parquets, 20.8.1979, in Mampunga, Jean Jacques Yoka (ed.), Codes Congolais de Procédure Pénale, Kinshasa 1999

France

Code de Procédure Pénale (Code of Criminal Procedure) 2005, 12.12.2005, available at: <http://wings.buffalo.edu/law/bclc/resource.htm> (English version)

Code de Procédure Pénale, Renucci, Jean-François/Allain, Emanuelle/Gayet, Carole (eds.), 49th edition, Paris 2008 (French version)

Code Pénal (Penal Code), 30.7.2008, available at: <www.legifrance.gouv.fr/html/codes_traduits/code_penal_soman.htm> (English version)

Code Pénal, Mayaud, Yves/Allain, Emanuelle/Gayet, Carole (eds.), 105th edition, Paris 2008 (French version)

Germany

Gerichtsverfassungsgesetz 1877, 17.12.2008, available at <http://bundesrecht.juris.de/gvg/index.html#BJNR005130950BJNE017301301>

Richtlinien für das Strafverfahren und das Bußgeldverfahren, 1.1.2008, available at <www.bmj.bund.de/files/-/2720/RiStBV%20Stand%202008-01-01.pdf>

Strafgesetzbuch 1871, 31.10.2008, available at <www.gesetze-im-internet.de/stgb/index.html>

Strafprozessordnung 1877, 31.10.2008, available at <www.gesetze-im-internet.de/stpo/index.html>

Völkerstrafgesetzbuch, 26.6.2002, available at <http://bundesrecht.juris.de/vstgb/index.html>

India

Code of Criminal Procedure 1973, 25.1.1974, available at <www.laws4india.com>

Penal Code 1860, 6.10.1860, available at <http://punjabrevenue.nic.in/crime1.htm>

Kenya

Criminal Procedure Code 1987, revised edition 2007, chapter 75, Shollei, Gladys Boss (ed.), The laws of Kenya, Grey book, Nairobi 2007

Penal Code 1985, revised edition 2007, chapter 63, Shollei, Gladys Boss (ed.), The laws of Kenya, Grey book, Nairobi 2007

The Constitution of Kenya 2001, revised edition 2008, Shollei, Gladys Boss (ed.), The laws of Kenya, Grey book, Nairobi 2007

Norway

Criminal Code of the Kingdom of Norway, 22.5.1902, Act No. 10 amended by Act No. 50 of 1.7.1994, available at: <www.legislationline.org/documents/section/criminal-codes/country/11>

Criminal Procedure Code of the Kingdom of Norway, 22.5.1981, Act No. 25 amended by Act No. 56 of 17.7.1998, available at: <www.legislationline.org/documents/section/criminal-codes/country/11>

South Africa

Constitution of the Republic of South Africa, Act No. 108 of 1996, 8.5.1996, available at: <www.info.gov.za/documents/constitution/1996/index.htm>

Criminal Procedure Act, Act No. 51 of 1977, 22.7.1977, in Du Toit, Etienne et al. (eds.), Commentary on the Criminal Procedure Act, revision service 40, Cape Town 2008

National Prosecuting Authority Act, Act No. 32 of 1998, 3.7.1998, available at: <www.assetrecovery.org/kc/node/fe8a6008-2685-11dd-a5fa-994fad0d9d1f.2>

NDPP prosecution policy, 1.12.2005, available at: <http://us-cdn.creamermedia.co.za/assets/articles/attachments/02475_npaprosecutionpolicy.pdf>

Sudan

The Code of Criminal Procedure, 1994, Laws of the new Sudan, Secretariat for Legal Affairs

The Netherlands

Directives for the Public Prosecution Service re international crimes: Aanwijzing afdoening aangiften m.b.t. de strafbaarstellingen in de Wet internationale misdrijven, extended until 31.12.2011, Staatscourant 22.12.2003, no. 24

Wetboek van Strafvordering/Strafprozeßordnung der Niederlande, 31.10.2002, Scholten, Hans-Joseph, Freiburg 2003

Uganda

Agreement on accountability and reconciliation between the government of the Republic of Uganda and the Lord's Resistance Army/Movement, 29.6.2007, Juba (Sudan), available at: <http://northernuganda.usvpp.gov/downloads.html>

Criminal Procedure Code Act 1950 (Chapter 116), available at: <www.saflii.org/ug/legis/consol_act/cpca1950116220>

Penal Code Act 1950, 15.6.1950 (Chapter 120), available at: <www.ugandaonlinelawlibrary.com/files/free/The_Penal_Code_Act.pdf>

The Constitution of the Republic of Uganda, 22.9.1995, available at: <www.unhcr.org/refworld/category,LEGAL,,,UGA,3ae6b5ba0,0.html>

The Magistrates' Courts Act 1971, 1.8.1995 (13/70), reprint authorised and approved by the Attorney General as per S.I 107/95 under powers conferred upon him by S. 14 of the Acts of Parliament Act Cap. 15, Kampala 1995

The Trial on Indictments Decree 1971, 1.8.1995 (22/71), reprint authorised and approved by the Attorney General as per S.I 107/95 under powers conferred upon him by S. 14 of the Acts of Parliament Act Cap. 15, Kampala 1995

United Kingdom (England and Wales)

Code of Practice, Criminal Procedure and Investigations Act 1996 (s.23(1)), available at: <www.xact.org.uk/information/downloads/CPIA/Disclosure_code_of_practice.pdf>

Police and Criminal Evidence Act 1984, available at: <http://police.homeoffice.gov.uk/operational-policing/powers-pace-codes/pace-code-intro/>

Prosecution of Offences Act 1985, available at: <www.opsi.gov.uk/RevisedStatutes/Acts/ukpga/1985/cukpga_19850023_en_1>

The Code for Crown Prosecutors, available at: <www.cps.gov.uk/publications/code_for_crown_prosecutors/index.html>

USA

American Service-members' Protection Act, 30.7.2003, available at: <www.state.gov/t/pm/rls/othr/misc/23425.htm>

Table of Cases

1. International

European Court of Human Rights

Langborger v. Sweden, ECtHR judgment, 22.6.1989 (11179/84)

Findlay v. United Kingdom, ECtHR judgment, 25.2.1997 (22107/93)

Pullar v. United Kingdom, ECtHR judgment, 10.6.1996 (22399/93)

International Criminal Court
(respectively in chronological order)

Prosecutor v. Abu Garda, Decision on the confirmation of charges, 8.2.2010 (ICC-02/05-02/09-243-Red)

Prosecutor v. Abu Garda, Decision on the Prosecutor's application under article 58, 7.5.2009 (ICC-02/05-02/09-1)

Prosecutor v. Al Bashir, Second warrant of arrest for Omar Hassan Ahmad Al Bashir, 12.7.2010 (ICC-02/05-01/09-95)

Prosecutor v. Al Bashir, Second decision on the Prosecutor's application for a warrant of arrest, 12.7.2010, (ICC-02/05-01/09-94)

Prosecutor v. Al Bashir, Judgment on the appeal of the Prosecutor against the "Decision on the Prosecution's application for a warrant of arrest against Omar Hassan Ahmad Al Bashir," 3.2.2010 (ICC-02/05-01/09-73)

Prosecutor v. Al Bashir, Decision on the Prosecutor's application for leave to appeal the "Decision on the Prosecution's application for an arrest warrant against Omar Hassan Ahmad Al Bashir," 24.6.2009 (ICC-02/05-01/09-21)

Prosecutor v. Al Bashir, Separate and partly dissenting opinion of Judge Anita Ušacka, Decision on the Prosecutor's application for a warrant of arrest against Omar Hassan Ahmad Al Bashir, 4.3.2009 (ICC-02/05-01/09-3)

Prosecutor v. Al Bashir, Decision on the Prosecutor's application for a warrant of arrest against Omar Hassan Ahmad Al Bashir, 4.3.2009 (ICC-02/05-01/09-3)

Prosecutor v. Al Bashir, Warrant of arrest for Omar Hassan Ahmad Al Bashir, 4.3.2009 (ICC-02/05-01/09-1)

Prosecutor v. Bemba, Decision on the admissibility and abuse of process challenge, 24.6.2010 (ICC-01/05-01/08-802)

Prosecutor v. Bemba, Decision pursuant to article 61 (7) (a) and (b) of the Rome Statute on the charges of the Prosecutor against Jean-Pierre Bemba Gombo, 15.6.2009 (ICC-01/05-01/08-424)

Prosecutor v. Bemba, Decision adjourning the hearing pursuant to article 67 (7) (c) (ii) of the Rome Statute, 3.3.2009 (ICC-01/05-01/08-388)

Prosecutor v. Bemba, Mandat d'arrêt à l'encontre de Jean-Pierre Bemba Gombo remplaçant le mandat d'arrêt décerné le 23 mai 2008, 10.6.2008 (ICC-01/05-01/08-15)

Prosecutor v. Bemba, Décision relative à la requête du procureur aux fins de délivrance d'un mandat d'arrêt à l'encontre de Jean-Pierre Bemba Gombo, 10.6.2008 (ICC-01/05-01/08-14)

Prosecutor v. Harun and Kushayb, Request to United Nations Security Council members that are not States Parties to the Statute for the arrest and surrender of Ali Kushayb, 5.6.2007 (ICC-02/05-01/07-20)

Prosecutor v. Harun and Kushayb, Request to United Nations Security Council members that are not States Parties to the Statute for the arrest and surrender of Ahmad Harun, 5.6.2007 (ICC-02/05-01/07-19)

Prosecutor v. Harun and Kushayb, Request to States Parties to the Rome Statute for the arrest and surrender of Ali Kushayb, 5.6.2007 (ICC-02/05-01/07-18)

Prosecutor v. Harun and Kushayb, Request to States Parties to the Rome Statute for the arrest and surrender of Ahmad Harun, 5.6.2007 (ICC-02/05-01/07-17)

Prosecutor v. Harun and Kushayb, Request to the Arab Republic of Egypt, Eritrea, the Federal Democratic Republic of Ethiopia and the Libyan Arab Jamahiriya for the arrest and surrender of Ali Kushayb, 5.6.2007 (ICC-02/05-01/07-16-Corr)

Prosecutor v. Harun and Kushayb, Request to the Arab Republic of Egypt, Eritrea, the Federal Democratic Republic of Ethiopia and the Libyan Arab Jamahiriya for the arrest and surrender of Ahmad Harun, 5.6.2007 (ICC-02/05-01/07-15-Corr)

Prosecutor v. Harun and Kushayb, Request to the Republic of the Sudan for the arrest and surrender of Ali Kushayb, 5.6.2007 (ICC-02/05-01/07-14)

Prosecutor v. Harun and Kushayb, Request to the Republic of the Sudan for the arrest and surrender of Ahmad Harun, 5.6.2007 (ICC-02/05-01/07-13)

Prosecutor v. Harun and Kushayb, Background information – Facts regarding the situation in Darfur, Sudan, 2.5.2007 (ICC-PIDS-PR-20070502-214A)

Prosecutor v. Harun and Kushayb, Warrant of arrest for Ali Muhammad Ali Abd-Al-Rahman ("Ali Kushayb"), 27.4.2007 (ICC-02/05-01/07-3-Corr)

Prosecutor v. Harun and Kushayb, Warrant of arrest for Ahmad Muhammad Harun ("Ahmad Harun"), 27.4.2007 (ICC-02/05-01/07-2-Corr)

Prosecutor v. Harun and Kushayb, Decision on the Prosecution application under article 58 (7) of the Statute, 27.4.2007 (ICC-02/05-01/07-1-Corr)

Prosecutor v. Chui, Decision on the Joinder of the Cases against Germain Katanga and Mathieu Ngudjolo Chui, 10.3.2008 (ICC-01-04-01-07-257)

Prosecutor v. Chui, Prosecution's Observations on the Joinder of the Cases against Germain Katanga and Mathieu Ngudjolo Chui, 14.2.2008 (ICC-01/04-01/07-195)

Prosecutor v. Chui, Decision on the evidence and information provided by the Prosecution for the issuance of a warrant of arrest for Mathieu Ngudjolo Chui, 6.7.2007 (ICC-01/04-01/07-262)

Prosecutor v. Chui, Mandat d'arrêt à l'encontre de Mathieu Ngudjolo Chui, 6.7.2007 (ICC-01/04-02/07)

Prosecutor v. Katanga and Chui, Judgment on the appeal of Mr. Germain Katanga against the oral decision of Trial Chamber II of 12 June 2009 on the admissibility of the case, 25.09.2009 (ICC-01/04-01/07OA8)

Prosecutor v. Katanga and Chui, Motifs de la décision orale relative à l'exception d'irrecevabilité de l'affaire (article 19 du Statut), 16.6.2009 (ICC-01/04-01/07-1213)

Prosecutor v. Katanga and Chui, Public redacted version of the 19th March 2009 Prosecution response to motion challenging the admissibility of the case by the Defence of Germain Katanga, pursuant to article 19 (2), 30.3.2009 (ICC-01/04-01/07-1007)

Prosecutor v. Katanga and Chui, Motion challenging the admissibility of the case by the Defence of Germain Katanga, pursuant to article 19 (2) (a) of the Statute, 11.3.2009 (ICC-01/04-01/07-949)

Prosecutor v. Katanga and Chui, Decision constituting Trial Chamber II and referring to it the case of The Prosecutor v. Germain Katanga and Mathieu Ngudjolo Chui, 24.10.2008 (ICC-01-04-01-07-729)

Prosecutor v. Katanga and Chui, Decision on the confirmation of charges in the case of The Prosecutor v. Germain Katanga and Mathieu Ngudjolo Chui, 30.9.2008 (ICC-01/04-01/07-717)

Prosecutor v. Katanga and Chui, Decision on the Defence request for postponement of the confirmation hearing, 25.4.2008 (ICC-01/04-01/07-446)

Prosecutor v. Katanga, Decision on the evidence and information provided by the Prosecution for the issuance of a warrant of arrest for Germain Katanga, 5.11.2007 (ICC-01/04-01/07-55)

Prosecutor v. Katanga, Mandat d'arrêt à l'encontre de Germain Katanga, 2.7.2007 (ICC-01/04-01/07-1)

Prosecutor v. Kony et al., Decision on the admissibility of the case under article 19 (1) of the Statute, 10.3.2009 (ICC-02/04-01/05-377)

Prosecutor v. Kony et al., Prosecutor's response to observations submitted under Rule 103, 15.12.2008 (ICC-02/04-01/05-361)

Prosecutor v. Kony et al., Amicus Curiae submitted pursuant to the Pre-Trial Chamber II "Decision on application for leave to submit observations under Rule 103" dated 5 November 2008, 18.11.2008 (ICC-02/04-01/05-353)

Prosecutor v. Kony et al., Prosecution's observations regarding the admissibility of the case against Joseph Kony, Vincent Otti, Okot Odhiambo and Dominic Ongwen, 18.11.2008 (ICC-02/04-01/05-352)

Prosecutor v. Kony et al., Submission of observations on the admissibility of the case under article 19 (1) of the Statute, 18.11.2008 (ICC-02/04-01/05-350)

Prosecutor v. Kony et al., Observations on behalf of victims pursuant to article 19 (1) of the Rome Statute with 55 public annexes and 45 redacted annexes, 18.11.2008 (ICC-02/04-01/05-349)

Prosecutor v. Kony et al., Request pursuant to rule 103 (1) of the Rules of Procedure and Evidence for leave to submit observation as amicus curiae in the proceedings under Article 19 (1) of the Rome Statute of the International Criminal Court in the case of the Prosecutor v. Kony and others, 7.11.2008 (ICC-02/04-01/05-335)

Prosecutor v. Kony et al., Decision on application for leave to submit observations under Rule 103, 5.11.2008 (ICC-02/04-01/05-333)

Prosecutor v. Kony et al., Application by the Uganda Victims' Foundation and the Redress Trust for leave to submit observations to the Pre-Trial Chamber II of the International Criminal Court, pursuant to Rule 103 of the Rules of Procedure and Evidence, 31.10.2008 (ICC-02/04-01/05-330)

Prosecutor v. Kony et al., Decision initiating proceedings under article 19, requesting observations and appointing counsel for the Defence, 21.10.2008 (ICC-02/04-01/05-320)

Prosecutor v. Kony et al., Annex 2 to the report by the Registrar on the execution of the "request for further information from the Republic of Uganda on the status of execution of the warrants of arrest," 10.7.2008 (ICC-02/04-01/05-305-Anx2)

Prosecutor v. Kony et al., Submission of information regarding Vincent Otti, 8.11.2007 (ICC-02/04-01/05-258)

Prosecutor v. Kony et al., Prosecution's request that the warrant of arrest for Raska Lukwiya be withdrawn and rendered without effect because of his death, 22.3.2007 (ICC-02/04-01/05-230)

Prosecutor v. Kony et al., OTP submission providing information on status of the investigation in anticipation of the status conference to be held on 13 January 2006, 11.1.2006 (ICC-02/04-01/05-76)

Prosecutor v. Kony et al., Decision to convene a status conference on the investigation in the situation in Uganda in relation to the application of article 53, 2.12.2005 (ICC-02/04-01/05-68)

Prosecutor v. Kony et al., Decision on the Prosecutor's position on the decision of Pre-Trial Chamber II to redact factual descriptions of crimes from warrants of arrest, motion for reconsideration and motion for clarification, 28.10.2006 (ICC-01/04-01/05-60)

Prosecutor v. Kony et al., Warrant of arrest for Joseph Kony issued on 8 July 2005 as amended on 27 September 2005, 27.9.2005 (ICC-02/04-01/05-53)

Prosecutor v. Kony et al., Decision on the Prosecutor's application for unsealing of the warrants of arrest, 13.10.2005 (ICC-02/04-01/05-52)

Prosecutor v. Kony et al., Decision on Prosecutor's application for leave to appeal in part Pre-Trial-Chamber II's decision on the Prosecutor's application for warrants of arrest under article 58, 19.8.2005 (ICC-02/04-01/05-20-US-Exp)

Prosecutor v. Kony et al., Warrant of arrest for Dominic Ongwen, 8.7.2005 (ICC-02/04-01/05-57)

Prosecutor v. Kony et al., Warrant of arrest for Okot Odhiambo, 8.7.2005 (ICC-02/04-01/05-56)

Prosecutor v. Kony et al., Warrant of arrest for Raska Lukwiya, 8.7.2005 (ICC-02/04-01/05-55)

Prosecutor v. Kony et al., Warrant of arrest for Vincent Otti, 8.7.2005 (ICC-02/04-01/05-54)

Prosecutor v. Kony et al., Decision on the Prosecutor's application for warrants of arrest under article 58, 8.7.2005 (ICC-02/04-01/05-52)

Prosecutor v. Lubanga, Judgement on the appeal of the Prosecutor against the decision of Trial Chamber I of 8 July 2010, 8.10.2010 (ICC-01/04-01/06-2582)

Prosecutor v. Lubanga, Redacted decision on the Prosecutor's urgent request for variation of the time-limit to disclose the identity of intermediary 143 or alternatively to stay proceedings pending further consultations with VWU, 8.7.2010 (ICC-01/04-01/06-2517-RED)

Prosecutor v. Lubanga, Judgment on the appeal of the Prosecutor against the decision of Trial Chamber I entitled "Decision on the release of Thomas Lubanga Dyilo," 21.10.2008 (ICC-01/04-01/06-1487)

Prosecutor v. Lubanga, Judgment on the appeal of the Prosecutor against the decision of Trial Chamber I entitled "Decision on the consequences of non-disclosure of exculpatory materials covered by Article 54 (3) (e) agreements and the application to stay the prosecution of the accused, together with certain other issues raised at the Status Conference on 10 June 2008," 21.10.2008 (ICC-01/04-01/06-1486)

Prosecutor v. Lubanga, The Appeals Chamber gives suspensive effect to the appeal against the decision on the release of Thomas Lubanga, 7.7.2008 (ICC-CPI-20080707-PR338)

Prosecutor v. Lubanga, Decision on the release of Thomas Lubanga Dyilo, 2.7.2008 (ICC-01/04-01/06-1418)

Prosecutor v. Lubanga, Decision on the consequences of non-disclosure of exculpatory materials covered by Article 54 (3) (e) agreements and the application to

Situation in CAR, Decision assigning the situation in the Central African Republic to Pre-Trial Chamber III, 19.1.2005 (ICC-01/05-1)

Situation in Darfur (Sudan), Decision on the application for leave to appeal the decision on application under rule 103, 19.2.2009 (ICC-02/05-192)

Situation in Darfur (Sudan), Application for leave to appeal against decision on application under rule 103, 11.2.2009 (ICC-02/05-187)

Situation in Darfur (Sudan), Decision on application under rule 103, 4.2.2009 (ICC-02/05-185)

Situation in Darfur (Sudan), Annexes to application on behalf of Citizen's Organisations of the Sudan in relation to the Prosecutor's applications for arrest warrants of 14 July 2008 and 20 November 2008, Annex 7, Alex de Waal, The public application by the Chief Prosecutor of the ICC for an arrest warrant against Sudanese President Omar al Bashir: A critique, 12.1.2009 (ICC-02/05-171-Anx7)

Situation in Darfur (Sudan), Application on behalf of Citizens' Organisations of The Sudan in relation to the Prosecutor's applications for arrest warrants of 14 July 2008 and 20 November 2008, 11.1.2009 (ICC-02/05-170)

Situation in Darfur (Sudan), Prosecutor's application under article 58 (7), 27.2.2007 (ICC-02/05-56)

Situation in Darfur (Sudan), Decision assigning the situation in Darfur, Sudan to Pre-trial Chamber I, 21.4.2005 (ICC-02/05-1)

Situation in DRC, Judgment on victim participation in the investigation stage of the proceedings in the appeal of the OPCD against the decision of Pre-Trial Chamber I of 7 December 2007 and in the appeals of the OPCD and the Prosecutor against the decision of Pre-Trial Chamber I of 24 December 2007, 19.12.2008 (ICC-01-04-556)

Situation in DRC, Decision on the unsealing of judgment of the Appeals Chamber issued on 13 July 2006, 22.9.2008 (ICC-01-04-538-PUB-Exp)

Situation in DRC, Decision on the requests of the Legal Representative for victims VPRS1 to VPRS 6 regarding "Prosecutor's information on further investigation," 26.9.2007 (ICC-01/04-399)

Situation in DRC, Decision on the request submitted pursuant to rule 103 (1) of the Rules of Procedure and Evidence, 17.8.2007 (ICC-01/04-373)

Situation in DRC, Separate and partly dissenting opinion Judge Georghios M. Pikis, Judgment on the Prosecutor's appeal against the decision of Pre-Trial Chamber I entitled "Decision on the Prosecutor's application for warrants of arrest, article 58," 13.7.2006, reclassified as public on 23.9.2008 (ICC-01-04-169)

Situation in DRC, Judgment on the Prosecutor's appeal against the decision of Pre-Trial Chamber I entitled "Decision on the Prosecutor's application for warrants of arrest, article 58," 13.7.2006, reclassified as public on 23.9.2008 (ICC-01-04-169)

Situation in DRC, Judgment on the Prosecutor's application for extraordinary review of Pre-Trial Chamber I's 31 March 2006 decision denying leave to appeal, 13.7.2006 (ICC-01/04-168)

Situation in DRC, Prosecutor's application for extraordinary review of Pre-Trial Chamber I's 31 March 2006 decision denying leave to appeal, 2.5.2006 (ICC-01/04-143)

Situation in DRC, Decision on the applications for participation in the proceedings of VPRS 1, VPRS 2, VPRS 3, VPRS 4, VPRS 5 and VPRS 6, 17.1.2006 (ICC-01/04-101-Corr)

Situation in DRC, Decision following the consultation held on 11 October 2005 and the Prosecution' s submission on jurisdiction and admissibility filed on 31 October 2005, 9.11.2005 (ICC-01/04-93)

Situation in DRC, Prosecutors position on Pre-Trial Chamber I's 17 February 2005 decision to convene a status conference (redacted version), 11.3.2005 (ICC-01/04-12)

Situation in DRC, Decision to convene a status conference, 17.2.2005 (ICC-01/04-9)

Situation in DRC, Decision assigning the situation in the Democratic Republic of Congo to Pre-Trial Chamber I, 5.7.2004 (ICC-01/04-1)

Situation in Kenya, Decision pursuant to article 15 of the Rome Statute on the authorization of an investigation into the situation in the Republic of Kenya, 31.3.2010 (ICC-01/09-19)

Situation in Kenya, Decision pursuant to article 15 of the Rome Statute on the authorization of an investigation into the situation in the Republic of Kenya, Dissenting opinion of Judge Hans-Peter Kaul, 31.3.2010 (ICC-01/09-19)

Situation in Kenya, Decision requesting clarification and additional information, 18.2.2010 (ICC-01/09-15)

Situation in Kenya, Order to the Victims Participation and Reparations Section concerning victims' representations pursuant to article 15 (3) of the Statute, 10.12.2009 (ICC-01/09-4)

Situation in Kenya, Request for authorization of an investigation pursuant to article 15, 26.11.2009 (ICC-01/09-3)

Situation in Uganda, Decision assigning the situation in Uganda to Pre-Trial Chamber II, 5.7.2004 (ICC-02/04-1)

International Criminal Tribunal for the former Yugoslavia

Prosecutor v. Ademi & Norac, Decision for referral to the authorities of the Republic of Croatia pursuant to rule 11*bis*, 14.9.2005 (IT-04-78-PT)

Prosecutor v. Aleksovski, Trial judgment, 25.6.1999 (IT-95-14/1-T)

Prosecutor v. Babić, Trial judgment, Sentence, 29.6.2004 (IT-03-72-S)

Prosecutor v. Banović, Trial judgment, Sentence, 28.10.2003 (IT-02-65/1-S)

Prosecutor v. Blagojević & Jokić, Trial judgment, 17.1.2005 (IT-02-60-T)

Prosecutor v. Blaškić, Trial judgment, 3.3.2000 (IT-95-14)

Prosecutor v. Bralo, Trial judgment, Sentence, 7.12.2005 (IT-95-17-S)

Prosecutor v. Brđanin, Trial judgment, 1.9.2004 (IT-99-36-T)

Prosecutor v. Češić, Trial judgment, Sentence, 11.3.2004 (IT-95-10/1-S)

Prosecutor v. Deronjić, Trial judgment, Sentence, 30.3.2004 (IT-02-61-S)

Prosecutor v. Erdemović, Appeal's judgment, joint separate opinion of Judge McDonald and Judge Vohrah, 7.10.1997 (IT-96-22-A)

Prosecutor v. Erdemović, Appeal's judgment, separate and dissenting opinion of Judge Cassesse, 7.10.1997 (IT-96-22-A)

Prosecutor v. Erdemović, Trial judgment, Sentence, 5.3.1998 (IT-96-22T*bis*)

Prosecutor v. Furundžija, Appeal's judgment, 21.7.2000 (IT-95-17/1)

Prosecutor v. Furundžija, Trial judgment, 10.12.1998 (IT-95-17/1-T)

Prosecutor v. Galić, Trial judgment, 5.12.2003 (IT-98-29-T)

Prosecutor v. Hadžihasanović & Kubura, Trial judgment, 15.3.2006 (IT-01-47-T)

Prosecutor v. Janković, Decision on referral of case under rule 11*bis*, 22.7.2005 (IT-96-23/2-PT)

Prosecutor v. Jelisić, Appeal judgment, Partly dissenting opinion of Judge Wald, 5.7.2001 (IT-95-10-A)

Prosecutor v. Jelisić, Trial judgment, 14.12.1999 (IT-95-10-T)

Prosecutor v. Jokić, Trial judgment, 18.3.2004 (IT-01-42/1-S)

Prosecutor v Kordić, Decision on the review of the indictment, 10.11.1995 (IT-95-14-4)

Prosecutor v. Kordić, Trial judgment, 26.2.2001 (IT-95-14/2-T)

Prosecutor v. Kovačević, Decision on referral of case pursuant to rule 11*bis* with confidential and partly ex parte annexes, 17.11.2006 (IT-01-42/2-I)

Prosecutor v. Krnojelac, Trial judgment, 15.3.2002 (IT-97-25)

Prosecutor v. Krstić, Trial judgment, 2.8.2001 (IT-98-33)

Prosecutor v. Kunarac et al., Trial judgment, 22.2.2001 (IT-96-23 & 23/1)

Prosecutor v. Kupreškić et al., Trial judgment, 14.1.2000 (IT-95-16)

Prosecutor v. Kvočka et al., Trial judgment, 2.11.2001 (IT-98-30/1)

Prosecutor v. Limaj et al., Trial judgment, 30.11.2005 (IT-03-66-T)

Prosecutor v. Ljubičić, Decision to refer the case to Bosnia & Herzegovina pursuant to rule 11*bis*, 12.4.2006 (IT-00-41-PT)

Prosecutor v. Martić, Trial judgment, 12.6.2007 (IT-95-11-T)

Prosecutor v. Mejakić et al., Decision of Prosecutor's motion for referral of case pursuant to rule 11*bis*, 20.7.2005 (IT-02-65-PT)

Prosecutor v. Milutinović et al., Trial judgment, Volume 3 of 4, 26.2.2009 (IT-05-87-T)

Prosecutor v. Mrđa et al., Trial judgment, 31.3.2004 (IT-02-59-S)

Prosecutor v. Mucić et al. (Čelebići Camp), Appeal judgment, 20.2.2001 (IT-96-21A)

Prosecutor v. Mucić et al. (Čelebići Camp), Decision on the motion on presentation of evidence by the accused Esad Landzo, 1.5.1997 (IT-96-21-T)

Prosecutor v. Mucić et al. (Čelebići Camp), Trial judgment, sentence, 9.10.2001 (IT-96-21-Tbis-R117)

Prosecutor v. Naletilić and Martinović, Trial judgment, 31.3.2003 (IT-98-34)

Prosecutor v. Nikolić, Decision on interlocutory appeal concerning legality of arrest, 5.6.2003 (IT-94-2-AR73)

Prosecutor v. Nikolić, Trial judgment, Sentence, 18.12.2003 (IT-94-2-S)

Prosecutor v. Obrenović, Trial judgment, Sentence, 10.12.2003 (IT-02-60/2-S)

Prosecutor v. Orić, Trial judgment, 30.6.2006 (IT-03-68-T)

Prosecutor v. Plavšić, Trial judgment, 27.2.2003 (IT-00-39&40/1)

Prosecutor v. Rajić, Trial judgment, 8.5.2006 (IT-95-12-S)

Prosecutor v. Sikirica et al., Trial judgment, Sentence, 13.11.2001 (IT-95-8-S)

Prosecutor v. Simić, Trial judgment, Sentence, 17.10.2002 (IT-95-9/2-S)

Prosecutor v. Stakić, Trial judgment, 31.7.2003 (IT-97-24-T)

Prosecutor v. Strugar, Trial judgment, 31.1.2005 (IT-01-42-T)

Prosecutor v. Tadić, Appeal judgment, Sentence, Separate opinion of Judge Cassese, 26.1.2000 (IT-94-1-A and A*bis*)

Prosecutor v. Tadić, Decision on the defence motion for interlocutory appeal on jurisdiction, 2.10.1995 (IT-94-1-AR72)

Prosecutor v. Tadić, Trial judgment, Sentence, 11.11.1999 (IT-94-1)

Prosecutor v. Todorović, Trial judgment, sentence, 31.7.2001 (IT-95-9/1-S)

Prosecutor v. Todović & Rašević, Decision on referral of case under rule 11*bis* with confidential annexes I and II, 8.7.2005 (IT-97-25/1-PT)

Prosecutor v. Vasiljević, Trial judgment, 29.11.2002 (IT-98-32-T)

Prosecutor v. Zelenović, Trial judgment, Sentence, 4.4.2007 (IT-96-23/2-S)

International Criminal Tribunal for Rwanda

Prosecutor v. Akayesu, Appeal judgment, 1.6.2001 (ICTR-96-4-A)

Prosecutor v. Akayesu, Trial judgment, Sentence, 2.10.1998 (ICTR-96-4-T)

Prosecutor v. Bagaragaza, Decision on the Prosecution's motion for referral to the Kingdom of Norway, 19.5.2006 (ICTR-2005-86-R11)

Prosecutor v. Bagosora et al., Trial judgment, 18.12.2008 (ICTR-98-41-T)

Prosecutor v. Bikindi, Trial judgment, 2.12.2008 (ICTR-01-72-T)

Prosecutor v. Bisengimana, Trial judgment, 13.4.2006 (ICTR-00-60-T)

Prosecutor v. Gacumbtsi, Trial judgment, 17.6.2004 (ICTR-2001-64-T)

Prosecutor v. Kajelijeli, Trial judgment, 1.12.2003 (ICTR-98-44A-T)

Prosecutor v. Kambanda, Trial judgment, 4.9.1998 (ICTR-97-23-S)

Prosecutor v. Kamuhanda, Trial judgment, 22.1.2004 (ICTR-95-54A-T)

Prosecutor v. Kanyabashi, Decision on the Defence Motion on Jurisdiction, 18.6.1997 (ICTR-96-15-T)

Prosecutor v. Karera, Trial judgment, 7.12.2007 (ICTR-01-74-T)

Prosecutor v. Kayishema et al., Appeal judgment, 1.6.2001 (ICTR-95-1-A)

Prosecutor v. Kayishema et al., Trial judgment, Sentence, 21.5.1999 (ICTR-95-1-T)

Prosecutor v. Muhimana, Trial judgment, 28.4.2005 (ICTR-95-1B-T)

Prosecutor v. Munyeshyaka, Decision on the Prosecutor's request for the referral of Wenceslas Munyeshyaka's indictment to France, 20.11.2007 (ICTR-2005-87-I)

Prosecutor v. Musema, Trial judgment, 27.1.2000 (ICTR-96-13-A)

Prosecutor v. Nahimana et al., Trial judgment, 3.12.2003 (ICTR-96-11)

Prosecutor v. Nchamihigo, Trial judgment, 12.11.2008 (ICTR-01-63-T)

Prosecutor v. Ndindabahizi, Trial judgment, 15.7.2004 (ICTR-2001-71-I)

Prosecutor v. Ndindiliyimana, Decision on urgent oral motion for stay of the indictment, or in the alternative a reference to the Security Council, 26.3.2004 (ICTR-2000-56-I)

Prosecutor v. Niyitegeka, Trial judgment, 16.5.2003 (ICTR-96-14-T)

Prosecutor v. Ntagerura et al., Trial judgment, 25.2.2004 (ICTR-99-46-T)

Prosecutor v. Ntakirutimana, Trial judgment, 21.2.2003 (ICTR-96-10 & ICTR-96-17-T)

Prosecutor v. Nzabirinda, Trial judgment, 23.2.2007 (ICTR-2001-77-T)

Prosecutor v. Rugambarara, Trial judgment, Sentence, 16.11.2007 (ICTR-00-59-T)

Prosecutor v. Ruggiu, Trial judgment, 1.6.2000 (ICTR-97-32-I)

Prosecutor v. Rutaganda, Trial judgment, 6.12.1999 (ICTR-96-3)

Prosecutor v. Rutaganira, Trial judgment, 14.3.2005 (ICTR-95-1C-T)

Prosecutor v. Semanza, Trial judgment, 15.3.2003 (ICTR-97-20)

Prosecutor v. Seromba, Trial judgment, 13.12.2006 (ICTR-2001-66-I)

Prosecutor v. Serugendo, Trial judgment, 12.6.2006 (ICTR-2005-84-I)

Prosecutor v. Serushago, Trial judgment, Sentence, 5.2.1999 (ICTR-98-39)

Prosecutor v. Simba, Trial judgment, 13.12.2005 (ICTR-01-76-T)

Prosecutor v. Zigiranyirazo, Trial judgment, 18.12.2008 (ICTR-01-73-T)

International Court of Justice

Certain Expenses of the United Nations, Advisory Opinion, 20.7.1962, available at: <www.icj-cij.org>

Legal Consequences for States of the Continued Presence of South Africa in Namibia (South West Africa) notwithstanding Security Council Resolution 276 (1970), Advisory Opinion, 21.6.1971, available at: <www.icj-cij.org>

Questions of Interpretation and Application of the 1971 Montreal Convention Arising from the Aerial Incident at Lockerbie (Request for Indication of Provisional Measures), Libyan Arab Jamahiriya v. United States of America, Order, 14.4.1992, available at: <www.icj-cij.org>

2. Internationalized

Extraordinary Chambers in the Courts of Cambodia

Closing Order indicting Kaing Guek Eav alias Duch, 8.8.2008 (002/14-08-2006)

Special Court for Sierra Leone

Prosecutor v. Brima, Kamara and Kanu (AFRC trial), Appeals judgment, 22.2.2008 (SCSL-04-16-A-675)

Prosecutor v. Brima, Kamara and Kanu (AFRC trial), Sentencing judgment, 19.7.2007 (SCSL-04-16-T)

Prosecutor v. Fofana and Kondawa (CDF trial), Decision on the preliminary Defence motion on the lack of personal jurisdiction filed on behalf of the accused Fofana, 3.3.2004 (SCSL-04-16-PT-026)

Prosecutor v. Fofana and Kondawa (CDF trial), Judgment on the sentencing of Moinina Fofana and Allieu Kondawa, 9.10.2007 (SCSL-04-14-T)

Prosecutor v. Sesay, Kallon and Gbao (RUF trial), Sentencing judgment, 8.4.2009 (SCSL-04-15-T)

3. National

Canada

R. v. Campell [1999], 22.4.1999 (1 S.C.R. 565)

R. v. Mack [1988], 15.12.1988 (2 S.C.R. 903)

R. v. Magder Furs Ltd. [1989], 4.10.1989 (49 C.C.C. (3d) 267)

R. v. Power [1994], 14.4.1994 (1 S.C.R. 601)

R. v. St. Jean [1995], 9.11.1995, 1995 Canadian Legal Information Institute 1427 (BC S.C.), available at: <www.canlii.org>

Germany

BGHSt 38, 214 [1992], 27.2.1992 (5 StR 190/91)

OLG Stuttgart, Beschluss vom 13.9.2005 (5 Ws 109/05)

Kenya

Crispus Karanja Njogu v. The Attorney-General [2000], Criminal application no. 39 (unreported)

Crispus Karanja Njogu v. The Attorney-General & others [2005], Civil suit 574 of 2002, available at: <www.kenyalaw.org>

United Kingdom (England and Wales)

Associated Provincial Pictures Houses v. Wednesbury [1948], 10.11.1947 (1 K.B. 223)

Marshall v. DPP [2007], 24.1.2007 (WL 2866)

Patrick John Lewin v. CPS [2002], 24.5.2002 (EWHC 1049)

R (on the application of Da Silva) v. DPP [2006], 14.12.2006 (EWHC 3204)

R (on the application of Joseph) v. DPP [2001], 21.12.2000 (Crim. L.R. 489)

R v. DPP, ex p. Burke [1997], 12.12.1996 (C.O.D. 169)

R v. DPP, ex p. C [1995], 15.2.1994 (1 Cr. App. R. 136)

R v. DPP, ex p. Jones (Timothy) [2000], 23.3.2000 (Crim. L.R. 858)

R v. DPP, ex p. Kebilene and others [2000], 28.10.1999 (2 A.C. 326)

R v. DPP, ex p. Manning [2001], 17.5.2000 (Q.B. 330)

R v. Panel on Takeovers and Mergers, ex p. Fayed [1992], 3.4.1992 (B.C.C. 524)

The Queen on the application of Peter Dennis v. DPP [2006], 29.12.2006 (EWHC 3211)

United States

Attica v. Rockefeller [1973], 18.4.1973 (477 F.2d 375)

United States v. Armstrong [1996], 13.5.1996 (517 U.S. 456)

Index